MORE SECRETS

More Inside Information

Revised Edition
10 9 8 7 6 5 4 3 2

Boardroom® Classics publishes the advice of expert authorities in many fields. But the use of a book is not a substitute for legal, accounting, or other professional services. Consult a competent professional for answers to your specific questions.

Library of Congress Cataloging in Publication Data
Main entry under title:

More Secrets. More Inside Information.

1. Life skills—United States. I. Bottom line personal.
ISBN 0-88723-062-8

330 W. 42nd Street, New York, NY 10036

Contents

3 • MONEY MANAGEMENT FOR TOUGH TIMES

4 • CAR SMARTS

5 • CONSUMER SAVVY

6 • TAX-SAVING STRATEGIES

7 • A MORE POWERFUL YOU

8 • INSURANCE TRAPS AND OPPORTUNITIES

9 • HOME SMARTS

10 • AN INVESTOR'S GUIDE TO RETIREMENT PLANNING

11 • EDUCATION

12 • YOU AND YOUR FAMILY

13 • SEXUAL SECRETS

14 • SHREWD CAREER PLANNING

15 • FITNESS AND EXERCISE

1

A Healthier You

What Would You Do If Illness Or Injury Left You Unable To Work For An Extended Period Of Time?

If you think that your chances of suddenly becoming disabled are remote, be aware that…

• The probability of a 30-year-old being laid up for more than three months before age 65 is one in two.

• Those in their 40s are three times more likely to become disabled than to die before age 65.

And if you think that your job benefits will cover your bills for the time that you're laid up, think again. Very few employers offer adequate protection.

And Social Security, another source of financial help, is available to only approximately one-third of those people who apply for it.

Solution:

The answer for many is private disability insurance. Drawback: It's not cheap. It runs as high as $2,000 a year. But by following this advice—with some smart shopping—you can find comparable coverage for as little as $500.

Why the big spread? Because many insurance companies take advantage of consumers' lack of knowledge. To be sure you get the best insurance policy at the best rate, here's what you should do…

• Determine exactly how much money you'll need to cover your living expenses in the event of disability. Tax break: Payments of insurance claims are tax-free. Also, if you are forced to cash in your Individual Retirement Accounts or Keogh plans, you are exempt from the 10% penalty because of your disability.

• Factor in what you will get from company benefits and other sources of income. Your goal is to have a monthly income that's equal to 60%–80% of your current take-home pay.

You will need enough insurance to cover the gap that you've computed between your financial needs and the income you can count on. Critical:

The critical part of a disability policy is the definition of disability.

The best policies—but not necessarily the most expensive—let you collect if you're unable to return to the specific type of work that you were employed at before you became disabled.

The least-attractive policies don't provide benefits unless you are unable to do any work at all.

Many policies are ambiguous on this point.

Urgent: Make sure you clearly understand the definition of "disability" contained in any policy you consider, so you know under what circumstances you can collect from it.

If your work is less specialized—such as a job in general management or sales—you may be willing to accept a less rigorous definition of disability. But remember, that doesn't guarantee a lower premium. Also, be sure payments will replace partial loss of income if you must take a lower-paying job.

Don't consider policies that aren't described in writing as *noncancelable* and *guaranteed renewable*. This assures that your individual premium can't be raised or the policy canceled unless you stop paying. However, it does not prevent the insurer from raising the premiums on all policies in your class. Also, make sure the policy excuses you from paying premiums during the period of time that you're disabled.

One thing that will reduce your premium cost is a waiting period after the time you are disabled before policy payments begin. Arrange to have payments kick in only when salary and benefits from your job end.

Once you've determined what you want in the policy, start to shop for price, limiting your consideration to insurers that are relatively large and rated by the insurance-industry monitor, A.M. Best, as *A+*. You can find the latest Best reports in most public libraries.

Buying point: Disability policies generate sales commissions—about a third that of life insurance policies. Don't expect salespeople to be as accommodating when they sell disability products. In fact, expect the salesperson to quickly move into a pitch for life insurance.

Resist buying any insurance extras, or riders, that provide extra types of supplemental coverage. Most aren't worth the extra cost.

One thing you don't have to worry about is being pressured into buying more disability coverage than you need. Reason: Insurers don't want to make it more financially advantageous for clients to resist recuperation—and thus sit home and collect claim checks—than to get back to work.

Source: Robert Hunter, president of the National Insurance Consumer Organization, a consumer-advocacy group headquartered at 121 N. Payne St., Alexandria, VA 22314.

How To Get The Government Aid That You Are Entitled To For Health Care & Medical Bills

Given the skyrocketing costs of medical care and health insurance, it is particularly important to make sure you receive the benefits you're entitled to...and to minimize the expenses for which you are liable.

The primary federal health-care programs are *Medicare**...and *Medicaid*—for the needy.

Other government programs, for which fewer people are eligible, include Veterans Administration (VA) benefits and Supplemental Security Income (SSI), which assists the low-income aged, the blind and the severely disabled.

Medicare and Medicaid aren't charity programs. They are tax-funded insurance programs you have paid annual premiums for—through Social Security—and that you are entitled to. Most beneficiaries of Medicaid, which now covers half of the US nursing-

*The largest program for the largest population—those 65 and over, the severely disabled and those with severe kidney damage.

home population, have paid premiums for most of their working lives.

Even with an employer-provided health insurance plan—and we recommend you keep any plan you have—you should enroll in Medicare Part A (hospital insurance), when you turn 65...and purchase Part B (doctor insurance) within three months of your 65th birthday. Otherwise you will have to pay an additional 10% premium for every year you wait. Enrolling keeps that cost to your employer down and maximizes the benefits of your existing plan.

Medicare was never intended to cover all of its beneficiaries' health costs. Everyone's share is rising. Today, the elderly spend up to 20% of their income on health care, even with Medicare. The Medicare premium rises every year, and in 1988, the Part B section rose a staggering 35%—and is still rising.

Money-saving solutions: Make the most of Medicare. Make sure you have supplemental private insurance (medigap coverage)...and try to keep all medical costs as low as possible.

How to get the most from Medicare:

Maximize your coverage by tuning into Medicare's best-kept secrets...

• Doctors' fees are very negotiable. A doctor who accepts Medicare assignments agrees to accept the fee that it pays for the procedure or treatments provided, and handles the paperwork. You remain responsible for your deductible and 20% co-payment.

Only 40% of doctors accept assignments for all of their Medicare patients. But 70% accept assignments for some of their patients or for some services. So it is up to you to persuade your doctor to accept Medicare assignments on all of your bills.

Helpful approach: "I believe that Medicare pays a fair rate, and I hope you will respect my request, as I cannot afford more than the 20% co-payment. However, if you do not accept assignments, perhaps you could refer me to another practitioner who does." Doctors do not like to lose clients. Most people who take the trouble to negotiate assignments are successful.

• You never have to pay more than the Maximum Allowable Actual Charge (MAAC) for any service, even if your doctor does not take assignments.

Medicare has set a maximum fee (MAAC) for all services that doctors who do not take assignments may charge Medicare patients. To find out a specific MAAC, call the Medicare carrier in your area. If your doctor bills you for more than the MAAC, neither you nor your insurance company has to pay the difference.

Example: Your doctor charges $3,000 for a procedure. Medicare pays $2,000 for the same procedure, and has set the MAAC at $2,500. Medicare will pay 80% of the $2,000 "reasonable cost," or $1,600. If your doctor accepts assignments, you would only have to pay the 20% co-payment, or $400. If the doctor does not take assignments, you must pay the difference between $1,600 and the $2,500 MAAC, or $900, and the doctor must absorb the other $500. But if you haven't bothered to check the MAAC, you may be billed for the full $3,000, less Medicare's $1,600, and unknowingly pay the $1,400 difference.

• The fact that Medicare refuses payment does not necessarily mean that you must pay. You are not responsible for any medical bill that you could not reasonably have been expected to know wasn't covered. You must be informed in writing from an official source, such as a Medicare notice or pamphlet, that a service isn't covered. If your doctor tells you something is covered by Medicare and it isn't, then the doctor—neither you nor your insurer—is responsible.

• You cannot be discharged from the hospital before you are medically able to go. You cannot be discharged because your Medicare payments or "DRG" (Diagnosis-Related Group system) days have been used up. When you are admitted to the hospital, you will be issued a form outlining your rights as a Medicare patient. If you think you are being discharged too soon, request a review by your state's PRO (Peer Review Organization), a group of doctors who review Medicare cases. The PRO will decide if your Medicare coverage can be extended, based on medical necessity.

Shopping for medigap insurance:

Employer-provided retiree health insurance

is usually as good as the available high-option medigap policies, and often better. But more than five million older Americans are paying an unnecessary, duplicative insurance that they mistakenly believe supplements their Medicare coverage. If you have an employer-sponsored plan, you may not need more coverage. If you do not, consider supplemental insurance. What to look for:

The federal government certifies medigap policies as meeting minimum standards for Medicare supplemental insurance if the company requests it. To check on an individual policy, call your state insurance office.

Under Part A, supplemental policies are required to cover $78.50 per day co-insurance for care in a skilled nursing facility through the 100th day, when Medicare stops paying. A generous policy will provide coverage past the 100th day.

Under Part B, supplemental policies must pay the 20% co-payment not covered by Medicare, but only up to $5,000 total, and only after you have paid the $100 deductible and the first $100 of co-payment.

Key: A good policy will cover doctors' fees in excess of Medicare-approved amounts.

It is against the law for a policy that calls itself a Medicare supplement to exclude any preexisting conditions for more than six months.

Choose a policy that has a stop-loss provision, or ask your agent to add a rider (usually for a small extra fee).

Make sure the policy is automatically adjusted to increases in Medicare deductibles or co-payments.

Saving on out-of-pocket expenses:

You can minimize your co-payments and keep premiums down by trying to keep your medical expenses as low as possible.

- Take advantage of low-cost or free health services offered by counties, organizations or health fairs.

Examples: Inoculations, screenings.

- Make sure you are aware of your health plan's limits and exclusions.

Example: Number of chiropractic visits.

- Shop around for prescription prices, and buy generic drugs when possible.
- Guard against unnecessary or excessive testing. Many physicians have adopted new, costly tests while continuing to administer the old ones—often less expensive, and as effective.
- Avoid hospitalization and surgery unless absolutely necessary. Avoid for-profit hospitals—they're up to 23% more costly. Avoid weekend admission.
- Bring your own food, vitamins and drugs.
- Specify in writing that surgery or invasive procedures must be done by the person you are paying, i.e., your fully-trained physician, not a resident or intern.
- Keep track of all bills and services while hospitalized.

Common errors to check for: Type of room...number of days (look for an extra day on checkout day)...tests actually received, medications actually taken, physician's visits that actually occurred, as opposed to routinely billed.

Source: Charles B. Inlander, president of the People's Medical Society, a nonprofit consumers' health organization, 462 Walnut St., Allentown, Pennsylvania 18102. 800-624-8773. His book, co-authored with Karla Morales, is *Getting the Most for Your Medical Dollar,* Pantheon, 201 E. 50 St., New York 10022.

Could Your Doctor Be Wrong? How To Know

In this age of modern medical technology, we sometimes expect our doctors to be able to accurately diagnose and successfully treat every single disease. But no doctor is always right. Many people spend years suffering from ailments that have defied the efforts of even highly trained medical specialists.

Doctors have particular trouble dealing with ailments whose symptoms fail to "add up" to a known disease. Show up at the emergency room with a broken leg or a heart attack, and odds are strong that you'll get prompt, professional treatment. Show up complaining of fatigue or vague aches and pains, though, and you'll probably have problems. Reason: Most doctors like to "cookbook" their way through their cases. If you don't fit the recipe, the doctor has no idea of what to make of you or your ailment.

If your physician seems to be unable to solve your particular ailment, don't hesitate to seek out a second opinion—or even a third...or fourth opinion.

Many commonly misdiagnosed and mistreated ailments are controllable if you find a physician willing to make the effort.

Crucial: A willingness to consider all the possible causes of an ailment, not just the usual causes.

Commonly misdiagnosed ailments:

• Chest pain. Chest pain that cannot be linked to heart disease or some other familiar cause is often put down to a bad case of the "nerves."

But good doctors realize that once heart disease is ruled out, there remain several other possible culprits for the pain. They include spasms of the chest muscles and—more common—gastroesophageal reflux. This condition results when stomach acid splashes upward into the esophagus. It can cause pain that closely resembles that caused by heart disease.

However, unlike most chest pain caused by heart disease, pain from gastroesophageal reflux is not made worse by exertion. Gastroesophageal reflux is usually made worse by a big meal, while heart pain is only occasionally linked to eating. Eating less and avoiding aspirin and other medications that irritate the stomach are effective against gastroesophageal reflux, as is keeping the head elevated during sleep.

• Fatigue. Many different ailments, from anxiety disorder to parasitic infections, can cause chronic fatigue. Doctors are usually quite adept at treating fatigue that can be linked to one of these ailments.

But doctors unable to pinpoint an underlying cause are too eager to blame fatigue on stress, depression or another psychological problem. In such cases, another possible culprit—chronic fatigue syndrome (CFS)—is frequently overlooked.

Once thought by many to be merely a "fad" disease, CFS is now broadly recognized as a real and often debilitating ailment. Yet only a minority of doctors are adept at diagnosing and treating it. Unlike most other forms of fatigue, CFS is often accompanied by flu-like aches and pains, sore throat, mental "slowing" and other vague symptoms. CFS fatigue is typically made worse by exercise. Other forms of fatigue are little affected by exercise.

While there is no "magic bullet" for treating CFS, many drugs are effective at treating its symptoms.

Key: Finding a physician willing to work with you to keep your symptoms in check. In most cases, CFS disappears spontaneously after two and a half to three years.

• Headache. Many so-called "stress" headaches are really caused by muscular fatigue stemming from nighttime clenching of the teeth (bruxism)...or by chronic tension in the muscles at the base of the neck (trapezius muscles). Unfortunately, few doctors ever take the time to examine these muscles, so many people wind up taking drugs when behavioral therapy aimed at reducing stress would be far more beneficial for them.

Alternate treatments: In some cases, these headaches may also be relieved by treating the affected muscles with massage, electrical stimulation, or even injections of saline solution or by a combination of these treatments.

• Impotence. At one time, doctors thought that nine out of every 10 cases of impotence were psychogenic—caused by psychological factors, including depression and anxiety. Now we know that only about half of all cases are psychogenic. The other half are caused by specific physiological (organic) problems, including poor blood circulation to the penis.

Problem: Many men suffering from organic impotence are treated as if they have psychogenic impotence. These men waste time in psychotherapy or taking mood-altering drugs when their problem could be quickly and easily treated with minor surgery or with other, appropriate drugs.

Bottom line: Any man suffering from impotence should make sure his physician considers both possible causes before accepting treatment.

• Sleepiness. Daytime sleepiness not caused by insomnia is often blamed on depression or emotional stress, and is often treated with sleeping pills. In fact, many people troubled by daytime sleepiness are really suffering from sleep apnea. That is a condition in which sleep is disrupted scores or even hundreds of times nightly—and which cannot be controlled by sleeping pills.

Sleep apnea strikes all kinds of people but is most common among obese men who snore heavily.

Mechanism: Loose tissue inside the throat sags during sleep, eventually pressing upon and blocking the windpipe, disrupting breathing and causing the person to wake up.

In many cases, a sleep apnea sufferer's bed partner is well aware of these waking episodes—and may be instrumental in helping with the diagnosis.

Caution: Sleep apnea is more than an annoyance. It can cause fatal heart irregularities. Anyone suffering from unexplained drowsiness should suspect this condition. There are many effective methods of treating it.

• Sore throat. Doctors often treat a sore throat as if strep throat were the only possible cause. In fact, there are many other potential causes, and the antibiotics that are so effective against strep do nothing to control them. Other possibilities: Mononucleosis, tonsillitis, chlamydia, chronic fatigue syndrome, thyroid inflammation and more. In some cases, sore throat is caused by tenderness of the carotid arteries, a condition known as carotodynia.

Important: Don't take antibiotics unless your doctor has ruled out other possibilities. Insist that the true cause of the sore throat be found before you accept treatment.

Source: Jay A. Goldstein, MD, founding director of the Chronic Fatigue Syndrome Institute and author of *Could Your Doctor Be Wrong?*, Pharos Books, 200 Park Ave., New York 10166. Dr. Goldstein has residency training in both psychiatry and family medicine. He practices in Anaheim, CA.

Health Quackery Self-Defense

If a medical treatment or "cure" has not been prescribed by your doctor but you want to check it out, call...

• The National Cancer Institute at 800-422-6237.

• The Arthritis Foundation Information Line at 800-283-7800.

Regarding other suspicious health products, send questions about specific products to the Consumer Health Research Institute, 3521 Broadway, Kansas City, Missouri 64111. Include a self-addressed, stamped, business-sized envelope and $1.

And if you think you have been harmed by a quack remedy, contact the National Council Against Health Fraud, William Jarvis, PhD, Evans Hall, Room 204, Loma Linda University, Loma Linda, California 92350.

Source: AARP, 601 E St. NW, Washington, DC 20049. The *AARP Bulletin* is distributed to members, ages 50 and over, monthly.

What You Should Know About The Most Misunderstood Cardiac Condition

Mitral valve prolapse is an often misdiagnosed heart condition that occurs when the mitral valve, which lets blood drain from the top to the bottom chamber of the heart, buckles back during the heart's contraction.

Mitral valve prolapse syndrome (MVPS) refers to a cluster of symptoms that often occur when the heart has this abnormality.

Common symptoms: Heart palpitations, chest pain, dizziness, fatigue, anxiety or panic attacks, headaches, mood swings. Symptoms may be made worse by physical or emotional stress, caffeine, dehydration, skipping meals or being in a hot, dry environment.

MVPS affects 4% to 18% of Americans—as many as 40+ million people. It afflicts about three times as many women as men.

The physical abnormality is believed to be inherited.

Whether it actually causes the symptoms associated with it—and if so, how—is unknown.

Other physiological changes associated

with mitral valve prolapse include:

• High sensitivity to catecholamines, the adrenaline-like substances released by the nervous system to help the body deal with emergencies.

• Problems with the body's salt-regulating mechanism.

• Decreased intravascular volume—the amount of blood circulating through the body.

• In some people, the buckling back of the valve is accompanied by a murmur, during which a small amount of blood flows back into the top chamber of the heart. (The blood doesn't stay there, but gets pumped out on the next beat.)

Not all physicians are familiar with MVPS. Too often, symptoms are not taken seriously by doctors, or are wrongly attributed to other conditions—usually hypoglycemia, chronic fatigue syndrome, an inner ear problem or anxiety disorder.

Many people with the condition go from doctor to doctor, terrified they're on the brink of a heart attack—only to be told there's nothing wrong with them or that the problem is psychological.

The good news:

Despite being classified as a heart condition, mitral valve prolapse does not cause heart attacks, and it's believed that the majority of people with MVPS have a normal life span.

Sometimes, just learning that the condition has a name—and that it's not life-threatening—is enough to make the syndrome manageable.

However, patients with mitral valve prolapse are advised to use antibiotics when undergoing "dirty surgery"—procedures, such as root-canal work, during which bacteria could be released into the blood, making the valve more vulnerable to infection.

Diagnosing MVPS:

In addition to noting the presence of symptoms, a physician can usually diagnose MVPS by listening to the patient's heartbeat for a click (made by the buckling back of the valve)—or murmur (the swooshing sound caused by the flow of blood back into the top chamber). These sounds, though, aren't always detectable. The diagnosis may be confirmed with an echocardiogram, or ultrasound examination.

Living with MVPS: There is no cure for mitral valve prolapse. Fortunately, the symptoms can usually be controlled through changes in diet, exercise and other life-style habits.

Nutrition management:

• Avoid caffeine and other stimulants. Because MVPS patients are sensitive to adrenaline-like substances, stimulants can aggravate symptoms. Cut out coffee, tea, chocolate, caffeinated soft drinks and over-the-counter drugs containing caffeine, such as Anacin and Vivarin. Also avoid drugs that contain the stimulants ephedrine and pseudoephedrine, including Actifed, Benadryl, Chlor-Trimeton, Sudafed and many other antihistamines.

• Increase salt and fluid intake, especially if you feel dizzy when you stand up. People tend to think, *Heart problem—cut down on salt*, but the opposite is true of MVPS. The condition is often accompanied by problems with salt regulation and circulating blood volume, so taking enough salt and fluids—at least eight glasses of water or juice a day—is important.

Exception: People with high blood pressure should not add salt to their diet.

• Eat a well-balanced diet, not too high in calories or sweets. A high caloric intake—and the metabolization of simple carbohydrates and fats—can greatly increase the activity of the sympathetic nervous system, the body's "accelerator," making symptoms worse.

• Never go on crash or fad diets. Not only are they ineffective over the long term, but most of the weight loss achieved is through water depletion—just the opposite of what someone with MVPS needs.

• If you suffer from migraine headaches, avoid tyramine. Tyramine is a food component that has been associated with migraines. It is found in chocolate, citrus fruit, avocados, raspberries, pickled herring and some foods that have undergone fermentation, such as cheese and wine.

Exercise management:

My research has shown that many MVPS sufferers experience a dramatic improvement in symptoms simply by following an exercise program. For best results, workouts should be:

• Aerobic (brisk walking, bicycling, swimming, etc.).

• Done a minimum of three times a week, preferably on alternate days.

• Twenty to 45 minutes long, plus time to warm-up and cool down muscles.

• Performed at a level where work load feels somewhat difficult but not too intense. Taking pulse rate to measure workout intensity is not recommended for people with MVPS. If you feel out of breath, overexerted or dizzy, you're exercising too hard.

Very important: Start slow. If you're out of shape, begin with a 10-minute session and add a few more minutes each time. And don't expect symptoms to vanish overnight. Our research subjects didn't begin to show improvement until they'd been exercising regularly for six weeks or more.

Coping with panic attacks:

A number of people with MVPS have recurrent anxiety attacks accompanied by heart palpitations, light-headedness, shortness of breath, extreme apprehension or fear, chest pain and/or the feeling that they're about to pass out.

For many, the unexplained presence of frightening symptoms, such as a pounding heart, triggers an outflow of anxiety. The person may think, *I'm having a heart attack*, and these kinds of thoughts further intensify the physical symptoms.

Panic attacks rarely come from nowhere. If you think about it, you may be able to identify a source of anxiety—or remember eating a type of food you're sensitive to—preceding the attack.

Helpful: Cognitive therapy, as described in books by Dr. David Burns of the University of Pennsylvania.* You can change the way you react to events by altering how you perceive them. Key steps:

1. Be aware of automatic thoughts—*there is a clutching in my chest...I'm about to die.*

2. Identify the cognitive distortions, or irrational patterns of thinking, that lead to anxiety or depression.

Examples:

• Catastrophizing—*I'm going to pass out in the middle of the supermarket. I'll be humiliated.*

• Overgeneralization—*This panic attack will make me late for work and ruin my whole week...and my boss will probably fire me.*

• *Should* statements.

• Focusing on negative information and discounting the positive.

• Expecting the worst—*This must be a heart attack.*

• All-or-nothing thinking—*I can't take control of my health. I must be a total failure.*

3. Challenge your irrational thoughts with rational, contradictory evidence. Write your argument down if you have to.

Unfortunately, it's hard to think clearly enough to use cognitive therapy techniques when you're in the middle of a panic attack. Good on-the-spot measures:

• Get up and move around. By lying in the dark worrying, you'll only make it worse. Focus your attention on something else, such as housework or an absorbing book. Call a friend and touch base with reality.

• Breathe. Pursed-lip breathing is very effective in combating shortness of breath. Don't worry about taking a deep breath—just breathe in, then slowly exhale through your mouth with your lips pursed, as though blowing out a candle. Repeat three or four times until you can breathe comfortably.

Medications:

The non-drug interventions just described can bring about great improvement for the vast majority of people with MVPS. However, if excessive symptoms continue to interfere with the activities of daily life, medication may be helpful.

Most commonly prescribed: Beta-blockers and anti-anxiety drugs. Both have side effects, so discuss them with your doctor and make sure he/she carefully monitors their effects.

Source: Kristine Scordo, PhD, RN, clinical director of The Cardiology Center of Cincinnati and Mitral Valve Prolapse Program of Cincinnati, 10525 Montgomery Rd., Cincinnati 45242. She is the author of *Taking Control: Living with the Mitral Valve Prolapse Syndrome*, Camden House, Inc., Drawer 2025, Columbia, SC 29202.

**Feeling Good: The New Mood Therapy* and *The Feeling Good Handbook*, William Morrow & Co., Inc., 1350 Ave. of the Americas, New York 10019.

Heart Disease Myths/ Heart Disease Realities

Because cardiovascular disease is so familiar to all of us, we tend to think we know all about it. In fact, many ideas about heart disease commonly held by laypeople and physicians alike are nothing more than myths. Included:

• Myth: That an aspirin a day prevents heart attacks. Reality: A daily aspirin tablet does seem to help people who have had one heart attack from having another—but there's very little benefit for those without preexisting heart disease.

Recent study: For every 1,000 otherwise healthy people who took a daily aspirin tablet, heart attacks were prevented in only eight people. In contrast, 991 people experienced neither harm nor benefit...and one person suffered bleeding into the brain from the aspirin.

Aspirin has also been linked to stomach ulcers. And there is no evidence that taking a daily aspirin boosts life expectancy—people simply die from something other than a heart attack.

Self-defense: Do not take aspirin if your heart is healthy. If you have had a heart attack, take no more than one aspirin tablet a day—preferably children's aspirin.

• Myth: That we should all try to lower our cholesterol levels. Reality: Special diets and cholesterol-lowering medications make sense only for certain people—hypertensives, smokers, diabetics, people with cholesterol levels 280 or above...and those already diagnosed with heart disease.

Others who try to lower their cholesterol readings may be wasting their effort. Lowering your cholesterol level does nothing to increase your longevity, even if it does reduce your risk of heart attack.

Note: Elevated cholesterol readings should be of little concern in healthy people aged 65 or older. Studies have shown that these elderly people are no longer at increased risk for heart attack—if cholesterol hasn't led to heart disease by this age, it is probably no longer a threat.

• Myth: That a prudent lifestyle prevents heart attacks. Reality: Adopting a healthy diet, losing weight, and giving up smoking help prevent heart attacks, but nothing can guarantee a healthy heart.

Despite all kinds of precautions, some people wind up suffering a heart attack...just as others eat all the wrong foods and never exercise and remain healthy.

Bottom line: There is no way to eliminate your risk of heart disease entirely, even with the most aggressive preventive measures.

This does not mean a healthy lifestyle is of no value. I am a strong advocate of exercise and sensible diets, but primarily from the standpoint of improved self-image. Odds are your lifestyle will have little effect on your overall risk of heart disease.

• Myth: That all hypertensives should avoid salt. Reality: Only about half of all cases of hypertension respond strongly to salt reduction. About 30% respond weakly. In about 20% of all cases, salt intake plays no role at all.

• Myth: That a normal electrocardiogram (EKG) means a healthy heart. Reality: The EKG is an imperfect tool.

Although it's highly effective at pinpointing electrical disturbances in the heart and whether the patient is having or has ever had a heart attack, it reveals little about the health of the coronary arteries (the ones that sometimes clog and cause heart attacks).

Even hearts with severe blockages often appear normal on an EKG. I've had patients who had severe heart attacks within a week after having a normal EKG.

Alternative: The stress test. In this procedure, EKG readings are made during rigorous exercise on a treadmill. Stress tests are more likely to uncover potentially serious heart problems than are standard EKG's. However, even stress tests are not fail-safe.

• Myth: That heart murmurs are always dangerous. Reality: Although heart murmurs can be symptomatic of potentially deadly heart valve defects, they're often harmless.

In fact, a murmur means only that a physician using a stethoscope can hear blood rushing through the heart. This could mean a defective heart valve, but it's more likely the result of some other factor—a thin chest wall, pregnancy or even a highly conditioned heart.

If you are diagnosed with a heart murmur, make sure your doctor explains its nature—and whether or not you need to curtail physical activity.

• Myth: That a normal blood-pressure reading means a healthy heart. Reality: There is no such thing as normal blood pressure. The lower your blood pressure, the lower your risk of stroke and heart disease. So even a very low blood pressure reading is generally a good thing.

But blood pressure readings are notoriously inaccurate. They can be thrown off by many things, including illness, anxiety, medications...even posture.

Doctors should always take several readings before confirming a case of hypertension. In some cases, the physician may ask the patient to wear a 24-hour blood-pressure monitor for a day.

• Myth: That bypass surgery restores the heart to good health. Reality: All it does is restore blood flow to parts of the heart that had been blood-deprived.

Bypass surgery may lower the risk of subsequent heart attacks and increase life expectancy. It can't undo the effects of a previous heart attack. Damaged heart muscle remains damaged.

And unfortunately, the effects of bypass surgery do not last forever. Grafted blood vessels tend to clog back up within five to 10 years after surgery. Second and even third bypass operations are sometimes necessary.

If your physician recommends bypass surgery, find out how many blood vessels are diseased. If there are three or more, odds are that you can benefit from a bypass. For blockages in one or two coronary arteries, however, nonsurgical intervention is usually just as beneficial—and safer and less expensive.

Source: Bruce Charash, MD, assistant professor of medicine, Cornell University Medical College. A frequent lecturer on heart disease, Dr. Charash is the author of *Heart Myths*, Viking Penguin, 375 Hudson St., New York 10014.

How To Protect Yourself From Antibiotics

Antibiotics are broadly viewed as a cure-all. But...antibiotics only fight bacterial infections. They are useless against viral infections...and when taken improperly, they can have troublesome side effects.

Antibiotics work well against these bacterial illnesses:

• Bladder infections and gallbladder infections.

• Pneumonia.

• Strep throats—not all sore throats.

• Skin infections.

Viruses, however, cause most infections. Do not use antibiotics for viral illnesses, including:

• Colds.

• Influenza.

• Intestinal infections and diarrheas of most sorts.

• Bronchitis—in many cases.

Both doctors and patients contribute to the problem of antibiotic overuse.

Patients' errors:

• Self-medicating—using antibiotics prescribed at one time to treat current illnesses. When you treat yourself, you cannot be sure that you have a bacterial illness. But even if you do have a bacterial infection, all antibiotics are not the same. Your doctor knows which drug works best against your specific illness.

• Passing antibiotics around to friends and family. This can cause unexpected harm. Tetracycline, for example, prescribed for an adult, can stain teeth brown when taken by a child.

• Taking antibiotics without a doctor's supervision. All antibiotics, except those applied to the skin, are prescription drugs. It's important that you take the right dose...of the right drug...for the right length of time. Low levels of antibiotics taken too briefly help bacteria grow more resistant.

Where doctors go astray:

Sometimes doctors, without performing tests to confirm that an illness is bacterial, prescribe antibiotics anyway. Many physicians believe that patients want prescriptions and that antibiotics are harmless drugs and may help and can't hurt. But there are potential side effects and, usually, the doctor ought to test with a culture of the patient's blood, urine or throat mucus.

Consequences:

Antibiotic misuse takes a toll on both individuals and society...

- Allergies to antibiotics are common. Penicillin is one of the drugs that most often causes fatal allergic reactions.
- Antibiotics can kill natural bacteria that the body needs. Particularly worrisome: Those living in the intestines.
- Developing a new bacterial illness while already on antibiotics—makes the new problem much harder to treat.
- Antibiotics are expensive. Some new ones cost $2 per pill.
- Bacteria keep growing tougher—as more people take antibiotics. Problems once treatable with penicillin now require stronger drugs that have more side effects—and are more costly, too.

Self-defense:

If your doctor says you need an antibiotic, ask if your illness is definitely bacterial. Also ask if tests can confirm it.

Use antibiotics only with your doctor's supervision. Take them for the length of time prescribed unless you experience any side effects—if you do, tell your doctor. It may be wise to change the prescription. Also important: Take the prescribed dosage.

Recognizing antibiotics:

Most antibiotics (and all the older ones) are derived from natural products of fungi or bacteria. Some new antibiotics are "designer drugs" fashioned in the lab for maximum bacteria-fighting power. Major oral antibiotics:

- Penicillins: Including ampicillin and amoxicillin.
- Sulfa drugs: Sold under names including Bactrim and Septra.
- Erythromycin—and derivatives.
- Tetracycline—and derivatives.
- Cephalosporins: Natural and synthetic relatives of penicillin.
- Quinolones: New drugs—including ciprofloxacin—that fight many bacteria.

Source: Henry S. Fraimow, MD, Department of Infectious Diseases, Thomas Jefferson University, 1025 Walnut St., Philadelphia 19107. Dr. Fraimow researches ways to improve antibiotics and new mechanisms through which antibiotics can attack bacteria.

Vitamin C Danger

Don't chew vitamin C tablets. They damage tooth enamel. Reason: They are highly acidic.

Source: Sheldon Nadler, DDS, 25 W. 54 St., Suite 1D, New York 10019.

The Pill—What We Know & What We Still Don't Know

The birth control pill celebrated its 30th birthday in 1990. While the continuing flow of information shows the Pill to be effective, safe and ultimately beneficial to women's health, misconceptions and fears about oral contraceptives persist...

- Sixty million women worldwide currently use the Pill. Eleven million of them are in the US. Among American women, 82% of those who have used the contraceptives have used the Pill at some time in their lives.
- The Pill is the most popular form of birth control in the US, the choice of 28% of American women at risk of unintended pregnancy. Tubal sterilization is the next most common at 25%, followed by the condom at 13%. Average duration of Pill use is four to five years.
- Using any form of contraception, including the Pill, is safer and healthier than using no birth control. Contraception prevents about 1,500 hospitalizations per 100,000 women annually, and saves 120 to 150 lives per 100,000.
- The Pill protects against ovarian cancer. The risk is lowered by 30% for women who have used the Pill for four years or less, com-

pared with women who have never used it. Among women who have used the Pill for five to 11 years, the risk is decreased by 60%...and by 80% after 12 years of use. The protection is detectable within a few months of starting the Pill, and lasts for at least 15 years after use is stopped.

• The risk of being diagnosed with breast cancer by age 55 is the same for women who have ever used the Pill and never-users, when all age groups are taken together.

Women who first used the Pill at age 25 or later have the same incidence of breast cancer as never-users, regardless of duration of Pill use. But risks and benefits differ for women in different age groups.

Young women: Current or former Pill use is associated with a slightly higher risk of breast cancer for women under 35, when the disease is relatively rare.

Older women: The Pill is associated with a lower risk of breast cancer among women aged 45 to 54, when the disease is much more common.

The statistics: According to a study by the Centers for Disease Control, women aged 25 to 29, who have used the Pill for at least 10 years, will have nine diagnoses of breast cancer per 100,000 per year, compared with six cases for never-users of the same age. Long-term or current users in their 30s and early 40s will have seven to 11 more cases of breast cancer per 100,000 than never-users. But women aged 45 to 54 will have 19 to 21 fewer breast cancers per 100,000.

Cancer perspective: Overall, the net impact of Pill use on cancer is small. By age 55, there will be 500 fewer annual diagnoses per 100,000 of all cancers of the reproductive system for women who have ever used the Pill, compared with never-users.

• Pill use compounds the risk of heart attack, two kinds of stroke and venous blood clots for heavy smokers (those who smoke 25 or more cigarettes a day). The added risk to women under 30 is extremely small, but increases with age. Important: At all ages, the key risk is smoking, not Pill use.

However, the Pill is not recommended for women who have risk factors for cardiovascular problems (diabetes, obesity, high blood pressure, family history and sedentary lifestyle) which are more frequent among older women.

• Pill users have 93 more hospital admissions per 100,000 for gallbladder disease compared with other women at risk of unintended pregnancy. The risk virtually disappears after the first year of use.

• The Pill protects against benign breast disease—the longer the use, the lower the incidence—can prevent hospitalizations for ovarian cysts and reduce by half the incidence of pelvic inflammatory disease (PID), or infection of the upper genital tract.

What we still don't know:

• The exact relationship of the Pill to breast cancer. Hypothesis: Pill users may be screened for breast cancer more often than non-users, resulting in earlier detection. The hormones in the Pill may accelerate the growth of certain kinds of breast cancer, but do not initiate or cause the cancer, an effect that would be consistent with the temporarily increased risk of breast cancer during pregnancy. Women who use the Pill for long periods may have other health or behavioral characteristics that increase the risk of breast cancer.

Example: Deferred childbearing.

• Why the failure rate for the Pill, although relatively low, is still higher than clinicians believe it should be. Problem: Many women fail to use the Pill correctly. (The pregnancy rate in the first year of use is thought to be about 0.1% for women who use the Pill correctly, but it is 6.0% among current users.) Research is examining ways to improve ease and compliance of use.

Source: Jacqueline Darroch Forrest, PhD, vice president for research at the Alan Guttmacher Institute in New York City and co-author of *Preventing Pregnancy, Protecting Health: A New Look at Birth Control Choices in the United States*, The Alan Guttmacher Institute, 111 Fifth Ave., New York 10003.

Antacid Danger

Magnesium-induced diarrhea can affect people who take high-dose supplements or certain over-the-counter magnesium-containing antacids. Diagnosis of magnesium-induced diarrhea requires a stool analysis.

Source: Researcher Kenneth Fine, MD, Baylor University Medical Center, Dallas.

AIDS Defense

Circumcision and AIDS. Uncircumcised men may be up to eight times more susceptible to the AIDS virus during heterosexual intercourse than men who are circumcised. Theories: The intact foreskin may provide the warm, moist environment that the AIDS virus needs in order to survive...the foreskin may be traumatized during intercourse, enabling the virus to enter the body...the foreskin may contain cells that have receptors for the AIDS virus.

Source: Alan Ronald, MD, head of the Department of Internal Medicine, University of Manitoba, Winnipeg, Canada. Dr. Ronald is working in conjunction with Francis Plummer, MD, who is the Canadian head of the Cooperative Sexually Transmitted Disease Research Program in Nairobi, Kenya.

Cancer Test Failure

The usual test for cancer of the colon and rectum fails to find existing cancers 70% of the time. For this reason it may not be useful as a primary screening tool. The test looks for blood in the stool. But early-stage cancers of the colon and rectum do not cause bleeding and may have no overt symptoms at all—making the test a poor method of detecting them.

Source: A National Cancer Institute study of the test's effectiveness on more than 12,000 people, led by David Ahlquist, MD, Mayo Clinic, Rochester, MN.

Pneumonia/Self-Defense

Pneumonia/hospital connection: About two-thirds of all elderly pneumonia patients studied had been hospitalized within the past four years—for one illness or another. Recommended: Because many of these pneumonias are caused by pneumococcal infection, all people older than the age of 65 should have a pneumococcal vaccine following a hospital stay to protect against pneumonia. Advantage: The cost of a vaccination is approximately one-third the cost of hospital care for unvaccinated patients who are readmitted suffering from pneumonia.

Source: David S. Fedson, MD, professor of internal medicine, University of Virginia School of Medicine, Charlottesville.

Alcohol Dangers

High alcohol intake—particularly beer intake—has been shown in a recent study to be associated with an increased risk of rectal cancer among men. Reason: Unknown. Possible explanations: Alcohol may stimulate an increase in bile acids, which now seem to be involved in both colon and rectal cancers ...beer contains a high level of nitrosamine, a known carcinogen...ethanol has been linked to rapid cell growth in the rectum. At highest risk: Men who drink two or three beers per day—or men who drink a total of four alcoholic drinks per day. This group was shown to have an 85% increased risk of rectal cancer. (In women, the association between alcohol and rectal cancer could not be confirmed because those women studied did not drink as heavily as the men.) Note: Approximately four percent of all new cancers in the United States are rectal cancers.

Source: Jo L. Freudenheim, PhD, assistant professor of social and preventive medicine, State University of New York, Buffalo.

Dangers Of Herbal Teas

Some types may be bad for your health. Comfrey tea has been implicated in liver disease...lobelia can cause vomiting, breathing problems and convulsions...sassafras causes cancer in rats when taken in large amounts.

Source: *FDA Consumer*, US Superintendent of Documents, Washington, DC 20402.

Coffee Dangers

Is coffee really all that dangerous? Here's what our expert told us...

Although coffee has no nutritive value, its use is so common that no one thinks of it as what is really is—a recreational drug.

Problem: Coffee contains several potent pharmacological agents categorized as methylxanthines—caffeine is one of them. Coffee plants use these as natural pesticides. Scary: Some insects that eat coffee beans die immediately.

Because we're bigger than insects, the effects on people are less noticeable...but may, nevertheless, be harmful in the long run.

Coffee and the heart:

Large-scale studies on coffee's effect on the heart contradict each other. Some conclude that coffee is dangerous...others find it safe. Common sense suggests that it is a hazard. Reason: Coffee activates our adrenergic system—the fight-or-flight mechanism that produces adrenaline.

In addition to making us alert—usually the effect we seek—this adrenaline accelerates our heart rate and constricts the blood vessels, often for hours.

Result: If you drink four cups of coffee each day, your heart will beat thousands of extra times. And to overcome the constriction of the blood vessels in the periphery, it will beat harder, raising your blood pressure.

These extra, harder beats strain the heart and increase the risk of heart disease and heart attack.

In addition, coffee can provoke cardiac arrhythmia in people prone to this problem. And if a person has another factor that could cause arrhythmia, that factor will be compounded by caffeine. Result: Caffeine greatly increases the person's risk of developing cardiovascular problems.

More trouble: Because coffee is so bitter, many people counter that taste by adding sugar. This creates a host of additional problems for the cardiovascular and other systems.

Other negative effects:

In addition to causing heart problems, coffee can...

- Increase cholesterol levels.
- Magnify the effects of stress on the cardiovascular system.
- Cause ulcers and prevent ulcers from healing.
- Provoke or exacerbate anxiety disorders.
- Induce fibrocystic breast disease—a benign condition that scares many women by creating lumps in the breast.
- Generate migraines.
- Increase the risk of stroke. This risk has shown to be even greater when caffeine is consumed in combination with phenylpropanolamine, a drug found in nasal decongestants and over-the-counter diet preparations—many of which also contain caffeine.

How to give up coffee:

If you're addicted to coffee, don't stop cold turkey. This could make you extremely irritable...perhaps even cause a migraine headache. And such an unpleasant experience would make it less likely that you'd try to quit again, if your first attempt fails.

Better: Decrease consumption by a quarter cup to a half cup every few days. If you start getting headaches, increase your dose slightly, and then start decreasing it again—slowly.

Switching to tea or decaffeinated coffee is not the answer. Reason: Although decaffeination removes caffeine from the beverage, several other methylxanthines are still present. These naturally occurring pesticides can be found in decaffeinated coffee, decaffeinated teas, black tea, colas and chocolate.

Although it is reasonable to use decaf and these other beverages as a transition from drinking coffee with caffeine to no coffee, your mental and physical health can be greatly improved by eliminating the consumption of these beverages as much as possible.

Only the fact that these beverages are so widely consumed has made us lose sight of just how dependent we are on drugs.

Source: Richard M. Carlton, MD, a psychiatrist who has discovered that many psychological as well as physical problems can be solved through proper nutrition. He maintains a private practice at 333 W. 57 St., New York 10019.

Water Mix-Up

Any water except distilled water or purified water can be labeled mineral water in most states because all water naturally contains minerals. Mineral count: The levels in bottled water are too low to affect most diets. Purity: Some bottled water is simply municipal tap water that has been filtered.

Source: *Good Housekeeping*, 959 Eighth Ave., New York 10019.

Beware Of Using Paper Cups

Paper cups are more harmful to the environment than plastic foam cups (Styrofoam), contrary to popular belief. Study: The chemicals and energy used in making paper cups and the emissions from burning or burying them afterward have a more harmful impact on the environment than making and disposing of plastic foam cups. Making paper cups uses 12 times more steam and 36 times more electricity than making foam cups.

Source: Martin B. Hocking, chemistry professor at University of Victoria, British Columbia, quoted in *The Wall Street Journal*.

Understanding Food Labels

Low-calorie foods can contain no more than 40 calories per serving and 0.4 calories per gram...reduced-calorie foods must contain at least one-third fewer calories than a similar food in which the calories are not reduced...enriched foods have nutrients added to replace what was lost during processing...fortified foods contain added nutrients that are not normally present in the food.

Source: *Dr. Jean Mayer's Diet & Nutrition Guide*, Pharos Books, 200 Park Ave., New York 10166.

Lowering Cholesterol

Lower cholesterol by adding fiber supplements to your diet—but they must be the right type of fiber. Of the three common fiber supplements, only psyllium significantly lowers LDL (bad) cholesterol. Calcium polycarbophil and methylcellulose don't lower LDL cholesterol significantly...in fact, they may actually increase it.

Source: Study led by James Anderson, MD, University of Kentucky and Veterans' Administration Medical Center, reported in *The Medical Post*, 777 Bay St., Toronto, Ontario M5W 1A7.

Allergy Trap

Milk allergy alert. Children allergic to cow's milk might be ingesting small amounts of it by eating packaged foods—even when the food is labeled "nondairy." About 2½% of children have milk allergies. Symptoms include: Stomachaches, wheezing, hives and vomiting. Children with this allergy sometimes require hospitalization. Suspect foods: "Nondairy" frozen desserts...tuna fish...bologna...hot dogs. Researchers found that the frozen desserts had been processed in dairy-processing plants...and meats containing sodium caseinate, a milk protein, did not always have it listed on the label. Helpful: Have your children's foods tested, even if labeled "nondairy," when allergic reactions occur.

Source: Hugh A. Sampson, MD, Division of Pediatric Allergy/Immunology, Johns Hopkins University School of Medicine and Johns Hopkins Hospital, Baltimore.

Health And Eating Out Self-Defense

Avoid breaded or fried foods...chicken Kiev, southern fried chicken and Wiener schnitzel. Avoid foods in buttery sauces.

Order fish broiled with lemon instead of butter. For seafood and vegetables, eat those that are baked in foil, grilled, broiled, steamed or en brochette.

If you want steak, limit yourself to a four- or six-ounce serving—about the size of your palm.

Order dishes that have been marinated—they offer more flavor and need less oil or butter.

• Italian food. Avoid pastas with cream sauces, sausages and fatty cheeses, including Gorgonzola and fontina. Also avoid parmigiana dishes, fettucine Alfredo, spaghetti carbonara and dishes in béchamel (white sauce).

• Chinese food. Oriental stir fry is cooked with a minimum of oil, meats are used sparingly and they contain lots of vegetables. Avoid Peking duck, egg rolls, spring rolls, ribs, fried rice and deep-fried dishes.

• Thai and Vietnamese food. Avoid fried dishes.

• Japanese food. Most dishes are extremely low-fat. Exceptions: Tempura and fried, breaded pork.

• Mexican food. Avoid sour cream, cheddar or Jack cheese and fried tortillas. Use guacamole sparingly.

• Indian food. Avoid foods made with ghee (clarified butter) and layered breads, including paratha. Best: Tandoori chicken.

• French food. Low-fat dining is very difficult in a French restaurant. Best: Food cooked *en papillote*—wrapped in a parchment or foil case that preserves all the flavors and juices.

• Fast food. Between 40% and 50% of the calories in most fast foods come from fat. Much fast-food fish and chicken contains more fat than a hamburger.

• Take-out food. The cheese used in pizza contains a lot of fat. Blot it with a paper towel. With barbecued chicken, remove the skin.

• Salad bars. The biggest problem is the dressing. Use a small amount of those labeled *lite*. And avoid adding bacon bits, buttered croutons and other high-fat ingredients.

Plastic Surgery Problems

Whether it's an ordinary nose job or the removal of a rib to achieve a smaller waistline, cosmetic surgery performed by a qualified surgeon is usually safe and effective.

As with any medical procedure, however, cosmetic surgery occasionally results in complications in a small portion of all procedures. And when complications occur, the results can be devastating.

Cosmetic surgery risks:

• Persistent infection. This is the most common complication—and usually the easiest to correct. Antibiotics are effective in most cases, although implants sometimes have to be removed.

Exception: Cartilage infections, especially those that follow a nose job (rhinoplasty), rarely may persist for a year or longer even with aggressive antibiotic treatment...and they can destroy the nose's shape.

Self-defense: Choose a qualified surgeon—one who has performed the same procedure dozens of times.

• Silicone granulomas. Silicone gel implants are generally safe, although some experts contend that in the case of breast augmentation, they make mammography more difficult.

When large amounts of liquid silicone are injected into the breasts or other parts of the body, however, silicone granulomas sometimes develop. These lumpy, oozing lesions distort the shape of the surrounding skin...and they sometimes progress to open, draining wounds.

Self-defense: Injected silicone should be used only for small, superficial defects—not large ones.

• Nubbin nose. Nose jobs involving excessive cartilage removal can cause big trouble later in life. As the patient ages, the skin thins, and the nose appears to shrink—sometimes to little more than a tiny nubbin.

In extreme cases, a nubbin nose causes not only acute embarrassment, but also breathing difficulties. The only way to correct the problem is to transplant cartilage taken from elsewhere in the body.

Self-defense: The less tissue removed during any cosmetic surgery, the safer.

• Lumpy skin. Surgeons performing liposuction must wield the cannula (fat-sucking instrument) very deftly, since uneven removal of fat results in lumpy or rippled skin. These defects are difficult or impossible to fix, even with additional liposuction or fat transplantation.

In very rare cases, fat cells liberated during liposuction cut off the supply of blood to the heart or brain. Although rare, some fat embolisms are fatal.

Also in rare cases, liposuction can result in inadvertent damage to the spleen or other internal organs. A ruptured spleen usually necessitates emergency surgery to control bleeding.

Self-defense: Use an experienced surgeon. Check on the doctor's reputation, enlist word-of-mouth recommendations, and directly ask the doctor questions about his/her background.

• Barbie Doll hair. Hair transplantation is safe and effective, but the process takes months or even years to complete. Impatient patients who fail to see it through to the end often wind up with obvious plugs of hair arrayed in regular rows across the scalp.

Self-defense: Start hair transplants only if you intend to see them through.

• Distorted eyes. Surgeons performing eye tucks (blepharoplasties) must be careful to remove just the right amount of tissue around the eyes. Otherwise, the patient may be left with eyes that seem to turn downward or outward, or with an exposed mucous membrane around the eyes.

Sometimes the eyelids are stretched so tight by surgery that the eyes cannot fully close. Botched eye jobs can also result in acute glaucoma...even blindness.

Self-defense: Choose a highly experienced surgeon.

• Lopsided face. In rare instances, facelifts damage the facial nerve. Result: Diminished muscle tone or even partial paralysis. The patient may develop a crooked smile, sagging cheeks or may have difficulty blinking.

Similarly, implants in the chin, cheeks and other parts of the face must be firmly attached to the bone, or over time they may become mobile. More than an annoyance, mobile facial implants can result in a lopsided appearance.

Self-defense: Make sure the surgeon plans the implants so that they are placed on bone.

• Rashes and redness. Collagen used to fill in acne scars and other skin defects can cause severe rashes and persistent redness. Theoretically, collagen injected directly into a blood vessel rather than just under the skin could interrupt the flow of blood to an eye—resulting in blindness.

Self-defense: The doctor should make sure the patient is not allergic to collagen before large quantities are injected. This can be done by test injections, introducing a small amount of collagen into the body in an inconspicuous place.

• Bad nose job. The problem of rhinoplasty is that the removal of too much bone or cartilage can result in the collapse of the tip of the nose, which impairs breathing and creates an artificial-looking nose.

Self-defense: The patient must emphasize that they want a natural-looking nose with a minimal amount of bone and cartilage removed. An experienced surgeon would already be aware of this.

• Too-tight face lift. This usually occurs on repeat face lifts and strictly skin lifts. Newer face lifts include both deeper layers and skin and give a more natural look.

Self-defense: Ask what technique the surgeon uses and how much experience he/she has with the procedure. Ask to see other patients...or their photographs.

Source: Linton A. Whitaker, MD, chief of the Division of Plastic Surgery, the Hospital of the University of Pennsylvania, and professor of surgery, University of Pennsylvania School of Medicine. Dr. Whitaker specializes in facial surgery.

How To Protect Kids From Burns

Each year, over 200,000 children in the US are burned. Most of these burns could be prevented. We all know that children should be kept away from ovens, irons and other hot appliances. But kids are also at risk from...

• Electrical devices. A big problem for kids at the chew-everything stage. Be especially careful of:

Extension cords. Children may find an unused extension cord that's plugged in and stick the free end in their mouths or bite the cord.

Electrical sockets. Burns—and sometimes electrocutions—are caused by poking metal objects into unprotected sockets.

The small plastic plugs commonly used to top these sockets are choking hazards. Better: Special plates that cover the outlets until an adult slides open an access door. Cost: About $3 at child-safety specialty stores and at larger hardware stores.*

• Gasoline. Every gallon has the explosive power of 14 sticks of dynamite. At temperatures above –45°F, gasoline produces poisonous, flammable vapors.

Store gasoline out of children's reach, in tightly sealed containers. They should be filled no more than three-quarters full. Reason: Gasoline expands as it warms.

• Hot surfaces outdoors: Beyond the obvious dangers—barbecue grills, etc.—lie sun-baked pavements, burning hot sand, sun-heated metal playground equipment and other hazards. Problem: A child's skin is much more sensitive than an adult's.

Especially dangerous: Fireworks. Sparklers can reach temperatures above 800°F.

• Hot water. Small children are especially sensitive to scalds because their skin is so tender and their reactions are slower than an adult's. Most scaldings are caused by hot-water heaters set above 140°F. At that temperature, it takes water less than five seconds to cause a serious burn.

Safer temperature settings for water heaters: Lower than 130°F—125°F is better and will provide sufficient hot water for household conveniences. At 130° it takes less than 30 seconds to get badly burned. At 125°, it takes less than 90 seconds to two minutes.

• Microwave ovens. To decide if a child is old enough to use a microwave, consider:

Height. If the child's face is at or below oven level, he is too short to use it safely.

Maturity. The child must be old enough to read and understand directions.

Source: Matt Maley, The Shriner's Burn Institute. He is the author of *Burn Prevention Tips*. For a free single copy, write to The Shriner's Burn Institute, 202 Goodman St., Cincinnati 45219.

*Recommended: Plates made by We Care Incorporated, 605-224-5304.

Dubious Dentistry: How To Protect Yourself

The incidence of tooth decay has fallen dramatically in recent years, thanks largely to the fluoridation of the nation's water supplies. That's great news for families. But many dentists, faced with fewer cavities to fill, are looking elsewhere for income...and, too often, even well-meaning practitioners have begun pushing dental care that is unnecessary, expensive or downright fraudulent. Inappropriate dental care now costs Americans more than $1 billion a year.

Good news: A little of the right knowledge is all that's required to protect your family's health and pocketbook from inappropriate dental care. Suspect treatments:

• Alternate root canal therapy. Standard root canal surgery involves drilling out diseased root tissue and replacing it with an inert filler material—usually gutta-percha. But as many as 30,000 dentists in the US and Canada rely instead on a faster, cheaper, but unsafe method, in which the root is replaced not with gutta-percha but with a chemically unstable formaldehyde paste.

Danger: That paste sometimes seeps into the tissue below the tooth root, resulting in pain and disfigurement and in some cases necessitating corrective surgery. In one case, a Florida woman endured 40 additional dental procedures and the removal of part of her jawbone after bungled root-canal work.

Self-protection: If you need a root canal, find a dentist or endodontist with considerable experience...and make sure he uses the standard method.

• Alternate gum disease treatment. Standard treatment for advanced periodontal disease (pyorrhea) usually involves gum surgery. Since the late 1970s, however, some dentists have relied instead on a nonsurgical technique, in which the gums are examined under a microscope and then cleaned with a paste of salt, baking soda and peroxide. Many patients prefer it because it's nonsurgical—and because it costs a third of what conventional surgery costs.

Problem: There is no evidence to suggest that it is effective. For severe periodontal disease, stick to surgery.

• Inappropriate TMJ therapy. Temporomandibular joint (TMJ) disease—a legitimate ailment whose symptoms include facial pain and a stiff jaw—usually responds to simple treatments including moist heat, jaw exercise, over-the-counter anti-inflammatory drugs and a temporary soft diet. But some unscrupulous dentists seem to diagnose TMJ at every turn...and to treat it they prescribe treatments that are expensive, bizarre and often harmful.

Example: The MORA (Mandibular Orthopedic Repositioning Appliance), a plastic mouthpiece that's worn continuously for many months. It can shift the position of the teeth so markedly that patients are often forced to wear braces or have their teeth crowned just to eat and speak normally again.

If you experience chronic facial pain, consult a dentist to rule out tumors, cysts and other serious problems—then try moist heat and other simple techniques. If pain persists, you may need a neurologist rather than a dentist. Some dentists work with neurologists and other pain specialists who would also be appropriate for patients whose pain does not respond to simple reversible therapies. Note: Some plastic appliances are appropriate for some dental conditions. If your dentist prescribes one, make sure it covers all the teeth, and that it can be removed for eating and sleeping.

• Improper implants. When properly inserted, dental implants are safe and effective. But many dentists lack the training to perform implants successfully, in some cases getting their "expertise" from a single one-hour "video course."

Common problem: Poorly fitted implants fail to attach firmly to underlying bone, resulting in loose or painful implants. To make sure implants are appropriate for your case, and to make sure the job is done well, seek out a periodontist, oral surgeon or dentist who has completed a legitimate course (they can last several months)...and who has completed at least 50 implant procedures. Also, insist upon a Brannemark or Core-Vent implant or some other implant approved by the American Dental Association.

• Inappropriate bonding and bleaching. Bonding is terrific for improving a patient's appearance. But it is not a panacea. The teeth to be bonded should be healthy, with good gum and bone support. Bonding should not be used as a treatment for loose teeth (a symptom of periodontal disease).

Bleaching done in the dentist's office is usually safe and effective. However, unsupervised bleaching done in the patient's home has not been proven safe and thus should be avoided.

In many cases in which a dentist uses bleaching, the use of porcelain laminates would be more appropriate.

• Mercury toxicity. All major health organizations recognize the safety of silver/mercury amalgam fillings, but some dentists are recommending that these fillings be removed and replaced with either plastic, porcelain or gold—a very profitable recommendation for these dentists.

If your dentist recommends removing your silver fillings because of the mercury in them, find another dentist. Reason: This is an unscientific position that can lead to extensive, unnecessary dentistry.

Source: John E. Dodes, DDS, president of the New York State chapter of the National Council Against Health Fraud and a member of the New York State Health Department Fraud Advisory Council. Dr. Dodes, who practices dentistry in Woodhaven, New York, is the author of *Dubious Dental Care*, a newly published report on dental fraud. For a copy, send $3.85 to the American Council on Science and Health, 1995 Broadway, 16th floor, New York 10023.

Quit-Smoking Success Rates

Success rates for the various methods used by smokers to quit smoking...how to invest your time and energy.

Method	Success Rate
Nicotine gum plus counseling	47%
Group therapy/quit clinics	28%
Aversive behavior therapy	21%
Acupuncture	15%–20%
Hypnosis	15%–20%
Self-help brochures	15%–20%
Nicotine gum alone	8%–20%
Doctor's advice	5%
Self-determination alone	3%–5%

Source: Data from Public Citizen Health Research Group, reported in *Executive Female*, 1041 Third Ave., New York.

Safer Telephone Use

Don't use telephones while you're near water—doing dishes, bathing, etc. If the phone gets wet, it can give you—and the person you're speaking to—an electrical shock. Also: Avoid using the phone during an electrical storm—lightning can travel through phone lines.

Source: *Rodale's Complete Home Products Manual*, Rodale Press, 33 E. Minor St., Emmaus, PA 18098.

Questionable Medicines

For better or worse, Western medicine relies heavily on pharmacological treatment for ailments great and small. But all drugs have the potential to cause adverse reactions...any drug can be misused...and, because the human body is a complicated network of interrelated systems (circulatory, respiratory, nervous, digestive, etc.), all drugs can provoke responses in the body beyond what they are designed to do. These responses are known as side effects.

While most of the medications on the market today are quite safe and effective, there are many drugs—several among the most commonly prescribed drugs in the United States—that can be classified as questionable. What makes a drug questionable?

A drug is questionable if...

• It is ineffective in treating the condition it is supposed to treat.

• It can have harmful side effects...and safer alternatives exist.

• It is often overprescribed or inadequately monitored by doctors, misused or abused by patients.

The most questionable drugs in the US:

• Ulcer drugs (Zantac, Tagamet). These best-selling drugs work great—if you have an ulcer.

Problem: They are usually prescribed in large doses. But most ulcer patients fare very well after a few months on half the dosage, and some can stop taking the drug after two months—once the ulcer quiets down. If the ulcer recurs (and many won't), the drug can be resumed.

Worse problem: These drugs are widely prescribed to people with mild heartburn, indigestion or other vague, poorly defined abdominal pain not due to an ulcer. These conditions are often "self-limiting." They get better by themselves in a few days. This leads many patients to credit their recovery to whatever medication they are using. But 40% of these patients also get better when given a placebo. Better: Avoid pepperoni pizza and beer.

• Arthritis drugs (Indocin, Feldene, Motrin). The nonsteroidal anti-inflammatory drugs that are usually prescribed for arthritis do work to diminish pain and inflammation.

Problem: They are often prescribed indiscriminately when other alternatives exist. They can be costly and they can have dangerous side effects, such as gastrointestinal bleeding and kidney damage.

Example: Feldene has caused numerous deaths from internal bleeding, especially in older adults.

Better: Coated aspirin works well. And a recent study published in the *New England Journal of Medicine*, found that acetaminophen (Tylenol) is just as effective for many arthritis patients.

Key: It must be used regularly to provide

consistent relief, control symptoms and prevent flare-ups.

Caution: Some physicians may have a bias against older or over-the-counter drugs. Look for a doctor who will work with you to find the best dosage levels for you.

• Cholesterol-lowering drugs (Mevacor, Colestid, Lopid, Questran). These relatively new drugs are helpful for patients with extremely high cholesterol levels, especially in combination with a low-fat diet, regular exercise and weight control. But studies have shown many patients do well with diet and exercise alone.

Problems: The drugs are very expensive and can cause side effects, such as gastrointestinal problems. And the effects of their long-term use are still unknown.

Worse: Due to recent "cholesterol hysteria," these cholesterol-lowering drugs are being widely prescribed to people whose cholesterol levels are not high enough to warrant drug treatment, and for whom they are ineffective. They can even be counterproductive, if people who believe they are controlling their cholesterol by taking a pill avoid diet and exercise.

Many patients also respond well to supplemental niacin (Vitamin B_3), although supplemental niacin, too, can have side effects ranging from skin flushes to liver damage.

• Pain control (Darvon, Darvocet). The popularity of Darvon is mystifying, since it is known among physicians to be a "bad drug"—having overdose potential and also being potentially habit-forming.

Problems: It is no more effective than aspirin or Tylenol and it can be habit-forming. Additionally, the risk of overdose is greater and it costs more.

• Alzheimer's drugs (Hydergine, Pavabid, Vasodilan). These drugs have been prescribed as cerebral vasodilators, which allegedly open the arteries to improve blood flow to the brain and improve memory.

Problem: They don't do anything at all. One study found that Alzheimer's patients treated with Hydergine—the 11th-most-prescribed drug in the world—deteriorated faster than those given placebos.

Note: Vasodilan and Pavabid are also completely ineffective in treating vascular problems in the legs. Pavabid has been of limited benefit to some people when used to treat impotence.

• Insomnia and anxiety drugs (Valium, Xanax, Librium, Halcion, others). While tranquilizing drugs work well to relieve severe anxiety, they are often prescribed for too long a period of time and they are used excessively to treat insomnia.

Problems: These insomnia and antianxiety drugs are addictive, they become ineffective with long-term use (repetitive use merely prevents withdrawal symptoms) and their side effects can include drowsiness, mental confusion and rebound sleeplessness.

Better for insomnia: Go to bed at the same time every night, take a walk after dinner, don't drink coffee at night and, if you're over 60, avoid napping during the day. If all else fails, visit a sleep disorder clinic.

Caution: Some doctors are reluctant to recommend nondrug solutions to insomnia—and some patients demand medication.

• Depression (Prozac). Prozac clearly works for many patients with severe clinical depression.

Problem: Due to a combination of fashion fad and excessive marketing, it is being used far more widely than is prudent with a new drug.

Trap: It is being prescribed, unmonitored, for patients with mild symptoms.

While there is some concern about scattered reports of patients who became violent while taking Prozac, no conclusions have been reached, particularly since physicians tend to try new drugs on patients when illness has been hard to control.

Recommended: Rather than being used as a drug of first choice, Prozac should be reserved for patients with severe symptoms who don't respond to or cannot tolerate other antidepressants. Patients taking Prozac should be monitored closely.

• Blood pressure drugs. This is an area in which medication is underused.

Problem: Physicians are often reluctant to treat hypertension in the elderly. However, a recent study has shown pharmacological treatment of high blood pressure in the elderly to be safe, effective and very desirable.

Dosages: As people age, their sensitivity to certain drugs increases, their livers become less able to metabolize drugs, they generally have more body fat in which drugs can accumulate and their kidneys are less efficient at clearing drugs from the system.

In addition, they are more likely than younger people to use one or more prescription medications. Therefore, older adults are more likely to have an adverse reaction to a drug or combination of drugs.

Caution: Recommended dosages, even on drugs commonly used by the elderly, are often calculated too high. Whatever your age, ask your doctor to monitor your medications slowly. Aim: Fewer drugs at lower dosages.

Source: Jerry Avorn, MD, an internist and geriatrician. Dr. Avorn is associate professor of medicine and director of the Program for the Analysis of Clinical Strategies, Harvard Medical School, Boston, MA.

Leukemia Link

Electric blanket warning. Childhood leukemia risk increased 70% in children who used an electric blanket or whose mothers used an electric blanket during pregnancy. Leukemia risk did not increase from exposure to any other electric appliance studied (heating pad, heated water bed, television, portable heaters, bedside electric clock). Recommended: Although it's not certain that electric blanket use actually causes leukemia, if you want to warm up your bed with an electric blanket, avoid exposure by turning off the blanket before you get in.

Source: David Savitz, PhD, associate professor, Department of Epidemiology, University of North Carolina, Chapel Hill.

Simple Secret Of Weight Control

Last year Americans spent $32 billion on diet books, products and programs—and every cent of that vast expenditure was wasted. Dieting simply doesn't work. Dramatic, lasting weight loss—like that touted by the many weight-loss programs*—is essentially mythical.

Reality: 98% of these "successful" dieters regain all the lost weight within five years... and 33%–73% wind up with metabolic changes that cause them to grow even fatter.

Typical scenario: A woman's weight is stable at 150 pounds on a diet of 2,500 calories a day. She goes on a 1,500-calorie-a-day diet until she loses 10 pounds. When she returns to 2,500 calories a day, her body continues to burn calories at the reduced—1,500-calories-a-day—rate. Result: She regains all the lost weight—and probably more.

This woman feels like a failure, but in truth it's the diet that has failed. Even if she holds her post-diet weight gain to the original 10 pounds, she is worse off than she was before dieting.

Reason: Although her weight has not changed, the percentage of her body composed of fat is now significantly higher, because the slight amount of muscle tissue inevitably lost while dieting is usually replaced in part by new fat cells. Each time a weight loss/weight gain cycle recurs, this increase in fat cells makes getting back to the desired weight harder.

Recent evidence has found that this "yo-yo" dieting is more harmful to a person's health than being consistently overweight.

Weight-control secret:

The key to weight control—known by 4.5 billion instinctive eaters—is to eat only when you're hungry, and not to eat when you're not hungry. That sounds simplistic, but it is the only surefire technique for controlling weight.

Dieting doesn't work because it forces people to reverse the process by which instinctive eaters avoid weight gain—that is, eat little or nothing even when they're famished and then stuff themselves when they really aren't hungry. Dieters spend so much time thinking about eating that they fail to heed the

*Fourteen commercial weight-loss programs are currently under investigation by the Federal Trade Commission for possible fraud.

hunger/satiety signals that are the crux of weight control.

Obesity myths:

Before you can become an instinctive eater, you must shed common misconceptions about obesity. Many believe that fat people are fat because some psychological defect caused them to overeat, or because they lack willpower or simply because they're gluttonous.

Fat people themselves get so much criticism that they too begin to believe these misconceptions.

Reality: Obesity is often hereditary. If one or both of your parents are fat, odds are that you too will be heavy—and there isn't a great deal you can do about it.

Self-defense: Naturally heavy people must realize that while they might want a model's body, they do not need such a body. They can be happy and successful with the body they have. And, contrary to what most people believe, there are no health reasons to lose weight—so long as their weight remains stable.

Exception: People who are extremely overweight—those more than 50% above their ideal body weight—should see a doctor about how they can control weight gain.

Most overweight people whose weight is constant have no more health problems than thin people. It's when they start starving themselves that they get into trouble. Yo-yo dieters are at increased risk for diabetes, heart disease and other serious ailments. Someone whose weight stays a constant 190 pounds faces fewer health risks than a person whose weigh fluctuates between 120 and 160.

Most people have a sense of how much they should weigh, but this perception is often far off the mark. Problem: They confuse ideal and optimal weight.

- Ideal weight is that which each of us, for reasons of vanity, would like to reach. Unfortunately, many of us would have to literally starve ourselves to reach this weight...and once we reached it, we would probably be unhealthy and miserable.
- Optimal weight is that at which our bodies feel and function best. For a few fortunate people, ideal weigh coincides with optimal weight. For many, optimal weight is several pounds above ideal weight.

Principles of instinctive eating:

Learning to eat instinctively does not guarantee that you will reach your ideal weight. But it does ensure that you will reach your optimal weight, and that is more than good enough.

Illustration: One woman who attended one of my seminars had ballooned from 110 pounds to more than 200 pounds. She learned the principles of instinctive eating but for the following six months remained as heavy as ever. Then, almost imperceptibly at first, her body began to shrink. Now, several years later, she is down to a size 14. She may never again reach her ideal size four, but she has stabilized her weight at an acceptable level. More important, her self-disgust at being overweight has ended.

To eat instinctively...

- Learn to recognize hunger. Different people feel hunger differently—some people feel a gnawing sensation in the stomach...some get a feeling of tension in their chest...others get a headache or feel weak.

Unfortunately, many signals taken to be signs of hunger are really symptomatic of illness, fatigue, sadness, nervousness or some other condition. To eat instinctively, you must learn to tell the difference.

Self-test: If you think you feel hungry but are unsure, have a bite to eat. Wait several minutes. If the sensation is somewhat alleviated, you truly were hungry. If the sensation persists, however, you were not. Do not continue eating if not hungry. Instead, go for a walk, call a friend, take a nap or do something else not involving food.

At first, it may be difficult to tell hunger from other sensations. Eventually, the process will become automatic.

- Determine what you're hungry for. The body is a machine, and, like any machine, it requires different kinds of maintenance (food) at different times. Hunger is the body's way of requesting fuel. To make sure you feed your body the right fuel, run through a mental checklist.

Protocol: Instead of grabbing the first thing

that looks appetizing, break foods down into their specific attributes.

• Temperature—do you want something hot, cold or room temperature?

• Taste—do you want something sweet, sour, bitter or salty?

• Texture—do you want something smooth, crunchy, chewy or fibrous?

In many cases, you will be just as satisfied by a low-calorie, nutritious food as by a calorie-dense, nutrient-poor food. This checklist cannot reduce how much you eat or how often, but it can reduce your caloric intake and make your diet more wholesome.

Example: A hungry overeater heads to the freezer for ice cream. But after running through the food-attribute checklist, she finds that she really craves not cream, but sweetness. So instead of a bowl of Rocky Road, she enjoys a ripe pear—thus providing her body with nutritious food and saving herself several hundred calories.

• Eat sitting down. Eating while standing or on the run not only encourages you to eat more often, but also makes it more difficult to tell how much you are eating. Pick one spot in your home and always eat your meals there. Don't eat in bed, while watching television, while talking on the phone or while involved in any other activity.

• Eat slowly. After the first bite of food, it may take 20 minutes or so for the body to "realize" that it is no longer hungry. Unfortunately, the average American meal is consumed in under seven minutes. By the time we feel full, we've already consumed hundreds of calories more than we needed or even wanted.

Helpful: Never rush your meal. To indulge your sense of anticipation, look at your food before eating. Chew thoroughly. If you have trouble pacing yourself, make it a point to chew with empty hands—place your knife and fork on the table while you chew and swallow. Eating slowly sounds easy, but for many people it is the single most challenging aspect of instinctive eating.

• Learn to recognize satiety. Just as instinctive eaters know how to tell when they're hungry, they're also able to recognize when they are full. Again, the process depends upon paying close attention to the signals your body gives you.

Procedure: After each mouthful of food, pause briefly to ask yourself if you are still hungry. If so, continue eating. But if you no longer feel hungry, stop eating at once. Do not let yourself eat out of habit. Do not let yourself be pressured into eating for social reasons.

• Don't be tyrannized by numbers. Many overweight people pay such close attention to their weight, calorie counts and other numerical measures of diet that they lose sight of the natural hunger/satiety mechanism.

Helpful: Get rid of your scales, listen to your body and forget about calorie counts.

• Don't accept criticism of your body. Few of us tolerate attacks on our religion, ethnic heritage, profession, etc. Why put up with comments like, *You could stand to lose a few pounds?* Accepting such criticism not only makes obese people feel bad, it engenders a sense of hopelessness that reinforces and encourages overeating.

Better way: Love yourself at your current weight, even if that weight is well above your optimal weight. If someone puts you down for your weight, just ignore him.

Source: Steven C. Strauss, MD, a board-certified internist practicing in New York City and author of *The Body-Signal Secret*, Rodale Press, 33 E. Minor St., Emmaus, PA 18098. Dr. Strauss's *Lighten Up* seminars, given in New York City and Washington, DC, teach participants to control their weight permanently without dieting.

How To Get A Good Night's Sleep

Worrying about insomnia is the most common cause of insomnia. That excessive concern about sleeping habits can actually create problems. People who have had difficulty falling asleep go to bed anxious about whether they'll have trouble falling asleep again, and worrying about what will happen the next day if they don't get enough sleep.

Result: It's the anxiety about not getting to sleep that keeps them awake.

Other people may carry out complicated

sleep rituals involving relaxation tapes or special mental or physical exercises, not realizing that most of these efforts are counterproductive. Counting all those sheep is really a mental stimulus, not a relaxation technique!

The stress and anxiety that people experience when they try so hard to fall asleep are the very factors that tire them out the next day.

When they get up in the morning after a restless night, they're exhausted from the struggle to fall asleep (rather than the lack of sleep itself). But they actually may be getting enough sleep.

Trap: Their anxiety increases and causes them to struggle even harder the next night, creating a vicious cycle of anxiety and insomnia.

Break the circle: You can probably function better than you think with less sleep than you're accustomed to getting. Just knowing this can help to turn down your anxiety about getting "enough" sleep.

Working on your night moves:

Our sleep disorders experts tell patients to reduce their active efforts to fall asleep at night. Cut out the tapes, relaxation exercises, etc. Simply accept the fact that the body will naturally seek the amount of sleep it needs, and that your body will sleep when it's ready to.

Don't be a slave to the clock. People get used to the idea that 10 o'clock is bedtime and think they must be in bed by 10 p.m. to get the amount of sleep needed.

Result: A lot of people are forcing themselves to get into bed before they're really ready to sleep. Their "biological clock" has not yet come around to the time at which the body is ready to sleep, so they lie in bed awake, which increases their anxiety about insomnia and makes it even harder to get to sleep.

What can you do while you're waiting for your body to get tired? Stay up? Read in bed? The issue of whether or not to read in bed is actually a subject of much debate among experts.

One theory: People who read in bed excessively acquire an association between the bed and wakefulness rather than sleep.

Alternative: Some people who get drowsy reading on the couch wake themselves up when moving to the bedroom.

Bottom line: It's an individual issue. If you can get into bed and read for just a few minutes, and that's all it takes to make you sleepy, keep your book on the night table. But reading in bed for hours and hours is not a good idea. It's essential to have your brain associate the bed with sleep, not with activity.

Another important factor in establishing and maintaining healthy sleep habits is to make sure you carry out all your normal activities the day after a night of suboptimal sleep.

Many people will say things like, I slept badly last night, so I'm not going to exercise today, or I'm going to cancel this appointment, and make changes in their normal lifestyle.

Trap: The changes will create anxiety about not sleeping the next night. (Look at all the terrible things that are happening in my life because I'm not sleeping.) Most of these last-minute changes are not really necessary—a generally healthy body is probably up to the normal activities of daily living.

How much is enough?

Much of the anxiety about getting enough sleep stems from the myth that everybody needs eight hours of sleep every night. While eight hours is what most people need, many need far less. Cases of individuals requiring less that one hour of sleep a night have been documented.

Realistic sleep requirements for adults range from five to six hours to nine to 10 hours. Children, of course, need more sleep than adults. But probably the greatest discrepancy between sleep need and sleep amount occurs in teenagers. They still need almost as much sleep as children do, but they begin to adopt adult sleep schedules. (That's why they fall asleep in algebra class.)

Catching up:

Is it possible to "catch up" on lost sleep with a catnap? Most true insomniacs can't nap during the day, but for other people, a quick 40 winks probably isn't harmful. If, however, your nap lasts too long, you can expect it to disrupt your sleep that night.

Advice from our experts: Keep naps short. If you sleep too long during the day, it can throw off your sleep rhythm and may even cause your natural sleep rhythm to "flip," so you sleep during the day and not at night.

"Safe" catnap: Less than 30 minutes.

The consequences—helpful or otherwise—of a nap also depend upon the time of day. The closer to bedtime, the more disruptive its effect.

More sleep do's and don'ts:

• Don't engage in strenuous exercise too late at night. Vigorous aerobic exercise accelerates the body's metabolic rate, which remains "charged" for several hours.

• Don't sleep late on weekends. It can disrupt your sleep schedule.

• Avoid big, heavy or spicy evening meals. However, a light, high-carbohydrate snack may be helpful. This kind of snack increases insulin secretion, which appears to be associated with sleepiness.

About that glass of warm milk:

Most people don't like the idea of taking a drug to help them fall asleep, especially now that concerns have been raised about the side effects of a widely prescribed sleeping pill. But what about the old-fashioned remedies, like a glass of warm milk or a hot toddy?

It is probably not surprising that no controlled clinical studies have been done on the effect of warm milk. Theories do exist about why warm milk should be an effective sleep aid, but the issue is unresolved.

As for the hot toddy, the use of alcohol is controversial issue in terms of sleep benefits. Alcohol has been shown to have a disruptive effect on sleep. Although it may sometimes help people to get to sleep a bit more easily, it's also likely to cause them to wake up during the night, or to have more fragmented sleep. Therefore, alcohol is not an insomnia remedy that a sleep disorders clinic would recommend.

If lack of sleep or concern about your sleep habits is disrupting your life, consider seeking help at a sleep disorders clinic.

Source: Mark Chambers, PhD, a clinical psychologist at the Stanford University Medical School, Sleep Disorders Clinic, 211 Quarry Rd., Stanford, CA 94305.

How To Eat Safely

Many people are concerned about food safety—worrying about ingestion of pesticides, herbicides and other man-made chemicals. But the idea that our foods are tainted by dangerous toxins is completely mythical.

Reality: There is not even a single documented case in which illness has been caused by the regulated and approved use of these chemicals. The American food supply is safer, more varied and less expensive than food anywhere else in the world. Other food myths:

• Myth: Organic foods are better. Organic foods are no more wholesome than conventional foods. Nutritionally, they are equivalent. With regard to appearance, organic produce often has more blemishes. The only thing especially healthy about organic foods is their markup—they are far more expensive than conventional foods.

• Myth: Processed foods are not as safe as home-cooked foods. Home-cooked foods may taste better than pre-cooked foods, but they're no safer. Few households could stand up to the rigorous inspections required for institutional food processors.

Example: A friend of mine was dead-set against feeding her baby foods from cans or jars, arguing that food prepared in her own home would be safer. One day I watched as she pureed her baby's meal. When my friend turned to feed her baby, the cat was licking the blender that contained the baby's next meal!

In an effort to recreate the charm of the old-fashioned general store, many supermarkets have begun selling nuts and other goods from open bins. But packaged foods are just as wholesome, and they are much less likely to be dirty or contaminated. If you have a choice, opt for prepackaged foods.

• Myth: Local produce is best. Produce purchased at a local farmer's market often tastes better and costs less, but it's no better for you. Many people prefer local produce because it lacks the wax coating found on store-bought produce. In fact, all the evidence suggests that eating small amounts of wax is safe.

• Myth: Seafood is often contaminated with mercury and other deadly toxins. Despite the recent concern, commercially sold seafood is generally safe—and quite healthful. Exception: People with severe seafood allergies should obviously avoid seafood.

• Myth: Preservatives are unsafe. Many people shun foods that contain BHT* or other common food preservatives—even though repeated testing has proven these chemicals safe. Irony: Recent studies suggest that preservatives retard the food's aging process and also help prevent cancer—at least in laboratory animals. While others try to avoid preservatives, I try to avoid foods that do not contain preservatives.

• Myth: Artificial sweeteners are unsafe. Decades of testing and more than 100 years of widespread use have proven conclusively that saccharin, for example, is safe for humans, even though the government continues to require warning labels for foods containing saccharin. These labels, required after studies revealed that male rats whose mothers ate huge amounts of saccharin sometimes developed bladder cancer, are not applicable to humans. The same test on animals have also shown that mustard and edible mushrooms are carcinogenic.

• Myth: Sulfites are unsafe. For the vast majority of people, these compounds—used to prevent discoloration and retard bacterial growth in dried fruits, shrimp and wine—are perfectly safe.

Exception: A small percentage of the population—including 5% to 10% of asthmatics—is allergic to sulfites. If you are, be sure to check labels for sulfite content.

• Myth: Mayonnaise promotes food poisoning. Chicken salad and other mayonnaise-containing dishes are associated with food poisoning not because the mayonnaise somehow "goes bad," but because the chicken itself is contaminated with salmonella or other disease-causing bacteria. For safer picnics: Keep meats well chilled until it's time to eat.

• Myth: Salad bars are unsafe. Many salad bars used to lack plastic "sneeze guards" and other features that ensured clean, wholesome food. Today, any salad bar that looks reasonably clean and well maintained most likely is so.

*An antioxidant that prevents food spoilage.

• Myth: Avoiding cholesterol is essential to good health. Only people with dangerously elevated levels of cholesterol need worry about cutting back. Those with normal levels can safely eat foods containing cholesterol as part of a balanced, varied diet. Irresponsible packaging: Peanut butter, cooking oil and other vegetable products are often labeled "no cholesterol," as if to suggest that the food were specially processed. In fact, cholesterol is found only in animal products—meats, eggs and dairy products. Vegetable foods, by themselves, never contain cholesterol.

• Myth: Avoiding fats is essential. Although recent research suggests that excessive fat consumption helps promote cancer, the real culprit is not dietary fat but excessive calories. Overweight people are more vulnerable to diabetes, heart disease, uterine cancer and many other ailments than are people of normal weight—and far too many Americans are overweight. To maintain proper weight... exercise regularly and keep within your caloric needs.

Proper handling, preparation and storage of food:

• Handle food carefully. Fruits and vegetables should be thoroughly washed to remove soil particles and pesticide residues. Use warm water (soap is unnecessary). Exercise special care when handling meats, especially poultry. Uncooked, these foods are often contaminated with salmonella and other bacteria that can cause illness if ingested.

Precautions: Wash your hands after handling raw meat...when barbecuing, do not put cooked meat onto the same platter that held the raw meat..if you toss a salad after making hamburger patties, be sure to wash your hands first.

• Prepare food carefully. Cook all meats. Poultry and pork should be cooked until all the pink is gone. Beef and other meats are generally safe with somewhat less cooking. Note: Home canning can be a more complicated procedure than most people realize. To prevent food-borne illness (namely botulism), and spoilage, follow USDA guidelines.*

• Store food carefully. Keep hot food hot and cold food cold. If you use something from the refrigerator, put it back immediately after taking what you need. Do not eat refrigerated food that has been left out more than a couple of hours. If you are uncertain about a particular food, throw it out.

*These can be found in the *Complete Guide to Home Canning*, available from the Resource Center, Cornell University, 7 Business and Technology Park, Ithaca, NY 14850. Order Number: 399-USDA-539.

Source: Elizabeth M. Whelan, ScD, MPH, president of the American Council on Science and Health, 1995 Broadway, New York 10023. Dr. Whelan is the author of 21 books, including *Toxic Terror*, Jameson Books, 722 Columbus St., Ottawa, IL 61350.

You, Too, Can Beat Common Colds—The Simple Secrets

There is no cure for the common cold—but there is a bewildering array of over-the-counter remedies that promise to relieve all its symptoms. I personally don't believe in the multi-ingredient remedies currently available. You get better results with medications that attack symptoms individually...

Decongestants:

If you have nasal congestion and a runny nose, use nose drops or a nasal spray with decongesting drugs, such as Neo-Synephrine, phenylephrine or oxymetazoline hydrochloride. These decongesting drugs, known as vasoconstrictors, really do the job.

How they work: They shrink the blood vessels and open breathing passages in the nose. Side effects: Increased blood pressure and pulse rate. Warning: Don't use oral decongestants. Because they work not only on your nose, but also on the blood vessels throughout your entire body, the concentrations of the drug are necessarily weak and therefore not as effective as topical decongestants.

Warning: If you use topical decongestants for more than three days, you get what is called a rebound effect—it takes more and more drops or spray to open your nose. Eventually the nose will not open without the use of a decongestant. I've seen patients who've used nose drops for weeks, and when they try to stop they can't breathe or sleep. Sometimes we have to give them steroids to get them off the decongestants.

Recommended: Don't use decongestants for longer than three days. In most colds, the worst part is over by then anyway.

If your nose is still stopped up, use salt-water drops. You can make your own by dissolving a teaspoonful of salt in eight ounces of warm water.

Myth: You shouldn't stop your nose from running, because that will cause the cold to last longer. Reality: There is nothing beneficial about a runny nose. And since it doesn't help clear up your cold, there's no reason to endure the discomfort.

Nasal secretions are irritating to the skin of the lips and nose. To avoid these skin irritations, use a petrolatum-based ointment such as ChapStick or camphor ice to keep the secretions off the skin and allow it to heal.

Cough medicines:

Two kinds of cough medicines...

• Expectorants, such as guaifenesin, supposedly loosen your sputum and make you cough more. It's difficult, if not impossible, to prove that expectorants do much of anything.

• Suppressants help if your cough is keeping you awake at night or bothering you during the day. They usually contain dextromethorphan or codeine.

Myth: Suppressing a cough can cause pneumonia. Reality: This is a danger only for people with chronic lung disease such as emphysema—not for normal, healthy people with a cold.

If you have a sore throat, use topical analgesics such as throat lozenges. But gargling with salt dissolved in warm water several times a day is about as effective as anything you can buy. It's much less expensive and it will give you some temporary relief.

Muscle aches and fevers:

Although these symptoms are not usually part of a true cold, people often think of colds and flu as the same thing. Recommended: Aspirin for adults and acetaminophen for children. We don't like to give children aspirin because it can lead to Reye's syndrome, a neurological disease. People are now also using ibuprofen for colds and flu.

Other remedies:

• Steam vapor machine. This supposedly cures colds by blowing hot steam up the nose. It may work, but it hasn't been scientifically proven effective. Reason: It's hard to set up a double-blind study to test it. (Can people only think they're getting hot steam up the nose?) Related statistic: There's a strong placebo effect with the common cold. If you give lactose, which does nothing, to a group of people with colds, a third if them will say it was helpful.

• Vitamin C and zinc. Neither of these "natural" remedies has been proven effective. Research has shown that zinc gluconate tablets, the most recent fad, are basically ineffective. In addition, zinc causes very unpleasant side effects, such as a sore mouth, an upset stomach and a bad taste.

• Antihistamines. These counteract the body's production of histamine, a substance that causes allergic diseases, such as hay fever. But studies show that the nasal secretions of people with colds don't contain elevated levels of histamine and that the effect of antihistamines on colds is minimal. They may have a slight drying effect on the nose, but you'd be better off with a decongestant.

• Antibiotics. Most people know that antibiotics do nothing for a cold and can have unpleasant side effects, like stomach upset and vaginal yeast infections. But antibiotics are helpful if there's a complication like a sinus infection or a middle ear infection. How do you know if you have an infection? It's more likely if you're a smoker, have had previous cold complications or a cold lasts longer than usual. If you suspect a complication, see your doctor. Problem: It's not always easy to diagnose sinus disease. X rays are expensive, and the best in-office technique, holding a light to the sinuses, is only somewhat reliable. Doctors often prescribe antibiotics just in case—so if you want to avoid taking them unnecessarily, insist on X rays.

• Bed rest. There is no scientific evidence that you'll get better faster if you stay in bed. However, since you'll feel better if you don't push yourself, I recommend bed rest for patients who feel really sick. Common courtesy: If you do stay in bed, you won't give your cold to other people.

Source: Jack M. Gwaltney, Jr., MD, professor of internal medicine at the University of Virginia School of Medicine, Charlottesville, VA 22903. He is one of the leading researchers of the common cold.

How To Lower The Fat In Your Diet And Still Eat The Foods You Love

The average American's diet is much too high in fat. Although no more than 30% of our calories should be from fat, it makes up 40% of the calories in most people's diets.

Example: Someone accustomed to eating eggs and bacon for breakfast...perhaps a roast beef sandwich for lunch...and a steak for dinner can easily be taking in up to one half of his/her calories in fat.

Such eating habits place us at high risk for a number of deadly diseases, particularly heart disease, stroke, breast cancer and colon cancer.

Although many people know that a low-fat diet can help prevent these diseases, most think low-fat means low-flavor. But it doesn't have to. There are many delicious low-fat foods that can be enjoyed both at home and in restaurants.

How to start:

• Keep a food diary. Write down everything you eat for four or five days, including a weekend. Next to each food, record the number of calories and the number of grams of fat it contains. Use an inexpensive calorie counter, available in most bookstores.

This diary will show how many calories you consume daily, and how many of those calories come from fat. It will also help you identify high-fat foods.

• Determine your fat allowance. This will tell you the maximum number of fat grams you can eat on a daily basis.

Use your food diary to calculate the average number of calories you eat each day.

Take 30% of that number—that's the maximum number of calories that should come from fat.

Convert those fat calories into grams by dividing by nine (one gram of fat contains nine calories).

Result: The maximum number of fat grams that you should eat each day.

Example: If you eat an average of 1,800 calories a day, 30% of that—540 calories—can come from fat. Then, 540 divided by nine equals 60. Result: You should eat no more than 60 grams of fat per day.

Think of these grams as an allowance, and limit the number you spend daily.

One option: Spend half the fat grams on two meals and a snack...and the other half on your favorite meal.

• Trade-off. It's okay to indulge in high-fat foods on occasion...if you make up for it by being prudent the rest of the day. Use your food diary to differentiate high-fat from low-fat foods. High-fat foods should be limited or avoided, while low-fat foods can be eaten frequently.

Also, identify high-fat foods you know you "can't" give up. Make up for them by giving up the many high-fat foods you can live without.

• The portion problem. It's very important to control not just what you eat, but how much. Tripling the size of a portion can turn a low-fat meal into a high-fat meal.

How to lower your fat intake:

There are many things you can do to reduce the number of grams of fat you eat each day. What to do for...

• Breakfast. Instead of cream in coffee, use low-fat milk. Sourdough bread is made without fat and makes fabulous toast. Whipped butter contains less fat because it has water beaten into it. When making pancakes or French toast, use skim milk and substitute an egg white for one egg.

• Lunch. Eat sandwiches made with tunafish, turkey breast, small amounts of lean roast beef or sliced chicken breast. Instead of mayonnaise: Mustard, lettuce, tomato or cucumber for moisture.

• Dinner. Trim as much fat off meat as possible...then use herbs, spices and aromatics—garlic, leeks, etc.—to make up for fat's flavor. Use recipes that require smaller quantities of meat. And when serving chicken, don't eat the skin. Best: Remove it before cooking. Instead of hot butter on vegetables, use a butter substitute. Instead of sour cream, use nonfat yogurt mixed with chopped scallions or blended with cottage cheese and chives.

To sauté onions and garlic, use a non-stick pan and either a tablespoon of olive oil and chicken broth or just chicken broth. Use prepared, low-fat salad dressings. Or cut the calories in regular salad dressings by extending them with lemon juice, water or low-fat buttermilk and herbs. If you prefer to make your own dressings, beat in a lot of mustard to cut down on oil. And use balsamic vinegar—or rice wine vinegar.

• Snacks. Better than potato chips: Bread sticks, matzo and plain popcorn.

• Desserts. Bake cakes with two egg whites instead of one whole egg. Instead of two eggs, use three egg whites or one egg plus one white. Cut the amount of nuts in recipes in half. And angel food cake is virtually fat-free. Instead of ice cream: Low-fat frozen yogurt, ice milk, sherbet or sorbet.

How to shop:

Read food labels carefully. Many are deliberately misleading. Examples:

• 95% fat-free can mean the product contains 5% fat by weight. This does not tell you the percent of fat in calories, which may be as much as 50%.

Better: Read the fine print on the label. Find the number of grams of fat per serving. Multiply that number by nine to find the number of calories per serving that come from fat. Divide this number into the total number of calories per serving to figure the percentage of calories that come from fat.

Example: A package of turkey is marked "95% fat-free." But reading the label tells you that one serving contains two grams—18 calories—of fat. And since there are 35 calories per serving, about 50% of the calories come from fat.

• Part-skim milk does not mean a product is low in fat.

Example: A ricotta cheese labeled part-skim milk contains almost as much fat—five to six grams per two-ounce serving—as whole-milk ricotta. Better: *Lite* ricotta—it has only four grams of fat per two-ounce serving.

Many brands of microwave-ready rice, packaged rice and potato mixes and microwave popcorn contain hidden fat. Avoid foods processed with palm, palm-kernel, coconut, hydrogenated or partially hydrogenated vegetable oils.

More foods to avoid:

• Peanut butter—two tablespoons contain 16.2 grams of fat.

• Potato chips—eating eight ounces is like pouring 12 to 20 teaspoons of vegetable oil and a teaspoon of salt on a potato.

• Crackers contain saturated fats in the form of tropical oils and partially hydrogenated vegetable oils.

• Hot dogs—even all-beef varieties—contain about 13 grams of fat each...chicken franks contain eight grams.

• Non-dairy creamers and flavored instant coffee mixes contain tropical oils as primary ingredients.

• Prepared granolas are high in fat.

Source: Ruth Spear, author of *Low Fat and Loving It*, Warner Books, 666 Fifth Ave., New York 10103.

Foot Pain Prevention

Many people over 50 experience foot pain. Common cause: Loss of metatarsal fat pads.

Problems: The fatty pads that cushion the foot diminish with age.

Solution: Replace the lost cushioning. This often can be accomplished by buying shoes with thick rubber soles and installing sort insoles, available at drugstores.

If this doesn't help, see a podiatrist for customized orthotics—custom arch supports that correct improper foot function.

And if this doesn't help, it may mean that the distribution of weight over the bones in the foot has become uneven. This can be corrected with surgery.

Source: Kenneth Meisler, DPM (doctor of podiatric medicine), 35 E. 84 St., New York 10028. He is director of podiatry at the Preventive and Sports Medicine Center, New York.

How To Protect Your Lungs From Yourself... From The World

The Lung Line provides information to callers about asthma, emphysema and other respiratory diseases. Questions callers ask most often:

What's the best way to quit smoking?

There's no single way that works for everyone, but we encourage smokers to attend group programs—the support of other people boosts success rates. Local chapters of the American Lung Association have lists of nearby programs.

We also suggest that people identify the times when they are most likely to smoke, and substitute another activity.

Example: If you're used to lighting up after a meal, go for a walk, do the dishes...anything to break the pattern.

How dangerous is secondhand smoke?

Evidence shows that people who live with smokers have a significantly higher incidence of emphysema and other lung diseases than people who don't.

Smoke is a respiratory irritant. It's a trigger for asthma. And it's especially harmful to children two and under. Youngsters living with parents who smoke get more bronchitis, colds and other respiratory infections.

If you smoke and have children living with you, stop! At the very least, quit smoking in the home and car.

What is asthma? What causes it?

Asthma is a disease associated with the obstruction of air passages in the lungs, resulting in wheezing or labored breathing. The obstruction is usually the result of inflammation, although a muscle spasm or mucus can also be the cause of blocked airways.

A number of triggers can set off an attack. Included: Stress, exercise, allergies (especially to molds and dust mites), sinus conditions, cigarette smoke, changes in the weather and viruses.

We also know that a predisposition to the disease can be inherited—although asthma also develops in some people with no family history of it. We don't yet know what causes the predisposition.

How do I know if I have asthma?

Wheezing, coughing or shortness of breath are associated with a number of respiratory conditions, not just asthma. Your doctor would need to take a detailed medical history, and possibly perform a simple spirometry test—a breathing test—to make a diagnosis.

What are the treatment options?

Obviously, triggers should be avoided if possible. There are many safe and effective medicines—either inhaled directly into the lungs or taken in tablet form. Your doctor can work with you on an appropriate treatment program based on your condition.

I've been taking theophylline for asthma, but I recently read an article claiming it's dangerous. Is it?

Theophylline, a pill that dilates the bronchial tubes, has been around for many years. It's in the same family as caffeine and can cause nervousness and sleep disturbance in some people. At too-high dosages, reactions can include stomach upset, vomiting, headache and, in extreme cases, seizures.

Theophylline should only be taken under a doctor's close supervision, and a blood test should be given periodically to monitor theophylline levels in the blood. When used correctly, it is still a safe and effective asthma medication.

I think I might be allergic to pollen. What kind of allergy testing do you recommend?

Skin testing, recommended by the American Academy of Allergy, is a highly accurate and reliable testing method.

The doctor places drops of allergens on the skin of the patient's arm or back and scratches each spot. He then watches for a reaction. Results are usually available in a few minutes.

Blood tests are more expensive, less reliable and take longer to get the results.

Antihistamines put me to sleep. How can I get rid of hay fever symptoms and stay alert on the job?

Several prescription antihistamines, including Seldane and Hismanal, are long-acting and don't cause drowsiness.

Certain nasal steroid sprays can relieve symptoms by decreasing inflammation and swelling in the nasal passages. Unlike some nasal decongestants, steroid sprays don't cause dependence. Because they're topical—they don't get absorbed by the body—they carry very little risk of side effects.

Will an air filtration system help improve my respiratory problems? What kind do you recommend?

Filtration systems filter out many of the substances in the air that can cause allergic reactions or asthma.

The type of filtration system we recommend most often is the HEPA (High-Efficiency Particulate Air) filter system. It's effective but expensive—$400 to $600 for a room model.

Central air conditioning in a house where doors and windows are kept closed usually filters out 80% of pollens. So if you have air conditioning and your symptoms are not severe, a filtration system may not be worth the investment.

Also, filtration doesn't work for everyone. Discuss this option with your doctor, taking into consideration your symptoms, sensitivities and environment.

Source: Audrey Cohen, manager, and Epi Mazzei, RN, and Michelle Freas, RN, lead nurses of the Lung Line, National Jewish Center for Immunology and Respiratory Medicine, 1400 Jackson St., Denver 80206. Lung Line nurses are available to answer questions 9 a.m. to 6 p.m., Eastern Time, Monday through Friday. Many free booklets are also available—call for information: 800-222-LUNG.

How To Reduce Stress

The very best way to reduce the amount of stress in your life is to keep it from building up in the first place. Taking a few small actions can do a world of good. Suggested:

• Get up 15 minutes earlier in the morning. The inevitable morning mishaps will be less stressful.

• Don't rely on your memory. Write down appointment times...when to pick up the laundry...when library books are due, etc.

• Make duplicates of all keys. Bury a house key in a secret spot in the garden. Carry a duplicate car key in your wallet, apart from your key ring.

• Be prepared to wait. A paperback book can make a wait in a post office line almost pleasant.

• Plan ahead. Don't let the gas tank go below one-quarter full...keep a well-stocked emergency shelf of home staples...don't wait until you're down to your last bus token or postage stamp to buy more.

• Don't put up with something that doesn't work right. If your alarm clock, wallet, shoelaces, windshield wipers—whatever—are a constant source of aggravation, get them fixed or replace them.

• Relax your standards. The world won't end if the grass doesn't get mowed this weekend.

• Ask questions. Taking a few moments to repeat back directions, what someone expects of you, etc., can save hours.

• Say *No.* Turning down extra projects, social activities and invitations you know you don't have time or energy for takes practice, self-respect and a belief that everyone needs some quiet time each day to relax and be alone.

Source: Seymour Diamond, MD, executive director of the National Headache Foundation, and director, Diamond Health Clinic, 5252 N. Western Ave., Chicago 60625.

Mighty Milk

Milk protects the heart. In a 10-year study, only 1% of men (ages 45 to 59) who drank at least a pint of whole milk a day had heart attacks compared with 10% of non-milk-drinkers. Theories: An ingredient in whole milk lowers cholesterol...or men who drink milk may have healthier lifestyles.

Source: Researchers in the epidemiology unit, Medical Research Council, Landough Hospital, Penarth, Wales.

Is It A Heart Attack? Or...Just A Chest Pain?

A phenomenon, known as Syndrome X, refers to exercise-related chest pains experienced by people who have chest pains that seem cardiac related but who have no blockages in the main arteries. In such cases, the chest pains may be attributed to one or more causes. Included:

• Acid reflux. Acid from the stomach backs into the esophagus.

• Abnormal nerve sensitivity. Nerves leading from the heart and the esophagus to the central nervous system are inappropriately activated.

• Anxiety disorders. Panic attacks, in particular, can be associated with chest pain.

• Microvascular angina. A disturbance of the small blood vessels of the heart.

A routine angiogram can't detect microvascular angina. What can: Radionuclide angiography—measures function of the heart during exercise and at rest...or Positron Emission Tomography (PET)—a nuclear scan measuring blood flow in the heart.

Treatment: Calcium channel blockers can help chest pains caused by microvascular angina.

Source: Richard Cannon III, MD, senior cardiology investigator, National Institutes of Health, Bethesda, MD.

Beware of Lyme Disease

Lyme disease is a growing summertime hazard. Although it has been known in Europe for more than a century, this tick-spread disease is a relative newcomer to this country. It gets its name from a cluster of cases reported in the town of Old Lyme, Connecticut, in 1976. Since then, the disease has spread to 43 states, with more than 8,000 cases reported through 1990.

It's not know why the incidence of Lyme disease is increasing, but reports have been going up steadily for more than a decade, with overall incidence and geographical spread on the rise. Undetected and untreated, Lyme disease can cause crippling arthritis, heart disease and brain and nerve damage. And it can show no signs of infection until major symptoms appear weeks after the initial tick bite.

Good news: Some simple measures can prevent the disease, either by deterring tick bites or detecting them as soon as they occur.

Caught early, Lyme disease is easily treated with antibiotics. And the serious symptoms, such as arthritis, are seen in only a small percentage of cases.

Danger zones: The great majority of cases have been reported in only a few areas of the US, almost invariably form May to October, when the Lyme disease tick is found in woody and grassy areas.

Through 1990, more than 90% of cases were reported from nine states in the Northeast, Midwest (Wisconsin and Minnesota especially) and Pacific regions.

The two hottest spots are Nassau and Suffolk Counties on Long Island, New York, where more than half the total cases have been reported. But because the disease is spreading, caution is needed in almost any wooded or scrubby area, particularly in regions where infections have been reported.

A local health department will know whether Lyme disease is present in a community.

Prevention: Lyme disease is spread by the deer tick, which is roughly the size and color of a poppy seed. Feeding on blood, the tick can pick up and transmit the microbe that causes the disease. The tick is found not only on deer but also on field mice and other rodents that inhabit wooded regions.

Note: Pets can pick up the Lyme disease tick in the woods and bushes. Anti-tick collars are recommended in infested areas.

The first line of defense consists of measures to avoid tick bites. Included:

• Wear protective clothing. When walking in wooded or grassy areas where ticks are known to live, wear shoes, a long-sleeved shirt and long pants tucked into socks. Best: Light-colored clothes, which allow ticks to be spotted more easily.

• Use insect repellents. Best: Those that contain the active ingredient DEET are highly effective at keeping ticks away.

Caution: Insect repellents can cause adverse reactions, especially at high concentrations, when sprayed on the skin. Read the label before spraying.

A product containing more than 25% DEET shouldn't be used for children. For adults, the limit is 50% DEET. Spraying repellent on clothing reduces the risk of adverse effects.

• Inspect yourself carefully. The most effective prevention is a thorough self-inspection after being outdoors. Ticks can grab hold anywhere, but most of them are found on the lower body.

Look for a dark-colored insect a bit larger than a pinhead. Check especially at cuffs and collars—any gap where a tick can reach the skin. Cats, dogs and other pets should be groomed carefully after an outdoor romp to see if they've brought ticks indoors.

If a tick is found, it should be pulled out with a set of tweezers as close to the skin as possible. Don't yank quickly or crush the tick. Pull steadily and carefully.

Total removal isn't necessary. A couple of black dots left in the skin after tick removal won't be harmful.

Multiplying the problem: At least half of all tick bites aren't noticed at all. The bite is painless, and the tick falls off the body after feeding for 24 to 48 hours.

If you are bitten:

A visit to the doctor isn't mandatory even after a tick bite is noticed. Reason: Not all ticks carry the Lyme disease microbe, a spirochete (a spiral-shaped bacteria related to the organism that causes syphilis). Watchful waiting most often is the best course of action, rather than a quick demand for medication.

A few years ago, it was common to give antibiotics to all persons bitten by the tick, but that procedure has not proven helpful. Today, antibiotic therapy is indicated only when signs and symptoms appear.

Danger signs: Most infections are marked by a rapidly expanding red rash at the site of a bite. The rash is three to four inches across, sometimes with a clear area in the center.

The Lyme disease rash can be distinguished from the rash of a mosquito bite because it doesn't cause pain or itching and is much bigger.

Although the rash is the surest sign of Lyme disease infection, there's no rash in about a third of Lyme disease infections. But other symptoms are common.

What to look for: A progression of symptoms—aches...pain...fever...chills...swollen glands...headaches...lethargy...and general malaise typical of viral diseases such as the flu.

In days to weeks after infection, most patients develop muscle and joint pain, with redness and swelling affecting the knees and other large joints. One or two sites are affected at a time, and symptoms last for a few hours to several days.

Most of the time, Lyme arthritis—as this symptom is called—goes away by itself. But a small percentage of patients develop acute arthritis, which usually affects the knee or other large joints.

Because most virus-like symptoms really are caused by viruses—not by the Lyme disease spirochete—Lyme arthritis and other conditions are the most important symptoms that people should watch for.

Without treatment, 50% of Lyme disease patients eventually develop arthritis...15% develop meningitis or painful nerve conditions within three months of infection...and 8% of adult patients develop heart problems that can be life threatening—at least one death has been reported.

Clinical diagnosis:

The standard way to diagnose Lyme disease is a blood test that detects antibodies to the microbe that causes the disease.

Unfortunately, the blood test isn't perfect. It misses about 40% of cases in the first month of infection, because the body isn't producing detectable levels of antibodies. But the test does catch almost all cases by the end of the second month, as antibody production is stepped up.

False alarm: The Lyme disease blood test sometimes can indicate infection when none is present, since related (but harmless) spirochetes are often found in the body.

In practice, the diagnosis frequently is made on the basis of the distinctive rash that follows a tick bite, or when arthritis or one of the other major problems caused by Lyme disease becomes apparent.

Treatment: Antibiotic therapy should be started as soon as an infection is confirmed. Note: It's never too late to treat Lyme disease. Antibiotic treatment can be effective weeks or months after an unsuspected infection.

Standard courses of treatment have emerged over the past few years.

• For children. Amoxicillin, a form of penicillin.

• For adults. Amoxicillin with probenecid, which increases its effect. Or doxycycline, a tetracycline.

The usual course of treatment is three weeks. Although antibiotic treatment almost invariably cures the infection, antibiotics won't reverse any damage that has been done by Lyme disease.

Examples: Damage to knees or other joints caused by Lyme arthritis won't go away even after the infection is conquered.

This makes it important for someone who lives in an area where Lyme disease is endemic to consult a physician as soon as the suspicion-raising sequence of symptoms occurs.

Since the key to limiting the damage is early detection, diagnosis and treatment, any obvious sign or symptom of Lyme disease should be taken seriously.

Bottom line: Overall, people are more afraid of Lyme disease than they should be. Although the disease can be nasty, bad outcomes occur only in a minority of cases. Caution is advisable, panic isn't.

Source: Raymond J. Dattwyler, MD, associate professor of medicine and director of the Lyme Disease Clinic at the State University of New York at Stony Brook.

Skin Exams Are Very Important To Your Health

Since the 1930s, a person's lifetime risk of developing malignant melanoma, the most common form of skin cancer, has risen from one in 1,500—to one in 150 today.

Self-defense: The American Cancer Society now recommends that people receive a total-body skin examination once a year. And people at high risk for skin cancer should be examined even more often. Risk factors include:

- Light hair, skin, eyes.
- Tendency to sunburn.
- History of blistering burns.
- Having lived or spent time in sunny, warm areas.
- Family or personal history of skin cancers or precancers.
- Many moles or congenital moles (present at birth).
- Exposure to X rays.
- Exposure to certain chemicals.

People who have actually had skin cancer should be examined every three months in the first year after treatment, every six months in the second year and once a year after that.

Skin exams are important for many reasons. Included:

- You may be unaware of a dangerous growth (on your back, for instance) that you cannot see.
- Even if you see a premalignant or malignant growth, you may not realize it is dangerous.
- Your skin may subtly reveal the existence of other disorders, including thyroid conditions and diabetes.

Physician's exams: A total-body skin exam takes only a few minutes. A physician checks every inch of your skin including areas that you can't easily see yourself.

Complete disrobing is vital. A study of more than 2,000 people showed that doctors found malignant melanomas six times more often in patients who disrobed completely than they did in those who chose only a partial exam.

Self-exams: In addition to an annual exam by a doctor, people at high risk should perform a self-examination every two months. Patients who don't receive a skin exam annually should perform a self-exam once a year.

Look for spots resembling a mole that may be black, brown, pink, purplish or a mix of colors. They are often smaller than a dime and do not hurt, itch or bleed. What to do:

1. Get ready. You'll need a brightly lit room, a full-length mirror, a hand mirror, a seat and something on which to stretch out your legs. Disrobe completely.
2. Check your hands, inner forearms and the outside of your upper arm.
3. To check the inside of your upper arms, raise your arms above your head and look in the full-length mirror.
4. Examine your face and the front of your body in the long mirror.
5. Turn sideways to the mirror. Lift your arm and check your side. Repeat with the other side.
6. Turn your back to the mirror. Then look over your shoulder at your reflection to examine your buttocks and the backs of your legs.
7. Remain with your back facing the mirror. Use the hand mirror to completely check your shoulders and back.
8. Maintain that position. Using the hand mirror and aiming it at the long mirror, check your scalp.
9. Sit down and stretch out one leg. Use the hand mirror to examine the length of the inner leg. Repeat with other leg.
10. Still seated, examine the soles of your feet.

Source: Deborah Sarnoff, MD, FAAD (Fellow of the American Academy of Dermatology), assistant clinical professor, Department of Dermatology, New York University School of Medicine and a dermatologist in private practice in Hicksville, NY.

Mail-Order Pharmacies—Pros And Cons

Fueled by rising prescription costs, the number of mail-order pharmacies has grown dramatically since the 1980s. Few sell directly to individuals but many people have access to them through group health insurance plans. Advantages:

- Cost. Drugs by mail are potentially cheaper than drugs from the corner pharmacy. It's difficult to determine exactly how much cheaper because costs depend on the person's health insurance plan.
- Convenience. You save a trip to the drugstore—important for the disabled or seriously ill.

What to be wary of...

- Quality. Mail-order pharmacies—large and automated—can make mistakes. But so can drugstores. The nine mail-order pharmacies studied have elaborate quality-control systems. And the drugs themselves are produced by major manufacturers.
- Pharmacist-patient relationship. Some people want an ongoing relationship with a pharmacist. But mail-order pharmacies have toll-free numbers and include written information with the drugs.
- Time. Mail-order pharmacies ship within two days of receiving an order, so do not try to fill a prescription that you need quickly. These services should only be used for drugs that treat chronic conditions—arthritis, hypertension, etc.
- Waste. Most mail-order pharmacies fill orders for extended periods—often 90 days. If you don't need that much, you're stuck with drugs you can't use.

Source: Constance Horgan ScD, research professor, Bigel Institute for Health Policy, Heller Graduate School, Brandeis University. She was principal investigator for a mail-order pharmacy study funded by the Health Care Financing Administration.

Low Blood Pressure Can Be Very Serious

People taking medications to lower high blood pressure should be aware of blood pressure that is controlled at a very low level.

While a treated diastolic blood pressure below 85 mmHG appears to protect against strokes, it may increase the risk of heart attack in certain people.

To prevent heart attack and stroke, some doctors increase medication to the point where diastolic blood pressure falls to 60 or 70. This may be beneficial in some people, but others may not need such aggressive control.

Some people become symptomatic when their pressure is lowered excessively.

Symptoms: Dizziness going from lying down to sitting or sitting to standing, fainting, fatigue, feeling cold. These symptoms usually appear when diastolic pressure dips below 70. But most people with diastolic levels between 70 and 80 don't have any symptoms.

Each patient's therapy must be individualized to take into account other medical problems. And doctors should inform patients of their blood-pressure goals.

Self-defense: People taking high-blood-pressure medicine should have their blood pressure checked every few months.

If your diastolic blood pressure remains below 85 for a prolonged period of time, ask your doctor about adjusting or changing your medication if you do not require aggressive therapy...treating your high blood pressure without drugs—through weight loss, diet and exercise.

Source: Lisa Farnett, PharmD, clinical professor at the University of Texas Health Science Center, and author of a recent report about low blood pressure that appeared in the *Journal of the American Medical Association.*

How To Avoid Breast Pain

Up to 70% of all woman experience breast pain, from mild sensitivity a few days a month before their periods to severe pain so intense that it hurts to put on a bra or a blouse.

Most common: Cyclical pain caused by hormonal variations.

Although some studies have suggested that avoiding caffeine and taking vitamin E could relieve breast pain, subsequent research has not corroborated this.

Most effective now: Treatment with the hormone Danazol. Unfortunately, it requires high doses and produces undesirable side effects, including facial hair and weight gain. It is also extremely expensive—about $200 a month.

More promising are several treatments that have the potential to relieve breast pain...but require further study. Included:

• Low-fat diet. Hormonal variations may have some relationship to how the body handles fat in the diet. A group in Toronto has found preliminary evidence that cutting fat intake reduces breast pain. Important: Fat intake must be cut to 15% to 20% of total calories.

• Pain management. Meditation and visualization, or over-the-counter drugs such as aspirin or other analgesics, can provide relief.

• Progesterone gel. Rubbed on the breast, it is absorbed into the breast tissue—not into the entire body—so it can improve breast symptoms without side effects.

Many women fear that breast pain is a sign of cancer, but that's true only in rare cases. To rule out the possibility, women over 35 should have a mammogram and examination by a breast specialist.

Source: Susan Love, MD, director of the Faulkner Breast Center in Boston and clinical assistant professor of surgery at Harvard Medical School. She is the author of *Dr. Susan Love's Breast Book*, Addison-Wesley Publishing, One Jacob Way, Reading, MA 01867.

Recovery After Surgery Faster...Better

At one time, doctors thought that general anesthesia rendered surgical patients unconscious—incapable of hearing events or conversations that took place in the operating room.

No longer...some researchers now believe that there are many levels of consciousness, and that even during deep anesthesia patients can hear things spoken by doctors and nurses in the operating room.

Even more surprising: What a patient hears during surgery can profoundly affect his/her recovery following the operation. Patients who hear negative comments—about the surgery or even about seemingly innocuous topics such as the weather—tend to recover slowly and painfully.

In contrast, those patients who hear positive comments both before and during the surgery tend to recover promptly and with little pain or bleeding.

Recent study: Surgical patients were divided into two groups. Members of the first group were told prior to surgery, *You will bleed less as a result of surgery.* Members of the second group were given no such reassurance. Results: Members of the first group experienced far less bleeding than those of the second group.

Recommendations:

Surgeons traditionally have used cloth barriers to protect the sterile field. This also keeps the patients from seeing the incision site or anything else that might prove disturbing.

I and other researchers recommend that an aural barrier also be set up to prevent the patient from hearing potentially unpleasant or disturbing things during surgery.

The best way to do this is through the use of a Walkman. Listening to an appropriate tape during a surgical procedure not only blocks potentially distressing operating room conversations, it can also replace them with positive, upbeat messages.

What you can do:

Surgical patients should take a Walkman and a tape to the hospital with them and listen to the tape during surgery. Before they enter the hospital, patients should tell their surgeon and their anesthesiologist that they would like to use a Walkman.

What to listen to:

Some people prefer soothing music, while others may opt for meditation or relaxation tapes.

But homemade tapes that contain the reassuring voices of loved ones are generally the most effective at reducing stress and speeding a patient's recovery. To make such a tape, ask friends and family members to record simple statements of reassurance.

Example: The fact that you are hearing my

voice means that the surgery is going well and you will recover quickly...You will have a speedy recovery and will feel no pain...I love you, and I look forward to seeing you after surgery.

The closer your emotional ties to the people on the tape, the more effective it will be. No one knows precisely why listening to these tapes is so powerful, only that they do work.

Source: Clinical psychologist John Hudesman, PhD, professor of student affairs, City University of New York. Dr. Hudesman is conducting pilot research on the role of spoken communication in recovery from surgery. He maintains a private practice in New York.

Better Summer Care For Your Skin

As you head outdoors this summer, be prepared to protect your skin from permanent damage. Don't fall for these myths:

• Myth: That a slight tan is a safe tan. Even a slight tan indicates that the skin has been damaged and is at risk for developing premalignant and malignant lesions.

• Myth: That sun blocks prevent long-term damage to the skin. Suntan lotions that contain sun protection factors (SPFs) protect against burning...but the sun's rays continue to penetrate and damage the skin.

Trap: People slather themselves and their children with sun blocks...and then spend hours in the sun, thinking they're safe.

• Myth: That the sun can help improve acne. The sun actually causes only a short-lived cosmetic improvement in acne. Ultimately, the sun dries out the skin, stimulating the oil glands to start pumping, pumping, pumping, worsening the condition.

Because exposure to the sun toughens the skin, it also causes enlarged pores and blackheads.

• Myth: That ocean water is good for the skin. Salt from the ocean depletes the skin's moisture, and makes it dry and prone to wrinkles.

Source: Mary Ellen Brademas, MD, assistant clinical professor of dermatology at New York University School of Medicine...and chief of dermatology at St. Vincent's Hospital...and director of the Venereal Diseases Clinic at Bellevue Hospital. All are in New York City.

New No-Drug Cure For Tinnitus

Tinnitus—chronic, disabling ringing in the ears—afflicts one in five people in the US at one time or another. It disrupts their ability to converse, concentrate and sleep.

Because today's standard medical treatments—drugs, sometimes surgery—for tinnitus address its symptoms but not its causes, they are usually highly ineffective.

My new treatment approach works very differently. And, as studies on 2,000 patients have shown, it provides a lasting cure 90% of the time.

The sick-ear personality:

Conscientious, driven people who exhaust themselves by setting very high standards for themselves are more likely than others to suffer tinnitus and related problems.

Included: Sudden deafness—usually in one ear—and Meniere's disease...vertigo and dizziness, often accompanied by vomiting.

Ear disease often sets in when the fatigue and constant inner stress these people create is further aggravated by a sudden outside stress—a death, divorce or career setback. By falling ill, the body forces the patient to attend to his/her body and its need for rest.

Ironic: For work-centered people, vacations, with all their unstructured time, can be highly stressful. Many people first experience ear disease during such holidays.

Today's treatment:

Doctors usually see some measurable symptom—such as a circulatory problem in the ear—and then treat it as the cause of the illness. They prescribe drugs or, in extreme cases, perform surgery.

But such methods seldom provide relief. In fact, the cause of the illness usually lies much deeper—in life-style and personality problems.

Breakthrough treatment:

I do not try to change to patient's personality—that is too slow and difficult. Instead, I...

• Make patients aware of dangers. I explain how inner and outer stressors affect the body to cause the hearing problem. I help patients learn to relax.

• Teach patients to reorder their lives. They need a healthy balance between work and leisure.

• Introduce biofeedback methods. These teach patients to become conscious of how the ear is functioning and how the blood circulates there. They can learn to control these processes.

• Employ healing hypnosis. Suggestions of heaviness and warmth induce feelings of wellness and relaxation in most patients. I also teach my patients to use self-hypnosis.

• Introduce progressive relaxation techniques. These include tensing and relaxing all of the body's muscles from the toes up.

• Prescribe breaks. For the first six months of treatment, I have my patients take at least one 20-minute break for biofeedback practice of deep relaxation during the workday.

What you can do:

Although I do not practice outside of Germany, people in the United States who want to try this kind of therapy can benefit by following the advice in my book.

More information: VDG, Box 1197, FDR Station, New York 10150.

Source: Hans Greuel, MD, a physician who specializes in both psychology and otolaryngology in Dusseldorf, Germany. Dr. Greuel is the author of *Up to the Ears: Sudden Deafness, Vertigo, Tinnitus* published by VDG (address above).

The Truths About Alcohol Are Only Coming Out Now

Health-conscious people think they know all about the dangers of alcohol—and that a drink or two a day is okay. But alcohol affects the body far more severely and pervasively than most of us imagine.

Alcohol—even in limited quantities—damages practically every part of the body—the brain, the liver, the heart, the sensitive tissues lining the mouth and stomach. And it does so in two distinct ways...

• By directly poisoning the cells with which it comes in contact.

• By altering the metabolism of fats, carbohydrates, other nutrients and drugs. This leads to nutritional imbalances—and it also makes it hard for doctors to prescribe medications.

How much is too much?

Just how much alcohol is too much has been the focus of debate for years. There does not seem to be any threshold level. Some changes occur in the body even after a single drink.

The most prudent advice is to abstain completely, although serious problems seldom arise in people who limit themselves to no more than one or two drinks a day.* More than that and the body is placed at risk of chronic and potentially life-threatening damage.

Alcohol vs. health:

• Brain damage. The brain and spinal cord are particularly vulnerable to the effects of alcohol. A drink or two too many results in confusion, loss of coordination and giddiness. More drinking may result in epileptic-like convulsions (rum fits), coma or even death. Chronic, long-term drinkers sometimes go on to develop debilitating central nervous system syndromes.

Example: Victims of Korsakoff's syndrome are forced to confabulate—that is, make up stories about themselves and their environments—because their short-term memory has been destroyed. Korsakoff's often leads to institutionalization.

• Nerve damage. Chronic alcohol abusers also experience nerve damage to their peripheral nervous system.

This damage may show up initially as a slight loss in the hands or feet. In some cases, sufferers develop great difficulty in walking. In other cases, alcohol-induced nerve damage causes chronic impotence.

• Delirium tremens (DTs). This syndrome—which occurs when chronic drinkers suddenly quit drinking—often lasts for several days. Symptoms: Severe shaking, fever, sweating, hallucinations and dehydration that

*Some people are less vulnerable to the visible effects of alcohol—that is, they can drink a fair amount without becoming intoxicated. Evidence suggests that tolerance for alcohol may be genetically based.

is severe and occasionally life-threatening. At one time 10% to 15% of all people who experienced DTs died. Today, the mortality rate is much lower. However, without proper medical care, DTs still kill.

• Liver damage. Because the liver contains the enzymes necessary for metabolizing alcohol, it sustains more damage than most other organs in the body.

Someone who drinks too much risks developing acute alcoholic hepatitis. This condition, characterized by jaundice and a buildup of toxins in the blood, is difficult to treat and potentially fatal. If the drinking continues, the liver damage may progress to the point of cirrhosis. Although it strikes only about 10% of chronic drinkers, cirrhosis is now one of the most common causes of death in this country.

Simply put, cirrhosis occurs when the liver has become so scarred that blood flow through the organ is impaired. This impairment causes a dangerous back-pressure in the veins. To compensate, veins elsewhere in the body—especially in the stomach and esophagus—swell like aneurysms and sometimes rupture...and a ruptured varicose vein can be deadly.

Cirrhosis can also lead to ascites, an accumulation of fluid in the abdominal cavity. Eventually, cirrhosis leads to complete liver failure. This irreversible condition leads inexorably to hepatic coma and death.

• Pancreatitis. Chronic drinking causes this painful inflammation of the pancreas. Typically, pancreatitis hampers the body's ability to digest fats and certain other nutrients. If the drinking continues, crucial insulin-producing islet cells in the pancreas sustain permanent damage. Result: Diabetes.

• Mouth and throat cancer. Chronic drinkers face a significantly increased risk of cancer in the mouth and throat, presumably because of the direct toxic effect of alcohol.

• Low body weight. People often associate heavy drinking with a beer belly. But chronic drinkers are more likely to be rail-thin than obese. Reason: They stop eating almost entirely and survive on alcohol's hollow calories.

• Vitamin deficiencies. Nutritional deficiencies that are almost unheard of in the general population—scurvy, beriberi, etc.—sometimes show up in long-term drinkers because of their poor nutrition.

• Heart failure. Although some research suggests a drink a day benefits the heart, the risks of drinking far outweigh any possible benefits.

Indeed, chronic drinking causes a pathological enlargement of the heart. This condition sometimes progresses to congestive heart failure and, from there, almost certain death.

• Social problems. Fifty thousand fatalities a year on our streets and highways can be directly attributed to alcohol abuse.

Similarly, alcohol abuse costs the US economy billions of dollars a year in reduced productivity and employee absenteeism. And alcohol abuse causes countless cases of spouse and child abuse.

• Stomach pain. Alcohol irritates the delicate mucosal cells lining the esophagus and stomach. Although this irritation seldom leads to ulcers, it can cause a generalized stomach inflammation—gastritis. Symptoms: Pain in the gut, vomiting, vomiting of blood.

• Hormonal irregularities. Men who drink to excess over a period of years often lose body hair. Alcoholic males also often experience a benign, but embarrassing, enlargement of the breasts, known as gynecomastia.

And males who abuse alcohol often experience atrophy of the testes and, consequently, reduced fertility. Those who are chronic alcohol abusers often produce lower levels of the male hormone testosterone.

• Reddening of the skin. Chronic drinking dilates small blood vessels just below the skin, causing them to show through to the surface. This condition—acne rosacea—often results in a reddish rash on the nose and cheeks.

• Muscle damage. Chronic drinkers often develop pain and tenderness in the skeletal—voluntary—muscles. This condition—skeletal myopathy—is generally not threatening in itself. However, breakdown of these muscles floods the bloodstream with proteins, severely damaging the kidneys.

Source: Ralph M. Myerson, MD, clinical professor of medicine, Medical College of Pennsylvania, Philadelphia. As a practicing gastroenterologist, Dr. Myerson has been treating alcohol abusers for more than 40 years.

How To Increase Your Iron Intake

Iron deficiency is a common nutritional problem—and may be a special concern among women on low-cholesterol diets who avoid such iron-rich foods as red meat and liver.

Problem: Although there is ample iron in many vegetables and grains, it is less efficiently absorbed by the body than is the iron in animal foods.

Solution: In a recent study, a group of borderline anemic women raised their iron level significantly when ascorbic acid (vitamin C) supplements were added to their fruit juice at each meal. The women improved their retention of iron from plant foods by more than 40% over a control group which did not receive the added vitamin C.

It is more nutritious to get vitamin C through foods than from supplements.

Plant foods rich in iron: Whole grains, nuts, beans and legumes.

Foods rich in vitamin C: Citrus fruits, tomatoes, cantaloupes, broccoli, strawberries, cabbage, potatoes.

Source: Janet Hunt, PhD, RD, a research nutritionist for the US Department of Agriculture's Human Nutrition Research Center in Grand Forks, ND.

For Much Less Painful Gallbladder Surgery

More than 600,000 gallbladder operations are performed in the US each year, making it the most common surgery. In a conventional gallbladder operation, a six- to nine-inch incision is made in the abdominal wall and the gallbladder and any gallstones are removed.

Problems: Patients must stay in the hospital five to eight days and miss work for a month or longer. In addition, they receive a large scar and are often in intense pain because muscles must be cut. Troublesome infections follow 1.5% of all cases.

Breakthrough: Doctors can now perform laparoscopic gallbladder surgery. Instead of one long cut, they make four ½-inch-long punctures through which they insert special instruments that can both explore and remove the organ.

Advantages: Patients go home within 23 hours (anything less than 24 hours is considered a short stay by insurance companies)... return to work in three to seven days...have minimal scarring and pain. And there is little risk of infection. Most general surgeons have learned or are learning this procedure. Although complications from this procedure are rare, patients can experience bleeding, infection and organ injury.

Self-defense: Find a surgeon who has performed this operation at least 10 times...and ask him/her if any patients have developed complications.

Source: Eddie Joe Reddick, MD, assistant clinical professor of surgery at Vanderbilt University at Nashville, and a surgeon in private practice at 2201 Murphy Ave., Suite 101, Nashville 37203. He is the developer of laparoscopic gallbladder surgery.

More TV Dangers

Many children who watch too much TV have high cholesterol levels.

Watching two hours or more of television a day doubled the risk of having a cholesterol level of 200 or more...those who watched four or more hours a day had nearly four times the risk of high cholesterol, compared with children who watched less.

Family influence: 90% of heavy TV watchers who had a family history of heart attack or high cholesterol had cholesterol levels over 200. (In children, a cholesterol count of 200 mg/dl or higher increases the risk of having high cholesterol in adulthood.)

Problems: Kids who watch a lot of television eat more junk food, and are less physically active.

Source: Kurt V. Gold, MD, resident in pediatrics, University of California–Irvine.

24 Ways To Cut Hospital Health-Care Bills

Most of the money spent on health care in this country is spent in hospitals. The cost is staggering: $890/day on average...and going up steadily.

Even with good insurance coverage, it's a rare patient who doesn't end up paying between 10% and 20% of that bill. That percentage is bound to increase as more employers, dismayed by rising premium costs, have employees pick up more of the health-insurance tab.

You can do a lot to keep your own hospital bill down. Key: Be an assertive and savvy medical consumer. Don't be cowed by the medical bureaucracy. You're the customer and you are entitled to do anything within reason to save money on health care.

Is this trip really necessary?

Biggest moneysaver: Stay out of the hospital in the first place. One long-term study put the number of avoidable hospitalizations of nonelderly adults at an astounding 40%.

So, the first thing to do when your doctor wants to put you in the hospital is to ask about other options.

Is an ambulatory surgical center, for instance, a feasible alternative? Such centers now perform more than 1,500 different outpatient procedures, from knee surgery to gallbladder removal.

Savings: Between 25% and 50% on a given procedure. And—of course—no charge for a room or hospital overhead costs.

The right hospital:

If you really must go to a hospital, start thinking about cost right away, beginning with your choice of a hospital.

• Avoid for-profit hospitals. They tend to be more expensive—20% more according to some reports.

• Avoid teaching hospitals. Costs can be twice as high as a nonteaching hospital. You shouldn't pay for their technological marvels if you have an ordinary, low-tech ailment.

• Check into room rates in advance. Rates do differ from hospital to hospital. Some hospitals offer three- or four-bed rooms that are cheaper than semiprivate rooms.

• Go to a hospital with expertise in the procedure you need. Ideally it should perform at least 200 such procedures annually. You're less apt to suffer expensive complications. A call to the hospital administrator or medical chief of staff will give you this information.

• Avoid weekend admission. In most cases you'll get no medical care. It's cheaper and more comfortable to stay at home.

• Avoid admission during the Thanksgiving and Christmas holidays. Staffing is low and you will be paying room and board just to wait.

• Time your arrival. Find out at what hour daily billing begins and arrange registration accordingly.

• Refuse to pay an admitting or release fee to your doctor. This is a common but unjustifiable practice.

Keeping nonessentials in check:

Charges for laboratory services have risen dramatically over the past two decades and often account for as much as 25% of a patient's total hospital bill.

You can cut costs here without cutting medical corners. One study of 2,000 patients slated for elective surgery found that 60% of approximately 20,000 "routine" presurgery blood tests were unjustified.

• Refuse preadmission tests that have nothing to do with your condition. If you're in for foot surgery, you probably don't need a chest X ray.

• Have necessary and diagnostic tests done before you sign in—if your health insurance covers them. Nearly every test can be done on an outpatient basis to save time and money.

• Insist on approving the use of specialists. Sometimes specialists are necessary, but often doctors call each other in (and bill for consultations, of course) on the basis of, *You scratch my back, I'll scratch yours.* These physician bills can be the biggest out-of-pocket hospital costs for well-insured and Medicare patients.

You can take it with you:

Everything in a hospital is more expensive than it is in the real world and nothing is free. Take most of what you'll need with you. Don't buy so much as a tube of toothpaste in the hospital or hospital gift shop if you can possibly help it.

Tell the hospital what you plan to do and be sure your doctor notes the instructions on your chart.

• Bring your own food—unless, of course, your doctor plans to put you on a special diet. Prepare ahead and have friends or relatives bring in containers of food and beverages. Negotiate for a discount deal or rebate and get it in writing. You'll save money and eat better. Not only is hospital food notoriously bad, but it usually isn't very nutritious.

• Bring your own vitamins and mineral supplements. Also: If your doctor says you can use aspirin, bring your own.

• Bring your own medication. Savings over the hospital costs of insulin, for instance, is 90%.

• Insist that your physician prescribe generic drugs whenever possible. They're 30% cheaper on average than brand-name drugs—and up to 70% cheaper than more expensive medicines.

• Bring your own cellular phone. This charge adds up during a lengthy stay. Some hospitals actually charge you for incoming calls.

• Bring your own portable TV.

Saving on baby:

Having a baby is the second-highest medical expense in most people's lives. It costs between $3,000 and $7,000. Only dying is more expensive. What you can do:

• Choose a hospital that encourages "rooming in" and early discharge. That means keeping the baby in the hospital room with its mother and leaving after 24 hours rather than the usual three days.

• Use a nurse-midwife or family practitioner as your birth attendant. They charge less and generally will not recommend expensive high-tech interventions unless they believe it's absolutely necessary.

• Avoid caesarean-section deliveries. Not all caesareans are avoidable, but a good many are. Be sure the doctor knows your wishes.

• Get your baby out of the hospital as soon as possible. Upper respiratory and staph infections are common in hospital nurseries. You may end up paying a lot for extra care to combat them.

Checking out:

• Leave early. Check out before new-day room rates begin.

• Do not take any drugs home from the hospital unless they are free of charge. Fill prescriptions at your own drug store.

• Request an itemized bill—and review it carefully. One study of 40,000 hospital bills found errors in 97% of them, with overcharges exceeding undercharges by three to one. Another study put average overbilling at $1,254 per hospital stay. That's almost equal to average per capita medical expenditures for one year.

Do not pay a hospital bill as you're leaving. It's the worst possible time to decipher such a complicated document, replete with all its abbreviations and obscure entries. Look it over carefully at home. Ask for explanations of items you don't understand.

Keep a hospital log. It is the best way to be sure the bill is accurate. Keep details of doctors' visits (how long), tests and medications. If it's not possible for you to do so, get a friend or family member to help.

This diary of daily events will jog your memory of what happened to you. The more detail, the better chance of spotting overcharges and other charges you—or your insurance company—shouldn't have to pay for.

Go over questionable items with the hospital. If you don't get satisfaction, tell your insurance company not to pay the bill and ask for an audit review.

If you don't have health insurance coverage or have only minimal coverage, it's obviously vital to scrutinize the bill closely. But even if you have superb coverage, don't think you won't pay eventually—in higher insurance premiums or reduced coverage—because the insurance company pays this bill. Furthermore, your insurance may have a lifetime cap of $100,000 or so.

Bottom line: Work to keep your bill down. If everybody did that, insurance rates wouldn't go up as much or as fast as they do.

Source: Charles B. Inlander, president of People's Medical Society, 462 Walnut St., Allentown, PA 18102. Annual membership: $15, includes a subscription to the *People's Medical Society Newsletter*. Mr. Inlander is also the co-author of *Take This Book to Your Hospital With You* and *Getting the Most for Your Medical Dollar*, Pantheon Books, 201 E. 50 St., New York 10022.

2

The Shrewd Traveler

How To Get Satisfaction From Travel Companies

Every year, Americans experience thousands of problems with travel arrangements. Travel and recreation are ranked sixth on the US Department of Commerce's list of the products and services consumers complain about most—up there with other such "top ten" headaches as cars, banks and insurance.

Here's how to register a meaningful complaint in the travel industry and how to pursue it until you get results.

Before you complain:

• Ask questions beforehand. Be extremely specific about your wants and needs when making arrangements. Aim: to accommodate special needs and avoid disappointing "mismatches."

Example: A couple instructed their travel agent to book them for a cruise they'd seen advertised. Although their cabin was comfortable and the food delicious, they didn't have much fun because most of their fellow passengers were retirees. They were expecting a younger, livelier group.

• Keep expectations realistic: A certain amount of inconvenience is an unavoidable part of life, whether you are at home or traveling. Problem: People may expect their vacations to be perfect. They often complain about hitches that occur while they are traveling that they would not attach blame to at home.

Example: A bus tour is held up in traffic due to an accident on the highway. The delay is clearly not their agent's nor the carrier's fault.

• Make sure your complaint is legitimate: Specifically, if a service promised in your contract is not delivered, and/or if you suffer damages due to some negligence on the part of the party you are complaining against, you have a legitimate complaint.

Example: A bus that was chartered to take a group to a Broadway show is delayed due to a flat tire. The driver grumbles that he has repeatedly advised the bus company to replace the worn tires. The delay causes the group to miss the entire first act and was clearly caused by the bus company's failure to provide a reliable vehicle.

If your complaint is minor:

The majority of travel complaints are minor problems that can be easily corrected.

Examples: You don't receive the double room, nonsmoking table or aisle seat you reserved.

Best: Complain politely immediately. In most cases, the personnel in charge will resolve your problem right away. If necessary, call your travel agent for extra clout.

In the event you are asked to put up with a minor inconvenience, such as taking the window seat or keeping the single room until a double becomes available, avoid becoming angry or rude.

Better: Ask for a concession that will satisfy you—a price reduction, a complimentary bottle of wine, a voucher for a future service. You may need to speak to the management to get your request honored.

Don't expect to collect a refund if you accept the unacceptable. For instance, if the air conditioner in your hotel room is too noisy, but you don't change your room or your hotel.

Helpful: Inform the management or company representative of problems you encounter as a courtesy even if you expect no recompense.

Examples: Tell the tour guide that he/she's talking too quickly...tell the hotel manager that the pool furniture needs cleaning.

Handling serious complaints:

Step one: Collect the names of witnesses and company employees you deal with, copies of contracts, reservations, tickets or receipts, photos and/or witness statements if appropriate and any other material that can document the incident and any losses.

Step two: Write directly to the president of the firm, by name. Your letter should be brief and clearly typed. Include the following:

• Who you are. Include any identification that may add weight to your complaint (you are a steady, old customer, a stockholder, a member of the travel industry, the chairperson of a travel committee).

• An objective description of what happened. Do not whine! Include: Your assertions as to why what happened was their fault, and a description of the damages caused, if any.

• What you expect in the way of compensation. This can be a refund, reimbursement of damages, voucher for future service, etc.

• Wait thirty days. If you receive no reply, follow up with a copy of the letter along with a note requesting a response. Also send copies of your letter to the Consumer Protection Division in the office of the Attorney General of your state (use his/her name), and to any other governing body responsible for regulating the company or service in question.

Accept the settlement offered if you believe it is in good faith. Unless your losses have been great, your complaint is probably not worth the time and expense involved in a lawsuit.

Last recourse: Talk to an attorney to see if your case is worth litigating.

Source: Herbert J. Teison, editor and publisher of monthly newsletter *Travel Smart*, 40 Beechdale Rd., Dobbs Ferry, NY 10522.

Trip Cancelation Insurance

Trip cancelation insurance can help recover deposits or advance payments if travel plans change. Important: Read the policies very carefully. Some policies limit coverage...some do not repay anything on specified portions of trips (for instance, airfare or land travel)... some repay when medical conditions force cancelation but not if the conditions are considered preexisting. Recommended: Pay for travel with credit cards—card issuers can sometimes help recover some money.

Source: Attorney Thomas Dickerson, reported in *Travel Law*, Law Journal Press, 111 Eighth Ave., New York 10011.

The Smart Way To Order Airline Tickets

When ordering airline tickets, pay for them with credit cards. Along with attractive sale prices as airlines try to lure flyers, the industry is experiencing a spate of bankruptcies. People who pay cash are in danger of losing their money if a carrier goes under. Credit card customers usually can get a refund.

Source: *New Choices for the Best Years,* 28 W. 23 St., New York 10010.

How To Keep Film Fresh

Keep film fresh by refrigerating it inside a sealed plastic bag. For longer storage: Put the bag inside the freezer—this will extend the expiration date by several months. Important: Always let the film warm to room temperature before using it.

Source: *Reader's Digest Practical Problem Solver,* by the editors of *Reader's Digest,* Reader's Digest Association Inc., Pleasantville, NY 10570.

How To Win At Blackjack... Without Counting Cards

Of all the casino games, only blackjack allows a player to gain a long-term advantage over the casino.

The big edge comes from mastering intricate card-counting techniques. This entails hours of practice, intense mental concentration and the risk of detection. (In Nevada, casinos can evict card-counters from the premises.)

But there is an easier way for beginning players to win at blackjack...a set of principles based more on common sense than higher mathematics. If you follow these principles, you can reduce the casino's advantage to a bare minimum—less than .01%. At those odds, you have a fighting chance to win at any given session.

Follow a good basic strategy. This tells you when to...

- Stand (refuse any more cards).
- Hit (take another card).
- Double down (double your bet and receive one and only one more card).
- Split (double your bet by playing each of two equal-valued cards—two aces, for example, or two 8's—as a separate hand).

You can find a basic strategy chart in almost any book on blackjack.*

- The fewer decks in play, the better your chances of winning. In Nevada, make a point to seek out single- or double-deck games. In Atlantic City, virtually all games are six or eight decks.
- Seek out a casino with the most favorable rules. Some rules—such as a 3-2 payoff for a player's blackjack—are universal. But others vary from house to house.

Examples: When a casino allows you to double down after you split a hand, it cuts the house edge by .14%. Also advantageous: The "surrender" option, which enables a player to sacrifice half the original bet (and retrieve the other half) before drawing any additional cards.

- Gauge the mood of the table before you play. If players are smiling and betting more than the minimum, the cards are probably flowing their way and against the dealer.
- Manage your money with betting progressions. For best results, beginning players should vary their bets according to general card-counting principles but without keeping a cumulative count of every card that has been played.

Example: If you sit down at a $5-minimum table, begin play with a $10 bet. Watch all cards exposed by both players and dealers. If you see more small cards (2's through 7's) than large cards (9's, 10's and aces), and you win the hand, increase your wager to $15...and start a fresh count of small and large cards.

As long as the small cards predominate on each hand, and as long as you keep winning,

*Most reliable sources: Lawrence Revere (*Playing Blackjack as a Business*) and Jerry Patterson (*Break the Dealer*).

continue to increase your bet as follows: $20, $30, $45. Stay at $45 until you lose or until the dealer shuffles, then revert to a $10 bet and begin again.

If you lose a hand and the large cards predominate, reduce your wager to $5. Keep it there win or lose until you reach a hand where the smaller cards come out ahead, then return to $10.

Limitations:

This system works best with single- or double-deck Nevada games. In Atlantic City and Nevada, where there are six- and eight-deck games, the large number of decks makes counting less valuable—begin at $10 or double the table minimum. If you win, increase your wager as follows: $15, $20, $30, $45, $60. Remain at $60 until you lose or the dealer shuffles, then go back to $10.

Source: "Mr. Blackjack," a professional gambler who has made his living at the tables for more than 10 years. For professional consultations or further information, he can be contacted through any gambling-book store in Nevada.

How To Profit When You Play State Lotteries

The trick to making state lotteries a better gambling proposition is to carefully choose unpopular numbers—numbers that are selected less often than the norm by the lottery-playing public.

When you hit a jackpot with unpopular numbers, you have a chance of being the only winner. And if you do have to share your jackpot, you'll probably share it with fewer people. This makes a significant difference.

Example: If a $1-million jackpot is split four ways, each winner takes only $250,000. Assuming a 20-year payout (typical for state lotteries), a single winner would receive $50,000 a year (minus taxes). In a four-way split, the winner would receive only $12,500 a year.

How to pick unpopular numbers:

• Play numbers higher than 31. Many lottery players choose numbers based on birthdays and anniversaries and other special dates—making the numbers 1 through 31 more popular than the rest.

Note: Don't make all six of your choices higher than 31. Reason: Many savvy players are already doing this. If you hit a jackpot with six numbers of 32 or higher, you'll probably have to share it with several of them. Better: Play a blend of three lower numbers (below 32) and three higher numbers.

• Avoid numbers in the visual hot zone. For psychological reasons, players who mark their lottery cards purely on visual impulse often use numbers from the third horizontal row down to the middle. They avoid numbers located in the outside vertical columns.

• Restrict your plays to large hold-over jackpots that are not heavily promoted. After the big jackpot goes uncollected for several games in a row, it can grow to five or six times the normal size. But when jackpots are at their largest, media-induced lottery fever generates much heavier betting by a larger player pool—which dilutes your advantage.

Watch for oversized jackpots in states that do relatively little lottery promotion. Other opportunities: Giant jackpots that are overshadowed and pushed out of the newspapers by major news events.

Source: Gambling authority Mike Caro (a.k.a. "America's Mad Genius"). He heads a national brain trust of experts who quote odds on current events and broadcast them over Las Vegas radio superstation KBEG. Caro has written six books including *Caro on Gambling,* Gambler's Book Club, Box 4115, Las Vegas 89127.

Cruise Selecting Mistakes Not to Make

Not all cruises are created equal. It's important to check them out very carefully...before you book.

Traps to avoid:

• Trap: Being stuck on a ship that's less than shipshape. The US Department of Health and Human Services publishes a biweekly assessment of the cleanliness of 75 or more ships. The ships' galleys (kitchens), bars, deck pantries and water systems are appraised. Evaluation is based on a 100-point rating system. The passing score is 86.

For latest assessment: Vessel Sanitation Program, Center for Environmental Health and Injury Control, 1015 North America Way, Room 107, Miami 33132.

• Trap: Not doing your homework. Cruise ships vary widely. Before you book, get a list of on-board facilities, events and sample menus.

Best source of information: Look in the Yellow Pages for a travel agent who's a member of the Cruise Line International Association. These agents have copies of *The CLIA Cruise Manual,* which gives complete cruise-ship information.

Also helpful: *Cruising: Answers to Your Questions,* CLIA, 500 Fifth Ave., Suite 1407, New York 10010. Free with a self-addressed, stamped envelope.

• Trap: Picking a cruise that caters to the wrong crowd. Some ships cater to older passengers. Others attract crowds of swinging singles. Still others encourage families by offering baby-sitting services and kiddie pools.

• Trap: Picking a cruise that doesn't offer activities you enjoy. On some ships, a hot night is dining, dancing and casino gambling. On others, it's a bridge tournament. Also consider: When the ship docks, activities vary from beach parties to tours of local museums.

• Trap: Not dealing with a travel agent who is a member of the National Association of Cruise Only Agencies (NACOA). These agents specialize in arranging cruise vacations.

For a list of members in your state: NACOA, Consumer Dept., Box 7209, Freeport, New York 11520. Free with a self-addressed, stamped business-size envelope. (Two-state limit.)

• Trap: Paying too much because you're single. Most cruise lines charge an extra fee for a single cabin...but supplements vary widely—anywhere from 125% to 200% of the twin-occupancy fare. Alternative: Stick to a cruise line that offers a roommate-finding service.

Source: An industry insider who has been rating and writing about cruises for many years.

Great Travel Deals For The 50+ Set

One of the nice things about getting older is the many travel discounts now available for people over 50. Included:

• Free cruises for single men. Because unattached males of a certain age are very scarce, two cruise lines offer free travel to single men over 50 who will act as unpaid hosts to the many single women on board the ship. Duties include dancing, serving as dining partners and mingling with female passengers. No favoritism, no romantic entanglements.

Royal Cruise Lines, Host Program, 1 Maritime Plaza, Suite 1400, San Francisco 94111. 415-956-7200.

The Delta Queen Steamboat Co., Robin Street Wharf, New Orleans 70130. 504-586-0631. Attention Tracey Schreiber.

• Great Britain blanket admission. Great British Heritage Pass is good for admission to more than 600 castles, palaces, homes and gardens. Included: The Tower of London and Windsor Castle.

British Tourist Authority, 40 W. 57 St., New York 10019. 212-581-4700. Prices: $45 for a 15-day ticket, $67 for a one-month ticket.*

• Great Britain by rail. Most European railroads offer senior discounts. But few can match those in Britain. Passes offer reduced rates on unlimited first-class travel throughout England, Scotland and Wales. Note: Passes must be purchased through a travel agent in the US.

BritRail, 1500 Broadway, Suite 1000, New York 10036. 212-575-2667. Prices: $289 for eight days, $429 for 15 days, $539 for 22 days, $619 for one month.

• National parks passport. Golden Age Passport provides free lifetime admission to all the the federal government's parks, monuments and recreation areas for people over 62. Users also get half off on all fees—camping, boat launching, parking, tours, etc. The pass covers the holder and any passengers in a single-family vehicle.

Not available by mail. Passports can be

*All prices listed are per person unless noted.

obtained at any national park where an entrance fee is charged. Proof of age required. More information: National Park Service, Box 37127, Washington, DC 20013.

• The big discount. Most airlines, car-rental companies and hotels offer discounts of 10% or more to travelers over 50. When you make reservations, always ask if a senior discount is available. Required: Some form of identification—a driver's license is usually sufficient.

Warning: Sometimes rates even lower than the senior discount are offered. Ask if the rate you're getting is the lowest one.

Special tours...and more:

People over 50 also have access to tours and packages not available to others. Included:

• Back to school. A worldwide network of schools, colleges and universities. Participants (who must be over 60) spend a week or more taking up to three courses from a selection of subjects in liberal arts and sciences. Classes are taught by the host institution's faculty and are not for credit. Students sleep in dormitories—accommodations range from rustic to urban.

Elderhostel, 80 Boylston St., Suite 400, Boston 02116. 617-426-8056. In Canada: Elderhostel Canada, Corbett House, 29 Prince Arthur Ave., Toronto M5R 1B2. Prices: Average $240 per week (in the US and Canada).

• For the truly adventurous. Desert backpacking, canyoneering, mountain expeditions, canoeing and sailing around the US. Four- to nine-day excursions help participants exceed self-imposed physical and mental limits. Campers sleep in tents and cook their own food.

Outward Bound USA, 384 Field Point Rd., Greenwich, CT 06830. 800-243-8520. (203-661-0797 in Connecticut). Price: $75 to $100 per day.

• Mild tours of wild Alaska. An eight-day *soft adventure.* Wildlife tours through national parks and refuges, whale watching and visits to historic bush towns. Nights are spent in comfortable lodges. And except for a few picnics, all meals are indoors.

Alaska Wildland Adventures, Box 389, Girdwood, AK 99587. 800-334-8730. Price: $1,850.

• Other cultures. Stay with families in other countries. Escorted groups spend three weeks in Japan or Scandinavia or four weeks in Australia/New Zealand.

Seniors Abroad, 12533 Pacato Circle N., San Diego 92128. 619-485-2696. Attention Evelyn Zivetz. Prices: $2,325 to $2,775.

• You and your grandkids. Vacations intended to strengthen the bonds between generations. Itineraries appeal to both age groups. Included: Tours of England, African safaris, trips to Washington, DC and Alaska and barge cruises in Holland. Escorted trips of seven to 14 days. Note: Uncles, aunts and other surrogate grandparents are welcome.

GrandTravel, The Ticket Counter, 6900 Wisconsin Ave., Suite 706, Chevy Chase, MD 20815. 800-247-7651 (301-986-0790 in Maryland). Prices: $1,995 to $4,700.

Source: Joan Rattner Heilman, author of *Unbelievably Good Deals & Great Adventures That You Absolutely Can't Get Unless You're Over 50,* Contemporary Books, 180 N. Michigan Ave., Chicago 60601. 312-782-9181.

To Take Some Of The Gamble Out Of Las Vegas Gambling

More than one million people visit Las Vegas each month...and most don't get their money's worth. Reasons:

• They are unaware of the many freebies and services that are available to casino customers.

• They fail to use the game strategies—many of them simple and straightforward—that greatly increase their odds of winning in the casinos.

Inside information about comps:

Because of the economy, there aren't as many high rollers as there used to be in Las Vegas. Result: Casinos are luring people with comps—complimentary meals, free rooms...even free plane tickets.

To take advantage of this, you must be willing to gamble a reasonable amount of money for several hours a day during your stay.

Example: If you play for as little as an hour, betting between $10 and $25 per hand, you can get a free meal at most casinos. For bigger perks, you must gamble at least five hours a day.

- $25-minimum bets* can earn you a casino rate—usually about half-price—on your hotel room.
- $75-minimum bets can earn you a free room.
- $150-minimum bets can earn you a free room, food and beverages.
- Bets that exceed $150 can earn you a free room, gourmet meals and possibly a round-trip plane ticket between your home and Las Vegas.

Before you start to play, register your name with the floor supervisor in charge of your table. He/she will monitor how long you play and the size of your bets. If you move to a different table, be sure to alert the new supervisor.

Another way to obtain comps is by establishing a $5,000 line of credit at a casino. To do so, you'll need either $5,000 in cash or in a pre-authorized checking account.

One type of casino comp is available to anyone who has the nerve to ask for it—even people who don't gamble at all. A line pass gets you into the nightly shows without having to wait in the long lines. If you have tickets to a casino's show, ask any floor supervisor to give you a line pass.

To get a good seat, when you get into the theater, tell the maître d' that you want to sit ringside, and that you'll take care of the captain. Then tip the captain who seats you—but only after you're given a seat that you like.

Inside information about table games:

- Baccarat. Many players are intimidated by the upper-class origins and elegant trappings of baccarat, but it is one of the best—and easiest—games to play.

The house advantage is only slightly more than 1%. What that means: If the average player sits down to play with $100 in his pocket, he can expect to leave with almost $99.

And there are no strategies to learn—you win or lose by pure chance. Your only decisions are whether to bet with the player or the banker—an arbitrary choice—and how much to wager.

*Minimum bets vary from casino to casino.

Bet to avoid: The tie—where you bet that the player's and the banker's hands will tie. The house advantage is far greater because this happens so rarely.

- Blackjack. The house advantage on blackjack is 4% to 5%.

Best bet: Doubling your wager when your first two cards total 10 or 11, since chances are one in three your next card will be a 10.

Bet to avoid: Splitting 10s. If you're dealt two cards of equal value, you can split your hand in two and play both hands. But if you have two 10s, you already have a probable winning hand. Why throw away one good hand for two possibly bad ones?

- Craps. The fastest game in town. The house advantage is slightly more than 1%—but only for the most favorable bets.

Best bet: The Pass Line. You bet that the shooter will win. Bet with the highest odds (or multiples of the original pass-line wager) you can get.

Bet to avoid: Proposition bets, such as Any Seven, where the house advantage can rise to 17%.

- Roulette. This is an unpopular game in Las Vegas...and for good reason. Roulette can be painfully slow, and the double-zero wheel—in contrast to the fairer single-zero wheel favored in Europe—gouges out a house advantage of more than 5%.

Inside information about other wagers:

- Slot machines. Very popular...but one of your least advantageous bets. Most nickel slots in Las Vegas return only 80% to 85%...quarter machines return 88% to 92%...and dollar machines return 90% to 97%.

Even the million-dollar jackpots offer less than fair value. To win one you must insert enough coins to light all the lines—it's the last coin that earns the biggest jackpot—and wind up with four sevens. If the machine paid out according to actual odds, your return would exceed $29 million. The biggest slot jackpot ever hit in Nevada was $6.8 million on a Megabucks Progressive at Reno's Cal-Neva Club in 1988.

- Poker. Here you play against other players, not against the casino. But the house gets its money with a 10% rake of every pot in small games or a flat chair-rental fee of $75 an hour in big games.

Best: The player's advantage is greater with the large-game rake.

• Race and sports books. Betting on sports evens is perfectly legal in Las Vegas—but the standard house advantage ranges from 2% on baseball to 5% on football.

Bets to avoid: Multi-game parlays. The odds against winning a 10-team parlay are more than 1,000 to one—and the payoff is only 600 to one.

Source: Barney Vinson, a casino executive and author of *Las Vegas Behind the Tables!* and *Las Vegas Behind the Tables! Part 2*, both published by Gollehon Press, 3680 Linden SE, Grand Rapids, MI 49548.

Make Vacationing Without The Kids Easier On Them

Before you leave, schedule play times or dinner dates for your children and their friends...give the names and telephone numbers of these friends and their parents to your babysitter...ask your children if they have a favorite snack food they would like while you're away or if there is a special meal they could prepare for themselves or that the babysitter could prepare for them.

Source: *How to Stay Lovers While Raising Your Children—A Burned-Out Parents' Guide to Sex* by Anne Mayer, Price Stern Sloan, 360 La Cienega Blvd., Los Angeles 90048.

Managing Foreign Currency

Before you go on a trip abroad: Buy a small amount of foreign money in order to pay for porters, taxi drivers and a meal upon arrival... get to know the money—study the bills and coins and their denominations. During the trip: Don't keep money and traveler's checks in the same place...have some cash on hand. When you return: Exchange unused foreign currency immediately—the dollar may continue to fall and money loses value daily in countries where inflation is prevalent.

Source: American Express, reported in *Cosmopolitan*, 224 W. 57 St., New York 10019.

Cheaper Tickets For London Shows

Order tickets directly by calling individual theaters from the US and charging the tickets to your credit card...instead of using local ticket-broker services, which usually charge $10 to $15 for commission. Find London theater listings and phone numbers in the Sunday edition of the *Times of London* at any newsstand that handles out-of-town newspapers.

Source: *Consumer Reports Travel Letter*, 256 Washington St., Mt. Vernon, NY 10553.

Get The Best Car-Rental Deal

Ask yourself: What kind of car do I want?... (the smallest that suits you will save money). When, and for how long, will I rent...(weekly and weekend-only rates are much lower). Where will I pick up and drop off the car? Will I need insurance? What add-on charges will I incur?...(mileage costs, airport surcharges, additional-driver fees, etc., add up). Am I eligible for any discounts?... (travel agents and hotels often can help you get them).

Source: *AAA World*, 12600 Fair Lakes Circle, Fairfax, VA 22033.

To Find Airfare Bargains

Check newspapers daily—not just on Sundays—for the best buys...keep calling airlines that advertise low-fare promotions, using your phone's automatic redialer if you have one...be flexible with time, date, even airport (if you can fly to a nearby alternative one)... always ask whether a quoted fare is really the lowest one available—and, if then quoted a lower one, keep asking.

Source: *Travel Smart*, 40 Beechdale Rd., Dobbs Ferry, NY 10522.

Cheap Airfare Strategy Threatened

Airlines are getting more vigilant about the "hidden-city" strategy used by bargain hunters. Airlines are now screening hidden-city tickets—when travelers purchase tickets that have the connecting point as their final destination on a longer route that is cheaper (they just get off at the connecting point and don't continue on the rest of the trip). Hidden-city tickets are against airline policy—and airlines now charge you full fare if you're caught.

Source: *Consumer Reports Travel Letter*, 256 Washington St., Mt. Vernon, NY 10553.

Don't Doze While An Airplane Is Landing

Stay awake to keep your ears unplugged. Reason: You swallow and yawn less frequently while you are asleep. Yawning is more effective than swallowing.

Source: *Travel-Holiday Magazine*, 28 W. 23 St., New York 10010.

Swimming Hazards

Dangerous swimming off the coasts of France, Spain and Italy in warm weather months. Polluting chemicals in these waters have recently killed 100 dolphins. Safer: Hotel swimming pools.

Source: *The Travelore Report*, 1512 Spruce St., Philadelphia 19102.

Family Vacations Can Really Be Wonderful

The most common vacation clash is between Type-A, *If-it's-Tuesday-this-must-be-Belgium* people...and Type B, *I-want-to-catch-up-on-my-reading* people.

There is no hard rule about which kind of vacation is better—as long as the whole family agrees. But serious problems can arise when even one family member wants a different type of vacation from what is planned.

Vacation types:

• Type A. The frenzied vacation where you're up at dawn and have to see everything. Focus: To make every minute count... to be stimulated...to learn.

People who set up this kind of vacation are generally compulsive, workaholic types. Even on vacation, they don't allow themselves time to relax. Deep down they believe that relaxing means loafing.

Downside: Type-A vacationers are exhausted...other family members resent them.

Upside: They learn a lot...have great stories to tell and pictures to show.

• Type B. The laid-back vacation, where everyone sleeps late and spends lots of time doing nothing. Focus: To relax.

It's not just less-ambitious people who choose this type of vacation. It's also popular among people who spent their childhood vacations at resorts or country houses. They've learned that long periods of time with little or no activity is the way to relax.

Upside: Type-B vacationers feel more rested...spend less money.

Downside: They have fewer stories to tell...never get to see a lot of things—the pyramids, the Parthenon, etc.

Resolving vacation conflicts:

The real problem arises when people with

different needs go on the same family vacation. Most affected: Kids.

Type-A parents often overplan for their kids. They want them to experience everything while they're on vacation. They see vacations as a teaching tool. Common motivation: Guilt.

At home, some of these people spend very little time with their kids. They try to make up for it on vacation by showing their kids the world.

Problem: Children don't respond well to hectic schedules. Even on vacation, they need some unstructured time to unwind. Recommended: Regular breaks from touring.

Example: After a few days at Disneyland with my family, I noticed that my kids were getting that glazed-over look. I decided we should spend a day at the hotel pool. The kids initially objected, because there was so much they hadn't seen yet. But it became clear as the day wore on that they needed a day to relax. The break made the next few days much more enjoyable.

A summer home or family resort is probably the best vacation for kids. Kids don't remember the blur of experiences traveling from one place to another. But family vacations at a regular summer place or favorite resort become treasured memories.

Example: My kids can detail every stretch of time we've spent at our country house. They have fond memories of special friends there, a dog who visits them and smells and sights they love.

Helpful experiment: Don't have a television at the house or resort. Although the children may complain about this initially, they'll discover more about what's around them.

Secrets of a happy vacation:

There are a few very important keys to making a family vacation a happy one. Included:

• Compromise on your plans. Recognize that people have different personalities and needs, and that extends to vacations as well as life at home.

What not to say: How could you just want to laze around when we only have a week? How could you want to run around so much...when are we going to relax?

• Plan for trouble in advance. Talk about how you would handle several possible problems. For instance, what would you do if one person wants to sightsee and the others want to relax?

• Book comfortable lodgings. Of all the expenses, this is the most important. With a family, a lot of time is spent in a hotel. The kids have to be in bed early and you may be eating meals there.

• Make other plans for teens. Adolescents have their own needs. They're more interested in the cute girl or boy they saw at the pool than in the sights.

Vacation is where teenagers often act out their rebelliousness. Unless they really want to go and you get along well, it's best to let them go somewhere else while you take the younger kids.

Good alternatives for teens: Teen tours... counselor-in-training programs at summer camps...visits with a friend's family.

• Hold daily conferences during the vacation. Talk together even when things are going well. This will head off trouble. Set the tone for a democratic discussion of the issues.

• Be willing to split up. There's nothing wrong with one adult visiting a museum while the other stays at the beach. Or with one parent taking a child on a tour while the other remains at the hotel and splashes in the pool with the other kids. Myth: That on a family vacation the entire family must stay together the entire time.

• Plan distractions for long car trips. Play games, such as looking for license plates from different states or counting drivers with mustaches. Bring along: Auto bingo...tape players and favorite tapes...portable computer games.

Positive reinforcement: Offer a treat in exchange for an hour of cooperation and quiet, the rule being that if any child is troublesome they all lose. This way, each pressures they other to act cooperatively.

• Have kids take pictures and keep diaries. Both enhance memory and help children *own* the vacation. Encourage them to write about their feelings and their interactions with family and friends—as well as about where they've been and what they've done.

Source: Barry Lubetkin, PhD, director of the Institute for Behavior Therapy in New York. He is co-author of *Bailing Out: The Healthy Ways to Get Out of a Bad Relationship and Survive*, Prentice Hall Press, 15 Columbus Circle, New York 10023.

How To Get The Most Out Of Disney World

Walt Disney World in Orlando, Florida, is the most frequently visited man-made tourist attraction on the planet. Although it can be overwhelming, a little planning will increase your enjoyment immensely.

Not every ride at Disney World is a winner. To fully enjoy your visit, know what to see, what to avoid and what to see only if you have the time.

The park is relatively empty until about 11 a.m. By noon, however, the lines for the best rides are horrendously long.

Best advice: Arrive early—at least a half hour before the park's opening time—and head straight for the most popular attractions you absolutely want to see. Then spend the afternoon visiting the less-popular attractions that are, nevertheless, high on your priority list.

The Magic Kingdom:

Not to be missed...

• Space Mountain. The ultimate roller coaster. The most popular ride in the park. Warning: Too intense for children under seven...and for some adults. Very crowded.

• Pirates of the Caribbean. A spooky boat ride through a seaport overrun by pirates. Too menacing for children under four. Moderately crowded.

• Big Thunder Mountain. A railroad-inspired roller coaster. Very crowded.

• Country Bear Vacation Jamboree. A fun, furry hoedown. Moderately crowded.

• Parades. The 3 p.m. parade down Main Street stars all the popular Disney characters. Very crowded.

Best for kids under seven...

• Peter Pan's Flight. Ride miniature pirate ships through scenes from the movie. Moderately crowded.

• It's a Small World. The classic visit to children of many different lands. Moderately crowded.

• Dumbo, The Flying Elephant. Passengers control how high the Dumbo ride flies by pressing a button. Fun for kids...but parents may not find the 90-second ride worth the one-hour wait. Very crowded.

• Mickey's Starland. A musical stage show that lasts 15 minutes. Have your picture taken backstage with Mickey. Moderately crowded.

Worthwhile—if you're staying two days or more...

• Jungle Cruise. A boat ride. But the jungle animals look stiff and fake compared with Disney's newer figures. Moderately crowded.

• Haunted Mansion. More funny than scary. It too looks dated. Moderately crowded.

• Mad Tea Party. A gussied-up spinning-top ride like those found at any carnival. Still, kids love it. Moderately crowded.

• Hall of Presidents. The lifelike figures of US presidents are impressive, although the dry patriotism bores young children. Moderately crowded.

• Swiss Family Tree House. The ultimate tree house. Tough for small children to navigate. Not crowded.

Skippable...

• Tomorrowland. The prototype for Epcot Center...which is much better. Exception: The Space Mountain ride is still worth a visit. Not crowded.

• Starjets. A circular thrill ride with passengers riding in Flash Gordon era rockets.

• Grand Prix Raceway. Drive scaled-down versions of race cars on an enclosed track. Kids love it, although there's probably something very much like this a lot closer to home. Moderately crowded.

• Snow White's Adventure. Too scary for young children. Moderately crowded.

• Mr. Toad's Wild Ride. Maybe wild for Mr. Toad...but much too tame for the rest of us. Moderately crowded.

• 20,000 Leagues Under the Sea. A submarine ride that doesn't quite compare with the Living Seas exhibit at Epcot. Very crowded.

• Enchanted Tiki Birds. Tired old mechanical birds that look stiff and unreal. Not crowded.

• Magic Journeys. A 3-D film that's quite dated. Not crowded.

• Boat rides. There are a number of boat rides at the Magic Kingdom, including canoes, river boats and keel boats. All circle Tom Sawyer Island. The pretty views aren't worth the wait if you're on a tight schedule. Moderately crowded.

Epcot Center:

Not to be missed...

• Spaceship Earth. A ride that traces the history of communication, from cave drawings to computers. Marvelous special effects. Very crowded.

• Body Wars. A high-speed thrill ride through a giant human body. Very crowded.

• Captain EO. A 3-D movie starring Michael Jackson. Too intense for younger children... and some adults will find the rock music loud and annoying. Very crowded.

• The Living Seas. Ride in cars that travel beneath a man-made sea. Visit myriad marine animals. Moderately crowded.

• The American Adventure. A multimedia salute to the heroes of US history. Moderately crowded.

• Maelstrom. Passengers on a Viking ship encounter storms, a three-headed troll, a waterfall and other adventures. Very crowded.

Worthwhile—if you're staying two days or more...

• CommuniCore East and West. Two crescent-shaped plazas full of shops, restaurants and interactive exhibits. Play with robots, computers and touch-sensitive TV screens. Not crowded.

• Films. The CircleVision 360 films are entertaining and informative...but time-consuming. Moderately crowded.

To save money:

Take advantage of discounts not available elsewhere by becoming a Disney stockholder (NYSE:DIS. Recent share price: $119¾). Even if you own only one share of stock, you're automatically enrolled in the Magic Kingdom Club. Members receive discounts of up to 40% on rooms in Disney-owned hotels and varying discounts on admission.

In addition, Disney has opened two on-site budget hotels—The Caribbean Beach Resort ($88–$99 per room per night) and Port Orleans ($84–$99 per room per night). Prices include free shuttle buses to the park entrance.

Source: Kim Wright Wiley, author of *Walt Disney World with Kids*, Prima Publishing, Box 1260, Rocklin, CA 95677.

Vacation Picture Mistakes To Avoid

Even the most technologically advanced camera isn't goof-proof. And mistakes are particularly disheartening when you lose photos from a long-awaited vacation. Common mishaps...and how to avoid them:

Pre-trip:

• Mistake: Not checking the camera before you go. Shoot and develop a roll of film at home to ensure that everything is working. Take at least one shot in each mode—flash, normal light, close-up, etc. This is particularly important if you don't use the camera regularly.

• Mistake: Taking too much equipment. Overloading yourself with lenses, tripods and other geegaws will make photographing your trip a chore. Best: Take two lenses (wide angle zoom in the 28–80 millimeter range, and a telephoto zoom in the 70–210 millimeter range), a primary camera body and a compact autofocus as backup. If you'll be shooting at night, add a lightweight tabletop tripod.

• Mistake: Not packing extra batteries. Batteries sold at souvenir stands often aren't fresh. And many of today's cameras use hard-to-find three- or six-volt lithium batteries. Also remember to bring extra film.

On vacation:

• Mistake: Shooting without film. This can happen in one of two ways:

You forget to load the film. Solution: Check the little window in the back of most cameras to see if it's loaded.

You improperly loaded the film onto the

take-up spool. Solution: Rewind the film a little bit to see if the crank handle turns. Some newer cameras also have a display that blinks if the film is loaded improperly.

If these measures don't help, take the camera into the darkest closet or room you can find, open the back and feel for the film. Expect to overexpose at least five or six shots if any light hits the film.

• Mistake: Using the wrong film at the wrong time. Load the primary camera with the film you'll use most often. For instance, use ISO 100 for bright daylight and ISO 1000 or higher for night-time photography. If you're only using one camera, ISO 200 or 400 speed film is a good compromise.

• Mistake: Photographing distant subjects with a flash at night. Even the very best flash has a range of only 10 feet to 15 feet. Solution: When you are shooting a well-lighted subject (a monument, sporting event, etc.) at night, use ISO 400 or faster film and prop the camera on a steady surface. Helpful: Use a tabletop tripod.

• Mistake: Thinking your subject is closer than it is. Things look closer in real-life than they do in a photograph. Solution: Move closer if possible. If you can't, move around, find something interesting in the foreground—some trees, an arch, etc.—and use it to frame the picture. Professional trick: Stand at what you think is a good distance from your subject...then take two big steps closer.

• Mistake: Shooting through the closed window of a moving car. With an auto-focus compact camera, the window glass will fool the camera's built-in brain. Result: An out-of-focus print. Even with an open window or a sophisticated SLR, the car's movement may result in a blurred or shaky shot. Solution: Stop the car and get out to take the picture.

• Mistake: Taking only postcard shots. If that's what you want...buy a postcard. For more personal shots, find details that strike your fancy and make your pictures special.

Example: Everyone knows what the Statue of Liberty looks like. More interesting: Photograph the faces of the children as they wait in line to enter.

• Mistake: Leaving film in a hot car. During the summer, a car's interior can quickly top 120°F in a parking lot, baking exposed film left inside. Result: Prints with an overly green cast. Solution: Take the film with you.

Source: An industry insider who has been involved with photography for more than 20 years.

Pre-Travel Health Precautions

Before an overseas trip, have your doctor write out prescriptions for any medications that you may need using the generic or scientific names. Foreign druggists may not recognize (or stock) American brand names of these drugs.

Source: *Tips for the Savvy Traveler* by Deborah Burns, Storey Communications, Schoolhouse Rd., Rd #1, Box 105, Pownal, VT 05261.

Overseas Driving

International driving permits are required for driving in foreign countries. Availability: From local auto clubs or the American Automobile Touring Alliance, 888 Worcester St., Wellesley, MA 02181. Applicants must be 18 years old. Required: Application...two recent passport photographs... valid US license...$5 fee.

Source: *Travel Tips International* by Deborah J. Hill, Renaissance Publications, 7810 Barkwood Dr., Worthington, OH 43085.

Airlines Raise More Than Just Ticket Prices

Latest ploys: Bigger charges for checking excess baggage and for changing the return portion of a non-refundable ticket. Some of these fees are now approaching $100.

Source: *The Wall Street Journal.*

Vacation Eyewear

Take a second pair of glasses along with you when you go away on vacation. Alternative: Carry a copy of an up-to-date prescription so you can, if necessary, get new glasses or lenses at a quick-service store.

Source: *Parents*, 685 Third Ave., New York 10017.

Talk Yourself Into First Class

With ticket sales down, airlines are more willing to upgrade their best customers—business travelers—into first or business class. Strategy: Chat up the gate attendants and, when boarding begins, ask if there are any upgrades available. Hints: Dress sharply and toss in some airline jargon—ask, *What time is pushback?* instead of, *Is the plane departing on time?*

Source: Bob MacDonald, chairman, LifeUSA Insurance Co., quoted in *USA Today*.

Unused Frequent-Flyer Mileage

Frequent-flyer mileage is considered company property at only one in four firms. Important: Companies could save up to 20% on air-travel costs if they claimed awards from employees. Since the inception of award programs in 1981, flyers have earned 875 billion miles or points—but 630 billion of these wound up unclaimed or unused.

Source: *Runzheimer Reports on Frequent Flyer Programs*, Runzheimer International, Consulting Services Division, 555 Skokie Blvd., Northbrook, IL 60062.

Traveling With Arthritis

Traveling with arthritis can be made easier by packing as lightly as possible...using lightweight luggage and always carrying it by the shoulder strap, never the handle...using luggage that has wheels...using luggage carts or porters when available—and carrying an ample supply of dollar bills to use as tips.

Source: *Taking Control of Arthritis* by Fred G. Kantrowitz, MD, HarperCollins, 10 E. 53 St., New York 10022.

Better Vacationing

Get away when the daily grind starts to wear you down, not when you are totally fatigued or depressed. Vary vacations. Take long weekends somewhere new—if you enjoy it, come back for a longer stay. At least add new activities if you always go to the same place. Useful: A one-day buffer between end of vacation and return to work—allowing time to readjust.

Source: Psychotherapist Steven Shapiro, PhD, quoted in *Secrets of Executive Success*, Rodale Press, 33 E. Minor St., Emmaus, PA 18098.

Getting Cash Abroad

Many foreign automated teller machines (ATMs) will not accept personal identification numbers (PINs) with more than four digits. If yours is longer, contact your bank for a new one...keypads on foreign ATMs often contain only numbers. If your PIN contains letters, use a standard touchtone telephone keypad as a guide to convert them to numbers...for a list of foreign ATMs that will accept your card, contact your local bank.

Source: Herbert J. Teison, editor, *Travel Smart*, 40 Beechdale Rd., Dobbs Ferry, NY 10522.

Foreign Coin Conversion

Foreign coins are harder to convert back into US currency than bills. Defense: Study the coins of a foreign currency—how to recognize them, what each is worth—as soon as you change your dollars. Learn to use these coins confidently so that you won't be left with an expensive handful on your return. (Some travelers always pay everything with bills, so they won't have to use change in a foreign currency.)

Source: *Tips for the Savvy Traveler* by Deborah Burns, Storey Communications, Schoolhouse Rd., Rd #1, Box 105, Pownal, VT 05261.

Safety Of Frequent-Flyer Miles

Frequent-flyer miles earned at financially troubled airlines are probably safe—for now. Significance: No pressure now to rush to use them on a trip you wouldn't otherwise make. Such frequent-flyer miles usually are honored by an acquiring airline that picks up the troubled airline's business, and by competing airlines that are looking for new customers.

Source: Randy Peterson, editor, *Frequent* magazine, quoted in *Kiplinger's Personal Finance Magazine*, 1729 H St. NW, Washington, DC 20006.

Car-Rental Agencies' Collision Damage Rip-offs

Loss damage waivers (LDW)—formerly known as collision damage waivers—make a lot of money for automobile rental companies...more than $1 billion a year, according to New York Attorney General Robert Abrams. New York is one of three states that ban the sale of the LDW.*

Some rental companies push the LDW aggressively and give employees commissions for selling it. Good salespeople can make it sound tempting to pay up to $15 a day for the peace of mind of knowing that any damage to the car is fully covered—even if you have an accident that is your fault. But the coverage is almost always a waste of money. Reasons:

*Illinois and Maryland are the others.

• Your own auto insurance usually covers damage to rental cars. Ask your agent. If you are not covered, find out about adding the coverage—for a lot less money than the rental companies will charge you.

• Many credit cards automatically include loss and collision coverage when you use them for rentals. Included: American Express (express corporate cards), Carte Blanche, Diners Club, Gold MasterCard and Visa Gold.

• If your credit-card company does not provide insurance automatically, it will usually sell you the coverage—for pennies per use.

LDW horror stories:

Some rental companies try to take advantage of infrequent or unsophisticated travelers.

At greatest risk: Travelers on vacation, or those traveling for small business (large corporations often negotiate inclusion of the LDW in their corporate rental rates).

Tactics: Requiring renters to sign a form at time of rental agreeing to assume full damage liability if the credit-card company does not... demanding payment for any damages immediately on return of the car...charging loss-of-use fees while a damaged car is being repaired.

Self-defense: Check with your credit-card company and insurance carrier to find out how you are covered—and which coverage is primary and which is secondary. Ask the primary insurer what to do if you have a rental-car accident and the firm demands immediate payment.

Remember that you are in control of credit-card purchases—even after you sign for them. In the emotional aftermath of an accident, you may be vulnerable to unfair pressure from rental firms.

But even if a firm charges thousands of dollars to your credit card, all you have to do is write the card issuer and explain the circumstances. The charges will be designated disputed and removed from your bill until the dispute is resolved.

Advantage: This forces the rental firm to deal directly with the credit-card company for payment—instead of you.

Source: J. Robert Hunter, president, National Insurance Consumer Organization, Alexandria, VA, and Harold Seligman, president, Management Alternatives, Inc., travel-expense-management consultants, Stamford, CT.

Offbeat Vacations—Cheap And Healthy

If your idea of the perfect vacation involves strenuous activities—hiking, biking and cross-country skiing—there is a world of opportunities you may not even have considered. Terrific offbeat jaunts, easy on the wallet but hard on the joints...

• Cross-country skiing in Vermont. The original low-cost honeymoon. The basic investment in skis, boots and poles is much less than is required for downhill skiing, and after that you merely pay modest trail fees (starting at $8–$12 per person per day) rather than the high prices of downhill lift tickets.

Stay at Edson Hill Manor, an unusual brick manor house located on a 200-acre estate in Stowe (800-621-0284). Also recommended: The popular Trapp Family Lodge in Stowe (800-826-7000) and elegant Blueberry Hill Inn in Goshen (802-448-0707).

• Hiking hut-to-hut in the White Mountains of New Hampshire. If the weather on blustery Mount Washington cooperates, you can enjoy some of the best views in the East, with vistas of pristine lakes and towering mountain tops speckled with alpine tundra that can't be glimpsed from the highway. All you have to carry in your packs are a change of clothes, and winter- and foul-weather gear. The eight huts, which are operated by the Appalachian Mountain Club (AMC) and stand a day's hike apart along the Appalachian Trail, provide hearty family-style meals in season (from June to Columbus Day—during off-season bring and cook your own food) and bunk-bed lodging (though you have to wait until you get back to civilization for a shower). You can visit just one or two huts over a weekend, or devote a full week and do them all. The cost is minimal—starting at $40 for adult AMC members. Make sure you're in top physical condition.

For reservations and membership information call 603-466-2727.

• Touring the Mayan ruins in the Yucatan Peninsula of Mexico. Travel in Mexico is a bargain. The dollar goes much farther than north of the border. After sightseeing, settle down for some serious relaxing, skipping the high-rises of Cancun for the remoteness of Playa del Carmen, a small dock village across the bay from Cozumel. Enjoy walking the miles and miles and miles of deserted, unspoiled beach.

• Bicycle touring through Vermont. Two- and three-day bike trips through the hills and valleys of pastoral Vermont never fail to refresh the spirit and rev up the heart. Bike across romantic covered bridges, visit cheese factories and dairy farms, browse at antique and craft shops, and cool off in burbling waterfalls and crystal-clear lakes.

The trips, organized by Vermont Bicycle Touring (the original bike tour operator, now copied by many others), are distinguished by stays at charming country inns that provide gourmet dining. A choice of three different bike routes is offered every day, and experienced tour guides (equipped with spare tires and bike-repair equipment) accompany the trips. Visits to attractions along the way vary depending on the tour leader and group. Prices for two- to five-day summer trips range from $269 to $779 a person.

Further information: Call VBT at 802-453-4811.

• Family camping at Echo Lake on Mount Desert Island in Maine. The camp, operated by the Appalachian Mountain Club, is situated on a pristine lake in Acadia National Park—with wonderful swimming and sailing. Though many singles attend, it is ideal for families because of the wide range of activities available for both children and adults. An optional daily program is conducted by an experienced leader who usually offers a hike or boat trip to one of the outer islands. Biking on the carriage roads of the park is another popular activity. Campers live in tents that have board floors and are supplied with beds, sheets and blankets. Hot showers are available. Three family-style meals a day are provided, including a clambake and lobster picnic. Given the modest prices ($260 a week for adults) and wonderful location, the camp is so popular that a lottery must often be held to determine who will get in.

Further information: Write to Echo Lake

Camp, Mt. Desert, ME 04660, or call 207-244-3747 (seasonal).

• Touring the Grand Canyon—and the Navajo and Hopi Indian reservations in the high desert of Arizona. Your family can hike three-fourths of the way down the canyon to get a glimpse of the turquoise Colorado River, stay at a motel on a Hopi reservation where you can have blue corn flakes for breakfast, visit the oldest inhabited village in North America—perched at the edge of a mesa in the midst of the desert, witness the holy Kachina dances ushering in the spring planting season and visit the centuries-old cave dwellings of the Anasazi Indians. Total cost: Less than $1,000—plus airfare.

• Touring Greece—by bus and boat...the native kind, not the tourist variety. Using indigenous transportation provides an unforgettable taste of local customs. Where else can you board a bus on which travelers provide their own seating (folding lawn chairs), the passengers include chickens and everyone gets an unscheduled souvlaki break? The high points include a visit to the site of the original Greek Olympics, and a stay at the little known island of Kos, off the Turkish coast, where the Greeks themselves vacation. While getting there can be pricey, once you arrive on Greek soil, expenses are minimal.

• Hiking the national parks of the West, including Rocky Mountain National Park, Zion, Grand Teton, Yellowstone and Glacier. Try to stay at hotels operated by concessionaires within the parks so that you can concentrate on exploring the splendors of our country's natural beauty. You can climb some of the highest peaks in the Colorado Rockies, marvel at the spectacular rock formations of Utah's canyons, come nose-to-nose with moose browsing along Wyoming's Jenny Lake and gawk at bison and geysers in Wyoming. Take a combination backpacking, rafting and fishing trip to the remote backcountry of Montana, using the Glacier Wilderness Guides (800-521-RAFT), the only licensed outfitter for Glacier Park.

• Learning to sail. The top-of-line approach is Steve Colgate's Offshore Sailing School, which provides a week of instruction at South Seas Plantation on Florida's Captiva Island (Cost: $895 to $1,388 for a single, offseason) ...or a five-day summer course at Wequassett Inn on Cape Cod ($1,195 to $1,265 for a single). They also offer three-day courses at City Island, just north of Manhattan ($415 to $425, not including accommodations). For further information, call 800-221-4326.

• Family-oriented sailing at the unpretentious but popular Linnekin Bay Resort in Boothbay Harbor, ME. (During winter, call 413-584-4554. Call 207-633-2494 April 15–August 31.) A converted girls' camp with the largest sailing fleet in New England, it provides three meals a day at better rates than most resorts. It's such a great deal that people return year after year.

• Hiking inn-to-inn in the Swiss Alps. Yes, getting there is expensive, but the views, cuisine and lodging at the four-star hotels in charming mountain villages are superb.

Further information: Ryder/Walker Alpine Adventures, 5 Lake Fort Junction, Box 947, Dept. S, Telluride, CO 81435, 303-728-6481 in summer from 1 p.m. to 4 p.m. Mondays through Fridays, or Alpine Adventure Trails Tours, 783 Cliffside Dr., Akron 44313.

• Playing—not listening to—chamber music in Europe...or on a cruise ship in the Bahamas. A wonderful opportunity for amateur musicians to immerse themselves in great music and do some sightseeing as well. Amateur Chamber Music Players (545 Eighth Ave., New York 10018, 212-244-2778), while it does not organize such weekends, is a good source of information on such trips and publishes a directory of musicians both in the US and abroad.

• Sierra Club trip to Alaska. Designed for the adventurous of all ages, abilities and interests, these trips range from a water tour via ferry, kayak, canoe and float plane that retraces the travels of John Muir, to fishing along the Alaska Range and a van and ferry tour from Denali (formerly Mount McKinley) National Park through Valdez and the Kenai Peninsula. Costs range from $995 to $2,130, per person, not including travel to Alaska or charter air costs.

Further information: Contact the Sierra Club

Outing Department, 730 Polk St., San Francisco 94109, 415-923-5630, for a complete list of outings.

Trip Cancellation Insurance

Trip cancellation insurance can help recover deposits or advance payments if travel plans change. Important: Read the policies very carefully. Some policies limit coverage...some do not repay anything on specified portions of trips (for instance, airfare or land travel)... some repay when medical conditions force cancellation—but not if the conditions are considered preexisting. Recommended: Pay for travel with credit cards—card issuers can sometimes help recover some money.

Source: Attorney Thomas Dickerson, reported in *Travel Law,* Law Journal Press, 111 Eighth Ave., New York 10011.

Telephone Safety Overseas

Some overseas pay phones require tokens ...some don't accept coins until the connection is made. Recommended: Check out how to use pay phones for local calls—it's very expensive to use your hotel telephone. For international calls, use a telephone credit card at an International Telephone and Telegraph Office—often in the post office—or, if it is available, dial direct from a pay phone using your credit card or by calling collect.

Source: *Tips for the Savvy Traveler* by Deborah Burns, Storey Communications, Schoolhouse Rd., Rd #1, Box 105, Pownal, VT 05261.

When Kids Fly Alone

Make sure they carry ID cards, itinerary and names of people meeting the plane...teach them how to make collect phone calls—and give them at least $2 in coins for pay phones... Best: Book them on non-stop flights—and ask for seats near the front door. Once they are on the plane, stay in the terminal until it takes off. When meeting a child, go to the gate and bring identification to prove you are designated to meet him/her.

Source: Travel columnist Peter Greenberg, quoted in *Travel Smart,* 40 Beechdale Rd., Dobbs Ferry, NY 10522.

Avoid Traveler's Diarrhea

Take two tablets of Pepto-Bismol four times a day, beginning 24 hours before leaving and two days after returning. Warning: Don't use longer than 21 days. Also: In high doses, Pepto-Bismol may cause a ringing in the ears. Cut back the dosage until the ringing stops.

Source: *Gastrointestinal Health* by Steven R. Peikin, MD, HarperCollins, 10 E. 53 St., New York 10022.

Traveling In Style Cheaply

You can take a luxury trip without paying exorbitant prices for tickets and hotels. Keys: Common sense and persistence in pursuing a bargain.

How to use your travel agent:

Travel agents are a surprisingly good resource for savings:

- If you're trying to save money by utilizing the consolidator market—where companies buy large blocks of seats from airlines at a discount and sell them at low prices—use an agent. Reason: Travel agents weed out frauds in this market, who may advertise to sell tickets they really don't have. Also, if the consolidator can't provide you with the promised ticket, the agent will often honor that price and issue the ticket.

•To find the cheapest package for a vacation, find three travel agents who are familiar with your destination and have them price the package. Let the agent with the cheapest package make your travel arrangements.

Advised: Ask the agent if there will be any extra charges and get the reply in writing. Beware: Don't trust the travel agent who tries to book you into a trip you don't want. The agent may just be after a commission.

Important: Ask the agent to explain the conditions clause in your package. Potential rip-offs: Cancellation penalties...the sponsor maintaining the right to cancel and keep your money...the right to raise the charter price...the right to substitute hotels or destinations.

Also: Read the fine print in package brochures yourself. Brochures may feature pictures of sports activities or beaches that aren't included in the package price or are far away from the hotel.

Hotels:

Most travelers don't think to cut costs here, but there are several ways to save money:

•Weeks before you leave, make a reservation for the cheapest room available. A few days before your departure date, call the hotel again to see if cheaper rooms have become available because of cancellations.

•If you're staying in a small hotel that has vacancies, try bargaining for a lower price or getting your room upgraded without paying extra. Best bargaining times: Off-peak seasons.

•Presenting your business card may entitle you to the corporate rate, which is much cheaper than the normal rate.

Airlines:

Ninety percent of airline passengers fly at discounted fares. How to get the cheapest one:

•Well before your departure date, call the airline and ask the reservations operator for the cheapest fare available to your destination. Make a reservation and write down the reservation number. Hang up and call again so you can speak with another operator. Because of the sheer number of ways data are listed, you'll often get a better price and can make another reservation.

As your departure date nears, make one last call to find out if any cheaper fares have become available because of price wars or unreserved seats. Then, go with the cheapest reservation and cancel the rest.

Cruises:

•Position crossings: You can take a wonderful cruise at bargain fares on a ship that is sailing from its home port to the port where it is scheduled to pick up passengers for a cruise. Availability: In Europe, the South Pacific, the Caribbean and Alaska. Call individual cruise lines for details. Average discount: 75% off the price of similar-length cruises.

•Regular cruises: Ask if reduced-price or free flights to the departure city are available. About 75% of cruise passengers take such flights.

Discount travel clubs:

Discount travel clubs offer last-minute flights and vacation packages at lower prices. When you join, you get access to a secret phone number, which is answered by a recording listing all the trips available to club members. Assured: The annual cost of membership in a discount travel club ($35–$65) will easily be made up the first time you travel with the club. Join a club whose trips depart from an airport near you. Sometimes the air fare offered in a club's package is so inexpensive that you can stay in a luxury hotel not included in the package and still save money.

Source: Marion Joyce, author of *The Frugal Traveler*, G.P. Putnam's Sons, 200 Madison Ave., New York 10016. Ms. Joyce writes the nationally syndicated column "Consumer Corner" and will answer questions about frugal vacationing when you write *The Frugal Traveler*, Box 116, Tuckahoe, NY 10707.

Tactics For Very Fearful Flyers

Avoid ingesting caffeine, sugar and alcohol before—and during—the flight...meet the crew and ask questions—even silly ones... walk around the cabin and talk to other flyers...put a rubber band around your wrist and snap it when negative thoughts pop up—

the sting will condition you to avoid upsetting thoughts...take deep breaths and lean back.

Source: Jerilyn Ross, president of the Anxiety Disorders Association of America, Box 42514, Washington, DC 20015. For more information, send a postcard to the above address.

How To Fly With Your Kids...Without Jumping Out

A little planning and common sense can prevent most problems from even starting.

•Give children window seats. It keeps them entertained and puts a parent between them and the temptation to run up and down the aisle.

•Let a child stand as much as possible before take-off.

•Set rules before you start. For instance, everyone must use his/her quiet voice...a 10-minute period of absolute silence will be required every hour.

•Bring along a teddy bear, favorite blanket or pillow. It will help a child feel comfortable in a strange, exciting place.

•Pack a diaper-changing pad in your carry-on luggage.

•Have a bottle ready for take-off and landing. The sucking will reduce the pressure on baby's ears. Give older children gum.

Source: *USA Today.*

The Missed-Plane Trap

If you miss your plane, don't wait in line at the ticket counter to book another flight—it may fill up while you're waiting.

Instead, go to the nearest phone and book yourself a seat on another flight using the airline's telephone reservation service. Then go to the ticket counter to pick up your ticket.

Source: James Samuel, former associate director of the Marriott Business Travel Institute, quoted in *Sales & Marketing Management,* 633 Third Ave., New York 10017.

How To Protect Yourself When Traveling Abroad

International travelers often encounter health hazards that cause real trouble. Some follow them home.

How to protect yourself from...

•Contaminated food. If you prepare your own food, the basic self-defense rule is: Boil it, cook it, peel it or forget it.

If you eat in restaurants, avoid cold platters, buffet dishes, pastries, custards and mayonnaise-based spreads. Refrigeration in much of the world is less than perfect. Be wary of dairy products and be very suspicious of highly spicy foods—seasoning masks spoilage.

To judge a restaurant: Look at the condition of the restroom. If there are inadequate facilities and supplies for washing hands, food is being handled unhygienically.

If you have doubts about local eateries, find a Chinese restaurant. The meals are generally wholesome and well-cooked and the premises are adequately maintained.

•Contaminated water. There are many myths that have made many people very sick. Examples:

•Myth: That freezing water makes it safe. Reality: Ice used in drinks is always suspect. Avoid ice served on board flights that originate in developing regions.

•Myth: That alcohol will decontaminate the water and ice in a mixed drink. Reality: It won't. Also, avoid draft beer. Order wine only by the bottle because when you order by the glass there's the risk that it was diluted with contaminated water.

Self-defense: Boil drinking water for five minutes. If you can't do this, use water-purification tablets or add five drops of iodine to a quart of clear water (10 drops if cloudy). Be suspicious of bottled water and avoid bottles with broken seals.

Unexpected hazard: Singing in the shower. Even small amounts of water swallowed accidentally can cause gastrointestinal disease.

•Diarrhea. Take two Pepto-Bismol tablets three to four times a day to prevent traveler's diarrhea. If you do develop symptoms: It's best to avoid antimotility drugs (Imodium, Lomotil) because the body is attempting to purge itself of a noxious, toxic or infectious substance. Exception: If you become dehydrated. If your itinerary keeps you away from lavatory facilities, it may be better to change your plans.

Best diet when diarrhea strikes: Clear soup, salted crackers, dry toast or bread and sherbet. As symptoms decrease, add rice, baked potatoes and chicken soup with rice or noodles. As stools begin to retain shape, add baked fish or poultry, applesauce and bananas. Protracted bouts of diarrhea can often be abated with a short course of antibiotic therapy.

Toilet horror: Cruise ships, airlines and other facilities use vacuum toilets. People who might be accustomed to flushing the toilet while still seated can sustain severe pelvic damage (particularly if buttocks and thighs completely cover the opening) when a surge of air carries away the bowl's contents. Even worse: The force of the vacuum has been known to suck portions of the intestine out through the anus.

Self-defense: Don't flush until you stand up.

• Flight problems.

• The bends. Decompression sickness can develop if you fly soon after you've gone scuba diving. Guidelines: If no decompression diving was done, you can fly the following day. In the case of decompression, wait 36 hours.

• Cast problems. If you have a leg or an arm in a cast, cabin pressure changes en route can result in injury or discomfort. Self-defense: Have the cast evaluated by a doctor before you fly. It may be necessary to have the cast vented.

• Heat. The older the traveler, the longer it takes to adjust to dramatic temperature increases. What to do:

• Don't take salt tablets. Too much sodium actually retards the adjustment process and can lead to medical problems in certain people. Better: Slightly increase salt consumption at the table if you have experienced excessive sweating.

• Drink fluids. Drink enough to keep your urine nearly colorless (this is particularly important for people who have a history of kidney stones). Rule of thumb: When active, drink one glass of water for every 20 minutes of exertion.

• Avoid alcohol. It hampers fluid balance and climatic adjustment...and it causes heat gain in warm climates and heat loss in cold ones.

• Avoid antihistamines. They're found in many over-the-counter allergy pills, cold preparations and sleeping aids and in some prescription drugs. They decrease your ability to sweat.

People who take any prescription drugs should review their travel plans with their physician.

• High altitude. Most people adjust to the reduced oxygen found at high altitudes in a day or two. Rest, limited activity, aspirin, light carbohydrate-packed meals, supplemental oxygen and time usually take care of the hangover-like symptoms. If symptoms don't improve after 48 hours, descend.

To combat altitude problems: The prescription drug Acetazolamide, taken prior to ascent, will usually prevent most symptoms. Side effects: It acts as a diuretic.

Some people should consult a doctor before they travel to high locations. This includes anyone who has had heart, lung or blood-pressure problems...retinal disease... an attack of high-altitude, cerebral or pulmonary edema...sickle-cell anemia...diabetes...or is obese.

• Malaria. Most malaria infections can be prevented by taking the prescription drug Chloroquine. When you travel to areas where Chloroquine-resistant strains of malaria exist, additional prescription medication will be necessary. Start to take the pills two weeks before you enter a risk area, and continue for six weeks after you leave.

To minimize the chance of mosquito bites, stay in well-screened areas when possible—especially at dusk and dawn. Avoid aftershave lotions, perfumes, etc. Wear clothing that covers limbs. When outdoors, apply mosquito repellent to clothing and exposed areas of skin.

• Motor-vehicle accidents. People who drive in foreign countries are confronted with strange cars, unfamiliar rules, unreadable signs, poorly engineered roads, non-defensive drivers, driving on the other side of the road and unique road hazards. And travelers who use taxis or buses to avoid driving are at risk too. Problem: Public vehicles are involved in ghastly accidents as often as private cars.

Self-defense: Drive defensively. Always give another vehicle the right of way. Rent larger cars (they're safer) and insist on one with safety belts. Don't drive more than six to eight hours a day—it's too tiring. And avoid driving at night and on weekends, when most accidents occur.

Source: W. Robert Lange, MD, MPH, who helped establish the Travel Medicine Clinic at Johns Hopkins Hospital, Baltimore. He is also the author of *The International Health Guide for Senior Citizen Travelers,* Pilot Books, 103 Cooper St., Babylon, NY 11702.

Good Friends

Good friends may not make good travel companions. Questions to ask before you plan a trip together: Are you a day person or a night person...do you prefer being active or relaxing, being physical or intellectual...are you interested in socializing or staying to yourselves...how much do you hope to see...do you sightsee in depth, or wander through... are you punctual or consistently late?

Source: *Travel Tips International* by Deborah J. Hill, Renaissance Publications, 7819 Barkwood Dr., Worthington, OH 43085.

Low-Cost Luxury Cruising

Most cruise lines accept stand-by passengers.

Advantages: Discounted rates, cabin upgrades on undersold sailings, no cancellation fees.

The downside: The great deals depend on last-minute cancellations, so you may not know whether you'll get on a ship bound for Mexico, Bermuda or the Caribbean.

How to go standby: Check on departures from the port nearest you—New York, Miami, Ft. Lauderdale, Los Angeles, Seattle, etc. Cruise line brochures, available at travel agencies, list itineraries and departure locales.

Choose a day when several cruise departures are scheduled.

- Target specific ships. Discounted rates vary widely, depending on destination, duration of cruise, and class of stateroom.
- On the day of sail, register with the reservation clerk at the pier, for the specific cruises you choose.

The clerk determines the price of the cruise depending on what needs to be filled, and how low they're willing to go on price to fill it.

Caution: Standby rates, though discounted, sometimes are not better than other discounted fares.

Chandris Inc. (Fantasy and Celebrity lines) set standby rates at the minimum published tariff, but then will give upgrades of up to two levels.

Carnival Cruises standby fares can be the same as the "C-saver" (which is equivalent to a "super-saver" airline rate) discounts they offer on undersold cruises just before the sailing date.

On ships more fully booked, standby savings can be greater. On a recent three-day cruise from Port Canaveral to Nassau, a $555 inside-twin cabin was knocked down to $359—the cruise line's rock bottom "C-Saver" rate.

Many travel agencies offer discounted group rates of up to 30% and slash discounted group rates of selected undersold cruises, starting about a month before the day of the sail, up to 50%.

Source: Carnival Cruise Lines, 800-327-7373. Chandris, 800-635-3363. Princess Vacations, 800-432-2294. Royal Caribbean, 800-327-6700.

Shrewd Travelers

Shrewd travelers don't carry a lot of cash (they use travelers checks instead)...they don't take expensive jewelry with them...but do carry a medical summary including generic names of medications they are taking and doses and a list of things they are allergic to. They also buy travel insurance through their travel agents...bring an extra pair of glasses... leave an itinerary with friends and relatives—and check in regularly...find out about special health precautions they should take before they leave.

Source: *The Senior Citizens' Handbook* by Wesley J. Smith, Price Stern Sloan, 11150 Olympic Blvd., Los Angeles 90064.

When You Take A Night Flight

When you take a night flight across the US or overseas, bring a small flashlight or battery-powered reading lamp with you. Overhead lights may be weak, not shine where directed, or bother passengers who are trying to sleep.

Source: James Samuel, former associate director of the Marriott Business Travel Institute, quoted in *Sales & Marketing Management,* 633 Third Ave., New York 10017.

How To Travel Like A Travel Agent

You can get benefits and perks of a travel agent without changing careers.

How: Act as an outside agent on behalf of a travel agency. Arrange trips for friends and relatives through the agency.

Many agencies will provide shell literature—flyers and brochures that explain the attractions of various trips, with blank space for you to fill in trip dates, etc.

Outside agent benefits:

- You receive up to half of the agency's commissions. Agencies typically receive 10% of the cost of airline tickets and receive 15% of the cost of ground arrangements.
- Commission income establishes a profit motive for your activity, entitling you to claim a tax deduction for all outside agent expenses—including trips you take to resorts to familiarize yourself with them before you arrange future trips.
- You can get free trips—usually one for every 15 full-rate fares you arrange.
- If you earn $6,000 in commissions during one year, you may qualify for free and discounted airline tickets and familiarization trips around the world at a discount of up to 75%.
- Presentation of a travel agent's business card at hotels and restaurants will often result in discounted prices or upgraded service from proprietors who hope you will refer business to them.

Source: Charles Givens, author of *Wealth Without Risk,* Simon & Schuster, 1230 Ave. of the Americas, New York 10020. Mr. Givens has been an outside agent since the early 1970s.

When Changing Money Overseas

Beware. High fees may be charged by banks offering an attractive exchange rate. Structure exchanges with fees in mind. Examples: If a fee is charged for each traveler's check, exchange your largest checks first. If fees are charged per transaction, make a few large exchanges rather than many small ones.

Source: Dianne Marshall, editor, *The Savvy Shopper,* 12 Rambling Road, Northport, NY 11768.

To Get A Hotel Room Rate Discount

Shop for rates through large travel agencies—or call the specific hotel and talk with the assistant manager. If the hotel has rooms available, the assistant manager may be open to bargaining. Best: Whenever you call to make reservations, ask what special rates are available at that time, and which organizations (such as the American Automobile Association) get discounts.

Source: *Money,* Rockefeller Center, New York 10020.

Keep Your Car From Ruining Your Vacation

Car trouble can bring a vacation to a standstill and eat up money earmarked for fun.

To avoid nasty surprises, inspect your car and have any needed work done at least two weeks before the trip. This way adjustment problems can be discovered—and repaired—before you're on the road. What to check:

•Alignment. Load the car with weight equivalent to what you'll be carrying when you travel. Don't forget to allow for passengers. Then have the alignment checked. The extra weight will greatly affect tire wear and car handling.

•Good ideal: If you carry a great deal of weight in the back—enough to raise the nose of the car—have the garage install helper air shocks. These replace regular shocks and are inflated with an air hose. They will jack up the back of the car to distribute weight more evenly. Cost: Simple models cost about $100. Models that operate from a switch inside the car cost more.

Obvious but worth repeating: Eliminate unnecessary baggage and trunk junk. The more you carry, the worse your mileage.

•Battery. Buy the biggest battery with the longest-rated life that will fit in your car. It will do a better job and your alternator won't work as hard.

•Belts and hoses. Inspect belts for appearance and tension. Buy a new belt if: Cracks, grazing or the threads woven into the belt are visible...a belt is loose or squeals (it'll drain a battery)...a belt hasn't been replaced in four years or 50,000 miles.

Check hoses for cracking, bulges and seepage. They too should be replaced every four years or 50,000 miles.

•Brakes. Brake fluid should be changed every two years. Old fluid is more likely to boil when you go down hills, causing brakes to fade. The brake-fluid level should remain constant—low fluid could be a sign of worn brake pads. Check the fluid level two weeks after changing the pads to make sure the level hasn't dropped. Any drop means a leak, which is bad and must be investigated.

Brake test: In a deserted parking lot, make several quick panic stops. Then get out of the car and check for skid marks—there should be four clear ones. Any fewer—or if brakes pulled to one side—means your brakes need to be checked. Other tip-offs: Pulsating brake pedal...squealing upon application...chattering or spongy-feeling brakes.

•Engine. Have it checked for proper tuning. Important: Consult your owner's manual or dealer to find out the minimum fuel octane required for your car. Your regular brand may not be sold where you're traveling, and you may have to buy based on octane level alone.

•Headlights. If the car carries a lot of weight in the back, have the angle of the lights adjusted. Otherwise, your regular lights will seem like high beams to oncoming traffic.

•Radiator. Clean it with a garden hose, spraying from front to back to clear the fins of grease, dirt and debris. Replace the radiator cap if it's four years old or hasn't been changed in 60,000 miles. The same goes for the thermostat. Coolant should be changed every two years or 30,000 miles and be mixed 50/50 with distilled water.

•Shocks. Put your weight on the fender and move up and down until you get the car bouncing. Then jump off, and count how many times the car bounces. If it bounces up once and then stops, the shocks are fine. But if it keeps bouncing, get new shocks.

Another test of shocks: Hit the brakes hard when driving 15–20 miles per hour in a deserted parking lot. If the car stops and bounces, you need new shocks.

Cars with front-wheel drive: Check the axle boots (the rubber stocking over the constant-velocity joint) for cracking or tearing. Damage will allow grease leakage and prevent normal functioning of the joint.

•Steering. Have your steering checked if you experience a pull to one side...excessive wandering, vibrating or shaking at highway speeds...tire wear...or you hear a clunk when starting or stopping the car.

•Tires. Rotate them. Wheel lug nuts should be replaced using a torque wrench, not an impact tool (typically used in garages). Lug nuts replaced with an impact tool will warp the brake rotors and make the brakes pulsate.

Check tire pressure before you go and when you arrive at your location. Reason: Temperature affects pressure—one pound for every 10 degrees of temperature.

Example: If you leave New York on a 50° day and travel to Florida where it's 100°, your tire pressure will change five pounds—enough to damage them.

Let tires cool for an hour after driving before checking them.

•Windshield. If it is heavily pitted, replace it. Excessive pitting can cause night-blindness.

Source: Dré Brungardt, member of the Automotive Hall of Fame and of the Society of Automotive Engineers. He is publisher and editor of *Nutz and Boltz,* Box 123, Butler, MD 21023.

The Most Valuable Safety Advice For International Travelers

Even a seasoned traveler may leave gaps in planning for unexpected mishaps. Best defense: Getting advance warning about conditions where you will be traveling...and bringing along items that can make your trip faster and more convenient.

Information resources:

To learn about particular dangers or possibilities for unrest in any country you plan to visit, contact:

•The US Department of State. On country-specific travel hazards call the Traveler Advisory lines: 202-647-5225 or 202-647-0900. Know the details of your trip so you can respond to touch-tone instructions.

•The Regional Security Officer (RSO) at the US Embassy in the country you'll visit. Get the US Embassy number and name of the RSO from the State Department Country Desk Officer (202-647-4000). Note and keep the Embassy/RSO number and name for emergency use during the trip.

•The US Department of Commerce can offer insights about the business climate that may have safety implications. Example: Bribery is a crime in some places. Call the department's Trade Information Center (800-872-8723) or the desk officer for the country you'll visit (202-377-2000).

•American Chamber of Commerce. Call the Washington headquarters (202-463-5460) for the number of the affiliate in your destination city.

•A knowledgeable travel agent. Ask someone you know who travels regularly to your destination which travel agent they prefer to use.

Often-overlooked items to take:

Leave time before you leave home to obtain...

•Traveler's health insurance: Many emergency medical facilities abroad provide care only when paid immediately, in cash. Special travelers' policies provide ready cash...tie in to doctors worldwide...offer around-the-clock emergency response via a toll-free number...and provide assistance in any language. Cost: About $4/day for $100,000 of coverage.

Bonus: The insurers provide blood that has been checked for AIDS or evacuation to a facility that has such blood.

Best-known providers: TravMed Medical Assistance (800-732-5309)...International SOS Assistance (800-523-8930)...Travel Assistance International (800-821-2828).

•International drivers permit: This license lets you leave your passport stored safely when you go out. Passports are thieves' top target around the world—more than 25,000 are lost or stolen every year. When you must carry your passport, carry the license, too—in a separate pocket or bag. If the passport is stolen, you still have an identity document. Valid for one year, they can be obtained at any central AAA office at a cost of $5 for AAA members. Also, take extra passport photos on your trip in your case you need a replacement.

•Communications links: It can be hard to find good telephone service abroad. Public phones are often out of order, affected by bad weather, inconveniently placed and not secure for confidential discussions. Practice using them ahead of time and always carry the proper change or tokens. Hotel phones are more reliable but can be very expensive—especially for international calls.

Solution: US phone companies offer services that allow you to immediately access a US operator who then routes your call within the US. You receive a free, wallet-sized card listing the special codes you'll need to place calls from various cities. More information: ATT USA Direct (800-444-4000)...or MCI Call USA (800-444-4000). You can use these services from public phones or hotels. Hotels often charge fees—up to $15 per call—when you use your hotel room phone and won't disclose ATT or MCI direct access codes upon request.

Technical problem—and solution: Many overseas phones are rotary and may not have * or # tones. If you need touch tones to use your equipment—a voice mail or message machine back home—buy a pocket phone dialer (Recommended: Radio Shack item number 43-139). It imitates tones through the receiver. Cost: About $50.

• Emergency escape smoke shield: If you pull this transparent, heat-resistant head made of Kapton plastic over your head during a fire, its special breathing filter keeps out many of the toxins in smoke. With it on, you may gain additional time to escape a fire on a plane or in a hotel.

Convenience that counts: It weighs three ounces and folds into a 3" by 5" x ⅓" pack so it fits into a purse or pocket. Order from: Survival Products, Inc., Box 100428, Fort Worth, TX 76185, 817-923-0300. Cost: $46.70 (includes shipping and handling).

• Little things that can be a big help: A small flashlight that looks like a pen, which is handy for finding the keyhole in a dark hallway...a pocket flashlight that includes an alarm for protection on the street...thong sandals with stiff soles to keep at your bedside to prevent stubbed toes that come with stumbling around unfamiliar sleeping quarters... dropper bottle of tinctured iodine or Halazone tablets for water purification (one drop/pint of water for at least three minutes)... about $50 in US five-dollar bills to use where local currency may be familiar to you. The bills may serve as a tip or taxi fare where permitted by local law. Also: Lots of business cards.

One American businessman arrested by mistake in an Argentine police raid hurled business cards at onlookers and screamed for somebody to call the US Embassy. Someone did and embassy officials were able to quickly track him down and get him released.

Minimize terrorist risk:

Book nonstop flights whenever possible. Whenever you can, try to avoid airports in hub cities like Paris or Frankfurt where many US military personnel fly in and out.

Note: Although most of the time publicity centers on acts of terrorism that occur in the Middle East, more than 50% of all anti-US terrorist acts occur in Latin America.

Source: Peter Savage, a former foreign service officer and crisis-management planner with the Parvus Co., 1700 Elton Rd., Silver Spring, MD 20903. He is the author of *The Safe Travel Book: A Guide for the International Traveler,* The Free Press, 866 Third Ave., New York 10022.

3

Money Management For Tough Times

Recession Strategies From Frank Cappiello

We're looking for this recession to end sometime in the fall of this year. A bell won't go off, but some positive numbers will begin to come in for autos, housing and durable goods.

The reason we think that this will be about an average year-long recession is because there haven't been the kind of excesses that cause longer recessions—huge inventories, lots of expansion and speculation.

The Federal Reserve Board has been fighting inflation for the past two years and the only excesses have been in real estate and in banks and savings and loans. But those were created over a decade's time, so we expect a gradual unwinding, not a big shock.

Our scenario accords with one of the most venerable cycles we have on Wall Street—the Presidential cycle—which says that the economy rises and falls on a four-year cycle. The first and second years of a new President's term are when he gets a lot of the bad stuff out of the way, the third year (1991) becomes a transition year and the fourth year (1992) is usually a good one for the economy as reelection time approaches. Why this cycle works is open to a lot of interpretation, both cynical and scholastic, but it does work. Most likely: The Administration, Congress and even the Federal Reserve do everything they can to improve things before elections.

Assuming our scenario is correct, the stock market—which has a fantastic record of anticipating recovery four to six months before it happens—could start to move up as soon as March or April. The market's big rise after the 1980–1982 recession started in August, and the recession wasn't clearly over until year-end.

Since individuals can't do very much once we're in a recession, the appropriate strategy is to start planning now about how to capitalize on the recovery. The turnaround will happen because interest rates have come down enough to stimulate the economy.

That means that you should be buying

long-term bonds and stocks, mainly the big capitalization stocks favored by institutions and foreigners and groups that did well after the last recession.

Early candidates: Transportation issues like Yellow Freight and Consolidated Freight, as well as American Airlines and United. Retailers have been pounded, but we can't have a recovery without them. First buy WalMart and K Mart, then later on take a look at Carter Hawley Hale and Tiffany, a great franchise whose stock has taken a beating lately.

Cyclicals that should do well: Reynolds Metals and Geneva Steel (the reorganized Kaiser Steel).

Companies that look good in just about any climate: Boeing and Eastman Kodak. If the recession drags on: Look into Blockbuster Entertainment (videocassettes are now filling the role that movies played during the Depression) and Jostens, maker of high school rings and educational systems.

Later this year, we'd begin to look for a long overdue move in small cap stocks, those with $750 million or less in capitalization. Safest: Companies involved with health care and the aging of Americans. We like Health Images and Healthdyne.

Source: Frank Cappiello, president, McCullough, Andrews & Cappiello, Inc., 1 Greenspring Station, 10751 Falls Rd., Lutherville, MD 21093.

Recession Strategies From William E. Donoghue

Before the Bank of New England was taken over by the government, I predicted a major money center bank failure this year. Now I think that there could be more.

I also expect the failure of a major life insurance company—and a greater than zero possibility of a national bank holiday. (The problems Rhode Island had when a bank president took off with $30 million and caused many small banks to fail is an example.)

Message: Given the deteriorating condition of America's most trusted financial institutions, exercise extreme caution.

Stick with strictly credit-risk-free investments. Whether the recession turns out to be shallow or deep, I like Benham Target Maturity Trust portfolios for 2000, 2010, 2015 and 2020, which are invested only in US Treasury bonds maturing on those dates. These are zero coupon bond funds, which can be volatile on a day-to-day basis (that's market risk as distinct from credit risk). The yield is guaranteed if you hold to maturity, but if you sell before that, you could wind up with a big profit...or a big loss.

How this could work: If interest rates were to decline 150 basis points (1.5 percentage points) in a year, the longest term bonds in Benham Target Maturities—2020—would earn you a total return of 62%. If rates were to rise the same amount, your loss would be only about 30%. But this year, the odds are tilted in favor of falling rates.

Note: Although zero coupon bonds, which are sold at a big discount, pay no cash dividend, you are liable for annual income taxes on what the IRS calls imputed interest.

Caution: Reconsider keeping your money in government-insured bank accounts. The Federal Deposit Insurance Corp. (FDIC) had—before the Bank of New England takeover—reserves of only $.60 per $100 of bank deposits. Steps are underway to improve that to $1.25 per $100 of deposits by 1995, but that's still only marginal protection.

The good news: You can put your money in money market mutual funds that invest 100% in US Treasury bills. These funds are not insured by the FDIC...they're safer because they have $100 in reserves backing up $100 in investments. Top choices:

- Dreyfus 100% US Treasury Money Market Fund LP.
- Fidelity Spartan US Treasury Money Market Fund.
- Benham Government Agency Fund.
- United Services Government Savings Fund.

The last two funds invest in direct obligations of four agencies backed by the full faith and credit of the United States government, as well as Treasuries.

Bonus: These funds are exempt from state

income taxes in 40 states, so they have a tax equivalent yield higher than other money funds. Moreover, their sponsoring companies have not been charging management fees.

Though the next 15 to 21 months could present the stock-buying opportunity of a lifetime (see *Personal Advantage/Financial*, November 1990) I would be conservative and stay out of stocks right now.

Because the odds overwhelmingly favor further interest-rate declines, we are now recommending intermediate bond funds, including...

- Fidelity Government Securities, L.P., which allows the pass-through of state and local tax-free income, so it is not suitable for tax-deferred plans like IRAs.
- T. Rowe Price New Income, a big, conservatively managed fund that is largely invested in US government obligations plus some AAA corporates and a few Canadian government bonds.

Now is also a good time to look very carefully at every insurance company with which you're doing business.

For a nominal charge, you can get insurance guru Martin Weiss's safety rating on a specific insurer by calling our company, WEDCO, at 800-642-4276.

If the Weiss rating is A+ or A, you can be sure that you have a solid company protecting you. Anything better than B+ is OK. A C rating is neutral. But if the rating is D or less, you should definitely reevaluate your situation now.

Reason: Several experts whose opinions I respect now believe that a deep recession could wipe out as many as 20% of all US insurance companies.

Finally, for an investment that's almost completely credit-risk-free, consider a mutual fund that has a managed basket of foreign currencies to protect against a decline in the value of the dollar.

I like International Cash Portfolios (Pasadena, California. Maximum load: 4¼%) which is invested for total return, high income and hard currency.

Source: William E. Donoghue, publisher of *Donoghue's Moneyletter*, Box 6640, Holliston, MA 01746.

Smart Investor's Money-Market Calendar

The yields paid by tax-exempt money market funds tend to move up and down following a predictable pattern. Reason: Supply and demand. States tend to issue tax-exempt bonds at set times during the year. The increased supply leads to a reduction in rates. Investors also tend to withdraw funds at set times (Christmas, tax season) reducing demand and boosting rates.

Months	Rates
January–March	Decrease
April	Increase
Early May	Decrease
Late May–Early June	Increase
Late June–July	Decrease
August	Increase
September–November	Decrease
December	Increase

Strategy: Time investments with the rate pattern in mind. For instance, if you are planning to make a purchase using funds in a money market account, you might delay the purchase from April until early May, to get maximum benefit from seasonally high rates.

Source: William E. Donoghue, editor of *Donoghue's Money Fund Report*, Box 540, Holliston, MA 01746.

How To Buy Into Mutual Funds That Are Impossible To Buy Into

Some of the most successful no-load mutual funds are impossible for small investors to buy. Reason: They require prohibitively high minimum investments—up to $500,000.

The back door: By going through a discount brokerage that maintains a master account with such funds, you can often bypass the large minimum that would be imposed if you were to go directly to the fund.

Although these funds require a large

amount of money to open the account, most allow investors to deposit far smaller amounts of money after that.

Because many discount brokerages maintain omnibus accounts with no-load mutual funds, new shareholders buying into the funds through a discount brokerage are treated as if their investments were subsequent investments.

Example: The Gabelli Asset Fund, run by renowned stock picker Mario Gabelli, has a $25,000 initial minimum. Since subsequent investments can be as modest as $250, small investors can gain access fairly easily by going through a discount brokerage.

Even though the funds may not impose a minimum for subsequent investments, discount brokerages generally set their own minimum transaction fees.

And of course, you must pay the transaction fee on such trades, even though they involve no-load funds. Our transaction fee on trades of less than $50,000 is $20 plus .002 (2/10 of 1%) of the principal.

Source: Jack White, president of Jack White & Co., 9191 Towne Center Dr., Suite 220, San Diego 92122. 800-233-3411. One of the first discount brokerages, it pioneered the concept of secondary trading in mutual funds.

The Best Municipal Bonds Now

Although this is a good time to buy municipal bonds, it's very important that investors do so with their eyes wide open. It's particularly important to limit purchases to the best quality issues.

These are dangerous times. Corporate profits are crumbling—and so are the abilities of many states and local governments to raise enough tax revenue to keep functioning adequately.

Stick with general-obligation bonds—ones backed by tax revenues collected by the issuer...or revenue bonds—ones whose income comes from receipts of the actual project being financed, such as a toll bridge or a public-transportation system.

Then make sure that the bonds are rated double A or triple A by Moody's or Standard & Poor's. It's simply not worth the risk—that the issuer could default—to get a slightly higher rate of interest by purchasing lower-rated bonds.

I think many feasibility studies for publicly funded projects that were conducted when business was booming are not in tune with today's realities. I'm afraid that, in many instances, the worst-case scenario of such studies won't be bad enough for the tough times we face.

I'm not a fan of insured bonds. Reason: The reserves of the insurers that guarantee such bonds have yet to be tested by a large-scale failure. Yes, there were some insured bonds in the Washington Public Power Default, and purchasers did get their money back. But the amount involved was relatively small in relation to the outstanding issue.

I'm frankly concerned about the Municipal Bond Insurance Association (MBIA), which guarantees many municipal bonds, including some issued by cities that are in trouble. One indication is that MBIA's publicly traded stock has deteriorated much more rapidly than the market as a whole. This makes me worry about the company's reserves should there be a major failure.

I'm not as impressed as I once was by enhancements, such as bank letters of credit, that were supposed to serve as a secondary source of repayment should the bond issuer encounter trouble. Reason: The banks themselves are struggling to stay afloat, so their letters of credit are no longer as reassuring as they once were.

My favorite municipal bonds are those that are escrowed to maturity with Treasury bonds. Nicknamed ETMs, these bonds were issued in the early 1980s and have been refunded now that interest rates have come down.

Refunded bonds mean the issuers have taken some of the proceeds of the new issue and bought Treasury bonds that sit in an escrow account and guarantee both the interest and principal payments of the original issue. Hence, we have a municipal issue guaranteed with US Treasury bonds.

Investors receive tax-free interest that is backed by the full faith and credit of the US government. The bad news: You can't lock up this dream of a deal long-term. Most of the ETMs out there are short-term, with five years and less remaining until maturity.

I think anyone with $25,000 or more to invest should purchase individual bonds, rather than open- or closed-end funds or unit-investment trusts. Reason: You get a known, steady income stream, with none of the surprises that can crop up when you purchase a package of securities that you may not know as much about as you think.

Example: You may find some of the bonds in the fund or unit trust have early call features. Result: The high interest rate you were so delighted with disappears after the first few years.

When you buy municipals, a lot depends, of course, on where you live. Attractive now if you live in...

• California. Los Angeles Department of Water & Power Revenue Bonds. Double-A-rated intermediate-term bonds issued by the city's utility. One of the best bonds California residents can buy because, even in a recession, people need power and water. Coupon: 6%. Due: April 15, 2000. Yield to maturity: 6.35%.

• Illinois. Illinois State General Obligation Bonds. Triple-A-rated bonds. Coupon: 6.75%. Due: June 1, 2009. Yield to maturity: 6.9%.

• New York. New York State General Obligation Bonds. Single-A-rated bonds. Coupon: 6.5%. Due: June 5, 1995. Yield to maturity: 6.35%.

• Texas. Texas State General Obligation Bonds. Triple-A-rated ETMs. Coupon: 6.7%. Due: July 1, 1995. Yield to maturity: 5.8%.

Source: Marilyn M. Cohen, co-founder (with Jay Goldinger) and president of Capital Insight, Inc., a full-service retail and institutional brokerage firm. The company publishes *Jay Goldinger's Early Warning Wire*, 190 N. Canon Dr., Beverly Hills 90210, for the financial industry.

Questions To Sidetrack A Scam

When a person calls to sell you an investment, use the following questions to tell a swindler from a legitimate salesperson...

• Where did you get my name? Insist on a specific answer, not "from a list of qualified investors."

• Will you explain the risks involved in this investment?

• Can you send written materials backing up your claims?

• Will you explain your proposal to my accountant or lawyer?

• What regulatory agencies supervise your activity?

• How long has your company been in business?

• How much of my money will go for fees and commissions?

• Where and how will my money be held, exactly?

• What types of written statements do you provide and how often?

• Who are your firm's principals? Can you provide references for them?

Honest salespersons will answer these questions—in writing if you request it. Con artists may try to lie, but it's much more likely they'll quickly give up on you and try to find someone more gullible.

Source: *Modern Maturity*, 3200 E. Carson St., Lakewood, California 90712.

How To Avoid The Traps In Misunderstood Investments

Although most investors are now looking for higher returns when they invest, many still don't understand the risks involved in their investments.

As the renowned Bernard Baruch once said: "I'm not so concerned about the return *on* my money, as I am about the return *of* my money." All investors should take heed. But there are risks that are not so obvious to all...

• Treasury bonds and AAA-rated bonds. Many investors buy these thinking there is nothing safer—and then can't believe it when the bond's market value drops.

Explanation: What's safe about these bonds is the issuer's promise to pay a set rate of interest on them. Not safe: How this rate of interest will compare with general market rates, which change over time. That depends on broad economic factors like inflation, economic growth and the supply of credit.

When interest rates go up, a bond's market value goes down because the bond then pays less compared with other investments. So while the US Treasury may never default on a bond, a $1,000 Treasury bond could have a current market value of only $500 in a period of rising interest rates, leaving you with a big loss on this "safest" of investments if you had to sell before the date of the bond's maturity.

Of course, changing interest rates have the same impact on other high-rated "safe" bonds, such as municipal bonds and AAA-rated corporate bonds.

Opportunity: The same market forces also work in reverse—when interest rates go down, bond values go up. So it is possible to invest in high-rated bonds to obtain capital gains, as well as a secure source of interest income.

• Ginnie Maes. Ginnie Mae stands for the Government National Mortgage Association. They are pools of federally insured mortgages that are resold to investors. These are offered to investors as certificates that represent shares in a pool of home loans. As an investor, you receive part of the homeowners' monthly mortgage payments—a combination of interest and repayment of principal.

Trap: Ginnie Maes have often been advertised as offering "government-guaranteed" high yields. But only the principal of the mortgage loans is guaranteed. This leaves it possible to lose in two ways...

When interest rates rise, the market value of outstanding Ginnie Mae securities will fall, just as in the case with bonds, explained above. But with Ginnie Maes, you can also lose...

When interest rates fall, because homeowners may refinance their mortgages, causing your Ginnie Mae investment unit to be liquidated years before you expected. You'll get the principal back, but will then have to reinvest it at lower prevailing rates. And if you paid a premium (more than the face value of the underlying mortgages) to buy a Ginnie Mae investment that paid an unusually high interest rate, you will lose the amount of the premium as well, in spite of the government guarantee.

• Unit investment trusts. Many individual investors buy tax-free municipal bonds in the form of unit investment trusts. They are simply packages of a variety of municipal bonds. The trust itself may have millions of dollars worth of bonds. The units are sold to individual investors, usually in $1,000 amounts. If you are buying a tax-free unit investment trust, try to buy it during the original public offering.

Reason: When interest rates fall, many bonds may be called by their issuers—redeemed early to save on interest expense. And, of course, the highest-yielding, most attractive bonds are likely to be called first. If a trust's units have been outstanding for several years...and have been through periods of up and down rates, you no longer can determine the holdings of the trust's investments from looking at a unit's market price. It's best to buy a unit trust during its initial offering because at that point you know what you're getting.

• Zero coupon bonds. Zero coupon bonds pay no interest but are sold at a deep discount to face value. You get your return entirely through appreciation in the bond's value, realized when it is cashed in on maturity. The benefit of this is that zeros let you lock in a compound rate on interest on your investment.

Example: A 12% zero coupon bond accrues 12% compound interest until maturity, even if interest rates drop. In contrast, a normal $1,000 bond paying 12% pays $120 cash interest each year. If rates drop, you have to reinvest the $120 at lower rates, reducing your return.

But zero coupon bonds can sometimes be risky...

Trap #1: Although these bonds pay no actual cash dividends, you must pay taxes on the amount they appreciate each year. To avoid this tax problem, invest in tax-exempt municipal zeros, or buy zeros through tax-sheltered accounts—IRAs and/or Keogh plans.

Trap #2: The market value of zero coupon

bonds is much more sensitive to interest rate changes than that of regular bonds. A small change in rates can produce a big price move, up or down. That volatility means there's a real danger of taking a hit if you should have to sell before maturity.

Best protection: Obtain liquidity by investing in zeros through no-load mutual funds that buy only US Government Treasury zero bonds, such as Benham Capital Management's Target Maturity Funds 2005, 2010 and 2015.

If interest rates drop and your fund investment increases in value, you can always lock in your profit by switching into their money-market fund.

You might even consider buying back into zeros when interest rates rise again. That's a strategy for traders, but most people should be willing to hold zeros until maturity—don't invest money that you might have to withdraw when prices are low.

- Limited partnerships. These let you invest as an owner in a project such as a shopping center, hotel or oil well. The sales pitches for these deals promise returns much larger than you would expect from the stock or bond market. But remember that the partnership organizers often take hefty fees and commissions off the top of your investment.

Another trap: Because partnership interests are not traded the way stocks and bonds are, it can be extremely difficult to get out of a partnership. If the investment is a loser, or you need to raise cash in an emergency, you may find it impossible to cash out.

Advice: Scrutinize the business prospects of the partnership carefully before you make an investment. And don't invest any money you may need to withdraw prematurely.

Source: Terry Savage, a registered investment adviser and Emmy-award-winning financial journalist. Her new book, a comprehensive guide to personal and family finance, is *Terry Savage Talks Money*, Dearborn Financial Publishing, 520 N. Dearborn St., Chicago 60610.

Shrewd Timing

Buy US Savings Bonds at the end of the month. Reason: No matter when the bond is purchased, interest is credited from the first day of that month...so you get most of the month's interest for free.

Source: *The Super Saver: Fundamental Strategies for Building Wealth* by Janet Lowe, Dearborn Financial Publishing, 520 N. Dearborn St., Chicago 60610.

Money-Market Account Trap

About 99.9% of banks and thrifts pay below market rates to their money market account depositors. Better: Money funds. They have the same liquidity as money market accounts and offer higher returns.

Source: Norman Fosback, president, Income and Safety, 3471 N. Federal Highway, Fort Lauderdale, FL 33306.

Mutual Fund Tactic

Before investing in a fund, ask if the fund's managers invest their own money in it. If they do, they'll have personal reasons to hold down expenses, resist fee hikes, and focus on long-term results. Other managers may boost expenses (such as their own salaries) or take risks to make a "big score" that can lead to a better job elsewhere. Catch: Mutual funds are not required to disclose how their managers invest, but when one of them refuses to answer, you can safely guess the answer is no. Funds usually are eager to advertise the fact when they receive investments from their own managers and employees.

Source: Donald Phillips, editor, *Mutual Fund Values*, quoted in *Forbes*, 60 Fifth Ave., New York 10011.

How To Make Your Children Money-Smart

Most parents believe children learn about money naturally, the same way they learn to tie shoelaces or ride a bicycle. But finances are much tougher, and teaching kids about taking care of finances can be very hard work.

Challenges: Children who grow up ignorant about money run serious financial risks as adults. Not only are they unable to save, but they also lack the ability to appreciate value—and they lack the ability to postpone gratification. Those are vital talents in an age where ads scream at us to spend and indulge.

As soon as kids can pick up a coin, tell them it's money...and that it can be exchanged for something else—including peace of mind. At two years old, they probably won't understand what you mean, but you'll be laying the groundwork for what should begin at age three—the first lessons in finance.

There are no precise ages for teaching specific aspects of money, but here are some useful guidelines...

Age three:

- Give them a small allowance in exchange for doing simple chores—picking up their clothes, keeping the tricycle off the driveway, etc. The object is to introduce the concept of work for pay.
- Use trips to restaurants to show how money is used to pay for goods. Show them prices on the menu, the total of the bill and the payment that you make at the end of the meal.
- In stores, point out prices and sizes. Make it a game, and see whether they can find certain prices or items.

Age five:

- Now when you go to a restaurant or grocery store, give money to the kids so they can have the experience of paying a bill. It's a practical application of arithmetic that may reinforce what they're taught in school.
- For the first time, let children use their allowance to save for something they want to buy. Don't start with big items like a bicycle that will take years of savings, but something simple that can be bought after two or three weeks.
- Explain the meaning of charity. To show them how people must be responsible for each other, point out how much you, as parents, are giving them. Then encourage your children to give part of what they have to a charitable organization or someone who has less than they do.
- Open a small bank account for them. This is the opportunity for introducing the concept of investing.

Age seven to eight:

- When you're in a store, give the kids about $5, and ask them to find certain products with such-and-such ingredients. Then let them keep the change if they're able to find the products for less than $5.
- As children grow, increase their allowance, and help them save by paying them for bigger and bigger chores.

Age nine to 11:

- Make children responsible for their own budget. First figure out what you spend monthly on the children for clothing, entertainment and other discretionary items. Then give them control over that amount each month. If there's any left over at the end of the month, they can save or spend it as they wish.

This is when life changes for kids. If they used to ask for designer jeans and $100 sport shoes, chances are they'll stop when the money comes from their own budget.

Caution: Don't give in and supplement the budget if one month one of your kids has holes in his/her shoes. The embarrassment is a small price to pay for learning how to save and plan ahead.

Teens:

- In the early teens, consider opening a joint brokerage account and teaching teenagers about serious investments. Don't push, however, if they are simply not interested at this time.
- If you're saving for college expenses, insist that children also make a contribution.
- Get the kids involved in family finances. Give them responsibility for paying part of all of the insurance on cars they drive. If the family is going through tough economic times, explain the situation and ask for a sacrifice on their part.

The longer you wait, the harder it will be to teach children about money, but it's never really too late. If you've neglected these lessons, start with the basics, regardless of how old the child is. True, a 12-year-old may resent being put on a tight budget for the first time, but it's a lot easier to learn at 12 than 22.

Source: Neale S. Godfrey, chairman of Children's Financial Network, which runs workshops to help children learn about finances, 70 Tower Hill Rd., Mountain Lakes, NJ 07046. Ms. Godfrey is also author of *Kids' Money Book*, Checkerboard Press, 30 Vesey St., New York 10007.

Your Safe Deposit Box Can Be Much Safer

Don't keep anything in a safe deposit box that may be needed quickly when the owner dies. At that time, a bank normally seals the box until legal proceedings (sometimes lengthy) take place.

Don't store:

• Original will, cemetery deeds or burial instructions. (Keep them in a safe place at home or in a vault belonging to your lawyer, executor or accountant.)

• Large amounts of cash. Money in a safe deposit box is not working for you and suggests intent to evade income tax.

• Unregistered property (such as jewelry or bearer bonds) belonging to someone else. Courts presume these items to be your property and proving otherwise might be difficult.

Do store:

• Personal papers, such as birth and marriage certificates, military service or citizenship papers and important family records.

• Original signed family or business documents, such as house deeds, mortgage papers, trust agreements, contracts, leases, court decrees.

• Securities, registered or bearer.

Final check: Make sure someone knows where the safe deposit box is and where the key is, too.

Important: Safe deposit boxes taken out in a corporate name don't get sealed upon the death of one of the principals. This could be very useful for closely held firms.

Source: David Ellis, editor, *The Book of Money Secrets*, Boardroom Classics, Box 736, Springfield, NJ 07081.

Claude Olney's Money-Making Secrets

Claude Olney started his first multimillion-dollar venture from his kitchen table, selling a mail-order study tape for college students, *"Where There's a Will, There's an A."* Olney made the tape to help his own children do better at school.

A lawyer by training, Olney is a professor at Arizona State University because he loves teaching. His successful contracting, collecting and investing have been done on the side. We asked Olney to talk about his secrets for success...

• Write down your goals. This is the first step to accomplishing anything. List them... copy them, draw a picture...but put them on paper. If you don't, they'll probably never happen.

Example: A student who had put herself through college selling cleaning supplies door-to-door arrived at Olney's house in a 450SL Mercedes. She had carried a picture of that car in her wallet for several years. Now that she was making well over $100,000 a year from four hours of selling a day, she owned her dream car. The picture was her constant reminder of her goal.

• Make your goals very specific. Don't just write that you're going to study harder. Write that you will take a computer course, or that your will get an A in economics this quarter or master a particular skill. The student soap seller had a specific goal of selling 13 gallons of cleaner a day.

• Put your goals in a time frame. Don't say you'd like a new car. Picture yourself in a red Corvette within 12 months. Promise yourself you'll get your next promotion in six months or look for another job. Tell yourself you'll sell a particular number of units a week within three months.

• Don't be afraid to change your goals. As you grow and learn, you may find that last month's goals no longer apply. Perhaps you can do more, or you may want to do something different.

• Write down the reasons why you haven't

acted yet. Maybe you're afraid of starting or afraid of possible setbacks.

Example: One friend wanted to sell a particular kind of taffy with logos imbedded in it, but was afraid he wouldn't have enough money to pay the manufacturer for the rights to sell it, so he put off the call. He finally got up the courage after seeing his problem on paper. Then he found the company was willing to work with him, and his business was launched.

• Listen and get ideas from others, but make your own decisions. Talk to everyone who can help you. Go to the library and find out all you can. This can save you from making the mistakes others have made—but in the end you must take responsibility for your own actions. Then you can savor your own rewards.

• Go one step at a time. Sam Walton started the Wal-Mart empire with a single store in Roger, Arkansas. He had to make that store work before he could add the next one.

• Use your creative IQ. This is your capacity to be innovative, different, imaginative or just plain clever in solving life's big and little problems—in school, at home or in business. It can generate a good idea for a useful product.

Example: A friend of mine who saw telephone operators on television using headsets that left their hands free launched a successful mail-order business selling headsets to consumers.

The creative IQ is the part of you that says "yes" when a customer needs something that's not in stock and you can figure out a way to find it or make it.

Example: Another of my friends molded custom-fitted plastic skylights in his backyard so that a good customer would not be disappointed.

And the creative IQ is the force that finds a new use for a product that has become obsolete.

Example: Turning wire mesh that once was used to plaster walls into portable snow-traction pads for cars.

• Work at what you enjoy. If you are only putting your time in until retirement, change jobs. If you go to work because you want to and not because you need to, you'll be much more creative and bold. You'll contribute more and be better appreciated. People thrive on activity. When they are not busy, they get sluggish. There are 25,000 different kinds of jobs in the United States...there must be at least one that suits you.

Source: Claude Olney, whose most recent book is *The Buck Starts Here: How to Turn Your Hidden Assets into Money,* William Morrow & Co., 105 Madison Ave., New York 10016.

Investment Mistakes

Most investors have psychological time horizons that are too short. This is particularly true of retirees.

Retirement usually begins by the time a person reaches his/her mid-60s, but few of these retirees realize how many years they have ahead. People who live to their mid-60s will probably live at least another 20 years. So it's extremely important that they keep their money working for them.

Problem: Whether in their 60s or late 50s, retirees develop a deep conservatism born of the realization that they're no longer participants in the economic mainstream. They know they must now rely on their accumulated assets and respond to this realistic concern by getting out of stocks—which they perceive as risky—and into fixed income investments like bonds, CDs and money-market funds.

Trap: That's exactly the wrong thinking because inflation and taxes remain even as our income declines.

Stocks have the proven ability to grow with inflation, both in terms of share prices and dividends paid.

Bonds, issued with fixed interest rates, guarantee a certain income and return their face value at maturity. But they tend to lose value with inflation because bond prices decline as interest rates rise.

If you have to sell a bond before maturity, you could lose part of your principal. This is particularly troublesome with so-called zero-coupon bonds, which are sold at a deep discount from face value and actually pay no cash interest—although you must pay tax based on the portion of the bond's yield accrued during the year.

Better: Graduate the maturities in your fixed-income investments—bonds, CDs, municipal bonds, money market funds—so that some will always be coming due to meet your income needs for the coming three, four or five years. That will enable you to afford the long-term risks of equity investments, which can make more money for you over the long haul.

Owners versus creditors:

Retirees, as creditors (bondholders), will just barely get back the money they loaned. Owners, however, have the potential to greatly increase the value of their holdings. At the very least, they should be able to keep abreast of inflation.

What to own: Stocks are the most convenient and liquid form of ownership. They're traded every day on the stock exchanges and even if the market takes a tumble, you can always realize quick cash. That's not the case with artworks, antiques and real estate.

How much of your portfolio should be in equities is determined by your living expense needs...and how much time you realistically expect to live. If you have a million dollars in assets, for example, and are only spending $25,000 a year during your retirement, you don't need stocks. But if your assets total only, say, $800,000 and your life-style demands an income of $100,000 a year, you need not only stocks—but growth stocks.

Many retirees in their 50s and 60s will want to have 50%, 60% or even 70% of their portfolio assets in common stocks.

For the safety provided by diversification and professional management, use no-load mutual funds with a long and consistent track record. Don't try to hop aboard the latest fad and buy or switch into a new fund. Funds that have done well in the current cycle probably won't be the winners in the next cycle.

Consider the fund's management, its philosophy, the services it offers and its expenses. Buying the fund with the lowest management expense is especially important when investing in a fund that's indexed to the Standard & Poor's 500 or some other broad market average where management plays no real role.

Funds that allocate assets among different investment areas, such as real estate, precious metals and foreign stocks, make a lot of sense in terms of having a broad base of ownership potential, as opposed to putting your money in bonds, which makes you a creditor.

IRAs and other retirement plans are good vehicles to hold your long-term common stock investments because you have considerable flexibility in withdrawing the funds—and paying income tax on them. You don't have to start making withdrawals until you reach the age of 70½. Then you can base withdrawals on the life expectancy of yourself and your spouse, recalculated each year to stretch out your payments.

Home ownership:

Since many retirees have paid down most of their home mortgage, the question arises whether or not to hang on to the home. The problems of upkeep, etc., are really life-style decisions. But all things being equal, ownership of your current home or some other piece of real estate carries tax benefits that aren't available from other investments. You can refinance your home to get cash to live on or take out a home equity line of credit. Either will give you the tax advantage of deductible interest that is also generally low.

Option: Homeowners with low mortgages can often find a bank willing to finance a so-called reverse mortgage. This is really an annuity—in which the bank gives you an interest free (and tax free) loan, usually in the form of monthly payments, with the promise that when you die or the house is sold, the bank will be repaid with interest before any money goes to your heirs. Reverse mortgages are becoming more widespread and could offer future retirees a sensible way to recapture the equity they have built up in their home to pay for their retirement years.

Insurance:

Typically one's need for life insurance decreases with age and the accumulation of other assets. However, you should consider hanging on to your policy(ies) if your spouse will need that money to maintain his/her lifestyle. Other reasons: To provide needed liquidity to pay estate taxes or to avoid a distress sale of a family business or other illiquid assets.

Insurance can also be a shrewd but somber investment if you have any reason to think that you might not outlive the mortality tables upon which the premiums have been based.

Source: Tim Kochis, partner, Kochis & Fits, personal financial consultants, 450 Sansome St., San Francisco 94105.

The Case For Safe Investment Strategies For These Tricky Times

The world of investing is generally divided into bulls and bears. Bulls, the optimists—and bears, the pessimists.

I'd like to add a third category—the chickens. They don't want to risk any of their assets betting that things will get better—or worse. Chicken money is money you simply can't afford to lose. That money doesn't belong in the stock market, where one must make a forecast about the future. It belongs in insured CDs, money-market accounts and Treasury bills.

You won't get rich in those investments. You may barely beat inflation. And then income taxes cut into any profits. But—you won't lose any of your principal.

Know yourself:

The first thing each investor must do is to know himself/herself. Understand your "chicken" feelings—about funds that you must keep safe for some specific purpose. It's nothing to be ashamed of—being rationally unwilling to accept risk. Even if you can afford to take some risks in the stock market, it's not worth it if you can't sleep nights.

Self-discipline is the best way to avoid letting emotion overcome reason—when natural greed tempts you to jump in and make a big killing as the stock market hits new highs—or when fear paralyzes you from taking any investment action. It's important to know exactly what you're doing—and why.

Knowing yourself and your needs is much more important than just blindly following the advice sold by "experts."

Old rules no longer work:

Recognize that many of the old standby financial rules may not be good rules to follow in the 1990s.

Example: Home ownership. Sure, it's nice to own the house you live in...and there are tax benefits too—since home-mortgage interest is one of the few tax deductions still available. But don't fall into the trap of thinking of your home as an investment that's going to keep on increasing in value. Or that it will bail you out when it comes time to retire or put a child through college.

As we've seen in many parts of the country today, it's no longer realistic to assume that your home will increase in value every year. Ask yourself: What if its value goes down? Where will that leave me financially? You've got a big problem if you live in the Northeast, for example, where real-estate prices are crumbling—and you want to retire to a popular resort area where prices are still rising.

Another old standby that's no good for the 1990s—debt. It worked well in the 1980s when inflation was high and loan interest was tax deductible. But consumer finance charges are no longer deductible and the price being charged to carry debt is simply too high. Amassing 20% debt on credit cards, for example, simply puts one into a big deep hole, from which it is very, very difficult to escape.

Have a cushion:

Everyone should have a cushion before taking financial risk.

In today's insecure job world, many personal finance experts recommend three to six or even nine months of expenses, but it's hard to establish any general rule. Find your own comfort point and then respect that.

If you're young and making a good salary, you have lots of time to build your nest egg. You can usually afford to risk more than an older person, who is retired and no longer has a stream of income, or someone who knows his savings will be required to put a child through college in a couple of years. Those people have to be more conservative.

Over the long run, the stock market has always outperformed chicken investments. But the trick is picking the right timeframe.

During the 1980s, which began with the Dow Jones Industrial Average at 846, and ended with it near 3,000, it was hard to make a mistake. But if you had bought into the market in the late 1960s, when the DJIA hit a high of 1,000, you could have lost a lot as the market declined to 570 in 1972.

Defensive strategies:

#1. Pay yourself first. A great way to build up a reserve fund of cash for emergencies is to make regular contributions to a money-market mutual fund. Do this before the money hits your checking account, where you will almost surely spend it.

My trick: When I make a deposit in my money-market fund one month, and the computer printout statement comes back with a deposit stub and a return envelope, I put that return envelope and deposit slip right on top of next month's bills.

Safe/solid money market choice: Capital Preservation Fund (800-4-SAFETY). It is a no-load fund and buys only US Treasury bills.

Other good opportunities: Take full advantage of a company 401(k) plan by contributing the maximum allowed. This will be tax-deferred until you start withdrawing it after the age of 59½.

I also recommend using payroll deductions to buy Series EE US savings bonds. These now pay market-based floating interest rates, but you must hold them for five years to get the full advantage of that feature.

#2. Build a long-term diversified investment in the stock market. If you're put off by the big minimums required by many stock mutual funds, look into United Service Funds (800-873-8637). It's a new family of no-load funds with minimal service fees and is going after the small investor. It has an ABC (Automatically Building Capital) Investment Plan that lets you open an account in any one of their 13 mutual funds with as little as $100, and then add to it $20 at a time.

Remember: You must authorize the fund to automatically deduct your regular monthly investment from your checking or money-market account. That's actually a good discipline. This fund also charges $5 for switching between funds. My advice:

Choose five different funds and put $20 into each one every month. United Services' All-American Equity Index Fund, for example, allows you to effectively buy the whole stock market, because it's indexed to the S&P 500.

Speculations for the 1990s:

If you do have a cushion and want to speculate in the 1990s, here are ideas that I consider to be risky but potentially rewarding...

- Residential real estate. Because of changed tax laws and the recession, you can negotiate good deals now. This may provide shelter or rental income. As distressed sellers have found, it's not always easy to sell property, so look for property that can be rented out for income.
- Junk bond funds. If you believe that the 1990s will bring prosperity, and that some highly leveraged companies will survive, now may be a good time to put some speculative money in high-yield bond mutual fund. They've been moving up smartly lately, and even some pros are getting back into the market.
- Listed stock options. The Chicago Board Options Exchange has a new type of option investment called LEAPs (Long-term Equity Appreciation Participations) that offers investors the chance to own or control a stock, via its options, from six months to two years.

How it works: An option allows you to leverage a relatively small investment to control the future gains in a stock's price over the life of the option.

The risk: If the stock's price falls below the striking price of the option, you lose your original investment. For a descriptive brochure, call 312-786-5600.

Source: Terry Savage, recently elected a director of McDonald's Corp., and a registered investment advisor who appears regularly on Chicago's WBBM-TV. She writes a weekly "Smart Money" column for *The Chicago Sun-Times* and is also author of *Terry Savage Talks Money*, Dearborn Financial Publishing, 520 N. Dearborn St., Chicago 60610.

Alexandra Armstrong Tells How To Protect Your Assets No Matter Which Way The Economy Moves Next

With the experts disagreeing on whether the recession is still here, or over or getting worse, I don't want to bet on anything but continuing uncertainty. What do I do to conserve the value of the investment portfolio I've been building up?

Actually, a time of uncertainty is the best time to make investments. When everybody is sure things are going well, everything is bid up. But when there's uncertainty, there's opportunity to pick up bargains. That's how fortunes are made.

My basic advice now to conservative investors is to be wary of investments that promise a yield much above average. When people offer you a high yield, there's an offset—and that offset is greater risk.

With interest rates dropping, is there a temptation to reach for yields right now?

Definitely. I had a client yesterday who asked what I thought of her investing in some offshore securities that projected much higher returns. And I said, "Yes, you might. But you're not going to do it with me. There's a tax question and other questions about the risks you would be taking." And she said, "That's a relief. I really didn't want to do that anyway."

Well, how do you feel about overseas investing now?

Investing in overseas securities is essential for anyone nowadays. We recommend you invest at least 10% of your total portfolio overseas. If you only invest in US stocks, you are overlooking opportunities in 70% of the world-wide market.

Whether you invest in foreign stocks or bonds depends on your overall investment goals and tolerance for risk.

The way to minimize risk in foreign investments is via international mutual funds—either equity funds or bond funds. Pick those whose managers have good track records in coping with currency risks—as well as skill in selecting the soundest companies. Few individual investors have the experience and the information needed to deal with the risk of currency values shifting against one another. That can have a substantial effect on your total return.

These funds are excellent vehicles for dollar-cost-averaging. Putting a set sum into the fund every month over a number of years will even out the fluctuations.

And I also don't encourage individuals to use country funds for their foreign investing—funds that buy securities in just one country—Germany, for instance. I prefer to let the professional managers of an international fund decided which countries are most likely to prosper.

What about the risks in equities?

Study after study has shown that you will make money in the long term without undue risk by investing conservatively in stocks.

But you can't look at results year by year—short term. You must be able to live with the volatility over at least five years—and preferably 10 years. If you can't—because you have a specific need for the money a year from now—then you can't afford to put it in stocks. You can't time the market that way. It could be sharply down just at the time you have to raise cash. When that's your situation, you really should put the money in a money-market fund and be satisfied with the lower-than-average yield for the benefit of liquidity.

We see the stock market running between 2700–3000 on the Dow Industrial Average through the end of the year—no big upward breakthrough.

If you buy values—companies with increasing earnings, good balance sheets without excessive debt—your risks are reduced. You won't make as big gains but you're not likely to lose. I wouldn't buy companies without earnings or buy companies that need financing, because credit is very tight out there right now.

More and more of my friends in their mid-fifties are encouraged to move out of their jobs *and take early retirement—winding up with lump-sum payments of $200,000 or even more from savings, profit-sharing and retirement accounts. Some have put substantial sums in investment products they don't seem to understand very well. What would you recommend?*

We recommend for most people in that position to roll the money over into an IRA invested in a balanced portfolio. A 50/50 combination of stocks and bonds seems to do very well over the long term. Don't gamble on high-risk investments with retirement money. Funds work best, we think, because dividends and interest can be so easily reinvested with a minimum of fuss. And in later years, when these people might want to begin withdrawing money, funds can send a monthly check.

The biggest mistake I see these individuals make is focusing only on what they need right now, in their late 50s, or after 65. Too few seem to take account of the fact that they are likely to have to live on that money for 25, 30 and even 40 years.

What sort of inflation—and interest rates—do you anticipate people will have to deal with over the next decade or so?

It's very difficult to predict for that long a period of time. However, near term, we don't see interest rates going up—even with recovery—more than one or two points above where they are now. We see no signs of a return to the high interest rates and high inflation we had in the early 1980s.

People are genuinely more cautious now than they have been for years. They're not taking chances. They are not buying things. They aren't borrowing. That's going to take its toll on business expansion.

And taxes?

Our best information is there won't be any tax action from Congress this year. But in the years to come, we certainly see taxes taking larger chunks out of everyone's income—property taxes, state and local taxes, sales taxes. For those people still working, higher Social Security taxes.

How about the troubled financial condition of so many of the nation's banks. Is that going to keep the economy under a lid?

No. When you think of the particular functions banks have provided, you see the attractive alternatives now. In the past, most people thought only of banks when they considered where to put their savings. But we have clients who have moved their money from bank to bank as bad news broke—and they certainly don't think of banks as safe places to put their money any more, with or without deposit insurance. They use money-market funds instead. And keep only small checking accounts in banks.

Many more people are now aware that there is a price to pay for easy loans and offering high yields to attract deposits. They are willing to take less now for less risk. And there will be continuing bank consolidation. That's certainly not all bad.

Finally, what do you tell clients who express concern that their adult children are having a hard time financially and ask your advice on helping them out?

Frankly, I think as a nation we've spoiled the younger generation. They expect to have in their 30s and 40s what their parents weren't able to afford until their 50s. Parents used to think their expenses for children would be completed once they paid for college. But now financial requests continue with graduate school tuition and the down payment on a house and help in getting started in a business.

I caution many of these parents that they have to pay attention to what they are going to need over decades of retirement.

And I now see signs that changes are occurring. The daughter of a fairly wealthy client of mine lives with her husband and children on a really humble income. She just inherited some money from her grandparents. And she told me, "I really prefer for this money to be invested so I can't touch it. I want to invest it for our children's' education and our own retirement. I may inherit something from my parents but I can't count on that. They may have to spend it all."

Source: Alexandra Armstrong, CFP, chairman of Armstrong, Welch & MacIntyre, Inc., financial advisers, 1155 Connecticut Ave. NW, Suite 250, Washington, DC 20036.

Balancing Your 401(k) Plan...Advice from Brian Ternoey

It's time to update the investment strategy for your 401(k) plan. The investment decisions you made during the eighties may no longer be appropriate.

The most important question to ask yourself is...*When will I need the money?*

If you won't need the money immediately, invest for the long-term. The majority of people put their money into investments that are too short-term. While they think this is a conservative strategy, it isn't because it allows their pension assets to be worn away by inflation.

Guaranteed Investment Contracts (GICs) became the most popular investment vehicle in 401(k) plans during the 1980s—and for good reason. GICs gave investors a 6% to 7% return after inflation.

Now, however, you'll be lucky if you get 3% to 4% over inflation from a GIC—or if you get more than 2% over inflation in a money-market fund.

But equities will return 5% to 7% after inflation if you're willing to invest for the long-term and ride out the inherent volatility.

Caution: Keeping all your money in GICs doesn't give your investment portfolio enough diversification. Some people feel uneasy with the quality of insurance companies.

Best strategy: Diversify your 401(k) assets into a mix of equity and index funds, as well as money-market and other fixed-income investments.

Note: Usually you can switch out of a GIC into another investment option in your company's 401(k) plan "menu" without incurring penalties.

Trap: A lot of people spend too much time looking at their account balance, worrying about whether it's going up or down. If you won't be withdrawing your money in the near future—and that accounts for most people up to age 60—don't waste your time worrying.

Trap: Many people mistakenly assume they should move their money out of long-term investments, like stocks, into short-term investments as soon as they retire. This strategy, however, can deprive you of thousands of dollars in tax savings. You don't have to begin taking money from your retirement account until you're 70½. If you have other assets in taxable sources, such as personal savings, stock brokerage accounts or an inheritance, get income by liquidating those assets first. That will allow your retirement money to keep building up tax deferred.

On the other hand: If the inherent volatility of equities causes you to lose sleep, you may never live to enjoy your retirement. In that case, move back into more liquid investments.

Source: Brian Ternoey, a partner at Foster Higgins, a benefits consulting firm, 212 Carnegie Center, Princeton, NJ 08543, 609-520-2543.

Financial Planning Opportunities...Mistakes

Over the years, I've helped hundreds of clients dig themselves out of disastrous financial predicaments. In many cases, the situations were preventable. The most common mistakes I've seen can all be turned into opportunities:

- Mistake: Blindly chasing higher yields. With interest rates dropping, everyone is looking for higher yields. But many are buying high-risk investments without understanding the dangers.

Example: Looking for higher yields, Janet bought several municipal bonds rated below investment grade. She didn't realize that the economic decline had brought the municipality to the brink of fiscal disaster. And even if the municipality keeps making interest payments, lower bond ratings would reduce the value of the bond.

- Mistake: Clinging to cash. Many people, scared by economic uncertainty, are keeping too much of their money in cash and fixed-income investments. As a result, they are missing out on tremendous opportunities available in conservative long-term investments.

Rule of thumb: Keep six months worth of living expenses in an emergency cash fund... and invest the rest for the longer term.

• Mistake: Buying investments you don't understand. Never buy an investment without thoroughly understanding how it works.

Example: Many people bought real-estate partnerships in the early 1980s without realizing that the projected returns were based on inflation-rate assumptions of 10% to 15%. They also didn't understand their liability as a limited partner. Now some of the partnerships are going bankrupt, and they are getting hit with big tax bills.

• Mistake: Maintaining an unbalanced insurance portfolio. Many people buy more life insurance than they need, but they neglect to purchase any disability insurance.

Unless you're over 65, the chances of being disabled are far greater than the chances of losing your life. And unless you're properly insured, your family could be left destitute if you suffer a stroke, heart attack or other disabling illness.

• Mistake: Investing hastily. People who bow to high-pressure sales tactics often buy investments without first taking the time to properly research them. This happens to even the most conservative investors.

There's no investment that can't wait until tomorrow. If a broker calls with a tip, say you'll think about it overnight and call in the morning. Then find out what you can about the investment on your own.

• Mistake: Being stubborn. The essence of good investing lies in being flexible. But many people refuse to cut their losses when an investment declines in value.

Example: A family that has moved to a new town still has its old house on the market at a highly inflated price...what it might have sold for two or three years ago. Reality: The real-estate market in their area is not going to turn around soon. And selling the house at a lower price would be a lot cheaper than paying an expensive mortgage for another year.

• Mistake: Caring too much about taxes. Some people will do anything to save taxes—even if it loses them money in the long run.

Example: John owned a stock that had risen 100% and wasn't likely to go higher. But he refused to sell it because he was worried about the capital-gains taxes he'd have to pay. While he procrastinated, the stock dropped in value, and he was out real cash.

Similarly, many people take on huge mortgages, reassuring themselves that the interest payments are tax-deductible. They forget that although the government may give them back up to a third of that payment, they're still paying two-thirds of the cost out of their own pocket.

• Mistake: Following the crowd. Many people rush into investments based on something they hear at a cocktail party. More often than not, hot tips turn out to be wild exaggerations.

• Mistake: Poor record-keeping. People who can't put their hands on the proper records at tax time miss out on valuable tax deductions.

Also important: Keep back tax records for five years. If you're audited, poor record-keeping could cost you thousands of dollars in additional taxes, interest and penalties.

Source: David Himmelreich, a partner in the financial counseling firm of Hynes, Himmelreich & Glennon, 1 Dock St., Stamford, CT 06902.

The Secrets Of Safe Investing

Safe investing doesn't have to mean earning lackluster returns. My top safe-investing suggestions in these worrisome times:

• Get high yields on the world's safest investments. People who are concerned about the safety of their bank deposits have a very good alternative—government money-market funds.

Bonus: Some of today's safest funds also pay the highest dividends. My favorites:

• Benham Government Agency Fund. Benham Capital Management Group, 1665 Charleston Rd., Mountain View, CA 94043. 800-472-3389. No load. Minimum initial investment: $1,000.

• Dreyfus 100% US Treasury Money Market

Fund L.P. Dreyfus Service Corp., 144 Glenn Curtiss Blvd., Uniondale, NY 11556. 800-645-6561. No load. Minimum initial investment: $2,500.

• Fidelity Spartan US Treasury Money Market Fund. Fidelity Distributors Corp., 82 Devonshire St., Boston 02109. 800-544-8888. No load. Minimum initial investment: $20,000.

• U.S. Government Securities Savings Fund. United Services Advisors, Inc., Box 29467, San Antonio 78229. 800-873-8637. No load. Minimum initial investment: $1,000.

These funds all invest only in direct obligations of the United States Government, which are backed by the full faith and credit of the US Treasury.

Included: Treasury bills and the obligations of just four federal agencies—Ginnie Mae (GNMA), Sallie Mae (SLMA) the Farm Credit System and the Federal Home Loan Bank.*

The funds' dividends are 100% exempt from state income taxes, giving you an additional .40% to 1% yield on a tax-equivalent basis.

And the companies that manage these funds have waived all or a portion of their management fees and expenses, giving the funds an additional yield of .70%. Result: A tax-equivalent yield of 8% or more.

Many people pass up these funds' 8% tax-equivalent yield in order to invest their money at 5% at their commercial banks, because it offers them a guarantee from the Federal Deposit Insurance Corp. (FDIC). But three percentage points is quite a bit of money to pay for FDIC insurance.

It makes even less sense when you realize that every $100 that's invested in a commercial bank is backed by only 28 cents in FDIC reserves. But every $100 that is invested in a government money market is backed by $100 in government securities.

• Earn 30% on a riskless investment. How can you get such a juicy opportunity without an illegal insider's tip or a huge hidden risk?

It's simple. Pay down your credit-card balances now. Those monthly service charges are costing much more than you think. You pay for them with after-tax dollars, and the interest payments aren't deductible.

If you pay down your balances, you'll be able to increase your wealth as much as if you'd discovered a 30+% riskless investment.

Example: If you live in Massachusetts, pay 31% in federal tax, 12% in state tax and 12% interest on your credit card, you'd have to find an investment earning 34.6% that would pay you as much as you'd save by paying down your credit-card balance.

• Trade nondeductible high-interest loans for deductible low-interest loans. If you can't find the money you need to pay down your credit-card balances, transfer your debt to an investment portfolio account at a brokerage house and borrow against the assets in your investment portfolio.

Your broker will give you a line of credit that is worth up to about half of the value of your stocks, bonds and mutual funds.

The rates are usually lower than the prime rate paid by banks—about half the rate you're paying on your credit card—and the interest is tax-deductible.

Because it's a fully collateralized loan, you can't be turned down. And you won't have to give up any of your long-term investment positions.

Be aware, however, that you can't use money from your IRA or your Keogh as collateral.

Source: William E. Donoghue, host of the syndicated radio show, *Donoghue's Strategies*, and publisher of *Donoghue's Moneyletter*, Box 8008, Holliston, MA 01746. Call 800-445-5900 for a free sample issue.

Advantages Of Stock Ownership

Owning even one share of stock in some companies can generate big savings on the company's products and services. Marriott gives registered shareholders significant hotel discounts...Brown Forman/50% discounts on Lenox china...Tandy/10% discounts at Radio

*Beware of government money-market funds that buy repurchase agreements and other securities. They are backed by weaker government guarantees. And they may only be partially tax-exempt.

Shack...Pfizer/discounts on cosmetics...General Mills/25% discounts at Red Lobster restaurants.

Source: *Investing at a Discount: Saving on Commissions, Management Fees, and Costs* by Mark Coler, New York Institute of Finance, 2 Broadway, New York 10004.

CD Interest Rates

Falling CD interest rates (20% in six months) are pushing money into government bond mutual funds where yields are now 7.5% to 8%.

Source: Mutual Fund News Service, Box 937, Bodega Bay, CA 94923.

Analyzing The Analysts

When your broker pushes a stock, ask the name of the analyst who made the recommendation. Then follow the stock's performance. Over time, you'll learn which analysts to trust...and which to avoid.

Source: *Medical Economics*, 5 Paragon Dr., Montvale, NJ 07645.

Bill Donoghue On A Great New Opportunity... Full Service Banking Without Banks

It's time to make a change from your bank to lock in competitive rates on safe investments, cheap checking and savings accounts.

Big problem for banks now:

Banks are in the throes of downsizing to meet regulatory capital requirements. Most simply don't have enough capital to insulate you from their problems. Banks are reducing their deposits by offering less and less competitive interest rates...making fewer and smaller loans...and even calling in and/or refusing to renew good loans. This is to increase their capital as a percentage of deposits to make up for operating and bad-loan losses. They are doing everything they can to increase profits, such as adding on new fees to existing services.

Savings account options:

No-load (no-sales charge) mutual funds are the best substitute for banks. There are quite a few safe no-load mutual funds with higher-than-bank returns.

My favorite mutual funds for savings account substitutes...

- United Services Savings Government Securities Fund (800-US-FUNDS). It delivers the highest money-market returns on safe investments and it is exempt from most state and local income taxes (current yield: 5.98%, worth a taxed equivalent return of 6.3%–6.8% in states with state income taxes) with a constant price per share.
- Blanchard Short-Term Global Income Fund (800-922-7771). Current yield: About 9.4% with a principal risk of about plus or minus 2% of the net asset value of the fund due to market fluctuations—a great trade-off, in my mind.

Checking accounts:

Money funds and a few selected mutual funds including the United Services and Blanchard Fund (above) offer free checking services, in these cases with $100 and $500 minimum checks, respectively.

United Services Treasury Securities Cash Fund (also 800-US-FUNDS) however, offers no-minimum balance and unlimited free checking, although it does pay a lower yield than the Savings Fund and is only about 50% exempt from state and local taxes.

The company that you work for can deposit your paycheck each week into the fund of your choice. Make sure, though, that the fund will allow you to draw checks immediately. Most will if paid electronically. A short discussion of what you are doing with the manager of your local supermarket will help you cash checks when you need to. (Some supermarkets have a policy against out-of-state checks, so you need to arrange for approval.)

With this method, you can be earning as much as 9% or more on your checking balance. And you will be earning daily dividends in the fund of your choice until your check clears.

Borrowing on investments rather than from the bank:

If you have an investment portfolio (stocks, bonds and/or mutual funds) shift those securities into your brokerage account and borrow on margin—at rates between 8% and 10%. By borrowing on margin from your portfolio, you can pay down expensive debt, such as your credit card debt. Credit card rates run about 19%—and with combined federal and state income tax rates of, say, 37% (31% federal plus 6% on average state income taxes)—you have to earn 30% or more before taxes to earn the 19% after taxes to pay the nondeductible credit card interest.

If you borrow against your investments, you may even be able to deduct the interest on the loan as an investment-related expense.

Deductibility secret: To be deductible, the interest must be on loans for investment purposes and is limited to the amount of net investment income. A safe strategy is to sell one investment to pay off the credit card balances and borrow to buy back a similar investment. That gives you the chance to sell an investment that is "underwater" and get a tax break for a realized capital loss as well. Discuss this tax strategy with your tax advisor to execute it correctly.

Source: William E. Donoghue, publisher of *Donoghue's Moneyletter* and the new audio cassette service, *Moneytalk*, 800-642-4276.

Reporting Fraud Pays Off

The False Claims Act of 1863—with added 1986 changes—offers hefty rewards to private citizens who spot and report fraud against Uncle Sam. Example: An eye surgeon recently won almost $700,000 in an out-of-court settlement when her report that another eye surgeon was charging Medicare $1,000 for glaucoma treatments that actually should have cost less than $400.

Source: *Business Week*, 1221 Ave. of the Americas, New York 10020.

Alexandra Armstrong Says Saving Is Especially Important Now

Many couples in their 40s are sandwiched between their needs to provide for their children's college education in a decade or so and their own retirement further down the line. Can you help?

A couple in their early 40s has $65,000 of after-tax income today. Twenty-five years from now, this same couple will need $220,000 after taxes (assuming 5% a year inflation) to buy the same things they are buying today with their $65,000 income.

And to generate that income just from their investments, they would need $3,386,000 in capital, assuming it yielded 6.5% after taxes.

To accumulate that much capital, the couple would have to set aside around $46,000 a year—starting now. Remember, that's out of $65,000 net income. We're assuming 8% annual appreciation.

What about Social Security?

Social Security might help but no one knows what that will be 25 years from now. My personal theory is that Social Security will be used for health care and won't be available for income needs.

Wouldn't those figures put a scare into most 40-year-olds who were figuring they were doing pretty well financially right now?

Yes. And the picture is harsher still for couples now in their 50s who dream of retiring in their late 50s. At the rate many 50-year-olds save, even those with ample incomes, early retirement is unrealistic. Many would run out of money some time in their 60s.

That's just retirement. What about financing college?

Most couples with $65,000 after taxes like to think they will send their kids to private colleges. That's $20,000–$30,000 a year today—and going up 10% a year.

To give you an idea of what that means, a couple with an eight-year-old and a 10-year-old at present would have to start putting away about $29,000 a year now to fulfill that dream.

Well, putting that much aside for retirement and college is clearly impossible with an after-tax income of $65,000. What are these people supposed to do?

Youngish couples are going to be facing projections like these over and over again in the years ahead. You can't let these projections paralyze you into doing nothing, which, too often, is just what happens.

There's only one sensible course. Recognize that the financial outlook is tough and that you must start doing something about it—fast. The earlier you start, the less you have to put away—regularly, every week or month—without fail.

So, it won't be $30,000 a year. It will be less. And there won't be as much as you would like in the future...but it will be something.

You cannot just say we'll just put enough aside now for the children. Then, when we're 50 and they're out of school, we'll be able to start saving for our retirement. For most people, there will not be enough time left to do something substantial then.

If you can't meet those retirement and college goals, what can you do?

Start making tough choices—now—because the figures show you what is and is not possible.

On college, for instance, don't let your children build up unrealistic expectations. Figures like these often start couples thinking—and talking to their children—about good public universities rather than private colleges. Some people with "portable" careers deliberately move to states with top public colleges.

What can people do about having enough money to see them through retirement?

One strategy...they should start early to explore a move to a less expensive part of the country after retirement.

And they don't have to assume they must keep their capital intact to hand over to the children. They can carefully plan to prudently deplete capital, if needed, during their retirement years.

What about tapping the equity some couples might have in their homes?

It is a viable short-term option for many. From my professional experience, I know that more people have substantial amounts of equity in their homes than the press reports would have you believe. As long as the law allows interest on home equity loans up to $100,000 to be deducted, this has to be considered.

Eating into home equity to meet college expenses leaves a family with that much less when they do retire, of course, because their mortgage payments will be higher than they would be otherwise.

What about putting money in the children's names?

I feel strongly that people should keep the money in their own names, and not their children's. The tax benefits for keeping money under your children's name have dwindled over time, with little tax benefits available right now. However, the chief reason is that if you give the children the money, they may not use the money to go to college.

How about investing those savings right now? Do you think interest rates are bottoming out?

This is just the time in the interest rate cycle when investors are tempted to reach for yields. And it's also the time when that runs a good chance of getting them into trouble.

So we're now advising clients to be as liquid as they can with their fixed-income holdings—in money-market funds even though the yields are low. We anticipate interest rates will be higher a year of so down the road.

We think it would be a mistake to go for the higher yields in longer-term securities right at this time. If rates do go up, those securities will fall in value.

Source: Alexandra Armstrong, CFP, chairman of Armstrong, Welch & MacIntyre, Inc., financial advisors, 1155 Connecticut Ave. NW, Washington, DC 20036.

How To Know When It's The Right Time To Sell Your Mutual Fund Shares

Now may be the time to consider selling your mutual fund shares. Reasons:

• Basic indicators: If they are correct, the market is overdue for a price drop.

• Tax planning. If you have a loss on another investment, for example, that loss could be used to offset the gain from selling shares in a mutual fund.

The key signals:

Few people who invest in mutual funds review their holdings often enough.

Result: They miss chances to make a profit, or they suffer unnecessary losses.

Consider selling when...

• Performance drops. Look at how the fund performs in relation to other funds of the same type—growth funds, technology funds, etc. Then look at how share prices are doing in comparison with funds of the same type and the same strategy, such as aggressive growth funds, biotechnology, etc.

In both cases, consider dropping a fund if it's not in the top 25% of either category.

Exception: If a price drop resulted from situations beyond the control of the fund.

Example: Funds that invested heavily in the auto industry have recently been hurt by the credit crunch. Nevertheless, these funds may be worth holding because virtually no one could have anticipated tight credit.

Apart from a comparative price drop, make sure to review holdings when all equities suffer. If interest rates begin rising, for instance, it may be more profitable to switch to bonds or bond funds.

• The fund closes to new investors. This action usually means the fund managers feel they can no longer find investments that fit the strategy that's outlined in the fund's prospectus.

Example: Janus Venture Fund, which specializes in companies with small capitalization, recently closed. To do otherwise would have meant continuing investment in what the fund's managers considered a very treacherous segment of the market.

When a fund closes, its share price is usually at or near the fund's high.

• The fund's portfolio manager leaves. That usually foreshadows a change in the investment philosophy that attracted you to the fund in the first place.

Exception: If the former manager trained a successor and gradually handed over the reins, it can make sense to keep your shares despite a shift at the top.

If professional investors have doubts about the successor, their opinions will immediately be reported in *Barron's* and *Forbes*. Reliable brokers may also be helpful.

• The investment no longer meets your personal objectives. Example: At age 35 you might have invested heavily in growth funds. But if you're now 55, it probably doesn't make sense to take the risk associated with that type of fund. It may be more prudent to switch to capital appreciation funds, zero-coupon bonds or another investment that will build up cash for retirement.

Source: Jack Walsh, editor, *United Mutual Fund Selector*, an investment advisory service that tracks over 1,100 mutual funds, 101 Prescott St., Wellesley Hills, MA 02181.

Lessons In Minimizing Personal Financial Risk From Alexandra Armstrong

More and more families have been reducing their equity stake in their homes—for many, their major form of savings—by taking out home equity loans. How risky is that?

Well, people have to be aware of two risks on such loans. First—most home equity loans have a variable rate, which is fine now with mortgage rates declining. But once interest rates begin to pick up again, some homeowners might find themselves financially pressed within a couple of years by substantially higher monthly payments.

Now would be a good time to lock in a fixed rate on such a loan, if you can negotiate it with the lender.

And if you're about to take out a home equity loan, be sure to shop carefully. Typically, in every area there is one bank that is aggressively going after home equity loans—and is ready to make the best deal. Self-defense: Ask potential lenders what fees will be charged—and negotiate to eliminate those fees. Otherwise, you can be unpleasantly surprised by appraisal expenses, closing costs, settlement costs and so forth.

And the second risk?

Whether or not interest paid on such debt will continue to be tax deductible. Currently, interest up to $100,000 of home equity debt—whether you tap that equity via refinancing, a second mortgage or a home equity line of credit—is fully deductible. But as long as Congress is desperate to raise tax revenues, there's a lot of talk around town about cutting the limit to $50,000—and even eliminating the deduction. If that does happen, it is not certain that the existing loans would be "grandfathered"—that is—have the deduction still allowed.

Are there good—and bad—ways to use the cash a family raises from a home equity loan?

My advice to clients is that they should never borrow money for anything except a long-term investment that is expected to appreciate in value. If you use the money from a home equity loan to buy a car or pay off credit-card debt—just because auto-loan interest or credit-card interest is no longer tax deductible—you're pouring the cash into a depreciating asset.

But, if you use the money to pay college bills, you could consider that a long-term investment in your children's future. And certainly if you use the money to improve the home, that's fine. We feel that you can be reasonably confident that homes will be appreciating assets.

Really? Might people still be overestimating the value and appreciation potential on their homes?

Actually, many people are now underestimating the value of their homes and the prospects for appreciation. Of course, we can't expect the 10%–15% a year appreciation some homeowners enjoyed in the 1970s and 1980s. But it's reasonable for a homeowner to expect the value of a home to increase more or less in line with the inflation rate.

What risk-reducing advice do you have for people who suddenly find they have a lot of cash because they've been eased out of their jobs by early retirement programs and need to make investment decisions? Many of them are wary about putting a lump sum into the stock market.

Don't try to time the market. True, we've had about a 20% gain in the stock market this year. So it's reasonable not to expect much more from this level. But that doesn't mean that well-selected issues can't appreciate substantially. Look for companies whose price/earnings ratios and other fundamentals make sense—companies that don't have excessive debt.

Cautious strategy: Select a family of funds that consistently perform above average. Put the lump sum into a bond fund and then use dollar-cost-averaging by gradually moving a set amount each month from the bond fund into a stock fund or several stock funds within the fund family.

Another cautious strategy: Select an equity stock fund that has had a reasonably good track record during past bull markets and that doesn't lose much when the market swings down. Many investors who are wary about going into stock funds think that fund managers are fully invested all the time. Of course, that's not true. A manager with a good long-term track record makes better-than-average judgments about the right time to move some of the portfolio into cash—anticipating a drop in an overvalued market.

What typical investment mistakes do you find when you take over the portfolios of new clients?

They are either too widely diversified—or not diversified enough.

Is not being diversified enough very common?

Yes. Often, portfolio holders will have too much stock in the company they work for—or worked for. It's almost as if they have a need to be attached to the company.

However, they would have a tremendous tax bill if they sold these shares of stock that they have been holding for so long. So when we begin to reconstruct these portfolios to increase their investment returns, it can take some time to shift out of these stocks.

And sometimes it's a very sound strategy not to sell because the stock is a good one.

Source: Alexandra Armstrong, CFP, chairman of Armstrong, Welch & MacIntyre, Inc., financial advisers, 1155 Connecticut Ave. NW, Washington, DC 20036.

Ed Mrkvicka Tells How To Get The Best Loan Deal You Possibly Can

Getting a car loan or a personal loan is simple. But to get the best possible terms, you need to know a few things that your banker isn't going to tell you...

1. Get a copy of your credit report. Go to your local credit bureau—you can find it in the Yellow Pages. Alternative: Call your bank to get the phone number of the credit agency they use.

Check your credit report to make sure that the information is accurate.

Beware: An estimated 40% of all credit reports contain inaccurate information that may prevent you from getting a loan.

If there is negative, but accurate, information on the credit report, such as a payment you refused to make (because an item you bought was a lemon and the company wouldn't take it back), bring it to the attention of the loan officer. Being "up front" about it will show you to be a responsible and honest prospective client.

2. Shop by phone. Call a minimum of three banks in your area and request to speak to a loan officer. Ask him/her to enumerate the fees associated with the type of loan you need as well as the interest rates being offered. Compare the costs of all three. Include credit unions and your local savings and loan institution in your survey.

3. Sit down with a loan officer and structure the loan you want—once you've found the institution with the most favorable rates. Warning: Quite often the loan vehicle the bank offers is not the least expensive option available.

Example: Many banks use an installment loan vehicle which is based on an add-on interest rate installment plan. Than means that you are paying interest on the total of the loan (say $10,000) every month rather than paying interest on the declining principal. This is called a front-end loaded loan, and is not a good deal for you.

Best: Ask for a simple interest, single-payment note than allows for monthly payments or an installment loan calculated on a simple interest basis. This loan vehicle charges interest only on the remaining amount of the principal you're paying off.

4. Negotiate a better position. Push to get a point—or at least a half point—shaved off the interest to be paid on the loan. Bargaining chips:

- If you've been with the bank for a long time, you can reason with your loan officer that you've given them steady business, and should get something a little better than the guy who just walks in off the street.
- If you're at a new bank, offer to let them handle a Certificate of Deposit for you, or tell them you'd be willing to move your checking account to their bank to get a better loan deal.
- An excellent credit rating is also a bargaining point—that's worth a lot to a bank. You are the kind of customer whose business a bank wants.

Look to shave off loan fees, such as application fees, credit-check fees, document or secretarial fees, lawyer's fees, title-search fees, etc.—not just points on the interest of the loan. If you are negotiating a loan with many up-front fees, such as a home equity line of credit, negotiate with the bank to waive a few of these fees.

You stand a much better chance of getting a better deal if you are negotiating with a smaller institution than with a large bank. A smaller bank will work harder for your business.

5. Calculate the total cost of the loan. You should know exactly how much the loan will cost you in fees and interest over the life of the loan. A bank, for example, that has a higher fee structure, but a slightly lower interest rate, may look more expensive at first glance. But if you calculate out a loan from another bank that has very low fees and higher interest rate, it may turn out that the former bank's loan is actually cheaper than the low-fee/high-interest combination.

Source: Edward F. Mrkvicka Jr., author of *The Bank Book: How to Revoke Your Bank's License to Steal,* HarperCollins, 10 E. 53 St., New York 10022, 800-331-3761. He is also publisher of *Money Insider,* a financial newsletter for consumers, Reliance Enterprises, Inc., Box 413, Marengo, IL 60152.

Twelve Ways To Avoid Being Ripped Off By Your Bank

I have the highest regard for the banking system. Without it, our economy could not exist today.

But what I have no respect for are banks and bankers that manipulate the system for their own aggrandizement. Unfortunately, those types have taken over.

That's why banks no longer meet the moral imperatives of their charters, and why the Federal Deposit Insurance Corporation (FDIC) has reported that a substantial number of forced bank closings are the result of illegal insider transactions.

I have no objection to banks making money. In fact, they have an obligation to their shareholders to make a fair return on their investments. But I'm very troubled that so much of the money that they make is through deception, withholding of information and planned intimidation.

Banks function according to one principle—you can make the most money from the people who can afford it the least...meaning the average family.

My own experience over the last 20 years in the banking business indicates most consumers will overpay their bank more than $100,000 during their lifetime, through mortgages, credit cards, loans, checking and savings accounts. Self-defense...

1. Never borrow on a typical installment loan basis. These loans are front-end loaded. That is, you pay interest on the original balance of the loan through the entire term of the loan, even though your are reducing the amount you owe every month through your repayments. A much better route is to ask your bank for a loan on a simple-interest, single payment note that allows for monthly repayments or an installment loan calculated on a simple-interest basis. This method charges interest on the balance outstanding at any point in time. On a modest $7,000, four-year loan, this approach can save you hundreds of dollars in interest.

Many banks will claim that they do not make such simple-interest loans, but that's simply not so. What they really mean is that they don't make these loans to consumers—who are usually not smart enough to ask for them—but they do to businesses (which are savvy about the cost of borrowing).

2. Never buy credit life and disability insurance from a bank. Banks often try to sell this insurance to mortgage or loan borrowers. This insurance pays off debt in the event that the borrower dies before the loan term is up. Problem: This coverage is much more expensive than what you could buy independently from an insurance company...and, in many loans, the costly premium is subject to an interest charge.

3. Negotiate before taking out a mortgage. Don't assume such items as interest rates, "points" (prepaid interest) and closing cost are set in stone. You have to speak up. Most people who have tested my advice tell me they were amazed at how easy it was to convince their banks to reduce their interest rates or the points they were required to pay.

Negotiating pays off. A one-percentage-point cut on a $100,000, 30-year mortgage will save you almost $27,000...a half-point cut will reduce your costs by $13,500. If your bank won't budge, then try several others. Chances are, you'll find one of them hungry enough for your business that it will make some concessions—you'll just have to look a lot harder right now.

4. Consider paying off the principal on your mortgage early. Most banks offer residential mortgages for a standard term of 29 or 30 years. That's because banks make much more money with longer payment periods than with shorter ones. What they don't tell you: By simply increasing your monthly payments by a modest amount, and/or making your payments early, you'll be able to shorten the repayment term significantly...and lower your total costs.

Example: If you have a $100,000, 30-year mortgage at 9½%, the standard amortization schedule calls for monthly payments of $840.86. This results in total repayments of $302,709.60 over the entire life of the loan.

But by adding just $50 per month to your regular payments, you'll repay that 30-year loan in only 23 years and three months...and you'll reduce your costs by a total of $68,109.66.

5. Don't allow the bank to force you to make payments into a bank escrow fund for your home insurance and property taxes. Banks will claim that such accounts ensure that all the bills on "their" property are paid on time. But the real reason is profits—their profits. They can make large sums of money by investing the amounts that are in your—and thousands of other customers'—escrow accounts until the very day that they pay those tax bills. But many institutions pay little or no interest on their escrow accounts, which means you are giving them an interest-free loan every day your mortgage is in existence.

Solution: Tell your bank that your will not agree to an escrow account unless it pays a fair-market interest rate on the funds in that account. You should also insist that the account be under your name and control, and that you—not the bank—pay the bills as they come due. If your bank balks, check with the appropriate state or federal bank supervisory agency. In almost all cases, a bank's requirement of an escrow account is bank policy, not law.

6. Never, ever borrow through your credit cards. Too many people are seduced by the convenience of bank credit cards, and wind up with stratospheric interest rates to finance non-essential purchases. To put the level of credit card rates into perspective, what would you do if your mortgage was approved, but at 19%, or your car loan was okayed, but at 22%? You'd immediately withdraw your application and take your banking business elsewhere.

Also helpful: Do some comparative shopping to locate banks that charge low or no annual fees, impose reasonable interest rates and don't charge interest from the date of the charge transaction even though you pay off your bill in full by the due date.

7. Know the pitfalls of bank safe deposit boxes. You may think your bank safe deposit box is safe, but it isn't. Bank vaults are not impervious to break-ins, fires or floods. If anything happens, the contents of the box may not be insured under the bank's insurance policy.

Additional vulnerabilities: If you have an unpaid delinquent tax obligation, the federal or state government can obtain a warrant to invade your safe deposit box and confiscate its contents to pay its claim. The bank has no alternative but to comply.

Solution: Buy a home safe that meets or exceeds the fire rating of a bank vault. For a one-time cost of about $250, you get the same protection that you do with a safe deposit box, and you need pay only once, not year after year after year. With proper documentation, contents can be insured under your home insurance policy.

8. Avoid automatic teller machines (ATMs). Banks duped consumers into using ATMs by telling them it would cut labor costs by eliminating expensive human tellers. But now that consumers are hooked, banks want to make these ATMs profit centers. It's a rare bank these days that doesn't charge customers for the privilege of using such machines. Furthermore, ATMs can be dangerous to your physical as well as your financial health. Despite repeated robberies, most banks do not provide security guards for customers using after-hour ATMs.

9. Beware of overdraft checking. This service allows your to write checks for more than you have in your account. It's based on customers' fear that their checks will bounce. While it may sound like a bargain, overdraft checking is often nothing more than an expensive way to get you deeper into debt.

Due to the way many banks have designed the service, you may wind up borrowing (and paying interest on) more money than you actually need to cover your checks. Under one method, for example, a bank will deposit an amount equal to the next $100 that is needed to cover your overdraft. Say you overdraw your account $105. The bank will deposit $200 in your account and charge you interest on this amount, even though you're only using $5 of the second $100.

Solution: Have your bank "red flag" your account so you're called if you have an overdraft. This way, you can go to the bank and make a deposit to cover the check without paying an overdraft—or overdraft protection—fee.

10. Avoid bank Individual Retirement Accounts (IRAs). While IRAs are a fine idea, banks rarely offer the best deal in town. Usually, their rates on certificates of deposit are not competitive with other institutions, and may be one to three percentage points below the market. Even though banks promote the advantage of Federal Deposit Insurance, if people accumulate the large sums the banks claim they can by stashing their retirement savings in an IRA, any funds in excess of $100,000 are not covered by FDIC insurance.

Best: Check out rates at several brokerage houses before you turn your IRA money over to a bank.

11. Do preventive maintenance on your personal bank account. It's always smart to get on a first-name basis with the manager and several tellers of the branch of your local bank. That way, should a need for VIP treatment arise in the future—if, for example, your business needs a large loan or you need an out-of-town check cashed immediately—you're much more likely to get a sympathetic hearing than if you've never before introduced yourself.

12. Use a small bank rather than a big one. At big banks, the attitude often is, *We do it our way or we don't do it at all.* But smaller banks tend to be more flexible, and rarely have a large bureaucracy for you to contend with. Furthermore, while your business might be considered insignificant at a big bank, it could represent an important contribution at a small bank.

A $10,000 CD at huge Citibank, for example, probably wouldn't even be noticed, while the same deposit at a community bank could have a big impact on its weekly deposit figures...and give you bargaining leverage for things like a service-charge-free checking account.

Source: Edward F. Mrkvicka, Jr., author of *The Bank Book: How to Revoke Your Bank's License to Steal,* HarperCollins, 10 E. 53 St., NY 10022, 800-331-3761. He is also publisher of *Money Insider,* a financial newsletter for consumers, Reliance Enterprises, Inc., Box 413, Marengo, IL 60152.

4

Car Smarts

New-Car Options: What To Buy And What Not To Buy

The right optional equipment can transform an automobile that's okay...into one that's truly outstanding—not only in terms of safety, comfort, and convenience but also in terms of resale value. Which new-car options are good choices, and which are a waste of money?

• Air conditioning. Except if they're to be used exclusively in frigid climates, all cars should be equipped with air conditioning. Besides raising your comfort level during warm weather, air conditioning boosts a car's resale value. Cost: $700 to $1,500.

• Automatic transmission. This feature simplifies driving, especially in urban areas. Like air conditioning, it usually boosts a car's resale value. Drawbacks: Increased cost, reduced fuel economy, more sluggish performance. Before deciding which transmission to order, test drive cars equipped with each. Cost: $700 to $1,500.

• High-performance engine. A decade ago, many standard-equipment engines were so underpowered that they made driving unpleasant and, at times, unsafe. Today's base engines are usually more than adequate...and any increase in performance afforded by a power plant with turbocharging or extra cylinders must be weighed against the higher cost ($200 to $2,000), and the reduction in fuel economy and the potential for higher insurance premiums.

Bottom line: Unless you need extra power for specialized application, order the base engine.

Note: If you tow a trailer, inquire about special trailer-towing packages that combine a larger engine with automatic leveling, beefier shocks and springs, heavier-gauge wiring and special engine-cooling equipment.

• Anti-lock brakes. These make driving safer, and in many cases they qualify owners for lower insurance premiums. Well worth the money. Cost: $500 to $1,500.

• Rustproofing. Most new cars have adequate protection against the elements, thanks to standard factory-installed rustproofing. Dealer-applied rustproofing is not only unnecessary, but also potentially harmful to a car's corrosion resistance.

Similarly, special dealer-applied paint protectants and upholstery treatments generally are not worth the cost. Cost: Anywhere from $200 to upward of $1,000.

• Rear defroster. This low-cost option—now mandatory in Michigan and some other states—dramatically improves rearward visibility in inclement weather. Worth the money. Cost: $200 or less.

• Heated windshield. This sounds great to everyone tired of scraping snow and ice. However, heated windshields are coated with a thin metallic heating film that subtly cuts visibility—especially at night. And, they cost more to replace than standard windshields. They also reduce the range of radar detectors.

Bottom line: Unless you frequently leave your car outside in icy or snowy weather, save your money. Cost: $200 to $300.

• Sunroof. If you want one, make sure it is factory-installed. Dealer-installed sunroofs are more vulnerable to breakdowns. Warning to taller drivers: Sunroofs limit interior headroom. Cost: Approximately $550.

• Power controls. Power locks make it easier to lock a car's doors, so they're sensible from a safety standpoint ($250). Power windows are more of a trade-off. While more convenient, they are more expensive to repair if they break down ($300). Power seats, though expensive, may help you to get more comfortable in a car, especially if you are smaller or larger than the average person ($250–$1,000). Power rearview mirrors make sense only for cars driven by several people (usually part of the package—$75). Power steering is now standard on all but the tiniest economy cars.

• Adjustable steering wheel. A wheel that tilts upward for easier ingress and egress is well worth the small additional cost—typically under $100.

• Handling packages. Stiff springs, beefier shocks, stabilizer bars and larger tires dramatically improve a car's ride and handling—if you prefer a stiff, responsive ride. If you prefer a softer ride, opt for the standard suspension. If you're not sure, arrange for extended test drives in cars equipped with one type of suspension. Cost: About $150.

• All-wheel drive. Many cars and mini-vans are now offered with a "full-time" all-wheel drive option, in which power is applied to the road through four wheels instead of the usual two. It improves traction on ice, snow or sand, giving an uncanny sense of surefootedness, and may be worth the additional expense—about $2,000.

• Active suspension. Infiniti offers this option, which uses computer-actuated springs to "iron out" road bumps. Sounds great—but not worth the current exorbitant cost—$2,200 in the case of the Infiniti Q45 and the cost of reduced fuel efficiency.

• High-performance tires. Many drivers pay extra for super-high-performance tires—not realizing the tiny additional improvement in dry-weather handling is often outweighed by the big decline in wet-weather handling. Unless you live where it almost never rains or snows, go for the standard all-weather rubber. Cost: $50–$100.

• Special seats. Performance-minded motorists spend hundreds of dollars on seats made to hug the body. Surprise: Most motorists find standard-equipment seats more comfortable, especially for extended stints behind the wheel. Cost: $500.

Source: An industry expert who has been evaluating cars and options for 10 years.

Gas Rip-off

Service stations are selling regular gas under the higher-priced premium label. Where to watch out for this: States where agencies do not inspect service stations—Indiana, Michigan, Missouri, Montana, Oregon, Tennessee and Washington.

Source: US General Accounting Office.

Best Ways To Protect Your Car From Thieves

A quality security device installed on your car will more than pay for itself on insurance premium savings alone.

• Many insurance companies provide premium discounts for cars with anti-theft systems.

• One of the best ways to reduce premiums is by increasing the deductible on your insurance policy. A good anti-theft device will help cut premium costs by increasing your deductible—while reducing the risk that you will ever have to pay it.

Anti-theft basics: You want the car thief to know that you do have a security device on your car. Therefore, make sure you let your system show—the little red light under the dashboard is an excellent deterrent—also, you should put a sticker advertising the alarm system in a window.

But you also want to make it difficult for the thief to figure out what he has to do to beat your system, and give him very little time to do it.

Trap: Thieves are very familiar with the most popular security systems, such as those installed on new cars at the factory, and can defeat them quickly.

Self-defense: Start by hardening your car's "soft spots." Thieves know the vulnerable spots on your car better than you do. Examples:

• Many GM cars are stolen by "peeling" the steering column casing, a technique used to expose a little rod that can then be moved almost as easily as a key to start the engine. If your GM car has a plastic steering column casing or one made of lightweight metal, buy a reinforced collar—either one that you have to remove every time you start the car or one that is permanently installed. (One source that specializes in fitting columns to GM cars is Steadfast. Call 800-342-5911 for information on your nearest dealer.)

• On many Japanese-made cars, key mechanisms are vulnerable—namely the steering column and trunk. The Japanese don't have a serious car-theft problem, so they don't put much effort into improving the quality of their locks. A lock shield may deter a thief skilled in taking advantage of this weakness.

It's a mistake to rely entirely on a sturdy bar that locks the steering wheel in place so the car can't be driven, as many people do. Under US auto-safety standards, the steering wheel must collapse easily in a crash.

Result: Thieves find it easy to cut into the steering wheel and remove the bar.

Some simple security steps that work:

• When you park against a curb, turn the front wheels sharply to the right—or left—and make sure the front of the car is not pointed outward, which would make it too easy to tow away. The thief would then have to tow the car from the rear—and won't because the angle of the front wheels makes the car almost impossible to control.

• Buy a car alarm that sounds when a car is tilted, again to defeat towing.

• Have all the windows and major parts (doors, fenders, bumpers, tops and fancy wheels) etched with the car's Vehicle Identification Number (VIN). Body shops that know they are subject to search by the police won't accept parts that are marked this way—and thieves know that. Most effective: Put a sign in the window noting that the parts have all been marked.

• Install a simple toggle switch (Cost: Less than $5) on the wire that runs from the ignition to the starter and hide it amid the wires under the dash or run it under a car seat. Turn the switch off when you leave the car. Catch: Read the warranty on a new car first. Some manufacturers make it difficult to buy anything but a dealer-installed system by voiding the warranty on the car's electrical system if a wire is cut to install a security device.

To learn about a range of more sophisticated devices that won't be familiar to most thieves, call the Vehicle Security Association* for its brochure on selecting an alarm system and a list of its member manufacturers—the upper echelon of the industry. Also read the ads and articles about security systems in reli-

*202-828-2270. 2101 L St. NW, Washington, DC 20037.

able trade magazines—*Car Audio and Electronics*, etc.

Recovery strategies for already stolen cars: There are sophisticated security systems that will track your car after it has been stolen.

• Lo-Jack system, now operating in Massachusetts, New Jersey and southern Florida, hides a tracking unit about the size of a chalkboard eraser somewhere in your car. If your car is stolen, you call the local police and give them your Lo-Jack code number. They then use the Lo-Jack tracking system to locate your car.

• Teletrac, soon to be available in the Los Angeles area, does not depend on a call to the police. A thief who hot-wires the car or tows it initiates the tracking system automatically.

• Code-Alarm's Intercept system that will use the Coast Guard's Loran C Navigation System to track cars, will be available next year in several coastal areas.

One California company has recently announced a system that will use satellites to hunt down stolen vehicles.

Meanwhile, don't forget the simplest and most effective auto-theft prevention system of all: Always take the car keys with you when you leave the vehicle. One out of five auto thefts occurs because the keys were left in the ignition.

Source: Ken MacKenzie, an investigator with the Richardson, TX, police department and officer of the International Association of Auto Theft Investigators, 255 S. Vernon, Dearborn, MI 48124. Barnet Fagel is first vice president with the Vehicle Security Association, 2101 L St. NW, Washington, DC 20037, and public safety liaison manager, International Teletrac Systems, 9800 La Cienega Blvd., Inglewood, CA 90301.

Car Rental Trap

Those big rental discounts apply only if you rent a car for exactly as long as you say you will when you're taking the car out. Traps: By returning a car early, you may increase the cost of the rental due to a loss of the discount. Similarly, if you rent a car for a few days and then decide to extend the rental period, there's usually no chance of getting a discount for the longer period. And an extended week-long rental may cost significantly more than the discounted weekly rate the company advertises.

Source: Jan Heffington, president, JBH Travel Management, 200 Union St., Suite 318, Denver 80228.

Repair Scam

Secret warranties between auto manufacturers and dealers (called good-will adjustments in the industry) may be costing you money. How they work: Manufacturers notify dealers of a widespread defect in a car model and authorize them to make free repairs for people who complain. Problem: Dealers often don't tell you that the repair is covered by the manufacturer—and they charge you for it. Self-defense: Ask the dealer if the repair is a good-will adjustment. To find out for yourself, write to the Center for Auto Safety. Give the make, model number and year of your car, describe its problem, and enclose $1 and a stamped (52¢), self-addressed, envelope.

Source: Center for Auto Safety, 2001 S St. NW, Washington, DC 20009.

Safety Statistics You Should Know

Vehicles with the highest occupant death rates: Chevrolet Corvette Coupe...Chevrolet Sprint two- and four-doors...Chevrolet Camaro...Ford Mustang...Nissan 300ZX...Yugo two-door...Chevrolet Spectrum two-door...Pontiac Fiero. Models with the lowest rates: Volvo 240 station wagon...Saab 900 four-door...VW Vanagon...Olds Cutlass Cruiser station wagons...Pontiac Safari/Parisienne station wagon...Volvo 740/760 four-door...Volvo 240 four-door...Acura Legend four-door...Audi 5000 four-door...Lincoln

Town Car...Mercedes SDL/SEL...Toyota Cressida.

Source: Insurance Institute for Highway Safety, 1005 N. Glebe Rd., Arlington, VA 22201.

Car Sense

There's no good reason to buy a Porsche, Infiniti or other expensive car. Beyond their high-status image and interior bells and whistles, most are bad values. These cars require premium gasoline, get poor mileage, are expensive to maintain, carry higher insurance rates, don't necessarily handle that well and aren't any safer than less-expensive cars.

Source: An auto-industry insider who regularly test-drives the newest cars.

Parking Lot And Garage Owners

Parking lot and garage owners are responsible for damages and losses to your car when it's in their care—if they are in possession of the keys. Extra protection: Notify the attendant if there is something fragile about the car or something valuable inside it.

Source: *The Business of Living* by Stephen M. Pollan, personal finance commentator for CNBC/FNN, Fireside Books, 1230 Ave. of the Americas, New York 10020.

How To Get The Most Mileage From Your Tires

Tires must be carefully maintained to yield maximum mileage. The basics:*

• Rotation. Because drive-axle tires wear more evenly than non-drive-axle tires, rotating them helps to equalize wear. Not rotating tires can cut their life in half.

*For a copy of the booklet *How to Take Care of Your Tires,* send a self-addressed, business-size envelope to Atlantic Tire, 7307 Pulaski Hwy., Baltimore, MD 21237.

Rotate tires about every 7,500 miles (more frequently for heavy city driving, less frequently for heavy highway driving). To rotate:

• Two-wheel-drive cars: Cross the non-drive-axle tires and keep the drive-axle tires on the same side of the car.

Example: In a front-wheel-drive car, the right rear tire is rotated to the left front...the left rear tire is rotated to the right front...the right front tire goes to the right rear...and the left front tire goes to the left rear.

• Four-wheel-drive vehicles: Cross the tires only if they are showing heel-toe wear. To tell: If, when you run your hand around the tire, it feels smooth in one direction and sharp or chopped in the other, it is suffering from heel-toe wear. Otherwise, simply switch the right front and back tires and the left front and back tires.

Note: The rules on tire rotation have changed. For even wear, radial tires should be crossed when rotating.

• Balancing. Balance the tires that are moved to the front of the car with each rotation to help ensure even wear. If there is any sign of uneven wear, balance all four tires.

• Alignment. Poor alignment causes a tire's edge to wear faster than the rest of the tread. Uneven wear reduces driving safety and increases cost per mile as a result of shorter tire life and decreased fuel economy. Causes of misalignment:

• Driving over something very hard—a pothole, etc.

• Hitting the curb with your wheels turned when parking. This can be even more damaging than hitting a pothole.

• A change in the vehicle's height. After 20,000 to 30,000 miles, the car's springs start to sag. A change as small as ¼ inch can cause alignment problems.

For best alignment results, bring your car in with half a tank of gas—a full or empty tank will throw it off. Also, people who often carry a very heavy load (salespeople, carpoolers, etc.) should notify the mechanic so that the extra weight can be compensated for.

• Tire pressure. Underinflation causes tires to wear faster...lowers the tires' weight capacity...cuts fuel economy...decreases maneuverability...and may lead to a blowout.

Ideally, pressure should be checked twice a month. At the very least: Check when the seasons change. Also check pressure before taking a trip where you'll be driving the car for several hours at highway speeds.

Source: Ralph Schissler, a 21-year veteran of the tire industry. He is the owner of Atlantic Tire, an independent tire dealership in Baltimore, and president of the Maryland Tire Association.

Stop Driving Yourself Crazy

Driving can make your pulse race and your blood pressure soar. About 40% of Connecticut's one million commuters, for instance, are troubled by stress while on the road, according to a recent survey by that state's Department of Transportation. Although you can't do anything about the traffic, you can keep it from getting to you.

Self-defense:

- Join a car pool or take public transportation to work. The conversation and companionship will take your mind off the commute, even when it's your turn to drive. When you're a passenger, you have the freedom to work, read—or sleep.
- When you drive alone, visualize your car as a refuge, not a battleground. Use this as getaway time to recharge your batteries and relieve the pressures of the day.
- Listen to soothing music. Play your favorite tapes. If you listen to the radio, do so without constantly switching stations. If you don't want to hear a particular song or commercial, just lower the volume.
- Buckle up. Somewhere in your subconscious you know it's safer—and therefore less stressful—when you drive with a seat belt. Also: Be a safe driver. Don't tailgate, make quick lane changes, run yellow and red lights, etc. You'll not only feel safer, you'll be safer.
- Give yourself extra time to reach your destination. Eliminate the need to rush. And remember, everyone is sometimes late...people will understand.
- Don't be a traffic judge and jury. If another driver does something stupid, stay calm. Don't let it bother you.
- Don't fight the traffic. Give in. Go with the flow. You can't prevent the flooding or the jackknifed tractor-trailer and anxiety about it isn't worth it.
- Believe that you are the master of your own behavior. Exercises: Drive using your brakes as infrequently as possible. Keep several car lengths between you and the car in front of you.
- Know when not to drive. Never, ever drive after drinking alcohol or taking antihistamines or other drugs that can impair your performance.

Source: Martin Brenner, MD, an authority on driver stress and freeway violence and a recovering Road Warrior. His Stress Care Driving Program was developed for the Connecticut Department of Transportation. To receive a free copy, send a self-addressed, stamped business-size envelope to Connecticut Department of Transportation, 24 Wolcott Hill Rd., Drawer A, Wethersfield, CT 06109.

Auto Odors

Odors your car gives off are clues to mechanical problems. Burning plastic: Short circuit in the electrical system. Burning oil: Low oil, transmission overheating or oil leaking onto a hot engine part. Burning rubber: Hot tire because of locked brake shoe or a rubber hose touching the hot engine. Exhaust odor in car: Puncture in exhaust pipe under passenger compartment. Gasoline odor in car: Defective evaporation-control canister, leaking or disconnected vapor or fuel line.

Source: Shell Oil Co., Hammond, IN.

Dying Car Dilemma: Fix It? Get Rid Of It?

Many families have an older car that they use just for driving to the train station or for quick trips to the grocery store. Question: At what point does it stop making sense to keep the car alive?

Before you authorize major repairs on an older car, determine how its value compares with the cost of the needed repairs.

Check the newspaper classifieds to see what cars comparable to yours are selling for...and ask your mechanic how much the repairs will cost.

• If the value of your car is less than the repair costs, get rid of the car. Options: Trade it in and buy a new one...sell it...donate it to a technical school (and use it as a tax write-off)...or junk it.

• If repair costs are roughly equal to the value of your car, it still may not be worth the cost of getting it repaired.

Ask yourself: Have I already spent a great deal on repairs? Are all the other parts still okay? How many miles are on the car?

A four-cylinder car that has been properly maintained will last about 100,000 miles...six-cylinder, 150,000...eight-cylinder, 200,000. Note: The life expectancy is much shorter for cars used primarily for stop-and-go city driving.

If you decide against the repairs, and simply want to get the car into working order to sell it or trade it in, buy junkyard parts.

A junkyard engine, for instance, costs one-half to one-quarter the price of a remanufactured engine,* which averages about $2,000. The junkyard will usually install the remanufactured engine for you or recommend an outside installer. Check the Yellow Pages under "Automobile, Wrecking."

If the repair looks worthwhile:

If it makes financial sense to go ahead and have the car repaired, there are still some important points to consider. Included:

• Are the parts available? The 2.6-liter Mitsubishi engine, for instance, once used in the Mini Dodge Caravans and in many Mitsubishi models, had an inherent defect and is failing all across America. Because the demand is so great, it's very hard to find replacement engines.

• How long will the repairs last? Based on the warranty of the added parts (normally one year or 12,000 miles), decide whether the expected added car life justifies the repair costs. Note: There's a good chance that the repairs will last longer than the warranty...but don't count on it.

• What does your mechanic say? If your car has been regularly serviced by a reliable mechanic who knows it well, he/she can offer useful advice about whether or not to repair it.

Source: Dré Brungardt, a world-class auto technician and member of the Automotive Hall of Fame and of the Society of Automotive Engineers. He is editor and publisher of *Nutz & Boltz*, Box 123, Butler, MD 21023.

*A remanufactured engine is a used engine that has been brought back to original specifications. Replacement engines are nearly always remanufactured.

Best Time To Buy A New Car

The weeks before Christmas—business is usually very slow, so you should be able to negotiate a lower price. Also good: January and February, when weather is bad and people stay home...at the end of any month, when dealers are struggling to reach sales quotas. Worst time to buy: March through June, when people begin planning summer vacations.

Source: *Reader's Digest Consumer Advisor: An Action Guide to Your Rights*, Reader's Digest Association, Pleasantville, NY 10570.

Dozens Of Ways To Improve Your Car's Mileage

Suddenly, the price of gasoline is soaring... again. But there are ways you can cut your gas bill. To drive more efficiently...

Things to do to your car:

• Keep your car properly maintained. Follow the manufacturer's recommended tune-up program. Also helpful: Keep a log of your gas mileage. When mileage drops, have the car checked. Particulars:

• Oxygen sensor. If your car was made after 1980, it probably has an oxygen sensor. This wears out at about 60,000 miles.

• Tire alignment. Misalignment wears out tires and lowers mileage.

• Radiator thermostat. Change it if it's five years old or older. Recommended: Install the hottest temperature thermostat possible to allow your engine to warm up fast. The sooner it warms up, the more efficiently it runs.

• Air filter. Make sure it's clean. Best: An oil-wetted foam air filter.

• Front brake rubber hoses. If your car is 10 years old or older, change the hoses. Old hoses cause front brakes to drag and decrease mileage.

• Thermostatic air-control system. This brings preheated warm air into your engine when it's cold outside. When it's not working properly, the car takes too long to warm up and burns more gas. Have your mechanic check its operation.

• Keep tires properly inflated. Check tire pressure monthly. According to a Firestone study, we waste 600 million gallons of gas each year because of underinflated tires. Helpful: Install pressure indicator caps (available at auto-part stores) in the valve stem to warn at a glance when the pressure is low. Cost: About $10/set of four.

• Use synthetic motor oil lubricants instead of those refined from petroleum. Synthetics provide less friction and are less affected by changes in temperature than petroleum products.

Switching to synthetics normally yields a 2%–5% increase in mileage, but can yield up to a 25% increase in mileage. If everyone in the US switched to synthetics, we would need less oil from the Middle East.

• Use fuel with the correct octane. Helpful: Keep a logbook and see which octane gives the best fuel mileage for your car without causing ping.

• Test your fuel for alcohol.* Use brands that contain the smallest amount. Problem: Alcohol, used as a cheap way to achieve octane, has only half as much energy as gasoline. Although the amount of alcohol added per brand varies by region, Chevron, Exxon, Mobil and Texaco are best overall.

• Don't overfill the tank when you pump your own gas. The pump automatically clicks off when the tank is nearly full. Continue to pump until it clicks off the second time, then stop. Any more gas will be wasted because it will contaminate the evaporative canister (an emissions device), possibly running onto the ground.

• Install the biggest battery that will fit in your car. A large battery helps the car start faster when it's cold and lowers the charging-system work load.

• Eliminate unneeded weight. The heavier the car, the worse the mileage. Take out sand bags when it's not snowing, remove the roof rack when it's not in use, etc.

• Use radial tires. They roll with less friction than regular tires.

• Install oversized tires. Larger tires yield a smaller rear axle ratio—the ratio of engine revolutions to wheel revolutions. A smaller ratio translates to better mileage. Note: Remember to have the speedometer recalibrated. Important: Only use larger tires if space permits in the wheel well.

• Park your car in the garage if you live in a very cold climate. If you don't have a garage, install an engine-block heater to preheat the engine in freezing weather. The faster the engine warms up, the better your fuel economy.

• Install a locking gas cap.

Things to do when you drive:

• Accelerate and decelerate slowly and smoothly. Avoid quick starts and stops. Helpful: Install a motor minder vacuum gauge on the dashboard. It connects to the engine's vacuum to show when gas is being used most efficiently.

• Use cruise control for highway driving. Accelerating and decelerating wastes gas.

• Don't speed. A steady 55 mph truly is best for fuel economy.

• Coast as much as possible.

• Do not downshift. Use your brakes instead.

• Keep your foot off the clutch as much as possible. Let the engine idle without pushing

*Alcohol test kits are available from *Nutz & Boltz*, Box 123, Butler, MD 21023. $3.

the clutch, which can cause the automatic idle to speed up the engine.

• Don't drive with one foot on the brake and the other on the gas. It's likely that your left foot will push on the brake slightly, causing drag.

• Don't turn on the heater until the temperature gauge starts to move. Waiting about two minutes lets the engine warm up more quickly...and the car's interior will heat up just as quickly.

• Start the car properly. Fuel-injected cars: Don't give it any gas. Carburetor cars: Pump the pedal once, then start the engine.

• Use the parking brake at least once a week. Without use, the cables can rust, causing the brakes to drag.

• Don't let the car idle. If you won't be moving for more then two minutes—even if you're stuck in traffic—turn off the motor.

Other things you can do:

• Join a carpool. Take public transportation or bike or walk to your destination.

• Buy a fuel-efficient car. Don't buy a bigger car than you need.

• Plan drives carefully. Choose the shortest, least-congested route. Combine trips.

• Avoid city driving.

• Travel by train. They use less fuel per person than cars or planes.

Source: Dré Brungardt, a world-class auto technician and member of the Automotive Hall of Fame and Society of Automotive Engineers. He is editor and publisher of *Nutz & Boltz,* Box 123, Butler, MD 21023.

Posted Speed Limits

Posted speed limits are often set at up to 10 miles per hour lower than the prevailing speed. Unsurprising result: Only one in 10 speed zones has a better than 50% compliance rate. On average, seven out of 10 motorists exceed the posted speed limit in urban areas. Danger: By ignoring posted speed limits with impunity, drivers' respect for the law becomes diminished.

Source: Driver Speed Behavior on US Streets and Highways, Federal Highway Administration, McLean, VA, reported in *Car & Driver,* 2002 Hogback Rd., Ann Arbor, MI 48105.

To Handle A Highway Breakdown

Stay calm...put on your right-hand flasher and get in the right lane so you can pull off the road onto the right-hand shoulder on a straight section of the road where other cars can see you...get out of the car on the passenger side...open the hood (a universal signal of distress)...at night, light flares—put them 25 to 50 feet behind your car...wait for help a safe distance from the car (or stay inside the car with your seat belt on if there is nowhere to get out)...ask strangers to call for police help—don't accept a ride.

Source: Dré Brungardt, editor, *Nutz & Boltz,* Box 123, Butler, MD 21023.

Car-Accident Basics

Stay calm and turn on your hazard lights... determine if anyone is injured—if so, call 911 or your local emergency number for an ambulance and the police...get the names of all those involved and their automobile registration and license numbers...get the names, phone numbers and addresses of any eyewitnesses...note the street names, the location of any traffic signals, markers or warning signs... write down the weather and road conditions...write down any "people" conditions (the sobriety of other drivers) that may have contributed to the accident...when the police arrive, cooperate fully with them...report the accident to your insurance company as soon as possible.

Source: *AAA World,* 12600 Fair Lakes Circle, Fairfax, VA 22033.

Traps To Avoid When Selling A Used Car

Selling a used car on your own often makes more financial sense than offering it to a dealer as a trade-in. Reason: A used car's resale (retail) value far outstrips its trade-in (wholesale) value. But selling a used car exposes people to many pitfalls...

• Trap: Setting an inappropriate price. Pricing a car above its true value alienates potential buyers, stretching the span of time required to sell it.

Pricing the car below its true value amounts to throwing money away.

To determine a car's value, check the National Automobile Dealers Association (NADA) Official Used Car Guide (*The Blue Book*), which can be found at your local library, bank or credit union...scan the local newspaper for prices of similar cars...and take the car to a used-car lot to see how much they'll offer.

Rule of thumb: Decide on a rock-bottom price, then add 10% to 15% to allow room for negotiation.

• Trap: Failing to prepare the car for sale. A thorough cleaning greatly enhances the value of a car, regardless of its true condition. Clean the car inside and out. Don't forget the trunk.

Have the engine steam-cleaned. Wipe corrosion from the battery terminals. As you clean the car, tighten any loose fittings. Even minor rattles can discourage buyers.

• Trap: Making extensive repairs before the sale. Making major mechanical repairs or body work usually does not pay. In most cases, the increased price you'll get for the car is less than the cost of the repairs.

Instead, be honest and straightforward about the car's shortcomings, especially in a classified advertisement.

Example: 1985 Ford Escort, runs like a dream, looks like an ugly duckling.

If the car looks worse than potential buyers were led to believe, they will be less likely to buy.

• Trap: Ineffective or inappropriate advertising. Your ad should be clear and honest. List the year of manufacture, model, body style, engine size and type, total mileage and color.

Use attention-getting adjectives, such as clean, low-mileage, one-owner, excellent fuel economy, etc. Skip flowery phrases. List your telephone number, along with good times to call. Don't list your address.

Post your ad on neighborhood bulletin boards, in employee publications and in community shopper newspapers. Post a for-sale sign on the car itself—if it is legal in your community.

If these free sources of advertising do not work, place a classified ad in the local newspaper. Try to word your ad differently from those for similar cars.

• Trap: Trusting potential buyers. Always accompany potential buyers on test drives—not only to prevent theft but also to demonstrate all the car's features.

Warning: Sharp potential buyers may squirt oil under the car and say it leaks or even fiddle with the engine while looking under the hood. These techniques are used by masquerading professionals eager to buy and then resell the car.

• Trap: Negotiating ineffectively. Set a minimum price, say $8,000, and try not to go below it. If someone makes an offer below that figure, say you've already turned down an offer of $8,000 and that you'll entertain offers above that.

Always take down names and telephone numbers of potential buyers. If you have trouble getting your minimum price, you can phone these people later.

• Trap: Accepting personal checks. Accept cash or certified checks only. Personal checks are too risky.

Give the buyer a receipt specifying that the car is being sold as is. Sign over the title to the purchaser.

To eliminate your liability for subsequent accidents or traffic tickets, notify the state department of motor vehicles of the sale. Retain your license plates.

Source: Jack Gillis, director of public affairs for the Consumer Federation of America and author of *The Used Car Book*, HarperPerennial, 10 E. 53 St., New York 10022.

How To Trade In A Used Car

Selling a used car on your own inevitably brings more money than unloading the same car as a trade-in. However, if you're too busy to sell your car independently, steps can be taken to maximize your car's trade-in value...

• Know the approximate value of your trade-in car. To get an idea of your car's value, check the prices listed for similar cars in your local paper's classified ads. Also: Consult *The Blue Book*, available at local libraries and banks. It lists the high price and low price for every car. Unless your car is in particularly bad condition, aim for the higher price.

• Discuss a trade-in only after you've agreed on a purchase price for the new car. Be sure to get it in writing—verbal contracts are meaningless. Otherwise, the salesperson will likely "pad" the price of the new car by the estimated value of your trade-in. If the salesperson asks if you plan to trade in your present car, say you haven't yet decided...and that you'll discuss that possibility later.

• Wash, wax, and vacuum your trade-in car. Clean cars sell better than dirty cars. However, performing extensive repairs wastes time and money. Never clean under the hood. That suggests there's an engine problem you're trying to hide. If your car's exterior finish is hazy or cracked, consider having it repainted. Cost: As little as $300.

• Have your trade-in car appraised at night. Scratches, dents and other flaws are harder to spot in dim light. Important: Do not drive your trade-in car onto the dealer's lot until you've settled upon a price. Have a friend drive you...or park a couple of blocks away and walk. Otherwise, the dealer may surreptitiously appraise the value of your car as you and the salesperson negotiate.

• Bring your service records when having your trade-in car appraised. Cars with detailed service records are more valuable than cars without such records.

• Beware of cash rebates. Because they are taxable as personal income, they are less desirable than a higher trade-in offer. If the salesperson offers you $500 for your trade-in car and a cash rebate of $1,000, ask instead to forgo the rebate and get a trade-in of $1,500. Bonus: Getting the money "up-front" reduces the purchase price of the new car, thus minimizing the sales tax you must pay.

Source: Dré Brungardt, editor of *Nutz & Boltz*, Box 123, Butler, MD 21023.

New-Car Buying Strategies...

It's possible to cut dollars off the cost of a new car by getting the lowest price the salesperson can offer. Helpful:

• Show the salesperson that you have alternatives. Bring brochures of other dealers with you, or carry the classified ads with circles marked around cars for sale.

• Don't be too eager. Have a family member who comes with you look reluctant and mention "other deals."

• Shop at the end of the month. Dealers may be anxious about excess inventory, and salespersons may be eager to meet their quotas.

• Buy from stock. You can get a better price by helping the dealer cut inventory costs.

Example: You like a particular car but not the "extras" that have been installed on it. The dealer may throw in the extras for free just to get the car off the lot.

• Don't leave a deposit. You'll feel pressured to rush your shopping. And if you find a better deal elsewhere, you'll have the awkward task of facing the salesperson to get your money back.

• Don't trade in. Although it's more work to sell a used car on your own, you can usually get a better price by finding your own buyer and cutting out the middleman.

If you do trade in your old car, keep the buying and selling separate. First negotiate the best price you can get on the new car. Then negotiate the best trade-in price on the car you're selling. That way you'll know exactly what you're paying.

Source: *The Car Book* by Jack Gillis, HarperCollins, 10 E. 53 St., New York 10022.

15 Easy Ways To Save On Auto Insurance

Home and automobile insurance are major budget items for most Americans.

The bill for this combined coverage comes to more than $2,000 a year for the average family. On an aggregate basis, American consumers spend more than $100 billion a year to insure their homes and cars.

It's important to do everything possible to suit your bill for this expensive protection. Fifteen surefire ways to save on the auto-insurance portion of this coverage:

• Shop around for the lowest rate. Don't assume all insurance companies charge identical premiums. There are at least 3,500 different auto insurers, and it is a very competitive business. You may be able to save hundreds of dollars annually by comparison shopping.

Example: Recently, a New York State survey found an enormous range in rates for a 35-year-old male driver purchasing the minimum amount of coverage required by the state law. Of the 20 companies queried, rates ranged from a high of $655 to a low of $362—a difference of almost 81%.

• Select the largest deductible you can afford. The deductible is the amount you agree to pay out of your pocket before the insurance company pays a claim. Increasing your deductible to $500 from $200 could reduce your collision premium as much as 30%. And agreeing to pay the first $1,000 of expenses could slash your collision premium by 40%. Savings will vary from company to company.

• Drop collision and comprehensive coverage on older cars. These are optional coverages that may wind up costing you more than you'll ever recover. Collision pays when your car is damaged in a crash, while comprehensive pays if your car is stolen, or damaged by fire, flood, hail or wind. If your car is worth less than $2,000, it probably isn't cost-effective to purchase such protection.

• Buy a large, American-made, four-door car. Reason: Such cars are safer, less expensive to repair and less attractive to thieves than flashy sports cars or top-of-the-line luxury models. This translates into fewer, less expensive claims for insurance companies and lower premiums for policyholders.

• Install anti-theft devices in your car. Companies in some states will cut 5% to 15% off the cost of comprehensive coverage for cars that are equipped with a hood lock and an alarm or disabling device that prevents the vehicles from being started. Such discounts are mandatory in New York, Rhode Island, Massachusetts, Illinois, Michigan and Kentucky.

• Insure all household cars with the same company. You can save between 15% and 25% by consolidating your car insurance with the same company.

• Insure your teenagers on the family policy. Such coverage is usually cheaper, under the theory that teenagers who are covered under their parents' insurance drive the family car less frequently than if they were insured independently. And if your young driver is away at school (at least 100 miles from home), companies may grant another discount that can range from 10% to 40%.

• Have your teenager complete a driver-education course and take a defensive-driving course yourself. Many companies offer discounts of 5% to 15% for completing such courses. And if your child maintains B grade or better in high school or college, he/she may qualify for a good student discount that can save as much as 25%.

• Make use of the senior-citizen discount. Drivers age 50 or 55 and older may qualify for discounts of as much as 10% to 20%. Driving habits, employment and other factors will affect the size of the savings.

• Buy a car with passive restraints. Most companies offer discounts of 10% to 30% for factory-installed automatic seat belts and/or air bags. Full front-seat air bags may cut the no-fault and medical portion of your premium by as much as 40% to 60%.

• Car pool with friends or colleagues. Sharing the driving (and the related car-maintenance and fuel costs) to and from work may also enable you to qualify for discounts of 5% to 25%.

• Drop medical coverage from your policy

in states where such coverage is not required—if you have good protection through your company's health-insurance plan.

• Be abstemious. A few companies offer discounts to non-drinkers and/or non-smokers. But you must sign a pledge that you intend to say no when offered a cigarette or cocktail. If you slip and are involved in an accident, your insurance policy may not be renewed.

• Take advantage of female-driver discounts. Some companies offer discounts of 10% and over to women who are the only drivers in a household. Theory: They are safer drivers, and less likely to be involved in an accident than their male counterparts.

• Investigate package deals. Many carriers offer discounts of 5% to 15% if you insure your home and auto with the same company. Such a move also simplifies the family bookkeeping.

Caution:

There's one area that you should never skimp on with auto insurance, and that is liability protection.

This covers your responsibility to others should you be involved in an accident. Personal injuries suffered in an accident, or damage done to another person's property, can result in catastrophic lawsuits. For a few more dollars a year, you can increase the liability limits on your policy to $300,000 from the standard $100,000. It's one of the best investments you can ever make.

Source: Barbara Taylor Burkett, consumer consultant, Insurance Information Institute, 110 William St., New York 10038. She is the author of *How To Get Your Money's Worth in Home and Auto Insurance*, published by the Insurance Information Institute.

To Avoid Overheating Problems

To avoid overheating problems check hoses for cracks and sponginess. Check to see that connections are tight and leak-free. Inspect fan belt for cracks and proper tension... fluid level and radiator for leaks... thermostat for proper operation, and radiator grill for obstructions. If your car overheats: Don't turn off the engine. Rather, shift to neutral and race the engine moderately for 30 seconds at two-minute intervals. Shut off the air conditioning. And then turn on the heater for a few minutes—that increases coolant flow.

Source: Auto Club of NY.

Child Safety Seats

Don't use seats with rusted or loose fittings or with worn or discolored straps...replace a seat that has been in an accident...do not buy or use a seat manufactured before January 1, 1981 (when federal regulations for seats went into effect)...face seats intended for infants to the rear of the vehicle, seats used by toddlers to the front.

Source: Information from the American Automobile Association.

Reasons To Fix Up An Older Car

It is less likely to be stolen than a new car...parts cost less...cost of operation is low. Reasons to get rid of it: It needs a lot of body or mechanical work...it is a gas guzzler... parts are becoming hard to find...it has a safety flaw.

Source: Dré Brungardt, editor, *Nutz & Boltz*, Box 123, Butler, MD 21023.

No More Auto Mysteries

You can differentiate between the many fluids that may leak from your car by determining their color, smell and texture. Some leaks will stop by just tightening a bolt or clamp. Others require a mechanic's attention.

To determine what the leaking fluid is,

place a plastic container under it. To gauge the color of a very small leak, catch it on white paper.

- Antifreeze/coolant. Usually green or yellow with a slightly sweet smell. Poisonous.
- Automatic transmission fluid. Light red, oily.
- Battery acid. Smells of sulfur, highly corrosive.
- Brake fluid. Clear, almost watery. A danger sign—see a mechanic immediately.
- Gasoline. Obvious by its familiar odor. Highly poisonous.
- Gear oil. Heavy and oily. Tan when fresh. Later, dark or black.
- Grease. Very sticky and thick. Slight leakage after a grease job is normal.
- Power steering fluid. Automatic transmission fluid is commonly used and is often red.
- Shock absorber fluid. Usually appears as a dark stain on the shock body itself. Check all shocks. If leakage is found, replace the shock.
- Water. Clear water is simply normal condensation from the air conditioner.
- Windshield washer solvent. Bluish. Smells like a detergent or alcohol. Poisonous.

Source: *The Family Handyman,* 7900 International Dr., Suite 950, Minneapolis 55425.

A Car Complaint Letter

A car complaint letter should outline clearly the major problems with your car and your attempts to have them fixed within the system. Be concise and demand action. Include copies of key documents—major repair bills, admissions of the problems by dealers, etc. Address the letter to the president or chairman of the board of the manufacturer and note at the bottom that copies are being sent to the dealer and the manufacturer's zone office. Helpful: Also send copies to your state consumer protection agency, the Better Business Bureau and any other interested parties.

Source: *The Lemon Book* by Ralph Nader and Clarence Ditlow, Moyer Bell Limited, Colonial Hill, RD 1, Mt. Kisco, NY 10549.

Preventive Maintenance

To save your car, change the oil every 3,000 miles or every three months, whichever occurs first, even if you don't drive it very much. Reason: This is the manufacturer's recommendation for severe driving conditions—short trip stop-and-go town driving at high/low speeds, driving in temperatures below freezing...or above 90°F...or in high humidity.

Source: *Keeping Your Car Running Practically Forever* by Mort Schultz and the editors of Consumer Reports Books, 101 Truman Ave., Yonkers, NY 10703.

5

Consumer Savvy

Questions to Ask Before Retaining a Lawyer

Before you hire a lawyer to handle even a simple matter like an uncontested divorce or a fender-bender case, follow these steps to be sure that the lawyer will accomplish exactly what you want, and that you're not surprised by the final bill.

Start your search for a lawyer by getting recommendations from respected friends and associates.

Other helpful resources: State and local bar associations—a lawyer with experience and expertise in a particular field is especially needed.

Then, conduct telephone interviews with several candidates who "feel" best. Ask:

- Are you taking cases?
- What is your experience in the field?
- What are your fees and what are the fee options?

Lawyers' fees are generally negotiable, based on one of the following four fee structures:

- Flat fee. You know exactly what the cost will be, regardless of how long the matter drags on.
- Hourly rate. If a lawyer is unsure how much work will be incurred on a case, he/she will often quote an hourly fee. Caution: Unless some limits or controls are placed on this practice, a case can become extremely expensive.
- Contingency fee. When you are suing for a sum of money, the lawyer may ask for a percentage of the award. The percentage may be steep (often 30% to 40%) but the lawyer gets paid only if he wins. You avoid large payments up front, and the lawyer bears the risk of loss in the case of a small (or zero) recovery.
- Percentage fee. Such an arrangement is usual for a probate case, where the lawyer takes a share of the estate being settled. Again, the amount of the percentage is negotiable.

The lawyer may be willing to combine some

types of fee options. This can reduce the lawyer's economic risk and your overall cost.

Examples: An up-front fee combined with a limited hourly rate, or an up front fee combined with a smaller percentage fee.

Making a choice:

Arrange in-person interviews with two or three lawyers who sound the best suited to your needs. Most will not charge for the initial consultation, while some will charge a modest fee. Questions to ask:

- How long will the case last?
- What is an educated guess of the outcome?
- Does the lawyer recommend any options other than litigation?
- Who will pay expenses (court fees, expert witnesses, etc.)?
- Is the lawyer willing to sign a client-attorney agreement that spells out all this information?
- What happens if the two of you fall into a dispute?

Most disputes with lawyers center on fees. Expect the lawyer to agree to give the dispute to arbitration. Even though most arbitration panels are composed of bar association lawyers (some also have nonlawyers on the panel), their decisions are usually fair because they try very hard not to show bias.

Important: Be wary if a lawyer is not willing to explain the strategy he will adopt for the case, or if he is not forthcoming about fee structures or seeking ways to save you money.

Source: George Milko, the director of the education department at HALT, a Washington, DC, group that advocates legal reforms. For more information about dealing with lawyers, consult the book compiled by the HALT staff, *Using a Lawyer*, Random House, 201 E. 50 St., New York 10022.

How to Protect Yourself From Banks' New Services

Banks are offering an avalanche of "new" services that are just old services—repackaged. And, they are charging you for them.

Charges for some bank services have gone up 400% since the banking industry's deregulation in the mid-1980s.

How your bank may be squeezing you:

- Controlled disbursement services—your ability to transfer money electronically to cover checks. This used to take only a call to your bank. Now many banks charge customers $1 or more for these offsite transactions.
- Overdraft service. In the good old days, you could call your bank and ask to be notified if a check came in that your funds couldn't cover. Then, they would give you a chance to deposit money that day to cover the check. Now, overdraft services cost consumers a hefty service fee—plus, if you have overdraft "protection," interest on the "borrowed" funds.
- Automatic Teller Machines (ATMs) used to be a free service—but now many banks charge 50 cents to $1 for each transaction.
- Calling in for balances—and a record of checks cashed. You once could call your friendly teller for this service, free of charge—but it now may be costly.
- Home equity lines of credit are just repackaged second mortgages...with a bundle of additional service fees tacked on.

When you shop for a bank—compare the fees on new services. Go with the bank that has the lowest fees for the services you use most...and stay away from the routine use of ATMs.

Don't immediately opt for the checking and savings account packages that have a lot of services attached.

If you only write a few checks a month, ask the bank for its low-cost, minimum standard checking account. And if you're a student, or disabled or a senior citizen, ask for a service-charge-free checking account. Most banks make these available, although few promote this service.

If you know your banker, go to the bank and ask him/her to phone you to let you know when an overdraft occurs—instead of paying for an overdraft "service." And, if you know your banker, you are much more likely to get a loan...be able to negotiate service charges, fees and loan interest rates...or get a dispute with the bank solved quickly and favorably. You should know at least one teller, a loan officer and a vice-president at your bank. These are the people that can solve virtually every banking problem you encounter. I call this preventive maintenance.

Source: Edward F. Mrkvicka Jr., author of *The Bank Book: How to Revoke Your Bank's License to Steal*, HarperCollins, 10 E. 53 St., New York 10022, or 800-331-3761. He is also publisher of *Money Insider*, a financial newsletter for consumers, Reliance Enterprises, Inc., Box 413, Marengo, IL 60152.

Bargain Hunters' Bonanza: Secrets of Buying Government Seized Property

The federal government has always been a gold mine for savvy shoppers. But today—thanks largely to the recession—it now offers bigger bargains than ever before.

Government agencies that sell and finance real estate, meanwhile, have recently created unique opportunities for people who want to buy a house at a bargain price.

Unfortunately, bargain hunters are still confronted by a bureaucratic maze that often makes it difficult to find out which property is for sale...and when and where merchandise will be auctioned. How to steer through merchandise bargains:

• US Marshals Service: Auctions property seized by the IRS, FBI, Immigration and Naturalization Service and the Drug Enforcement Agency. They now have a backlog of $1.4 billion in vehicles, boats, household goods and even works of art.

Rules: Bidding starts at about 90% of the fair market value and auctioneers rarely let it go lower. Bidders can usually inspect the goods before auction, but the extent of inspection varies from sale to sale. Bidders often must pay all or part of the price in cash or a cashier's check.

Latest information: The Marshals announce upcoming sales in *USA Today* on the third Wednesday of each month. Auction information is also available from Marshals Service offices in 94 major cities and from the agency's headquarters...202-307-9221.

• General Services Administration: Auctions off surplus automobiles, computers and office equipment, laboratory supplies, manufacturing machinery and farm equipment. It also handles many sales from the overburdened Marshals Service.

Rules: Bidders have a limited right to inspect goods from one to three days before the auction. The minimum bid can be above or below market value, depending on what the auctioneer believes the item will bring. Bidders customarily must pay all or part of the price in cash or a cashier's check. But unlike most other government agencies, the GSA lets bidders pay with Visa or MasterCard. It also lets buyers return the goods within 15 days if they don't match the catalog description.

Latest information: Available from the GSA's headquarters...703-557-0384. GSA regional offices usually print catalogs about three weeks before an auction. The offices are located in Atlanta, Auburn (Washington), Boston, Chicago, Denver, District of Columbia, Fort Worth, Kansas City, New York, Philadelphia and San Francisco.

• US Postal Service: Each year millions of unclaimed and undeliverable items wind up on the auction block, including those from mail order companies. Merchandise includes virtually anything that gets sent through the mail—from fur coats to plungers. Auctions are usually held every six weeks in Atlanta, New York, Philadelphia, St. Paul and San Francisco.

Rules: Minimum bids can be as low as 25% of the fair market value, but this and other rules vary from city to city. All wrapping is taken off the merchandise, and bidders usually have two hours to inspect the goods before an auction. Merchandise can't be returned.

Information: Contact the main post office in the five cities where auctions are held.

How to find real estate bargains: The collapse of savings and loan institutions throughout the country has put billions of dollars in homes and commercial property on the market at distress prices.

Very good news for buyers: The Resolution

Trust Corporation, which sells the property, is now under pressure from Congress to speed up the sales. That means in many areas the RTC is lowering prices even further. That's in addition to price reductions already made because of the recession.

The RTC makes information on its more than 40,000 pieces of property available in complete catalogs, regional listings, city listings and computer databases. Prices vary from about $5 for a city listing to $50 for a regional listing on a floppy computer disk to $600 for the entire list on CD-ROM disks.

You can also look at the list free of charge in any of the nearly 1,400 government document depositories around the country. Phone 800-431-0600 to find the nearest one.

Listings are essential for prospective buyers because they name the real estate agents who handle the properties. But the listings often have only sketchy data about properties.

Buyers of RTC property must pay cash or get their own financing.

Latest information: Phone 800-782-2990 or 703-487-4068.

• Many other real estate opportunities: While the RTC tries to sell off property of failed S&Ls, the Department of Housing & Urban Development, the Federal Home Loan Mortgage Corporation, the Federal National Mortgage Association, the Government National Mortgage Association and the Department of Veterans Affairs are dumping more property on the market as homeowners default on loans that the agencies guarantee.

Rules: Houses that these agencies sell usually come with easy financing. With good credit you can probably get a 30-year, fixed-term mortgage with a 10% downpayment. The interest rate is currently just under 10%.

Latest information: Phone your local realtors association to find out which ones handle repossessed federal properties. In many areas there are brokers that now specialize in them. You can also phone the federal agencies directly at the following offices:

HUD regional offices: Atlanta/404-331-5136, Boston/617-565-5234, Chicago/312-353-5680, Denver/303-844-4513, Fort Worth/817-885-5401, Kansas City/913-236-2162, New York/212-264-8053, Philadelphia/215-597-2560, Seattle/206-442-5414, San Francisco/415-556-4752.

One step ahead: Ask for HUD's "pink sheet." It lists properties that have been on the market for months and are now selling at deep discounts.

• Special opportunity: The Farmers Home Administration will lend potential buyers 100% of a home purchase price if their income is less than about $25,000 a year. Although the rules eliminate middle- and higher-income individuals, the loan plan can help many of their children buy a home.

Despite the name of the agency, most of the Farmers Home properties are in the suburbs and semi-rural areas. The current mortgage rate is just over 9.5%.

More information: 202-447-4323.

24 Ways to Stretch Family Income Without Cutting Your Standard of Living

With recession looming, people are looking for ways to save money that won't seriously affect their standard of living. Best: Enlist the entire household and make money-saving a family project.

Example: Post each month's electric bill on a bulletin board so everyone can see the result of his/her efforts. And reward yourselves—perhaps with a special dessert—for a job well done.

• Consolidate your checking, savings and money-market accounts at one bank. Banks continue to increase the minimum-balance requirements for free checking and other services.

Consolidating all your funds at one bank makes it easier to meet the minimum balance. Caution: Deposits are insured only up to $100,000 per person. Potential savings: $25 per month.

• Buy from fee-only or discount life-insurance brokers. A relatively new development in the life-insurance game, these brokers sell life insurance for 20% to 30% less than traditional brokers.

The Council of Life Insurance Consultants can provide you with the names of fee-only or discount brokers located in your area. More information: 800-533-0777.

• Trade with a discount stock broker. If you do most of your own investment research, a discount broker can save you up to 50% on commission costs.

• Raise the deductible on your automobile collision insurance. Increasing it from $100 to $500 can cut your car insurance costs by 25%. Also: Consider eliminating collision coverage entirely once your automobile loan is paid off—if you're willing to bear the risk of repair costs.

• Refinance your mortgage. A recession will probable result in lower interest rates. Rule of thumb: If the difference between your current mortgage rate and the new rate is two percentage points or more, and you plan to stay in your home for at least three years, it will pay to refinance your mortgage. Potential savings: Thousands of dollars over the life of the loan.

Best: Try to refinance through your current mortgage lender. You could save additional money on points, title research and other closing costs.

• Pay off your credit cards promptly. In addition to avoiding interest charges of up to 20%, none of that interest is tax deductible.

• Be an informed car buyer. Knowing what the dealer paid for the car puts you in the best bargaining position.

Helpful: Carputer International lists actual dealer costs (not the inflated invoice cost touted in car ads) on hundreds of automobile models and thousands of options. Cost: One dollar per minute, with the first minute free. More information: 800-722-4440.

• Get good investment advice. Subscriptions to investment newsletters cost hundreds of dollars a year, and even trial subscriptions are not cheap.

Better: For $11.95, Select Information Exchange offers trial issues of newsletters you select from a free catalog of more than 350 titles with descriptions. Choose newsletters with good track records, then check them out to see which one best suits your needs. More information: 212-874-7333.

• Lower your thermostat setting. Rule of thumb: For each degree it's cut back, you'll reduce your fuel bill 2%.

• Have your phone bill audited. Some long-distance companies offer auditing services. You send them several monthly bills and they determine what you would have paid had you used their service.

Have your long-distance bill audited by several different firms, and choose the least expensive. Note: Rates change...have your bill audited at least once a year.

• Use the phone book to find phone numbers. Most phone companies offer several free calls to directory assistance each month... then charge 30 cents or more for each additional request.

• Do it yourself. Sewing machines, ice-cream makers, even the new bread-making machines are worth the money if you use them often enough.

• Buy generic. Supermarkets aren't the only places that sell money-saving generic brands. Store-brand cosmetics, available at many drug stores and at beauty-supply houses, are often just as good as expensive designer brands. And you can save as much as 70% on lipstick and other cosmetics.

• Clip coupons. But only for products that you usually buy. This will keep you from spending more rather than less at the supermarket.

• Buy bargain underwear. Hanes (L'eggs) offers discounts on slightly imperfect merchandise. Twelve pairs of slightly imperfect pantyhose, for instance, cost $11.28—a savings of $11.40. More information: 919-744-1790.

• Take in boarders. College students are often looking for clean, safe rooms to let. Bonus: In exchange for reduced rent, many will perform chores such as babysitting or cooking—even some light housecleaning.

• Skip first-run films. All but the biggest blockbusters are available on video three months (sometimes even sooner) after release.

• Dine out early. Many restaurants offer

early-bird specials for people willing to eat a little earlier than usual.

• Go to the public library. This is much less expensive than buying books. By paying taxes, you've already helped pay for the books in the library...why not take advantage of them?

• Buy bridge, tunnel or tollway tokens in bulk. Some mass-transit systems also sell discounted monthly commuter passes.

• Take mass transit. Even if you do this just one day a week, you'll substantially cut your commuting costs.

• Pay cash...and pump your own gas. By taking advantage of discounts on self-service gasoline (about five cents per gallon) and cash transactions (about four cents per gallon) you can save nine cents per gallon.

• Use last-minute travel bargains to vacation. Cruise lines, charter services and hotels would rather fill cabins, seats and rooms with travelers paying bargain rates than not fill them at all.

Travel "clubs" sell these bargains, but usually charge a membership fee. Better: Make friends with a well-connected travel agent who will alert you to upcoming bargains simply for the commission he receives.

• Cash in your frequent-flyer miles. Recent air-fare hikes make free travel that much more valuable.

Source: Terry Savage, a registered investment advisor. She is the author of *Terry Savage Talks Money*, Dearborn Financial Publishing, 520 N. Dearborn, Chicago 60610, 800-621-9621.

How To Be The Best Construction Boss For Your Home Renovations

Summer and early fall, when windows can be left open for ventilation, are the best times to redo your kitchen, paint the living room, or—even more ambitiously—close in the porch or add an extra bedroom or bath to your house.

However, the most important job takes place long before the first nail is hammered. You guarantee good work with careful planning and research.

You can ensure the success of your renovation by learning what it takes to accomplish the project and then overseeing it yourself.

• Check with your local building inspector to see if the work you want to do requires a building permit—or a zoning variance. Local ordinances differ from community to community, so don't assume you know what they are without asking.

• If your project requires any structural changes to your house, hire an architect to draw up plans whether they are required by the building inspector or not. An architect will invariably bring ideas you haven't thought of to the project and make it better.

• Don't look in the Yellow Pages for the craftsmen you need for the job. The best carpenters, masons, painters and paper hangers don't advertise there. Ask friends and neighbors for recommendations. When you see a particularly attractive construction-in-progress, stop and talk to the owners and to the contractors. Most owners are delighted to talk about their projects. And follow up on flyers you receive.

• Interview as many good contractors as you can find. You will learn something every time you discuss the project with a new person. Don't feel guilty about taking up their time. Good craftsmen want you to appreciate their expertise. Make it clear at each interview that you are looking for the best workmanship.

• When you choose the contractors you want, ask for a written contract. Be sure that it covers all the work to be done, a time limit and costs. For a big project, have your lawyer go over the contract.

• When the work starts—be there. Don't be a pest or get in the way, but show your interest and be available for consultation. And don't be afraid to ask questions if you don't understand why something is being done a certain way.

• Beware of verbal "change work orders" as the project progresses. This is a trap for owners and contractors alike. As work progresses, you—or the contractors—may suddenly realize that if you add something or do something a different way, it will be better. That's fine, but put it in writing and, just as you did in the original contract, spell out the costs and the time limits. (You can both initial the additions written into the original contract, if that is easier.)

• Expect problems. There will always be something that goes wrong—the weather, supplies that come late, a paint color that looks different on the wall. Be prepared to be flexible. There has to be give and take on both sides and very few projects are finished exactly on time.

Source: Mary Weir, a specialist in renovating and restoring old houses. Based in Rumson, NJ, she supervises all of the work herself.

Everything You Need To Know About Credit Cards

Most people carry around a wallet full of credit cards, but few give any thought to these powerful pieces of plastic after they say, *Charge it.*

Questions to consider: Are you getting the best deal for your money on your credit card? How do you guarantee that your rights as a consumer will be protected if there's a problem with your bill? Should you sign up with a credit card registration service as protection against theft or misuse of your cards?

• Travel and entertainment (T&E) cards (like American Express and Diners Club), are not issued by banks, and the card issuer requires monthly payment in full of all charges.

• Bank cards (such as Visa and MasterCard) essentially provide access to small, generally unsecured, personal loans that are repaid, with interest, over time. Because bank cards are really just personal loans granted by a bank, it pays to shop around for the best terms, just as you would for a mortgage or home equity loan.

About 6,000 different banks around the US issue Visa and MasterCard. Unlike American Express, which is one big company, Visa and MasterCard are more like franchise organizations that license agents—in this case, banks—to issue cards. Each bank is then free to develop its own annual fees, interest rates and additional charges (late charges, bounced check charges and cash advance charges), as well as its own package of useful extras (travel assistance or credit card registration, for example). A bank can even set its own acceptance standards. If you've been turned down by an individual bank, feel free to take your business elsewhere.

Shopping for a bank card is really shopping for a bank. Potential pitfalls: Don't be lured into applying for a particular card because the issuing bank promises you a great package of extras. That's like choosing a savings institution because they give you a four-slice toaster.

Some consumers will decide to apply for a card issued by a bank in their town, thinking, *If there's a problem with the bill, I want to be able to walk in and talk to someone.* But under federal law, if you have any disputes about your bill, you must put your complaint in writing or you completely lose your rights to withhold payment without penalty. So it doesn't make much sense to choose a local bank for the walk-in convenience. But you should also be wary of the big banks that tout a flashy array of cardholder services—24-hour toll-free customer-service hotlines, for example. It's easy to get lost in the crowd at one of these megabanks.

Key: Focus on the financial terms—interest rates, annual fees and other charges. Bankcard Holders of America publishes a list (updated quarterly) of the best deals in bank cards—those with annual interest rates of 16.4% and below.

Current interest rates on bank cards range from a low of 10.5% to an awesome 24%. Most people pay about 18.8%.

About two-thirds of consumers use the revolving credit option with their credit cards. So, for most people, the interest rate is the biggest bank card cost factor.

If you don't carry a balance over from month to month, it's best to get one of the "free," no-annual-fee cards. They are listed in another of our quarterly updates.

Pick a safe bank:

Many consumers have been concerned

about whether a particular credit card issuing bank is a "safe," financially stable institution. You might think that you don't have to worry about that issue because, as a credit card holder, you owe the bank money, they don't owe you.

Trap: Your account may be sold. And credit cards are not like any other type of bank loan. A fixed interest rate does not always mean a fixed rate in the credit card business. A bank—your current bank or a new bank that buys your account—can raise its credit card interest rate at any time, to whatever level is legal in the state in which its credit card operations are located. All it has to do is give you 15 days advance written notice. Then the bank can apply the new rate to your outstanding balance, as well as to new charges.*

To err is human, but to fix a credit card billing error can seem to require divine intervention. In reality, laws can usually rectify the situation—if you know the laws.

The federal Fair Credit Billing Act specifies that, to assert a billing error, you must state your complaint to the credit card issuer, in writing, within 60 days of the postmark date of the statement on which the disputed charge first appeared.

Problem: Most people call their bank's customer service representative, who makes a note of the complaint and promises that someone will look into the matter. But if the card issuer can't get reimbursement from the merchant, or if there's some other problem, they can come back to you three months later and inform you that you're responsible for the charge after all. By then, it's too late to exercise your right to dispute the charge.

Self-defense: Complain to the bank—or other card issuer—promptly, and in writing. It's particularly important if you think you're dealing with a questionable merchant, or if you can't get a credit slip from the merchant immediately, or if a large dollar amount is in dispute, or if you anticipate any kind of problem. You may find that if you contact the merchant and not the card issuer, the merchant will promise to rectify the error—but then not do it. By the time you find out, it's too late to dispute the charge properly. If you call first, follow up the call with a letter summarizing the discussion. Important:

• Send your letter by certified mail, with a return receipt requested.

• Include your name (as it appears on your credit card), your current mailing address, and credit card account number.

• Identify the type of error that you're disputing, the dollar amount, the merchant and the date of the billing error.

• Send the letter to the address listed on your statement for billing errors and inquiries. This is probably a different location than the address to which your payments are sent.

Within 30 days of receiving your letter, card issuers must inform you, in writing, that they are either still investigating the dispute, or that they have resolved the matter.

They are obligated to tell you, in writing, the way in which a dispute has been resolved. During an investigation, you may withhold payment of the disputed amount and any related finance charges—without penalty.

The card issuer must, within 90 days, either correct the error, or provide you with a full written explanation that no billing error has occurred.

Trap: During an investigation, the disputed amount is "frozen" against your credit limit, so if it's a large amount, it will leave a dent in your credit line.

Credit card services typically keep records of all your credit card accounts. If your cards are lost or stolen, you call the registration service and the service notifies all your credit card issuers. Some of these services promote themselves by claiming to "insure" you against loss—but they really don't provide much insurance because, under federal law, you're not liable for that much money even if your card is stolen and used fraudulently.

Self-defense: If you decide to register your credit cards with a service, make sure that the company you're dealing with is reputable. Be sure that the service has a toll-free telephone access number, preferably with international

*Exception: In the state of Delaware, under Delaware law, consumers have 30 days to decline acceptance of the new terms. If they then stop using the credit card, they can pay off the existing balance at the old rate.

access, and that they'll accept collect international calls.

Generally, these services are not recommended—unless they are offered free or at very low cost from the bank or company that issued your credit card.

A credit card issuer can cancel your credit card at will—at any time—for any reason.

These seemingly arbitrary cancellations are happening more and more frequently nowadays, as credit grantors are closely scrutinizing their current customers.

When your card comes up for renewal, most banks do a full credit analysis. If you're not as good a credit risk now as you were when you applied for the card, the creditor can lower your credit limit, freeze your line of credit or revoke your card privileges altogether.

Travelers beware: Many credit card companies are cutting back on free car rental insurance coverage...so check with your issuer before you rent.

Also: When you check into a hotel or rent a car, the merchant will—completely legally—put a "hold" on your credit card for the estimated amount of the rental or the stay, so that there's money available (for them) when you check out. But these holds can remain on your account for as long as two weeks. If you're traveling for an extended period of time, you could easily freeze up your entire credit line.

Solution: Use two different cards when you travel—one for hotels and car rentals, one for important purchases or emergencies.

Source: Gerri Detweiler, education coordinator for Bankcard Holders of America, 560 Herndon Pkwy., Suite 120, Herndon, VA 22070. Bankcard Holders of America was founded in 1980 as a national, nonprofit consumer credit education and advocacy organization that provides its members with information and one-on-one assistance regarding credit card problems. A low-rate, no-fee credit card list is available for $4.

How To Protect Yourself From Credit Thieves

At a time when more and more borrowers are defaulting on their loans, a good credit rating has become an increasingly valuable commodity.

Danger: Your credit rating is vulnerable to theft—by people who use phony data to "buy" items while charging them to other people's credit card accounts.

- The easiest route for credit thieves is to obtain a carbon copy of a credit card sales draft, which gives them all the information they need: A person's name, address, account number and account expiration date. The thieves can then purchase items over the phone for delivery to any address they please.

Prevention: Always shred and dispose of your carbons so that they cannot be used.

Big problem: Thieves that work in collusion with store employees can get the data they need from the store's carbon copy.

- Alternatively, a credit thief can tap into your credit history by using your Social Security number, a primary identifier (along with name and address) for credit card issuers. In this way, the thief can open a new account (with a fresh spending limit) in your name. Sources: Many people reveal their Social Security numbers on ID cards, pay stubs and paychecks, and office badges.

Prevention: Whenever possible, omit your Social Security number on forms which request it (aside from IRS returns, where it is mandatory). Under federal law, you cannot be penalized for this refusal.

Even more insidious are the "credit doctors," professionals who sell credit histories of innocent third parties to their clients.

These practitioners will often even advertise their services in newspapers, promising to quickly "fix" credit ratings, no matter how bad the ratings may be.

How the doctors operate: Their favorite ploy is to find an individual in the same locale with a name that is similar to their client's.

Example: The innocent Robert Tomasson's credit history may be pillaged for a customer named Bobby Thompson. The credit doctor will unearth Tomasson's birth date, and possibly his Social Security number, which will then be used by Thompson to create a new credit history, combining the two people's personal data.

The most sophisticated credit doctors may even access computer codes (with the help of an accomplice in the financial services industry), and draw their information directly from a credit bureau.

What victims can do: A credit theft involving unauthorized charges to a legitimate account is a relatively quick and easy matter to resolve.

But if a bogus account has already been set up and used in your name, it can take anywhere from four to eight weeks to establish the fraud and clear your credit rating. In the meantime, you may not be able to borrow money from a bank.

Helpful: Check your credit history twice a year through one of the credit reporting agencies. If a phony charge shows up, you'll be able to nip the fraud early on.

Source: Bill Esham, a special agent for investigations for First USA Bank, one of the nation's largest issuers of credit cards, 201 N. Walnut St., Wilmington, DE 19801.

Warning for Bank Borrowers

Rates on loans are often not fixed until the money is actually transferred—no matter what the written documents say. If market rates rise between the time the documents are signed and the time you borrow the funds, your rate probably will go up—and your only recourse is to refuse the loan and start again.

For business borrowers: Loans are almost always callable on demand—even if you have a perfect payment record. Banks insist on this right—if you do not agree, you probably will not get the money.

Source: *How to Make Your Shrinking Salary Support You in Style for the Rest of Your Life* by Michael Evans, PhD, chairman, Evans Economics, Inc., Random House, 201 E. 50 St., New York 10022.

How to Make Your Own Non-Toxic Cleaning Products

Cleaning house should not be harmful to your health. Yet many of the most popular cleaning products are extremely toxic.

All you really need is baking soda, distilled white vinegar, table salt, lemon juice, water and borax. With these inexpensive and easy-to-find products, you can make everything you need to clean the whole house...without harming the housekeeper or the environment.

- All-purpose cleaner. Most cleaners contain ammonia, which attacks the skin and irritates the eyes and lungs. Better: Mix one teaspoon of a vegetable-based liquid soap* or one teaspoon of borax into a quart of warm water. Add a squeeze of lemon or a tablespoon of vinegar to cut through grease and grime.
- Dishwasher detergent. Avoid dishwasher detergents that contain chlorine. It gives off irritating fumes when it comes in contact with water.

Better: Use one part borax and one part baking soda.

- Dishwashing liquid. Use a vegetable-based liquid soap. Or rub a damp sponge on a bar of all-natural soap.**

Add a few slices of lemon to the dishwater to cut grease and impart a lemony scent. If dishes are not greasy, clean them in very hot water with a sponge or dish brush.

- Drain cleaner. Pour a handful of baking soda and a half cup of vinegar down the drain. Cover immediately, and let the fizzing chemical reaction eat through the blocked matter. Rinse with plenty of hot water. Also effective: Pour a half cup of salt and a half cup of baking soda down the drain, followed by lots of hot water.
- Glass cleaner. Avoid glass cleaners that contain ammonia.

*Use a biodegradable soap, such as Dr. Bronner's available at natural-food stores and some supermarkets.

**Choose a soap that contains no added scent, color or deodorizer. Good alternative: A natural glycerin soap or one made from olive oil.

Better: Combine equal parts vinegar and water. Sponge or spray it on windows and glass. Wipe it off with a clean, lint-free cloth. The wax buildup from chemical glass cleaners sometimes causes streaking the first time vinegar is used. Simply rub a little alcohol on the glass first, then use the vinegar and water.

• Oven cleaner. Standard oven cleaners contain lye, which irritates the skin. All contain ammonia, even those that claim to be free of fumes.

Better: Mix together in a one-quart spray bottle two tablespoons vegetable-based liquid soap, two teaspoons borax and enough warm water to fill the bottle. Spray the mixture on the oven interior, holding the bottle close to the target so the mixture doesn't get into the air or your eyes. Leave it on for 20 minutes, then scrub with steel wool and a scouring powder that does not contain chlorine. Rub pumice onto stubborn baked-on spots.

• Scouring powders. Most scouring powders contain talc and chlorine bleach. Talc may be contaminated with asbestos. As you sprinkle the cleaner, a small amount of asbestos may go into the air—and your lungs.

Better: Use a wet sponge sprinkled with salt, baking soda or borax.

Source: Leslie Cerier, a personal fitness consultant, RFD 2, School House Rd., Amherst, MA 01002.

Software Purchasing Trap

Many retailers now have shrink-wrapping machines, and can repackage returned goods to make them look new. This is a special danger when buying computer software because returned software may be "infected" with computer viruses, or otherwise have been harmed by a previous user in a way that a visual inspection cannot detect. Always be sure of the integrity of the dealer you buy from, and verify that you are getting new, from-the factory-goods.

Source: Harry Newton, publisher, *Teleconnect,* 12 W. 21 St., New York 10010.

Safest Air Fresheners

An open box of baking soda or natural cedar blocks do a good job without harming you or the environment. Problem: Aerosol air fresheners contain volatile organic compounds (VOCs)—a major source of smog. Solid air fresheners are less troublesome than aerosols, but still contain some VOCs.

Source: *The Earth Care Annual 1991,* edited by Russell Wild, Rodale Press, 33 E. Minor St., Emmaus, PA 18098.

Old TV Warning

If you own a set over five years old, have a repairman take out its instant-on feature—its special light bulb can explode and cause a fire.

Source: *Kovel's Antiques & Collectibles Price List 1991* by Ralph Kovel and Terry Kovel, quoted in *1,001 Home Ideas,* 3 Park Ave., New York 10016.

How To Protect Yourself When You Are Buying By Mail...Or By Phone

Everybody's dread: Buying what looks like a great product by mail or phone and then never receiving it...or getting a product that doesn't work...or something other than what was ordered.

Just like other companies, the vast majority of mail-order firms are honest and competent. When problems arise, it's usually because of unintentional errors or the customer's unfamiliarity with the seller's policy. But fraud, though rare, can indeed occur.

The law: If a mail-order company doesn't specify a date, it must ship the goods within 30 days after it receives your order form and payment. Alternatively, it must inform you if there will be a delay and also give you a new shipping date. You then have the option of canceling the order. However, if you go ahead with it, and the company fails to meet the new shipping date, you again have the option to cancel.

If you cancel, the company is legally required to credit your credit card account within one billing cycle or, if you paid by check, issue you a check within seven business days.

As for fraud, of course, the product must live up to claims made in the ad or by the telephone salesperson. Mail-order fraud is outlawed by both federal and state laws.

The best protection:

• Look closely at the company's guarantee and return policies. They may vary widely from company to company. If you have questions, call the company. Don't do business with a firm that doesn't have a satisfaction-guaranteed policy or that can't fully explain its policies when you phone.

• Phone protection: If you haven't done business with a firm that phones you with a sales pitch, ask the salesperson to send you information on the product. You may also check out a company by contacting the local Better Business Bureau for the area where the company has its headquarters. Don't do business with companies that refuse your requests.

• Keep all records of mail and phone purchases. It may not be necessary to photocopy the paperwork before you mail it in, but doing so can help speed the resolution of problems. When the goods arrive, keep the box they came in until you're satisfied that the product lives up to your expectations. Some companies require you to return goods in their original boxes.

• Avoid doing business with companies that...

• Phone you and ask for a credit card number. As a general rule, don't give credit card numbers to companies that initiate a call. If you're interested in the product, ask the salesperson for a phone number you can call back. Never do business with a company that doesn't have a number for you to phone.

• Sell products with names that sound like better-known brands.

• Don't give a full description of the product either in an ad or when you phone for more information.

• Tell you that a purchase will automatically enter you in a sweepstakes. By law, you don't have to buy anything to be eligible in a sweepstakes.

When protection doesn't work:

• Contact the company. Give the firm details of the transaction, and offer to send photocopies of the paperwork. Reputable companies will usually clear up the problem within a few days, but if a mailer doesn't solve it within 30 days...

• Write to the Direct Marketing Association's Mail Order Action Line at 6 E. 43 St., New York 10017. Send a complete description of the transaction and photocopies of the paperwork. Action Line personnel run interference for consumers by getting to the right people in the mail-order companies and asking them to resolve the problem within 30 days.

Except in cases where the mail-order firm has gone bankrupt, their success rate is high, largely because mail-order companies know that if they don't get satisfaction, the matter will be turned over to legal authorities. But if Action Line isn't able to help...

• Contact your state's consumer protection agency. It's usually part of the state attorney general's office. Though they have heavy case loads, these authorities can often put pressure on stubborn companies.

Source: Lisa Caugherty, director of Shop-at-Home Information at the Direct Marketing Association, 11 W. 42 St., New York 10036.

Bait-And-Switch Self-Defense

Shop around before buying equipment—hi-fi, telephone, TV, etc. Decide on the exact make and model number you want before you buy, and stick to that decision no matter what the salesperson says...write down the prices quoted...open the box to make sure the model number on the item matches that on the box.

Source: Roundup of consumer affairs experts, reported in *Condé Nast Traveler*, 350 Madison Ave., New York 10017.

How To Haggle

Haggling over prices has never been an American tradition. But this recession has made many retailers happy to negotiate.

How to do it:

The first rule of haggling is—don't be afraid to ask. In today's tough market, you won't be the first person to request a discount—and you won't be the last.

Basic rule: The worst thing a salesperson can do is say, *No.*

Haggle gently. No one likes to be threatened, so don't demand a discount on an item. Try playing the innocent. Ask... *Is this the best price you can offer?*

Alternate: *I've heard that you might be able to give me a better price on this item...*

If the clerk refuses, your comeback might be, *Well, if I could get it for $X, I'd buy it right now.*

Alternate: *My husband/wife won't let me spend more than $X.*

If the clerk still refuses to budge, ask when the item is scheduled to be marked down and if he/she will call you when it is. If you let it be known that you plan to spend a lot of money on a particular product, many stores will be happy to alert you when something you've expressed interest in is going on sale.

Where to haggle:

Most stores are flexible on prices—but some are much more flexible than others.

Most flexible: Small, single-location mom-and-pop stores. Here, the salesclerk is probably also the store's owner. He'll know what the profit margin is on a particular item and how much he can cut the price and still make money. Or, he may be very happy to get rid of the item at cost to reduce a swollen inventory. Even better, this person is the boss...so he doesn't have to clear any discounts with his supervisor.

Least flexible: Larger shops—and stores that are part of a chain. These stores track inventory by computer. An item sold for less than the marked price will send up a red flag that has to be explained to management. Tipoff: Price tags that list computerized inventory numbers.

But that doesn't mean these stores won't negotiate. If the salesclerk doesn't have the authority to cut prices, ask to speak to a department manager or store manager who does.

For discounts on damaged goods or items that are the last in stock, take the merchandise to the customer-service desk.

What to ask for:

Don't be greedy. Most stores have already cut their profit margins due to increased competition. If you ask for too much, you might close the door to all possible negotiations.

Rule of thumb: 20% off the marked price usually represents a fair discount. Money, however, isn't the only thing worth haggling over. Instead of price cuts, you can often negotiate for goods and services.

Example: When I recently bought a washer, dryer and refrigerator, the store wouldn't negotiate because, they said, as a discount house, they were already giving me their best prices. So I asked, *Well, how about a thank-you gift?* We haggled and they eventually included several blank videotapes in the deal.

Delivery charges on furniture, major appliances and other large and expensive goods can also be negotiated. Ask for a reduction.

Admitting defeat:

Even the most determined negotiator needs to know when to call it quits.

If I can't get a salesperson to come down in price, I politely say thank you and humbly make it clear that, in light of the store's attitude, I'll take my future business elsewhere.

Source: Suzy Gershman, consummate shopper and author of the *Born to Shop* series of books. Her most recent edition is *Born to Shop: Florida,* Bantam Books, 666 Fifth Ave., New York 10103.

Hidden Costs Of Quality

To measure the effectiveness of efforts to improve product or service quality, the company must break down everything it does to reduce defects, enhance component quality, fix defective products before they leave the plant, etc. Trap: It's easy to measure the costs of functions like product inspection and employee training. But hidden costs, such as a purchasing manager's time spent screening vendors...or marketing people's time spent resolving customer complaints, are also quality costs. If the obvious costs are high, it may mean the company isn't spending enough on hidden elements of quality.

Source: Karen Muse, senior consultant, Grant Thornton, quoted in *Manufacturing Issues*, 800 One Prudential Plaza, Chicago 60601.

Smarter Shopping For Superior Savings

- Always make a list of what you need—and don't add to the list once you're in the store.
- Watch for sales or bargains in newspapers and flyers that are distributed at the stores. Then check for sales prices on the items that you buy regularly.
- Only use cash. Paying by credit card or check doesn't hit the consumer as much as handing over cold, hard cash—until it's too late.
- Take advantage of coupons and rebates.
- Avoid buying plastic bags—you can get them free in the produce section of your supermarket. Also reuse grocery bags.
- Check the checker. Note the price on the items you're buying, and make sure the checker is totalling the same prices.
- Keep non-food items off the grocery list.

Source: The National Center for Financial Education, San Diego. For more information, send a self-addressed, stamped, business-sized envelope to Box 34070, San Diego 92103.

Funeral Fees: How Not To Get Ripped Off

It's not easy to be an experienced, sophisticated buyer of funeral services. We do it so few times—usually at the last minute. And the decision is fraught with emotional confusion.

Practical advice*...

Picking a funeral parlor:

- Decide how much you can—or want—to spend. The average cost of a funeral is about $3,200...but there is a wide variation. Some people—often out of guilty feelings for what they did or didn't do when the person was alive—think they must spend a lot. Don't let emotions obscure your bottom line.
- Ask for recommendations. This is the best way to ensure that the funeral home you choose will be reliable. Good sources: Friends, family, clergy, lawyer, doctor, banker.
- When you inquire about services, have someone who is less emotionally involved accompany you. Many people find it difficult to concentrate, to express themselves or even to remember key details in the arrangements when they're overwrought by feelings of loss and grief. This person will provide emotional support and help ensure that you ask the right questions and make the right choices.
- Check out more than one facility. Prices vary greatly—often by hundreds of dollars—for the exact same services.
- Get price information up front. The Funeral Rule, passed by the Federal Trade Commission (FTC) in 1984, requires funeral providers to give the consumer an itemized written price list of offerings. The rule also requires funeral providers to quote prices over the phone, upon request.
- Consider all costs. All charges are *à la carte*, so be sure to review each item on the list with the funeral director and make sure you understand every cost you will incur.
- Communicate clearly. Most problems that arise result from poor communication, because making these arrangements is such an emotional experience. Asking questions and asserting preferences can be uncomfortable. Having somebody with you helps ensure your desires are expressed.

*Several useful, free brochures on funerals are available from the American Association of Retired Persons—*Cemetery Goods and Services* (#D13162), *Funeral Goods and Services* (#D13496) and *Pre-Paying Your Funeral* (#D13188). Send your request on a postcard (include the item number) to AARP Fulfillment, 601 E St. NW, Washington, DC 20049. Also send for *Consumer Guide to the FTC Funeral Rule* (#457-W), Consumer Information Center, Dept. 457-W, Pueblo, CO 81009.

Common traps:

According to the Funeral Rule, funeral providers are prohibited from...

...tying the purchase of any funeral good or service to the purchase of any other funeral good or service. You are not required to take any services except those mandated by state law.

Example: Having the body embalmed is not required by state law if you are planning an immediate burial (within 48 hours), but is required if the body is being shipped across state lines.

Trap: An item on the price list may appear to be optional when it is not. Although a funeral home is permitted to offer a package deal, you are not required to take it.

Examples: If the body is being embalmed, there may be a separate charge for using the embalming room—but you can't embalm without using the room...if you plan a visitation for friends and family to view the body a day before the funeral, there may be a charge for outside facilities (the parking lot)—but it's difficult to have a visitation without using the parking lot.

...making false claims about a casket's preservative value. Casket prices run from about $400 to $10,000, so some funeral directors push high-end models, which are made to seal out air and water to "retard corrosion." According to the FTC, the body decomposes no matter what kind of casket it's in.

...charging for embalming—unless it has been authorized by a family member or is required by state law.

...misrepresenting the requirements of cemeteries and crematories.

Examples: Not all cemeteries require an outer burial container (vault) in addition to the casket. And a casket is not required if the body is to be cremated immediately.

Contact the cemetery or the crematory to find out its regulations...don't rely on the funeral parlor for this information.

Making things easier for your loved ones:

Pre-arranging your own funeral will save a great deal of emotional pain for your survivors. Helpful: Discuss your preferences with friends or family. The sooner you do this the better, since no one can predict a sudden illness or serious accident.

A good way to broach subject is to say, *I read an interesting article about funeral services. That's something that we've never discussed*...or, *Do you remember going to Aunt Susan's funeral? How did you feel about the way it was arranged?*

Or write a letter stating your preferences. Give copies to a few people, and review it with at least one of them in case there are questions.

If someone else—especially someone who is ill—raises the subject with you, listen to what the person has to say, no matter how difficult it is to hear. You'll both be happier knowing that you can arrange a funeral according to the person's wishes.

About prepaid funeral services:

Although preplanning your funeral is highly beneficial, the AARP recommends using great caution if you decide to pre-pay for it. Reasons:

- There's no guarantee that the funeral home will still be in business when you die. A funeral director may, for instance, make bad investment decisions that force the operation out of business.
- There's no guarantee that the funeral director is honest. The person may just pocket the money and disappear.
- Consider the time value of your money. You may not earn any interest on money you've given a funeral parlor...they will. Better: Invest the money yourself. The interest you earn will surpass what you may save in funeral costs.

Source: John DeBerry, administrator, Funeral Service Consumer Assistance Program, 1614 Central St., Evanston, IL 60201 (a free brochure is available describing its services), and Lee Norrgard, investigative analyst, American Association of Retired Persons (AARP), 1909 K St. NW, Washington, DC 20049.

Protect Your Privacy From Merchants

Don't give a merchant your address or telephone number on a credit-card sales slip. Demands for such information violate your privacy. Visa, MasterCard and American Express prohibit merchants from refusing to do business with people who won't provide this information. What's going on: Many merchants believe that this information can help them locate a credit-card holder if there is a problem with the transaction (exceeded credit limit, etc.). The truth: If the merchant correctly processes the transaction, financial responsibility is automatically assumed by the merchant's bank.

Source: Elgie Holstein, director of Bankcard Holders of America, a nonprofit consumer-information organization.

How To Get The Most Out Of Your Accountant... Lawyer...Doctor

Our society is now so structured that it's almost impossible for people to take care of themselves. We all need professionals to help us solve legal, medical, financial and other problems.

When a relationship with a professional works well, it is productive and enjoyable for both parties. Trap: Many professionals are overburdened, disinterested, incompetent, too big for the problem—or downright dishonest—to give you the service you want and need.

To protect yourself, carefully choose the professionals you hire—and then monitor them even more carefully.

Define your needs:

Before you approach any professional, figure out exactly what you need him/her for. Trap: If you rely on someone else to define your needs, you open yourself to exploitation.

Costly errors: Giving an accountant a shoebox full of receipts...crying to an attorney that you've been mistreated without clearly defining your problem.

If you're having trouble defining your problem, talk to someone who has been though what you're going through. Super resource: People who have been burned by a professional are the best experts on what you need to know.

It's also important to figure out whether you're ready to pay the cost of hiring the right professional. And money is only part of it. Also involved: Time, energy and the ability to take direction from someone else.

Example: Getting your teeth capped is very expensive and time-consuming...and you have to be willing to follow the time-consuming daily dental-hygiene procedure at home, forever.

Find the best:

To locate the best doctor, lawyer, etc., find out who the professionals use themselves. The best attorneys are those used by other attorneys...the best dentists are those used by other dentists...and so on.

The second-best source of information is friends, relatives and other people whom you trust who have used a professional successfully.

Interview at least three professionals in your problem area. Present your clearly defined problem and watch how he addresses it...and how you are treated. Get a sense of what it would feel like to work with him. In each meeting you'll learn a lot about how to deal with your problem.

Questions to ask: Is this an area in which you're both experienced and interested? What kind of results have you had with problems similar to mine? Do you have the time to deal with my problem?

Pick the person who seems the most competent—and who makes you feel the most comfortable.

Most professionals will do their best to please you in an interview. So unless there's a real solid click, continue to shop around.

If you hire someone despite bad intuition, it may take years for you to find out why your gut instinct was right. Better: Choose someone who may be less qualified...but with whom you feel absolutely safe.

How to work with a professional:

Many people who work with a professional never give him any feedback about what he's doing—whether they think he's right or wrong, too aggressive or too passive, proceeding too slowly or too fast, etc.

But professionals need your feedback. Reason: Only you are in the middle of your problem...they're working on it from the outside.

Pay attention to your intuition all through the process. And communicate your feelings in a polite but assertive manner.

The best professionals realize that what starts out as a small discomfort to a client can turn into a major mistake if it's continually ignored. This is especially true if solving your problem is a long, drawn-out procedure—as the solutions to almost all tax or legal problems are these days.

Trap:

The age-old purpose of professionalism is to provide a person-in-need with a knowledgeable, strong and trusting relationship.

The dark side of that positive function is that people who are starved for a parent figure or for a close relationship often use professionals as paid parents and friends. They rely on them for advice in areas in which they are not experts. Although this is most obvious in the case of therapists, it can occur with a variety of professionals.

Trying to use the wrong type of professional to solve a personal problem corrupts the relationship. What happens: The professional either takes advantage of the situation or ignores it.

Example: Lawyers who practice domestic law don't know how to deal with the emotional intensity of many divorce and custody disputes.

The only way to protect yourself is to be clear about your needs. If you feel at all vulnerable or needy because of your problem, you need two professionals—one to tackle the nuts-and-bolts problem...and another to counsel you on the emotional issues.

Source: Martin G. Groder, MD, a psychiatrist and business consultant in Chapel Hill, NC. His book, *Business Games: How to Recognize the Players and Deal With Them,* is available from Boardroom Classics, Box 1026, Millburn, NJ 07041.

Clothing Money-Savers

Clothing sample sales, held by designers in their showrooms to make room for new collections, offer prices at wholesale or lower. Best times to shop: November and December for fall clothes...April and May for spring styles. Samples are generally size eight. If you're not a size eight, look for stock sales. Important: Sales are final...many are cash only...try-ons may not be permitted.

Source: *The S&B Report,* 112 E. 36 St., New York 10016.

6

Tax-Saving Strategies

Tax Planning That Boosts Cash Flow

Thoughtful tax planning boosts the company's cash flow by reducing taxes and/or deferring the time when payments are due.

Estimated taxes affect the cash flow of all profitable businesses. And, the recently enacted Deficit Reduction Act increases the cost of underpaying estimated taxes by adding an extra two percentage points to the IRS interest rate that applies to underpayments (the normal IRS interest rate is set quarterly).

Corporations generally must pay 90% of their final tax bill for the year through equal quarterly estimated tax payments (22.5% of the final tax bill each quarter). However, there are ways to reduce the size of quarterly payments and defer the tax bill.

"Small" businesses (those that have not had more than $1 million of taxable income in any one of the last three years) can base estimated payments on the previous year's tax liability. Thus, each quarterly payment need be no larger than 25% of the prior year's final tax bill, even if this year's bill will be much larger.

Catch: Payments can be based on the prior year's tax bill only if the company owed some tax for the prior year. If no tax was owed, estimated payments must total 90% of the current year's tax bill.

Strategy: A company that sees it may owe no tax for the current year should consider taking steps to generate a small tax bill just before the current year's end to slash the following year's estimated tax liability.

Example: The company could sell a piece of equipment for which an investment credit was claimed in an earlier year, and thus incur a small recapture tax on part of the credit's value.

The few dollars of tax incurred right away by the company could produce big-dollar deferrals of estimated payments the following year.

A company that expects to derive most of its income during the last half of the year may defer a large portion of its estimated tax obligations by reporting income on an annualized basis.

Under this method, the company takes income-to-date at the end of each quarter, projects a year-end tax bill on the basis of income coming in at the same rate for the rest of the year, and computes estimated taxes accordingly.

Result: Tax payments that are due for the early, low-income quarters in the year are reduced.

This method is particularly valuable for growing businesses, seasonal businesses that earn most of their income near year-end (such as many retailers) and firms that expect management changes or improving markets to have a positive financial impact near year-end.

Annualizing income provides an extra benefit by allowing flexibility in choosing the period on which annualized income may be based...

- The second quarter payment may be based on income received during the first three or five months of the year.
- The third quarter payment may be based on the first six or eight months.
- The fourth quarter payment may be based on the first nine or 11 months.

Tactic: A company that receives most of its income during one part of the year and wishes to minimize the cost of estimated taxes may adopt a fiscal year that ends just after the busy season. For example, many retailers have fiscal years ending on January 31, just after the Christmas shopping season.

New opportunities for cutting the cost of Tax Reform's uniform capitalization (unicap) rules are the hot tax topic of the moment.

Background: Tax Reform required that inventory-related overhead costs of manufacturers, wholesalers and retailers be capitalized (added to the value of inventory) rather than deducted immediately. Such costs include storage rent, insurance, repairs, maintenance, utilities, a portion of salaries and other items related to storage of inventories. The bottom-line impact is that the deductions for these items are deferred—they cannot be deducted until the inventory items are sold...so the current tax bill is increased.

Snag: While Tax Reform required companies to adopt unicap rules on their 1987 tax returns, the IRS did not provide guidelines as to how the new rules were to be applied. Companies were left on their own to figure out the complicated new rules.

Recently, however, the IRS has issued a series of announcements that companies can use to simplify unicap accounting and reduce their tax bills.

Problem: Many companies are not in compliance with the new IRS procedures. They set up their accounting methods before the more favorable procedures were announced by the IRS.

Opportunity: By coming into compliance with the new procedures, many companies may simplify their accounting methods and regain large deductions that previously were lost.

Unicap should be seriously looked into by...

- Manufacturers with large amounts of raw materials in inventory.
- Companies with temporarily idled property, plants or equipment.
- Retailers with handling costs at facilities where goods are sold on site.
- Wholesalers and retailers with repackaging costs.
- Companies using LIFO (last-in, first-out) accounting and electing LIFO's simplified capitalization method.

We recommend that all companies using unicap accounting review their current accounting procedures...almost all will find tax-saving opportunities.

Unicap accounting procedures can be extremely complex, however, so be sure to consult with a capital-cost accounting specialist.

Accounting methods can have a major impact on the company's cash flow...

- Cash-basis accounting provides greater flexibility than accrual-basis accounting. An accrual-basis firm must report income when it is earned (for example, when goods are shipped) whether or not it has received payment. Similarly, it must deduct expenses when they become due, regardless of whether they have been paid. Cash-basis firms, however, report income and expenditures only as cash is exchanged, giving them greater leeway to time income and deduction items by accelerating or delaying payments and billings.

Caution: Not all firms qualify to use cash-basis accounting, so consult a tax advisor for details.

• LIFO (last-in, first-out) accounting can generate a large tax deferral for an indefinite period of time when both inventory costs and inventory levels are rising. LIFO accounting treats the last, and most expensive, item added to inventory as the first one sold, thus increasing the company's deduction for cost of goods sold.

• Real estate. A company that's about to take a large gain on the sale of real estate may be able to postpone the tax due indefinitely by trading the property in a like-kind exchange instead of selling it for cash. Requirements: Within 45 days of disposing of old property, the company must designate a specific replacement property to be received. And it must actually take possession of the replacement property within 180 days.

If the company can't find another firm with which it wants to make a straight swap of properties, a commercial real estate broker may be able to arrange a three-way exchange or other multi-party transaction.

At the future date when the company finally wants to dispose of the replacement property, it may be able to defer tax again with another like-kind exchange.

• Bonus payments. The 1990 Tax Act increases the salary base subject to the Medicare portion of Social Security taxes from $51,300 to $125,000. This tax is imposed at a 1.45% rate on both the employer and the employee. Result: An extra 2.9% of tax is imposed on income earned in this range starting in 1991.

Tactic: Beat the tax by accelerating employee compensation from next year into this year by paying year-end bonuses in lieu of standard payments that would be paid during the early part of next year.

• Depreciation: Companies should time the acquisition of depreciable equipment for the best tax impact. Normally, a "mid-year convention" applies so that the company gets a half-year's worth of depreciation deductions for new equipment no matter when it is placed in service during the year. This can be costly for property acquired at the beginning of the year, and favorable for property acquired toward year-end.

If more than 40% of all property is placed in service during the last three months of the year, a mid-quarter convention applies—depreciation deductions are allowed from the middle of the quarter in which property is placed in service.

The company's tax advisor should consider how tax benefits will be affected by the simple timing of equipment acquisitions, and plan accordingly.

Source: David W. Jessen, partner and director of entrepreneurial services, Ernst & Young, 3600 Glenwood Ave., Raleigh, NC 27612.

How To Reduce Property Taxes

When most people complain about taxes, they tend to think in terms of federal income taxes. Yet property taxes are the stiffest of all, and rising faster than any other type of levy. In some areas of the country, they have skyrocketed by nearly 50% in the last five years. And—according to the headlines—they'll be going up further...fast.

Many Americans are overpaying their property taxes—needlessly. When faced with an enormous property tax bill, homeowners generally take a defeatist attitude. They think there is nothing they can do about it. Nothing could be further from the truth.

For about 60% of American homeowners, there is sufficient evidence to warrant a tax reduction.

There are a wide variety of reasons to justify a tax cut.

Examples: There could be arithmetic errors in the records of the local taxing authority...or you could be taxed for a two-story house when in fact you own a one-story residence...or your residence may be listed as 10 years old when in fact it is twice that age...or the dimensions of your land may be overstated...or you may not have been given a special exemption to which you are entitled, such as a veteran's exemption...or property values may have declined significantly in your area.

It makes sense to complain about your property taxes when you can demonstrate that you have been wrongfully overcharged. More than half of the homeowners who do protest their assessments get them reduced...according to the International Association of Assessing Officers, an organization dedicated to property valuation for assessment purposes.

It isn't quite as easy as walking into the tax assessor's office, informing the official that you think your taxes are high and expecting a reduction on the spot.

You must take the time to collect the necessary information that will support your case.

Next, you need to present your appeal in an organized, convincing fashion that will leave the tax officials little choice but to agree with your contention that your tax bill is incorrect.

This approach will take some time—generally between six and 10 hours of research and writing. But the time you spend will be well worth your effort. In addition to reducing your tax bill for the tax year in question, you'll be reducing your property taxes for years to come, since future tax bills are based upon past records.

Step one: Obtain what is called that tax list. This document, which is available in the local tax assessor's office, is simply a list of property owners in your area. It lists blocks and lot numbers or property identification numbers, assessed values of the properties...and what their property taxes are.

Next step: Obtain your own property record card. This document, also available in the tax assessor's office, is the assessor's official worksheet that is used to determine the assessed value of your property. It contains information that is unique to your property—the dimensions of the house and lot, list of unique features, etc.—as well as a top-view drawing of the residence with dimensions.

Usually, it's simple to obtain a copy of your property record card. But, in a few states, these cards are not considered public records and assessors are not required to furnish you with a copy until a week to 10 days before a formal appeal. This policy may put you in the position of having to file an appeal before knowing all the facts. And, if the assessor decides to go by the letter of the law, you may not even be allowed to photocopy the card when you do get your hands on it.

Self-defense: Take carefully handwritten notes on the information you need from the card while you are still in the assessor's office.

Regardless of whether you get a photocopy of the property record card, or have to transcribe it by hand, you should scrutinize it carefully. Often, there are many errors in these records. Most common:

- The dimensions of your land are wrong. You may own 1½ acres, but you are being taxed on two acres.
- The dimensions of buildings or improvements are wrong. If your house is rectangular, the length on one side may be listed as 20 feet, while the length on the opposite side is given as 25 feet. Or you may have a 1,800 sq. ft. house and are being taxed for a 2,500 sq. ft. house.
- The description of the building is wrong. Your house may be listed as being made of brick when it is less expensive frame construction.
- The description of your land is wrong. Perhaps the description includes part of your neighbor's land and you are wrongfully being taxed on it.
- Finished areas of your house are listed incorrectly. Your record may indicate that your basement is completely paneled, with an acoustical ceiling and hardwood floors, when in fact it is unfinished.
- The grade and quality of improvements are wrong. Perhaps you put gravel stones on

your driveway, but you're being charged for a paved drive.

• The depreciation factor—the assessor's opinion of the condition of your house—is wrong compared with houses whose condition is similar to yours.

You may find enough errors on your property card to justify a meeting with the assessor on those mistakes alone.

Is your house being assessed at a higher value than "comparable properties"? These are properties that are similar to your own residence in location, age, design, size and construction. Goal: Unearth data that will support a lower assessed value for your property.

Example: If you can show that a property comparable to yours is assessed at only $120,000 while your house is assessed at $145,000, you have solid grounds for an appeal.

Ideal: Have your house compared with a twin of your own house that was sold during the current tax year. This establishes the comparable's "market value"—the best indicator of the property's true worth. If you live in a development, for example, the ideal comparable would be the house next door that is identical to yours. To find a comparable:

• Begin by looking for comparables in your neighborhood—within a few blocks of your home rather than across town. Then, compare similar styles.

• Compare such items as square footage of living area, number of bathrooms and bedrooms, whether the houses have air conditioning, fireplaces or unfinished basements, garage capacity, etc.

Since it's unlikely that another house is completely identical to yours, you probably will have to make adjustments.

• After you gather information on three comparable properties—and take photos of them if possible—you must come up with an adjusted value for your property and the three others. You then take the square footage for your house and the comparables, divide by each property's adjusted value and come up with adjusted value per square foot for each house. This gives you the basis on which to compare the assessments on all the properties. Presumably, your research will indicate that your house has been assessed at a higher value than the three comparable properties.

When presenting your case, remember the rules of successful negotiating:

• Let the assessor make the first offer.

• Never say yes too quickly.

• Don't be vague about what value is acceptable. Suggesting—and supporting—a specific assessed value for your property is essential. Without your input, the assessor's own conclusion may not be satisfactory.

Bear in mind that determining the value of a property is partially subjective. It is an opinion that is supported by facts—but there can be a difference of opinion about those facts. So, to avoid disappointment, recognize that you may not get total agreement from the assessor about the value you are proposing.

Though it's possible to take your appeal to a local review board or to court, you may wish to accept a reasonable compromise offer. It is better to accept a slightly higher valuation than to risk a worse outcome.

Source: R. Harry Koenig, owner of King Associates, a Chester, NJ, tax-consulting firm. He is the author of *How to Lower Your Property Taxes*, Fireside/Simon & Schuster, 1230 Ave. of the Americas, New York 10022.

Tax Loopholes For Hobbies

Most people have a hobby of one kind or another that they pursue for enjoyment. Opportunity: If the hobby is set up with taxes in mind, the government will subsidize some of the costs.

For tax purposes, there are two kinds of hobbies—those where you collect things, and those that are more active, such as photography, painting and weekend farming.

• General rule for hobbies that involve collecting: Gains on the sale of items in your collection are taxable. Losses can be offset only against the gains from the sale of items in your collection.

Loophole I: If you take big gains in one

year, remember to also take some losses that year. Use the losses to offset the gains.

Loophole II: Suppose you want to keep your collection intact, and you also want to sell loss items to offset gain items. You can repurchase the items you sold, but you must wait 31 days before doing so. Your losses will be deductible as long as you avoid the *wash sale rule* by waiting 31 days.

Loophole III: Take advantage of tax-free swaps. Tax on any gain will be deferred if you trade items in your collection for other collectible items.

Loophole IV: Change your status from hobbyist to investor so you can take deductions for your losses.

• How to maintain investor status for your collection. There are three tax categories of collectors—hobbyist, investor and dealer. Tax differences:

Hobbyist: When you sell items in your collection, the gains are taxable. Losses can be written off against gains, but otherwise they're not deductible. The stamp hobbyist can't take stamps he sold at a loss and apply them against the stock he sold at a gain.

Investor: Profits are capital gains. Losses qualify as capital losses and can be used to offset other types of capital gains, such as gains on the sale of stock. If your losses exceed your gains, they are deductible against your other income, subject to the $3,000 per year limit, until they are used up.

In addition, your investment expenses are deductible. These include insurance, investment advisory fees and travel costs, safe-deposit-box rent, subscriptions to collectors' journals, appraisal fees and depreciation on safes and other security systems.

Dealer: Profits are taxable income. Losses are deductible as ordinary business losses.

For most collectors, the best category to be in is investor. Whether or not you're an investor is a question of intention and facts. Things you can do to maintain investor status:

• Make necessary sales. If you never sell items from your collection, you're a hobbyist. As an investor, though, you would sell when items in your collection don't meet your investment needs or goals.

• Buy investor grade items—such as stamps and coins that are sold in two grades—collector and investor—depending on their condition. Buy items that you expect to appreciate in value.

• Keep detailed records. If you do this, you're obviously not just a hobbyist. The extent of the detail may be the deciding factor in whether an item is bought for hobby or investment purposes.

• Be well informed about this field. Subscribe to trade journals and publications. Buy auction house catalogues and follow the trends.

Caution: To be an investor—don't make sales at the retail level, and don't advertise in trade journals. If you do, you might be considered a dealer.

If you want to be treated as a dealer, you should open a separate bank account, register a trade name, obtain a resale certificate, be listed as a dealer in trade publications and join a trade society.

You may be able to operate your hobby as a business. If that is the case, your expenses are deductible and any losses you incur can be used to offset other income. Key: You have the intention of making a profit.

But if the activity is not carried on for profit, your deductions are limited and no loss is allowed to offset other income.

Factors the IRS considers in determining whether an activity is carried on for profit include...

• The time and effort you put into the activity indicate whether you intend to make it profitable.

• You carry on the activity in a businesslike manner.

• You are depending on income from the activity for your livelihood.

• Your losses from the activity are due to circumstances beyond your control or are normal in the start-up phase of your type of business.

• You change your methods of operation in an attempt to improve the profitability of the activity.

• You, or your advisors, have the knowledge needed to carry on the activity as a successful business.

• You have been successful in making a profit in similar activities in the past.

• The activity makes a profit in some years.

• You can expect to make a future profit from the appreciation of the assets used in the activity.

An activity is presumed to be carried on for profit if it produced a profit in at least three of the last five tax years (two out of the last seven years for activities that consist primarily of breeding, training, showing or racing horses).

If you are just starting out in an activity and you do not yet have three years of profit, you can take advantage of this presumption at a later time.

Loophole: File IRS Form 5213, *Election to Postpone Determination as to Whether the Presumption That an Activity is Engaged in for Profit Applies.* Filing this form postpones any determination that your activity is not carried on for profit until five (or seven) years have passed since you first started the activity.

Impact: The IRS will not question whether your activity is engaged in for profit until three or five years are up. It will not question your deductions relating to the activity.

If you have the choice of receiving a valuable collection either as a gift or an inheritance, it's best to take it as an inheritance. You'll pay less capital gains tax when you ultimately sell the collection.

Reason: When you inherit property, the basis, or tax cost, is stepped up to its value on the date of the donor's death. But when you take property by gift, your basis is the basis of the person who gave you the property, which is usually its cost to that person.

Source: Edward Mendlowitz, partner, Mendlowitz Weitsen, CPAs, Two Pennsylvania Plaza, New York 10121. Mr. Mendlowitz is the author of several books, including *Aggressive Tax Strategies*, Macmillan Publishing Co., 866 Third Ave., New York 10022.

How To Deduct Your Summer Travels

There are a number of ways to get income tax deductions for your summer travels. Key: Arrange a trip that has business as its primary purpose. It needn't be what you usually think of as a business trip—a trip to look after your investments can also be considered a "business trip."

• Travel for business and pleasure within the United States. As long as the trip is primarily for business purposes, the cost of getting to and from the business location will be fully deductible even though you tack on a few days of recreation. Expenses at your destination that are incurred for business purposes are also fully deductible, but expenses that are incurred for purely personal agendas are not considered deductible.

Example: You work in Atlanta and make a business trip to New Orleans. During the return trip home, you decide to stop in Mobile to visit friends. You spend $450 for the nine days you are away from home for travel, meals, lodging and other travel expenses. If you had not stopped in Mobile, you would have been gone only six days and your total cost would have been $400. You can deduct $400, including the full cost of round-trip transportation to and from New Orleans.

Even if a trip is primarily for vacation, you can deduct any business-related expenses you incur during the trip.

Example: You take your family on a vacation to Disney World. While there, you take a one-day side trip to see a supplier in Miami. Result: Any cost related to the side trip is deductible.

Scheduling incidental business activities during a trip won't change what is really a vacation into a business trip.

• Foreign travel for business and pleasure...the rules are tougher. Where business and pleasure are mixed, the full cost of getting to and from your destination is deductible only if...

Travel is for one week or less, or...

Less than 25% of the time is spent in non-business activity.

Caution: If too much time is spent on personal activities, it will be hard to prove to the IRS that the trip actually was a business trip. Remember, the trip must be primarily for business.

If the trip lasts more than seven days, or 25% or more are non-business days, you must reduce your transportation reduction accordingly on a day-to-day basis between business days and personal days.

Example: You take a 30-day trip to London, but only 20 days are spent on business. You can deduct only two-thirds of the cost of getting there and back. In addition, though, you can deduct expenses in London for the 20 business days.

Business days are days in which you actually do some business as well as days you spend traveling to and from the place of business (if the days before and after are business days). In counting business days for purposes of the week-or-less and less-than-25% rules, remember to include travel days. Keep trips within these limits if possible.

Tricky counting: If you take a seven-day business trip and tack on a weekend of vacation, the weekend will not be treated as business days, since the days after the trip are not business days. But if you leave on a Wednesday and come back on a Tuesday, the weekend in between will be counted as business days.

Travel to US possessions, such as Puerto Rico and the Virgin Islands, is considered to be travel outside the country.

• Expenses of your spouse. The cost of having your spouse accompany you on a business trip is nondeductible unless you can show that his/her presence on the trip has a bona fide business purpose. Incidental services—for example, the occasional typing of notes—are not sufficient. Cases where a spouse's travel expenses have been held to be deductible:

• Where the spouse's presence helped an executive to promote the public image of his firm and to cultivate business relationships.

• Where the spouse contributed directly to the success of a taxpayer's sales activities.

Hotel deductions: If your spouse accompanies you on a business trip without a bona fide business purpose, your deduction for lodging is what it would cost you if you had traveled alone.

Example: You stay at a hotel where a single room costs $100 per night. With your wife along, you take a double room for $140 per night. Your deduction is not limited to half the room's cost ($70). You can deduct the full $100 that you would have paid if you had gone alone.

Source: Laurence I. Foster, tax partner, middle market practice, KPMG Peat Marwick, 599 Lexington Ave., New York 10022.

Tax-Filing Loopholes

Deductions and credits aren't the only way to save taxes. How you complete and file the return itself at tax time can also save you big money.

Extension loopholes:

If you can't get your return done on time, you'll have to apply for an extension. You do this by filing Form 4868, *Application for Automatic Extension of Time to File*, by April 15. This gives you four months, until August 15, to file your tax return for 1991.

Trap: Form 4868 extends the time for filing, but not the time for paying the tax. You'll be penalized if the total tax you've paid, including withholding, estimated payments and the check that accompanies your extension request, doesn't equal 90% of the tax you owe for 1991.

If you fall short, your extension will not be valid and you may be charged late payment and late filing penalties in addition to interest.

Loophole: If you're self-employed, you may have a good reason to get a filing extension. Tax-deductible contributions to a Keogh plan or a Simplified Employee Pension (SEP) can be made until the extended due date of the return. By getting an extension, you give yourself an extra four months to come up with the money to make the Keogh or SEP contribution.

Loophole: Apply for an extra two months' extension—and file your return at the last minute, just before October 15. People who file in the fall, just before the October 15 deadlines are, in my experience, less likely to be audited than those who file by April 15. Reason: Most targeted returns are selected for audit during the summer months. By fall, most of the year's quota of returns to be audited has been filled.

Short-of-cash loopholes:

If you don't have the money to pay your taxes...you cannot apply for an extension. The best thing to do is to file your return on time—just don't send in the money. By doing this, you avoid penalties for late filing.

Problem: The IRS will come after you for the taxes. This usually takes about six weeks. If you still can't pay the full amount of tax, when the IRS comes after you, you should write to an office asking that someone contact you to arrange for installment payments. Better: Go to your local IRS office to set up an installment arrangement.

Loophole: Apply for an extension for payment of taxes. In cases where you can't pay your tax because of an unusual hardship, you can apply for an extension of time to pay by filing Form 1127, *Request for Extension of Time for Payment of Tax.* Unusual hardship includes things such as the death of the spouse who owes the taxes, the loss of your job, serious illness or imminent bankruptcy. You must show that you will have a substantial financial loss if you pay your tax on the date it is due.

To get the extension, you must state why you can't borrow the money to pay the taxes. You must also provide financial statements. Extensions of time to pay are generally limited to six months.

Estimated-tax loophole:

The first 1992 estimated tax payment is due on April 15, and the next on June 15. You should check to see whether you're required to make estimated payments. Review the instructions to Form 1040-ES.

Loophole: One way to make your estimated tax payments is to credit an overpayment from your prior year's return to the current year's estimated tax. So when you make your extension payment, include the amount you would normally pay for the first estimated installment.

This strategy minimizes the penalties you could be subject to for miscalculating the amount of 1991 tax you owe. Because you've made a combined payment, increasing the amount of 1991 tax you pay, you won't need to worry about violating the 90% rule—your combined payment will put you above the 90% threshold. Your extension won't be invalidated, and you won't be assessed lateness penalties.

You may, however, be short on your first quarter's estimated payment for 1992 when the IRS applies your tax overpayment to estimated taxes. But the penalty for underpaying estimated taxes in a quarter is less than late payment and late filing penalties.

Loophole: You can avoid underpayment penalties entirely by having more tax withheld from your salary.

Joint- or separate-returns loophole:

A couple who are squabbling may have trouble agreeing about filing a joint return.

Loophole: The couple can file separate returns, then, if they patch things up later, they can amend those returns and file a joint return. This can be done up to three years after the filing of separate returns. Trap: You can't go the other way. When you file a joint return, you can't later decide to switch to separate returns.

Other reasons for filing separate returns...

- One spouse owes the IRS money. Suppose the husband owes money to the IRS from a prior year's activity and the wife is getting a refund. This couple might consider filing separate returns, even though they'll pay more tax. Reason: The wife will get her refund. If they file a joint return, the refund may be offset by the tax the husband owes.

Loophole: This couple might consider filing a joint return listing the wife as the taxpayer and the husband as the spouse. The wife's Social Security number will appear first on the return. It is my experience that IRS computers scan only the first Social Security number on the return against their records to see who owes them money.

- Lawsuits. If one spouse is facing substantial lawsuits, a couple might consider filing separate returns. This is a way of keeping the other spouse's sources of income private. It is much more difficult for the separate return of that spouse to be subpoenaed by the creditors of the other spouse.

Source: Edward Mendlowitz, partner, Mendlowitz Weitsen, CPAs, Two Pennsylvania Plaza, New York 10121. Mr. Mendlowitz is the author of several books, including *Aggressive Tax Strategies*, Macmillan Publishing Co., 866 Third Ave., New York 10022.

How To Deduct Nondeductible Expenses

The tax law imposes strict limits on personal deductions. But creative tax planners have found ways to get around these limits. With a little careful planning, you can turn nondeductible expenses into tax deductions.

• Interest deductions. Interest on personal debt is no longer deductible. This includes interest on car loans, college loans, credit cards, revolving charge accounts, installment purchases and late-paid taxes. But interest on home-equity loans of up to $100,000 remains fully deductible.

Loophole: Take out a home-equity loan on your first or second home and use the proceeds to pay off personal debts. Your interest payments will then be deductible. You will have converted nondeductible personal interest payments into deductible mortgage interest.

• Hire your kids. Instead of paying your child a nondeductible allowance, put him/her to work as a bona fide employee in your business. The wages are a deductible expense.

Loophole: If your business is unincorporated, you don't have to pay Social Security taxes on wages paid to a child who is under 18.

• Buy a vacation home. It can be a source of personal pleasure and valuable tax breaks. When you rent a vacation home to strangers for fewer than 15 days, the rental income is tax-free. This is one of the few instances in the Tax Code where income is considered nontaxable. You are not even required to report it on your tax return. Nevertheless, you are still entitled to full deductions for mortgage interest and property taxes.

When you rent your vacation home to others for 15 days or more, the income you receive is taxable. But expenses related to the property rental (including depreciation) are deductible, subject to certain limitations depending on the number of days you personally use the place. To get the full deduction, you yourself cannot use the place for more than the greater of 14 days or 10% of the number of days it is rented to others.

Loophole: Days spent fixing or maintaining the house do not count as personal use.

• Medical expenses of dependents. Even though you may not be able to claim a personal exemption for your contribution to the support of a relative because he/she had a gross income of $2,150 or more, you can still deduct any medical expenses that you pay on your relative's behalf. Key: You must provide more than one-half of the relative's support.

Loophole: Instead of giving your relative cash to pay medical bills, pay the bills yourself. This may give you a deduction.

If you are the one who is claiming a dependency exemption for a parent under a multiple support agreement (Form 2120) with other relatives, you should also pay the dependent's medical expenses. Reason: In determining qualification for the exemption, the payment of medical expenses is treated as part of the dependent's support. The payment is also deductible as a medical expense.

Impact: You get a double tax benefit for the same payment, a dependency exemption and a tax deduction.

Another way to get a double benefit is to make a charitable contribution on your parent's behalf. The payment is included in calculating support and you get a charitable deduction for it.

• Hobby losses. Expenses of activities that are primarily sport, hobby or recreation are not deductible. In order to convert these nondeductible expenses into allowable deductions, the activity must be changed to an activity carried on for the production or collection of income. This is not hard to do if you keep good records. Factors that the IRS considers include...

The businesslike nature of the taxpayer's records.

The extent of the knowledge and expertise of the taxpayer and the manner in which he/she uses them in the activity.

The history of prior income or losses connected with the activity.

The taxpayer's success in conducting other types of activities.

• Employee business-expense deductions. As an employee, you can deduct unreimbursed expenses for business-related travel, transportation, meals, entertainment and gifts.

Trap: Most unreimbursed employee business expenses come under the category of "miscellaneous itemized deductions" and, as such, can only be deducted to the extent that, in total, they exceed 2% of your Adjusted Gross Income (AGI). If your expenses don't come up to this floor, you get no deduction for them.

Loophole I: Have your employer reduce your salary by the amount you normally spend during the year on business expenses—say $1,000. Then have your employer reimburse you directly for the $1,000 of expenses. Impact: You no longer have to worry about the 2% floor. You get a deduction for the full $1,000 of expenses through the salary reduction. Caution: The salary reduction may affect your pension contributions.

Important: Be sure to adequately account for the expenses to your employer. If you don't, you could be required to pick up the entire amount of the reimbursement as ordinary income.

Loophole II (for anyone who is physically or mentally handicapped): Impairment-related work expenses are not subject to the 2%-of-Adjusted-Gross-Income limit on miscellaneous itemized deductions.

Loophole III: Beat the 2% floor on deductibility of employee business expenses by filing Schedule C (Profit or Loss From Business), where there is no such limitation. To qualify for reporting your expenses on Schedule C, you must fit into one of the following categories...

Self-employed individual or independent contractor.

Statutory employee. This is a category of worker that includes full-time life-insurance salespeople, certain agents and commission drivers and certain home-workers. Statutory employees are entitled to file Schedule C even though Social Security tax has been withheld from their paychecks and they have been issued W-2 forms.

Qualified performing artists. To qualify in this category, a taxpayer must have performed services in the performing arts for at least two performances in the tax year... and had performing-arts-related business expenses in excess of 10% of his/her performing-arts gross income...and had AGI of $16,000 or less. (Performing-arts expenses can be deducted even though deductions are not itemized.)

• Passive losses. Tax Reform produced the "passive loss rules" that generally limit the deductibility of losses from passive activities to the amount of income derived from such activities. Passive activities are defined as those activities involving the conduct of a trade or business in which the taxpayer does not materially participate.

Accordingly, you can avoid the disallowance of losses if you "materially" participate in the otherwise passive activity. Material participation in a trade or business activity means satisfying any one of a variety of tests.

Example: If you participated in the activity for more than 500 hours during the year, the passive loss rules would not apply to that activity.

Strategy: To prove material participation, keep an appointment book, calendar or narrative summary in which you record a listing of all the services you performed.

Loophole I: New IRS regulations for self-charged interest permit the matching of interest income (normally portfolio income) directly against passive losses to the extent that the loss includes self-interest charged through the entity by the S corporation shareholder or partner.

Loophole II: Amended returns can be filed to claim a refund going back to all open years from 1987 on.

• Small business losses. If you're operating a business as a regular corporation, any losses you suffer when you sell your stock in the company are usually treated as capital losses, deductible only against capital gains and up to $3,000 a year of ordinary income. Losses on the sale of Section 1244 stock are deductible in full against ordinary income.

Limits: $100,000 a year on a joint return ($50,000 a year if you are single).

To qualify under Section 1244, the corporation must have capital of $1 million or less. It must operate as a business. And the stock must have been issued for money or property.

Source: Edward Mendlowitz, partner, Mendlowitz Weitsen, CPAs, Two Pennsylvania Plaza, New York 10121. Mr. Mendlowitz is the author of several books, including *Aggressive Tax Strategies*, Macmillan Publishing Co., 866 Third Ave., New York 10022.

Tax Loopholes For People With Sideline Incomes

More and more people moonlight, consult...and have set up sideline businesses. The tax advantages of having a business of your own, even if it's only a sideline, are significant. Opportunities:

• Report income and expenses on Schedule C of Form 1040. There's a big advantage in doing this. Business expenses, such as transportation costs, are deductible in full on Schedule C. They are not subject to the 2%-of-Adjusted-Gross-Income limitation that applies when the same expenses are taken on Schedule A of the 1040.

If you get a commission, report it on Schedule C, even if you have no business expenses to write off against it. Reason: If the income qualifies as self-employment income, you can use some of it to set up a Keogh plan.

• Have bigger pension plans. The amount of money employees can put into tax-favored retirement plans is relatively modest. If they qualify under the new deduction rules, they can put $2,000 a year into Individual Retirement Accounts (IRAs) and deduct it, and put that and about $8,000 a year into 401(k) plans if their companies have such a plan.

But people who have sideline businesses can build bigger retirement nest eggs. They can open Keogh plans and SEPs (Simplified Employee Pension plans), which have more generous contribution and deduction limits. You can put up to $30,000 a year into a Keogh or SEP, or 13.043% of your earned income, whichever is less.

Super Keoghs: There's a kind of Keogh, called a defined benefit Keogh, where contributions are determined actuarially. You can contribute to—and deduct from—this kind of Keogh, an amount that will provide you with a retirement benefit of over $100,000 a year.

Loophole: Contributions to IRAs must be made by April 15 to be deductible on the prior year's return. But contributions to Keoghs and SEPs can be made after April 15, until the extended due date of your return, provided the plans were set up by the deadlines imposed by the Tax Code—December 31 for Keoghs and April 15 for SEPs.

• Depreciate business equipment. Depreciation deductions on equipment, such as a personal computer, shelter some of your income from tax. Instead of taking depreciation deductions, you may, under Section 179 of the Tax Code, write off up to $10,000 worth of business equipment in the year of purchase.

• Hire your children. A child who works in his parent's sideline business can earn up to $3,400 in 1992 without owing any federal income tax. The salary is deductible by the business. An additional $2,000 of the child's salary would escape tax if it was put into an IRA.

Loophole: If your business is unincorporated, you don't have to pay Social Security tax on wages paid to a child who is under 18.

• Deduct advertising expenses. These are deductible along with all other ordinary and necessary business expenses.

Example: A freelance computer consultant is drumming up business among his neighbors. He decides to sponsor the Little League team his child plays on. The cost of his sponsorship is a deductible business expense—it's advertising.

• Deduct home-office expenses. If you work out of your home and it is the main place of business of your sideline business, you can deduct a portion of your expenses—insurance, utilities, rent, etc.—as home-office expenses.

• Maximize your interest deductions. When you borrow money to put into an unincorporated business, the interest you pay is fully deductible as business interest on Schedule C. If you borrow money on your credit card to put into the business, the interest is business interest, not personal interest, and is fully deductible.

Compare: If you borrow money to invest in an incorporated business, the interest is only deductible as investment interest, subject to investment-interest limitations. These limit your interest deductions to the amount of investment income you have for the year.

• Hire independent contractors. When you hire people who are self-employed, as you are in your own capacity as the owner of a sideline business, they may be considered "independent contractors" for withholding-tax purposes, rather than employees. Benefit: You don't have to withhold income tax or pay the employer's portion of Social Security tax for independent contractors.

The key test for determining whether someone who performs services for you is an employee or independent contractor is this: Do you control what will be done and how it will be done? If you do, the person is an employee. If you don't exercise control over the methodology of services, the person is an independent contractor.

• Minimize Social Security taxes. When both spouses work in the business, and one spouse has a full-time, high-paying job, that spouse should be listed as the sole owner of the business. Business income paid to that spouse will not be subject to self-employment tax if the spouse pays the maximum Social Security tax on his salary from his job. (For 1992, the maximum amount of salary that Social Security tax is taken from is $53,400. However, the 1.45% Medicare hospital insurance tax is taken from salary up to $125,000.)

Compare: If the business was in the name of the spouse who did not have a full-time job, that spouse would have to pay self-employment tax on up to $53,400 (or Medicare hospital insurance tax up to $125,000) of business income.

• Write off your losses. If your deductions for the year are more than your income, your net loss can be used to offset other income.

Caution: Certain deductions can't be used to create a loss. These include home-office deductions and the expensing deduction under Section 179.

• Minimize estimated tax payments. If you have sideline income, you're required to make quarterly estimated tax payments to the government. You'll be penalized by the IRS if your payments fall short in any quarter.

Loophole: You can avoid making estimated payments on your sideline income by increasing the amount of tax that is withheld from your salary. You do not have to make estimated tax payments if your withholding for the year equals 90% of the total tax shown on this year's return, or 100% of the tax you paid last year.

Loophole: If you receive most of your income late in the year, use what is called the annualized income installment method to figure your quarterly estimated tax after you've received the bulk of your income. To calculate your payments, use the annualized income installment worksheet in Form 2210, *Underpayment of Estimated Tax by Individuals and Fiduciaries.*

Source: Edward Mendlowitz, partner, Mendlowitz Weitsen, CPAs, Two Pennsylvania Plaza, New York 10212. Mr. Mendlowitz is the author of several books, including *Aggressive Tax Strategies,* Macmillan Publishing Co., 866 Third Ave., New York 10022.

Tax-Free Living

A family self-incorporated and transferred its assets—including house, car and equipment used in the family business (a farm)—to the new company. The family then entered into an employment contract with the company, which required family members to live in their former house because their presence was required at all hours to run the business. The company agreed to pay the family's living expenses, including food and lodging. The family took the payments tax-free because the arrangement benefited their employer, and the company deducted its expenses. IRS ruling: The arrangement is proper even if it was adopted with the explicit intention of avoiding taxes.

Source: *Letter Ruling* 9134003.

Traps And Opportunities In The New Luxury Tax

The 1990 Tax Act imposed a new excise tax on high-cost cars, boats, airplanes, jewelry and furs. The tax is 10% of the excess of the sales price over specified threshold amounts. The thresholds are...

Jewelry and furs: $10,000
Passenger vehicles: $30,000
Boats: $100,000
Airplanes: $250,000

The seller of a taxable article is responsible for collecting the tax from the purchaser and paying it to the government. As a general rule, the tax is imposed on the first retail sale after manufacture or importation. It applies to new, not used, items. In some cases it works as a "use tax" and is imposed when you first use a taxable item.

• Trap: You can't avoid the luxury tax by buying an item, such as an expensive car, overseas. The tax will be imposed when you import the car into the US for your personal use. You'll have to pay the tax and file IRS Form 720, *Quarterly Federal Excise Tax Return*, for the calendar quarter in which you import the car.

Other traps and opportunities in the new law...

• Opportunity: Wait six months before you add parts and accessories to an article that is subject to the tax. Parts and accessories sold on or in connection with the sale of any article subject to tax are treated as part of the article. Their cost is included in the original purchase price for tax purposes. The law says that if parts and accessories are added within six months of the purchase of an article, they are treated as if they were included in the original purchase price. Implication: If you wait six months to add the parts or accessories, their cost and installation will escape tax.

Example: You buy a $40,000 car and want to add a high-powered stereo system costing $5,000. If you buy the stereo with the car, your luxury tax will be $1,500 ($40,000 + $5,000 – the $30,000 threshold × 10%). But if you wait six months to have the stereo installed, the luxury tax will only be $1,000 ($40,000 – $30,000 × 10%). Saving: $500.

• Trap: Substantial modification to jewelry and furs that alter the purpose or style of the item can trigger the tax. Repairs and slight modifications to an article are not subject to the tax. But substantial modifications are. The delivery of the modified item to you by the person who does the work is treated as a sale and is subject to tax. The tax is imposed on the value of the finished product in excess of $10,000.

Example: You inherit a diamond ring worth $15,000. You take it to a jeweler to be made into a necklace. The jeweler charges $5,000 for parts and labor, bringing the value of the finished necklace to $20,000. Impact: You'll owe a luxury tax of $1,000 ($20,000 – $10,000 × 10%) when you pick up the necklace. The tax applies to the market value of the necklace, even though the actual value that's been added is only $5,000.

The same principle applies to furs. If you spend $5,000 to recast a $15,000 fur coat into a more fashionable design, you'll owe $1,000 of luxury tax. (Altering hemlines and sleeves, however, is not considered substantial modification.)

• Opportunity: Foreign visitors are not subject to the tax. Tell your friends. The tax does not apply to articles sold for export. Foreigners who buy goods here and have them shipped home won't pay the tax. A foreign visitor who wants to use a taxable item while in this country can avoid tax by certifying that the item will be taken out of the country. He must show his passport along with a transportation ticket indicating that he will be leaving the country within six months.

• Opportunity: Spread the tax out over time. Leases are treated as sales, subjecting the leased item to tax. But the rules allow the tax on a leased boat, plane or car (if for at least one year) to be collected at the same rate that the lease payments are collected. This means you can pay a small amount of tax each month for the term of the lease.

• Trap: People who sell things that are subject to the luxury tax may be liable for the tax themselves if they use an article in their inventory for personal purposes before they sell it. Executives and salespeople of car dealerships could easily run into this problem. When a car is driven more than 200 miles for a dealer's personal use, the luxury tax will be imposed.

• Opportunity: Special rule for business airplanes. The luxury tax does not apply to an airplane if at least 80% of its use will be in a trade or business. The owner must provide proof of business use for the first two years after purchase. If proof is not provided and the purchaser fails to pay the tax, no depreciation deductions will be allowed for the aircraft. Note: This exception is only for planes. If a corporation buys an expensive car for an executive to use, it will have to pay the tax.

Source: Donald T. Rocen, tax manager, National Tax Consulting Group, Coopers & Lybrand, 1800 M St. NW, Washington, DC 20036.

Tax-Saver Gifts

• Pay tuition directly to a college or university. Parents or grandparents can give a child more than $10,000 a year by paying the child's tuition directly rather than giving the money to the child. Such payments are free of federal gift tax, over and above $10,000/$20,000 annual amounts. The only qualification is that the money must go directly to the educational institution.

• Make gifts to elderly parents. An annual gift-giving program also makes sense if you are supporting your parents. If your parents are in a lower tax bracket, you'll save on taxes by transferring income-producing assets to them.

Make the gift at the beginning of the year and you'll be able to shift a whole year's income. The same limits apply here—you are allowed to give up to $10,000/$20,000 to each parent each year free of federal gift tax.

Another way that you can make additional tax-free gifts to your parents is by paying their medical expenses directly to their health-care provider. The same wrinkle that applies to directly paid educational expenses also works for directly paid medical expenses.

Hitting-the-Jackpot Loopholes

Everyone dreams of a once-in-a-lifetime windfall of big money. Sometimes the dream comes true...but then there are taxes to consider.

How you handle the tax aspects can make a material difference in the amount of windfall you end up keeping.

First step: Figure out whether the windfall is taxable or tax-free.

Tax-free windfalls include:

• Gifts. The person who gives you the money must pay the tax. You, the recipient, get the gift free and clear.

• Inheritances. Recipients don't pay federal estate tax on the principal they inherit. The estate pays the tax before it is distributed to the recipients.

• Life-insurance proceeds. The beneficiary receives the proceeds free of tax. But the estate may be liable for estate tax on the proceeds.

• Custodian accounts. When the account is turned over to you—say when you reach 18 years of age—you get the money tax-free.

• Disability payments from accident or health insurance policies paid for by the taxpayer are generally not taxable. But they're usually taxable if your employer paid the premiums.

• Property settlements between spouses in a divorce. These are not taxable to the recipient. However, if the property has gone up in value, the recipient must pay tax on that gain when he/she sells the property.

Loophole: Plan to receive the property that has a high basis, or tax cost. That will minimize the gain—and the tax—when you sell the property.

• Damages from a lawsuit. Amounts received on account of personal injury or sickness are not taxable. This includes damages for age and sex discrimination and for libel and slander. However, punitive damages and damages for injury to business profits are taxable.

Loophole: Before you launch a lawsuit, have your attorney consult with a tax pro so the complaint is worded in a way that produces the lowest possible tax.

Taxable windfalls include:

• Lottery winnings. These are generally paid out over a period of time. They are taxable when you receive them. Those who pay must generally withhold 20% of the proceeds for payment of taxes.

Loophole: You can offset your winnings with gambling losses, which are deductible up to the amount of your winnings. Keep records of your losing wagers. Losses from one kind of gambling (losing race track bets) are deductible against winnings from another kind of gambling (lottery winnings).

Also, gambling losses of a husband and wife are pooled if they file a joint return, so that losses of one are deductible against the winnings of the other.

• Raffles and contests. The fair market value of your prize is taxable. You will get a 1099 for the fair market value as determined by the organization awarding the prize. This would be the list price of a car, for example, or the full cost of a trip.

Loophole: You don't have to report as income the amount shown on the 1099. You only have to report what the car or trip would have cost you if you had purchased it yourself. For example, if the car you win has a list price of $30,000, but you could have bought it for $27,000, you only need to report $27,000 on your return.

Helpful: Explain on your return why the amount you report doesn't agree with the amount on the 1099.

• Lump-sum pension distribution. This is taxable in the year you receive it. But there are loopholes...

Roll the distribution over into an IRA and defer taxes until a later date.

Apply 5- or 10-year averaging to the distribution, which reduces the tax.

Treat part of the distribution as a long-term capital gain taxed at a 20% rate.

Note: The return of any nondeductible, voluntary contributions is not taxable.

• Stock bonuses. The fair market value of the stock is fully taxable when you receive it. If the stock is subject to a substantial risk of forfeiture (that is, it is restricted) and cannot be transferred free of that risk, income is generally deferred until the stock is no longer subject to risk.

Loophole: A person who receives restricted stock can elect, under Code Section 83(b), to recognize income immediately instead of deferring it. This would be a smart thing to do if the stock has a very low value presently but is expected to have a high value in the future.

• Liquidating your business. Distributions in excess of your original cost are subject to capital gains tax.

Loophole: If you are near retirement, sell the assets of the business at book value, but keep the corporation intact as a personal holding company. Do not distribute the cash from the sale, but keep it in the corporation, invested in tax-exempt municipal bonds. When you die, the assets will pass to your heirs at their stepped-up, date-of-death value, and income tax on any gain will be avoided.

• Stock options. These are not taxable when you receive the option. They are taxable when the option is exercised. Exception: Incentive stock options are taxable only when you sell the stock.

Estimated tax loopholes:

To avoid underpayment penalties, you are required to pay estimated taxes during the year on your windfall. Loopholes:

Loophole I: If your total withholding tax for the year is at least as much as the amount of tax you paid last year, you're not required to make estimated payments.

Loophole II: If withholding equals 90% of the tax you will owe this year, estimated payments are not required.

Don't rush to make estimated payments on the windfall. You may already have paid in enough tax through withholding.

Source: Edward Mendlowitz, partner, Mendlowitz Weitsen, CPAs, Two Pennsylvania Plaza, New York 10121. Mr. Mendlowitz is the author of several books, including *Aggressive Tax Strategies*, Macmillan Publishing Co., 866 Third Ave., New York 10022.

Bankruptcy and Back Taxes

Virtually everyone you ask in the Collection Division of the IRS will tell you that federal income taxes are not discharged in bankruptcy.

This is not entirely true. Unpaid taxes for returns filed three years or more before the bankruptcy petition is filed are dischargeable. The bankruptcy rules are very tricky. Get expert advice.

Source: Ms. X, a former IRS agent, still well-connected.

Savings-Bond Loophole

For taxpayers in a certain income range, the interest on US Series EE savings bonds that are cashed in and used for educational expenses is tax-free. The bonds must be bought in the parents' name and they must have been issued after 1989.

To fully benefit from this tax break, the parents' Adjusted Gross Income can't be more than $60,000 (joint) or $40,000 (single) in the year the bonds are cashed in. (The figures will be adjusted for inflation, starting this year.) Partial benefits are available to parents whose AGI is less than $90,000 (joint) and $55,000 (single). But you get no benefit at all if your income goes above these figures.

Problem: The people who can best afford to buy savings bonds for their children may very well earn too much to get the benefit of the tax exclusion when their child gets to college.

Source: Edward Mendlowitz, partner, Mendlowitz Weitsen, CPAs, Two Pennsylvania Plaza, New York 10121. Mr. Mendlowitz is the author of several books, including *Aggressive Tax Strategies*, Macmillan Publishing Co., 866 Third Ave., New York 10022.

Home-Office Break

A self-employed professional worked 35 to 40 hours a week at various locations but kept his business records in a home office. The IRS disallowed his home-office deduction under long-standing rules because the office wasn't his principal place of business—he spent most of his working time elsewhere. But the Tax Court overruled the IRS and allowed the deduction because the office was essential to his business—the professional had no other place to keep his records. Now the Court of Appeals has affirmed the new ruling. Many more taxpayers may qualify for the deduction as a result.

Source: Nader E. Soliman, CA-1, No. 90-1807.

Before You Mail Your Return: A Checklist

- Recheck the arithmetic.
- Include your name, address and Social Security number on the first page of the return. If you use the IRS pre-addressed label, correct any wrong information.
- Write your name and Social Security number on every page and every form you send to the IRS.
- Attach copy B of your W-2 form.
- Sign and date your tax return. (Both spouses must sign a joint return.)
- Staple your check or money order to the return. Don't forget to sign the check and write on it your Social Security number, the form number, and the tax year.
- Make a copy of the return for your own records.
- Include every form and related schedule.
- Address the return to the Internal Revenue Service Center for your state. Many tax experts say that using the IRS envelope will speed up your refund check.
- Mail the return on or before April 15. Use certified mail, return receipt requested. Otherwise, the IRS may not accept proof of filing.

Source: Leon M. Nad is consulting editor of *Tax Hotline.*

Getting Control And Keeping It

IRS personnel who have contact with taxpayers—primarily, revenue agents, tax auditors and collection personnel—receive instruction in techniques designed to give them a psychological edge over taxpayers. They are taught to remain respectful at all times and to take control of the conversation and pursue the accomplishment of their mission. Counterattack: Take control away from the person you're dealing with. Insist on your mission. Your mission might be to end the audit sooner rather than later...or to delay the payment of tax...or to convince the auditor to accept your verbal representation concerning an issue which normally requires written proof. Steady insistence on your objective keeps you in control of the conversation. It gives you the opportunity to be assertive and thereby achieve your objective. Caution: Being assertive can, and should, be accomplished using a low-key approach, rather than abusive language.

Source: Ms. X, a former IRS agent, still well-connected.

How To Untangle IRS Red Tape

Dealing with the IRS bureaucracy can be very frustrating...especially when the IRS is wrong.

Here are some of the most common IRS mistakes—and what you can do to correct them...

Matching notices:

When the income that you report on your tax return doesn't agree with the 1099 information forms that have been submitted to the IRS by the payers of income, you will receive a "matching notice" from the IRS.

This is a computer-generated notice that summarizes the income you failed to report and recalculates your tax.

Problem: The IRS may be working with an incorrect 1099. Or, the 1099 may be right—and you reported the income—but not as you should have. Examples:

• Hidden items. You reported an item of miscellaneous income on Schedule C rather than on your 1040. IRS computers can't find it and you get a matching notice.

What to do: Write back to the office that sent you the notice, and point out exactly where the miscellaneous income was included on your return. Enclose a copy of your Schedule C and indicate on the copy, with red ink, where the item was reported.

• Dividends. You reported a dividend as being received from XYZ company when your broker reported it to the IRS as being paid by the broker as your nominee. IRS computers can't find the dividend as it was reported on the 1099.

What to do: Write to the IRS. Include a copy of your brokerage statement showing you hold XYZ stock. Show how it was reported on your return.

• Custodial accounts. You have a custodial account for your child, but your Social Security number, not the child's, is on the account. Or, the IRS may pick up your name and your child's Social Security number. That creates a mismatch. You get a notice saying that you failed to report the account's interest.

What to do: Send a copy of the bank passbook to the IRS with a letter explaining that the account is your child's and that you are merely the custodian. Ask the bank to correct its records to avoid future notices. When you open a custodial account, ask the bank to put your child's name up-front, rather than yours, so your won't run into matching notice problems.

To avoid getting a matching notice: Check all 1099 forms when you receive them to be sure they're correct. Check to see that the forms are in the right name, that the taxpayer identification numbers are correct, and that the dollar amounts are correct. If you find a mistake, send a copy of the 1099 back to the source to have it corrected before it goes to the IRS. You have a month in which to do this. 1099s are required to be mailed to your by January 31 of each year, but they do not go to the IRS until the end of February.

Automatic penalties:

Always check penalty notices carefully to make sure you really are liable for the penalty. You may not be. But it's up to you to get yourself off the hook. Possible problems:

• Estimated tax. When withholding and estimated tax payments don't total at least 90% of the tax owed (or 100% of last year's tax), the IRS automatically assesses a penalty on the underpayment.

You may, however, qualify for one of the tax law's exceptions to the penalty. If, for example, you received most of your income late in the year, you may qualify for the annualized income exception.

To avoid the penalty: Fill out Form 2210. Underpayment of Estimated Tax by Individuals. There's a worksheet in the instructions for Form 2210 which you may use to calculate your qualification for the annualized income exception.

• Waiver of penalties. You may also apply on Form 2210 to have the underpayment penalty waived. One reason given in the waiver section of the instructions to Form 2210 is "the underpayment was due to a casualty, disaster, or other unusual circumstances, and it would be inequitable to impose the penalty."

Penalty reduction: If you're charged and underpayment penalty, you should work the figures through on Form 2210 to see if you can reduce the amount of the penalty.

• Late-filing penalties. Penalties are assessed automatically when you file a tax return late. But you may have a legitimate excuse for late filing. Send the IRS a letter explaining why you have "reasonable cause" for filing late and should, therefore, be excused from the penalty.

Self-defense: Always send your tax return by certified mail—return-receipt requested. That gives you proof that you mailed it on time and proof that the IRS received it.

Other mistakes:

• Math errors. You get a notice saying there's a math error on your return. Don't automatically assume that the IRS is right. Check the return. Did you make a mistake? Or, did they?

An IRS clerk may have transposed figures when punching in your return. If the IRS made a mistake, write to them and explain the mistake.

If you made a mistake, correct it and pay any extra tax as soon as possible to prevent interest from piling up. Point: For 1991, none of the interest on unpaid taxes will be deductible.

• No return filed. You get a letter from the IRS saying that no return was received from you, even though you filed one.

What to do: Write to the IRS enclosing a copy of your return. Tell them to cancel your first check and enclose a new check. If you sent the original return by certified mail, return-receipt requested, enclose a copy of the certified mail receipt and/or the return-receipt. (If you can prove that the IRS received your return, they shouldn't charge you interest for late payment.) Early warning: If, after two months, your check to the IRS hasn't cleared your bank, write to the IRS asking why. Alert them to a potential problem.

• Audit errors. Check the agent's figures after you've agreed to an adjustment to your tax bill. Agents are only human and may very well make math mistakes. Be sure the agent is using the right figures, charging the correct amount of interest, and not overlooking a tax break you're entitled to, such as five- or 10-year averaging on pension payouts.

• Withholding mistakes. Review W-2 forms when you get them to make sure there are no mistakes. Check them against your pay stubs. Write to your employer for a corrected W-2 if you find an error.

• Missing schedules. You may have forgotten to enclose a schedule, or the IRS may have lost it. Send in a copy. they generally give you 30 days to furnish them with a copy without penalties being imposed.

• Incorrect refunds. Sometimes the IRS sends a taxpayer somebody else's refund. Eventually it asks for the money back—with interest!

Precaution: If you receive a refund check that you know you're not entitled to, don't keep it. Return the check and ask for an explanation. Keep copies of the check and your cover letter.

Problem solving:

If you can't get a mistake corrected through normal IRS channels, take the matter to the IRS's Problems Resolution Office (PRO). This section of the IRS is staffed with people whose job is to cut through IRS red tape. To get the PRO working on your case, you must have written to the IRS twice, or 90 days must have gone by without results.

• Write to the PRO in your district. (Every IRS district and all Service Centers have a PRO.)

• Make your letter simple and direct.

• Enclose copies of your previous correspondence with the IRS.

• Summarize your problem and explain what should be done to correct it.

You'll generally hear from the PRO within 15 days, saying they've received your letter. Most problems are resolved within a few weeks.

Source: Marvin Michelman, specialist in IRS practice and procedure, Deloitte & Touche, One World Trade Center, New York 10048. He held various positions with the IRS for 19 years, including senior regional analyst for examinations.

50 Of The Most Easily Overlooked Deductions

• Accounting fees for tax preparation services and IRS audits.

• Acupuncture fees.

• Air conditioners bought to alleviate allergies.

• Alcoholism and drug abuse treatment.

• Amortization of premiums on taxable bonds.

• Appraisal fees for a casualty loss or charitable contribution. (They are deductible as miscellaneous itemized deductions.)

• Appreciation on property donated to a charity. (When you give appreciated property to charity, you get a deduction for the full fair market value of the property.)

• Auto license fees if you live in a state where the fee is based solely on the value of the car.

• Braille books and magazines.

• Breach-of-contract damages.

• Business gifts of $25 or less per recipient.

• Commissions on the sale of property.

• Contraceptives, if bought with a prescription.

• Depreciation on home computers to the extent they are used for investments.

• Dues to labor unions.

• Education that maintains or improves skills required in your present line of work.

• Electrolysis by state-licensed technicians.

• Employee moving expenses, including those related to house-hunting, selling your old home or settling an unexpired lease, and travel (including lodging and meals).

• Entertainment expenses in connection with taxable investments.

• Fees for safe deposit boxes used to hold investments (stock certificates, for instance).

• Foreign taxes paid.

• Gambling losses to the extent of gambling gains.

• Hair transplants.

• Hearing devices.

• Impairment-related work expenses for handicapped individuals.

• Job-hunting expenses, including employment agency fees, resume preparation, and travel and transportation expenses.

• Medical transportation, including the standard mileage deduction of nine cents a mile.

• Mortgage prepayment penalties on home mortgages—deductible as home mortgage interest.

• Orthopedic shoes.

• Out-of-pocket expenses relating to charitable activities, including the standard mileage deduction of 12 cents a mile.

• Passport fees for business trips.

• Payments into a stock fund.

• Penalty on early withdrawal of savings certificates.

• Phantom, or forgone, interest expense on loans with below-market interest rates.

• Physical examinations required by employer.

• Plastic surgery fees for a facelift. Note: Beginning in 1991, cosmetic surgery which is not medically necessary will not be deductible.

• Points on a home mortgage and certain refinancing.

• Postage related to investment activities.

• Seeing-eye dogs.

• Special equipment for the disabled or handicapped.
• Special diet foods.
• Special schools.
• Theft of embezzlement losses.
• Trade or business tools with a life of one year or less.
• Trustee's fees for your IRA, if separately billed and paid.
• Uniforms and work clothes not suitable as ordinary wearing apparel.
• Used clothing and household goods donated to charity.
• Weight-loss programs for treatment of a specific disease, such as hypertension or obesity.
• Wigs essential to mental health.
• Worthless stock or securities.

Source: William G. Brennan, partner, Ernst & Young, CPAs, 1225 Connecticut Ave. NW, Washington, DC 20036. Mr. Brennan is the editor of the *Ernst & Young Financial Planning Reporter.*

Helping The Agent Conduct An Audit

Helping the agent conduct an audit can lead to a better result than if the agent does everything by himself. An inexperienced agent may have difficulty understanding how the company's books and records are organized. Although every double entry set of accounting records contains debits and credits, each company seems to do things their own way.

Instead of letting the agent wrestle with the books and the adjusting journal entries, it makes sense to prepare a worksheet for those items the agent wants to examine. The worksheet should show precisely which numbers were added up to agree with the amount shown on the tax return.

Benefit: The agent will not stumble across something you would rather he not see, as he might if he had to tackle a different reconciliation of the numbers.

Source: Ms. X, a former IRS agent, still well-connected.

Saving Money

It's expensive to hire a tax professional to represent you before the IRS. IRS agents, for the most part, are not sensitive to the hourly fees charged by tax pros. Typically, they are not in a hurry to finish the audit. But there are ways to speed things up. Here's one strategy to talk over with your adviser...figure out which items the agent is likely to be interested in auditing. Prepare worksheets that summarize the expenses that make up those items. Hand the agent a copy of the worksheets. Ask him to select those items he wants you to back up with canceled checks and/or receipts.

Source: Ms. X, a former IRS agent, still well-connected.

Missing Records

Sometimes you just don't have the original records to give the auditor. For example, it's not uncommon for a business to incur costs each week for small, out-of pocket items, like coffee and sandwiches for the office and other expenses that are paid from the petty cash fund. Although receipts are supposed to be kept, it is common for many of these expenses to get paid without obtaining a receipt. Best approach: Reconstruct the amount of money typically spent each week and multiply it by the number of weeks your office was open during the year. Hand the reconstructed list to the revenue agent and explain how you arrived at the numbers. The written list brings credibility to your position.

Source: Ms. X, a former IRS agent, still well-connected.

Best Ways Now To Shelter Income From Tax

The old-fashioned tax shelter is now very much a thing of the past—but there are still plenty of ways to shelter income from tax.

The best...

• Base estimated tax payments on last year's tax. If you had a bad year last year, this is a smart thing to do. Reduced estimated tax payments will keep cash in your pocket in the current year, at a time when you most need it. You can put the money that would otherwise go to taxes to work earning more for you.

• Accelerate deductions into the current year. The more deductions your take, the less tax you'll pay this year. And, you can put the tax money to work. To accelerate deductions:

• Pay your fourth quarter state estimated tax payment during this year (in December).

• Pay real estate taxes in December.

• Prepay your January mortgage interest payment in December.

Caution: When you accelerate deductions, you must always beware of the Alternative Minimum Tax.

Bonus: Reducing the tax you pay this year will reduce the amount of estimated tax you pay next year, since estimated payments can be based on this year's tax. As a result, accelerating deductions improves your cash flow next year.

• Keep your Adjusted Gross Income down possibly by investing in municipal bonds. Tax-exempt income is not included in AGI. If you can keep your AGI below $100,000, you won't suffer the 3% disallowance of deductions that the new law requires. A lower AGI will also increase deductions that are based on percentage-of-income limitations. And increased deductions will shelter more income from tax.

• Borrow wisely, with tax deductions in mind. Interest on personal debt is no longer deductible. But mortgage interest, investment interest, and business interest are generally deductible.

Strategy: If you're buying a new house, borrow as much as you can. Use any unused money set aside for a down payment for personal expenditures, such as furnishings for the house.

• Manage your investment interest expense. Your deduction or investment interest expense is limited to the amount of net investment income you have for the year. A way to boost your deduction is to boost your investment income by selling assets that produce capital gains. The gains will be tax free if you have excess investment interest expense to write them off against.

• Bunch medical expenses and other expenses that are subject to percentage-of-income limitations. For example, have voluntary medical or dental work done before year-end to beef up your medical expenses this year. Your hope in bunching expenses is to get over the percentage limitation and secure a deduction.

• Donate appreciated securities to charity. A donation of appreciated securities gives you a deduction for the securities' full fair market value. What is more, you don't have to pay tax on the appreciation.

Caution: Donations of appreciated securities can trigger the Alternative Minimum Tax, so, be careful. Exception: For 1991 only, the appreciation in gifts of tangible personal property, such as works of art, is not subject to the AMT.

• Contribute to an Individual Retirement Account. Contributions are at least partially deducible even if you're covered by a company pension plan, as long as your Adjusted Gross Income is below $50,000 (joint) or $35,000 (single). The contribution reduces your tax and reduces your AGI, which may increase other deductions that are based on a percentage of AGI. Tax is deferred on the income your contribution earns. The benefit of tax deferral is available even if you don't get a deduction for your contribution. To maximize the benefit of tax deferral, contribute IRA money as early in the year as possible.

• Give children under age 14 assets that produce up to $1,100 of investment income. The first $550 of a child's investment income escapes tax entirely, and the next $550 is taxed at the child's rate, generally 15%, rather than yours (if higher).

Give children age 14 and over assets that produce up to $20,000 of income. The first $550 is not taxed. And the nest $20,000 is taxed at 15%.

Problem: you must give up control over assets you give to your children.

• Take full advantage of the tax breaks that homeowners are entitled to...

• Interest on up to $1 million of acquisition indebtedness plus $100,000 of home-equity debt is fully deductible. (Interest on any amount of acquisition debt incurred before October 13, 1987 is fully deductible.)

• Points, or loan origination fees, paid to secure a mortgage to buy a home are deductible up front in the year they're paid.

• Tax is deferred on the sale of a home if you buy a new, more expensive home within two years of selling the old one.

• If you're 55 or older, up to $125,000 of gain on the sale of a home is tax free. This is a once-in-a-lifetime tax break and a married couple is entitled to only one exclusion.

Strategy: If you and a friend are both 55 or older and are planning to marry, sell your houses before you get married so both of you can take a $125,000 exclusion.

• Take advantage of the like-kind exchange rules. If you trade a business asset—equipment, land or a building—for similar property, you don't have to pay tax on the exchange. Tax is deferred until you sell the asset your received in the exchange. The rules on tax-free exchanges are tricky, though, so, see your tax advisor.

• Buy US Series EE bonds. You have the option of paying tax on the interest each year or accumulating it and paying the whole amount when you redeem the bonds.

EE bonds issued after December 31, 1989, are tax free if the proceeds are used to pay for education expenses. To get the full benefit though, your income in the year you redeem the bonds can't exceed $60,000 (indexed for inflation).

• Buy life insurance. The income that builds up on investment-orientated life insurance products is tax deferred.

• Maximize contributions to your company's 401(k) plan. Tax is deferred on the salary you put into the plan, and income your money earns in the plan is tax deferred. Maximum contribution for 1991: $8,475.

• Maximize contributions to tax sheltered annuities. If you're a teacher, or you work for a charity or church, you can put up to $9,500 a year into a tax sheltered annuity. You don't pay tax on the money you put in and the income it earns is tax deferred. If your employer also has a 401(k) plan, you can put $8,475 into the 401(k) and $1,025 into the annuity. The total can exceed $9,500.

• Know the rules about Social Security benefits. If you're under age 65, you can earn $7,080 this year without losing any benefits. For amounts above that figure you lose $1 of benefit for each $2 you earn. IF you're between 65 and 69, the earnings limit is $9,720. You lose $1 of benefit for each $3 you earn above that. If you're over 69, you can earn an unlimited amount of income without losing any of your benefits.

Strategy; If you became eligible for Social Security benefits in 1991, but you find that you won't get any benefits because you earned too much money, you can disqualify yourself and elect to start collecting benefits in the following year. When you put off the starting date, you'll increase your benefits by 3½%. Warning: Sign up for Medicare when you're 65, or you'll run into problems.

• Consider filing separate returns rather than a joint return. This will save taxes when one spouse has much larger deductions relative to income than the other, and the deductions are subject to percentage-of-income limitations. Examples: Medical expenses, casualty losses, miscellaneous deductions. A bigger deduction will shelter more of your income from tax.

Caution: You may lose out on other benefits by filing separate returns.

Source: Laurence I. Foster, tax partner, personal financial planning practice, KPMG Peat Marwick, 599 Lexington Ave., New York 10022.

Emergency Tax Advice For Any Friends Who Are Newly Unemployed

People who never expected career problems are finding themselves out of work these days. It may happen to a good friend of yours, or a relative. Here is some very good financial and tax advice for them.

• Apply immediately for unemployment insurance. Don't be shy about it. You've indirectly paid for it over the years and you're entitled to it.

Tax impact: Fully taxable.

• Negotiate a severance pay package with your employer. Act quickly to take advantage for the employer's guilt and negotiate the best severance package possible.

Tax impact: Severance payments are fully taxable in the year they're received.

If your friend has the option of taking the payment in one lump sum of in monthly installments, it's usually best to take the lump sum. He can invest the money so that it earns interest for him.

Exception: If the termination happens near the end of the year, arrange to receive the severance more advantageously—perhaps in two payments, one in one year and one in the next, so as to minimize taxes.

Tax-free fringe benefit: The value of job placement counseling if included in the severance package, is nontaxable income. In a recent moment of magnanimity, the IRS withdrew a 1989 ruling that found out-placement counseling to be taxable income. For now, it's not taxable as long as it's offered on a non-discriminatory basis to all employees.

Two kinds of severance: If severance pay is given in lieu of notice of termination, your friend won't qualify for unemployment insurance until the notice period is up. But if the severance is given in return for past service as an employee (example: one week's severance for each year's employment) your friend should qualify for unemployment insurance immediately.

• Maximize home-equity borrowing. Your friend may not have borrowed up to the limit on his/her home-equity line of credit. Now would be the time to do so.

Tax advantage: Interest on up to $100,000 of home-equity borrowing is fully tax-deductible, no matter how that money is spent.

• Don't cash in retirement funds. The money is taxable and, if your friend is under age 59½, he'll pay a 10% penalty in addition to the tax. This is too great a price to pay. Better: Roll the pension distribution over into an IRA. It can be moved from there into another company's pension plan when he finds work.

A smart thing to do is to arrange with the employer to postpone distribution from the pension plan, and, in the meantime, take out a "hardship" loan from the plan. This will defer taxation until the time the pension plan trustee is required to distribute the plan funds. If your friend is short of cash at that time, he can take a distribution of part of the funds and roll the rest over into an IRA. He'll pay tax and penalty on the amount distributed to him, but the tax on the amount rolled over will be deferred until he takes money out of the IRA. Problem with rolling money over into an IRA: Loss of a significant tax benefit—the right to five or 10-year averaging. Also, borrowing from an IRA is prohibited.

Opportunity: If your friend put his own after-tax money into the plan, he can take that out without paying tax or penalty. One option would be for your friend to roll over the employer's contribution into an IRA and take out his own contributions.

If he has a choice whether to leave his money in the plan or take it out, he's best advised to leave it with the company. Reason: The money continues to grow on a tax-deferred basis and distributions qualify for five- or 10-year averaging which reduces the tax that will ultimately have to be paid.

Your friend may have no choice but to leave his pension money in the plan. Many plans require that employees leave their pension money in the plan until they retire.

• Don't use pension funds to pay off a home mortgage. This is often a knee-jerk reaction of people who lose their jobs. But people who do this lose a major source of liquidity (the pension money) at a time when they most need it. In addition, they have to pay tax on the pension funds. They're also losing one of the cheapest kinds of borrowing they can get...and mortgage interest payments are generally fully tax deductible.

• If bankruptcy is a possibility, the best situation to be in is to have a home mortgage but no personal debt, such as credit card debt. A person's home is protected in bankruptcy proceedings, so he won't lose that. And he should be able to reestablish credit relatively easily, despite the fact that personal bankruptcy shows up on a person's credit history. What hurts chances for future credit is to file for bankruptcy with large amounts of personal debt outstanding.

• Consider borrowing from family. Parents and other relatives can give up to $10,000 ($20,000 if the gift is made jointly by a husband and wife) each year to any number of recipients without having to pay gift tax. In addition, parents or grandparents can pay tuition and medical bills for family members without being subject to gift tax as long as the payments are made directly to the institution or medical care provider.

Other sources of borrowing:

• IRA accounts. Your friend can get a very short-term interest-free loan by rolling over the money in his IRA. Trap: The money must be redeposited in the IRA within 60 days or it will be taxable and, if your friend is under age 59½, subject to a 10% penalty.

• 401(k)s. Your friend may be able to borrow from his company's 401(k) plan. The money would not be taxable and the interest would be nondeductible.

• Life insurance. Another source of borrowing that should be considered is life insurance policies. The borrowed amounts would generally not be treated as taxable income, and the interest payments would not be tax deductible.

Source: Jack Porter, partner, national director of tax practice, BDO Seidman, CPAs, 1707 L St. NW, Suite 800, Washington, DC 20036.

Your House And The IRS

The chances of the IRS seizing your principal residence for nonpayment of income taxes are reasonably low. IRS Code section 6334(e) requires that the district director or assistant district director personally approve all such seizures. Revenue officers tell me that they are reluctant to go after a principal residence unless the taxpayer absolutely refuses to pay the tax and no other assets are available to seize. But what if you have equity in your house and you owe the IRS? They will expect you to borrow as much as the bank will lend you against the equity. If you don't, all bets are off. They may very well go after the house.

Source: Ms. X, a former IRS agent, still well-connected.

Hard Times

IRS Form 911 has been used by many taxpayers to hold off IRS action that is about to cause them financial or emotional hardship. But if your request for a Form 911 order is turned down and the IRS is ready to proceed full steam ahead...a few options still exist...

• Ask the Problem Resolution Officer to reconsider your request.

• If that fails, contact the office of the district director for assistance,

• Finally, be prepared to file a petition with the US Bankruptcy Court. A bankruptcy filing automatically brings a halt to all collection action by the IRS even if the unpaid taxes are not dischargeable in bankruptcy.

Source: Ms. X, a former IRS agent, still well-connected.

Paying Your Taxes With Post-Dated Checks

If you owe a large amount of money to the IRS, usually the best course of action is to work towards securing a part-payment plan under which you agree to pay the tax bill in installments. Problem: The revenue officer you're dealing with may insist on a substantial downpayment before he is willing to consider an installment arrangement. You can help the process along by handing the revenue officer two or three postdated checks for the amount you are able to pay in installments. Call these checks your downpayment. Caution: If any check bounces, your chances for securing a formal part-payment agreement are considerably reduced.

Source: Ms. X, a former IRS agent, still well-connected.

How To Deal With The IRS: Self Defense Tactics

The IRS is a gigantic organization that handles billions of pieces of paper a year with antiquated equipment and systems.

It is very prone to error. Dealing with the agency can be akin to Chinese water torture at times...the IRS drips pieces of paper on your desk until you get so frustrated that you can't stand it anymore.

Fortunately, there are steps to take to cut the risk of getting caught up in this bureaucratic machine.

1. Keep logical, well-organized records. This is extremely important. If you do get questioned on an item, you'll need to be able to substantiate what you did on your return. An IRS auditor, when confronted with a taxpayer who has made an effort to keep organized records, will have a different reaction than when confronted with a taxpayer who presents a shoe box full of unsorted and generally messy papers.

2. Check all 1099s and W-2s when you receive them. They're not always right. The Social Security number may be wrong, or the name, or the amount. The time to correct these records is when you receive them. If you don't, the error will show up on the IRS's records and it will generate a notice to you saying that their records don't match what you put down on your return. This can result in considerable aggravating, and sometimes fruitless, correspondence with the IRS.

3. Follow IRS directions to the letter. The more careful you are, the less chance the IRS will soul things up on their end. IRS processing systems are designed to accommodate the instructions they give.

Examples:

- When you file your return, organize the forms and schedules in the sequence in which they're numbered. All the forms and schedules have an IRS sequence number in the upper right hand corner.
- Use the IRS preprinted label to mail your return.
- Put whatever symbols the IRS put on its correspondence on your response letter. (They tell you what number, name or office to refer to when you respond.) A letter addressed to "Dear Service Center" won't get you very far.

4. Never ignore any paper you get from the IRS even if it appears to be irrelevant or stupid. Throwing notices in the wastepaper basket can only lead to trouble. Always reply, even if you know that you're right and they're wrong.

5. File your return as early in the year as you can. The IRS is much more likely to make a mistake in processing your return if you file at the peak of the season close to the deadline, as most people do. Your odds if getting audited are exactly the same no matter when you file. Returns aren't picked for audit until about eight months after the filing deadline. Selecting returns for audit is a separate process, and it has no relationship to when the return was filed.

6. Always use the forms the IRS provides. It's less likely that they will make a mistake in processing their own form as opposed to a made-up form.

Example: The correct way to change your address is to use the IRS form for that purpose, Form 8822. They may make a mistake if you simply send in a letter changing your address.

Exception: Instead of using Form 8275 to make a disclosure to avoid the substantial understatement penalty, make the disclosure in a written statement attached to your return.

7. Explain any discrepancies between 1099 amounts and what you show on your return. Suppose, for example, that you have a joint bank account with your brother. The interest earned in the account should be split between you. But you get a 1099 reporting all the interest under your Social Security number. What to do: On your return, show the full

amount of interest as it appears on the 1099. Under that, deduct one-half of the amount, stating "one-half reported by my brother (and give your brother's name and Social Security number)."

8. Make sure the entry on your return agrees with the 1099. If the 1099 reports interest from First National Bank, list the bank that way on your return. Don't list it as "1st Nat." or some other abbreviation. That may create a computer mismatch and prompt the IRS to send you a notice. You will wind up having to explain the discrepancy.

9. Use certified mail for all important correspondence to the IRS. Put the certified-receipt number on the document you're sending, and keep the receipt. This gives you a record that the document, if the IRS loses it, was mailed on such and such a date. This is especially important if the mailing is time-sensitive, such as responding to a penalty notice.

10. Act quickly when responding to penalty notices or anything remotely threatening. The faster you can get something back to them, the more likely it is that you will prevent the system from moving to the next unpleasant step in the process.

11. Remain calm and courteous in your dealings with the IRS, no matter how difficult it is. Remember that IRS personnel are not out to get you, the systems are just messed up. Nasty, angry calls and letters won't help your case. If you find it impossible to keep calm, let your accountant or lawyer handle things for you. Professionals are less likely to get bent out of shape by whatever the IRS is doing...and less likely to give up something that the IRS would like. And, it often makes good sense to let your representative handle an audit for you. Taxpayers who go it alone are too likely either to clam up, which is provocative...or to gush, which can get them in trouble.

12. Turn matters over to the Problem Resolution Office in your district if you can't straighten things out yourself. The purpose of this office is to deal with bureaucratic tie-ups. To get the PRO working on your case, you must show that you tried twice to solve the problem through normal channels and failed. Call the IRS's toll-free number for your district's PRO.

Source: Peter K. Scott, director for IRS policies and practice, Coopers & Lybrand, 1800 M St. NW, Washington, DC 20036. Mr Scott was formerly deputy chief counsel with the IRS.

The Biggest Mistakes Taxpayers Make At IRS Audits...And How To Avoid Them

Audits are a part of life. They are neither something to be feared—nor something to be offended by. If you've prepared a correct and accurate return, an audit is going to reveal that.

Common mistakes people make at audits:

• Mistake: Being too defensive. Some taxpayers are so defensive at an audit that they seem to deny the government's right to ask them questions about their return. This attitude only leads to trouble. It can cause the examiner to think that there must be something wrong on the return. His natural response will be to ask more probing questions than he otherwise would, and to go more deeply into things. That's the last thing you want.

The right attitude to have at an audit: Be cooperative and forthcoming. Avoid showing hostility and fear.

• Mistake: Volunteering information. In your effort to be cooperative and forthcoming, you must remember never to volunteer information. Answer only the questions that are asked...nothing more.

And...produce only those records that you've been asked to produce. The IRS will inform you in the audit notice what items are being investigated on your return. If the agent brings up any items other than what you expected, explain that you don't have them with you since they were not relevant to the audit notice. Ask the agent if the audit could be adjourned until such time as you can produce the additional records.

• Mistake: Trying to handle technical issues yourself. Know your limits. If the audit involves nothing more than providing proof for your deductions, you can probably handle it yourself.

But if technical or legal issues are involved, particularly if you had to seek advice in the first place for the treatment on your return, you should be represented at the audit by an experienced tax professional. The problem with doing it yourself is that you won't be equipped to field specific technical questions the auditor will ask.

• Mistake: Not preparing ahead of time. Taxpayers who show up unprepared run the risk that the agent will interpret the lack of preparation to mean that there is something wrong on the return.

Helpful: Bring an adding-matching tape and a worksheet that show how you arrived at the figures you claimed on your return.

If you're missing a significant number of cancelled checks, you should prepare for this advance by getting corroborating evidence for the expenses.

Example: If you've made a contribution to a charity and you don't have the cancelled check, you should try to get a statement or a receipt from the charity indicating that you made the contribution. Another way to approach this is to see if your bank keeps photocopies of cancelled checks.

• Mistake: Not asking for relief under the IRS's repetitive audit procedure. If you've been audited in either of the last two years on a particular item and the audit resulted in no change in your tax bill, you can request that you not be audited on that same issue again.

Self-defense: As soon as you receive your audit notice, write to the IRS to claim an exemption under the Repetitive Audit Program. Enclose a copy of your audit notice and "no change" letter from the previous audit.

• Mistake: Not reviewing your rights. Along with your audit notice, you should be sent a copy of IRS Publication 1, Your Rights as a Taxpayer. Read this pamphlet carefully, so that you know your rights. Remember, you're dealing with someone—a revenue agent or tax auditor—who does audits every day.

• Mistake: Not drawing attention to items you could have deducted but didn't. If you come across deductions you're entitled to, but failed to take, you should bring them to the IRS's attention. Use these items to offset any deficiencies the IRS finds during the audit. Some people actually wind up getting refunds as a result of an audit.

• Mistake: Not trying to talk the auditor out of penalties. Penalties may be brought up by the agent during the audit. These penalties are really judgment calls on the agent's part. They don't have to impose them. You should make every effort to convince the agent that the penalty shouldn't be applied.

• Mistake: Not asking to speak to the auditor's manager when you can't reach an agreement with the auditor about adjustments to your tax bill. The Internal Revenue Manual requires that whenever there's an unagreed case, the IRS manager should offer to speak to the taxpayer to try and resolve the matter.

It's a good idea, though, for the taxpayer to initiate the meeting...if the IRS doesn't.

Source: Marvin Michelman, specialist in IRS practice and procedure, Deloitte & Touche, One World Trade Center, New York 10048. He held various positions with the IRS for 19 years, including senior regional analyst for examinations.

Benefits Loopholes

Here are some ways to get the most mileage from the noncash benefits your company provides.

• Pension and profit sharing plans. Your employer contributes money on your behalf and the money accumulates on a tax-deferred-basis. You don't pay tax on the money until you withdraw it. These are the basic tax advantages, but there's more...

Loophole: Take a tax-free loan from the pension of profit sharing plan. You can do this if the plan permits borrowing—not all do. Plans that allow borrowing usually make it easy on the participant—no need to justify why the loan is needed.

Tax law limits: The amount you can borrow

is limited to your vested balance up to the greater of $10,000 or one-half of your vested account balance, with a maximum of $50,000.

Loophole: Put some of your own money into the plan—many plans allow employees to make voluntary contributions. Such contributions are not tax-deductible, but the money accumulates income on a tax-deferred basis.

Loophole: If your company's plan is inactive, in that no additions are being made and no benefits are accruing on your behalf, you are eligible to contribute to an IRA.

• 401(k) plans. You contribute part of your salary to a company-sponsored savings program. You pay no income tax on the dollars you contribute until they're withdrawn. Interest, dividends, and other earnings accumulate tax deferred until you take them out.

Loophole: Though the amount you can contribute each year is limited by the tax law, it's far more than you could put into an IRA. Maximum 401(k) contribution for 1991: $8,475, up from $7,979 in 1990.

• Company-paid life insurance. As long as the coverage doesn't exceed $50,000, you are not taxed on the premiums the employer pays. But if it is more than $50,000, you are taxed on part of the premiums.

Loophole: The taxable amount is figured from IRS tables and is less than the actual premiums the employer pays. You pay some tax for the extra coverage, but it is far less than it would cost your to buy similar life insurance coverage outside the company.

Loophole: The first $5,000 of death benefits paid by an employer to an employee's beneficiaries are tax-free to the beneficiaries..

• Medical and disability insurance. Company-paid insurance is not taxable to the employee.

Loophole: Even if the employee's dependents are covered by the insurance, the employee does not have to pay tax on the premiums.

Drawback: Disability payments received are taxable income to the employee.

• Cafeteria plans allow employees to choose between cash and a shopping list of benefits, including group medical insurance, disability, child care, and the like. The employees choose their own menu of benefits. The benefits do not have to be included in the employee's taxable income.

Loophole: These plans are very easy to set up and administer.

• Employee loans. Employers can make interest-free loans of up to $10,000 to their employees. The employee does not have to report the forgone interest as taxable income.

• Use of an apartment by an employee. This is taxable to the employee at fair market rent.

Loophole: Fair market rent for this purpose is a price that is consistent with the apartment's value to the employee. If an employer puts an employee up in a three bedroom apartment, but the employee only needs a one bedroom apartment, the employee would only have to pay tax on the value of a one bedroom apartment.

• Stock with cash in tandem. If a company gives stock to an employee as an incentive or bonus, the fair market value of the stock is taxable to the employee in the year it is received. The tax cuts deeply into the true value of the bonus. But the company gets a tax deduction for the stock's full value.

Loophole: In addition to the stock, the company gives the employee cash to cover his tax liability on the stock and the cash together. Assuming the company and the employee are in roughly the same tax bracket, the transaction will be a wash. The amount the company saves in taxes will be about equal to the amount the employee owes.

• Incentive stock options. When a company gives an employee what are know as "nonqualified stock options," the employee must pay tax when he exercises the options. But if the company gives "incentive stock options," tax does not have to be paid until the employee sells the stock. No taxable income is recognized by the employee when the option is granted or exercised.

Trap: The difference between the option price and the fair market value at the time an incentive stock option is exercised must be included in calculations for the Alternative Minimum Tax. It's complicated, so look into it with your tax advisor.

Loophole: The employee can, if he chooses, elect to pay tax on the value of the stock in the year that he gets the stock, not in the year it becomes available to sell. This is an election made under Section 83(b) of the Tax Code. In many instances, if the company is expected to grown very rapidly, it would be advantageous to make this election.

• Phantom stock, also called stock appreciation tights, are sometimes issued to employees. No actual stock is give but payments are made as if actual stock had been issued. If any dividends are paid to stockholders, they are also paid to the phantom stockholders. This money is taxed as compensation, rather than as dividends.

Loophole: The employee doesn't pay tax until there is an actual payment to him as a phantom stock holder. No tax is payable when he first receives the phantom stock.

• Secular trusts. These trusts have been developed to ensure that companies pay employees the deferred compensation that has been promised them. How they work:

The company puts money into an irrevocable trust for the employee and gets an immediate deduction for the contributions. The employee is taxed currently on all contributions credited to the trust. But, the company makes a payment to the employee to cover his tax liability. When benefits are eventually paid, the employee gets them tax free.

Loophole: A secular trust is less expensive for a company to establish than its relative, the Rabbi trust.

Source: Edward Mendlowitz, partner, Mendlowitz Weitsen, CPAs, Two Pennsylvania Plaza, New York 10121. Mr. Mendlowitz is the author of several books including his latest, *Aggressive Tax Strategies*, Macmillan Publishing Co., 866 Third Ave., New York 10022.

Preparing Your Tax Return When You've Lost Your Records

Preparing your tax return when you've lost your records is not impossible. First, to the extent possible, obtain copies of 1099 forms from banks and brokerage firms. At least interest and dividend income will be reported accurately. Expenses for mortgage interest and real estate taxes can also be easily documented by getting copies of statements. Business expenses for entertainment and travel can be estimated by reconstructing them from your daily calendar. Self-defense: If a substantial portion of your tax return has been reconstructed, attach a note to your return disclosing that fact. In the event of an audit, and a large disallowance, such a disclosure may help in having a penalty for substantial understatement of tax liability excused.

Source: Ms. X, a former IRS agent, still well-connected.

The Biggest Tax Mistakes Investors Make— How To Avoid Them

Tax planning for investors is truly a year-round proposition. It's not something you can leave until the end of the year. Best: Keep taxes in mind at all times.

Here are the biggest tax mistakes investors make...

• Mistake: Not keeping good records. The amount of tax you save often depends on the soundness of your record-keeping. Examples:

• Is a capital gain long-term or short-term? Long-term gains are gains on assets held for more than one year. They're taxed at a favorable rate. But can you prove that your gain is long-term?

• How many dollars worth of improvements have you made to your house? When it comes time to sell the house, the cost of improvements can be used to reduce your taxable gain.

• Is an interest payment you've made personal interest (not deductible) or investment interest (deductible up to the amount of investment income you have)? You need records of how you spent the money you borrowed to decide what category the interest falls into.

• Mistake: Not being able to specifically

identify stock you've sold. Record-keeping is the key when you sell only a portion of the shares you own in a particular company. If you can't specifically identify the shares you sell, the IRS imposes a first-in, first-out (FIFO) rule. They assume that the shares you're selling were the first ones you bought. But that may not result in the best tax treatment. The way to control your gains or losses on the sale is to tell your broker exactly which shares you're selling.

- Mistake: Not keeping track of your gains and losses throughout the year. There's good reason to know where you stand, especially as the year draws to a close. Capital losses offset capital gains dollar for dollar...and up to $3,000 of salary and other income each year. If you have an excess of capital losses, you may want to take some gains, since the gains will, in effect, be tax-free—wiped out by the losses. On the other hand, if you have an excess of gains, you may want to take some losses to shelter the gains from tax.

- Mistake: Failing to sell short against the box. This is a way to nail down the gain and defer taxes until the following year. To do this you borrow through your broker the same number of shares of a particular stock as the number of shares you own. You sell the borrowed shared now, then complete the transaction next year by delivering your own shares to cover your short position. The gain is locked it but not realized for tax purposes until your shares are used to cover.

- Mistake: Running into trouble with the wash sale rule. This rule prevents deducting a loss on a stock you've sold if you buy the same stock back within 30 days of the date you made the sale. But you may want to sell a stock to take the tax loss and buy it right back because you like it and expect it to appreciate in value. To do that: Wait 31 days before buying the stock back. Note: The wash sale rule does not apply to gains. If you sell stock at a gain, you can buy it back immediately.

- Mistake: Failing to consider bond swaps at year-end. Look for bonds in your portfolio that have gone down in value, sell those bonds, and repurchase ones that are not "substantially identical."

Example: The new bonds might have the same maturity, but have a different issuer...or a different interest rate. Or, they may be from the same issuer but have a different maturity...or a different interest rate. Safety: If you buy bonds from the same issuer, make sure there's a difference in maturity of at least 20% or a difference in coupon value of least 30%.

Impact: The sale will generate capital losses which you can use to offset capital gains. In addition, you may improve your portfolio by buying a better-performing bond.

- Mistake: Failing to take the passive loss rules into account. An investor who doesn't know the rules can end up the year thinking he has more deductible losses and less taxable income than he really has. "Passive losses" (generally, losses from an investment you don't materially participate in) are deductible only against passive income. They can't be used to offset ordinary income, such as salary, dividends, interest, and capital gains. One way to utilize passive losses is to look for investments that generate passive income (so-called PIGs). Passive losses can be used to offset passive income.

- Mistake: Not considering home equity loans. Interest on personal debt is no longer deductible. But generally interest on up to $100,000 of home equity borrowing is fully deductible, no matter what you spend the borrowed money on. If you used the proceeds of the loan to pay off personal debt, you will have converted nondeductible interest into deductible home-mortgage interest.

There are costs associated with taking out a home equity loan, but as interest rates come down these loans become more attractive.

- Mistake: Running into trouble with the Kiddie Tax. Don't forget that the investment income of children under the age of 14 is taxed at the parents' top tax rate after the first $1,100. Investments made on behalf of young children should either be ones that produce tax-exempt income or ones that emphasize appreciation rather than current income. The investments can be sold for capital gains after the child reaches 14 and the income is then taxed at his/her rate.

- Mistake: Failing to take advantage of the

annual gift-tax exclusion. You can give up to $10,000 a year ($20,000 if your spouse joins in the gift) to each of any number of recipients. You should take advantage of the exclusion if you want to reduce your taxable estate without running into gift-tax problems.

• Mistake: Failing to take advantage of IRAs and Keoghs. Many people who qualify for tax deductions for contributions to these retirement plans fail to utilize them. Check the rules. Contribute as early in the year as possible to take advantage of the tax-free buildup of money in the plan.

Source: Richard J. Shapiro, partner, director of taxes for the financial services industry practice, Grant Thornton, CPAs, 7 World Trade Center, New York 10048.

The Biggest Tax Loophole

The biggest tax loophole is most often overlooked because it is so simple. The loophole is the statute of limitations. In order for the IRS to collect additional tax, they must make an assessment before the statute of limitation expires. In most cases, the statute expires three years from the date a tax return was filed—or the due date of the tax return, if that date should be later. But the IRS won't tell you the statute has expired. It's up to you to discover this loophole. The statute of limitations has now expired on all 1987 individual tax returns filed on or before April 15, 1988. the limitations period for 1988 individual tax returns which were filed on or before April 15, 1989 will expire on April 15, 1992.

Source: Ms. X, a former IRS agent, still well-connected.

Education Loopholes

Tax-free scholarships. College tuition is not deductible. But any amount received by a degree candidate as a scholarship or fellowship is not taxable, provided that the money is used for tuition and related expenses—such as fees, books, supplies and equipment required for courses.

Any part of a scholarship that covers room and board, on the other hand, is taxable. Grants that represent payment for teaching, research, or other services performed by the student as a condition for receiving the grant are taxable too.

Loophole: Athletic scholarships awarded to students who are expected, but are not required, to participate in sports are tax-free.

• Gift tax loophole. Ordinarily you must pay gift tax when you give a child or grandchild more than $10,000 a year ($20,000 if your spouse joins in the gift). But payments made directly to a school to cover your child's tuition are not subject to the $10,000 limitation. Directly-paid tuition is gift-tax free no matter how large the amount is.

Caution: This exception covers tuition only. It does not include amounts paid for room and board.

• Appreciated securities loophole. You'll pay a steep capital gains tax if you finance your child's education by selling appreciated securities and using the proceeds for expenses.

Better way: Give the securities to your child and let him/her sell them. The gain will then be taxed at your child's low tax rate, not yours.

• Fund-building loopholes. It is still possible to save taxes by transferring income-producing assets to your children and having the income taxed on their returns. The tax savings will help you build a college fund. But you've got to watch out for the Kiddie Tax. Trap: Investment income of a child under the age of 14 is taxed at the parents' rate.

Loophole 1: the first $1,100 of investment income earned by a child who is under age 14 is taxed to the child at a very low rate. The total tax is only $82.50. (The first $550 is not taxed at all, because of the child's standard deduction. And the next $550 is taxed at 15%.) Strategy: Transfer to the child assets that will earn up to $1,100 of investment income a year.

Loophole: The Kiddie Tax does not apply to children who are 14 or older. From age 14 on, a child's investment income is taxed at his/her own rate, not yours. Strategy: Make bigger gifts to children who are 14 and older, so the income will be taxed at their low rate of 15%.

Problem: When colleges evaluate a family's finances to decide whether to give financial aid, they give a much greater weight to assets in the child's name than to assets in the parent's name. Transferring assets to the children may hinder their ability to get help from the school they choose to go to.

• Savings bond loophole. For taxpayers in an certain income range, the interest on US Series EE savings bonds that are cashed in and used for education expenses is tax free. The bonds must be bought in the parent's name and they must have been issued after 1989.

To fully benefit from this tax break, the parents' Adjusted Gross Income can't be more than $60,000 (joint) or $40,000 (single) in the year the bonds are cashed in. (These figures will be adjusted for inflation, starting this year.) Partial benefits are available to parents whose AGI is less than $90,000 (joint) and $55,000 (single). But you get no benefit at all if your income goes above these figures.

Problem: The people who can best afford to buy savings bonds for their children may very well earn too much to get the benefit of the tax exclusion when their child gets to college.

• College house loophole. One way to cut your cash outlays for college living expenses is to buy a house or an apartment near the college campus for your child to live in. The tax deduction the property generates will subsidize the expense.

If the property is your second residence, mortgage interest is fully deductible, as are real estate taxes.

If you rent part of the place to other students, it will qualify as a rental property. Your tax deductions, including depreciation, may exceed your rental income from the property, producing a loss. Up to $25,000 of these rental losses are deductible each year against your salary and other income, so long as your Adjusted Gross Income doesn't exceed $150,000.

Other education loopholes:

• Job-related education expenses are deductible—as miscellaneous itemized deductions. They are subject to the 2%-of-AGI limitation. To be deductible, though, the courses you take must maintain or improve the skills required in your present line of work. Courses that train you for a new trade or business are not deductible. Deductible items include tuition, books, registration fees, and local transportation expenses—the cost of getting from your job to school.

• Job-related seminars are tax deductible, including transportation costs. However, there are limits to the deduction if the seminar is held out of the country.

Caution: Travel, as a form of education, is generally not deductible.

• Reimbursed expenses. If your employer reimburses you for education costs, you do not have to include the reimbursement on your tax return as long as you account to your employer for the expenses, that is, submit bills and receipts.

• Child care credits. Generally,if one spouse is not working, a couple does not qualify for child and dependent care credits. But there's an exception if the nonworking spouse is a full-time student. If one spouse is a full-time student and the other works, the couple may qualify for child care credits.

The law assumes that the nonworking spouse had income—$200 a month if there is one child or $400 a month if there are two or more children—and calculates the credit accordingly.

For married taxpayers, expenses that qualify for the child care credit are limited to the lower earning spouse's income. That would normally be the income of the parent who is in school, with income calculated according to the figures above. The credit is a percentage of that income.

Source: Edward Mendlowitz, partner, Mendlowitz Weitsen, CPAs, Two Pennsylvania Plaza, New York 10121. Mr. Mendlowitz is the author of several books, including *Aggressive Tax Strategies*, Macmillan Publishing Co., 866 Third Ave., New York 10022.

Disclaimer Magic: How To Win By Losing

Through the use of a legal document known as a disclaimer, a person's beneficiaries can rewrite his will to accomplish tax savings that weren't anticipated when the will was drawn up.

Events may have changed between the time the will was actually written and the time the person dies. A disclaimer can be used to get better tax results based on the new situation. Or, the will may have had a mistake in it when it was written. A disclaimer can be used to correct the defect.

New facts:

A disclaimer can be used to capitalize on a change in circumstances...

Example: A husband of modest wealth writes a will leaving everything to his wife, or to his kids if she should predecease him. It is expected that little or no estate tax will be due when the wife dies, because the estate is so small. Then, the husband strikes it rich—but doesn't change his will to deal with his new economic status. When he dies, there is far more wealth than the wife could ever use.

Under these new circumstances, it would have been best from a tax standpoint if the will had said "I leave the first $600,000 to my kids." This amount would not be taxed because everyone has a right to leave up to $600,000 estate-tax free to beneficiaries other than their spouse. Unfortunately, the way the will is written, this $600,00 exemption is wasted. The widow gets an extra $600,000, which she does not need, and it's taxed in her estate.

Solution: The widow signs a disclaimer, a one or two page legal document, stating that she refuses to accept $600,000. The $600,000 then goes to the kids under the provisions of the will, as if the wife had actually died before her husband. Tax savings: Up to $330,000.

Another example:

A disclaimer might also be used to take advantage of the $1 million exemption to the generation-skipping tax.

The generation-skipping tax prevents grandparents from leaving everything to their grandchildren and thereby avoiding estate tax at their own children's level.

But there's an exemption to the generation-skipping tax: Grandparents can leave grandchildren up to $1 million without having to worry about the extra tax.

Most parents, though, leave everything to their children. This may not be the smartest thing to do tax-wise, and this is where the disclaimer comes in.

Example: A grandparent has a will that leaves everything to his child. At the time of the grandparent's death, the child is already wealthy in his own right and doesn't need the money. So the child disclaims $1 million worth of his inheritance. That $1 million passes, under his parent's will, to his own children—the grandchildren. It escapes tax in his estate because of the $1 million exemption to the generation-skipping tax. Tax savings: Up to $550,000, plus estate tax on the income and appreciation that occurs on $1 million from the time the grand parent dies to the time the parent dies.

Planning ahead:

The possibility that a beneficiary might give up an interest under the will should be planned for at the time the will is drawn up.

One of the problems with disclaimers is that the person who is disclaiming can't have any say regarding where the property goes. It must pass to other beneficiaries strictly according to the terms of the will.

But the person who is contemplating giving up an inheritance to save taxes might not approve of the way the will settles the estate. He/she might then refuse to do a disclaimer even though it saves taxes.

Example: A widow might not want her children to inherit money at age 21 which is what the will says. So, she refuses to disclaim her interest in the estate.

Planning ahead: Let the person who might disclaim an interest in the estate have a say in how the property passes under the will. Make sure it passes to children or other beneficiaries in a way that all the parties approve of.

Curing defects:

A will may give beneficiaries rights that cause tax problems. The beneficiaries can disclaim those rights and eliminate the problem.

Example I: A husband's will left $600,000 to a family trust that provided benefits to both the wife and kids. It was intended that this trust qualify for the $600,000 estate-tax exemption and not be taxed in the wife's estate when she died.

But the lawyer who drafted the will gave the wife a broader right to withdraw money from the trust than the tax law allows. He gave her the right to withdraw money for her "comfort." This was a broader right than the acceptable limits of withdrawing for reasons of "health, support, maintenance, and education." Because her right to withdraw was so broad, the trust was taxed in her estate.

Solution: The wife timely disclaimed her right to withdraw money for her "comfort." That limited her overall withdrawal rights to the legally acceptable ones, and the trust was excluded from her estate when she died.

Example II: I leave $600,000 to a family trust and the rest to my wife for her lifetime and then to my kids. My wife's interest is placed in what is called a Q-TIP trust—a Qualified Terminable Interest Property trust. This is a trust that provides all the income to my wife for life. If properly drafted, it qualifies for the marital deduction and avoids estate tax on my death.

To get the marital deduction, though, no one other than my wife can have any rights to the trust while she is alive. Suppose my will says that if my children need money for their education, the trustee can distribute it to them. Giving my children this right would disqualify my wife's trust for the marital deduction

Solution: The kids disclaim their right to receive money from the trust for education. That takes them out as beneficiaries of the trust. The trust then qualifies for the marital deduction and is not taxed on my death.

Legal requirements:

Disclaimers must strictly comply with the law. To be legally effective, a disclaimer must be...

- A written, irrevocable, unconditional refusal to accept a full or partial interest in money or property.
- Received by the estate's executor within nine months after the benefactor's death.
- The person who makes the disclaimer must not have accepted any benefit from the disclaimed inheritance.
- The disclaiming heir can't designate the recipient of the rejected interest.
- The rejected inheritance can't go into a trust that benefits the person making the disclaimer, unless that person is the decedent's spouse.

Most common traps:

- Not disclaiming soon enough. The disclaimer must be done within nine months of the person's death. If it's done too late, the person disclaiming will have to pay gift tax on the property he gives up in favor of others.
- Accepting benefits from the property that is disclaimed. That invalidates the disclaimer. In the case of stock, for instance, the person disclaiming can't have accepted any dividends.

Source: Ross W. Nager, tax partner and director of family wealth-planning, Arthur Anderson & Co., 711 Louisiana, Houston, Texas 77002.

Home Selling Tax Angles

Every profitable home sale must be reported in a timely fashion, meaning April 15th following the year of sale. Reporting basics:

- If you do not plan to replace your home after a sale: The tax on all gains will be due. Profits should also be reported on Schedule D, Form 1040.
- If you replace your home with one at a lower cost: A partial tax may be due. Report your gain not only on Form 2119, Sale of Your Home, but on Schedule D as well.
- If your home is not replaced by tax time: You must report the sale of a residence in the tax year in which the sale took place. This is true even if you plan on acquiring another residence, but have not done so. Fill out Part I and Part II, only, of IRS Form 2119.
- When you buy a replacement home after the sale return if filed: You must file an amended return on Form 1040X along with a completed Form 2119. Include a copy of the Form 2119 previously filed when you sold your former residence.
- If you pay the tax on the gain, then buy a replacement home during the replacement

period—two years before and after the sale—you can file an amended return. Attach Form 2119 giving details. You can claim a refund on any taxes paid which now may be deferred. Note: Deferral of gain and the postponement of any tax is not the taxpayer's option. If the deferral is allowable, it must be exercised.

• If you are divorced after filing a joint return and postponing the gain on the sale of your home...and you have not purchased a replacement home, but your former spouse has...you must file an amended joint return. If your former spouse refuses to sign this amended return, attach a letter of explanation.

Source: Jack Killough, affiliated consultant, McGladrey & Pullen, CPAs, One United Bank Center, 1700 Lincoln St., Denver 80203.

How To Avoid Showing The IRS Damaging Receipts

Suppose you've claimed deductions on your tax return that are personal and not tax deductible and ...you're being audited.

If this is uncovered, the information could lead the IRS auditor to expand the scope of the audit and possibly look closer at all your deductions. It may even tempt the auditor to examine your tax returns for the prior and subsequent tax years. Strategy:

Negotiate a settlement with the auditor. Offer to agree to the disallowance of a percentage of your total deductions—say 40%—if the auditor agrees to close the case without further investigation.

Source: Ms. X, a former IRS agent, still well-connected.

Dealing With An Abusive IRS Employee

Although they are, by far, the exception rather than the rule, there are a handful of abusive people working at the IRS. These employees are the kind who make up their own laws, lose your correspondence, serve you with a summons for information you have already agreed to furnish, and levy on your bank account though you have agreed to voluntarily pay the tax you owe. The first course of action when confronted with anyone at the IRS who is abusive is to go over their head and speak to their group manager. Should this be of no avail, find out who the group manager reports to. This is typically a branch chief. Address your grievance to that person. Good news: IRS management becomes offended when its employees get out of control. You can be sure that it will jump in when an abuse is reported.

Source: Ms. X, a former IRS agent, still well-connected.

Retirement Planning Tax Traps: How to Avoid Them

Retirement planning is an ongoing process. It's foolhardy and costly to think of retirement planning just at retirement time.

Think now about maximizing contributions to company plans—particularly 401(k) plans.

Important: Realize that retirement planning continues even after retirement, especially as to how distributions are taken from various plans.

The tax treatment governing distributions is very complex. Consider seeking the advice of a competent tax specialist to help plan the distributions.

Here are the biggest tax mistakes that people make in retirement planning...

• Mistake: Taking money from a plan before age 59½. As a general rule, there's a 10% penalty tax, in addition to income tax, when money is taken from a plan before age 59½.

Exception: The penalty doesn't apply when the money is withdrawn in the form of an annuity, that is, in a series of payments spread over the participant's lifetime.

Helpful: Use other monies, if at all possible, before taking money early from a retirement plan or IRA.

• Mistake: Failing to take enough money from the plan. Withdrawals must begin by April 1 of the year following the year in which the participant reaches age 70½. There's a minimum amount that must be withdrawn. Generally, it's an amount that will wipe out the account over the participant's life expectancy.

Trap: The penalty for not taking enough money out each year is 50% of the amount that should have been withdrawn but wasn't.

• Mistake: Failing to meet the 60-day deadline for rollovers. Tax and penalties on a distribution can be avoided by redepositing, that is, rolling over, the money into an IRA or other qualified pension plan. However, this must be done within 60 days of the time it is taken out. Failing to meet the 60-day deadline can be costly. Tax must be paid on the money and if the participant is under age 59½, a 10% penalty.

Worse: If the money is deposited into an IRA after the 60 days are up, rollover rights are cancelled and the money is treated as an excess contribution to the plan. This subjects the participant to an additional 6% penalty per year.

Escape hatch: If the money is taken out of the IRA before the extended due date of the participant's tax return, the 6% excise tax can be avoided.

• Mistake: Not electing special averaging for lump-sum distributions from qualified plans. Lump-sum distributions generally qualify for special five- or 10-year averaging, which dramatically reduces the tax, especially on smaller distributions. But many taxpayers are not aware of special averaging.

Trap: Special averaging is not automatic...it must be elected. To make the election, file IRS Form 4972 with your income tax return.

Important calculation: When a person gets a lump-sum distribution, he has the choice of taking the money now, and paying the tax, or rolling it over into an IRA. It is necessary to consider the net value of the two alternatives to determine which method is most advantageous.

• Mistake: Not knowing about capital gains treatment. Employees who were participants in their company's plan prior to 1974, qualify for tax-favored capital gains treatment on part of their distribution from the plan. Three choices:

• Ignore capital gains treatment.

• Have the capital gains part taxed at 20% (the capital gains rate in 1986).

• Include the capital gains part on Schedule D and have it taxed at today's rates with other capital gains.

• Mistake: Neglecting to take state taxes into consideration. In deciding whether to take the money now or roll it over, state income tax must be considered. This can affect the decision, especially when a taxpayer lives in a high-tax state. Each state has different rules governing plan distributions. Some have special averaging, some do not.

• Mistake: Rolling over into an IRA a distribution that includes voluntary contributions a participant made with his own money. This can subject him to the 6% excess contribution tax.

Reason: Only the taxable portion of a distribution can be rolled over. The portion of the distribution that is comprised of voluntary contributions is nontaxable...thus, it can't be rolled over.

• Mistake: Letting the company take withholding tax out of a distribution. This can cause a major problem if the participant later decides to roll the distribution over into an IRA. To be completely free of tax, the whole amount of a distribution must be rolled over.

However, if some of the distribution is taken out for withholding tax, the whole amount can't be rolled over. The employee will have to pay ordinary income tax on the amount withheld, plus a 10% penalty tax if under age 59½. The only way to prevent this from occurring is for the employee to come up with extra cash equal to the amount withheld so that he can roll over the full taxable amount of the distribution.

• Mistake: Taking too much from retirement plans in one year. There's a penalty for taking "excessive" distributions from retirement plans. Generally, a distribution is considered excessive if it's over $150,000 a year. All amounts withdrawn from an individual's different retirement plans are added together to determine whether the limit has been exceeded. The amount over $150,000 is subject to a 15% excise tax.

Better: Plan withdrawals carefully. Spread them over a number of years so that in no one year do they exceed the $150,000 limit.

Caution: Rolling lump-sum distributions into an IRA isn't always the best thing to do, especially if one is going to need a large amount of the pension money soon after retirement. The excess distribution rules may cause problems.

- Mistake: Failing to understand the nuances in the lump-sum distribution rules. One thing to know is that special averaging is only available if a person has been in the plan for at least five years before the year of distribution. If he fails this test, he'll have no choice but to roll the money over into an IRA—or pay the ordinary income tax.
- Mistake: Taking two distributions from two different types of plans in one year and choosing different tax treatments for each distribution. If one distribution is rolled over, the other must be rolled over too. Reason: The tax law says that all distributions taken in one year must be treated the same way.

Avoidance: Spread the distributions over two years. Roll one over and take averaging on the other.

- Mistake: Taking two rollover in one year from an IRA. The tax law permits one to make IRA to IRA rollovers. The money taken from one IRA won't be taxed as long as the funds are redeposited in the second IRA within 60 days of taking them out.

Rule: Only one rollover per year, per IRA. Transfers that violate this rule will be subject to income tax and penalties.

- Mistake: Taking "hardship" distributions from a 401(k) plan without realizing that the distribution is subject to ordinary income tax plus a 10% penalty if the participant is under age 59½. While the hardship provisions allow individuals to take money out of such plans, they won't avoid tax and penalties on those withdrawals.
- Mistake: Not creating a separate IRA for rollover distributions from company plans. When a distribution is mixed with an existing IRA, it can't be rolled over into another company's pension plan if the participant later gets a new job. By creating a separate IRA account for the rollover, the right to move it, tax free, from the IRA into a new company's plan is preserved.
- Mistake: Not understanding the new IRA rules. The new law didn't abolish IRAs, it just limited deductions for them. Taxpayers may still benefit by setting up nondeductible IRAs. Advantage: The account earns tax-deferred interest.

Source: Stephen Pennacchio, partner, KPMG Peat Marwick, 599 Lexington Ave., New York 10022.

Casualty And Theft-Loss Loopholes

The tax law allows deductions for losses due to casualty and theft. But to get a deduction on your tax return, your loss must be catastrophic. Reason: Personal casualty and theft losses are deductible only to the extent that they exceed 10% of your Adjusted Gross Income. In addition, you must reduce each separate casualty or theft by $100.

Loophole: The $100 reduction applies to each casualty or theft, no matter how many pieces of property are involved. If a hail storm damages your house, your garage and your car, you would need to deduct only $100 from your total loss.

Loophole: Losses to business, as opposed to personal, property are not subject to the 10%-of-AGI limit. If, for example, you suffer a loss to property you rent to others, the 10% limit doesn't apply, nor does the $100 per casualty reduction.

Loophole: Special tax treatment is available for losses of personal accounts in bankrupt or insolvent financial institutions. You have a choice of treating your loss as—

...a casualty loss, subject to the 10%-of-AGI limit—or...

...a nonbusiness bad debt, which is deductible as a short-term capital loss subject to the $3,000 limit on deductions of excess losses over gains—or...

...an ordinary loss incurred in a transaction entered into for profit. This treatment is available only if no part of your deposit is federally insured. If that is the case, you can deduct up to $20,000 of your loss—$10,000 for married individuals filing a separate return.

Important: Check with your tax advisor for help in deciding which method to choose.

• What is a casualty? It is defined as the damage, destruction, or loss of property resulting from an identifiable event that is sudden, unexpected or unusual.

• Sudden event: One that is swift, not gradual or progressive.

• Unexpected event: One that is ordinarily unanticipated and one that you do not intend.

• Unusual event: One that is not a day-to-day occurrence.

Deductible casualty losses include damage in earthquakes, hurricanes, tornadoes, fires, floods, shipwrecks, storms, and volcanic eruptions.

Accidents qualify as casualty losses, as do losses caused by theft, embezzlement or false pretenses.

• How to measure your loss. Your deduction is limited to the lesser for either the property's adjusted basis (usually cost) before the casualty, or its decline in fair market value as a result of the casualty.

Example: A ring that you received as a gift has been stolen. The ring cost the person who gave it to you $500. But its current value is $20,000. Your theft-loss deduction is $500, which is the lesser of tax cost or fair market value. When somebody gives you property, you take over the tax cost of the person who gives it to you.

If you inherit property, on the other hand, your tax cost is the value of the property at the time of the decedent's death or the value that's used on the estate tax return.

Loophole: If you have a choice of receiving an asset by gift or inheriting it, it's best to inherit it. This will give you a higher and more favorable tax cost in the property. Ask the person to lend it to you for the time being, and then leave it to you in their will.

For real estate, the measure of your loss is the difference between the value of the property immediately before the casualty and the value of the property afterwards. The difference is your deductible loss.

Loophole: The loss in value caused by damage to ornamental trees and shrubs can be much higher than the amount you actually spent on landscaping. Document your loss by getting a competent appraiser to supply before and after appraisals of the property's value.

• Figuring your deduction. You must reduce your loss by any insurance proceeds you receive or expect to receive from your insurance company.

Trap: If your are entitled to insurance reimbursement but do not request it—because you don't want your insurance premiums to go up, for example—you cannot claim a casualty loss deduction for the amount you would have been entitled to get from the insurance company.

Loophole: Any legal fees you incur to recover property that is stolen are added to the tax cost of the property and are deductible in that way.

• Proving your loss. To take a deduction for a casualty loss, you must be able to show that there was a casualty, and you must be able to support the amount of your loss.

If there's a theft, you should report it to the police. Keep copies of any insurance claims you make. Take photographs of losses caused by natural disasters, and keep newspaper clippings that report about casualties.

Suppose an uninsured piece of jewelry is stolen. You have no records showing that you bought in the first place. How do you prove that you were the owner of the jewelry? One way is to produce photographs showing you or your spouse wearing it. To establish the cost of the item, get an appraisal from a jeweler indicating what it would have cost at the time you bought it.

Remember that cost is the key figure in taking a casualty loss deduction. Your loss is the lesser of the cost or the decline in fair market value. The amount you have the property insured for is not an indication of cost.

• When is the loss deductible? As a general rule you may deduct casualty losses only in the year in which the loss occurred. But there are exceptions...

Loophole: Theft losses are deductible in the year you discover your property was stolen.

Loophole: Casualty losses from a disaster that occurred in an area the President of the United States declares a "disaster area" can be deducted either in the year the loss occurred or in the tax year immediately before the loss. Filing an amended return for the earlier year will give you a quick refund at a time you most need it.

• Recovered property. If property that is stolen is later returned to you, you have a choice of either amending your return for the year you claimed the loss or reporting the recovery as income in the year you receive it. You should figure your tax both ways to see which method is better for you.

Source: Edward Mendlowitz, partner, Mendlowitz Weitsen, CPAs, Two Pennsylvania Plaza, New York 10121. Mr Mendlowitz is the author of several books, including *Aggressive Tax Strategies,* Macmillan Publishing Co., 866 Third Ave., New York 10022.

How To Cut Through IRS Red Tape... When All Else Fails

Every IRS district office and every service center has a Problem Resolution Office (PRO).

The purpose of the PRO is to resolve taxpayer problems that have not been resolved through regular organization channels at the IRS.

Bogged down: The PRO is the office to turn to if there's been a bureaucratic mix-up and your case has become hopelessly bogged down.

Hardship: It's also the place to go to if IRS action against you poses a significant hardship.

Overlooked: It's the one office of the IRS where you can be sure your problem will not be overlooked. Your case will be assigned to a specific IRS employee for resolution, a person who has experience in various areas of the IRS.

Where to find the PRO: Call your local IRS district office and ask for the number of the PRO. Or, ask the IRS employee you've been dealing with to give you the number. You can also get a copy of IRS publication 1320, Operation Link, which lists the phone numbers and addresses of all the Problem Resolution Offices. (To get a copy of this publication, call the IRS toll-free at 800-829-3676.)

Sample problems for the PRO:

• Your tax refund is missing.

• You've received a notice from the IRS that you don't understand and nobody at the IRS will explain it to you.

• Tax payments you made were incorrectly posted by the IRS.

• The IRS says you owe tax on interest earned by your IRA.

• The IRS is attempting to levy on your bank account even though you've paid the tax.

PRO limits: The PRO cannot be used to contest the merits of any tax liability. The place to do that, if you've been audited, is the IRS appeals division.

PRO prerequisites: Before the PRO will take your case, you must have attempted to solve your problem through the normal IRS channels, without success. The PRO has different conditions for taking a case depending on the issue involved.

• Refund problems. First you have to wait 90 days from the date you filed your return. After that, you have to have made two or more unsuccessful inquiries about your refund and given the IRS a reasonable amount of time to respond.

• Inquiries. You've written the IRS asking for assistance or information on a tax-related issue and 45 days have gone by without a response. Or, you have not received a response from the IRS by the date they promised.

• Notices. You've received three or more notices from the IRS indicating a problem. You've responded to one or more of the notices but the problem hasn't been cleared up.

• Taxpayer assistance orders. You face significant hardship because of the way the IRS is administering the tax laws. You've tried without success to get the problem resolved through normal channels.

A system for dealing with the PRO:

• Call first to explain the problem and what steps you've taken to resolve it.

• Get the name of the officer you're talking to and the mailing address of the PRO.

• Tell the PRO officer you're going to send him all the information he needs to resolve your case.

• Call back to confirm that the PRO has received your letter.

• If you don't hear from the PRO in a couple of days, call to see if more information is needed.

Most cases are resolved quickly by the PRO, usually within 30 days...60 days at the outside. You'll first get a letter saying they have accepted your case into the PRO program and giving you the name and phone number of a person to contact. Faster action: Cases that involve significant hardship are required to be dealt with quickly.

Immediate taxpayer assistance. If you can show that you face significant hardship because of the IRS action against you, you can apply for immediate relief by filing Form 911 with the Problem Resolution Office. Form 911 is an application for what is called a taxpayer assistance order. Filing Form 911 immediately stops IRS action against you.

Most hardships occur during IRS action to collect tax. The IRS gives the following examples of significant hardships that could lead to a taxpayer assistance order being issued...

• Emotional stress.

• Threat of a poor credit rating caused by erroneous enforcement action.

• Imminent bankruptcy.

• Failure to meet payroll.

• Possible loss of employment.

• Pending eviction.

• Significant personal emergency.

Example: Counting on a refund check to pay for medical treatment.

To get a copy of Form 911, call the IRS toll-free forms-ordering number, 800-829-3676. You can also get the form from any IRS office or any practicing accountant's office.

Source: Marvin Michelman, specialist in IRS practice and procedure, Deloitte & Touche, One World Trade Center, New York 10048. He held various positions with the IRS for 19 years, including senior regional analyst for examinations.

What Do You Say To The IRS?

What do you say to the IRS when you have no money to pay your taxes but your spouse is wealthy? As long as you haven't filed a joint tax return with your spouse for the year that give rise to the tax liability, only you are liable. Generally, it is not advisable for your spouse to offer financial information to the IRS collection people. The fact that your spouse contributes assets or money for your mutual support does not legally require your spouse to pay off your tax bill. Caution: The IRS will try to make a case that assets which had been owned by you were fraudulently conveyed to your spouse. If successful, the IRS can effectively place those assets back in your name and then seize them from you.

Source: Ms. X, a former IRS agent, still well-connected.

When The IRS Is Wrong

It is not uncommon for the IRS to be clearly—and absolutely—wrong when they inform you that you owe money. Lately, they have been pretty good at correcting mistakes if you respond promptly with documentation to support your position. Caution: Some people look at an obviously incorrect IRS notice, see how wrong it is—and then throw it away. The IRS will not figure out that they have made an error unless you bring it to their attention and then document, to their satisfaction, that they are wrong. Be persistent and always have the IRS confirm, in writing, that the error has been corrected.

Source: Ms. X, a former IRS agent, still well-connected.

Recordkeeping Loopholes

The IRS has a rule about deductions—prove them or lose them. Without good records you won't remember what's deductible and what's not. Worse: You'll never survive an audit. Most important records:

• Deduction diary. Maintain a diary in which you record the details of all deductible expenses at or near the time you incurred them. Include a section for travel and entertainment expenses (T&E). Also record medical expenses, taxes, investment expenses, charitable contributions, etc.

Safest: Enter expenses in the diary within the same week that you pay them.

• Four Ws and a dollar sign. Special proof is required for travel and entertainment expenditures. It is necessary for you to include the following information in your T & E diary. I call this information the 4 Ws and a dollar sign to make it easy to remember...

• Who you entertained. Include the person's name, title, and occupation, to show the person's business relationship to you.

• When you were with them.

• Where the event took place.

• Why you entertained them. (Write down the business purpose of the event.)

• How much you spent.

Caution: You must also have a receipt for items of $25 or more.

• Charity records. Keep a list in your deduction diary of gifts you make to charity, especially the unusual ones that you might not remember when you are preparing your return. Examples:

• Donations of old clothes, newspapers, and similar items.

• Expenses for volunteer work at a charity. You can deduct actual car expenses for gas and oil or you can deduct the IRS's standard rate of 12 cents per mile.

• Parking fees and tolls incurred while driving your car for charity.

Your deduction for gifts of property to charity must be backed up by proof that the charity actually received the items you donated...and proof of the value of your gift.

• If the total value is $500 or more, you must attach Form 8283 to your return, showing how you arrived at the value you claimed.

• If the total value exceeds $5,000, you must have the property appraised by an independent appraiser.

Loophole: When you give capital gain property to a charity that uses the property in its charitable function, you can deduct the fair market value of the property. You don't need to keep a record of the property's cost, only its fair market value. (Capital gain property is property that would have resulted in a long-term capital gain if you had sold it.)

• Casualty losses. Keep records that show the cost of valuable items, such as jewelry, and when you bought them. Deductions for casualty and theft losses are limited to the lesser of the property's adjusted basis (tax cost), or its decline in fair market value as a result of the casualty. If you can't prove what the property cost, the IRS will estimate the cost for you. This may be a lower figure than what you actually spent.

Loophole: If you failed to keep a record of a lost asset's cost, you can reconstruct the cost. For example, get a jeweler to estimate what a stolen item would have cost you at the time you bought it.

• Inherited property and gifts. Keep copies of the estate-tax return or a letter from the estate's executor showing the date-of-death or estate's value of inherited property. You'll need this to calculate your gain or loss when you sell the property. Your gain is based not on the property's cost to the decedent, but on the value used on the estate's return.

Loophole: If the estate is under $600,000, no estate-tax return is required. But you should ask the executor to prepare one anyway so you'll have evidence of the property's date-of-death value.

The rule for property you receive by way of gift is different. Your gain is based on what the property cost the person who gave it to you. Get and keep a record of that cost.

• Hobby gains and losses. For tax purposes it makes a big difference whether you run a hobby, such as stamp collecting, as an investor, a dealer, or a hobbyist. Tax differences:

- Investor: Your profits are capital gains. Your losses are deductible as capital losses.
- Dealer: Your profits are taxable income. Your losses are deductible as ordinary business losses.
- Hobbyist: If you sell items from your collection at a profit, your gains are taxable. But your losses are not deductible.

To maintain investor status for your collection you should make occasional sales (hobbyists almost never make sales) and keep detailed records. If you pay cash for an item, get a receipt and keep it. Keep meticulous records of your expenses

- Sidelines. The IRS will be much more likely to allow sideline business deductions if you set up the sideline in a business-like way. Open a separate checking account for the business, and keep a separate set of bookkeeping records. The more detailed your records, the better chance you'll have with the IRS.

Source: Edward Mendlowitz, partner, Mendlowitz Weitsen, CPAs, Two Pennsylvania Plaza, New York 10121. Mr. Mendlowitz is the author of several books, including *Aggressive Tax Strategies*, Macmillan Publishing Co., 866 Third Ave., New York 10022.

How A Boat Can Help Reduce Taxes

The limitations on the deductibility of interest have left taxpayers scrambling to convert nondeductible personal interest into deductible home mortgage interest.

At first glance, you would likely assume that interest paid on a boat loan not purchased with the proceeds of a home equity loan could not be deducted. However, such interest can qualify as fully deductible residence interest if you meet these criteria...

1. The boat must qualify as a second residence. If you rent the boat during the year, then you or a member of your family must live on the boat for more than 14 days during the year, or more than 10% of the number of days you rent it out to others. However, if you don't rent the boat, you need not use it at all.

You may deduct interest on only one second residence per year. If you own a vacation home in addition to the boat, and the interest paid on the home's mortgage exceeds the interest on the boat, you will not benefit from this strategy.

2. The boat must contain sleeping space, a head, and cooking facilities.

3. The aggregate principal loan amount of your boat loan and primary residence loan should not exceed $1 million, as interest paid on acquisition indebtedness exceeding this amount is not deductible. This limitation is reduced by aggregate amounts of outstanding indebtedness incurred before October 13, 1987.

However, in most cases, you can deduct home equity indebtedness up to $100,000 even if you reach the threshold amount for acquisition indebtedness.

4. The boat must serve as collateral for the loan, and the lender's security interest must be recorded in the proper government office.

Special rules apply if you are married and file separately or if you lease your boat to others for a portion of the tax year. Aside from such circumstances, however, following these rules should help you minimize nondeductible personal interest when you buy a boat.

Source: Laurence I. Foster, CPS/APFS, tax partner, personal financial planning, KPMG Peat Marwick, 599 Lexington Ave., New York 10022.

Five Social Security Loopholes

Social Security taxes are rising. But there are still many forms of payments that are exempt from Social Security tax. Examples:

- Exempt: Wages paid to your children who are under 18 if your business is a sole proprietorship. Wages paid by a corporation, however, are subject to Social Security tax.
- Exempt: Any payments that are not compensation for services—dividends, interest, rent, pensions, gifts, inheritances, etc.
- Exempt: Loans from the company to an

employee or stockholder. But be sure the loan is fully documented to prove its legitimacy. If the IRS concludes that the loan will not be paid back, it will impose Special Security tax.

• Exempt: Fringe benefits, such as health insurance premiums paid by the employer, employer contributions to qualified retirement plans, educational benefits, etc.

• Exempt: Social Security benefits you receive are not subject to Social Security tax. (Don't confuse this with income tax. Depending on your income level, a part of your Social Security benefits may be subject to income tax.)

Source: Leon M. Nad, adjunct associate professor of taxation at Fordham University. He is a consulting editor of *Tax Hotline.*

Tax-Free Income... 10 Different Ways

• Gain from the sale of your home is exempt from tax if you reinvest it in another home within two years. If you're 55 or older, up to $125,000 of gain is tax free even if you don't reinvest.

• Children's wages. Up to $3,400 of wages a child earns is tax free in 1991.

• Children's investment income. In 1991, dependent children can receive up to $550 of investment income tax free.

• Vacation home rental. The income from renting for 14 days or less is tax free.

• Municipal bond income. The interest earned is exempt from federal tax and sometimes from state and local tax as well.

• Education savings bonds. Interest on special US savings bonds issued after December 31, 1989 is tax free to many taxpayers if the bonds are later redeemed to pay for education expenses.

• Federal income tax refunds are not taxable. (However, any interest the IRS pays on a late refund is taxable.)

• State income tax refunds if you took the standard deduction are tax free.

• Workers' compensation payments are tax free.

• Child support payments are tax free to the recipient.

7

A More Powerful You

17 New Lessons in Body Language

Reading other people depends very much on developing your ability to decipher nonverbal messages. In every exchange between people, messages are sent, through words and through the underlying dynamics of the nonverbal information—what I call subtext...

Subtext can reinforce and strengthen the spoken text, or it may contradict the text, canceling out any verbal promises or agreements. It is a mixture of many different elements, including...

- Each person's body language—posture, hand movements, eye contact, etc.
- How a person handles space.
- How a person uses touch.
- Tone of voice.
- How a person dresses and his/her overall appearance.
- What a person does outside a conversation that confirms or contradicts what is said during the conversation.

Identifying honesty:

What is there in the subtext of a person that tells you he's not being honest about who he really is? Or...what he really thinks? Or...what he feels? There can be any number of elements. Most important:

- Facial expression. Maybe he smiles at inappropriate times. A real, genuinely felt emotion causes a quick smile. If someone wants to fake an emotion, he'll hold the expression too long.

A genuine smile goes up into the eyes and involves the top of the face.

A false smile just involves the bottom of the face and is usually not as wide as a real smile.

- Physiological responses. There is no one gesture that gives away a lie. But there are a lot of little physiological responses that go with a lie—certain gestures that are used consistently by many people.

Example: When a politician is about to tell

a whopper, he'll usually rub the side of his nose with his finger. In the presidential debate between Carter and Reagan, both men did this at various points—Reagan, when he said he'd accomplish all his proposals without raising taxes! We don't know why this gesture is so consistent, but it is.

It's easiest to detect these bits of nonverbal information if you know the person well and you can identify abnormal or atypical behavior. Or, if you can observe his interactions with other people and compare them to his interactions with you.

• Look for discrepancies. Examples: Again, a smile that appears only on the lips, not on the rest of the face...smooth words backed by nervous mannerisms.

• Know your situation. If a business deal is a bad one, you're not going to find the flaws in the way the associate is behaving. You have to examine the deal itself. Abnormal behavior is really just a tip-off that you need to look at the situation more closely. You're not going to know that this person is putting over a phony deal unless you know what a good deal is and understand the whole situation.

In the same way, you're not going to become powerful by wearing power clothes. If you're a lawyer, you're not going to become competent by wearing an expensive gray suit. You become competent by knowing your job. Then the gray suit may help a little.

Intuition:

One term we use for this ability to read cues is intuition—but it's not really that magical—it's a computer in our brains adding up all the little things that are wrong in a situation, judging the subtext of the whole.

I don't believe in mysticism. And I don't believe that intuition is a leap into uncharted realms, through some telepathic power. It is the summing-up of all the little things that you know about a situation and drawing a conclusion.

Example: If your intuition tells you that you shouldn't trust your company's management team and their promises for the future, then start job-hunting immediately. Chances are you're picking up lots of tiny signals that your conscious mind doesn't even see, but your inner "computer"—the brain—does.

In general, women in our society are much more intuitive than men. Reason: Women are raised to be more nurturing than men. As a result, they take more time to learn about other people and to really understand what motivates them.

But anyone can cultivate their intuition. First step: Look for the subtexts in your interactions with other people—acquaintances and strangers. When you have a funny feeling about an individual or a situation, pay attention to it. Try and figure out exactly what bothers you and why. Often you can make an intuitive leap from there.

To improve your subtext:

It is possible to learn to cultivate your appearance and manage the impression you give to other people. This is why, for example, business people and politicians hire image consultants. Or why Donald Trump works so hard for publicity. If he didn't have that aura, I don't think that the banks would have given him the leeway to get himself into such financial trouble.

But while appearance is important, giving excessive importance to appearance doesn't make sense. There are people who aren't handsome who are really wonderful, lovely people. And a fancy exterior can't make up for an inner lack of ability or talent.

Although your appearance and subtext can help you communicate who you really are to others, the best message you can send in the world is that you're someone who knows what he's talking about. Understand your talents...and learn to use them at their highest levels. The self-confidence it gives you will be the best addition to your subtext that you can possibly make.

Source: Julius Fast, author of more than 30 books on the subjects of business and psychological communication, is most famous for his best-selling book *Body Language.* His latest book is *Subtext: Making Body Language Work in the Workplace,* Viking Penguin, 365 Hudson St., New York 10014.

Mindfulness Meditation... To Improve Your Life

Although meditation is a spiritual discipline that's estimated to be approximately 5,000 years old, it is still relatively new to the West.

More than just a set of mental exercises, meditation helps us understand on a deep level what it means to be human.

Although you don't have to be religious to benefit, you do need to be willing to embark on an intensely personal inquiry in an unfamiliar way.

Mindfulness:

We teach meditation as mindfulness—paying purposeful attention, becoming fully aware of the present moment.

Although we can't draw conclusions yet—too few controlled studies have been done—the evidence is strong that mindfulness meditation can have remarkable physical and psychological effects. It can be used to:

- Increase relaxation.
- Lower blood pressure.
- Decrease pain.
- Reduce secretion of stress hormones, including adrenaline and noradrenaline.
- Decrease the amount of excess stomach acid in people with gastrointestinal problems.

Patients with a wide range of chronic illnesses—from digestive problems to AIDS—attend our eight-session classes in mindfulness meditation. In addition, they make a commitment to practice on their own each day. Results:

- Virtually all patients, whatever their diagnoses, show dramatic reductions in physical symptoms over the eight-week period.
- Psychological problems—anxiety, depression, hostility—also drop over the eight weeks. Follow-up studies four years after completion of the course show that both physical and psychological improvements are consistent over time.
- Symptom reductions are greater than with other techniques, such as drug intervention, indicating that results don't come from a placebo effect. Somehow, the patient's inner resources for healing are being tapped.
- Patients' self-perceptions change. They view themselves as healthier and better able to handle stressful situations without suffering destructive effects. They feel more in control of their lives...view life as a challenge rather than a series of obstacles...feel they are living more fully.

Why mindfulness:

We live in an anxiety-producing, stressful culture. To cope with the strain, we seek out all sorts of chemicals to calm us down—alcohol, tranquilizers, illicit drugs, cigarettes. We use newspapers and TV addictively, regulating our mind-set so that we can justify our continuing race on the treadmill.

Mindfulness is a way of stopping outward activity so you can explore and refine your inner wisdom and learn to know your body and mind from the inside. Result: You develop a lifestyle that is more consistent with good health.

Most of us spend very little time aware of the present moment. We're usually absorbed in anticipating the future...planning strategies to ward off things we don't want to happen and to force outcomes that we do want...remembering who did what to whom and why.

All that mental manipulation leaves us enormously agitated. The meditative disciplines are avenues for reintroducing calmness and stability into our lives.

Sample mindfulness exercise:

Take three raisins and eat them one at a time, paying full attention to every part of the experience. Study the raisin as if you'd never seen one before. Feel its texture. Notice any thoughts you might be having about raisins and whether you like or dislike them.

Smell the raisin. Bring it slowly to your lips. Chew it carefully, noticing the taste. Experience the impulse to swallow, and imagine that your body is now heavier by the weight of one raisin.

What you'll learn:

The raisin exercise reminds us that anything can be done mindfully—eating, sitting, walking, breathing.

Paying full attention is the essence of mindfulness. We come out of automatic pilot and observe more deeply. This allows us to feel more connected to what's going on around us and develop a greater understanding of the order of things.

In a way, mindfulness is almost un-American—we are so oriented to running around doing. Yet it is not an easy or passive discipline—it requires effort, commitment and practice.

A receptive attitude—not blind belief, but openness—is essential. So are patience and trust. From this commitment can grow a deep sense of health and well-being.

Source: Jon Kabat-Zinn, PhD, director of the Stress Reduction Clinic at the University of Massachusetts Medical Center and associate professor of medicine in the medical school's Division of Preventive and Behavioral Medicine. He is the author of *Full Catastrophe Living: Using the Wisdom of Your Body and Mind To Face Stress, Pain, and Illness*, Delacorte Press, 666 Fifth Ave., New York 10103.

Perfectionism: In Yourself...In Others

People don't think of perfectionism as a problem. Striving for the best is generally considered a positive attribute.

Unfortunately, true perfectionists don't draw the line between striving to be the best they can possibly be in a given situation and expecting themselves and others to be flawless under all circumstances.

Destructive result: Unreal expectations create unhappiness for the perfectionist—and for those close to him. Fortunately, perfectionism is one of the easiest problems to overcome. Since perfectionists are quick learners, and are strongly motivated to change for the better, change comes easily to them.

Important: The ability to step back, observe and put things into perspective.

The roots of perfectionism:

Perfectionists are often created by perfectionist parents. These parents don't intend to be cruel or abusive...they just want the best for their children. But they don't realize the psychological pressures they're creating. Most affected: First children and only children.

Worst offenders: Carrot-dangling parents. Instead of setting a goal for the child that might be a little beyond him and then giving praise if the goal is reached—or expressing disappointment if it isn't—a carrot-dangler sets another goal as soon as the child reaches the first one.

Example: Telling a child who gets all A's and one B that you want to see all A's next time. Children of carrot-danglers learn to strive—but know they'll never really achieve.

Additional problems:

• Continued failure to be perfect lowers self-esteem. Only by being perfect can people with low self-esteem feel worthy at all. Lacking a sense of innate self-worth, they get caught up in the trap of needing constant affirmation from the outside.

• Societal pressures. As a society, we really do judge others on how they look or what they've accomplished. But perfectionists go overboard in judging themselves by society's impossibly high standards.

Example: A perfectionist in business who feels the quality of his work is inadequate may overcompensate and become a workaholic—producing tons of often mediocre work—trying to use quantity to hide lack of quality.

Are you a perfectionist?

• Do you go to almost any length to avoid making mistakes?

• Do you critique every performance or job you do, reviewing every minute detail, looking for mistakes?

• Do you wrack your brain for ways to correct or undo things you've already done?

• Are you always unsatisfied with the goals you reach?

• Do you feel a letdown after an achievement because you haven't anything new to strive for?

• Do you spend such an inordinate amount of time trying to excel in one area of your life that you ignore other areas?

• Do people call you a perfectionist?

• Do you procrastinate when you have to meet a deadline, or find yourself doing the same thing over and over?

• Do you avoid situations in which you think you won't perform or look the best?

If you answered yes to any one of these questions, you have perfectionist tendencies. If you answered yes to three or more questions, perfectionism is probably already causing problems in your life.

The four types of perfectionists:

- Performance perfectionists. Everything they do has to be flawless.

Symptoms: Trying so hard you trip yourself up...feeling that nothing you achieve is good enough...going from one goal to the next goal without appreciating your achievements...rationalizing away achievement by thinking someone else could have done it better, or it was easier than you thought or one little part was wrong so it wasn't perfect.

- Appearance perfectionists. They want everything to look perfect.

Symptoms: Being a neatness freak who gets nervous if everything isn't exactly in place... buying the perfect outfit but not wearing it because you're waiting for the perfect occasion...refusing to go to a function because you haven't got the right clothes... hating the way you look because you've gained five pounds. Extreme example: Anorectics who can never be thin enough.

- Interpersonal perfectionists. People who are terribly critical of others are usually perfectionists. As long as there's something wrong with everyone else, they don't have to face their own imperfections.

Symptoms: Never being satisfied with the behavior of those close to you...becoming enraged over small transgressions, like forgetting to put the cap on the toothpaste tube...finding flaws in everyone you meet...choosing friends and lovers based on how well they reflect on you.

- Moral/ethical perfectionist. These people can't ever bend the rules.

Symptoms: Their overly strict moral code makes them play by the rules all the time. Since they expect others to always "go by the book" too, they often get into trouble for not being flexible...but they don't know how to bend the rules.

Self-defense: Learn strategies to help you—and those around you—cope with your demanding nature.

How to cope with your own perfectionism:

Aim for balance. Bring back the aspects of your life that you've ignored or neglected.

Example: If you spend most of your time on your work, set aside some time every day to garden or bicycle, or something else you love but don't do anymore.

- Practice moderation. Set realistic goals and standards for yourself and others instead of lofty, unattainable ones.
- Lower your standards. Recognize when you've reached a point of diminishing returns. Find a way to get some of what you want in a way that will make you feel good and will help your relationships.

Example: Stop insisting that your mate put all his clothes away. Settle for getting the socks off the floor.

- Concentrate on the here and now. Don't obsess about the past and what could have been or what you should have done.
- Do things that don't require performance or evaluation, things you can do just for fun.

Example: Take long, meandering walks.

How to live or work with a perfectionist:

Unless you intend to cut yourself off from the perfectionists in your life, you'll have to deal with their nitpicking, obsessive worrying and controlling behavior. Coping strategies:

- Don't take their behavior personally. Remind yourself that perfectionists act out of habit. They're not out to get you...they're simply trying to manage their own emotions and boost their sense of self-worth.
- Avoid: Beating up on yourself for not living up to their expectations.
- Resist intimidation. Remind yourself that no matter how powerful and sure of themselves the perfectionists in your life seem to be, they're subject to the same laws of the universe as you. Stick up for yourself and don't automatically give in to their demands.
- Learn when and how to walk away. Spend less time with perfectionists who get to you. Or learn to overlook things that may be irritating but don't really hurt you.
- Resolve conflicts constructively. Helpful strategy...compromise. If you're married to a perfectionist, arrange to do things his way

one third of the time, your way one third and compromise creatively for the other third.

Example: Couples who are struggling for control of the kitchen can arrange it so that one of them cooks one night and the other cooks the next. On the third night, they can eat out or cook together.

Source: Psychologist Miriam Elliott, PhD, and social worker Susan Meltsner, MSW, co-authors of *The Perfectionist Predicament: How To Stop Driving Yourself and Others Crazy*, William Morrow & Co., 1350 Ave. of the Americas, New York 10019.

Mind Power Opportunities

There is increasing evidence that the mind has many more resources than the experts once thought.

There are hundreds of studies now that show how to use the mind more effectively—if we take the time to understand what is there for us.

Part of my interest in this area comes from the work of my grandfather, Edgar Cayce. Known as The Sleeping Prophet, he had an unusual mental talent: He could enter a sleep-like trance in which he accurately diagnosed the illnesses of thousands of people—whether they were in the same room or thousands of miles away.

You can train your mind to work more powerfully for you in these areas...

Healing:

The mind has a great deal of control over the immune system. Harvard psychologist Mary Jaznowski took 30 healthy students and divided them into three groups...

- One worked crossword puzzles.
- One was given relaxation training.
- One received relaxation training and visual imagery training—imagining their powerful and strong immune systems attacking weak flu and cold viruses.

Group One showed no increase in immune cells. Group Two showed a slight increase. Group Three showed a significant increase in immune system activity after only one hour of training.

We, too, can use the mind to teach ourselves to relax, to visualize changes in the body and to increase the probability of those changes actually occurring.

Problem-solving and creativity:

Our program teaches that if we simply pay more attention—more time energy—to becoming aware of our mental processes, we will be much more effective. One simple way of doing this is to work with your dreams. We all dream every night. If you aren't aware of your dreams, you are missing important messages from your inner mind.

Valuable habit: Put a pencil and paper by your bed and when you wake up, write down immediately what you recall from dreams during the night. If you do this consistently, you will find answers to problems from everyday life popping up in the dream state—how to deal with a situation at work, handle specific relationships, etc.

The presleep state is also valuable. Both Einstein and Thomas Edison got important insights while in the presleep period, and both found that the mind can function more creatively then—as opposed to when it is fully awake. Suggestions made during the presleep period can help you to reshape your behavior.

Example: One of my students was trying to stop smoking. He worked with presleep suggestion and visualization. He made a tape for himself, describing a number of situations in which he usually enjoyed smoking—but described them without the cigarettes. Every night for four months, he played this tape just before going to sleep. Then one weekend he threw away all his cigarettes and told himself that on Monday morning he would stop smoking. It worked. Months have passed... and he hasn't resumed smoking. He had tried other techniques, but none had ever worked before.

Stress reduction:

Meditation is one of the most vital tools used in reducing mental and physical stress. But recent research suggests that beyond these effects, the regular practice of meditation can enhance creativity and increase your attention span as well.

In meditation, you quiet the body and mind, and then place the mind on a single focus for a period of minutes. Harvard psychologist Herbert Benson found that the word one, or even a nonsense syllable, worked just as well as a mantra.

Benson showed that the body begins to change as we work with the meditation process—there is a decrease in oxygen consumption... the muscles relax and the general level of stress is reduced. In addition, I have found meditation helps to discipline and control the mind, which helps us focus our attention wherever we need to.

Intuition and ESP:

Intuitive ability is probably distributed normally in the population, just the way any other ability is—playing the piano or throwing a baseball accurately or running fast.

There are a few people who have a tremendous amount of abilities and a few who have almost none. Most of us are in the big bump in the middle on the bell curve. If we practice, we begin to see improvement, but we can't just sit down at the piano and play a sonata without training, as Mozart did.

Intuition can be very useful in your business life, your personal life and your health. Meditation, presleep suggestion, dreams and visualization can all enhance your ability to focus the mind in an intuitive way.

Helpful: Start now asking your inner self questions...Can I trust this person? Where did I leave my keys? Over time, the answers will get better and more frequent.

Developing our mind's capacity doesn't take much time. People generally begin to recognize results from these exercises after a month or so. Remember: In the Jaznowski study, results showed after only one hour of training!

Source: Charles Thomas Cayce, PhD, president of the organization founded by his grandfather, Edgar Cayce—the Association for Research and Enlightenment, Box 95, Virginia Beach, VA 23451. For information about Cayce's seminars and a tape and workbook course, call 800-428-3588, Monday-Friday, 9 a.m. to 5 p.m.

The Secrets Of Effective Thinking

The world is filled with success stories—very limited success stories...but few of us ever achieve success in even two of the following three life dimensions...

- Successful careers
- Satisfying work
- Rich personal lives

...and genuine "three-dimensional" success is extremely rare.

To learn more about three-dimensional success, I studied 1,200 people—lawyers, artists, blue-collar workers, teachers and students. All had successful careers, and so had achieved at least one-dimensional success.

My psychological tests gauged their success in the other two dimensions—job satisfaction and personal life satisfaction. Results:

- Fifteen percent enjoyed neither their jobs nor their personal lives. While they did a good job for their employers, their lives were empty. Their success was superficial—one dimensional.
- Eighty percent enjoyed their work but not their personal lives—and thus had achieved two-dimensional success. Sad: Most thought their successful, enjoyable careers resulted from a willingness to sacrifice their personal lives. One executive I asked to rate his personal life responded, Personal life? What is personal life?
- Four percent enjoyed both their work and their personal lives. These people had achieved three-dimensional success. They were good at their jobs...and they enjoyed their work...and they had fulfilling personal lives. I call these people Uncommonly Successful People (USPs).

To learn more about three-dimensional success, I subjected these USPs to additional psychological testing. I found that all USPs share three important traits...

- Inner calm that helps them to stay focused.
- Clear goals and a sense of purpose that guide their lives.
- Adventurousness that lets them laugh at

themselves and gives them the courage to take necessary risks.

Effective thinking:

That wasn't all they shared. All USPs also share an uncommon way of thinking—what I call effective thinking.

Effective thinking is not the same as positive thinking, although positive thinking can sometimes be effective. Effective thinking is any thought pattern that leads, directly or indirectly, to personal and professional success...to a rich and satisfying life.

Effective thinking is always result-oriented. There is an effective thought for every situation we encounter.

Note: Most USPs weren't born effective thinkers. They learned to think effectively, just as all of us can. What's needed:

- Finding out exactly what you want in each dimension of your life.
- Committing yourself to achieving those goals.
- Using this standard approach to effective thinking...
- Step one: Take notice. As you hurry through life, pause five or six times a day to take stock of your life.

Am I doing well? Am I moving toward my goal of three-dimensional success? If you can honestly answer these questions in the affirmative, no additional action is needed. Go back to what you were doing. But if the answer is no, you must pause to get back on track.

Uncommon success does not mean vast riches, nor does it mean you must enjoy every moment of your life.

Example: A meeting might not be fun, but enduring it might help land you that next promotion. Viewing such experiences as important steps along your way to uncommon success makes them easier to bear. What you think is entirely under your control. Don't blow minor or temporary annoyances out of proportion.

- Step two: Pause. If while taking notice you discover that you are not heading toward uncommon success, you must pause. This pause may last from just a few seconds to several months, while all the other aspects of your life continue as before. Whatever the duration of the pause, its purpose remains the same—to break your self-defeating mind-set.

Background: All humans approach life using certain mind-sets that have been programmed into our brains by parents, friends and teachers. At times these mind-sets are helpful...but at other times they make life needlessly difficult, interfering with our journey toward uncommon success.

Example: In my seminars, I ask participants if they're familiar with Ivan Pavlov, the Russian scientist who first demonstrated the conditioned response in which an animal's assumptions begin to control his behavior—a dog fed at the ring of a bell begins to salivate as soon as the bell is rung. Invariably, several participants raise their hands. When they do, I ask who told them to do so. Of course, no one did. They assumed they should raise their hands because they had in the past. Life works the same way. We behave in certain ways and think certain thoughts because we've been trained to do so. By pausing, we learn to break old habits and view life in fresh, creative terms.

- Step three: Identify effective thoughts. USPs always take responsibility for their life situation, shifting away from the external to the internal.

Example: A non-USP might think, *Pressures on my job make me nervous.* But a USP in the same situation thinks, *Pressures on my job do not make me nervous. My thoughts about these pressures make me nervous.*

In this way, USPs pinpoint defective thoughts and then identify—or create—effective thoughts with which to replace them.

Aids to effective thinking:

- Understanding anger. All anger stems from fear. Eliminate the fear, and you eliminate the anger. If you become angry, ask yourself what you fear. In most cases, fears are not justified. If you encounter an angry person, don't think, *What a terrible person!* Instead, ask yourself, *What is he/she afraid of?*
- Understanding depression. All of us experience depression at some time or another. Depression helps us cope with sadness and

then provides the impetus to get us back on track. Avoiding sadness or depression actually has a negative effect. The trick is not to spend too much time being depressed.

• Understanding failure. Think of setbacks not as failures, but as learning opportunities. People who have never had setbacks are most likely operating far below their true capabilities.

• Understanding intimacy. No matter how many friends you have, no matter how big and loving your family, each of us, alone, is responsible for him- or herself. This is especially true for uncommonly successful people, who operate at the upper echelons of business and society. Accepting the inevitability of occasional loneliness makes life more pleasant.

• Understanding neediness. People prefer to have all sorts of things—love, a nice house and car, a high-paying job, etc. In reality, they need only the basics—food, shelter and clothing. Realizing that you can make do without all your preferences helps you appreciate what you already have.

Paradox: In many cases, realizing that you don't need something makes it easier to get that something.

• Understanding resentment. Life is not always fair. Rotten people sometimes thrive, and nice people occasionally suffer. But being indignant about this unfortunate fact is useless.

Better way: Try to set right an unfairness when you can. When you cannot, mourn briefly, then get on with your life.

Once you have identified effective thoughts, all that remains is to implement them—by choosing to do so.

• Step four: Choose. The brain is capable of enormous tasks. Unfortunately, most people believe they have little control over their thoughts, and so are enslaved by them. As USPs already know, humans are unique among animals in that they can choose their thoughts.

In many cases, it's possible simply to choose to think of a particular effective thought to focus upon. If conscious choosing fails, however, there is an alternative...

Reverse psychology: Exaggerate whatever defective thought you are thinking until you grow weary of it. Then use this newfound sense of control to choose the effective thought. If you have insomnia, for example, try thinking thoughts that will wake you up. Once you tire of this, choose to think sleep-promoting thoughts.

Source: Gerald Kushel, EdD, Professor Emeritus of mental health counseling at Long Island University and president of the Institute for Effective Thinking. Lecturer and seminar leader, Dr. Kushel is the author of several books, including *Effective Thinking for Uncommon Success*, Amacom, 135 W. 50 St., New York 10020.

How To Work A Room

Working a room—meeting and greeting people you may or may not know in a business or personal situation—takes thoughtful preparation. Strategies:

• Adopt a positive attitude: Enthusiasm and a smile go a long way toward making any event more pleasurable.

It's extremely difficult to mask a negative attitude—even if you plaster on a smile, it will show in your eyes.

• Focus on the benefits of the event: Know what you stand to gain from leaving your home or office and working a room. These can include meeting new people, exchanging conversation and bringing back some business cards to expand your network contacts.

Example: I attend events sponsored by my local Chamber of Commerce and Convention and Visitors Bureau to stay visible and reconnect with my business buddies.

• Plan your self-introduction: The best are energetic and pithy—no more than 10 seconds long. They include your name and a tag line to tell others who you are, why they should remember you and perhaps something to spark the conversation. Your self-introduction should vary depending on the circumstances.

Example: John Doe, the director of Development for Memorial Hospital might use these variations.

• At his daughter's wedding: I'm John Doe, Mary's father.

• At a cocktail party sponsored by the hospital: I'm John Doe from Development.

• At his first meeting of the Development Directors' Association, where everyone attending is a directory of development: I'm John Doe from Memorial.

Don't be afraid to use a little humor. At the first meeting of a stop-smoking seminar try: I'm John Doe, and I consider myself this program's greatest challenge.

During the self-introduction, speak clearly and look people in the eye.

• Check your business cards: Bring enough so you don't have to write your name on a used napkin. If you want to give your card to someone but they haven't asked for it, ask for theirs first. Most people will respond in kind. Important: Do not pass out cards indiscriminately. Cards should be exchanged following a conversation during which rapport has been established. Before handing out your business card, ask yourself if you actually want this person to call you.

• Prepare your small talk: According to movie magnate Sir Alexander Korda, "Small talk should intrigue, delight, amuse, fill up time pleasantly. Given that, anything will do, from dogs to delicatessens. It's a game, like tennis, in which the object is to keep the ball in the air for as long as possible."

Prepare at least three pieces of small talk—a statement, a question or even a pleasant self-revelation. Topics: A local sports team, the organization for which you are meeting...yes, even the weather.

The old advice about avoiding controversial subjects like religion and politics should be heeded.

• Remember eye contact and smile: A roving eye gives the impression of an insincere, hand-pumping Mr. Sleaze. Too much eye contact may constitute glaring—and could be considered rude. In the US, a comfortable range is looking for seven seconds, and then looking away for the same amount of time.

If you look for more than seven seconds the "looking" may become a glare. "Looking away" may indicate a search for better opportunities.

• Practice your handshake: A handshake is the business greeting in America. Make sure yours is not...

• Too limp...they'll think that you're spineless.

• Knuckle breaker...they'll see it as a macho power player.

• Finger squeeze...they'll think you're prissy because your don't want to touch their whole hand.

• Covered handshake...they might be turned off if you put your left hand over the hands clasped in a handshake.

Source: Susan RoAne, keynote speaker and founder of The RoAne Group, 14 Wilder St., #100, San Francisco 94131. 415-239-2224. She is also the author of *How To Work a Room*, Warner Books, 666 Fifth Ave., New York 10103.

Secrets Of Unlimited Power: How To Use It In Your Personal Life... In Your Professional Life

Most of us would like to change many things about our lives. And most of us are able to get the results we want...some of the time.

But few people know how to achieve consistent results on an ongoing basis.

And even fewer people know how to make changes last.

Reading books and listening to motivational tapes can give you valuable information. But that information is useless unless you put it into practice...by changing your limiting beliefs and conditioned habits. Added trap: There's a big difference between knowing what to do...and doing what you know.

Tools for lasting change:

Powerful, consistent change requires three steps...

• Raise your standards: You need to believe that what you used to do is no longer acceptable. Your brain must register the conviction that change is a must, not a should.

• Change your beliefs: If you say, I want to lose weight, but on a gut level you don't believe you can, you're setting yourself up for sabotage. Before you can achieve something, you must believe it is possible.

• Enhance your strategies: You must come up with better strategies than you've been using to get the job done. It doesn't matter how enthusiastic and disciplined you are... how many affirmations you repeat. If your goal is to see the sunset, and you keep running east, you'll wind up disappointed.

One definition of insanity is doing the same thing again and again...and expecting different results.

• Key success strategy: Find role models—people who are consistently producing the results you want. Find out what they believe... what strategies they use...and copy them.

A good role model can save you months, even years, of trial and error.

• Example: Stu Mittleman broke a world's record by running 1,000 miles in 11 days. He slept just three hours a night and covered 84 miles per day...and ended in better condition than when he started. Stu Mittleman wasn't lucky. He applied the principles of personal power.

Mittleman trained physically for years—but one circumstance was especially powerful. Before undertaking the run, he spent time with a group of South America Indians who, as part of a celebration, ran 75 miles a day for fun. That experience transformed Mittleman's beliefs. He came to see that his goal of breaking the world's record was possible.

When I wanted to lose weight, I in turn used Mittleman as a role model. He had trained his metabolism to burn fat instead of carbohydrates so that his body functioned better, not harder, I copied his strategy and got into excellent physical shape.

Don't look for one perfect role model—there is no such person. Find a group of models. Look around for someone who has lifted himself out of depression...someone else who has turned her financial situation around...or found the mate of her dreams... then find out the beliefs and strategies that make these people effective. Apply those tools to your own life. And when you get results, share them with other people.

Mastering your emotions:

There are two powerful strategies you can put to use right now to change your emotional state...

• Change your focus: If you wanted to make yourself depressed, could you do it? Of course you could, easily—simply by thinking about a painful moment from your past...or something that you're worried might happen that hasn't happened. You probably do this already!

Most people would not see an awful movie a second time...yet they play the same bad memories, or worries about the future, over and over in their heads.

You can also change your focus in a positive direction. Remember a happy moment from your childhood...think of a cherished goal and imagine it already achieved.

What we focus on is controlled by the questions we ask ourselves.

Thinking is nothing but a process of asking and answering questions.

If you ask yourself awful questions, you'll get awful answers. And if you keep asking yourself the same questions, you'll continue to look at life in the same way.

If your usual questions are, How come this always happens to me? Why do people do this to me? Why can't I turn my life around? How come I can never lose weight? Your brain will answer, Because you're a jerk! You'll feel frustrated, angry, fearful, even humiliated on a regular basis. You will continue to see life as a series of events beyond your control.

To change your life, ask better-quality questions.

Example: How can I lose weight now—and enjoy the process? Your brain will say, Here's something you can try!...and if it's something you enjoy, you'll keep doing it.

Take advantage of the body's power over the brain. Simply trying to talk yourself into a better mood—by repeating affirmations, for example—is not effective by itself.

• What works: Change your physical actions. Depressed people have typical physical characteristics...slumped posture, downcast head and eyes, shallow breathing, slack facial muscles. By changing your gestures and facial expressions, you can instantly change the way you feel.

The quality of your life is the quality of your movement.

Emotion is created by motion.

Don't just repeat positive words. Breathe deeply and easily, lift your head, put on a silly grin. Your body will pass the message on to your brain, and your mood will improve.

If you're feeling down while sitting on an airplane, but are near a lively, enthusiastic person...copy his gestures...and begin to feel what he/she feels. You, too, can experiment with the incredible power of the body to enable you to experience new emotions.

Better relationships:

One very simple principle has the power to instantly transform your relationships. Go into every relationship as a giver, not a taker.

Most people are looking for someone to make them feel good. They walk in with demands, and if the other person has different demands, they reluctantly negotiate. The more you focus on giving to others, the more they'll want to give back to you—and the more you'll end up getting!

This attitude will improve not only your personal life, but your business life as well. Business is relationships, and every successful professional knows this.

• Example: The Home Depot chain of stores. In less than 10 years this company saw its stock rise 16,000%. It came to dominate the home-improvement industry, and continues to thrive despite the recession.

At Home Depot, salespeople develop relationships with their customers. This is drilled into all Home Depot salespeople. They learn customers' names...become familiar with their home-improvement problems...work with them on solutions. Result: People gravitate to their stores.

Mastering finances:

Most people run into trouble managing their finances—not because they don't have enough money, but because they have limiting beliefs about money. To improve your financial status, you must first change what money means to you.

Whether you make $2,000 per month or $1 million a year, it is within your power to develop a financial plan...one that will ultimately enable you to live a comfortable lifestyle without having to work unless you want to.

But that plan will not succeed if you have mixed emotions about what excess money means. It you unconsciously link money to pain, you will be sabotaging your efforts.

You may believe that money equals greed ...if I have more, somebody else has less...if I have lots of money, I won't be spiritual. If you are living with these false associations, you won't put real energy into your financial plan. You'll continue to make just enough to meet your basic needs, but not enough to obtain your real desires.

Exercise: Write *Excess Money* at the top of a piece of paper, and draw a line down the middle. On the left side, list your positive associations with money, on the right your negative associations.

Review this list to uncover your preconceptions about money. This is a good opportunity to reevaluate your beliefs and change your conditioned money habits according to your current needs.

Conquering fear:

Even when we know what we want and have a plan to achieve it, many of us stop ourselves from putting that plan into action.

Major barrier: Fear. And the most common fear is fear of failure. Fear will no longer stop you when you recognize this fundamental principle: There are no failures—only outcomes.

Success is the result of good judgment. Good judgment is the result of experience. And experience is often the result of bad judgment.

You can be sure that people who are more successful than other people got that way because they failed more than other people.

Failing—and learning from those failures and the failures of others—teaches us what works and doesn't work. The more areas in which you've failed—and learned from those failures—the greater your opportunities for successes.

Source: Entrepreneur and human-development trainer Anthony Robbins, author of *Awaken the Giant Within,* just published by Summit Books, 1230 Ave. of the Americas, New York 10020. His previous book, *Unlimited Power,* sold over a million copies and has been translated into 11 languages.

How To Uncomplicate Your Life...How To Improve It Significantly

The complaint I most often hear from friends and clients alike as a time-management and organization consultant is, *I just don't seem to have time for myself these days.*

But most of us don't really lack time, no matter how busy we are. Lack of time is a symptom. Real problems: Unclear priorities and lack of simple systems for dealing with everyday life.

Solution: Streamlining. Use streamlining to develop and maintain uncomplicated systems wherever life is driving you crazy—from your sock drawer to your social calendar.

Benefits: More time to do what you really want to do, improved relationships with people who really matter, increased focus on meaningful living, a sense of control. In my five-step plan for uncomplicated living, the first step is often the hardest, while the second is most important.

Adjust your attitude:

- Make a commitment to change: Streamlining is a change, so you must be willing to change. Most common obstacle: Fear of letting go of habits, possessions and people that are no longer relevant to your life.
- Take control of problems rather than letting them control you. Most common obstacles: An addiction to worrying—an addiction to feeling like a victim. Helpful: Put the same energy into solving problems that you would normally put into worrying...
- Resolve to be productive.
- Concentrate on one problem at a time.
- Take responsibility for your problems, but avoid thinking you should or must do everything yourself.
- When searching for solutions, ask others for advice. Find professional help when necessary. An accountant, a consultant, a teacher, a therapist.
- Learn to let go and move on from problems that are not within your power to solve.
- Control perfectionism: Striving for perfection can be counterproductive and self-sabotaging. Warning signs: Trouble delegating, frequent turnover among assistants—often due to unrealistic demands and expectations...inability to finish tasks quickly and simply. Most common obstacle: Failure to accept excellence in lieu of perfection. Helpful: Be willing to lower your standards. Often "good" is good enough.

Example: It's better to have a relatively clean house than to put off any cleaning until you have time to make it immaculate. Focus on results, not on how they are achieved or whether they are done your way.

- Stop procrastinating: Delay creates problems. Most common obstacle: Excuse-making, blaming others for why you're not doing what needs to be done, waiting for the "right time." Helpful:
- Divide large projects into manageable pieces. Do the hardest part first.
- Set deadlines and trick yourself into action if necessary.
- Reward yourself when you meet your deadlines.
- If you are putting off doing something you really hate or don't know how to do, hire someone to do it for you.

Prioritize and plan:

- Identify your life mission, goals and priorities. On the first page of a new loose-leaf notebook, briefly describe your purpose in life. What would you most like to be remembered for?

List your goals—one per page—everything from buying a house in the country to losing 20 pounds. People who write down their goals are far more likely to achieve them. Give each goal a realistic deadline, whether it's one week or five years. Next, make a "To Do" list of all of your unfinished business and projects: Take an exercise class...clean out the attic.

Review your mission, goals and list to determine project categories: Career, House, Finances, Self-Improvement, etc. Transfer "To Do" items to the appropriate category page, and prioritize each with a number.

- Plan and schedule regularly. Transfer errands and daily obligations to your calendar.

Then schedule time for work on your top-priority projects, including time for yourself. Helpful:

• Devote specific, uninterrupted periods to one project at a time, and finish what you start.

• Be realistic about the amount of time projects take. Use your calendar to schedule time for bill-paying, chores, volunteering, play.

• Build in some flexibility for the unexpected, but say no to unreasonable demands or invitations that don't interest you.

• Practice preventive maintenance.

Examples: Schedule regular checkups for your family, teeth, cars, etc.

• Continue to review your goals, priorities and schedule weekly. Aim: Increased awareness of what's really important to you...motivation to simplify and eliminate what isn't. Are you really spending more hours maintaining a finicky foreign car than reading to your children?

Eliminate the extraneous:

• Prioritize the people in your life. Time spent with people you don't care about means less time for those who are important to you. Clarify your priorities and learn to say no. Helpful: Improved communication skills can minimize time spent explaining, arguing, placating, etc.

• Reevaluate your possessions. Many people spend more time taking care of their "stuff" than they do taking care of themselves. Get rid of things you don't use or that no longer suit your lifestyle. Be ruthless.

Key: Separate need from want. You may want a gourmet popcorn popper, but you don't actually need it. Make an attempt to let go of the things that have accumulated from your "past lives."

Helpful: Give things away, right away. Someone else *does* need your extra china.

• Avoid fads, sales and shopping from habit.

• Rent rather than own equipment you seldom use.

• Don't store stuff in the garage!

• Evaluate what you do need to function efficiently.

Example: Keep scissors in the desk and in the kitchen.

Organize what's left:

• Establish a convenient place for everything: Tackle each area once and for all... kitchen, workspace, closets.

Stick to a system:

• Maintain systems at home and at the office: For ongoing efficiency and serenity, devise a system for handling the mail, keys, eyeglasses, shopping, cooking, filing, laundry, bills, etc. My books offer suggestions for organizational systems of every kind. Enjoy the newfound time and focused productivity of your streamlined life.

Source: Stephanie Culp, whose firm, The Organization, in Oconomowoc, WI, helps individuals and businesses develop systems to get—and stay—organized. Her latest book is *Streamlining Your Life: A Five-Point Plan for Uncomplicated Living*, Writer's Digest Books, 1507 Dana Ave., Cincinnati 45207. 800-543-4644 (in OH, 800-551-0884).

Chutzpah Lessons From Alan Dershowitz

Probably no one knows more about chutzpah than the undefeated grand master of the art, Alan Dershowitz. His reputation as Chutzpah champion of the American legal system has been spread by his spirited defenses in famous cases like Klaus von Bulow, Leona Helmsley, Rabbi Meir Kahane, Jonathan Pollard and Jim Bakker.

We asked Dershowitz, author of his best-selling book *Chutzpah*, to share his expertise...

What is chutzpah?

A polite word for it would be nerve. Chutzpah is not something you're born with...it's an acquired characteristic.

Chutzpah is a survival technique. Its goal is to level the playing field—when you are confronting someone who is more powerful than you in a situation.

Where does the word come from?

Nobody knows for sure. It's neither Yiddish nor Hebrew in origin, but is probably Aramaic, going back thousands of years. Today, its Yiddish and Hebrew meanings are different. In Yiddish it's more positive—a kind of assertiveness, a boldness, an aggressiveness. In Hebrew the meaning is more negative—arrogance and pushiness. The word has always had both positive and negative connotations, but I use it in the positive sense.

What is the value of chutzpah?

Chutzpah helps underdogs fight against bullies—people who have more power. It should never be used in a bullying way.

I believe that the reason chutzpah is considered a Jewish quality is that Jews, for centuries, have always been on the bottom trying to fight their way up.

Is chutzpah just for Jews?

Absolutely not! You don't have to be Jewish to have chutzpah. In fact, today, in America, chutzpah is needed, and used, by several less-advantaged groups—women, Asian Americans, African Americans, Hispanic Americans, etc.

You mean that any American can aspire to have chutzpah?

I have the sense that chutzpah is now the quintessential American characteristic. If you ask a native French person what Americans are like, they say we are too pushy—too aggressive...although they don't use the word chutzpah.

Mark Twain, who was able to put everybody down using his incredible wit, was one of the great chutzpahniks in history.

What's a chutzpahnik?

A chutzapahnik is one who possesses the quality of chutzpah.

Judge Wapner from TV's *People's Court* is the epitome of lack of chutzpah—quiet and soft-spoken. He told me that he was raised believing that chutzpah was negative and shouldn't be used. After reading my book, he realized that there was a positive meaning for it, and now he would be happy to call himself a chutzpahnik.

How do I develop chutzpah if I haven't got it?

The first rule of chutzpah is to constructively challenge authority. You have to think of yourself as equal to anybody else. You have to say over and over again in your head, I'm just as good as they are.

Also important: Understanding that everybody has different talents, techniques and weapons in this contest of life...and knowing where your special strengths lie. The next time someone looks at you with an aloof, smug look—because he's a foot taller than you, a million dollars richer than you, etc.—you can break through that veneer using your superior talent. That's chutzpah. That's what you have to practice.

To use chutzpah, you have to go against character. If someone is expecting you to raise your voice, for example, lower your voice.

One of the greatest acts of chutzpah of all time was author/Holocaust survivor Elie Wiesel, telling President Reagan not to go to Bitberg. He whispered to the point where Reagan had to lean over so he could hear what he was saying. Wiesel, a powerless little man, without an army, without a constituency, without a bank account, lectured the President of the United States on the immorality of Bitberg and of going to a cemetery where the victims of the Storm Troopers were buried.

Can chutzpah be misused?

Definitely. It's often misused. I think people use it promiscuously, as a way of dealing with everything.

You shouldn't use it with working-class people—taxi drivers, waiters, etc. And it should never, ever be used in your personal life. It's too potent a weapon to be used against a loved one. It's a contest. There's a winner and a loser. In love, there should always be a tie.

I have a friend who was married to a woman whom he loved very much for many, many years. But he dealt with everything by using chutzpah—by putting her down, by being funnier than she. My friend was a wonderful date, but a terrible husband. He had all the clever put-downs and the wonderful things that would have kept his wife laughing all the time—on a date. But you can't laugh 24 hours a day. There comes a time you have to have serious, direct discussions.

Can you be shy and still develop chutzpah?

Absolutely. You can develop a public personality that is very aggressive. I'm very shy at parties. I find it hard to begin a conversation with someone unless I'm spoken to first. But I am very successful using my chutzpah in my professional life.

Where did you learn chutzpah?

From my mother. But I never, never use it in relation to my mother! I learned it from watching my mother use it on other people.

My mother is a brilliant woman. I've always said, had my mother lived 30 years later, she probably would have been the first woman on the Supreme Court. She is almost 80 years old, and to this day, she has the quickest repartee of anybody I know. She could beat Jackie Mason and Alan King to the punch line every time.

Do you think that chutzpah has a future?

Without a question. My book has been very successful. I've been getting letters from people all over the country. It was even reviewed by the *Korean Times!* The sky's the limit.

Source: Renowned attorney Alan Dershowitz, Harvard Law School professor and author of *Chutzpah*, Little, Brown and Co., 205 Lexington Ave., New York 10016.

Dr. Norman Vincent Peale: How I Think Positively In These Increasingly Negative Times

In very troubling times, my mail gets very heavy...and it's quite heavy right now. So many people are writing for help dealing with their despair, anger and resentment.

In my 92 years, I've learned that, although pain is difficult to live through, the tougher the experience the more you learn and the stronger you become.

Prosperity follows adversity:

I lived through hard times during the decade of The Great Depression. All succeeding economic problems have been Sunday School picnics compared with that. We had long, long soup lines...and I saw formerly affluent people waiting in those lines for their day's rations.

But when I think about that Depression and other times of financial trouble in our country's history, I recall that every one was followed by a period of prosperity. And the prosperous periods always lasted much longer than the bad times.

So when adversity strikes, my message is: Even this will pass...and better days than we have ever experienced will come.

The question that follows naturally for most people is: *Can we live it out?* Well, you can if you have the will to survive...and if you share the burden with the people you love. Sharing the burden lightens the load.

There are too many cases of people who, feeling scared or frustrated after they suffer a tremendous loss, fall apart—or worse.

But no matter how bleak things may seem, we all have options. Instead of "blowing our brains out"...we can blow them up. And by that I mean using our intelligence to work our way out of our predicaments. We can use our brains to create.

I remember meeting a once-successful inventor during the 1930s. Fred told me he was unemployed and that, at the age of 42, nobody wanted to hire him because he was over the hill. But he had a new idea and plenty of time on his hands.

He left that meeting thinking that better days were coming...and they were. Fred perfected his invention. It succeeded and he became prosperous. Had it not been for adversity, Fred never would have found the opportunity to pursue his complex idea.

Moving past the down times:

Many people find it hard to believe that I go through down times, too. When I feel depressed, I give into it...for a while.

Like the sick sort of pleasure you get from jamming an aching tooth with your tongue, I wallow in my depression. But just as with a toothache, I won't let it hurt for too long before I do something about it.

To force myself to get out of the funk, I talk to myself, saying: You're a phony. You've written books and preached the gospel on the Power of Positive Thinking...now get with it and get out of the funk.

The toughest lectures I've ever heard are the ones I give myself. I always bow to my stronger self and I always get past the blue times.

William James, the father of American psychology, invented the *As If* principle. When you're feeling down...act *As If* you feel good. By acting it, you become it.

I employ the *As If* principle before every speech I make because I always become terrified right before it's time for me to go on. I talk to myself, saying I'm not afraid. I've done this many times before. I can do it because I've done it. So get out there. Then I find myself walking on stage, all of my fears behind me.

The great mistake:

The big mistake people in the United States have made is getting too used to prosperity. We had so much money after World War II that anything we did worked.

Now, 45 years later, we've gotten soft from generation after generation of people who never had to think to achieve. Trapped in those indulgent practices, we've forgotten how to actually deal with problems.

A woman I met told me she used to be the meanest woman in South Carolina. She said she was mean because she was poor, raised in poverty and married into poverty. She and her husband hated anybody who had anything.

But when I met her, they had their own business, a nice home and had managed to put three children through expensive colleges. Their secret: They had worked their way out of poverty by dropping their hate, which was an obstacle to clear thinking. Hate had shut off their minds.

By opening your mind, you can think your way out of just about anything. Talk the problems through...with knowledgeable friends. That's one of the real reasons we have friends. Talk. And talk. And let adversity be your teacher and your inspiration for positive change.

Source: Norman Vincent Peale, DD. His latest book is *The Power of Positive Living*, Doubleday, 666 Fifth Ave., New York 10103. His classic, *The Power of Positive Thinking*, has sold more than 15 million copies—so far.

Clear Communication Made Simple

Assume that the next message you send will be misunderstood. Then ask yourself, How can I convey this message to ensure that I will be understood? This process will help you communicate more thoughtfully and effectively...and you'll examine yourself first when you don't get your desired results.

Source: *Smart Moves* by Sam Deep and Lyle Sussman, Addison-Wesley, Route 128, Reading, MA 01867.

Late-Night Thoughts

Keep a notepad and pen with a built-in light by your bedside for when you think of a great idea in the middle of the night. Other key places for scratch pads: In the kitchen and the car.

Source: *Super Memory: A Quick-Action Program for Memory Improvement* by Douglas J. Hermann, PhD, Rodale Press, 33 E. Minor St., Emmaus, PA 18098.

How To Get Over Shyness

Most people think of shyness as a minor problem...but many people are so shy that they don't fully live their lives. By hiding from interactions that make them uncomfortable, they become increasingly lonely and unhappy.

People who are shy suffer from low self-esteem. Because they have no reserve of self-confidence, they see any rejection or social slip—no matter how small—as an indictment of their worth as a person. Over time, these rejections set the stage for a lifetime of shyness.

The truth about shyness:

- Myth: That far more women than men are shy. Truth: At least as many men—possibly more—say they are shy.
- Myth: That shy people are born shy. Truth: Many shy people report they weren't shy at all until adolescence. At that point, they became self-conscious—often about their looks—and had problems establishing their identity.
- Myth: That shy people are aloof and unfriendly. Truth: Most shy people actually crave companionship.

• Myth: That loners are shy. Truth: People can be reclusive without being shy. They simply choose to be alone.

How to overcome shyness:

• Make a list of social interactions that are difficult for you. Start with the easiest.

Example: Asking a clerk at the store if there is a shirt in your size.

Continue working on your list until you come to the interaction that you find the most difficult.

Example: Going to a business party where you don't know anyone.

• Take small steps to overcome the problems on your list. Start with the first—the easiest.

Example: If you're shy with store clerks, practice going into stores and asking simple questions: What time do you close? Does this come in red? Is this item on sale?

Concentrate on short interactions. That way, if you're overcome by shyness, you can back off quickly...and try again and again.

Goal: After repeated practice, you will be able to perform this interaction without feeling shy.

• Move on to the next challenge. Achieving each step will build self-confidence. Don't push yourself. If you try to take on too much too soon, you risk negative reinforcement.

Example: A person tries to overcome his/her shyness by forcing himself to go to a party...has a horrible time...and is very reluctant to try again.

Also helpful:

• Join a therapy group for shy people. This is one of the best treatments because you get support of others and have a laboratory in which you can take risks in a supportive environment.

• Make a list of major accomplishments. Pull it out and review it just before you go into a social situation. This will defuse your shyness by reminding you of the things you are good at.

• Give yourself permission to be shy in some situations. By accepting your shyness under some circumstances, you decrease your anxiety and you're more likely to enjoy yourself.

Helpful self-statement: I'm going to be shy at dinner tonight...and it's okay.

• Don't assume that other are judging you. Tell yourself that you refuse to give them the power to do so.

Helpful self-statement: I'm going to be myself, no matter what.

• Focus on others. Listen carefully and intently to what they're saying. It's impossible to be self-conscious while you're concentrating on someone else.

Source: Psychologist Christopher J. McCullough, PhD, author of *Managing Your Anxiety*, Jeremy P. Tarcher, Inc., 5858 Wilshire Blvd., Los Angeles 90036.

Words To Use To Protect Your Health. Words? Yes...Words!

With medical costs rising astronomically and no relief in sight, it's increasingly important for Americans to reduce their dependence on outside experts—and take at least some control of their own health care.

One of the best tools for doing so is also one of the most basic—language.

The language of health:

There are many ways that language can be used to affect our health—both for good and bad. Included:

• Messages that we give ourselves: Whether we're aware of it or not, most of us talk to ourselves continuously.

Pessimistic, helpless messages (I feel terrible, and there's not a thing I can do about it) tell the body to give up.

Positive message (I can stand this discomfort, and I will feel good again) help the body to fight illness.

• How we respond to others: Chronic exposure to hostility is a risk factor in many diseases—and the primary factory in heart disease. We can't always avoid hostility and conflict, but we can learn to use language to deflect a verbal attack and spare ourselves mental and physical strain (see below).

• Metaphors we use: Visualization can be an

effective healing tool in dealing with illness.

Example: Patients are advised to imagine the disease as an army of enemy invaders, and the immune system as a good army destroying the invading forces.

But warlike images are only helpful to people comfortable with military themes. For others, violent imagery may work against healing by equating illness with violence and slaughter.

As an alternative, focus on fixing rather than killing.

Example: Think of your immune system as a gardening crew pulling up weeds...or a road crew fixing potholes in the street...or a piano tuner restoring harmony to an out-of-tune instrument.

• Doctor/patient relationships: When doctors and patients don't communicate well with each other, patients wind up with poor health care.

A pain-phobic society:

What we tell ourselves about pain has a profound impact on our well-being. TV commercials bombard us with the notion that pain is terrible—that no one should ever hurt even a little. But pain is a normal part of life.

That doesn't mean that discomfort should be ignored. If running makes your shins hurt, rest...don't push on for another mile.

Pain alerts us to our limitations, and chronic discomfort may be an indicator of a physical condition that requires medical attention.

People who panic every time they're in pain end up spending a lot of money needlessly on doctors and drugs, without appreciable benefits. In fact, their fears—and the drugs' side effects—may make them feel even worse.

Coping with pain:

If you're plagued with chronic or acute pain, instead of telling yourself, I can't bear this, substitute the thought, I can stand this pain for 15 minutes.

Then spend 15 minutes doing something you enjoy—gardening, playing music, absorbing yourself in a challenging project at work. At the end of 15 minutes, you're likely to find that the pain is gone.

If not, say, I can stand this pain for another 15 minutes. You'll notice that the pain ebbs and flows. This attitude enables you to go on with your life, instead of focusing your life around the pain.

Another way to cope with pain is to keep a journal. Describe what the pain feels like and what sets it off. Give it a name. Compare it with something else that has a similar distinguishing feature.

Example: My pain is like an earthquake—sudden and unpredictable.

As you start to define your pain and give it boundaries, you will see it less as an overwhelming force that's controlling you, and more as an object...which you can control.

Deflecting attack:

We can relieve ourselves of a great deal of stress by learning not to get hooked into other people's hostility.

Verbal attacks aren't always easy to recognize. Someone can be smiling, or using words like sweetheart and darling, and still be sending a hostile message. Key: Verbal hostility has a characteristic melody in which many words are emphatically stressed.

Examples: Why do you always think only of yourself? Or: I'm only thinking about what's best for you.

There are several ways to deflect verbal hostility...

• Remember that nobody can fight alone. If you refuse to fight, even the most hostile verbal attacker will give up.

• When in doubt about how to handle an attack, try the boring baroque defense. Treat the attack as if it were a serious rational question or statement, and talk the other person into a coma.

The idea is to answer in such excruciating detail that the attacker has no fun at all. Example:

Attacker: Why can't you ever stick to your diet?

Boring baroque defense: You know, that's an interesting question. I think it has to do with when I was a kid in Wisconsin, and our family...no maybe it was when we were living in Illinois. Yes, it must be Illinois, because that's when my uncle was working for the Post Office, and...

This technique won't work if you let sarcasm creep into your voice. You must keep your tone serious.

How to talk to doctors:

It's easy to become resentful when dealing with doctors, especially if the doctor is brusque, uses jargon or acts condescending. Unfortunately, in our society, inequality is built into the doctor-patient relationship.

Acting resentful, however, will not help you achieve your health goals. The doctor is as trapped in the system as you are, and communicates in doctor-speak because he/she has been taught to.

Your doctor is a channel through which you get access to medicine, surgery and other treatments that affect your health. Annoying your doctor makes about as much sense as annoying your computer or arguing with a traffic light.

To get what you need, learn to interact with your doctor effectively...

• Before your appointment, make a list of things you want the doctor to know and any questions you need answered. Don't leave the meeting until those subjects have been covered to your satisfaction—even if you have to repeat your questions several times.

• Remember that a meeting with a doctor is not a social conversation. Don't worry about being entertaining or bouncing the conversational ball back and forth.

• Keep each question or statement to 18 seconds at most. Research shows that's the longest period of time doctors allow patients to talk before interrupting them.

• Don't try to talk like a doctor. If you've been feeling short of breath, say so—don't say you have dyspnea. Using medical jargon may be taken as a challenge—the doctor may try to top you by using even more technical language, and you won't get your questions answered.

Your goal is not to impress the doctor, it's to get the information and care that you need.

Source: Linguist Suzette Haden Elgin, PhD, who teaches communications skills to health-care professionals nationwide. She is the author of a series of books on verbal self-defense, most recently *Staying Well with the Gentle Art of Verbal Self-Defense*, Prentice Hall Business and Professional Publishing, Route 9W, Englewood Cliffs, NJ 07632.

Time...Precious Time How To Use It Very Wisely

I am a very organized person. As a result, I get more things done with less effort. And I make fewer mistakes.

When I work on a project, I start early and do it well. When I've finished, I never say to myself, I could have done it better if I'd had more time. I know it's the best I was able to do...and I move on to the next project.

My secret—the master list:

We're overwhelmed with so much information, our circuits are overloaded. We're overstimulated. Everybody is screaming for our immediate attention. Everything has become urgent.

Our projects are hanging in limbo, half done, and we can't decide what to do first. Most mistakes are self-inflicted, the result of negligence, improper planning or procedure.

To avoid these pitfalls that erode your precious time, write down all your unfinished work on a Master List.

You make lists all the time—grocery lists, lists of party guests, etc. If you make a Master List of all your current and pending projects, you'll find that it's the engine that makes your day run.

People jot down their chores, their projects, phone calls they have to return on little slips of paper. Result: They have 25 notes tacked to their office walls or sitting in piles on their desks.

Consolidate those notes onto one page, one that your can scan from top to bottom.

With that Master List, you know what you have to do and the time frame in which you have to do it. Without it, you're frantically trying to remember what needs to be done next.

The Master List is an inventory of all your unfinished work and ongoing projects. Go through all your papers. Ask yourself: Is there any work that must be done by me—a phone call...a letter or report? Write it on your Master list.

If it concerns someone else, send it on. If it's not important, get rid of it.

The simple act of writing things down on

your Master List gives you freedom—nothing will slip through the cracks, nothing will sneak up behind you and hit you on the back of the head. The more you write down, the less you have to remember.

Make a file folder for each project, and as soon as you make a note on that project, or get an idea concerning it, file it with the rest so that every folder is current and contains everything you need to know—every scrap of information about the project.

Make an appointment with yourself:

Use your calendar to schedule appointments with yourself to complete work.

If you need to meet with a person face-to-face, you schedule an appointment. If you have work to do for that same person, why not block out an hour on your calendar and treat it just like that face-to-face meeting? Hold all calls. Close the door. Allow absolutely no interruptions.

Plan for interruptions:

I anticipate emergencies. I don't know what they'll be, but I expect them. I do this by being ahead in my work, not behind.

There are two ways you can go through life. One is by figuring that everything will go as expected. When something unexpected happens, it takes you by surprise. The other is by figuring that anything that can go wrong will go wrong.

Expect unexpected detours and distractions, so you're not thrown for a loop when they do pop up.

Deal with the disorganized:

Many of the people I work with are disorganized. Therefore, I have to be even more organized in my dealings with them—otherwise I'll never get anything done.

If you give an assignment to someone, you must assume that they are not going to do it on time. You have to take it on yourself to follow up with them.

I try to maintain control and don't let the deadline slip through my fingers. That's where the Master List comes in again. Note the deadline on your Master List, since it's your responsibility to make sure the assigned work gets done.

When you're dealing with people who are chronically late to meetings and appointments, allow 50% more time and call to confirm how late they are running. Don't schedule appointments back-to-back. Give yourself a cushion between meetings...otherwise you're asking for trouble.

As a general rule, projects will take more time than you expect them to. If you need an hour, schedule an hour and a half.

Stay on top of your work. Expect and anticipate disorganization and lateness from others and you will take the nasty surprises out of your business day. Result: You'll complete twice as much work, in half the time.

Source: Jeffrey J. Mayer, one of the country's leading authorities on time-management and founder of the consulting firm Mayer Enterprises, 50 E. Bellevue Place, Suite 305, Chicago 60611. Its clients include Ameritech, Commonwealth Edison, Encyclopædia Brittanica, Sears Roebuck, Navistar and First National Bank of Chicago. He is the author of *If You Haven't Got the Time To Do It Right, When Will You Find the Time To Do It Over?* Fireside Books, 1230 Ave. of the Americas, New York 10020.

The Most Important Contributor To A Successful Life Is Self-Discipline

Without discipline, we can't improve ourselves or solve problems or be competent or delay gratification or assume responsibility.

Without discipline we cannot find reality and truth...we never evolve from children into productive adults.

Yet discipline is a trait that's in short supply these days, especially among young people.

To find why this is so—and what we can do about it—we asked the best-selling author of *The Road Less Traveled...*

Why is discipline so powerful?

Most people think that the point of life is to be happy. But life is really about self-improvement. We're not born perfect. It's our job to make ourselves as good as we can be.

As Benjamin Franklin once said, those things that hurt, instruct. Yet the concept that life can be difficult is alien to most people.

The only way we can improve ourselves is through discipline. Without it, we can't solve any problems. With some discipline, we can solve some problems. But with total discipline, we can solve all of our problems. Discipline makes us competent.

I used to tell my patients that psychotherapy is not about happiness, it's about personal power and competence. If you get hooked into therapy and go the whole route, I can't guarantee you'll leave one bit happier. But you will leave more competent.

The problem with competence is that there's a vacuum of it in the world. So as soon as people become more competent, either God or life gives them bigger problems to deal with.

There is, however, a certain kind of joy that comes with knowing you're worrying about the big problems and that you're no longer getting bent out of shape about the little ones.

How can people determine which problems are truly important?

Think about them. Most people don't. I spend the first hour of each day sitting in my bedroom thinking about my priorities. What should I be working on now? What can be put off until later?

Important problems are ones that affect all of us.

Example: I work with many organizations, businesses and agencies on how to better integrate psychiatry, religion and spirituality. That's a big problem.

It's impossible to think about big problems if you're spending your time worrying about what you're going to watch on TV or what you're going to say to someone. Spending time on that kind of problem is a waste of energy.

Isn't it true that some people think about the little problems to put off working on the important ones?

This relates to one of the main issues of discipline—delayed gratification.

This means doing the things in life that are unpleasant before those that are enjoyable. If you do what you have to do first, you'll be free to enjoy yourself later.

Most people—and I'm not just talking about children—dash to what they want to do, and then feel terrible trying to get around to what they have to do.

Why do so many people, especially young people, have so much trouble delaying gratification?

Gratification is something that must be learned. We rejoice in the spontaneity of small children. But in truth, children are all born liars, cheats, thieves and manipulators who don't know how to delay gratification.

It's hardly remarkable that many of them grow up to be adult liars, cheats, thieves and manipulators. What's even harder to explain—but what life is all about—is that some children grow up to be disciplined, God-fearing and honest.

There are many reasons why people grow up undisciplined. Most importantly, many children lack good parenting. Parents are role models. And kids with undisciplined parents have a much harder time growing up to be disciplined.

Discipline also suffers from an image problem in our culture. We think of discipline as something that's imposed by someone else rather than as a form of self-love.

Learning discipline requires real effort. But this is what it takes for people to find the most joy and lead the most productive lives. Delaying gratification means, ultimately, enjoying things more.

Does a person have to be completely unselfish to be able to accept discipline?

There's no such thing as an unselfish person. I myself am totally selfish. Strictly speaking, I've never done a thing for anyone else.

When I water my flowers I don't say, Look, flowers, what I'm doing for you...you ought to be grateful. I do it because I like pretty flowers. When I extend myself for my children, it's because I want to have an image of myself as a good father.

You could look at monks and nuns and think how unselfish they are. But they've decided that this is the best way to personal joy.

We need to distinguish between the path of smart selfishness and that of stupid selfishness. Stupid selfishness is trying to avoid all pain and all problems, while smart selfishness is learning the difference between unnecessary pain and that which is an inherent part of life.

Get rid of the unnecessary pain, but meet the necessary pain head on. Work it through and learn from it.

In what ways do people fail to accept discipline?

People often look to someone else to solve their problems. This is a natural tendency. Being disciplined requires assuming responsibility. And that means saying, This is my problem. You can't solve a problem until you admit that you own it.

Example: Three years ago, I had a sharp disagreement with my 18-year-old son. I raked him over the coals. The next morning I found an angry letter from him outside my door. I thought about it and decided he was right. So I apologized. It wasn't easy for me, but it was very healing for my son to have his father apologize.

Lesson: You can't apologize unless you accept responsibility for being at fault.

To take responsibility, you have to value yourself. And you have to have role models. Kids who don't assume responsibility undoubtedly have parents who won't either.

In the example with my son, one of the beauties of my apology was not just that it made peace between us and increased his self-esteem, but that it gave him a model of taking responsibility.

How do we get the discipline to accomplish what we set out to do?

It requires dedication to reality...the truth. The more clearly we see the world, the better equipped we are to make wise decisions.

But reality and truth are only things that we can approach. We can't get them tied in a nice little package and put it in our briefcase.

What else does it take for people to be disciplined?

People need deadlines. When I used to work with groups and they weren't getting anywhere, I'd impose a six-month deadline. It's amazing how a group of people who had been acting as if they had all the time in the world could get moving once they had a concrete deadline.

Death is the ultimate deadline. None of us has forever to accomplish what we want to.

Is it possible to be over-disciplined?

Yes, it certainly is. Our parents and our culture teach us that certain things must be done in certain ways. Result: We can become so disciplined that we're not able to stop and smell the flowers.

Example: I used to think that if I went into a fancy restaurant I had to order an appetizer, entrée and dessert. But sometimes I'd be attracted to two or three appetizers. Only now that I'm in my 50s can I order two appetizers and forget the entrée. It's more constructive for me to eat what I want than to please the waiter.

Lesson: You can fiddle around with discipline...as long as you're not doing anything that's harmful.

Source: Psychiatrist M. Scott Peck, MD. His latest book is *A Bed by the Window, A Novel of Mystery and Redemption*, Bantam Books, 666 Fifth Ave., New York 10103. His big bestseller is, of course, *The Road Less Traveled*. Much of Dr. Peck's time is now spent in management consulting. His office: Bliss Rd., New Preston, CT 06777.

The Angry Victim Syndrome

We think of victims as weak, powerless people who can easily be taken advantage of...but some victims aren't weak at all.

Some victims are strong-willed people who get angry when they can't control others.

These people, whom I call angry victims, want others to live up to their often unreasonable expectations...and then feel angry when people inevitably disappoint them.

In order to change, angry victims have to realize that the problem lies within themselves, and that controlling others is not the solution.

Who's an angry victim:

Angry victims, most of whom are women, swing between two poles—the desire to control and the desire to please.

Example: When Laura disagreed with her

husband, she would first suppress her anger in order to please him. Eventually, however, she would swing to the control pole and fly into a rage. But then, she would start to worry about losing him and backpedal, apologizing profusely for getting so angry. Result: He became confused and the relationship ultimately suffered.

Angry victims constantly flip back and forth in their emotions because they're not comfortable in either mode. They're afraid that if they exert too much control people will become distant and angry with them.

At the same time, they're afraid that if they try too hard to please, people will take advantage of them.

Whichever pole they gravitate to they're afraid of something...and sure to lose no matter what they do. Result: Angry victims live in a state of constant fear.

Since pain hurts more if you're already fearful and tense, angry victims are often stunned by the depth of the feelings generated by a minor disappointment. A normal domestic problem can seem like a tragedy.

Example: Len's wife, Nora, got tied up at the office one night. She came home late and forgot to call. Len felt rejected and flew into a rage.

Although angry victims expect a lot from their friends and loved ones, most have a limited tolerance for the expectations and desires of others. This allows them to blame others for their problems.

Example: Sue, who hadn't had a serious relationship in years, finally met a man who appeared to be perfect for her...but two months later, she was complaining about him. For one thing, he dropped in whenever he wanted to, which she thought was rude and demanding. After some counseling, Sue realized that she hadn't had a relationship for so long because she didn't want to put up with anyone else's schedules. The problems was hers, not his.

Are you an angry victim?

There are three aspects to the angry victim syndrome:

- Fear of abandonment
- Fear of engulfment
- Need to control

If you suspect you're an angry victim, give yourself these tests:

- Abandonment test: Fantasize that everyone in your life calls you on the same day and says they never want to talk to you again. How much rejection would it take—one person, two people, 10 people—for you to feel devastated?

If even one rejection would be extremely hurtful, you're probably trying too hard to please people.

- Engulfment test: Fantasize that everyone in your life calls you on the same day and invites you out to dinner. How many offers would it take to make you uncomfortable?

Again, the fewer people it would take, the more likely it is that you're afraid of being overwhelmed with a lot of love and attention.

- Control test: Think back to minor disappointments, when people who you depended on did something that you thought was wrong. What was your reaction to those incidents? Did you laugh or cry or get angry?

If you got angry or frustrated, you probably have a control problem. And the sooner you felt that way, the bigger the problem.

How to stop being an angry victim:

If the above test shows that you could be an angry victim, follow these steps:

- Go easy on yourself: Most angry victims are extremely self-critical. Don't beat yourself up because you've discovered the problem—understanding that you have a problem should be the first step toward overcoming it.
- Realize that your expectations are not unnatural: They come from our bedrock fears about the world—that we're not going to be loved and cared for...that we can't control what happens to us.

Instead of rejecting these fears, be aware of them and be honest about them...with other people as well as with yourself.

- Let others know how you feel: Talking things over with people you're close to is the best way to work out your angry-victim problems.

Example: Jody was upset because her friend Tina never seemed to have enough time for her. She fought the desire to get angry and told Tina how she felt. Tina explained that her idea of friendship was having a lot of casual friends to see occasionally for lunch. Although the two couldn't be close friends, the conversation helped Jody break out of her angry-victim cycle.

• Recognize when you're out of balance: Work to stay in the golden zone—where you feel adequately loved yet adequately free to do what you want and reasonably in control of your life.

This is a very hard balance to maintain, and you won't get there by pushing yourself. Better: Respect and acknowledge your needs for love, freedom and control.

Source: Martin G. Groder, MD, a psychiatrist and business consultant in Chapel Hill, NC. His book, *Business Games: How to Recognize the Players and Deal With Them*, is available from Boardroom Classics, Box 736, Springfield, NJ 07081.

It Pays To Be An Optimist Even When Almost Everyone Is Pessimistic

Pessimism is in fashion these days. With recession at home, unrest overseas and all the other bad news around us—optimists are suspect.

Fashionable or not, however, it pays to be an optimist. Reasons:

• Optimism fight depression.

• Optimistic people achieve more. They do better at school, work and on the playing field than they'd be expected to do based on talent alone.

• Optimists enjoy better health. They get fewer infections and chronic illnesses, age more comfortably and may even live longer than pessimists.

The current pessimistic wave is partly a reaction to the mindless American boosterism of the past.

Although positive thinking was once credited with the power to make everything better, simply repeating positive statements to yourself has little effect on mood or achievement.

Pessimism and depression:

We're now in the midst of a depression epidemic, fueled by a combination of disintegrating social ties, dissolving religious faith—two of the supports people traditionally turned to for solace—and pessimism.

Ten times as many people suffer from severe depression today as 50 years ago...and depression strikes them earlier in life.

Depression can be described as a disorder of helplessness and hopelessness in response to loss or failure.

Everyone experiences life's inevitable losses and defeats from time to time, but optimists and pessimists handle these setbacks very differently.

Pessimistic people see failure as long-term and general. They believe that their misfortunes are their own fault...and that they are powerless to change their lot. These helpless, hopeless feelings make them afraid to try again—so they never take the chances in their lives that could make them happier.

Optimistic people see failure as temporary and specific. They blame defeats on bad luck or other people. As a result, they bounce back from adversity relatively quickly.

Both optimism and pessimism are self-perpetuating. If you believe you're not going to be successful, your won't try as hard. If a goal is achievable, no matter how remote, believing you can achieve it might enable you to be the person who climbs Mount Everest. Human beings give up easily and need optimism to keep them in the game.

Pessimism does have one advantage—accuracy. Pessimists may not enjoy life, but they do see it more realistically than optimists.

Example: If an optimist and a pessimist are given a set of 20 problems and each gets 10 right and 10 wrong, the optimist will guess that he got 17 right, while the pessimist's estimate will be much closer to the truth.

Does this mean that people who value honesty should be pessimists? Absolutely not! I advocate flexible optimism.

Life is a balancing act, and no one should be a slave to either mind-set. Key: Know the consequences of each strategy. Use optimism to fight depression and poor health, or in a situation where achievement is very important. Use pessimism when the cost of failure would be disastrous.

Example: A pilot deciding whether or not to de-ice a plane should use a pessimistic approach, since the wrong decision could lead to the loss of life. If you're choosing stocks in which to invest your life savings, you should seek the advise of a pessimistic financial expert. But if you're thinking about walking up to an attractive person and introducing yourself, the consequence of failure is simply rejection. Be optimistic.

How to be an optimist:

If you're not an optimist you can learn to be one. Pessimism and depression are largely a result of explanatory style—what you tell yourself about what happens to you.

Changing your style is remarkably simple and can be done by learning a new set of skills. You don't need a therapist's help for this process. You will have to work at it, though. Don't expect to alter your entire patter of thinking overnight.

To make your job easier, these new thought patterns are self-reinforcing—once you start using the skills, you feel better right away—and you keep using them.

Caution: If your depression is severe or accompanied by thoughts of suicide, seek professional help.

To think like an optimist:

• Recognize your automatic thoughts. Look for negative things you say to yourself when you're feeling bad. These thoughts are so habitual they're often barely conscious. Be especially alert for statements that are general, self-blaming or that imply permanence.

Example: A woman in her 40s enrolls in college and becomes depressed over a poor grade on her final exam. She realizes she is telling herself, *I'm too old to be in school. I can't possibly learn this material. I don't belong here. I'm such a failure. I should give up this whole idea.*

• Dispute your automatic thoughts. You already have the disputing skill—you use it when you argue with someone about a topic in which you believe strongly. Treat your automatic thoughts as voices that are wrongly accusing you, and marshal contradictory evidence to defend yourself. Force yourself to examine the evidence, even if you don't believe it at first. Helpful: Write down your automatic beliefs and the evidence against them...or say them out loud.

Example: The woman going back to college writes, *Plenty of people have gone back to school in midlife and done fine. I can learn new things—I did a great job last summer learning to use a complicated camera.*

• Look for alternative explanations of events. Then add them to your arsenal of contradictory evidence. Focus on causes that are...

Changeable—*I didn't spend enough time studying*...Specific—*A couple of people said this exam was especially hard*...Non-personal—*The professor graded unfairly.*

Again, even if you find some of the alternatives hard to believe, remember that pessimists do just the opposite—they cling to the explanation that puts them in the worst possible light. That's a destructive habit, and fighting this habit is healthy.

• Question the negative assumptions that govern you. Substitute more realistic, workable beliefs.

Examples: Instead of, *I can't live without love*...tell yourself, *Love is precious but rare.* Instead of, *Unless I do this perfectly, I'm a failure*, think...*Success is doing my best.*

• Distract yourself from depressing thoughts. In some situations, you don't have time to go through the disputation process.

If it's not practical for you to take optimism-inducing steps at the moment—or if you catch yourself ruminating and not getting anywhere—tell yourself very firmly to *stop.* Then make an appointment with yourself to address the problem later on.

Meanwhile, write the upsetting thoughts down to get them off your chest. Then find something else to think about—even if you just pick up a nearby object and concentrate on it for a few minutes.

Source: Martin E.P. Seligman, PhD, UPS Foundation Professor of Social Science and director of clinical training in psychology at the University of Pennsylvania. He has received two Distinguished Scientific Contribution awards from the American Psychological Association and is the author of *Learned Optimism*, Alfred A. Knopf, 201 E. 50 St., New York 10022.

The Secrets Of Much, Much Better Problem Solving

We all start life as creative creatures. Think of how eagerly children fantasize, act out stories and apply crayons to paper.

As we grow older, however, many of us erect barriers to creativity. Result: Our personal lives and careers suffer.

What to do:

The best way to boost your creativity is to learn to recognize and to overcome these barriers.

Barrier: Apathy. This is usually not an intellectual problem, but an emotional one. Although many people may envision a creative solution to a particular problem, few are sufficiently motivated to take the initiative to do something to change the status quo.

To conquer apathy, redefine your goal in terms that engage you personally, or in terms that express basic human values.

Example: Your goal is to straighten out a badly disorganized office filing system. Goal redefined: Bring harmony to office workers' relations.

• Barrier: Fear. Many people smother their own creativity out of simple fear. Sensing risk in trying something new and failing, they opt instead to play it safe—and do nothing.

In reality, though, doing nothing at all is often riskier than trying something new. Reason: The world is constantly changing.

People and organizations that fail to adapt get left behind. Even mistakes can prove useful.

Example: The Ford Edsel sold poorly when it was introduced—it's still considered Detroit's most notorious failure. But the lessons learned from this fiasco helped Ford develop the Mustang, one of the industry's all-time best-sellers.

Thomas Edison said he never had any failures...just learning experiences.

• Barrier: Self-doubt. Self-confidence is crucial to the creative process. At some point along the road from having an idea to implementing it, however, you will doubt your ability to succeed.

To beat self-doubt: On note cards, write down five or 10 positive statements about your personal strengths (intelligence, resourcefulness, persistence, etc.). Post these cards around your work area. If you feel doubt creeping into your thoughts, let them reassure you.

If you feel foolish posting worded affirmations, devise a graphic symbol for each of your strengths, and write these on the cards.

• Barrier: Isolation. Many people searching for new ideas isolate themselves. This is a mistake. Human contact is a powerful stimulant of ideas.

Keep your office door open...visit friends and family regularly...attend meetings and conferences. Best: Interact with people you can learn from—people directly or indirectly related to your areas of interest.

Barrier: Failure to choose the right goal. Many imaginative people aren't creative because they apply their efforts inappropriately. They may, for instance, seek small-scale solutions to large-scale problems, or vice versa.

Helpful: Write your overall goal on a piece of paper. On the same paper, state why you seek this goal, and list the biggest obstacle in your path.

Examine all three statements. Compared with overall goal, the second will be broader in scope, while the third will be more specific. Make sure you're working on the most appropriate level.

Example: Your goal is to boost office efficiency. Why? To make the office a more pleasant place to work. What's the biggest barier to reaching this goal? The staff is too small. Now examine all three statements. Given your knowledge of the situation, decide on the most appropriate immediate goal.

Barrier: Limited thinking: Good ideas are plentiful, but workable ideas are very rare. To get a few good workable ideas, you must generate many ideas, then discard the bad ones.

Most people, however, approach their goals using a single way of thinking. In fact, there are four styles of creative thought. Each can be summed up by one question...

• Modifying style: How can I improve on what has worked before?

• Visioning style: What is the ideal solution over the long term?

• Experimenting style: What can I combine to develop a new idea?

• Exploring style: What basic assumptions can I challenge...and what new ideas would result.

Consider each of these questions in turn as you brainstorm ideas.

Example: To design a new car, I may use a combination of existing components (modifying style)...or I may decide to start from scratch (experimenting style).

All ideas are worthy of consideration at least initially—even ideas that seem foolish, unrealistic or impractical. An idea that isn't workable may spark one that is.

Barrier: Impatience: Although persistence often pays off, true creativity cannot be forced. Creativity is stifled by the sense of needing to be creative. It often pays to step away from the challenge for a breather. Take a nap. Go for a walk. Later, when you feel more energetic, return to your work.

Many of the world's most creative ideas have arisen seemingly by chance, during a rest period or even during sleep. Keep a pad of paper or a tape recorder by your bedside. And carry notepaper with you at all times.

Barrier: Faulty evaluation of ideas: Once you've generated several ideas, evaluate each. Use two types of thinking:

• Analytical: Devise a list of standards or rules that you want to use to evaluate your ideas, and write these in a column on a piece of paper. In a row across the top of the page write the ideas you want to evaluate. Rank each idea according to the standards you've devised.

• Intuitive: Take a broad view of the problem facing you, and use your gut feeling to evaluate your ideas. Ask yourself, Does this solution make sense in the big picture?

Don't confuse intuition with an emotional attachment to a particular idea. Intuition is usually correct, while emotional attachments are often wrong. Ideas must succeed or fail on the basis of their strengths, not on the basis of whose ideas they are.

• Barrier: Failure to listen to others: Creativity thrives on input from friends, family members and co-workers. Everyone views the creative challenge from a different viewpoint.

Example: A salesperson may view a sales slump in terms of selling techniques, while a machine operator might view the same slump in terms of quality control.

The greater the number of viewpoints brought to bear on a challenge, the easier it will be to find a creative solution.

If you're unable to see the problem from several viewpoints, seek out other perspectives. A large percentage of major product innovations come not from well-funded corporate research-and-development teams, but from customers.

Seek input from uninvolved parties. If creative ideas are to be discussed at a meeting, ask someone from outside the group to attend. A seemingly simplistic question asked by a naive genius can really pay off.

• Barrier: Failure to sell the idea: Even a brilliant idea is worthless if it's not accepted or implemented by other people.

Selling your idea means answering all the questions that people affected by the idea might have. The creative process does not end until your idea has been accepted or rejected by others.

• Barrier: Tentativeness: Some people are full of ideas. But they're so wary of troubling the people around them, their ideas never see daylight. Why people are troubled by ideas: The ideas usually result in changes in their jobs or in their lives.

But employers, co-workers, friends and family are less resistant to change than most of us think. Lesson: Always try to follow your creative strategies, after they have been carefully thought through and polished.

• Barrier: Failure to celebrate. Creativity takes a toll on the emotions. Even the most creative people risk burnout if they fail to celebrate the conclusion of a creative effort. Celebrating a creative effort brings a sense of closure that promotes creativity later on.

The celebration doesn't have to be a lavish party, although that might be part of the process. What it should involve is reflecting on what has been achieved and what has been learned...and rewarding those who were creative, as well as those who facilitated their creativity.

In our society, creativity is usually acknowledged with raises, promotions and other monetary rewards. We must remember, however, that intrinsic celebrations—personal fulfillment and the sense of having improved things for others, for instance—are equally important.

Source: William C. Miller, principal consultant, Global Creativity Corp., 453 Marin Dr., Mill Valley, CA 94941. It is a consulting firm that works regularly with many Fortune 500 companies. Miller is the author of *The Creative Edge: Fostering Innovation Where You Work*, Addison-Wesley, Route 128, Reading, MA 01867.

Verbal War Self-Defense Tactics

Verbal zaps and zingers are so much a part of our lives that we hardly ever notice them until we start feeling down—without knowing why.

Most vulnerable: People who are in any way different from the cultural ideal.

The first step in self-defense is recognizing that you've been attacked, however subtly. Simple signs: A queasy feeling in your stomach... or a depressed feeling after a conversation. Once you know you've been hurt, it's prudent to set up a self-defense system for future use.

What leads to sniping:

The roots of most verbal sniping lie in perfectionism. People who were constantly criticized as children end up believing that love and approval come to only those who are perfect. And since they can only be perfect by comparison, perfectionists throw a lot of hurtful comments at others.

To deal with perfectionists: Let them know that you think they are wonderful. But point out that you have different values and needs. Make it clear that you're unwilling to be unjustly criticized to make them feel better.

What to watch for:

People who throw verbal zaps do so in many ways. Included:

• Constructive criticism: Insulting comments disguised as helpful suggestions. They are usually preceded by certain phrases.

Examples: I hope you don't mind if I'm honest...This is for your own good...Please don't get mad at me but...

You end up confused because you're supposed to admire snipers for their honesty. But you're also reeling from the punch.

• Heirlooms: Criticisms passed down through the generations.

Examples: Fatso...selfish...good-for-nothing...troublemaker.

If we call people by labels long enough, they start to believe that the labels are true... even if the information has been proven invalid.

• Time-release zaps: Insidious comments you don't notice until much later.

Examples: You're so quiet no one knows that you're there...Your haircut looks great—you should have cut it years ago...You have such a pretty face, if only you'd lose weight.

• Body barbs: Negative comment about appearance. Perhaps the biggest category. Children are often the victims.

Examples: You'd better get that nose fixed or no one will marry you...You used to have such a nice figure...Too bad your hair is so thin.

• Family putdowns: Relatives sometimes think they can say things they wouldn't say to anyone outside the family.

Examples: You're just like your father—you'll never make it on your own...Your mother was so well dressed—what happened to you?

Good defenses:

Once you've identified the attack and the attacker, there are several defensive measures to take. Included:

• Determine what kind of attack you are facing. Ask yourself:

• Is the person upset with you for some reason?

• Is the issue competition with a friend?

• Are you dealing with an abrasive type of person...or a person with a different cultural style?

• Is some relative just repeating the family pattern?

Once you know where the remark is coming from, you'll be better able to deal with it.

Example: Your husband makes a nasty comment about the dinner you've cooked. You know he's had a bad day. Instead of getting defensive, tell him you know that he's upset...but you'd prefer he didn't take it out on you.

• Keep a record. Start a list to track where the barbs are coming from. Give them a rating from one to 10. Which hurt the most?

Just writing them down will give you perspective. It will also give you practice in identifying the worst offenders and a chance to plan advance strategies.

• Avoid personalizing the conflict. Strategy: Assume that these remarks bear no resemblance to you or to reality.

• Bury them: If you're feeling secure enough, dig an imaginary hole with your foot, drop the remark in and walk away. The ability to forgive and let go is an important survival skill.

• Make friends with your body. Stand in front of the mirror and make a list of all the body-image zaps you've picked up along the way. Acknowledge that most of them have long since become irrelevant to you.

If you can accept yourself as you are, it will be easier to handle the negatives people throw you.

• Acknowledge the remark. Confront it directly. Useful replies: I'm sure you didn't mean to insult me...Is there any reason you would want to hurt my feelings?...Are you aware how that remark would sound to some people?

Alternative: Ask the person what was meant by the remark. If the sniper was only being honest or just trying to help, explain that your prefer to get help in ways that don't hurt your feelings.

• Set up signals. These are especially helpful in close relationships.

Example: Jenny's husband constantly sniped at her in public. She started carrying a little hand towel everywhere..and every time he criticized her she put her head in it. He was so embarrassed he halted the criticism.

Family system: Stop nasty remarks at the dinner table by ringing a bell whenever someone says something negative.

• Analyze the remark. Divide an attack into its parts and respond to each without putting yourself into the position of being an aggrieved victim.*

Putdown #1: Even a woman should be able to understand this. Reply: When did you start thinking women were inferior?...*Putdown #2:* If you loved me, you would lose weight. Reply: How long have you thought I didn't love you?

• Resist. Write a letter or tell people who criticize you that you simply will not accept their criticism any longer.

*Adapted from *The Gentle Art of Verbal Self-Defense* by Suzette Haden Elgin, HarperCollins, 10 E. 53 St., New York 10022.

Source: Cultural anthropologist Jennifer James, PhD, a columnist, lecturer and TV talk-show host. She is the author of six books, including *You Know I Wouldn't Say This If I Didn't Love You,* Newmarket Press, 18 E. 48 St., New York 10017.

The Secrets Of Personal Power

The concept of power is often associated with authority and influence over others—rather than an understanding of ourselves. Self-knowledge and self-mastery are a lifelong quest that may begin in childhood, but certainly are the core of adult education. We become aware of the process of learning about ourselves when we make a decision to do what we believe instead of what we are told to do or are expected to do.

Kierkegaard, the philosopher, expressed the idea as the title of one of his books: *Purity of Heart Is To Will One Thing.* The exercise of will toward purity of heart is self-mastery.

Facing up to needs:

As a psychiatrist in training, I had to spend time at a major psychiatric hospital. I was designated leader of a team of experts including a psychiatrist, a psychologist, a social worker and a senior staff consultant. I was intimidated by the other team members' experience and found it impossible to express my own opinions in such august company.

My supervisor, thinking that I was not capable of leadership, suggested that I might be more comfortable in private practice.

I could have settled for what he said, but I decided to attack the problem. I didn't mind choosing not to do something because I didn't want to, but I did mind opting out because someone said that I wasn't capable of doing it. I wasn't sure how I was going to become a better leader, but I knew that it was important to me do it somehow.

I didn't attend any management seminars or read any books on the subject of leadership. Instead, what I did was work independently at another hospital for a year developing my skills and understanding of both psychiatry and myself.

I came back to the same hospital where I had failed in leadership before and took on the leadership challenge again. This time I asked for opinions and information from each of the team members and I told them what I thought. My new supervisor was impressed with my leadership skills.

The change was interior. I had learned to trust myself and my own opinions more in another setting, and now I could safely share them with others without being disrespectful of their ideas or intimidated by them. I had come to understand that I knew what I was doing—and that I could be effective much more often than not.

Self-mastery empowers you to take chances in your life and accomplish things you weren't sure that you could do.

Self-mastery also empowers you to accept that you're not always right. It allows you to ask for help whenever you need it, whatever the reason may be. Sometimes you need help because the situation is difficult. Sometimes it's because you are simply not at your best energy level or your interest has flagged.

Self-mastery is acknowledging weaknesses, giving up control sometimes and accepting assistance from other people.

The yoga connection:

Hatha-yoga exercises emphasize breathing and control during a series of slow movements that are all designed to develop flexibility, stamina and grace. These qualities I strive for psychologically as well as physically. In yoga as well as in life, I believe that strength and consistency are all-important.

Mastery of the body promotes mastery of the mind. There is a balance between the two that is worth pursuing.

One "practices" yoga the same way that one practices medicine or many other professions. What matters is daily discipline, the process and the effort.

Importance of imagination:

We must create our own visions of who we want to be. That is very hard to do, because for most of our lives, we have seen ourselves through the eyes of parents or spouses or teachers or mentors or even friends and colleagues.

It takes imagination to build your own vision of yourself as you not only want to be, but as you believe you should be. You can only create that picture of yourself through clear self-knowledge of your personal strengths and weaknesses.

An adult imagination is not the unbridled fantasy of a child. It is the disciplined energy of a growing person with experience, insight, curiosity and reason.

Freedom from "oughts":

Psychiatrist Karen Horney wrote about the "tyranny of the shoulds." These are all the do's and don'ts from childhood that prevent us from seeing the world for ourselves and making decisions and value judgments for ourselves.

I see the "oughts" limiting the imaginations of patients and I tell them to simply tell those voices from the past to shut up. I know it is a simplistic device, but it works more often than it doesn't, and it give them more power to develop their own visions of themselves.

We must imagine ourselves powerful so that we can become powerful. Conquering these archaic parts of ourselves may be the most important step toward self-mastery.

The Tao Te Ching contains these lines: "Knowing others is intelligence; knowing yourself is true wisdom. Mastering others is strength; mastering yourself is true power.

Source: Dr. Sue Chance, a psychiatrist on the staff at Willowbrook Hospital in Waxahachie, TX. She has lectured extensively on the subject of self-mastery and is currently working on a book on that subject.

8

Insurance Traps And Opportunities

Tricks To Watch Out For When Submitting An Insurance Claim

Whenever you file an insurance claim, the person who decides if, when, and how much you will be paid is the claims adjuster, not the agent or salesperson with whom you usually do business.

Because insurance companies are never inclined to pay what they don't have to pay, claims adjusters look first for a reason to deny or delay payment. Then, if they can't find one, they usually pay it. So it's important to present an airtight claim that leaves no room for excuses.

There are six traps to avoid that claims adjusters routinely look for.

• Trap #1: Unpaid premiums. Make sure you pay insurance premiums on time. Don't rely on a "grace period." Reason: If you suffer a loss after the due date but before you pay, or even a few days after you pay a late premium, the insurance company can say your policy had lapsed.

• Trap #2: Delay in reporting. Notify your insurance company at once if you intend to file a claim. In cases of theft, car accidents, etc., file a police report immediately. Reason: The insurance company will require independent verification of the circumstances of the incident, and may need to resolve questions of negligence. Failure to notify the police after a crime occurs can be grounds for denying a claim. Note: The company cannot refuse to pay simply because you are late with the paperwork, unless it can show the company has been harmed by your tardiness.

• Trap #3: Incomplete or incorrect information on claims forms. Probably the most common reason claims don't get paid—a lack of information is an excuse for delay, while misleading information can cause claims to be denied outright.

Example: A claims adjuster disallowed the claim of a man with a painful eye infection, because his ophthalmologist wrote eye examination on the claim form and check-ups were excluded under the policy. If the diagnosis and treatment had been accurately described, the adjuster would have understood that the procedure was medically necessary, and thus covered.

Best: Follow directions meticulously and submit paperwork within 30 days of a loss. If you can't yet estimate any part of your claim, notify the company that you will be making a further claim.

Example: Cleaning and redecorating costs following a fire or flood.

• Trap #4: Lack of documentation. Unsubstantiated losses or expenses are red flags to claims adjusters.

Example: A man received a Rolex watch as a gift and was unable to show a receipt when it was stolen. The claims adjuster disputed his ownership of the watch until he presented the box it came in and the warranty as proof of possession.

Recommended: Prepare documentation for all insurance claims in any way you can.

Examples: Photograph or diagram evidence such as skid marks and collect witnesses' accounts. Keep copies of contracts and bills for repair work to your home, auto, or property, receipts for alternate living or transportation costs, etc. It is up to you to show the necessity for repairs or expenses. When filing a property claim, take photos of damage or loss and wait for a claims adjuster to visit before making large, permanent repairs.

Important: Take all necessary measures to prevent further damage to your property. If you fail to do this, the insurance company can refuse to pay your claim.

Examples: Fix broken locks or windows to prevent further theft, repair leaks to prevent further water damage. Call your insurance company to authorize immediate repairs. Keep sales receipts for all major purchases in a safe deposit box, along with an updated inventory of your belongings.

Caution: Some claims adjusters are suspicious of photographs or videotapes used to document personal possessions, citing cases of fraudulent claims by people who staged the pictures.

Solutions: Keep all sales receipts. Give copies of the photos or tape to your insurance agent ahead of time. Ask the company to agree to the value of your possessions (a "stated value policy").

• Trap #5: Overstated losses. Claims adjusters are trained to be suspicious and are alert for inflated claims. Never file a false or exaggerated claim. That risks prosecution for fraud, cancellation of your policy, and it adds to the insurance industry's contention that consumers routinely try to defraud insurers.

• Trap #6: Incorrect or incomplete information on applications. Be honest and accurate, especially with your medical history. Reasons: Insurance companies normally check your records after a claim is filed. Nondisclosures on your application can be grounds for a claim to be denied—or even the policy rescinded—if the insurance company can show you had a pre-existing condition. However, an omission or untruth must be material.

Example: Forgetting to report you once sprained your ankle is not grounds for denying a claim for cancer surgery. But claiming you don't smoke could cost you your coverage for lung-cancer treatment if other information confirms that you smoke two packs a day.

There are several areas in which it is wise to keep an eye on your insurance company. When in doubt, don't be afraid to dispute their conclusions.

• Trick #1: Disagreement on cost of repairs. Most insurance companies recommend their own contractors, who may turn out to be less expensive than independent contractors. Recommended: Get estimates and descriptions of materials, etc., from both.

Caution: If you employ a contractor provided by your insurance company, be sure to get a guarantee of quality from the contractor and the insurance adjuster before work begins. Otherwise, hire your own contractor. In cases where there is a significant difference in estimates between the insurer's contractor and your own, most policies provide for a mediator to settle the difference.

• Trick #2: Disagreement on "reasonable and customary charges" for medical procedures. Often, a portion of a medical claim will be denied on the basis that the policy only covers set "customary charges."

Problem: Insurance companies often base these rates on old schedules or national averages that don't take regional differences into account, thereby chiseling away at the health claims they are obliged to pay. Most people don't contest the "small stuff," and adjusters know it.

Recourse: Survey health providers in your area, and present documentation of customary charges for your procedure. In the face of evidence, insurers usually back down.

Threat: A class action suit based on your research could cost them millions.

• Trick #3: Denial of preauthorized medical procedures. Preapproval of medical costs does not guarantee an airtight claim. Many current lawsuits concern the denial of claims after the treatments were precertified by the insurance company.

Examples: Hospitalizations the adjuster calls "custodial" rather than treatment-related, and heart transplants or bone marrow transplants for cancer patients, often costing $100,000 and up, that are determined to be experimental—after they were approved.

Trap: Often, a clerk will precertify a general medical procedure or course of treatment, which an adjuster will withdraw later.

Self-defense: Have your doctor write in for general precertification of any serious procedure, have it done, and fight later if you have to.

Always be courteous and cooperative with insurance claims adjusters. They are under continuing pressure to close many files...and their opinion is not final. If you feel your claim is not being handled fairly, kick it upstairs.

Source: William M. Shernoff, a specialist in bad faith lawsuits against insurance companies. He has been called "the lawyer the insurance industry fears the most." His latest book is *How To Make Insurance Companies Pay Your Claims & What To Do If They Don't*, Hastings House, Mamaroneck, NY.

How To Win The Long-Term-Care Insurance Game

The cost of nursing home care can drain an individual and his/her family of their life savings, if they haven't planned carefully—in advance.

Many people take out long-term care insurance to protect their assets for their children.

And...people with elderly parents are taking out long-term care policies to protect their own assets.

In order to protect yourself you must face the following facts...

• Two out of five people over the age of 65 will end up spending some time in a nursing home.

• Nursing home care can cost between $30,000 to $80,000 a year, depending on where you live.

• About half of those needing long-term care end up paying for nursing home expenses out of their own pockets.

Preparing for nursing home costs requires getting past commonly held myths.

• *Medicare will pay for my long-term care.* Medicare only pays for 2% of all nursing home expenses. It pays only for skilled rehabilitative care in a Medicare approved skilled nursing facility, and then only for the first 20 days completely, and partially for the next 80 days.

• *My family will take care of me.* For the most part, that's wishful thinking. Many wives who used to take care of older relatives now have careers of their own. And more people need care that requires specialized training.

• *I can "spend down" assets and go on Medicaid.* You must divest yourself of your assets thirty months before you apply for Medicaid. If you do spend down your assets to go on Medicaid, you may be leaving your spouse impoverished. Some states allow Medicaid applicants only $800 a month in income and $12,000 in assets. Moreover, you'll find yourself without financial resources if you recover and leave the nursing home.

Getting started:

Presently, there are more than 100 companies that offer a wide variety of long-term care products for every budget. Even though you might not be able to afford the optimum coverage, there are plenty of good choices available. However, it's important to consider the following points when selecting insurance.

Optimum coverage:

• Home care. The plan should pay for home health care in addition to nursing home expenses. Most policies will pay 50% of the nursing home benefit for home health care. This may be adequate in some parts of the country. But if you reside in a major metropolitan area where home health care costs are higher, try to get insurance that pays either 80% or 100%.

• Kinds of care. The plan should cover all levels of care...skilled, intermediate and custodial. Some older policies limit coverage to skilled or intermediate facilities.

• Length. You can usually choose how long the policy will pay for benefits once you enter a nursing home. The longer the coverage, the costlier the policy. Coverage periods are usually two, four or six years, or life. The average nursing home stay is two-and-a-half years, but I recommend at least four years of coverage.

• Waiting. Most plans won't cover pre-existing conditions for six months after you begin paying the premiums. However, the maximum waiting period should be no longer than six months.

• Adequacy. Make sure the coverage is enough to pay for the cost of nursing home expenses in the area where you live. Call your local community department of aging or some local nursing homes to find out.

• Nonescalation. Make sure your policy has a level premium that does not increase as you get older.

• Inflation. The company should offer an inflation benefit, preferably one that is compounded.

• Waiver premium. The policy has a clause waiving your premium if you're in a facility for more than 90 days. Consider getting one of the new policies that will waive the premium on your first day in a facility.

• Hospitalization. Make sure a hospital stay isn't required to get insurance benefits.

• Rating. Make sure the insurance company is rated A+ by A.M. Best or Standard and Poor's.

Watch out for:

• Any plan that requires going to a nursing home before getting home health care benefits.

• Any plan that pays benefits based on diagnostically related groups. These plans limit benefits by specifying exactly how much benefits you get for a specific illness. If it takes you longer than the allotted time to recover, you're out of luck.

• Renewability. Some policies offered through group plans allow the insurance company the option of not renewing your policy. A good plan should be guaranteed renewable for life.

When to buy:

Like life insurance, long-term care insurance is cheaper the earlier you begin buying it. I recommend starting when you reach age 45 to 50, when premiums are lowest.

Expect to pay $500 to $1,500 a year in premiums at age 50, $1,000 to $3,000 at 60 and $1,500 to $5,000 at 70. If you wait too long, you may develop a medical condition like rheumatoid arthritis that would prevent you from getting coverage at any price.

Most companies will sell these policies to those 40 and over. There are a few companies who will sell long-term care insurance through the age of 85. When the time is right for you, go to an independent insurance agent who specializes in insurance for the elderly.

Source: Ronni Greene, a specialist in insurance for senior citizens, Prager & Greene, 14 Chittenden Rd., Fair Lawn, NJ 07410, 201-791-8643.

Help A Friend Fight For Unemployment Insurance

Many people struggling with the financial burdens of unemployment fail to apply for unemployment compensation. They think they're not eligible...or they're afraid of the stigma attached to receiving benefits.

But unemployment compensation can be a significant source of cash—as much as $200 a week for 26 weeks—and can help a family get through a very difficult time.

Each state sets its own benefit amounts and its own requirements for eligibility and disqualification. To collect benefits, state authorities require people to demonstrate that they have worked for a certain number of weeks during the past year—usually 14 to 30 weeks.

Most states also require people to actively look for a new job and supply them with the names of all their job contacts each week. White-collar workers can often arrange to search for work by mailing résumés rather than applying for jobs in person, if this is customary in their fields.

People who are laid off should be able to draw benefits for up to 26 weeks.

People who are fired can only be denied benefits if their employers can establish that they were fired for just cause or misconduct.

Incompetence isn't misconduct. Neither is missing work or showing up late a few times. However, fighting with a supervisor, stealing or chronic tardiness is considered misconduct.

People who quit their jobs voluntarily can still collect unemployment insurance if they can show that they quit for a good cause.

Examples: Sexual harassment, unsafe working conditions, failure to pay overtime wages.

• Trap: Clerks often try to discourage valid claimants from applying. They are often simply trying to reduce their own workload.

Solution: Apply for unemployment benefits anyway.

• Trap: Some employers encourage people to resign instead of being fired. This, they say, looks better on a résumé. But people who resign under such circumstances usually aren't eligible to collect unemployment.

Solution: People who want to make certain that they can collect benefits should let themselves be fired rather than resigning.

• Trap: Some employers fight former employees who are trying to collect unemployment. This usually happens when people lose work for reasons other than layoffs.

Solution: People who think that they have been unfairly turned down for benefits should appeal their denial of their benefits before an administrative hearing. Hearings are generally short and informal.

A person's best defense at a hearing is documentary evidence—doctors' statements, job evaluations, etc.

Witnesses are also helpful. People discharged for not doing their jobs, for instance, should take along co-workers or union representatives to bolster their cases.

Source: Richard McHugh, associate general counsel, United Auto Workers, 8000 E. Jefferson Ave., Detroit 48214. He has helped hundreds of people collect unemployment benefits.

Insurance Companies And The Truth

Always tell insurance companies the truth. Very often, if you lie, a policy will be canceled—after you make a claim. In effect, the policy never existed, because it was written under false assumptions. Auto insurance will cost more if you admit accidents or traffic violations—but that's better than not having any insurance. Health insurance companies may charge more to cover problems you reveal, or may exclude some conditions from coverage—but a surprising number of insurers will cover the conditions if they know about them. Life insurers must normally pay if you hold a policy for at least two years—even if you lied to get it. Also: Smokers who claimed nonsmoking status to get policies may be denied no matter how long the policies have been in effect.

Source: Sam E. Beller, CLU, ChFC (chartered life underwriter and chartered financial consultant), author of *The Great Insurance Secret.*

Winning The Vicious New Health-Insurance Game

If you or your spouse changes jobs, if you move to another state or if you become self-employed, there's a good chance that you and your family may be left without health insurance. That can be a nightmare today as medical costs continue to skyrocket.

Though not widely known, there are places to find coverage. If you and everyone in your family are under 40 and in perfect health, you can probably call Blue Cross/Blue Shield and get coverage without delay. The process becomes harder, however, when someone is over 40...and in less-than-excellent health. Smart strategy:

• Buy an interim medical policy. Though rarely advertised, many insurance companies write policies for up to 12 months. These typically have deductibles of at least $500 and often lack the generous benefits commonly attached to company policies.

But interim coverage is usually very affordable. A middle-aged person in good health, for example, can expect to pay $100–$150 a month for an interim medical policy.

Where to find interim coverage: Ask your life insurance company if it offers interim coverage. Many of them do and there are also specialty insurance carriers in the business. If your life insurance company doesn't sell interim medical policies, call the state insurance commission for names of companies that do.

Limitation: Though most interim carriers say their policies can't be extended once they expire, many actually will extend them, especially if you haven't filed a claim during the initial period.

• Contact local health maintenance organizations. Generally, HMOs provide health care as good as, or better than, most company policies provide. The problem is that in many areas, HMOs screen applicants before accepting them. Then they either reject those who have serious health problems or exclude the problems from coverage.

Example: Someone with a serious heart condition may be accepted, but coverage wouldn't extend to their heart problems.

But don't give up on HMOs, even if you have a serious medical problem. Opportunity: Many HMOs, and occasionally Blue Cross/Blue Shield, have an "open season" for one or two weeks a year when they accept virtually all applicants without giving them a physical. If you have doubts about being accepted on the basis of an exam, wait for an open season (often advertised in newspapers and on television).

• Consider a separate policy for an existing medical condition. If one member of your family has a kidney problem, for instance, look for a general policy or an HMO to cover all but that ailment. Then buy a separate policy to cover dialysis or whatever else is needed for the kidney condition. The premiums, while high, might be less than what you'd have to pay if the condition worsened. You can find special high-risk carriers through state insurance commissions.

• Join an association that offers health insurance. Many fraternal and professional organizations—as well as clubs, alumni associations and civic groups—sell health insurance to members. Coverage can sometimes be bought even without a physical. Caution: Look carefully at the policies. A few are excellent, but others can be expensive—and the coverage minimal.

To find out which organizations you might consider joining, consult the *Encyclopedia of Associations*, available in nearly all public libraries. By looking up any of your special interests in the index, you'll find a list of organizations involved with that field.

Then phone the groups to find out if health insurance is one of the benefits they offer. In general, nationwide organizations are more likely to offer health insurance than local ones.

• State uninsurable plans. Twenty states, including most of the predominantly industrialized ones, have plans to insure people who can't get coverage elsewhere. Rates, however, are usually up to 50% higher than what carriers normally charge.

Advantage: These plans accept nearly everyone, regardless of existing medical conditions. This may actually make the coverage cheap for people with ailments that are expensive to treat.

Source: Robert J. Hunter, director, National Insurance Consumer Organization, 121 N. Payne St., Alexandria, VA 22314.

All About The Life Insurance Innovations

During the 1980s, insurers introduced two important variations on traditional whole life insurance policies...

• Universal life: Allows you to get market interest rates on the cash value in your policy.

• Variable life: Allows you to direct the investment of the cash value into various types of securities funds.

Like traditional whole life, universal and variable policies allow cash values to build up tax-deferred. Now insurers are offering two other interesting variations...

Second-to-die, or survivorship, insurance. Since 1981, changes in the tax law have allowed couples to postpone federal estate taxes until the death of the second spouse. But, at that point, the estate can be hit with estate taxes of between 37% and 60%. Quite often, heirs are forced to sell assets at a discount to meet these taxes.

Survivorship life insurance is a policy that pays a benefit when the second spouse dies, giving the couple's heirs the money to pay estate taxes just when they need it. It can be purchased as an option to whole, variable or universal life. Keep in mind:

• The first $600,000 of each spouse's estate can be given to heirs free of federal taxes. As a result, survivorship life makes most sense for couples having a total estate of $1.2 million or more.

• Second-to-die insurance does not replace the need for traditional life insurance. If the husband's earnings are the family's primary source of income, his family will still need traditional life insurance to replace his earnings if he dies.

Prepayment of Death Benefit options: Life insurance, by its nature, pays its benefit at death.

That doesn't do much good for people who need money at the end of their lives to pay for nursing homes or other kinds of medical care. They are usually forced to borrow against the cash value of their life insurance policies. Now, some insurers have come up with new options that allow you to get a "prepayment" of a portion of your death benefit during your lifetime. The options can pay up to 70% of the death benefit if you're terminally ill. That's significantly more than what you could get by borrowing against your policy's cash value.

Warning: These riders or options are not available yet through most of the major brand-name insurance companies. The tax consequences of these payments are still in question. Policyholders might be forced to pay income taxes on the money they receive from these policies, whereas death benefits are tax-free.

Bargain: These options may have no up-front cost, but the insurance company usually retains a portion of the death benefit in exchange.

Source: Jeff Franklin, president of Franklin Planning Associates, Inc., certified financial planners, 215 Lexington Ave., New York 10016.

Family Insurance Planning Pays

If you own your own life insurance policy, the proceeds paid on your death will be included in your taxable estate. If you're married, the proceeds will pass to your spouse free of estate tax. But, when your spouse dies, the proceeds will be included in his/her taxable estate—and may be taxed at rates as high as 60%.

Self-defense: To have the policy proceeds ultimately pass to your children, give the insurance policy to them. The policy proceeds will then be paid to them directly. You'll avoid leaving up to 60% of your insurance to the government.

Critical: Don't wait too long to make the gift. If you die within three years after making it, the policy proceeds will be swept back into your estate.

Source: Irving Blackman, a partner with Blackman Kallick Bartelstein, 300 S. Riverside Plaza, Chicago 60606.

Protecting Yourself From An Insurance Company Failure

The insurance industry is in the early stages of a major shakeout. In 1989 and 1990, a total of 73* life, health and annuity insurers failed—compared with a total of 53 failures for the preceding four years combined.

There are indications that failures are snowballing. It's posing a growing risk to consumers.

As public awareness of the problem increases, more people are moving their business to higher-rated insurers. Result: A drain of assets from lower-rated companies making their status even more precarious.

Given the complexity of insurance company finances, some consumers are making serious errors...jumping from the frying pan into the fire.

Example: One publicized factor in insurance company failures is excessive investment in high-risk "junk bonds." As a result, people might move from Company A, with 50% of its assets in junk bonds, to Company B, with only 20% in junk bonds. Problem: If Company A has a significantly larger capital pool, it may well be safer than Company B.

If unchecked, a wave of insurance failures could be more devastating than the S&L crisis. Reason: There is no equivalent to the FDIC to safeguard the investor's money. If your insurance company goes bankrupt, you may be out of luck. Witness the disaster at Executive Life Insurance Company of California, which was just taken over by the state commissioners, jeopardizing the policies and annuities of 400,000 Americans.

How to avoid a failing company:

In analyzing the health of a bank, an educated layperson can make two or three quick calculations and get a firm grasp on where the institution stands. But the task is more difficult with insurance companies...

While there are several acknowledged key indicators—the ratios of junk bonds and mortgages to capital resources—simple calculations can be misleading. To be safe, consumers must examine their insurance companies' stability by using a professional rating agency—and preferably more than one agency.

Complication: The consumer must know how to evaluate this information, since the same rating means different things at different agencies.

Examples: At A.M. Best & Co., the largest insurance rating specialist in the country, anything below its top rating, A+, is cause for caution.* An A rating is only fair, and an A– or B+ is a danger sign.

A.M. Best is supported with fees paid by insurance companies, and is notoriously slow to downgrade a favorable rating.

Example: Best gave Integrated Resources of Iowa an A (excellent) rating up to within a year of the company's failure in January, 1990.

Our ratings are quite conservative. Among the roughly 50 factors involved in rating insurance companies, these are the two questions Weiss considers most basic:

- How much risk is the company taking on with its investments and business operations?
- How much capital resources does the firm have to cover potential losses from that risk?

Based on these principles, a rapidly growing company is generally less stable than a more static one. Reason: A growth spurt is expensive, since it requires large up-front commissions to salespeople and increased field costs. Important safety indicator: A consistent pattern of profitability is a positive sign of good management and a solid bottom line.

See the box below for ratings of the strongest and weakest insurance companies. By our scale, A ratings are outstanding...and any firm at B+ or better is considered safe and we recommend it. Whereas a rating of C+ to C– represents a warning. If your insurance company is at the D level, we would advise that you consider shifting your policies elsewhere.

Note: Decisions to shift an insurance policy also hinge on other factors, including penal-

*This figure understates the problem, since it excludes companies that do all their business within a single state, and firms that have been resuscitated by their state governments.

*Even Best's A+ ratings can be suspect, since they are given to almost all companies with $10 billion or more in assets—regardless of investment risks or other possible weaknesses.

ties, reinsurability, customer's age and preexisting medical conditions.

In devising our ratings, we don't assume a very rosy economic scenario—nor do we assume a very dark one. A soundly managed company should be prepared for either contingency.

Source: Martin D. Weiss, president of Weiss Research Inc., an economic research and rating firm and publisher of investment directories, 220 N. Mango Rd., West Palm Beach, FL 33409. Directories include *Insurance Safety Directory*, which can be ordered through the Weiss Safety Hotline at 800-289-9222.

Strongest US Insurance Companies

Company Name*	State	Safety Rating
Combined Ins. of America	NC	B+
Commonwealth Life	KY	B+
Continental Assurance	IL	A–
First Colony Life	VA	B+
Hartford Life	CT	A–
Jefferson-Pilot Life	NC	A+
Liberty National Life	AL	B+
Lincoln National Life	IN	B+
Massachusetts Mutual Life	MA	B+
Metropolitan Life	NY	B+
Nat'l Home Life Assurance	MO	B+
New York Life	NY	B+
Northwestern Mutual Life	WI	B+
State Farm Life	IL	A+
United Ins. of America	IL	A+
Unum Life Ins. of America	ME	B+
The weakest insurers		
Anchor National Life	CA	D+
Equitable Life Assurance	NY	D+
Equitable Variable Life	NY	D+
Executive Life Insurance	NY	E–
Fidelity Bankers Life	VA	D+
First Capital Life	CA	D+
Kemper Investors Life	IL	D+
Monarch Life	MA	D+
Pruco Life	AZ	D+
Tandem Insurance Group	IL	D
Union Labor Life	MD	D+

*Insurance companies listed in alphabetical order. Each has more than $2 billion in assets.

Source: Martin D. Weiss.

The Truth About Mortgage Insurance For The Jobless

Mortgage insurance for the jobless may not be the best use of your money.

Insurance companies developed this new insurance product in response to fears of layoffs and firings due to the current economic downturn.

Trap: This type of insurance has a restrictive timetable and short benefit period that limits its effectiveness to provide any meaningful security. Better: Take the money you would use to buy mortgage insurance, and set up an emergency fund that can cover three to six months of living expenses.

Source: Margaret Miller Welch, financial advisor, Alexandra Armstrong Advisors, 1140 Connecticut Ave. NW, Washington, DC 20036.

How To Protect Yourself From Your Own Insurance Company

Insurance abuse—unjust practices on the part of our nation's insurance firms, large and small—has become a nationwide scandal. Abuses of policyholders are widespread throughout the insurance industry, and take many forms.

Examples: Insurance benefits that end up being uncollectable because of ambiguous wording in the policy...withholding of dividends due to policyholders...failure to lower premiums in the face of huge profits...habitual delay and/or unreasonable denial of legitimate claims.

We asked attorney William Shernoff, a specialist in insurance abuse, what we consumers need to know to protect ourselves against the companies we pay so dearly to protect us.

How to protect yourself from insurance abuse:

Don't assume it couldn't happen to you... even if you've been doing business with a "reputable" firm for many years. Reason: Insurance abuse is shockingly commonplace. Here are just a few of the cases I've handled involving large, prestigious firms...

• Sick fall: Michael Egan, a roofer, was permanently disabled in a fall. His insurance company cut off his benefits, claiming that his disability was caused by sickness rather than an accident, thus reducing a lifetime of coverage to a mere three months. Result: Financial and emotional devastation for the Egan family.

• Good news is bad news: John Sarchett was ordered into the hospital by his doctor, who suspected a life-threatening condition. Tests were negative and he was given a clean bill of health. His health-insurance company refused to pay his claim on the grounds that (after the fact) the hospitalization had not been medically necessary. Result: Time-consuming arbitration for both Mr. Sarchett and his doctor.

• Imposed suicide: Although a jury found that David Frazier's accidental-drowning death was caused by negligence on the part of a fishing boat's crew, his insurance company refused to pay his widow a double-indemnity benefit, claiming that their investigator's verdict was suicide. (It later became evident that they had instructed their investigator to find some motive for suicide.) Result: Inexcusable emotional anguish for the family.

• Tricky technicality: Morris Bronstein, completely disabled by heart disease, retired. On his doctor's advice, he began to take short daily walks. His insurance company discontinued his disability benefits on the grounds that he was not "confined to his house." (In a particularly ludicrous piece of testimony, the claims manager for this company testified that a quadriplegic who attended a baseball game in a wheelchair would likewise lose disability benefits under the same "house-confinement" clause.)

The good news: In all of these suits, the policyholder was vindicated. I've met all of the big companies in court—doing dirty little things—and have beaten them all.

Important: If an insurance company is found guilty of bad faith, the policyholder is permitted to recoup the benefits due under the policy, compensation for damages and emotional distress, inlcuding future damages, plus punitive damages assessed against the insurer.

How it works: Insurance companies are fiduciaries...they are founded on public trust. By law, a betrayal of this trust constitutes "bad faith."

Punitive damage awards are important in such cases, and should be upheld. Reason: Insurance companies find it more profitable to routinely deny legitimate claims and invest the money, until the policyholder...

• Gives up in despair.

• Is forced to settle for a reduced amount.

• Sues.

The interest earned on the withheld benefits more than covers court costs and attorney's fees. The risk of a high-dollar judgment is the only incentive that an insurance company has to modify its behavior. Until reforms are instituted in the insurance industry, the right to sue for punitive damages is the only effective weapon that consumers currently wield against insurance abuse.

Prime problem areas:

Punitive-damage awards have helped in some areas...but in others, insurance abuse is getting much worse.

Worst area: Health claims. Reasons: The US Supreme Court recently ruled that a federal law, ERISA (the Employee Retirement Income Security Act), preempts state laws that regulate the insurance industry. Effect: Individuals are who covered under an employee benefit plan are no longer permitted to sue their insurer for any damages, compensatory or punitive. They can only sue for the amount of benefits due under the terms of the policy plus attorney fees, which are discretionary with the court.

Result: Although ERISA was passed to protect American workers, the insurance industry is using it as a shield against employees' claims. As long as the industry enjoys legal immunity, abuses in the area of employee group-health plans will get worse. However, both Congress and the federal courts have recognized this problem and are beginning to move toward providing more appropriate remedies.

Other problem areas:

• Small claims. Insurance companies are more likely to dispute $200 or $2,000 claims. Actually, 95% of claims are small. And most policyholders give up. They feel powerless...or their lawyer is busy...or they believe that lawyers cost too much.

Recourse: Attorneys who specialize in bad-faith litigation will work for a contingency fee.

• Homeowner's insurance for victims of catastrophes. The deductible for many of these insurance policies is applied to the value for which a house is insured—not to the amount of damages the house has sustained.

Example: If a house is insured for $200,000 with a 10% deductible and an earthquake leaves $20,000 worth of damages, an unsuspecting homeowner might expect to pay $2,000 (10% of the damages) and be covered for $18,000. But he/she would be wrong...he would actually end up paying for all the damages. Reason: The fine-print clause on that particular contract specified that the deductible would be $20,000—10% of the amount the home is insured for ($200,000).

Many recent earthquake and hurricane victims learned the lesson of reading the fine print the hard way.

Recourse: Lawsuit...a possible class-action suit. Grounds: Courts have held that where language in an insurance policy is unclear, it will be construed in favor or the policyholder. Some courts go further in ruling in favor of the reasonable expectations of the policyholder, regardless of the fine print.

• Disability. This is an area in which there is a great deal of room for dispute. Reason: Your insurer may define disability differently than your state laws. Read your policy very carefully. Are you covered if you are unable to perform your usual work? Or only if you are unable to work at all? For your lifetime, or only for a year or two?

• Business policies. Many businesses don't pursue valid claims for which they are covered. Often overlooked: Coverage for business-interruption losses due to fire, theft, a recall, strike, etc. If you fail to file a claim, your insurer won't point out the oversight.

Example: Coverage for defense of a lawsuit. Often a corporation that is being sued will pay to defend itself, or fail to pursue the matter if its claim is refused. But its insurer's duty to defend a policyholder is broad. It applies even if the insurer reserves the right to contest the coverage at a later date. Case in point: The Los Angeles Raiders football team was sued for malicious prosecution. Even though they were clearly covered under the terms of their policy, their insurer claimed that they were not required to defend willful actions. But if this was so, why did they offer the coverage and accept the premiums? Outcome: The insurer did defend the lawsuit, reserving the right to contest the coverage. The insurer is now being sued for bad faith, for selling unusable coverage in the first place.

• Retirement policies. The elderly are particularly susceptible to abusive marketing practices. Recently, insurance agents have aggressively sold long-term-care policies to hospitalized patients, visiting them to collect their premiums. But when the patients enter nursing homes, their claims are denied on the grounds that the policies do not cover patients who purchased coverage while hospitalized.

One insurer denied the claim of a woman with Parkinson's disease who was discharged to a nursing home after 10 weeks of hospitalization. Grounds: The woman was not in the acute-care unit in the hospital—despite letters from the hospital and State Insurance Department certifying that she had indeed received acute care while in the hospital.

Families USA, a Washington, DC-based advocacy group, has documented similar, terrible abuses by some of the most reputable companies in the country. Common: Insurers arbitrarily deny claims for intermediate care for patients leaving a nursing home, claiming that custodial care (a lesser benefit) will suffice—despite the assurances of the medical personnel involved that intermediate care is required.

Very common: Overselling and other related shoddy-agent practices that are clearly sanctioned by the insurer.

Example: An agent fails to ask a client for certain medical data. Then the insurer denies claims, accusing the policyholder of failure to provide pertinent information.

Recourse: Insurance companies are legally responsible for the actions of their agents.

How to fight insurance abuse:

Protect your rights by supporting insurance reform, fighting to turn around ERISA and battling the powerful insurance-industry lobbies, who seek to limit or eliminate punitive damages and even jury trials.

Outrageous: Insurance lobbies—champions of bad faith in themselves—use the profits from our high premiums to fight legislation that favors our rights as consumers. They blame lawyers and high damages awards for the high premiums we all pay, when, in fact, they keep obscene amounts of cash in reserve.

Example: The insurance-industry standard for a prudent reserve of funds is $1 in surplus for every $3 in premiums. However, the nation's largest provider of auto insurance kept $1 for every $1.23 in premiums in 1988. (The industry average was $1:$2.17.)

Recourse: My firm is currently handling a national class-action suit against that insurer, demanding the return of $6.87 billion in surplus funds to its policyholders.

Source: Attorney William M. Shernoff, who specializes in "bad faith" insurance cases, some of which he describes in his book, *How to Make Insurance Companies Pay Your Claims...And What to Do if They Don't*, Hastings House, Mamaroneck, NY.

Insurance Costs: The New Self-Defense Basics

To get the best deal on the company's life and health insurance today, it's important to go beyond simply asking an insurance broker to put the company's business out for bids.

Before any decisions can be made concerning insurance, here are the tough challenges to keep in mind:

• Determining which of the new policy features and financial techniques for containing skyrocketing health insurance costs—being introduced every month—are best for the company.

• Finding and doing business with insurance companies that are financially sound, in today's environment of unprecedented financial instability.

Key: Getting the most thoughtful and professional advice on selecting insurers for the company's life and health insurance. Leaving this up to the company's conventional insurance broker is not necessarily the best policy in today's fast-changing world.

Sources of advice:

There are three categories of insurance professionals who provide advice on choosing insurers:

• Insurance agents: Likely to be legal representatives of a single insurance company, or a few companies. Some are agents for one insurer and also operate as brokers for other companies.

Advantage: An agent who brings considerable business to an insurer has influence with the insurer if your company runs into problems with a claim or service.

Drawback: The agent typically owes allegiance to one insurance company and will try to place your company's business with that insurer. There's nothing wrong with that—if the insurer's policy best suits the company's needs and is competitively priced. But that's not always the case.

• Brokers: They're not exclusive to a particular insurer and can shop the company's business around more widely than an agent.

Reality: Many brokers actually work closely—sometimes exclusively—with a single insurance company. Insurers offer incentives to encourage this—higher commissions, for instance, to a broker in their "A" category who writes more business with them than a broker in their "B" category, or by defraying some of a broker's office expenses, making a computer available, or picking up expenses for an industry convention.

Advantage of using a broker: More objectivity in reviewing insurance products and insurers than an exclusive agent. Even if the broker leans toward one or two insurers, that may be because he/she has monitored its performance with a number of customers and is convinced it's superior.

Drawback: The "objectivity" may be less real than it seems.

• Consultants: In the group life and health business, these are usually benefits consultants who also assist companies with their pension and profit-sharing plans.

Consultants collect a fee, charging by the project or by the hour, for specific services connected with selecting an insurer. Typically, once a company selects an insurer, the group policy will be written directly—with no commission. The consultant collects his fee from your company or, in some cases, the client may ask that the consultant accept the commission in lieu of a fee.

Consultant advantages: The advice is less colored by where the commissions are greatest because consulting fees can be charged instead, thereby eliminating the consultant's motivation to steer clients to insurers with the highest commissions. Consultants also may have experience with a larger number of insurers than some agents or brokers.

Drawbacks: Less "clout" with an insurer if problems develop than a very productive agent or broker might have. Anybody can call himself/herself a consultant, and some really operate as brokers, accepting as their primary source of income commissions from insurers they recommend to clients.

Ask direct questions:

Because commissions play such an important role in how certain advisors tailor the advice they provide to clients, it's critical to learn—before accepting an advisor's service—how he/she will be compensated.

Trap: If health insurance premiums go up 20% a year, a broker's commissions go up as well, each time the company renews its policy. Being unaware of this arrangement from the outset can be costly.

Trap: Insurance companies sometimes pay commissions to brokers on a sliding scale—highest in the first year (to attract new business), and substantially lower in subsequent years. This pressures brokers to move their clients' business around from one insurer to the next—simply to maximize commission income. For the company's employees, though, this is disastrous—if a serious illness exists before insurance coverage starts, the employee may not be eligible for benefits.

Recommended: If possible, use a consultant on a per-project or hourly-fee basis and use him/her as an intermediary, thereby cutting out commissions. This protects the independence of the consultant in shopping around.

If such a consultant isn't readily available, use a broker or agent who is completely straightforward about the commission arrangements he/she has with insurers. Use this knowledge to assess and, if necessary, challenge advice about policies or new insurers the broker or agent gives—to be sure of the best deal for the company, instead of just helping the broker or agent earn a bigger commission.

Specify insurance needs:

The next important step in screening insurance advisors is providing adequate information about the company's specific insurance needs. Examples:

• The company is in a financial squeeze and must cut costs, including insurance benefit costs.

• Our employees say they have a lot of problems with their claims. Can we get better service from another insurer?

• The people who manage benefits at the company spend too much time administering our health and life insurance benefits. Can we do better?

• Our employees and manager are very happy with what we have now. We don't want to rock the boat or drop any benefits, but we do want to know whether what we pay in premiums is reasonable.

Guideline: Be wary of any agent, broker or consultant who gives you a quick response, such as...

• Why don't we just try putting this out to bid and see what we can do.

• I know just the insurance company that can do the best job for you.

These are almost always self-serving attempts to give your business to an insurance company paying a fat commission.

Key: A serious advisor won't give a "solution" before looking carefully at all the information about current plans. A top advisor will ask for details about the company's current coverage because without it, he/she can't honestly look for a better deal.

What good advisors will ask for:

• Copy of the current insurance policy.

• Demographics on the work force—ages, dependents, geographical location.

• Claims and premiums paid over the last five years.

• Which carriers the company has been with and is now with.

• Latest renewal letters from the company's current carriers, with their explanation of premium increases, if any.

• How employees and benefits managers view current carriers' performance.

• Life or health benefits the company might consider modifying.

In discussions with prospective advisors, be clear about what the company's priorities are in providing these benefits. And redirect the advisor to those goals if he/she seems to veer off-track.

Danger-sign: You ask whether a specific policy feature would be good in the company's plan—and the advisor immediately dismisses it.

Important: Probe for good answers. Ask whether the advisor has introduced the idea to other clients...and what their experiences were...and if you can talk with them about it.

Key: When there are clear signs an advisor is being motivated by a promise of high commissions, challenge his advice...until there's no doubt you're getting the very best advice for the company.

Source: Arthur Dreschler, vice president, Martin E. Segal Co., consultants and actuaries, One Park Ave., New York 10016. Dreschler is an expert in benefits planning and previously worked 15 years for insurance companies, chiefly with group plans.

Insurance 1992: New Tricks...New Traps

A recent wave of concern about insurance industry solvency is prompting many people to investigate switching annuity contracts or life insurance policies to companies they perceive as unquestionably healthy.

While there are situations in which it may be advantageous to switch policies, in general, there is no need for concern. Most states have guaranty funds (similar to the FDIC) that protect these investments.

Depending on the type of policy you have, switching may cost far more in lost interest and surrender fees than the low risk of staying put.

Bigger problem: Policyholders have lost a great deal of money to deceptions and scams involving unnecessary replacement of their existing policies.

Life insurance switching:

• Term life insurance. Switching a term life policy is as straightforward as exchanging an auto or homeowners' policy. It is advantageous if you find a better deal. Most people are competent to judge whether a new rate compares favorably with their old rate, and encounter no significant problems switching policies.

• Cash value policies. The worth of an individual cash value policy is far more complicated and difficult to assess. It has a dual purpose. The policy serves as a death protection—and a savings plan. Furthermore, insurance agents are not trained to analyze the policies.

General rule: If you own an older policy that is paying dividends (and most do), it is best not to change. If you feel you need it, buy additional coverage rather than a replacement policy. Be wary if you are approached to trade in an old policy for new, broader coverage.

Trap: Unscrupulous agents routinely "rip off" clients by persuading them to cash in their older, relatively high-yielding policies for lower-yielding new ones. This is usually a ploy to boost sales commissions.

When it may be useful to switch: If your policy doesn't pay dividends. In a close call, it may tip the balance if you are now a nonsmoker, and you bought a policy before the early 1980s, when insurance companies began to make the distinction.

Most damaging time to switch: After the first two to three years, when surrender penalties are at the maximum. But there is likely to be some kind of surrender penalty for the first 10 to 15 years. Also: Switching to a new policy will activate new suicide and contestability clauses.

If you do decide to switch, both life insurance and annuities can be exchanged by tax-free transfer. (The succeeding company will ask you to fill out a "1035 Exchange" form.)

But if you cash in your policy, you will have to pay taxes on any gain. In addition, on recent single premium life policies and most annuities, there's a 10% penalty if you are younger than age 59½.

Annuities:

It is generally not possible to terminate an annuity contract once it has begun to pay. Of those not in payout:

- Annuities beyond the surrender charge period. It may be wise to switch annuities if you are no longer liable for a surrender penalty (that's usually after seven or eight years), if the interest rates are significantly better elsewhere.

Downside: With a new policy, you incur a new surrender charge period.

- Annuities within a surrender charge period. The current yield is composed of two elements...the interest rate being paid now... added to the decline each year in the amount of the surrender charge.

Example: If the annuity is currently paying 8%, and the surrender charge goes down by 1% per year, the current yield is the sum of the two, or 9%. Therefore, it would be foolish to switch to a company paying 8.5%.

Before considering a switch, ask the new company for its track record on interest credit. Do rates remain favorable? Are policyholders treated fairly and consistently?

One of the best deals around:

Compare any policy you are looking at with the life insurance annuity products offered by USAA Life (a subsidiary of United Services Automobile Association, headquartered in San Antonio, TX). It sells life insurance and annuities that are available to the general public.

Because USAA does not pay agents or brokers, it can offer a better deal than most companies. One advantage is low surrender charges—for example, 4% on annuities—that disappear after two years. USAA is a highly rated, efficiently run company with a good record on annuities.

Source: James Hunt, life insurance actuary, former state insurance commissioner and director of the National Insurance Consumer Organization, 121 N. Payne St., Alexandria, VA 22314.

Long-Term Disability Insurance

With nursing-home care now costing $30,000 to $40,000 per year, chronic disease in the elderly can easily impoverish an ill person and his/her family.

Solution: Long-term care* insurance. These policies are expensive...but worth it, because owners are very likely to collect on them. More than 25% of people over 65 years old will eventually need long-term care, as will 50% of people over 89.

Long-term-care insurance is recommended for anyone 50 or older who has a net worth of $200,000 to $1 million.

If your net worth is less than $200,000, the cost of the policy would probably interfere with your current quality of life. It would make sense not to purchase the insurance. If long-term care impoverished you, Medicaid would pay for your care.

If your net worth is more than $1 million, you could probably afford the cost of care. But you still might wish to purchase long-term-care insurance to preserve your estate for your children.

Note: Consider family finances. The spouse of an ill person must deplete a large portion of his/her savings before Medicaid starts to pay.

And children, although not legally required

*Long-term care lasts six months or longer. It is usually provided in a nursing home or in an adult congregate-living facility. People who require such care have debilitating chronic disease and need help performing everyday activities.

to pay for a parent's care, often feel obligated to do so. Because of this, some children purchase long-term-care policies for their parents.

Although many companies will not sell long-term-care policies for people under 50, it should be purchased at as young an age as possible. The longer you wait, the more likely poor health will disqualify you. Also, the younger you are when your policy begins, the less it will cost in the short and long run.

Example: A typical policy that would cost a 50-year-old $250 per year would cost a 60-year-old $550, a 70-year-old $1,450 and a 79-year-old $4,400. If they all live to 85, their total cost for the insurance would be $8,750 for the 50-year-old, $13,750 for the 60-year-old, $21,750 for the 70-year-old and $26,400 for the 79-year-old.

Like disability insurance, long-term-care policies provide a certain amount per day for a fixed period. Most have a waiting period before the insurance kicks in. You usually have to be in a nursing home 20 to 100 days before the policy starts to pay you.

All major policies are noncancelable—the insurance company cannot arbitrarily terminate your policy or raise your premium because of age or health. Exception: Although companies cannot cancel the policy, they can make changes in the premium for an entire group of people—say everyone in Florida over 60 years of age.

In recent years, long-term-care insurance has been greatly improved. Most insurers have dropped restrictions that made many of the early policies all but useless for most people.

Example: Many policies paid for long-term care only if you'd been in the hospital for three days first. But less than half the people who go into a long-term-care facility go into a hospital first.

How to pick a policy:

Long-term-care insurance is now being sold by more than 100 insurance companies. This includes most of the major companies that sell health or life insurance.

Current recommendations: John Hancock, Travelers and Amex Life. Although none of their policies is perfect, they are currently the best on the market.

Before you buy a policy, study it carefully to make sure it meets your needs. The basic policies...

• Pay at least $80 per day for three years. The average stay in a nursing home is about three years. Although some policies offer lifetime coverage, the probability of needing care for more than five years is minimal.

• Have a 100-day waiting period. Anyone who can pay for this type of insurance should be able to afford the first 100 days of care. And a 100-day waiting period will save you money on premiums.

• Have an inflation rider. This guarantees you can increase your coverage as the cost of care rises. Note: You will have to pay higher premiums to get greater benefits.

There are two types of inflation riders. One increases your benefits by 5% per year (simple, not compounded). Better: One that bases increases on the Consumer Price Index.

• Cover care in custodial facilities—not just nursing homes. Known as adult congregate living facilities, these are more residential than nursing homes. People have their own rooms and eat meals in a group dining room. They're best for people who can't manage on their own...but don't require full nursing-home care.

• Cover adult day care. This lets people stay at home and out of an institution much longer. Spouses or other caregivers can temporarily turn care over to others while they deal with their own lives.

• Start paying when you need them. Most policies start paying when you are unable to perform two or three activities of daily living (ADLs) on your own. ADLs include: Getting in and out of bed, eating, bathing, using the toilet and dressing. The higher the number of ADLs that help is needed with before coverage kicks in, the less desirable the policy.

• Are offered by companies that are exceptionally strong. The insurer should have a top rating from at least one of the four insurance-rating services—Standard & Poor's, A.M. Best, Moody's or Duff & Phelps. Reason: These policies are still relatively new. You want a company that could withstand heavy losses from them without going under.

• Are offered by companies that have stringent underwriting to lessen the risk of losses. Such companies take a great deal of health information from applicants, check it thoroughly and reject those in poor health. If a company takes only the healthiest clients, their claims will ultimately be low, and it's unlikely they'll raise prices as quickly in the future.

Of course, if you're not in the best health you'll be forced to go to a company with less stringent requirements, and it will probably cost you more in the long run.

• Are offered by companies with a long history of satisfied customers. Because long-term-care policies are changing rapidly, you want a company that will provide improvements to people who have already purchased coverage.

Example: Some companies allow people who hold old long-term-care policies to upgrade to new policies without a new medical evaluation. And the new price is based on the client's age at the time of the original application. Other companies require people who bought old policies to start from scratch to upgrade. They must reapply and pay rates based on their current age.

Source: Harold Evensky, CFP, a partner with the financial-planning firm Evensky and Brown, 2701 Ponce de Leon, Coral Gables, FL 33134. He is the author of *Planning for Long-Term Health Care*, Houghton Mifflin Co., 52 Vanderbilt Ave., New York 10017.

Life Insurance Can Be Collected Early

Almost 30% of all the money a person spends on health care during his/her lifetime is spent in the last 40 days of life. Reason: Terminal illness is expensive—and three out of five deaths in the US are caused by cancer or heart disease.

In response to this tremendous financial burden, the insurance industry has developed a way for people who are terminally ill to withdraw money from their life insurance before they die.

Under the new Accelerated Death Benefit (ADB) life-insurance rider, the money can be used to pay medical expenses or nursing-home bills without sapping family savings. Most insurance companies pay a one-time sum—usually a portion of the policy's face value.

Requirements vary by insurance company. Some limit the age at which the rider can be added to a policy. Some will pay the ADB only if a person has one of a number of specific illnesses or is expected to survive only for a certain period of time.

Although some companies now charge a one-time premium of up to $200 for the ADB, competition should eventually lead to the offer being made at no additional charge.

Even if you have an ADB rider, there are several factors a person should consider before taking advantage of it. Included:

• Other sources of cash. Unless a large financial gain would result, selling stock or other assets is often a better way to obtain cash. Reason: Life insurance proceeds—including interest earned over the course of the policy—will be tax-free at death, but capital gains tax on investments are taxed.

Remember, Medicaid provides key payments for eligible nursing-home residents... although some people don't want the stigma of being a government dependent.

• Tax implications. Life-insurance benefits are tax-free if received after the policyholder's death. We don't know yet if—or how—the government will tax pre-death receipt of benefits.

• Potential for abuse. Terminally ill people are very vulnerable and can't always think clearly. The decision to take the money early should be discussed carefully with family members. Beware of mentioning this option to health-care providers, who could take advantage by inflating their fees.

• Outliving the money. A person may live longer than expected and deplete all of the benefits collected early from the insurance policy. Consider: How will health-care bills be paid then? How will this affect the family's finances?

Important: Anyone who plans to withdraw benefits early should reexamine his will. Less life insurance may affect the way other assets are to be divided.

Source: Arthur Schechner, Schechner Lifson Ackerman Chodorcoff, Inc., insurance agents and brokers, 225 Millburn Ave., Millburn, NJ 07041.

9

Home Smarts

Consumer Alert: Adjustable Rate Mortgages

Two words of advice to owners of adjustable rate mortgages—watch out.

Some experts are now estimating that up to one fourth of all adjustable rate mortgages have been adjusted incorrectly.

In an attempt to streamline their operations, many banks are now lumping their older adjustable rate mortgages together with their newer ones. Consequently, the likelihood of an error increases if your mortgage is older or if it was made with a smaller institution.

Banks don't intentionally make these errors. But if you correct them, you may find hundreds or even thousands of dollars for yourself. A bank's mistake of even an eighth of a point could cost you $3,375 over the course of a 30-year mortgage. The important things to check each time your mortgage is adjusted...

• Was the mortgage adjusted on the proper date? Mortgages are adjusted upward or downward according to a particular index. Although the index changes on a particular day, your mortgage may not have to be changed until several days or weeks later. Make sure they've adjusted the mortgage on the date stipulated in your contract.

• Is the change in the index accurate? Make sure the index actually changed on that particular day. Check the financial pages of your newspaper. Or call Loantech Inc. (800-888-6781), which will provide you with a photocopy of the appropriate index for $12.

• Was the rate rounded off properly? Adjustments are usually rounded off to the nearest eighth or quarter of a percentage point. But banks make mathematical mistakes all the time. Make sure that they round it off correctly. Also: Make sure that the bank has not made other mathematical errors.

The documentation of most adjustable rate mortgages is often incomprehensible to the average homeowner. If you're uncertain about a change, call your bank and ask them to explain the adjustment to you.

If they can't, or give you answers that are ambiguous, consider a full audit. Mortgage Watch (800-642-5510) will perform a complete mortgage audit for $95.

If they don't find errors that are at least equal to their fee, they'll refund your money. Loantech will also provide a complete audit for $49. They do not provide a refundable guarantee.

Source: Edward F. Mrkvicka, author of *The Bank Book: How to Revoke Your Bank's License to Steal,* HarperCollins, 10 E. 53 St., New York 10022, 800-451-0643. He is also publisher of *Money Insider,* a financial newsletter for consumers, Reliance Enterprises, Inc., Box 413, Marengo, IL 60152.

How To Use Company Cash To Build Your Home

Here's a way to take cash out of your corporation without paying tax on it...and build or buy your dream home.

Loophole: Give the corporation a first mortgage on the home.

As long as you dot your "i"s and cross your "t"s you can nail down substantial tax deductions by letting your corporation finance your home. The interest you pay on up to $1 million of mortgage debt will be fully tax deductible home-mortgage interest.

Guidelines:

- Be sure the corporation charges market-rate interest on the loan.
- Document the loan with a promissory note.
- Record the mortgage at the courthouse.
- Adhere strictly to the payment schedule called for in the note.
- Correctly classify the loan and your subsequent repayments on the corporate books.

If you carefully follow these guidelines, you can dip into the company till and avoid paying any tax personally.

Source: Irving L. Blackman, partner, Blackman Kallick Bartelstein, CPAs, 300 S. Riverside Plaza, Chicago 60606.

Why You Shouldn't Pay Down Your Mortgage

Many financial planners are advising homeowners that they can save $150,000 or more in interest charges by accelerating payments on their home mortgages. They're only half right.

Although your interest costs will be reduced, you may be losing the use of money that could be better invested elsewhere. If you invested that money in a mutual fund...or in a new business...you could end up with more than you'd save in interest expenses.

Paying down your mortgage also forces you to give up a terrific tax deduction. Now that credit card and personal interest deductions are gone, your home mortgage is one of the last remaining sources of deductible interest. If you're paying 10% on a mortgage in a 40% tax bracket, the mortgage is only costing you 6%. Accelerate your payments and you'll lose that deduction forever.

Trap: If you pay down your home mortgage and then decide later to raise money by refinancing it, you may not be able to deduct all of the new interest expense or the points unless any increase in mortgage is used to improve your home. More problems: Although you'll still be able to take out a tax-deductible home equity loan for up to $100,000, Congress may very well act to restrict use of home equity loans in the near future.

Source: Attorney Martin Shenkman, 1086 Teaneck Rd., Teaneck, NJ 07666. He is the author of *How to Buy a House with No (or Little) Money Down,* John Wiley & Sons, 605 Third Ave., New York 10158.

Refinancing Your Mortgage: Pros and Cons

Mortgage rates are lower than they have been in years...but it doesn't necessarily pay to refinance. Reason: The loan application costs about 4% of the amount you borrow.

To recover those costs and start seeing some real savings, refinance only if:

• The new mortgage is two percentage points less than your current mortgage.

• You plan to stay in your present house three years or more.

It's important that you meet both of these criteria.

Example: If you have a $100,000 mortgage at 10.75%, you're paying $933 a month. If you can find a mortgage at 9.25%, you'll be paying about $823 a month, a savings of about $110. But since your closing costs will be about $4,000, it will take you 36 months just to break even.

Refinancing now makes most sense to people with mortgages at more than 11%. But most people with mortgages that high refinanced in 1987, when rates dropped to 9.25%.

If your mortgage rate is more than 10.5%, start shopping the mortgage market. You could see loans out there that are very attractive. Note: It may also be worth refinancing at mortgage savings of 1.5% if you plan to be in your house five years or more.

Key questions for loan officers: How much will it cost me to get a new loan? How much will my monthly savings be?

Caution: Make sure that the quotes include just the principal and interest, not insurance costs or any other mortgage expenses.

Source: Robert K. Heady, publisher of *Bank Rate Monitor*, Box 088888, North Palm Beach, FL 33408.

Hidden Mortgage Traps

Avoid: Banks that require you to obtain permission before you can get a second mortgage or home-equity line of credit...clauses requiring you to sell your old home before the bank will allow you to close on a new one...any add-on charges and fees.

Source: *Dun & Bradstreet Guide to Your Investments: 1991* by Nancy Dunnan, HarperPerennial, 10 E. 53 St., New York 10022.

The Larger-Mortgage-Down-Payment Challenge

The savings and loan crisis and the recession has given mortgage lenders a bad case of the jitters.

Financial institutions who purchase packages of mortgages from local banks are demanding mortgages with higher down payments.

Result: Many banks are reverting to their previous practice of requiring minimum down payments of 20% and 25%. The higher down payments also allow banks to hedge their bets if the real estate market moves farther south.

What to do:

Shop your local mortgage market carefully. Although some banks are asking for higher down payments, it's not universally true. There are still plenty of mortgage companies eager to do business in this real-estate slump.

Helpful: Don't just call the places recommended by your real-estate broker. Many real-estate brokers now have business relationships with mortgage brokers and may not help you get the best deal. You may also be eligible for a low down-payment loan from the FHA or another government source.

Source: David Schechner, Esq., partner at Schechner & Targan, 80 Main St., West Orange, NJ 07052.

Beware Of Mortgage Fraud

The increase in mortgages transferred from one holder to another has led to an increase in mortgage-transfer scams, where people are told to send future mortgage payments to a new—phony—servicer.

Self-defense: If you suddenly receive a letter from a new servicer, contact your original mortgage holder to confirm the change. In a legitimate transfer, you should receive a "goodbye" letter from your current lender naming the new servicing company.

Source: Warning from Mortgage Bankers Association of America, reported in *Changing Times*, 1729 H St. NW, Washington, DC 20006.

Mortgage-Payment Mistake

Don't use the 15-day grace period unless you have a very good reason—you're sick, out of town, etc. Reason: Always paying after the official due date will result in being listed as a chronic late payer on your credit-bureau history.

Source: Marvin Kaplan of the Associated Credit Bureaus in Houston, quoted in *Working Mother*, 230 Park Ave., New York 10169.

How To Cut Your Mortgage Costs

Most people think the only way to reduce their mortgage costs is to find a lower interest rate. They're only half right.

You can reduce the overall cost of home ownership by one simple technique—prepaying as much of your mortgage as possible. Many mortgages allow you to do so without penalties.

Paying even a modest amount more each month can cut your costs dramatically, because that extra money goes to paying off the debt...not interest.

Example: The monthly payment on a $100,000 30-year mortgage at 9.5% is $840.85. But if you pay another $50 a month, your mortgage will be paid off in 23 years and you'll save $54,698 in interest. If you paid $203 more a month, you'd pay off your mortgage in 15 years and save $114,747.

Common questions:

• Why should I put money into my mortgage when I could invest it in stocks or bonds? The rate of return you'll get for investing in your mortgage is probably higher than any other investment with comparable risk.

• If I prepay my mortgage, won't I lose my interest deductions? Yes, but your total costs will still be much less.

If you are in the 28% tax bracket, when you pay $100 in interest to your bank, you deduct 28% when you file your tax return, so you wind up paying $72 in mortgage costs. But if you prepay your mortgage, you don't have to pay anything to the bank. You'll pay $28 to Uncle Sam, but that's a lot better than paying $72 in interest to the bank.

Bonus #1: If you prepay your mortgage regularly, you'll have more equity in your house if you decide to move. You can transport that equity to your next house or use it to buy a bigger house.

Bonus #2: The more quickly you pay down a mortgage, the easier it becomes to get home-equity financing. This is the largest source of credit available to most people, and can be very valuable if you want to purchase a business or finance a child's college education. And the interest on a home-equity loan is usually tax-deductible.

Mistakes to avoid:

Many mortgages prohibit prepayments or charge a penalty if you do prepay. Self-defense: When you negotiate a new mortgage, make sure it includes the option to prepay—in whole or in part—at any time without penalty.

Don't make the mistake of signing up for a 15-year mortgage instead of a 30-year mortgage with a prepayment option. If you do, you'll be contractually obligated to come up with larger payments every month.

Prepaying with a 30-year mortgage gives you flexibility. If you have a good month, you can make a prepayment. If things get tight, you don't have to.

Source: Peter G. Miller, a Washington, DC–based real-estate broker and author of *The Common-Sense Mortgage*, HarperCollins, 10 E. 53 St., New York 10022.

How To Have A Successful Garage Sale

Garage sales are a resourceful way to make money and clean house, but make sure you take a professional approach for a maximum return with a minimum of problems.

Running a garage sale is quite similar to running any retail business—the difference is that you have only one or two days to get rid of your entire stock. The same rules apply as in any other business...you must know how to attract customers, price and display merchandise...and take security precautions.

To ensure that your garage sale goes smoothly...

- Learn from others' experiences. A month or two ahead of time, visit other garage sales in your area. Notice which items are in demand and how they're priced. Talk to the people running the sale—most will be glad to share information they learned the hard way.
- Have family and friends—or neighbors—help you out. A garage sale is physically demanding—you need to set up tables, carry merchandise and be "on" with the public for two full days. Consider joining forces with other families on the block or tenants in an apartment building. Group sales are usually very successful.
- Advertise. Attracting customers is probably the single most important element of a successful garage sale. The more people you draw, the greater your chances of having a customer fall in love with a particular item and pay the asking price.

Most newspapers have a section in the classifieds devoted to garage sales. The cost is minimal compared with the potential gain. A week before the sale, place notices on supermarket bulletin boards, trees and fences in the neighborhood.

- Make the atmosphere festive...with colorful signs, balloons and streamers. Some people spend the day driving from one garage sale to another. If all they see are just another two forlorn tables and a bored-looking salesperson, they may not bother to get out of the car.
- Display goods attractively. Wash and iron—but don't bother to mend—all clothing and linens. Organize items neatly by category. Another option: Pile goods randomly on a table. A hodgepodge spells "bargain" to most shoppers.
- Price merchandise wisely. Check Sears or discount catalogues for guidelines on merchandise you want to sell—and take into account wear and tear of the items. Examples:

Adult clothing: 10%–20% of original cost. Antique clothing or military uniforms may bring more.

Children's clothing: 40%–60% of retail price.

Wooden furniture: If well constructed and in good condition, it may sell for more than the original price.

Upholstered furniture: Doesn't sell well in the Northeast...but does better in other parts of the country.

- To bargain or not to bargain? Whether you allow room to negotiate depends on personality and circumstances. If you think you've priced an item fairly, stick to that price. You can always drop it later if customers feel it's too high.

If a potential buyer is very interested and wants to bargain, a 5% drop in price is reasonable, but don't offer a discount too quickly. Try not to haggle when other customers are within earshot—they'll be tipped off that the marked prices are negotiable.

- Watch for shoplifters. Thieves seek out garage sales—they know they'll find lots of small, easily-concealed items, and that the people in charge are reluctant to confront a possible shoplifter.

Assign at least one person to keep an eye on the merchandise. If you see someone walking off with an item, handle the situation in a nonconfrontational way: "You forgot to pay for that ceramic duck. It must have slipped your mind."

Tricks: Keep jewelry and other valuables in a glass case and have customers ask to see the pieces. Permit customers to view only one valuable item at a time. Arrange small items in a pattern so you'll notice immediately if a piece is missing.

If many people are participating in the sale, consider hiring a uniformed guard.

• Check local regulations. These are not often strictly enforced, but you should place a call to city hall to familiarize yourself with local laws.

Some communities require a license to hold a garage sale...some prohibit signs on public property.

If you hold garage sales often, the government may consider it a business and require you to collect sales tax or to pay tax on income. If you hold only an occasional sale, and sell items of your own below their original cost, you would not have to pay income tax on your receipts because they really represent losses, not gains.

Source: Robert L. Berko, executive director of the Consumer Education Research Center and author of *Holding Garage Sales for Fun and Profit,* Consumer Education Research Center, 350 Scotland Rd., Orange, NJ 07050.

Fireplace Safety

Fireplaces—a perennial source of warmth and good cheer—can turn destructive or deadly when people grow careless. Fireplace safety tips:

• Have your chimney inspected annually. Hire a professional chimney sweep. It doesn't hurt to ask if the chimney sweep is certified through the National Chimney Sweep Guild or the Woodheating Education Research Foundation (WHERF).

Modern chimney sweeps use special video equipment to check for dangerous accumulations of creosote. This black, tarry substance is extremely flammable and is responsible for most chimney fires.

Make sure the chimney sweep checks the outside as well as the inside of masonry chimneys. Cracks that leak creosote can cause harmless chimney fires to spread to the roof.

It takes about an hour to thoroughly clean a two-story chimney. Cost: About $75.

• Burn wood only. Burning paper speeds the accumulation of creosote.

Some woods "pop" more than others, sending out showers of sparks. These woods increase the risk of fire spreading outside the fireplace. High-spark woods: Oak, mesquite, dogwood, red cedar, white cedar, spruce. Safer, low-spark woods: Pine, cherry, maple, walnut, sycamore, elm, yellow poplar, Douglas fir.

• Don't use gasoline or other starters. These agents can cause a fire to spread uncontrollably.

Safe way to start a fire: Use only matches and newspaper—but only as much newspaper as it takes to start the fire, not as a source of fuel. If necessary, use a little kindling—also only as much as is required to start the fire. Reason: When a fire starts, it's burning at a low temperature. The resulting incomplete combustion leads to more fireplace emissions. Don't use anything but wood logs as your primary source of fuel.

• Keep fireplace screens closed. Glass doors are safest.

• Maintain a safety perimeter. Furniture, mantel decorations and other potentially combustible objects should be no closer than three feet from the fireplace opening.

Hidden danger: Wood exposed to heat begins to break down chemically—even though its appearance remains unchanged. Over time, this process can make the wood so unstable that it bursts into flame even without coming into direct contact with flame.

• Never leave a roaring fire unattended. If you have to leave the house—even briefly—or if you are retiring for the evening, make sure the fire is low, under control and properly screened. And children should be carefully supervised while a fire is burning.

• Dispose of ashes properly. Ashes often remain hot for days after the fire has gone out...and they can cause fires if they are disposed of in a garbage can. Always put ashes in a metal container with a tightly fitting top.

• Keep a fire extinguisher handy. And make sure everyone in your house knows how to use it.

Source: Geoff Wurzel, executive director, the Wood Heating Education and Research Foundation, 1101 Connecticut Ave. NW, Washington, DC 20036. For more information, write to the foundation, or call the National Chimney Sweep Guild at 301-774-5600.

The Simple Secrets Of Becoming A Natural Gourmet Cook

Today's natural gourmet serves low-fat, high-fiber whole foods in style. There are abundant natural-food cookbooks, but your imagination is all that you need to guide you as you vary cooking style, presentation and seasonings to elevate the simplest brown rice to high cuisine.

Whole grains are a mainstay of the new health-conscious diet because they are high in fiber and nutrients—with zero cholesterol. But plain grain gets boring. To liven it up:

- Brown rice and chestnuts. Adds sweetness to the meal. Soak ½ cup dried chestnuts overnight. The next day, drain the chestnuts. Rinse 2 cups brown rice. Pressure-cook the rice, chestnuts, a pinch of sea salt and 3 cups water for 40 minutes.
- Millet apple raisin cake. It's wheat-free, easy to prepare and delicious. Rinse 1 cup of millet until the water is clear. Combine it with 3 cups apple juice, a pinch of sea salt and 1 cup of raisins. Pressure cook or simmer for 20 minutes.
- Teff pancakes. Teff (found in natural food stores) is incredibly rich, chocolaty in appearance and flavor. Combine 1¾ cups brown teff flour, ¼ tsp. sea salt, 1 tbsp. baking powder and 2 tbsp. arrowroot. Add 1 cup apple juice, 1 cup amasake (a brown rice dairy drink also known as rice nectar), 2 tbsp. corn oil and 1 tbsp. vanilla. Mix together and cook in a hot oiled frying pan.
- Couscous with sautéed vegetable. A tasty complement to a seafood dinner. In a large frying pan, sauté onions and zucchini in olive oil. Add 1½ cups couscous, a pinch of sea salt and 3 cups boiling water. Cover and simmer for 5 minutes.

Other ways:

- Roast grains before boiling or pressure-cooking them to bring out a nutty flavor.
- Shape pressure-cooked grains into balls, burgers and croquettes, and serve with mushroom or onion sauce. Children enjoy shaping grains into balls and rolling them in ground roasted nuts, seeds and herbs to be served as appetizers at parties.
- Instead of using a pinch of salt, cook grains with an umeboshi plum, (a small pickled plum) or small piece of mineral-rich kombu (a sea vegetable). Both are available at natural-food stores.
- Fresh or sautéed vegetables, herbs, seeds and beans add color, texture and flavor to cooked grains.
- Add grains to your usual salads, soups, muffins and stews.
- Other grains to explore include barley, amaranth, corn, quinoa, whole oats, buckwheat groats, sweet brown rice, wild rice, whole grain noodles, wheat and rye berries.

Delicious beans:

Beans are the second-most-important component in today's healthy diet. There are a wonderful variety of beans available...adukis, chick peas, lentils, limas, kidney, pinto, navy, black beans, etc.

A tasty way to serve beans is to sauté vegetables and spices and add them to cooked beans as they soften. Hearty vegetable bean stews and soups also benefit from adding seasonings such as miso, mustard, curry, chili powder, garlic, ginger and dill. Delicious ideas:

- Fabulous hummus...blend 2 cups chick peas cooked with kombu seaweed, 1 sliced, raw red onion, 1 fresh bunch parsley, 3 cloves garlic, the juice of 1 fresh lemon, 1 tsp. tamari and at least ¼ cup of tahini. Or...let your intuition and taste buds tell you how much flavoring to add. Serve hummus with pita bread and long diagonal slices of carrots and celery.
- Marinated bean salads can be make colorful by adding red cabbage, red onions, radishes, carrots, scallions and red pepper.
- Tender-cooked kidney and pinto beans are scrumptious on corn tortillas topped with shredded carrots, lettuce and hot salsa.
- Beans can also be cooked with grains.

Still in the mood for meat and dairy? There are available plenty of substitutes for burgers, cheese, milk, hot dogs, sausage, bacon, bologna, margarine, dips and dressings that are all made from soy beans. All are cholesterol-free and taste close to the real thing.

Presentation:

To create an exciting meal, attractively arrange the foods being served by colors, textures—such as soft and crisp—and by tastes. Use beautiful serving dishes. Black beans will look stunning in a colorful bowl garnished with chopped scallions. For an even more stunning effect, add a carrot or radish cut like a flower.

The taste, texture and artistic presentation of brown rice is enhanced when garnished with fresh chopped parsley, scallions, toasted sunflower seeds or strips of toasted nori (a sea vegetable). Edible flowers such as rose petals and squash blossoms also add a creative and delicious touch. A sprinkling of nuts or fruit on top of a dessert will stimulate interest and indicate key ingredients of the treat to come.

For maximum enjoyment, use premium-quality natural and organic foods. They are more flavorful than those sprayed with pesticides or injected with hormones and other chemical preservatives. Be an educated and adventurous consumer. Sacrifice calories, sugar and fat. Go for maximum taste and nutrition. You'll discover that the foods that are good for you are also rich in flavor.

Source: Leslie Cerier, a natural-living consultant, RFD 2, School House Rd., Amherst, MA 01002.

Better Mattress Buying

Test mattresses by lying down and rolling around on each for a few minutes—with your sleep partner. If you choose well, a good mattress should last eight to 10 years.

Important: Wear comfortable clothes and shoes that are easy to slip on and off. Look for:

- Thickness: At least eight inches.
- Coils: More than 300 tempered-steel coils per full-size bed (375 for queen and 450 for king). Coil wire should be at least 13.5 gauge.
- Deeply quilted covering: You should not be able to feel the coils.
- Comfort: See how the mattress feels on your hips, shoulders and lower back when lying in your usual sleeping position. There should be no uncomfortable pressure. Your spine should be in the same alignment as when you are standing with good posture.

Note: Sliding a board between the mattress and box spring for extra firmness, or buying a firm mattress that feels like a board is not recommended. Mattresses today can provide firm support and a cushiony surface.

- Noise: Avoid mattresses that creak, crunch or make other suspicious sounds when you move on them.
- Movement: Avoid mattresses that sway from side to side, cause you to roll to the center or pull you in the opposite direction when you roll on them.
- Box spring: Buy the companion box spring when you buy a new mattress—they were engineered to work together.

Source: Sleep experts, quoted in *HomeOwner* magazine.

How To Unload Your Second Home If You Can't Sell It

While selling a rental resort home or apartment in a bad real estate market is difficult, there is a very attractive way to unload it—and save on taxes too. The secret: Trade it!

A bargain hunter looking for a white shirt will be attracted to a sale rack with a peach-colored shirt just because it's a bargain. Similarly, people will take property in trade that they wouldn't think of buying because it gives them tax benefits or other advantages.

Under IRS Code 1034, you can sell your primary residence and acquire a more expensive property without paying any capital gains taxes. But if you sell your investment property, you have to pay income taxes on any increase in the property's value. Trading instead of selling your investment property may allow you to maximize your reinvestment capital, because you have no tax to pay.

Example: You purchase a rental home for $50,000. A few years later, you sell it for $150,000, and pay 33% tax on the $100,000 capital gain. As a result, your net proceeds are $117,000. That's $150,000 less $33,000. But if you decide to trade your second home for another property, you may not have to pay any taxes—and you could protect the home's full value of $150,000.

By becoming an aggressive buyer, you can turn the current buyer's market to your advantage and trade your property on a more expensive investment.

Example: Using your rental property as a down payment toward the purchase of a small office building.

A real estate broker can help you find properties available for trade. If the property owner doesn't want to accept your property in trade, the broker may be able to find somebody who will. Real estate trades often involve multiple parties.

Example: Party A gives property to Party B, Party B gives property to Party C, and Party C gives property to Party A.

Warning: Very few real estate brokers fully understand trading techniques. Call your local board of realtors and ask for the professional real estate exchangers in your area or a list of members active in real estate exchanges.

Source: Jack Cummings, a broker who specializes in real estate exchanges, Cummings Realty, 3111 N.E. 22 St., Fort Lauderdale, FL 33305. 305-771-6300. Cummings is the author of *The Guide to Real Estate Exchanging,* John Wiley & Sons, 605 Third Ave., New York 10158.

On Air Conditioner Covers

Outdoor air conditioner covers are unnecessary. To keep out drafts, simply remove the inside front panel of the air conditioner and slip in a piece of plastic to cover the opening to the outside. Replace the panel. Then, next summer, just remember to remove it before you turn the unit on.

Source: *The Family Handyman,* 7900 International Dr., Minneapolis 55425.

Oven Energy Saver

Preheat no longer than 10 minutes—and turn off the oven ten minutes before a dish is done...food will continue to cook while the oven cools.

Clockworks

Restart an electric clock that has stopped by turning it on its head for a few days. Aim: To redistribute the clock's oil throughout the mechanism and lubricate frozen key parts.

Source: *Rodale's Complete Home Products Manual: The Best Guide for Using and Maintaining Your Appliances, Tools, Furnishings—and More!* by the editors of Rodale Press, 10 E. Minor, Emmaus, PA 18098.

Home-Buying Danger

Residue from misapplied pesticides that can last for years. Do not buy a house that was treated within the past 10 years with the now-banned pesticides chlordane, heptachlor, aldrin or dieldrin. Also, reject any house treated for termites more than three times during the past 10 years. For more information: National Pesticide Telecommunication Network's pesticide risk information line...800-858-PEST.

Source: Debra Lynn Dadd, author and environmental consultant, quoted in *Money Guide: Your Home* by the Editors of Money Magazine, Universal Press Syndicate Co., Andrews and McMeel, 4900 Main St., Kansas City 64112.

House Painting: How To Avoid The Standard Errors

A quality paint job on your house can last for many years. However, paint often fails prematurely because of mistakes made when it was applied. To help you take the best approach, we correct some of the misinformation that often causes homeowners to make money-wasting mistakes.

Setting the record straight:

• Misconception: A house has to be painted every five years.

• Fact: Two coats of today's top-quality latex house paint, applied to a properly prepared surface, can last up to 20 years.

• Misconception: Alkyd paint lasts longer than latex paint.

• Fact: Today's top-quality latex paint, properly applied, offers better durability than alkyd paint.

• Misconception: Alkyd paint has better gloss than latex paint.

• Fact: Initially, alkyd gloss may shine more than latex gloss. But in the long run, a gloss latex enamel retains gloss and color far better than alkyd paint.

• Misconception: There's no quality difference among paints.

• Fact: The type and proportion of binders and pigments, which remain after the paint cures, determine paint quality. Poor-quality paint wears out much more quickly.

• Misconception: All paints will fade.

• Fact: Paint colors fade from the sun's ultraviolet (UV) rays and because they're sometimes hidden by chalking. Generally, latex paints resist fading and chalking better than alkyd paints.

• Misconception: Alkyd paint should be recoated with alkyd paint.

• Fact: That depends. Latex paint is more elastic than alkyd paint. If an old house has a build-up of 10 or more coats of alkyd paint, using latex paint can cause severe peeling. Otherwise, remove or treat the alkyd paint chalk and apply a self-priming latex paint.

• Misconception: One thick coat is as good as two thin coats.

• Fact: Applying one thick coat can cause improper curing, premature failure and alligatoring. Two thin coats are better and should be applied at a coverage rate recommended by the manufacturer.

• Misconception: Sticky brown clear spots on new paint are from the wood underneath.

• Fact: Most likely, they are latex-paint additives that are extracted by rain or dew during the first one or two years after the paint has been applied. Remove them with a scrub brush and water. Or, they may be redwood or cedar oil stains and should be treated with a special primer prior to repainting.

• Misconception: Aluminum siding must be painted with paint that contains aluminum.

• Fact: The factory-applied coating on aluminum siding is similar to house paint formulated for wood siding. Special paint is not necessary.

• Misconception: Vinyl siding can't be painted.

• Fact: You can change the color and add a few years to the life of vinyl siding by painting it with the same paint you'd use on wood siding. Choose a color that's lighter than the color of the vinyl, or the siding may absorb excess heat from the sun and warp.

• Misconception: Overlap marks can't be avoided.

• Fact: Overlap marks are caused by letting the edge of one section dry before you paint the adjoining section. This problem occurs most often in latex paints. To avoid it, keep a "wet edge."

• Misconception: Paint should be applied when the temperature is between 50°F and 85°F.

• Fact: That's true for latex paints. Alkyd paints can be applied in almost any temperature. In either case, the dewpoint at the time of painting should be at least 15 degrees lower than the air temperature. Call a local airport or get a sling psychrometer (which measures humidity) to check it.

• Misconception: Concrete block, shakes and shingles should only be brush-painted.

• Fact: Concrete block is best painted with a pad applicator. Shakes and shingles are best covered with a latex or alkyd stain applied with an airless sprayer.

• Misconception: Only cheap paint peels.

• Fact: All paints can peel. Alkyd paint peels because it seals the surface, trapping moisture beneath it (latex paint "breathes"). The source may be uncured (green) wood siding, excessively moist interior air or no interior vapor barrier. Air vents, an exhaust fan or a dehumidifier can help. Back-priming the siding before installation can prevent it. Latex paint peels if it is applied to a surface that hasn't been cleansed of dirt, oil or chalk.

Source: An article by Matt Phair in *Home Mechanix* magazine. Copyright © 1991 by Times Mirror Magazines, Two Park Ave., New York 10016.

Mistakes People Make When Moving

Moving doesn't have to be a headache, as long as you can avoid making the following common mistakes:

Packing up:

- Mistake: Moving items that you don't need. Hold a garage sale to get rid of items you don't want to pay to move.
- Mistake: Not leaving enough time to pack. Figure at least two weeks to do the job right.
- Mistake: Failing to clearly label boxes. Label each carton with the room it is to go to—the master bedroom, bath, kitchen—so you and the movers know where to unload them.
- Mistake: Failing to separate items not going in the moving van. These can be anything you'll need until you get to your destination, including suitcases, a household inventory list, medicines, keys to your new home, etc. Also: Take valuables such as jewelry, important documents and irreplaceable keepsakes with you.
- Mistake: Having utilities turned off too soon. You'll still need the telephone and electricity on moving day. Arrange to have these disconnected several days after you're gone.

The physical move:

- Mistake: Not confirming hotel reservations. Also: Ask whether the hotels and motels will accept your pet.*
- Mistake: Driving too much. Better: Try to make the drive to your new home a semi-holiday, rather than a chaotic series of gas station stops. Limit your daily land journey to distances your family can easily tolerate.
- Mistake: Not tracking mileage and expenses. Most moving expenses are tax-deductible. Keeping careful records will make tax time much easier.

Source: The USAA Foundation, a nonprofit organization dedicated to promoting consumer awareness.

*For a brochure listing pet-friendly lodgings, write Quaker Professional Services, 585 Hawthorne Ct., Galesburg, IL 61401.

Avoiding Home Insurance Mistakes

Don't assume that all homeowner policies are alike...Don't assume that all insurers charge about the same...Remember to update coverage periodically.

Source: *Make Your Money Grow,* Theodore J. Miller, editor, Kiplinger Books, 1729 H St. NW, Washington, DC 20006.

Kitchen Remodeling Tips

To redo your kitchen successfully, first keep notes about what does and doesn't work in your current design—there aren't enough electrical outlets for appliances, you need more counter space near the oven, you really like the ice dispenser in the refrigerator, the roaster doesn't fit in the sink for washing, etc. Only after you know the little things that you want should you hire a planner to help you work them into a new design.

Source: *How to Be Your Own Contractor* by home renovators and national newspaper columnists Gene and Katie Hamilton, Collier Books, 866 Third Ave., New York 10022.

Home-Repair Scam

A crooked company sells products and services to long-term tenants of older homes. One paper signed is a trust deed, securing the loan for the products and services with the value of the home. Workers do a shoddy job or leave work unfinished. The owners refuse to pay for the work. The crook uses the trust deed to force the sale of the home to pay for the work—or forces the owners to take out another high-interest loan from him/her. Self-defense: Seek legal advice before signing papers.

Source: *Insight*, 3600 New York Ave. NE, Washington, DC 20002.

How To Conquer Clutter

Sooner or later, clutter invades nearly everyone's life. A key to clutter control is to have a place for everything. To figure out what belongs where...

• Organize the clutter in one complete area without stopping. Set aside a minimum of a half day—or tell yourself you won't stop until "two closets, the bathrooms or the garage" are clutter-free. Important: Avoid distractions.

Example: While cleaning her bedroom closet, Mary found something that belonged in the kitchen. But when she opened the kitchen cupboard she decided it needed to be organized as well—and never made it back to the bedroom closet.

Other distractions: Phone calls (take the phone off the hook)...old magazines, high school yearbooks, college term papers (do not stop to read anything)...errands (put them off until your task is complete).

• Set up large cardboard cartons. Recommended: One each for Elsewhere, Charity and Toss...

Elsewhere. For anything that goes in another room. Do not put away items from this box until the end of the day.

Charity. For usable items you no longer want. Do not put junk (torn clothing, broken toys than cannot be fixed, etc.) in this box—it will only tax the resources of the charity you're trying to help. Put this box into the car immediately and drop it off the next time you go out.

Toss. For the true junk. Suggestion: If you're the type of person who has a problem throwing things away, have another member of the family come by once every hour and empty this box in the trash.

• Empty the target area of clutter. Sort it into the three boxes as you go. Anything not sorted into a box should be temporarily put elsewhere—the hall or on top of the bed.

What doesn't go into a box goes back to where it came from—but stored neatly. Hint: Group like items together and keep in "clutter containers."

Examples: Underwear goes in the same drawer with drawer dividers to keep it separated...bobby pins and hair clips are stored in a covered container, etc.

• Reward yourself for a job well done. Have a nice dinner out, take in a movie...or spend a quiet evening in your newly clutter-free home.

To help keep your clutter from getting out of control in the future...

• Take 20 minutes a day to tidy up by putting everything in the right room. Toys go in the kid's room, papers and magazines go into a reading stack, etc. Later, when you have more time, you can put things away more specifically.

Examples: Toys in the toy chest, last week's unread newspapers in the trash, etc.

• Find effective clutter storage containers. Games can be stored in a trunk that doubles as a table on top of which children can play the games.

• Make an ongoing effort to get rid of things you never use. Keep a charity box on hand for usable items that you no longer want. The minute the box gets full, put the items in bags and take them to your favorite charity.

Source: Stephanie Culp, founder of The Organization, a company dedicated to helping people and businesses get organized and stay organized, and author of *How to Conquer Clutter*, Writer's Digest Books, 1507 Dana Ave., Cincinnati 45207. 800-543-4644 (in Ohio, 800-551-0884).

How To Build A Home Gym

When I tell people I'm a home fitness consultant, the first question they ask is, "If I buy just one piece of exercise equipment, what should it be?" There's no easy answer. It all depends on the individual.

Most important: Before you buy anything, make a serious commitment to exercise. Without a commitment, you'll probably waste hundreds—or thousands—of dollars on equipment that goes unused. How to shop:

- Consider your needs and wants. If you love outdoor biking but live in northern Minnesota, buy a stationary bike. If you sit behind a desk all day, choose a machine you can use standing up.

Other considerations: How much space you have...how much motivational feedback you need (don't buy high-tech options you'll never use)...who else will be using the equipment. Buy a unit with a timer and other performance readouts. Reason: Feedback gives goals and helps with motivation.

- Try the equipment out before you decide to buy. Don some comfortable clothes and athletic shoes and head to the store for test-runs on different types and models of equipment. Really work out for at least five to 10 minutes.
- Buy from a specialty store. They usually have the best selection and service and the most knowledgeable sales staff. Despite the money-back guarantees, I do not recommend buying through the mail.
- Buy quality. Don't buy cheap equipment, thinking that you'll upgrade it later with something better. A poor-quality machine that is uncomfortable to use will turn you off to exercise completely.

Aerobic equipment:

Treadmills

- Benefits: *Habit-forming*—they have the highest adherence of all home exercise equipment...*Healthful*—doctors say weight-bearing exercise helps prevent osteoporosis and also burns lots of calories...*Safe*—walking (not running or jogging) is easy on the joints.
- Drawbacks: *Expensive...Stressful*—running and jogging are hard on joints. If you want to run: Buy a shock-absorbing model. And don't run if you have an orthopedic problem...*Large*—they take up a lot of space.

Best basic: Pacemaster 870XE. 1.8-hp motor...0 mph–11 mph speed range...manual elevation 0°–10°...feedback includes calories burned, speed, time, distance and elevation...computer memory stores four workout programs. $1,425.* Source: Aerobics, Inc., 385 Main St., Little Falls, NJ 07424. 201-256-9700.

Top of the line: Precor 9.4sp. 2.2-hp motor...0 mph–10 mph speed range...electronic elevation from –3° to 12°...96 pre-programmed courses and up to 20 custom courses. Very sleek. $4,500. Source: Precor USA, 20001 N. Creek Pkwy., Bothell, WA 98011. 800-477-3267.

Stationary bikes

- Benefits: *Easy to use*—you can even read or watch TV while exercising...*Small*—they don't require much space. Exception: Recumbent models.
- Drawbacks: *Painful*—they can be a pain in the rear, literally, to use...*Limited*—they exercise only the lower body, unless you buy a dual-action model.

Best basic: Tunturi TEE. Top quality...unbeatable value...feedback includes workload, calories per minute, speed, distance and time remaining. $249. Source: Tunturi, Inc., Box 2470, Redmond, WA 98073. 800-827-8717.

Top of the line: Precor 8.7sp. Ultra-sleek, smooth and quiet...three-dimensional graphics simulate biking through three terrains—city, mountains and desert...race against other riders, or against yourself by storing a past ride in computer memory. $2,000. Source: Precor USA, 20001 N. Creek Pkwy., Bothell, WA 98011. 800-477-3267.

Cross-country ski machines

- Benefits: *Versatile*—they tone hips, thighs, buttocks and calves...*Rigorous*—a great aerobic workout.
- Drawback: *Hard to use*—the motion can be difficult to coordinate, especially with flywheel models.

Best basic: Fitness Master FM320. Sleek and very easy to use...adjustable resistance for legs and arms...electronic feedback on step count, time and calories burned...pacer to maintain rhythm....folds for storage. $349. Source: Fitness Master, 504 Industrial Blvd., Waconia, MN 55387. 800-328-8995.

*Prices listed are manufacturers' suggested list. Discounts of 5%–10% are sometimes available.

Top of the line: Nordic Track Elite. Made of walnut...elevation up to 10°...feedback includes time, distance, speed, pulse and performance index. $1,299. Source: Nordic Track, 141 Jonathan Blvd. North, Chaska, MN 55318. 800-328-5888.

Stair climbers

• Benefits: *Versatile*—they tone hips, thighs and calves, main trouble spots for most women. *Small*—they don't require much space, about the same as a bike.

• Drawbacks: *Limited*—they don't work the upper body (unless you get a dual-action unit). *Cheatable*—users tend to lean on the handlebars, which lessens the workload.

Best basic: Precor 718e. Solid construction...adjustable resistance. Feedback of time, speed, distance and pace. $399. Source: Precor USA, 20001 N. Creek Pkwy., Bothell, WA 98011. 800-477-3267.

Top of the line: Climbmax 150. Quiet and smooth. Features independent step action *à la* Stairmaster and electronic feedback on calories, time, distance, total floors climbed and horizontal equivalence to running. Also has race programs for competitive motivation. $3,195. Source: Tectrix, #6 Cromwell, Suite 102, Irvine, CA 92718. 800-767-8082.

Muscle-building and strength training:

Free weights

• Benefits: *Versatile*—the best, time-tested way to tone and strengthen all major muscle groups. And they require greater range of motion that machines...*Complete*—they work supporting muscle groups as well as the key muscle being developed in each exercise... *Inexpensive*—much cheaper than multi-gyms (see below) and single-station weight machines.

• Drawback: *Hard to use safely*—you should have someone assist you, specifically with heavier weights and bench-pressing. Highly recommended: A full-length mirror (for proper form).

Recommended: Excel, Parabody, Paramount and Universal. All offer complete lines of good quality free weights and benches. Weight starter set: About $100. Benches: $100–$150.

Multi-gym (strength-training) machines

• Benefits: *Safe*—you can train without supervision...*Easier to use than free weights.*

• Drawbacks: *Large*—they take up a lot of space...*Expensive.*

Low-end: Newport single-stack machine. Features high/low pulley, bench press, shoulder press and leg extension. $995 (additional $375 for pec-fly option and $100 for calf-raise option). Source: Pacific Fitness, 12349 E. Telegraph Rd., Santa Fe Springs, CA 90670. 800-722-3482.

High-end: Malibu double-stack machine. Features all of the above plus VKR (vertical knee raise), calf raise and pec fly. $2,400 (additional $1,295 for press option). Source: Pacific Fitness, 12349 E. Telegraph Rd., Santa Fe Springs, CA 90670. 800-722-3482.

Getting started/keeping going:

Developing a personal fitness program depends more on your fitness level than on your age. However, anyone over 35 should see a doctor—especially if you've had heart problems or if there's a history of heart problems in your family—before beginning a new fitness regime for a complete check-up.

Exercise minimum: Maintain your target heart rate* for at least 20 minutes three times a week. Other advice:

• Set specific fitness goals. Having a goal that is important to you (not your spouse or anyone else) provides needed motivation. Common trap: Picking a goal that is not attainable—if you have a large frame you'll never have the slender body of a runner...if your frame is slight, you'll never look like Arnold Schwarzenegger. Your doctor or personal trainer can help you set realistic goals.

Examples: Within a year, I want to reduce my body fat from 23% to 18%...run an eight-minute mile...lose two pounds a week.

• Distract yourself. Indoor exercise can be very boring. Make sure your exercise room has some sort of diversion—a stereo or a TV—or read.

• Diversify. Once you know you're committed, you may want to purchase additional pieces

*To determine your target heart-rate range: Subtract your age from 220. Multiply this number by 0.7 and 0.85. Your target heart rate, in beats per minute, is within this range.

of equipment to add variety to your workouts and to develop different muscle groups.

• Stretch. Muscles that are too tight are more easily strained—whether from playing sports or just getting out of bed in the morning. Typically, people feel old when their muscles lose flexibility. Recommended: Enroll in a yoga or stretch class...or follow a video or book on the subject.

Rules of safe stretching: Warm up with a couple of minutes of light aerobic exercise before your stretch...stretch in a slow, smooth motion—never bounce...stretch for a minimum of two to three minutes before you work out and three to 10 minutes after.

Source: An industry insider who continually tests the latest home exercise equipment.

Lightning-Protection Basics

Inside—during a storm, don't use telephones, hair dryers or washing machines... unplug televisions and stereos if they are fed by rooftop antennas...stay away from open doors, windows, stoves, metal pipes and sinks. Outside—stay away from trees. If there is no shelter, avoid the highest object in the area. If necessary, lie down in the open on the lowest spot of ground you can find...if you're in water, get out.

Source: Insurance Information Institute, 110 William St., New York 10038.

New Ultra Low-Flush Toilets

New ultra low-flush toilets require only one and a half gallons of water a flush—60% less than most water-saving toilets and 80% less than standard toilets. Available through plumbing supply houses. Cost: $100 to $250.

Source: *The New York Times.*

Appliance Cord Storage

Store detachable appliance cords in the cardboard tubes that paper towels come on. Label the outside with the name of the appliance.

Source: *Good Housekeeping,* 959 Eighth Ave., New York 10019.

Coping With Kids' Rooms

Adopt a different set of standards. Let them do whatever they want in their rooms—as long as it doesn't interfere with the rest of the house. Important: Stay out—don't even think about what it must be like inside. You will only upset yourself.

Source: Ron Taffel, PhD, author of *Parenting By Heart: How to Connect with Your Kids in the Face of Too Much Advice, Too Many Pressures, and Never Enough Time,* quoted in *Parents,* 685 Third Ave., New York 10017.

Toxic Antifreeze

Spilled antifreeze can be fatal to pets. Antifreeze tastes sweet and many animals will lap it up if given a chance. Defense: Wipe up spills...then hose the area down completely. Signs that a pet has ingested antifreeze include staggering or slow mental functions. If you think your pet has ingested antifreeze, take it to a emergency pet-care facility immediately.

Source: Mike Schaer, DVM, University of Florida College of Veterinary Medicine, quoted in *Woman's Day,* 1633 Broadway, New York 10019.

Beat Caller ID

Keep your unlisted phone number from being revealed by new "caller ID" devices. How: Make your call through the new Private Lines phone service. Dial 900-STOPPER. You'll get a second dial tone, when you can enter the number you want to reach. Your unlisted number will be masked out to ID devices. Cost: $2 per minute, with the charge appearing on your normal phone bill.

Source: *Inbound/Outbound,* 12 W. 21 St., New York 10010.

Upholstery Cleaning Guidelines

Cleaning codes for upholstery have been set by the furniture industry. Look for a letter code on the furniture label or in the consumer information pack that comes with it. W means the fabric can be cleaned with water-based products...S indicates you need a solvent-based cleaner...WS says you can use either...X requires professional cleaning. Self-defense: Always spot-test in an inconspicuous area before beginning a cleaning job, no matter what the label says.

Source: *How to Clean Practically Anything* by the editors of Consumer Reports Books, 101 Truman Ave., Yonkers, NY 10703.

Better Winter Heating

Think of south-facing windows as solar collectors. Remove summer screens and keep drapes and blinds open and the windows unshaded on sunny winter days. An average 10-square-foot, double-pane, south-facing window will gain almost 4,000 BTUs (British thermal units) of heat—more than it will lose on a sunny winter day. It costs about 40 cents to generate that much heat from natural gas—and even more from other fuels.

Source: Pat Huelman, University of Minnesota's Cold Climate Housing Center, St. Paul.

Make Your Old Home Feel Like New

Simple, inexpensive fix-ups can make an old home look almost new. And you don't have to be a home-repair whiz to do them. Some suggestions:

- Paper a room. A real easy job, especially with new, pre-pasted wallpapers. Cost: From $150–$300 per room, depending on the quality of paper. For walls that are marred, textured papers cover a multitude of sins.
- Kitchen face-left. A professional renovation can cost as much as $20,000. But simple, do-it-yourself tasks will bring new life to your kitchen. Easy possibilities: Paint the cabinets (use a good-quality enamel)...replace countertops with pre-made sections sold at building-supply stores...replace the sink...install a new floor using attractive vinyl squares. Total cost: Approximately $500.
- Redo the bathroom. Replace the old-style hanging sink with a modern pedestal sink or full vanity. Adding a vanity with drawers for storage allows you to replace an old-fashioned metal medicine cabinet with a full-wall-width mirror...making the room look twice as large. Cost:$500–$700.
- Refinish wooden furniture. Refinishing is much easier and more pleasant today than it was 10 years ago. Helpful: Nontoxic, odor-free refinishers have replaced the caustic, smelly products of old. New finishes are also easier to apply and much more forgiving. Cost: $15–$25.
- Replace gutters and downspouts. New vinyl gutters look much better than old, aluminum ones—and are easier to install. Segments snap together easily for a better water seal and can be cut easily using a regular hand saw. Easy-to-install mounting brackets hold gutters in place. Cost: Approximately $300 for an average-sized home.
- Install new storm doors. Usually the most visible part of a home. Old-fashioned anodized aluminum doors sag and fall out of alignment, resulting in a shabby look, a poor seal and wasted energy. Newer aluminum storm doors come in colors, have adjustable door frames for easy installation and fit snugly. Cost: $200–$300 each.
- Install a bay or bow window. A project that requires some—but not a lot—of expertise. Modern windows are pre-made and come in a variety of sizes and styles. Result: A

brighter, more "open" room. Trickiest part: Getting the window in place—they're heavy and bulky. Suggestion: Invite a few friends over for a "window-raising" party. Cost: $1,500–$2,500.

Recommended reading list:

• *Ortho's Home Improvement Encyclopedia* by Bob Beckstrom. Ortho Books, Box 5047, San Ramon, CA 94583. 415-842-5537.

• *Reader's Digest Home Improvement Manual.* Reader's Digest Association, Pleasantville, NY 10570. 800-431-1246.

• *Renovation: A Complete Guide* by Michael W. Litchfield. Prentice Hall, 200 Old Tappan Rd., Old Tappan, NJ 07675. 201-767-5937.

• *Popular Mechanics Home How-To* by Albert Jackson and David Day. Hearst Books, a division of William Morrow & Co., 1350 Ave. of the Americas, New York 10019. 212-261-6500.

Source: Arthur Rooze, senior editor, *The Family Handyman,* 7900 International Dr., Suite 950, Minneapolis 55425.

Piano-Tuning Guidelines

Tune your piano as often as you hear the need for it, or at least once a year. If you don't want to rely on your ears...tune it when seasons change. Not tuning a piano regularly can cause irreversible damage to it.

Source: Larry Fine, author of *The Piano Book: Buying and Owning a New or Used Piano,* Brookside Press, Box 178, Jamaica Plain, MA 02130.

Home Elevators

Home elevators are rising in popularity as the population ages. Uses: To accommodate older relatives or the disabled...to make it easier to keep a house into old age...to help when unloading groceries or moving heavy objects from floor to floor. Cost: $10,000 and up.

Source: Gopal Ahluwalia, director of research, National Association of Homebuilders, Washington, DC.

Check Background Noise

Check background noise before buying a house. Open the windows...sit outside on the porch or patio...stand on the front walk. Make sure the noise level will not be disruptive or make it unpleasant to sit outside. Reminder: Some noises vary with time of day. Highway noise, for instance, is louder during weekday rush hours than on Sunday mornings.

Source: *Home Safe Home: How to Make Your Home Environmentally Safe* by environmental reporter William J. Kelly, Avon Books, 105 Madison Ave., New York 10016.

For Warmer Feet

Footstools keep feet warm by lifting them off the floor where the coolest drafts swirl. Place a footstool at each comfortable chair in your home and you may be able to lower the thermostat a few degrees.

Source: *547 Tips for Saving Energy in Your Home* by Roger Albright, Storey Communications, Schoolhouse Rd., Rd #1, Box 105, Pownal, VT 05261.

Mortgage Refund Trap

If you were overcharged on an adjustable-rate mortgage and have received a refund from the bank, the refund is taxable income to the extent that it represents mortgage interest that you previously deducted. Safety: Be sure the bank provides you with a statement specifying how much of the refund is interest and how much is principal.

Source: David Ellis, editor, *Tax Hotline,* 330 W. 42 St., New York 10036.

Child-Guard Caps

Child-resistant pharmaceutical caps aren't child-resistant enough. Federal regulations consider 85% a passing grade—which means 15% of children may be able to open it. Added protection: Keep all medicine out of children's reach.

Source: *The Perfectly Safe Home* by Jeanne Miller, president, Perfectly Safe, Fireside Books, 1230 Ave. of the Americas, New York 10020.

Washing Sterling And Stainless

Washing sterling and stainless steel flatware together in the dishwasher will result in black spots on your good silver. Reason: The two metals have a galvanic—electrical—action when they touch, leaving the spots. The spots can be removed with silver polish. Better: Hand wash sterling silver.

Source: *Good Housekeeping*, 959 Eighth Ave., New York 10019.

Kitchen Energy Waster

An improperly set refrigerator/freezer can increase energy cost as much as 25%. Best: Set the refrigerator compartment between 38° and 42°...the freezer compartment between 0° and 5°.

Source: *The Student Environment Action Guide* by The Student Environmental Action Coalition, Earth Works Press, 1400 Shattuck Ave., Box 25, Berkeley, CA 94709.

The Auction Alternative For Selling Your Home

In today's tight real-estate market, many people are turning to auctions to generate the interest needed to sell their homes. An auction is a quick and efficient way to sell a house, a condo, even acreage, with no contingencies. Auction buyers are solid buyers, so financing is rarely a problem. Virtually 100% of auction contracts close.

To sell your property at auction:

- Contact a professional auctioneer who has experience selling property similar to yours. The National Auctioneers Association* publishes a national directory of auctioneers. Questions to ask...
- Will you do target-market research to determine what kind of customer my property should be promoted to?
- Are you willing to share your commission with local real-estate brokers to get the benefit of their advertising?
- Will you purchase the mailing lists needed to attract the proper prospects?
- The auctioneer inspects your property and sets a timetable and fees. It usually takes about 45 days to advertise and set up the auction.

Costs: In most cases, you will be asked to pay 1%–4% of the appraised value of your home to cover advertising expenses. In addition, you must pay a commission of 5%–10% to the auctioneer. A portion would be shared with the broker whose client buys the property.

- You decide what kind of auction to hold. There are two types:
- Absolute. The property sells to the highest bidder, period.
- Subject-to-confirmation. The seller establishes a minimum price that he/she will accept for the property.

Although the second choice sounds more beneficial to the buyer, the first generates more interest, because people love a potential bargain. Benefit: The more interest you get, the hotter the auction. Sometimes the price is driven higher than what you would get in a subject-to-confirmation auction.

- The listing agreement is discussed and signed. This is similar to the listing agreement you would sign with a traditional broker.
- A sign is put on your property to promote the auction. In addition, ads are placed in local papers and a brochure describing your property is distributed to prospective buyers.
- A preview of your home is scheduled before the auction. On this date, prospective buyers can inspect your property. Because

*For a free copy of the directory, write the association at 8880 Ballentine, Overland Park, Kansas 66214 or call 913-541-8084.

everyone comes on the same day, an auction generates more enthusiasm for and competition over your property. This also enables you to maintain some privacy while your home is on the market—you won't have brokers bringing people through at all hours.

• Another preview is held on auction day. This gives interested buyers a last chance to look at the property before the bidding begins.

• The auction takes place at your home. Prospective buyers bring cash or a cashier's check, the amount of which is designated in your listing agreement and is nonrefundable if financing falls through. The buyer then has 45 to 60 days to close on the property.

Source: Jim Gall, chairman of the board and founder of Auction Company of America, 100 N. Biscayne Blvd., Miami 33132.

How To Run Your Home Much Better

Whether you live in a large house or a small apartment, you can make your home more inviting. Ideas from America's best country innkeepers...

On overnight guests:

• Keep a flashlight handy in the guest room so guests can find their way to the bathroom in the middle of the night. Also put a flashlight by the front door so guests—or family members—who stay out late can find their rooms without turning on all the lights.

• Put a simple alarm clock in your guest room so guests can get a good night's sleep without the worry of oversleeping.

• Have a small book light available so a guest can read comfortably in bed without disturbing his/her partner.

• Place sample-size toiletries in a basket in the guest room in case guests forget something.

On entertaining:

• Give guests copies of the recipes for special dishes you serve. Write recipes on index cards and tie them with a ribbon.

• Chill champagne quickly by putting ice and water into the ice bucket. Submerge the bottle three-fourths of the way. The champagne will be ready to drink in just 15 minutes.

• Keep a scrapbook of activities to do in your area to help guests decide how they'd like to spend their time.

• Clean the powder room just before guests arrive even if you can't clean the whole house. If the bathroom sparkles, the whole house will seem clean.

• Set the table the night before a dinner party. Creating a gracious table takes time and you may not have enough if you wait until the last minute.

On food:

• Before preparing something gooey, place a plastic bag beside the telephone. If it rings, slip the bag over your hand before answering to keep the phone clean.

• Revive wilted salad greens by dousing them quickly in hot water, then in ice water with a little vinegar added.

• Prepare muffin batter ahead of time and freeze it in muffin tins. Bake frozen and uncovered five minutes longer than the recipe indicates. The muffins will be far better than if frozen after baking.

• Solid shortening is easier to measure by cold-water displacement.

Example: If you need ⅓ cup of shortening, put ⅔ cup of cold water in a one-cup measure. Add shortening until the water level reaches one cup. Then poor off the water.

• Include pineapple in a fresh fruit salad to prevent the other fruits from turning brown.

On special touches:

• Attract butterflies to your garden by planting zinnias and marigolds.

• For beautiful ice cubes, place one edible flower in each compartment of the tray, add water and freeze. Suggested flowers: Mustard flower, chrysanthemum, gladiolus, jasmine, squash blossom, honeysuckle, tulip, forget-me-not, day lily, rose.

• Make your house more inviting by tucking bunches of aromatic herbs—thyme, woodruff, marjoram, oregano, etc.—in corners. Or, boil apples, cinnamon and cloves on the stove. (Later, make applesauce by removing the cloves and mashing the apples with a potato masher.)

• Decorate a cake quickly by placing a doily on top of the cake and sprinkling it with powdered sugar. Remove doily.

• Keep electronic components (stereo, TV, etc.) inside antiques—an old cupboard, an armoire, etc.—if they don't fit with your antique décor.

• Dry flowers for potpourri by placing petals or blossoms in a shallow box in your car trunk. The heat will dry them and the darkness will help keep their color. In about a week, place petals in a plastic bag and mix with spices and essential oils.

• Tea tastes better when milk (not cream, which is too heavy) is poured into the cup before the tea.

On cleaning:

• Clean more efficiently by placing needed items—sponges, brushes, assorted cleaners, etc.—in a bucket and toting it to each room as you clean.

• Remove gummy buildup on wood with mechanic's waterless hand cleaner applied with fine steel wool. Wipe clean with a soft cloth.

• Clean the toaster daily. Burnt crumbs can set off the smoke alarm...and interfere with the toaster's thermostat.

• Remove mildew from a book by setting it in the sun and frequently fanning the pages. Brush off dried mold.

• Keep the kitchen drain unclogged by occasionally pouring in a quarter cup of grease-cutting detergent before going to bed.

• Remove wax from carpeting by placing a piece of tissue paper over the wax and applying a hot iron for a second or two.

On home improvements:

• Add 25% to 50% to a professional's estimate on renovations—extra costs often crop up.

• Stop putting off a project by planning an event for the room involved...and immediately mailing invitations. The forced deadline will provide needed incentive.

• Screws bite into wood more easily if they are first pressed into a bar of soap.

• Use yacht paint on porch decks and screen doors. It lasts much longer than conventional house paints in areas that get a lot of sun and rain.

• Install cedar paneling on bathroom ceilings to eliminate mildew problems.

• Remove paint from brass hardware by soaking the hardware in Lysol toilet-bowl cleaner.

• Tighten loose chair caning by applying rags soaked in hot water. Caning will tighten as it dries. If chair is soiled, gently rub with a mild detergent.

• Repair chipped crystal by filing the damaged area in a circular motion with a superfine emery board..

• If fireplace smoke backs up into the room, soak a wet towel in vinegar, wring it out and wave it around in the air to soak up odors.

Source: Gail Greco, author of *Secrets of Entertaining from America's Best Innkeepers*, The Globe Pequot Press, Box Q, Chester, CT 06412.

Dryers Cause 14,000 Fires A Year

Major cause: Dust and lint buildup in and behind the dryer cause overheating. Helpful: Clean the lint filter after every load...and make sure the dryer is operating properly. Important: Check the exhaust duct for lint buildup. Use only metal ducts, unless the manufacturer explicitly approves the use of plastic ducts. Also helpful: Remove clothes from the dryer right after the cycle finishes. Some materials will spontaneously heat in the confined space of the drum.

Source: *Consumer's Research*, 800 Maryland Ave. NE, Washington, DC 20002.

Fabric Protection

Spray-on fabric guards can protect upholstered furniture. Silicone sprays: Resist water-based stains—wine, etc. Fluorochemical sprays: Resist both water-based stains and oil-based stains—salad dressing, peanut butter, etc. Best: Fabric guards that have been applied by the manufacturer at the mill.

Source: *1,001 Home Ideas*, 3 Park Ave., New York 10016.

Home Fix-Ups: Should You Or Shouldn't You?

People who are interested in fixing up their houses often ask what kind of return they can expect on their investment.

Example: If I spend $7,000 on a new bathroom, will it add $7,000 to the value of my house?

Even if you can put a value on a home-improvement project (and I don't think you can), it's a mistake to rely on such general figures. There are many more things to look at than potential payback...especially in today's topsy-turvy real-estate market.

Questions to ask before you renovate:

- What am I going to do with the house? Unless you plan to sell it in the near future, don't make an improvement that you don't personally want.

An improvement that your family would truly enjoy may be worth it, even if you don't recoup the cost when you sell the house. How do you put a price on pleasure?

- What's happening in the neighborhood? If you're looking for a return on your investment, renovations would fit the trends in your neighborhood.

Example: My neighborhood consists primarily of older houses inhabited by young families with kids. Additional bedrooms and big, modern kitchens are highly valued. In a neighborhood of older couples with grown children, building another bedroom could detract from a home's value...but putting on a sun room may have great value.

- How would the improvement be made? If you're handy enough to do professional-quality work yourself, you can save 30% or more, and it is more likely that you will realize a good return when you sell.

If you're not handy but do have free time, you can save up to 20% by being your own general contractor and hiring each type of skilled worker that you need to get the job done.

- What are the market conditions? I built an addition on my house two years ago—at the height of the real-estate boom—when contractors were very busy. Three of the five companies I called wouldn't even talk to me. Today, however, because of the weak real-estate market, the same work would cost me 25% less.

If you are planning to sell:

There are fix-ups that will provide a good return if you plan to sell your house within a year.

- Repairs. Fix everything that isn't working properly. This will provide the biggest payback. Something as small as a leaking faucet can scare off prospective buyers who fear bigger, unseen problems.
- Unusual features. A two-bedroom house, an odd-colored room, a poorly finished basement, etc., probably need work to make the house sellable.
- Outdoor landscaping and painting. If your front lawn is overgrown, make it look attractive. If the paint is peeling, then paint.
- Energy-conservation improvements. These give an immediate return—by lowering your energy costs—and increase the value of your house when you are ready to sell. Add insulation if your house is not well insulated ...install energy-efficient heating and cooling systems...replace drafty windows, etc.

Source: Martin M. Shenkman, author of *How to Sell Your House in a Buyer's Market*, John Wiley & Sons, 605 Third Ave., New York 10158.

For Fresher Closets

Clear musty closet odors by keeping an open box of baking soda on a shelf. Also: Sprinkle a small amount of baking soda into shoes, boots and sneakers to absorb moisture and odors.

Source: *Good Housekeeping*, 959 Eighth Ave., New York 10019.

Kitchen Fire Protection

When you cook, wear tight-fitted clothing—loose clothes can be ignited by hot burners...never leave the kitchen when something is cooking on the stove...don't store extraneous items on the stove top...keep kitchen appliances clean and in good condition and turn them off immediately after use.

Source: National Fire Protection Association, Batterymarch Park, Quincy, MA 02269.

Best Time To Inspect A House

During or right after a rainfall, to see how water-tight the house is. When you can't wait for rain: Carefully examine the roof's condition. Important: A sloped roof (flat roofs hold water)...where sloped sections meet, water should be directed off the roof (bring binoculars to examine these areas)...flashing around the chimney and other vents should be intact...look for sections that have different-colored shingles—indicating repairs.

Source: *The Home Buyer's Inspection Guide* by James Madorma, Betterway Publications, Box 219, Crozet, VA 22932.

Cocktail Party Guideline

Ice per person for a cocktail party: One pound.

Source: *Do-Ahead Entertaining: Cooking in Advance for Any Occasion* by Malabar Hornblower, Globe Pequot Press, 138 W. Main St., Chester, CT 06412.

Faster Laundry

Instead of putting dirty clothes in a hamper, set up three bins labeled *whites*, *colors* and *badly soiled* so family members can sort as they toss. Keep a bottle of stain pre-treater near the bins so stains can be tended to immediately...use a fabric softener to cut down on ironing.

Source: *Woman's Day*, 1633 Broadway, New York 10019.

It Pays To Choose An Energy-Efficient, Cost-Efficient Washer & Dryer

Laundry appliances have continually evolved to keep up with changing lifestyles, fabric uses, technical advances and conservation regulations.

So if you haven't purchased a washing machine or dryer for the past 10 or 15 years, be prepared to face a bewildering array of choices that didn't exist the last time you bought appliances. Here's what's really important...

Capacity:

Manufacturers use general terms, such as "standard" or "super-capacity" to describe their appliances. Problem: One manufacturer's "standard" may not be the same size as another's.

Solution: Check poundage figures when comparing models. A washer or dryer labeled "standard capacity" may hold from 10 to 16 pounds of laundry. "Large" or "super-capacity" appliances handle 18- to 20-pound loads...while "compact" models handle eight pounds or less. (These measurements refer to loads of heavy denim work clothes. No home appliances are large enough for 20 pounds of sheets!)

Washers last an average of 13 years, and dryers 10. Many appliances last much longer. So be sure to consider your needs well into the future. Is your family expanding? Are your children nearing college age?

Don't buy too small a unit. Even if you live alone, you may want enough capacity for bedspreads, curtains, etc. Smaller appliances may cost less, but the difference is negligible over the life of the appliances because laundering multiple small loads can be time-, water- and energy-consuming.

Better: Choose a larger model with adjustable water levels for smaller loads.

Features:

Virtually all but the lowest-cost models offer a wide variety of settings, speeds and cycles. General rule: The more options, the higher the price. Most important:

• Water level: Look for infinite water level control, rather than high, medium, low. This allows you to save water by filling the tub only as high as needed.

• Water temperature: An energy-saving cold rinse cycle is now mandated on washers. But make sure you have several wash cycle settings as well—at a minimum, hot, warm, cold.

• Dryer temperature: Look for a no-heat or air-only setting. Also useful: A cool-down cycle.

• Fabric type: The most common settings are for delicate, regular and permanent press fabrics. Look for settings that meet your needs. For instance, a heavy-duty cycle for kids' jeans...a white cycle for uniforms...a light-soil cycle to conserve energy.

• Electronic controls: Computerized controls, found on the most expensive models, automatically select wash time, temperature, agitation and spin rate—or, on dryers, the combination of heat, tumbling and cool-down—to suit the type of load that has been selected. Some are preprogrammed, others will remember your customized instructions. Advantages: Electronic controls are the more precise. On dryers, electronic sensors that feel moisture will turn off heat when clothes are dry, saving electricity. Disadvantages: Electronic controls are the most likely parts to break...may need to be reset after power outages...add substantially to the price of the appliances.

• Other features: Avoid paying extra for options you won't use very much. Look for features that match your typical washloads. Examples: Pre-wash or soak cycle (great for heavily soiled work clothes or cloth diapers). Automatic dispensers for bleach and fabric softener (useful if you use these additives frequently). Mini-basket for delicates (great for fine lingerie, less useful if you only wear cotton briefs). Special dryer rack for sneakers.

• Ergonomics: Choose design features that meet your needs. Examples: If space is at a premium, look for a washer and dryer that can be stacked. Check the location of lint filters to make sure they are easily accessible. For the visually impaired, Whirlpool offers a large-graphics washer and dryer, and free Braille overlays for all its models.

• Appearance: As more and more laundry appliances are being used outside of the basement, they have become increasingly attractive. But if they are not going to be readily visible, you may not want to pay for designer colors. Unless it is important to you, they don't even need to match. It is perfectly acceptable to buy one manufacturer's washer and another's dryer. And you may have to replace one before the other wears out anyway.

Price and service:

Visit several stores and compare several brands and models. And be on the lookout for sales. Appliance prices are extremely competitive and volatile in this area. However, don't let price be the only, or even the most important, consideration.

Recommended: Start with the top-of-the-line models. Then eliminate features you don't need and buy the best model you can afford that has the features you do need.

Source: An industry expert with more than 20 years experience in the field of appliances.

10

An Investor's Guide To Retirement Planning

Pros and Cons of Tax-Deferred Annuities

Tax-deferred annuities are an increasingly popular investment. And now, they are being aggressively marketed by the insurance companies which sell them.

But, while annuities provide tax-saving opportunities—there are traps for investors as well. There are two kinds of tax-deferred annuities—fixed and variable.

• Fixed annuities: Provide a set investment return, which is determined by the return the insurance company earns on its investments.

Catch: The return on a fixed annuity may be guaranteed for a period of time (typically from one to five years), but it is not fixed for the life of the annuity. The return will vary with the insurer's financial performance.

• Variable annuities: In effect, mutual funds run by insurance companies. You select your own investments, and can change investments as you go along. Your return depends on your investment results.

With either type of annuity, you can withdraw your investment balance either in a single lump sum, or through payments made over a period of years.

However, with a variable annuity, you withdraw annuity "units"—the equivalent of mutual fund shares. If you withdraw your investment over a period of years, the value of these units may rise or fall, affecting your cash payout.

The main advantage of an annuity is that investment earnings compound on a tax-free basis as long as the money remains in the policy. Other advantages:

• You do not have to start making withdrawals at age 70½, as you would with an IRA or other retirement plan. Thus, money can stay invested in the annuity and earn tax-deferred interest for a longer period of time.

• You can make contributions to an annuity after the 70½ age limit set on IRAs and other kinds of plans.

Variable annuities also provide what can be a major tax advantage for mutual fund investors. They do not have to pay gains tax when they switch from one fund investment to another, as long as the money stays in the annuity. Thus, aggressive investors who try to time the market and frequently switch among various investment options may cut their tax bills significantly if they invest through a variable annuity.

Annuities hold traps for investors as well. The first mistake many annuity investors make is to overestimate the value of the tax deferral they get—if money is kept in an annuity for less than 10 years, the tax deferral may be the equivalent of less than 1% of yield. This is important because an annuity may pay less than other available investments.

Example: A fixed annuity will generally pay less than a taxable bond fund, and variable annuities typically impose annual charges of up to 2% of investment assets. That charge is more than that imposed by the average no-load mutual fund.

For the value of tax deferral to outweigh these costs, money should most often be held in an annuity for 20 years. This condition would be met, for example, if after a 10-year investment, annuity funds were withdrawn over a 20-year period, thereby providing a 20-year average investment period.

More annuity drawbacks...

- A 10% early withdrawal penalty applies to funds taken out of an annuity before age 59½.
- Most annuities impose surrender fees if you cash them in early. Typically, these start at 7% during the first year, decline 1% annually, and are eliminated after the seventh year. Details vary from policy to policy.
- Some policies impose other kinds of fees, such as "deferred sales charges" which are charged to your investment over a period of years.

Carefully check any annuity contract for all charges and expenses before buying, and be sure to consider how they will affect the net return compared with other investments.

Many people buy annuities with the financial goal of saving money which they intend to pass to the next generation—while keeping the money accessible should they need it. But there's a trap here. The increase in an annuity's value due to tax-deferred earnings becomes a taxable gain at death.

A better investment for many people in this situation is life insurance—which also provides tax-deferred status for investment earnings left in the policy, but which provides a tax-free death benefit. Even if an annuity provides a higher investment return than a life-insurance policy, the insurance may provide a much higher net return after tax.

Annuities and life insurance are both extremely complicated investments. The policies must be examined in detail to be sure you are getting the best deal.

Helpful: The National Insurance Consumers Organization's *How To Save Money on Life Insurance.* It compares various types of annuity and insurance programs from insurance companies. To order, write: NICO, 121 North Payne St., Alexandria, Virginia 22314, $13.95.

Source: James H. Hunt, a director of the National Insurance Consumers Organization, 121 North Payne St., Alexandria, VA 22314.

What To Do If Offered Early Retirement

As more companies streamline their operations, the chances are greater of being offered early retirement. When that happens, all too many people panic and make poor decisions. That hurts both their careers and their financial well-being.

Today there's no reason to feel pressured. The new federal laws encourage companies to let employees take up to 45 days to accept or reject the offer.

Evaluating early retirement is tricky—so take the time to examine and understand the provisions you're offered and consider the alternatives.

The majority of early-retirement packages offer...

- Better pensions. As an inducement to leave, pension payouts may be increased.

• Benefits that bridge the Social Security gap. These are typically supplemental monthly payments of $400–$600. They start upon leaving the company and end when you begin to collect Social Security at age 62.

• Limited health insurance. Caution: Unlike pensions, health coverage in an early-retirement offer is likely to be less extensive than what you have now. In most cases, you'll have to pay a larger share of the premium to cover your dependents under the company's medical plan.

Early-retirement offers are generally targeted toward older, longer service employees since they've already earned significant benefits under the existing pension plan. Employers attempting to motivate younger employees to leave usually offer some type of severance package. Offering a true early retirement would be prohibitively expensive.

Key question: If offered early retirement... it's important to ask yourself if continuing to work for this company is desirable. A majority of people make the mistake of not considering that:

• A company that offers early retirement is probably not in the best financial health. Some, in fact, may wind up in bankruptcy. If that happens, a lot of people will be out of work. A vested pension, though, will probably be secure.

• The employees affected are unlikely to be the employer's favorites. This means that your chances of earning a fat salary and finishing out your career with a generous pension may be in jeopardy.

If you still have doubts about accepting the offer...

• Calculate your likely alternative income after accepting—or rejecting—the offer. An accountant or financial planner can help you estimate the amount of your pension if you stay with the company. If you leave the company, don't forget to include income from a 401(k) plan, if you have one. These tax-deferred investment plans can be rolled over into IRAs or Keogh plans.

What isn't widely known is that they can also be paid out in annual cash installments.

Example: If you're 40 and the IRS estimates you'll live to 78, you can take out a 38th of the total in cash each year, paying tax only on what you withdraw. What you leave in your account continues to grow on a tax-deferred basis.

• Figure how much an individual health plan will cost. Turning to a private insurance carrier can be costly—$300–$350 a month is common for a family.

• Determine how you'd fare in the job market. Visit an employee counselor (included in some early retirement packages). Get an idea of what kinds of positions are available—also ask how long it would likely take to be rehired.

Answers can easily tip your response to accepting—or rejecting—an offer, especially if you're in your mid-50s. At that age, your pension may be under the amount you had planned to live on, but it also may be getting more difficult for you to market your skills.

• Consider the option of getting a part-time job or working for yourself as a consultant. Income from either source may be more than ample to fund your own supplemental retirement plan.

Working for yourself may also have tax advantages that could tip the scale in favor of accepting the offer.

Since calculating such things as pension income, tax consequences and IRA payouts is complex, it usually pays to consult a financial planner before making a decision.

Helpful: Under the new federal law, most early-retirement offers give you five days to change your mind.

Source: Jeff Strecker, an actuary and account manager with Hewitt Associates, benefit consultants, One Oxford Center, Pittsburgh 15219.

Retirement Tax-Planning Loopholes

The key to a successful and happy retirement is that you have enough money to satisfy your wants and needs.

Fortunately, there are a good number of tax

loopholes that will help you accomplish this goal. But there are traps to avoid, too.

• The amounts you receive as distributions from your company pension or profit-sharing plan are generally fully taxable.

Loophole: If you contributed to the pension plan with some of your own after-tax dollars, that contribution is not taxable when you take it out. Obligatory contributions to your employer's pension plan and voluntary non-deductible contributions to an IRA are not taxable when you withdraw them. (But 401(k) contributions, which are made with pre-tax dollars, are taxable when you take them out.)*

Important: Keep careful track of the amounts you contribute to a pension plan.

• Lump-sum distributions from pension and profit-sharing plans qualify for special tax breaks...

Rollover loophole: You can roll the money over into an IRA and postpone paying taxes until you take the money out of the IRA.

1936 loophole: If you were born before 1936, you can choose to treat a portion of the taxable part of a lump-sum distribution as a long-term capital gain taxable at a 20% rate. Also, you may elect to use tax-favored ten-year averaging for the ordinary income part of the distribution. This can further reduce the tax you pay.

59½ loophole: Regardless of when you were born, as long as you're at least 59½ years old, your lump-sum distribution qualifies for five-year averaging. You may end up paying a very low rate on the distribution.

• Don't miss the deadline for beginning to take money out of your IRA and pension or profit-sharing plan. Distributions from the plan must begin by April 1 of the year following the year in which you become age 70½.

Trap: If you miss the deadline, you'll be charged a 50% penalty tax on the amount you should have withdrawn, but didn't.

• Avoid penalties on excess distributions from your pension plans. You'll be charged a 15% penalty tax to the extent your annual distributions from all your plans exceed $150,000—or to the extent that you get a lump-sum distribution that exceeds $750,000. If you made a grandfather election on your 1987 or 1988 return, you might be exempt from the 15% penalty tax on part of your excess distribution.

Grandfather election loophole: Review with your tax advisor the way the election was made. You may be able to change the method of making withdrawals and, thereby, reduce the penalty.

Up to 50% of your Social Security benefits is taxable, depending on your total income. The calculation for taxing Social Security benefits includes tax-exempt interest you've earned from municipal bonds.

Taxable bonds loophole: You may be better off owning taxable bonds rather than tax-exempt ones since taxable bonds pay a higher interest rate.

Social Security benefits are based on your income. It's important to check periodically on your earnings record with the Social Security Administration. Errors more than three years old are hard to correct. If you catch a mistake early on, you'll be able to fix it.

To check: Fill out and mail to the Social Security Administration Form SSA-7004-PC, *Request for Earnings and Benefits Estimate Statement.*

Squeeze the maximum tax benefit from your home.

Home loophole: If you're 55 or older, you don't have to pay tax on the first $125,000 of profit on the sale of your home. This is a once-in-a-lifetime exclusion. Married individuals are entitled to only one exclusion per couple.

It's not a good idea from a tax standpoint to give the family home to your intended beneficiaries before you die. Reason: The recipients take over your tax basis in the property, which is generally its cost. When the recipients sell the property they will pay income tax on the full appreciation in value since you bought the property.

Inheritance loophole: Let your beneficiaries inherit the family home. They will receive it at its stepped-up, date-of-death value, and income

*Special loophole: Pensions from certain state governmental agencies are not subject to state income tax. Check with your tax advisor.

tax will be forgiven on the appreciation. This same loophole applies to other appreciated property. For instance, instead of selling stock and giving your children the proceeds, give them cash and let them inherit the stock.

A way to reduce your taxable estate is to make annual gifts to family members. You can give up to $10,000 a year to each of any number of recipients ($20,000 a year if your spouse joins in the gift) without having to pay federal gift tax.

Gift loophole: In addition to $10,000 or $20,000 amounts, you can also make gift-tax-free gifts for education expenses. To qualify a payment as a tax-free gift, however, you must make it directly to the college or other institution.

There are two ways to make gifts to children and still control the use of the money. Set up a trust for the children or a custodial account under the Uniform Gifts to Minors Act.

Trap: Don't make yourself the trustee or custodian of these accounts. If you do that, the assets will be taxed in your estate when you die.

• Life insurance. Premium payments on life insurance are not tax-deductible, and any proceeds that are eventually paid out are not considered taxable income. Many senior citizens have fully paid-up life insurance policies from which they receive dividends. They get 1099s from the insurance company for these dividends.

Insurance loophole: The dividends are not taxable until the cumulative amount of dividends received exceeds the total amount of premiums paid by the policy holder.

Source: Edward Mendlowitz, partner, Mendlowitz Weitsen, CPAs, Two Pennsylvania Plaza, New York 10121. Mr. Mendlowitz is the author of several books, including *Aggressive Tax Strategies*, Macmillan Publishing Co., 866 Third Ave., New York 10022.

IRAs—To Consolidate Or Not To Consolidate?

Taxpayers who have set up a number of IRAs over the years may be tempted to gather them together into one big IRA. There are definite advantages to consolidating accounts:

• Save on trustees' fees. Instead of paying separate administration fees for each account, you'll be paying only one.

• Simplify paperwork.

• Accumulate larger balances for investment. You get a greater rate of return on a $10,000 Certificate of Deposit (CD) than on a $1,000 CD.

Main disadvantages in consolidating IRA accounts:

• Problems with early withdrawals. When you consolidate accounts, you lose flexibility in making penalty-free early withdrawals.

• If you're under 59½ , you pay a 10% penalty tax on money you take out of your IRA. You can avoid this penalty, however, by taking money out in the form of an annuity—in substantially equal payments over your life expectancy. The simplest way to calculate this amount is to take the balance in your account and divide it by your life expectancy. This is done on an account-by-account basis. Impact: The more accounts you have, the smaller your substantially equal payments can be. This can be advantageous.

Example: Suppose you're 55 years old and have a 10-year life expectancy (for the purposes of this example). And suppose you need $10,000 a year from your IRA to make a mortgage payment. If you have one $500,000 IRA, your substantially equal payment figure would be $50,000 a year. This is five times the amount you need. But if you had one $400,000 IRA and one $100,000 IRA, you could take $10,000 a year from the $100,000 IRA and leave the $400,000 one untouched.

Reasons to use substantially equal payments:

• To make distributions to a divorced spouse.

• To make mortgage payments.

• To pay for college education.

Unrelated business taxable income. Although an IRA is exempt from current income tax, it may be subject to tax on what is known as unrelated business income. This is income from a trade or business involving the sale of goods or the performance of services. (An investment in commercial real estate which is mortgaged would be an example of an unrelated business.)

The first $1,000 of unrelated business income earned by each IRA account is tax-free. If you currently have only one IRA account, you'll get only one $1,000 exclusion. If you have five IRAs, and they each generate unrelated business income, you would get $5,000 worth of exclusion.

If you're over 59½ and you don't invest in anything that produces unrelated business income (for instance, you invest only in stocks and Certificates of Deposit), these disadvantages evaporate. You might just as well consolidate your accounts to capture the advantages mentioned above. Two ways to consolidate:

• Rollover. Take the money from one IRA and redeposit it in another IRA within 60 days. Trap: If you miss the 60-day deadline, the money will be taxable.

The courts and the IRS are not tolerant of individuals who miss the deadline. Furthermore, you can make only one rollover each year per account.

• Trustee-to-trustee transfer. Instruct the trustee of one IRA to transfer the funds to another IRA.

The money never comes into your hands. You can do this as frequently as you like, assuming the trustees will oblige.

Source: Deborah Walker, partner, KPMG Peat Marwick, 2001 M St. NW, Washington, DC 20036.

Pension Traps and Annuity Opportunities

Before collecting checks from your company pension plan or a single-premium deferred annuity, it pays to investigate your options.

By choosing an immediate annuity, you may wind up with hundreds of dollars more per month in your pocket—at no additional risk.

An immediate annuity is an insurance contract that, in return for a one-time payment, starts paying a fixed sum for your lifetime or for some other period right away.

A single-life annuity, for example, pays the agreed-upon sum every month until the purchaser dies. The payment doesn't have to stop at the first death. It depends on the option you select: Joint and two-thirds survivor, joint and 50% survivor, and joint and 100% survivor. A joint-and-survivor annuity for a married couple, by contrast, pays one larger sum while both spouses are alive, and a lesser amount after the first spouse dies. Payments continue at the lower level during the lifetime of the surviving spouse and end only when that person dies.

Comparison shopping in the immediate annuity market can pay off quite nicely.

Example: Recently, I checked out rates—which are expressed as monthly income per $10,000 of premium—for a 65-year-old woman. For a $100,000 investment, the monthly income ranged from a high of $915 to a low of $716—a difference of almost $200, or about 28%.

Trap: Don't automatically go for the highest monthly income figure. Given all the turmoil in the insurance industry these days, and the recent failure of Executive Life, in the example above I decided to not even consider the seven companies paying the top rates because I had reservations about their soundness. Bear in mind that you are purchasing something that you intend to last for the rest of your life.

I wound up recommending my client purchase an annuity that ranked 20th out of 100. It was offered by Northwestern Mutual, the solid, conservative and well-run Minnesota company. The annuity provided monthly income of $839. The median income figure was $809 a month.

Two common situations in which investigating what you'd receive with an immediate annuity makes sense...

• When you're retiring from your company. Before you automatically accept the monthly pension check your company plan offers, ask if the plan permits a lump-sum distribution instead. Many, but not all, plans do.

See what you can get in monthly income by purchasing an immediate annuity with some of that money. You may be surprised to discover that you'll get a much larger payment with the annuity than with your company pension.

• When you're ready to start annuitizing, or

receiving distributions, from a single-premium deferred annuity that you purchased years ago. Just because you purchased the annuity from Company A, don't assume that it now offers the best deal in terms of monthly income. You may do better by switching to Company B or C.

Caution: In either case, don't sink all your money into an immediate annuity all at once. You many be purchasing at a trough, and annuity rates may subsequently shoot up. I recommend that people purchase several contracts over time and that they not annuitize more than 50% of their total investable assets.

It's vital that you do your comparative shopping right at the point when you are ready to make your purchase.

Reason: The immediate annuity market is a very fluid one, and rates can fluctuate widely, even within a given company, depending upon the details of your individual situation.

Example: A particular company may post attractive payouts one month, but not the next. Or, it may be competitive at some ages but unattractive at others.

To check on the different rates offered by different companies, consult *Best's Retirement Income Guide.** It's published twice a year and available in many public libraries. The guide contains comparative information on many different types of annuities, both fixed and variable, offered by hundreds of different companies. To find out the annuity rate for an immediate annuity, you must consult the tables in the back, which give the monthly income you would receive if you paid a set sum to different insurance companies queried.

It's also possible to deal with a reputable broker who maintains a broad database of annuity rates paid by different companies. Sources:

- The Annuity Network, a subsidiary of the Laughlin group in Beaverton, Oregon (800-547-3257). The parent company evaluates the safety and stability of insurance companies. The Annuity Network works with about 300 insurance companies. The network is compensated on a commission basis from companies whose policies it sells.
- United States Annuities, Englishtown, New Jersey (800-872-6684). An insurance-brokerage and research firm that specializes in immediate annuities. It also works on a commission basis. The firm publishes the *Annuity Shopper*, a bimonthly newsletter that compares different insurers' ratings, rates and charges. US Annuities, 98 Hoffman Rd., Englishtown, New Jersey 07726. Six issues. $45/yr.

Of course, there are some drawbacks to opting for an immediate annuity, rather than for your company pension. Rejecting your pension might be unwise, for example, if your company has a history of increasing its pension payouts from time to time in order to offset inflation. The annuity check you get the first month is the same amount you'll receive 20 years from now—assuming you're still alive to collect.

And—pensions are insured by the Pension Board Guaranty Corporation, while immediate annuities are only as good as the company that issues them.

Before you jump at the highest available rate, you should always very carefully investigate the issuing company's financial health.

Aim: To be reasonably sure it will be able to make those payouts as long as you live.

Caution: Some, but not all, insurers require annuity buyers to pay upfront policy fees or other charges, which can range from $150 to $500. And about 10 states impose premium taxes that amount to 1% to 3% of the amount invested.

Source: Glenn Daily, a fee-only insurance consultant and author of *The Individual Investor's Guide to Low-Load Insurance Products*, International Publishing Corp., 625 N. Michigan Ave., Suite 1920, Chicago 60611.

*A.M. Best & Co., A.M. Best Rd., Oldwich, New Jersey 08858. $53/yr.

Protecting Your Assets From Creditors

As times get trickier and trickier, it's increasingly desirable to limit any losses that could be incurred if hit hard in the tough times ahead.

Key: The sheltering must take place well in

advance of declaring bankruptcy. Otherwise, under federal bankruptcy law, creditors can charge fraudulent transfer of assets and claim the money to pay your debts.

Although actual intent may be difficult to prove, courts recognize what are called badges of fraud.

Examples: Transferring property to a family member or a company insider without adequate consideration, removing or concealing assets, becoming insolvent as a result of a transfer.

All that a creditor's lawyer must do to establish constructive fraud is show that you transferred assets for less than fair consideration and this made you insolvent...or, it left you without enough capital to meet likely future cash needs of the company, or future debts as they became due.

Defense: Have your accountant prepare a financial statement proving that you were solvent at the time of transfer.

The best times to plan how to protect your assets are when you're first going into business—or when you're embarking on a new marriage, especially if both parties have children and assets. Lawyers can advise you freely then, whereas they're ethically constrained when either spouse is on the brink of bankruptcy.

Be aware that federal and state bankruptcy laws allow some exemptions so that people can make a fresh start after coming out of bankruptcy.

State laws vary widely, but many let you keep tools required to conduct your trade, often including a car. Most also allow you to keep some personal assets...but this ranges from as much as $30,000 in Texas, to as little as $1,500 in Utah.

Example: Florida is very liberal, protecting not only the homestead but salaries, annuities and some retirement, pension and profit-sharing plans from claims by creditors. The homestead is generally exempted, so people can sell non-exempt assets like stocks and bonds and put that money into their home, beyond the reach of creditors.

Nationally, it's unclear whether bankruptcy law or ERISA (Employee Retirement Income Security Act) law takes precedence when it comes to pension plan monies. Pension plans are probably safe from creditors, while IRAs and contributions to 401(k) programs are probably not protected.

Sophisticated lenders, such as banks, usually make sure they're covered with security, personal guarantees (personal assets, such as a home) and even spousal guarantees. So there's usually not much you can do to protect yourself from banks. But you can defend against judgment creditors. Steps to take:

- Incorporate your business. A corporation can protect your personal assets in the event of a lawsuit against the company. Professional corporations can also limit liabilities. A doctor or lawyer can't protect against malpractice suits, but in a group of professionals, Dr. A and Dr. C may be protected from Dr. B's malpractice claims.
- Spousal transfer trap. A widely used, but risky, procedure. If the timing is close, it's easily categorized as a fraudulent attempt to dispose of assets. And, giving up control of assets may mean trouble later if there's a divorce. Also, there's a danger that if you die, your spouse may not follow your wishes about who gets what.

Defense: Create a Q-Tip trust, which qualifies for the marital deduction and doesn't incur gift taxes. It provides income to your spouse, but you control the disposition of assets at your death.

- Set up a prenuptial agreement. Before getting married, both parties (with separate counsel) disclose their assets and liabilities. Then, depending on state laws about property rights, the lawyers help decide what should be in whose name.

Any time a major asset is acquired during the marriage, consider whose name it should be in—should it be in your name, your spouse's, or under joint ownership? Some types of joint ownership offer special protection.

Examples: *Tenants in common* provides that each partner's creditors can only attach that person's half (assuming there is no fraud). *Joint tenants with right of survivorship* varies greatly from state to state, but can be very attractive when the property is exempt from the separate debts of either spouse—as in Florida and Pennsylvania.

With any kind of trust, the amount of protection given directly correlates to the amount of control you're willing to give up.

To creditors, if you get all the income and retain the right to revoke the trust, it's the same as if you still owned it. Whenever the debtor himself sets up a trust, creditors can usually get at the income that is to be paid to him. If a relative is going to give you money, ask him to set up a trust with you as beneficiary.

Even better: Have a discretionary trust set up with a spendthrift clause, specifying that you not be paid any income if you owe creditors.

Example: A father set up a spendthrift trust for his son, a doctor. In the event that the son is involved in a malpractice suit, that money would be out of the reach of creditors and lawyers.

Another option: Set up a trust for your children. Trap: This is tricky to do without incurring either a gift or income tax, but it can be done.

Offshore trusts no longer carry tax benefits, but they can make sense for very wealthy people who want to take advantage of bank secrecy laws, and the fact that certain foreign governments make it hard to enforce US court judgments.

Life insurance won't help you, of course. However, it can provide money for the family because most states exempt it from creditors (with some limitations).

Source: Donna Barwick, an attorney and senior manager in charge of trust and estate planning, Ernst & Young, Atlanta. She is on the council of the Real Property, Probate and Trust division of the US Bar Association.

IRA Alert

Don't have your IRA invest in tax-exempt state or municipal bonds. Why: Any amount withdrawn from an IRA is taxable income, even if the withdrawn amount was earned from a tax-exempt bond. So, by having the IRA invest in tax-exempt bonds, you forfeit the tax exemption for them that would have been available had they been held outside the IRA.

Estate Planning Traps Today

We're all geared to estate planning for estates that are increasing in value. But that is not the case today. The downturn in the economy has brought to an end—at least temporarily—the era of large estates with rapid appreciation and growing potential.

The economic slowdown presents new traps—but it also presents big new estate planning opportunities. Main problems:

• Trap: Not setting up a gift-giving program at a time when asset values are low. Today's depressed asset values present taxpayers with tremendous gift-giving opportunities. Lifetime gifts are a way to transfer wealth to your heirs. The time to make gifts for estate planning purposes is when values are low and the appreciation potential in the property is high.

That's certainly the case today. Today, you can transfer property to your heirs at low gift tax cost and at the same time remove large amounts of potential appreciation on that property from your taxable estate. This reduces the estate tax you'll ultimately have to pay.

Limits to giving: You can give up to $10,000 per year gift-tax-free to each of any number of recipients ($20,000 per year if your spouse joins in the gift).

In addition, everybody has a $600,000 gift- and estate-tax exemption which can be used either during life or at death without incurring any federal gift tax. This makes it possible to make very substantial gifts free of federal gift tax. The full $600,000 might be given to one individual in cash or in property, or it might be split among a number of beneficiaries.

Caution: You must check state law. At least seven states now still have gift taxes which many conflict with the federal gift tax law.

• Trap: Not reviewing your will. This should be done every three to five years—

and any time there's a substantial change in family or finances. Because of the downturn in asset values, you may find that what you've done in your will is no longer consistent with your net worth. You may have made gifts in your will that exceed your current wealth. This can cause serious problems in your estate. It can cause legacies to be reduced and result in the people you wanted to benefit not getting what you intended to give.

• Trap: Not planning for adequate liquidity. Will there be enough liquid assets in your estate to pay the estate tax, which is generally due nine months after the date of your death? Assets that you had counted on to provide for estate tax may have gone down in value to the point where there won't be enough ready money to pay the taxes.

One solution: Increase your life insurance. The policy proceeds can supply the cash needed to pay estate taxes.

• Trap: Not rethinking generation skipping. When making their estate plans, wealthy people often skip a generation and leave property to their grandchildren or great-grandchildren, rather than to their children. This saves the estate tax that would otherwise be payable by the children's generation.

But your diminished estate may now not be large enough to provide for both your children and grandchildren. You may want to redo your estate plan to make your children, rather than your grandchildren, the main beneficiaries.

Caution: When giving to grandchildren, be aware of the implication of the generation-skipping transfer tax.

• Trap: Failing to revise your plans for charitable giving. When asset values were going up, you got the biggest tax benefit by giving the assets themselves to charity rather than selling them and giving cash. When you gave appreciated securities, for instance, you got a double tax benefit—you got a charitable deduction and you avoided paying capital gains tax on the appreciation. But it is not a good idea to give assets that have dropped in value since you acquired them. When you do that you waste a valuable capital loss deduction. The smart thing to do is to sell the securities first and give the cash to charity. That way you get a capital loss deduction on the sale and a charitable deduction for the cash you give.

• Trap: Having inconsistent—or inadequate—tax allocation clauses. The tax allocation clause in your will may not be consistent with the tax allocation clauses in trust documents that you've made during your lifetime. The documents may have been prepared at different times, or drawn by different attorneys, or drawn when you were a resident of a different state, one with different estate tax laws. This inconsistency can lead to costly litigation, especially when the beneficiaries under the will and under the trust are different people.

Your will and trust documents must be reviewed as a whole to make certain that there are no inconsistencies between them.

Estate and gift tax laws have changed a lot in the last 10 years. Many special provisions are now included in estate plans to cover surviving spouses, spouses who are not US citizens, intra-family transfers, large accumulations in pension plans, etc. All of these new provisions have major tax consequences.

Inconsistency and incompleteness in tax allocation can lead to disaster. You can end up with the estate tax coming out against the wrong person. Here again, it's important that your will be reviewed to clear up possible inconsistencies.

• Trap: Failing to take extra planning steps if your spouse is not a US citizen. The 1988 Tax Act bars the use of the unlimited marital deduction for property that passes to a spouse who is not a US citizen. Special planning is required to minimize the impact of this new rule.

One thing you can do is set up a Qualified Domestic Trust (QDT). If property left to the noncitizen spouse passes into this special kind of trust, it will qualify for the marital deduction. You might also set up a gift-giving program to reduce your estate and minimize the importance of the marital deduction. It is very important to work this out with your estate planner.

Source: Sanford J. Schlesinger, partner and head of the trusts and estate department, Shea & Gould, 1251 Ave. of the Americas, New York 10020.

"Free-gift" trap

Winners of sweepstakes and other promotional contests must pay tax on the value of the prizes. Trap: Contest sponsors report the value of prizes to the IRS at list prices—much higher than the "fair market" prices taxpayers are used to paying taxes on. Example: A couple won a trip worth about $1,400 from a radio station. But they were sent an IRS 1099 form with a value of $3,616 listed. Because the station got the air travel and hotel by bartering ad time for travel services, it valued the travel services at full retail value. Self-defense: See an accountant to obtain fair market values of prizes and pay tax accordingly.

Source: Jed Perkins, editor, *Consumer Reports Travel Letter*, 101 Truman Ave., Yonkers, NY 10703.

Important Estate Tax Avoidance Opportunities

The major tax issue for people of retirement age is not saving income taxes, but saving estate taxes. Federal estate taxes can take a huge bite out of even relatively modest estates.

Example: The combined estate of a couple with an estate of just over $1.2 million (a very easy level to reach for anyone who owns real estate that has appreciated over the years) is instantly subject to a federal estate tax of 37%. The tax rises to 50% on estates of more than $2.5 million, and reaches the maximum of 60% on estates of more than $10 million.

GRITs, GRATs and GRUTs

Recent changes in the tax law have created loopholes that enable your estate to escape the heavy hand of the tax collector. Under the Omnibus Budget Reconciliation Act of 1990, one section of the estate tax law has been repealed and replaced with another that allows the creation of what are called GRITs, GRATs and GRUTs—nicknames for grantor-retained income trusts, grantor-retained annuity trusts and grantor-retained unitrusts. They provide important new ways of saving estate taxes.

In these three types of trusts, you as grantor make a gift to the trust but retain an interest in part of the property that you give. The common denominator is that as long as you follow all the federal requirements when you make the gift, you can have the value of that gift reduced (for estate tax purposes) by the value of what you keep. That is, the tax tables measure the present value of the income that you keep, which is substantially less than the amount you've placed in the trust. In effect, you can have your cake and eat it, too.

Caution: You must be careful to follow all the rules or you may end up making a gift of the full amount rather than the reduced amount.

How the three trusts work:

• GRITs. The best of the three arrangements, although it only works with personal residences. How it works: You make a gift of the residence to an irrevocable trust for the benefit of your heirs, typically your children. You also retain the right to live in the house for a certain period. The value of the gift is reduced by your right to live in it during the trust period.

Example: You have a house worth $500,000 and give it to a GRIT, keeping the right to live in it for 15 years. Because you retain the right to live in the dwelling during that time, the IRS considers, based on its tables, that you are making a gift of just 16% of $500,000, or only $80,000, even if the house has doubled in value by the end of the period.

What if you live longer than 15 years? You must be prepared to rent the house from its owners (your children, who are the beneficiaries) after 15 years. But if you were prepared to turn the house over to them in the first place, eventually having to rent from them shouldn't be a problem. If, however, you die before the 15 years are up, the full value of the house is included in your estate and you haven't saved any taxes.

Another advantage: GRITs work with any personal residence. So you can make your kids a gift of the beach house or the ski condo, as well as the main family house.

• GRATs. This is the next best arrangement. The gift to the trust can be anything of value—other than a personal residence. Typically, parents give income-producing assets, such as securities or real estate, to the trust and retain a fixed dollar-amount from those assets, payable to them annually in the form of an annuity. The annuity is paid directly by the trust from the money that funded the trust.

The value of an initial gift is reduced by the value of the annuity payouts, and at the end of the period whatever is left goes to the beneficiaries.

Advantage: If you retain a large enough annuity interest, the value of the gift (as determined by IRS tables) is eventually "zeroed out" and reduced to nothing. For example, a gift of $500,000 in securities that paid an annuity of 13.5% for 15 years would result in a zero gift at the end of the period, even if it was necessary to invade the principal in order to make those annuity payments. Gifts that paid a 15% annuity over 12 years, or an 11.5% annuity over 22 years, would also result in gifts of no taxable value for estate purposes.

Reason: According the the IRS tables, keeping those percentages over those time periods will return to everything you put in, plus interest. Result: You've, in effect, given away nothing.

Note: These examples were computed using a rate of 10%. This rate is reset monthly and announced by the IRS. You must use the rate in effect at the time you create the trust.

• GRUTs. Under this variation, you also give income-producing assets to a trust. However, instead of taking out a fixed dollar amount each year, you take out a fixed percentage of the amount given. This may be less attractive than a GRAT, because it is impossible to "zero out" the value of the gift since the trusts assets are revalued every year, and you're only taking a percentage of them. But the advantage of refiguring the investment value of the assets annually and then taking a payout as a percentage of those revalued assets is that it provides you, as grantor, with protection against future inflation.

If inflation increases sharply, presumably the assets in the trust will also appreciate, and your annual income—which is calculated as a net percentage of those assets—will increase as well and allow you to maintain your lifestyle despite rising prices.

Other ways to cut estate costs:

• Never, ever make your estate the beneficiary of a life insurance policy or of company employee benefits, such as insurance. Doing so guarantees increased legal fees, ensures a time delay before the beneficiaries get their money, ensures the money will be taxable before they get it and exposes the insurance proceeds to the claims of creditors.

Better: Set up a trust as beneficiary of the proceeds. This way you avoid probate, minimize estate taxes and ensure that the assets will be distributed according to the judgment of the courts.

• Be especially careful if you own property in another state. Special trap: Vacation homes. They may lead to probate problems, particularly if the property is in the name of only one spouse.

Solution: Create a trust, and put an out-of-state property into that trust. This will avoid probate problems with the other state.

Source: Alexander A. Bove, Jr., a partner with Mahoney, Hawkes & Goldings, a Boston law firm that specializes in business and tax law. He is author of many books, including the *Medicaid Planning Handbook*, Little, Brown, 115 W. 18 St., New York 10011, and the *Complete Book of Wills and Estates*, Henry Holt, 34 Beacon St., Boston 02108.

Wonderful New Estate Planning Loopholes

Estate planning has become an area of major action in the tax-planning field. Federal estate tax rates run up to as high as 55%, which gives people a strong incentive to save.

Caution: Estate planning is a rapidly changing field. New opportunities:

• Life insurance trusts. If you own a life insurance policy at your death, or have any "incidents of ownership" in a policy, the proceeds will be included in your taxable estate when you die. Incidents of ownership include such things as the right to name a beneficiary of the policy.

Loophole: Set up an irrevocable trust and have the trust own the policy. This will get the proceeds out of your estate. Make your heirs the beneficiaries of the trust. If you wish, you can structure the trust so your spouse gets income from the proceeds for life. Don't pay the premiums directly—this may be considered an incident of ownership—but make annual gifts to the trust so the trustee has the money to pay the premiums.

Caution: If you die within three years of transferring a policy to the trust, the proceeds will be included in your taxable estate.

Strategy: Put cash or securities into the trust and have the trust buy a new policy. The three-year rule does not apply if the insured person never has any ownership rights in the policy.

- Employee-owned life insurance. In most cases, employees retain the right to name beneficiaries of employer-owned life insurance. Because of the incidents of ownership rule, the proceeds will be included in your estate.

- Life insurance pursuant to a divorce. Suppose a husband is required to buy two life insurance policies as part of his divorce agreement—one to benefit his ex-wife and another for his children.

Trap: The proceeds of both policies will be included in the husband's estate when he dies. Depending on the state law, it is possible that the estate tax on the proceeds will have to be paid out of the remaining assets in the husband's estate.

Loophole: Set up an irrevocable life insurance trust before the policies are purchased. Have the trust buy the policies. Result: Neither policy will be subject to estate tax when the husband dies.

- The $600,000 lifetime exemption. Everyone has the right to leave up to $600,000 to beneficiaries other than his/her spouse estate-tax free. Be sure to use the tax break. Leave $600,000 to your children or other beneficiaries.

Loophole: You can set up what is known as a credit-shelter trust in your will, leaving $600,000 to your children but giving your spouse the income from the trust assets for life.

Caution: The $600,000 exemption applies to federal state tax only. It does not apply to state inheritance tax.

- Section 303. This provision of the tax code applies to estates that are primarily composed of a closely held business or real estate. Estate tax does not have to be paid immediately. The executor can elect to pay the tax over a period of 14 years.

Bonus: The government allows low interest on part of the estate taxes that are deferred.

- Generation-skipping tax. Money left directly to your grandchildren skips a generation—your children's—and is subject to the generation-skipping tax if the amount is more than $1 million. The tax rate for generation-skipping transfers is 55%.

Loophole: Avoid leaving funds in excess of $1 million to grandchildren. Make gifts to them during your lifetime instead. You can give each grandchild up to $10,000 a year ($20,000 if your spouse joins in the gift.

- Charitable remainder trusts. This is a way to reduce your taxable estate while at the same time benefiting a charity. You set up a trust for your favorite charity and give securities or other assets to the trust. The trust pays you an income for life from the assets. The charity gets the assets when you die.

Tax impact: You get a current income tax deduction for the value of the interest the charity will ultimately get. This value is calculated from IRS annuity tables and depends primarily on your life expectancy.

Loophole: Give the trust assets that have appreciated in value since you acquired them. You'll get a charitable deduction for the full fair-market value of the assets at the time you put them into the trust, and you won't pay any income tax on the appreciation.

- Grantor-retained income trusts (GRITs). These are used to remove a person's personal residence from his estate at low tax cost. How they work: You give your residence to an irrevocable trust for the benefit of your heirs, typically your children. You reserve the right to live in the house for a period of years—say 10 years. At the end of that period, your heirs get the title to the house.

Tax impact: For gift tax purposes, the value of the house that you have given is reduced by the value of your right to live in it for 10 years. This will be far less than the market value of the house. For example, the transfer of a $300,000 house into a 10-year GRIT might be valued at only $116,000. This is the amount you pay tax on. Key: You will pay no gift tax as long as the gift-tax value is under $600,000.

Bonus: The value of the house is frozen at its gift-tax value at the time of the transfer to the trust. Any appreciation in value between the time of the transfer and your death is kept out of your estate.

Catch: If you die before the trust's term is up, the value of the property is included in your taxable estate.

- Grantor-retained annuity trusts (GRATs). This is a way to get securities and other assets out of your estate at a low gift-tax cost. You transfer assets you expect will appreciate in value to an irrevocable trust to benefit your heirs. You retain a fixed income from the assets for a period of years, payable annually in the form of an annuity. The gift-tax value of the gift is reduced by the annuity payments you will receive.

Loophole: If you retain a large enough annuity interest, the gift may result in no taxable value for gift-tax purposes.

- Grantor-retained unitrusts (GRUTs). Under this variation, instead of taking out a fixed dollar amount, you take out a fixed percentage of the amount given. The assets in the trust are revalued each year to figure out your income. In times of inflation, the assets will be valued higher and your income will go up.
- Living trusts. These are currently very popular, and they are often misunderstood. The living trust—a revocable trust into which you put all of your assets—avoids probate but does not avoid estate taxes. Your estate tax bill is the same whether you use a living trust or a will. Advantages of living trusts: The assets in a living trust avoid probate, which is a time-consuming legal process, and they avoid probate fees. An additional advantage is privacy. The court records of probate proceedings are open to the public. The terms of a living trust are private.

Source: Edward Mendlowitz, partner, Mendlowitz Weitsen, CPAs, Two Pennsylvania Plaza, New York 10121. Mr. Mendlowitz is the author of several books, including *Aggressive Tax Strategies*, Macmillan Publishing Co., 866 Third Ave., New York 10022.

11

Education

How To Improve Scores On Standardized Tests

No matter how smart you are, no matter how well-prepared, there are strategies you can use to improve your scores on any standardized test, including the SAT, GRE and MCAT. What to do:

• Get to know the test beforehand. Every standardized test is different. Important: Read the test booklet provided by the testing firm to find out what subjects will be covered, the precise form questions will take and the directions. If you have to spend two minutes reading the directions when the test is in progress, you're losing two minutes of valuable test-taking time.

• Review the subjects that will be covered. If the test you're planning to take has a mathematical section, bone up on math beforehand. Likewise with logical reasoning, science and so on. Start reviewing basic skills three or four months in advance.

• Take practice tests. Sample exams prepared and distributed by the testing organizations themselves are best. They will familiarize you with the material and give a fair indication of your actual exam score. If you are unhappy with your projected score, delay taking the exam until you have improved and are satisfied you can do well.

• Alert the test organization of any handicaps. Special provisions are made for students with hearing or vision problems, including dyslexia.*

• Get enough sleep. Not just the night before the exam, but for several nights beforehand.

• Eat sensibly. On test day, a light breakfast is best. A big meal can make you drowsy and exacerbate a nervous stomach. If you get hungry during the exam, eat a snack during the break.

• Come prepared. Bring your admission ticket, personal identification and six #2 pen-

*Dyslexics take the test in a separate room and have an unlimited time to complete it.

cils with dull points—they let you fill in the circles faster than sharp points and they don't break as easily. If you're prone to headaches, bring an aspirin or your favorite analgesic.

Arrive an hour in advance. If you're unfamiliar with the test site, make a trial run a few days beforehand.

• Keep anxiety in check. Cramming the night before the exam encourages anxiety. If you become anxious during the exam, breathe slowly and deeply. Get up and walk around during the break. A little anxiety is to be expected and can even help you do well on the test. But too much can bring your scores down. Remembering that you can always cancel your score and retake the test will also reduce anxiety. (See *Don't panic*).

• Use strategies. Answer short or easy questions first. Save long reading passages for last.

If you have trouble with one question, put a mark by it in the test book and go on to the next question. Then come back if you have time.

In reading comprehension sections, some find it easier to scan the questions before reading the passage. This will clue you in on what to look for as you read.

If you finish the test early, go back over your answers.

• Mark answers carefully. Make sure the circle you're marking corresponds to the question you intend to answer. Many students mark column after column of circles only to discover they're ahead or behind where they should be.

Self-check: Every five questions, make sure that question and answer numbers correspond.

• Know when—and when not—to guess. A few tests penalize you for wrong answers (the SAT, for instance), others don't. Find out beforehand whether your test does.

On tests where there is no penalty for wrong answers, fill in every blank—no matter how unsure of the answer you are. On tests where there is a penalty, guess only if you can rule out at least one of the possible choices.

In some exams, the SAT for instance, questions at the beginning of each section are usually easier than those toward the back. Thus, if on an early question you arrive at a quick, easy answer, and that answer is listed among the multiple choices, chances are you have the right answer. But if you come up with a quick, easy answer on a question deep into the exam, and that answer is among the multiple choices, watch out. There are no easy answers at the end of the test.

• Don't let difficult questions rattle you. If one section seems harder or less clear than the others, it could be an experimental section, being used to try out new questions, and will not count toward your score. Just do your best.

• Don't panic! If you think you bombed the test, notify the testing organization immediately (use overnight mail). For most tests you have a few days following the exam to ask that your test not be scored. You can take it again without penalty, although your record will show that you cancelled a previous test.

If your test is scored, and your performance falls shy of what you had hoped for, you can always take the test again. Most schools look only at the higher score. Exception: Most law schools average your scores.

Source: Stanley H. Kaplan, founder of Stanley H. Kaplan Educational Center, Ltd., 131 W. 56 St., New York 10019. Mr. Kaplan's company has coached more than 1.5 million test-takers over the past 50 years.

Reading Lesson: How To Absorb More...Faster

The first step toward reading more effectively is to be realistic about how much you really must read.

Getting a few good ideas out of the reading you actually do is much better than the intention of getting many more ideas from much more reading.

Piles of "interesting" books, magazines and reports put aside to read later inevitably remain unread. In fact, they can be a temptation to useless reading.

Before you start reading anything you pick up, ask yourself:

• Why am I reading this?
• What am I specifically looking for?

• What do I want to get out of this?

If you're looking for new ideas in an area where you've already acquired a great deal of information, for instance, and you find evidence in the first few paragraphs of conventional thinking and familiar notions, you can safely abandon the article, book or report right there.

The more experienced and informed you are in a field, the more selective you can be about your reading. There's absolutely nothing wrong in reading only the first and last paragraphs of a report or article, or just one or two chapters of a book.

Key: Don't slow down your reading by passively following the sequence in which most people write. Understand the difference so you can digest information or new ideas efficiently. A newspaper journalist puts all the new information right at the top of the article. You can skip the rest if you have no need for the details. In a non-fiction book or long article, the details are usually sandwiched in the middle, between the first section (setting out the problem to be discussed or solved) and the summary and conclusions at the end.

Take a speed-reading course if you really are burdened by masses of material you struggle to get through.

Caution: Be realistic about what you'll gain from the course. The average reading speed is about 300 words per minute. You might be able to push your rate up to 3,000 words per minute, or even more, by the end of the course. But you're not very likely to be able to maintain that pace unless you follow the technique all the time. Chances are you won't want to do that—certainly not if you also read for pleasure or recreation.

But you will learn a very useful skill…trusting your ability to absorb words by simply looking at them rather than sounding them out in your head (300 words per minute is about the rate at which we "hear" words and for most people, that becomes the limit on their reading speed).

By "looking" at the pattern of words on a page, rather than "hearing" each one, you're likely to be able to maintain a much higher reading rate after the course—not 3,000 words per minute but, perhaps, 800 words per minute.

Retaining what you read:

Next step: Learning to retain the information and ideas you absorb as you read and make them your own so they relate creatively to knowledge and experience you already have.

Draw an "idea map" of each article or book or chapter. Reason: The human mind does better with pictures of concepts than it does with words that describe the concepts. Words help individuals communicate with one another. But in the mind itself, pictures are what grab and hold attention and thereby enhance memory.

How to map ideas as you read: On a separate sheet of paper, or on the blank page of a book, draw a picture of the main concept being discussed. Use arrows, lines, circles, other pictures, question marks and any other devices that mean something to you, to illustrate relationships and cross-connections as the author develops them—and as you react to them. You might write down key words on the blank paper—"who," "what," "when," "how much." Then answer the questions as you read with pictures or trigger words, not long definitions or explanations. Also jot down the page numbers where you discover significant information or ideas. (This is actually more efficient than highlighting.)

When you're finished with the article or book, look at your idea map and think about it. Ask yourself: What does this do for me? How does this relate to the work I do? To a personal project? To my personal relations? Jot down ideas that come to you. Revise the diagram to reflect your reactions.

The book or article with your own personal outline in it of what you've learned from reading now becomes useful. By involving your hands and your imaging capacity, you'll have a much higher learning experience from your reading. And your idea map will be a quick reminder when you want to review the information.

Source: Eric M. Bienstock, PhD, consultant to executives on developing thinking and memory skills, 231 E. 76 St., New York 10021. He is author of *Thinking*, a Boardroom Special Report, 197 Mountain Ave., Springfield, NJ 07081, and *Success Through Better Memory*, Perigee, 200 Madison Ave., New York 10016.

Lessons In Learning For All Of Us From Asian Students

Contrary to popular opinion, Asians are not any smarter than Americans. Although most people think that Asians score higher on IQ tests, a study of the actual results proved that they are no more intelligent than Americans.

Nor is television the answer. For instance, Japanese students spend even more time in front of the set than do Americans.

No, Asians do better in school simply because they try harder...and because they believe that academic success results from hard work just as much as from intelligence. And this applies to people who have emigrated to the US from Asia as well.

What we can learn:

Although it's difficult to change our fundamental attitudes, Americans can learn from the educational successes of Asians. What Asian kids have that American kids don't:

• A positive attitude about achievement. In America, academic excellence is thought to depend heavily on innate ability. In contrast, Asians think that hard work makes the difference. In Asia, everyone—the gifted as well as those who are not—is assumed to be capable of success and achievement. Result: Asian students believe that diligence will pay off with good grades and greater opportunities for future employment.

Although most American parents know that it takes years of daily practice to become an Olympic athlete, they underestimate the role of practice in academics. Needed to succeed: Confidence and hard work...lots of it.

Example: The film *Stand and Deliver*, based on a true story, portrayed a group of Hispanic students who were convinced that they could not do calculus—until a dedicated teacher proved they could, if they believed in themselves and worked hard enough.

• Students of varied abilities in the same class. At one time, American educators thought all schoolchildren could and should learn the same curriculum. Today, American students are quickly segregated according to ability.

Fast-learners get challenging course work, while slow-learners are shunted along a remedial track. Sad result: Although separating children simplifies things for teachers, it's devastating to children...of both groups.

Slow-learners fall behind the other students until they figure it's not worth it to even try to learn. Fast-learners pull so far ahead that they find they can coast without any ill effect.

In Asia, every child masters the same curriculum because slow-learners and fast-learners stick together throughout their elementary schooling. In fact, the whole goal among Japanese educators is to foster conditions under which all children excel. Advantage: Fast-learners help teach slower classmates, helping themselves learn in the process.

By high school, however, students are competing with each other for top spots in the top universities.

• Better-prepared teachers. American teachers get too little time to prepare lessons. Chinese teachers are shocked to hear that American teachers spend almost the entire day in class. They ask, "When do they prepare for class or grade papers?" In China, no teacher spends more than three hours a day in the classroom—many spend only two. Gained: The teachers have time to present well-conceived lessons that are vivid and engaging.

• Interested parents. In Asia, parents believe the success or failure of a child is largely a measure of their ability as parents. Result: They have a much larger stake in seeing that their child does well...and this translates into heightened interest in the child's schooling.

Asian parents set aside time to discuss school matters with their children and help them with homework, if necessary.

• A place to study. Many Americans lack a quiet, well-lit place in which to study. Japanese and Chinese parents buy their children a desk and set aside a place to be used for homework.

Although it's true that children don't need computers, tape recorders and other expensive electronic gear to get good grades, they do need their own places to study.

• More homework. Asian students spend far more time on homework than their American counterparts. This starts in first grade and continues until graduation.

I recently polled mothers of schoolchildren in the US and Taiwan. In the US, first-graders spend about 70 minutes a week on homework, and fifth-graders spent about 252 minutes. In contrast, Taiwanese students spent about 494 minutes on homework in the first grade and a whopping 771 minutes in the fifth grade.

• Superior note-taking skills. Japanese students produce beautiful notebooks—clear, concise and intelligently underlined. Most American students take sloppy, incomplete notes that are of little value when it comes to studying for an exam.

• A different approach to television. Although most Asian children do watch a lot of television, they watch it differently. Where many American kids watch TV and do homework at the same time, Japanese children are allowed to turn on the TV only after their homework is completed.

• Positive role models. In Asia, children have a clear sense of just whom they should emulate. This is not the case in America. A generation ago, we had Neil Armstrong, John F. Kennedy, Martin Luther King, Jr., etc.—strong, vigorous, capable. Today, our children have a hard time finding such models.

• Better practice workbooks. Asian bookstores are filled with high-quality workbooks that cover all academic subjects. The comparatively few academic workbooks in American bookstores tend to be of poor quality.

• Relaxed schools. American schools are far more intense than those in Asia, where each 50-minute class is followed by a 10-minute recess. This gives students a chance to unwind after a period of intense concentration.

In America, students have few breaks and rush from class to class. Result: American students have more trouble concentrating.

Most children in Asia also stay after school to participate in activities or clubs—including those aimed at helping them perform well in school. In America, most students now leave school the minute the bell rings.

Bottom line: While most Asian students see school as central to their lives, most American students do not...and the difference is evident in academic performance.

Source: Harold W. Stevenson, PhD, a University of Michigan psychology professor who has studied extensively the differences between education in America and Asia. Dr. Stevenson is currently a visiting scholar at the Center for Advanced Study in Behavioral Sciences, Palo Alto, CA.

Biased College Admissions

College admissions practices—even at the best schools—are biased. Example: Harvard University's admissions office gives advice to recruited athletes and children of alumni. Harvard's view: Doing so is crucial to the functioning of the college. The acceptance rate is 35.7% for legacies and 48.7% for recruited athletes, while the overall admission rate is 16.9%. Note: Alumni children and recruited athletes score lower than other students in nearly every academic category the admissions office uses.

Source: *The Harvard Crimson,* 14 Plympton St., Cambridge, MA 02138.

Better Schoolbook Reading

When children bring home textbooks to read for school, teach them to preview the book before they read for better overall comprehension. What to preview: Look at the table of contents, which lists specific chapters being covered...read the preface to understand the author's goal...glance over the index, glossary and appendix...read the introduction...look at the bibliography.

Source: *Any Child Can Read Better—Developing Your Child's Reading Skills Outside the Classroom* by Harvey S. Wiener, PhD, Bantam Books, 666 Fifth Ave., New York 10103.

Benefits Of Reading Out Loud

Reading out loud lets parents (and teachers) check that children use proper pronunciation. During silent reading, repeated mistakes go unnoticed—and uncorrected. Added benefit: Better vocabulary building—children tend to skip over big words they don't understand when they read silently.

Source: *Marva Collins' Way: Returning to Excellence in Education,* Jeremy P. Tarcher, Inc., 5858 Wilshire Blvd., Los Angeles 90036.

How To Get Your Kids Into Harvard

A student seeking entry to Harvard or other Ivy League schools and their five cousins—Duke, Williams, Stanford, University of Virginia, etc.—is going to have just as tough a go of it this year as in the past.

This despite the fact that the pool of college applicants is shrinking due to fewer high school graduates nationwide—and will continue to do so for the next few years. The top schools always have four to five times more applicants than they can accept...and the majority of applicants have basic academic achievements at least equal to those who have been accepted.

Students must take a close look at their personal focus. It's no longer just the individual applicant's brains, record and leadership potential that gain him/her the coveted spot.

The colleges are looking now for a well-rounded freshman class rather than a class full of well-rounded individuals.

They want some real scholars, some exceptional athletes...and so on. They neither expect nor desire a long list of superior talents in a single student.

Key question: A candidate may be a swell, accomplished kid...but does he have that extra quality to enhance the freshman class as a whole?

What the Ivies want:

Colleges now pick their favorite candidates based on how well that applicant stands out in one of five categories.

Result: Applicants compete primarily against others in their own category (although some kids fall into more than one category), not against the entire applicant pool. Colleges look for:

• Intellects. Professors want real scholars... and the admissions officers listen to the faculty. Result: A certain number of students who demonstrate superior intellectual competence are always admitted...even if they show few other talents.

• Special talents. These run from prowess in football to talent on the oboe. It all depends on the university.

Example: Every Bowdoin freshman class has a super hockey goalie.

• Children of alumni. Private universities depend on their alumni to fill their coffers through contributions. To keep the alumni happy, family members receive an edge in the admissions process.

And the concept of family extends beyond alumni. Harvard, for instance, pays special attention to candidates from greater Boston.

• Affirmative-action students. Every college wants a representation of blacks, Hispanics and other minority students.

Because many of these students receive inadequate secondary schooling, they are judged as much on potential—how the student will look at the time of graduation from college—as an accomplishment this far.

• All-American kids. These are the well-rounded students who get good grades, play sports, edit the school newspaper and have lots of outside interests.

Most candidates fall into this huge group. Prestige colleges are swamped by them. This is where the competition is most intense.

The best way for candidates in this category to succeed is to have a foot in at least one of the other four categories. Occasionally, unusual factors—such as a candidate's geographic location or participation in significant political activities—provide the needed boost.

But wealth and position won't do it anymore. Many children of the rich and famous have not found the doors of the very selective colleges open to them.

How to help your child:

Although it's never too soon to start encouraging your child, the eleventh grade is the most important. It's the last full year in which a student's grades are reviewed by most admissions committees. Tell your child to...

- Take a challenging course load. It should be the most demanding load he can handle well. This is what the admissions committees look at first.

The schools are most concerned with grades in the most demanding courses taken in junior year. Sophomore grades are less important and freshman grades are less important still.

Warning: Senior-year grades are important. Colleges presume the student's level of achievement will remain constant. If his grades fall significantly, he could be unadmitted or admitted on probation.

- Communicate regularly with the guidance counselor. If the counselor is not spending enough time with your child or not offering advice that you think is good, hire an outside consultant who can offer advice on college goals and how to achieve them. Cost: $1,000–$1,500.

- Maintain a good grade-point average (GPA). It's usually more important than class rank...although a student with a high rank at a school where rank is weighted according to the difficulty of the course load looks very good to the college admissions board.

- Prepare for aptitude tests (SATs or ACTs) and achievement tests. The best way to do this is by reading extensively and doing well in the classroom.

By all means, students should take the practice tests provided by the College Board or ACT. Cram courses, however, are usually a waste of time.

Note: The importance of standardized tests has changed over the years. Test scores are now used as confirming evidence of a student's capabilities.

Mastering the admissions process:

There are several ways that even All-American kids can shine in the admissions process. Tell your child to...

- Concentrate on the application essay. It's the most important element colleges use to distinguish one student from another.

Don't tamper with your child's essay or let anyone else help. The strongest candidates do their writing on their own. Remember: A 17-year-old is an unfinished product. A slick, professionally packaged essay looks suspicious.

- Don't be pushy. Forget about gimmicks.

Example: One student sent pencils with his picture and the reminder "Admit me!" printed on them.

Such ploys are tacky. Pushy students or parents almost always lose out.

- Provide the recommendations the college requests. They will usually be school-related. The best ones come from a teacher who teaches a demanding course...who really knows the student...and can write well.

If your child has outside activities—part-time work, Outward Bound-type experiences, etc.—have him get recommendations from people who supervised him. But don't provide more recommendations than the school asks for. And avoid recommendations from your friends...they're death.

- Go for the campus interview. Most kids speak better than they write. If no campus interview is offered, seek out a hometown alumnus who will meet with your child and make an official report to the college.

- Be confident. Students should present themselves honestly but compellingly in the essay and the interview. One admissions officer said his main criterion was, "Whom do I want in the bow of my canoe?"

Best advice: Be yourself. Don't be what you think the college wants you to be. Be serious, but also be engaging. Remember that admissions officers are human. They have a sense of humor, a sense of fair play and huge imaginations.

Source: Richard Moll, who spent 30 years in college admissions at several Ivy League schools and lectures nationwide (with original music!) on how students can get into these schools. His is the author of *Playing College Admissions Games* and *The Public Ivies*, both published by Penguin Books, 375 Hudson St., New York 10014.

Good Grades Aren't Everything

Students need to focus on doing their best. Perseverance, endurance and diligence are essential qualities to learning. Effort is the central component of these qualities. Parents can help keep children interested in learning by teaching them to focus on the effort put into pursuing a goal, rather than just on the outcome.

Source: *Eager To Learn: Helping Children Become Motivated and Love Learning* by Raymond J. Wlodkowski, PhD, Jossey-Bass Publishers, 350 Sansome St., San Francisco 94104.

What You Can Do To Enhance Your Child's Education

Most Americans are all too familiar with the failings of our educational system—how test scores continue to drop, how our children are being outclassed by children of other nations, how the US is becoming ever less competitive in the global economy. Yet despite the good intentions of our elected officials, much-publicized education reform efforts and the expenditure of billions of dollars, the typical American public-school education remains haphazard and poorly focused.

Parents can make a big difference in their children's education—and not just by becoming politically involved to promote education reform. There are plenty of small but highly practical steps parents can take to change what their kids are learning and how they are being taught.

Encourage learning outside the classroom:

Ninety percent of a child's first 18 years is spent outside school, so it doesn't make sense to leave a child's education entirely to teachers. Recommended:

- Encourage your child to read books beyond those assigned in school.
- Take the family to museums, concerts, libraries and other cultural events and institutions.
- Discuss current events.
- Choose books for the family to read aloud. Follow readings with discussion.
- Be sure to provide for your children's ethical and moral education as well.
- Be a role model.
- Encourage participation in athletics, religious institutions, scouting groups, etc.

Monitor your child's progress:

Most parents have only a vague sense of what their children are being taught in any given week, so they have only a vague sense of what their kids are supposed to know.

Better: Determine exactly what your child must know to be promoted to the next grade, and also to perform well on a monthly, weekly, even daily basis. Then make sure your child is keeping up. If the class is studying fractions, for instance, informally test your child to make sure he's making progress in that area.

Helpful: If the teacher is hard to reach, suggest that he/she set up an answering machine with daily announcements about what's being taught. Parents can phone the machine each evening for an update. Those who have questions or comments can leave a message.

Help with homework:

Check your children's homework for completeness, correctness and neatness. Even if the subject material is unfamiliar to you or over your head, odds are you know whether the assignment "looks right." But remember, your role is to help check over homework, not to do it yourself.

Press for accurate information:

In a recent survey of results of standardized tests, 48 states claimed that their schoolchildren were performing at or above the national average. Clearly, something is amiss, since one would expect half the states to have scores above average and about half to have below-average scores.

Explanation: State educational officials and the companies that design these tests are eager to dispense good news. Everything is calculated to make the system look good. Sad result: In many communities parents never learn the truth about how their children are doing.

• Learn to interpret report cards. Teacher comments on report cards are always positive—or neutral. That's unfortunate, because the first step toward improving a child's academic performance in school is realizing when there is a problem.

Self-protection: Scrutinize report cards. Read between the lines. If your child's grade seems out of line with the teacher's overall assessment, or if there is some other puzzling aspect to the report, schedule a meeting with the teacher.

Become a school volunteer:

Many school districts welcome volunteers, yet few parents make the effort. If you can spare the time, ask school officials or individual teachers if there's anything you can do. If you have a particular area of expertise, work in a field that is of interest to students or have taken an interesting trip, offer to make an informal talk to students. Parents who are too busy to volunteer can ask grandparents to do so.

Planning ahead:

It pays to pick the best teachers and schools. Most parents are content to let the local school board determine not only what their children will learn, but also which school their children will attend and which teachers they will have. Better:

• Poll other parents to find out the best schools and teachers.

• Check results of standardized tests (usually published annually in the local paper).

• If necessary, petition school officials to reassign your children.

• While school administrators are understandably reluctant to honor special requests, in many cases the best schools and teachers are no more than a phone call or letter away. Note: In some cases, several different "schools" operate within the same building.

Source: Chester E. Finn., Jr., PhD, professor of education and public policy, Vanderbilt University, and director of the Educational Excellence Network, a nonprofit organization dedicated to improving education in the US. A close advisor to Federal Education Secretary Lamar Alexander, Dr. Finn is the author of *We Must Take Charge: Our Schools and Our Future*, Free Press, 866 Third Ave., New York 10022.

College-Aid Financial Myths

Many people don't apply for college financial aid, either for themselves or for their children, assuming incorrectly that they won't qualify for assistance. Common misconceptions...

• The money I have saved in my retirement account will count against my child's chances of getting financial aid. Money from 401(k)s, IRAs and Keoghs isn't counted in the formula for determining aid.

• If one child was rejected for aid, the other one will be, too. Families should apply for financial aid for all children who are attending college—even if a past application was turned down. Families with more than one child in school often have a better chance of being granted aid than those who only have one child in college.

• Older people returning to college—or those who are going to college for the first time—aren't financial-aid candidates. Older students are just as eligible for financial aid as traditional college-age students.

Source: Paula B. Redder, vice president, Student Loan Marketing Association (Sallie Mae), 1050 Thomas Jefferson St. NW, Washington, DC 20007.

Applying To College: Useful Financial Angles

Each year, tens of thousands of high-school seniors—many accompanied by a parent or two—make an early winter swing through "the colleges of their choice."

They're asked questions, stay overnight at dorms, listen in groups as admissions officers describe the schools' selection processes.

Too often missing in this picture: Honest, open and, when necessary, tough talk between the students and their parents about making realistic choices.

Decisions...decisions:

Racing far ahead of the inflation rate for more than a decade now, the increasing cost of education at the nation's leading private colleges now startles even well-to-do parents.

For high-income professional and executive families, the $90,000 or even higher bill for four years of undergraduate study and living expenses at the nation's elite schools most likely is well above the down payment they made on their homes—or, for many, even their current equity in those homes.

The decision whether or not to spend that much money should not be left to an 18-year-old. Especially not to an 18-year-old who has been left in the dark about the family's financial capacity. It's hard to believe that it has become customary for those students to make decisions substantially affecting their parents' finances.

Big mistake: Too many parents make the mistake of shielding their children from any clear understanding of the relation of family economics to their choice of college. Typical parental attitude: "You try to get into the best school you possibly can, and we'll find a way to pay for it."

Open up the discussion:

The purpose of the discussion is to make a sensible plan for the college admission process. And to reduce the great anger and resentment of children who get accepted into elite schools only to be told by their parents that they cannot afford it. Helpful:

• From the first year of high school—not starting with junior year—make clear to your children that you are interested in their choice of courses, their interests and what information or questions they have about possible college choices.

• No later than junior year, make clear what the family's contribution to college costs can be from its income and assets. Be specific, too, about the amount of debt you could undertake to fill the gap between actual school costs and your capacity to pay.

• Let your children express their feelings about taking on the burden of substantial student loans to fill any financial gap.

Application strategy:

Open discussions over the years widen the array of sensible choices:

• Apply to at least seven colleges—not the five that has been the standard recommendation for years. This can provide more choice if the first-choice school doesn't provide enough financial aid. And it might increase your leverage in negotiating for a lower family contribution.

• Overcome the pressure of thinking only the Top 20 private colleges are good enough to consider. If the child already has a clear interest in a subject, investigate course offerings in that subject at state universities. In environmental studies, for instance, state schools often have more complete programs than top private schools.

• Recognize the "tough schools." Getting into top state schools, such as Michigan, Colorado at Boulder and New York at Binghamton, is every bit as hard nowadays as getting into the Ivy League. They are not "safe" schools in your child's list of seven.

• Join your child on two or three of his/her school visits. Update your own impression of what colleges are really like today. Listen to—and respect—your child's feelings about a school...even if the reasons are not quite articulate. Compare notes and observations. This shared experience helps make clear that the ultimate choice must be a collective decision if parents are making a substantial contribution to the expense.

• Seek to close the financial gap. If your child is seriously interested in several high-cost schools, and has the academic credentials to make realistic bids for acceptance, learn whatever you can about how the gap might be filled. Use a good financial-aid consultant—one who'll do more than just fill out forms. Those with the right experience can give you a pretty good idea of what financial aid your family might qualify for at three or four colleges.

The best recommendation for finding a financial-aid consultant is by word-of-mouth—from satisfied customers. A college guidance counselor might prove to be a reliable source of who those families are.

The acceptance crisis:

The stress between college-bound children and their parents is rarely over nowadays when admission decisions roll in—especially if the "right" school says yes but the financial aid package offered isn't enough.

If you've used a financial-aid consultant or college consultant to make your choice, ask them for advice on negotiating for more financial aid. Or just go in and do it yourself—making clear that your child wants to go to that school but may have to select another because of the difference in costs—or aid package.

If the financial gap can't be breached at the top-choice school, you and your child should still be able to get the payoff from all the solid preparation and talk up to this point. Instead of recriminations, anger and heartbreak, child and parents together must make an adult choice among reasonable alternatives:

• Go into debt (family, child or both) to go to the top-choice school. This can be a deliberate decision. It should never be a reaction to a child's threat that he won't go to college at all if it's not this top one.

• Accept at the more affordable but perhaps less "prestigious" school that your previous research indicates offers its students top-quality education opportunities.

Source: Frank Leana, PhD, educational director of the New York office of Howard Greene & Associates, educational consultants, 176A E. 75 St., New York 10021. Dr. Leana is author of *Getting Into College*, Hill & Wang, 19 Union Square West, New York 10003.

How To Win The Public School Game

The best way to ensure a good learning experience for your child within the current system is to put time and effort into being an interactive parent. That means becoming a partner with the school and, most importantly, with your child's teacher.

Within every school, despite its problems, are good teachers who love their work and, with a little support, do a good job. Key: Find those teachers and make sure your child is in their classes.

Your message:

You don't want school personnel to see you as a troublesome busybody. As an interactive parent, you must convey a more constructive attitude. The basics of your message:

• I am seriously interested in my child's education.

• I think the best education comes from the joint efforts of home and school.

• I want to cooperate with the school in any way I can.

• I am a reasonable person, but I have strong beliefs about what makes for quality education.

Your responsibilities:

As an interactive parent, you must not only find your child the best teachers a school has to offer, you must support those teachers and enhance what they're doing in class. What to do:

• Supplement the curriculum. Find out what your child is studying. Check books out of the library that will enrich your experience. Take him/her to museums and other relevant places. If you or anyone in your family has relevant skills, collections, etc., offer to share them with the class.

• Work with the teacher to solve your child's problems. Listen to the teacher's ideas and analysis. Ask where you can help.

• Respect the teacher. Let your child see that respect. Send thank-you notes when your child has had a particularly rewarding experience.

Parents' calendar:

• August. Check in with the school secretary—a valuable resource person—to be sure your child is still assigned to the teacher you picked for him last spring (see *January* through *April*).

Find out the teacher's birthday, so you can celebrate it with a small remembrance. If you have not met the teacher, make a brief visit. Also visit the principal to establish or maintain contact and to express or reiterate your interactive-parent beliefs.

If your child is attending the school for the first time, take him for a visit.

• September. Get a copy of your child's curriculum and start to develop ideas for enriching his learning experience.

Consider what you might offer to the teacher as enrichment materials—an abandoned wasp's nest, an appropriate map, etc.

Send at least one thank-you note to the teacher about a classroom experience your child has enjoyed.

• October. Have a parent-teacher conference to review your child's progress and to see what else you can do to help. Discuss your child's standardized-achievement-test scores from the previous spring and the degree of balance among ability, achievement and expectations.

• November. Have a second parent-teacher conference to discuss your child's report card, the teacher's perceptions of your child's abilities and the progress and to find out about the upcoming curriculum. Do something special for the class that pertains to the curriculum.

• December. Work with your child to buy or make the teacher a small holiday gift.

• January/February. Have a third parent-teacher conference. Visit any special teachers your child has—music, gym, art. Start inquiries with other parents—and teachers—about teachers for the next grade.

• March. Keep up with the curriculum. Observe teachers in the next grade whom you may want your child to have.

• April. Make your formal request for next year's teacher through the principal. Continue to work with your child—and the rest of the class—on appropriate curriculum enrichments.

• May. Last teacher conference. Go over this year's standardized test scores and what they mean. Thank the teacher for a good year and ask for a summer reading list for your child. Preview the curriculum for the next year so that you can plan summer activities that will benefit your child.

• Summer. Monitor news of the school district so that you can help welcome new personnel and make new arrangements if the teacher you have chosen for your child is not coming back.

Read with your child. Take him to the library. Arrange for outings that will help him in his next year's work.

Source: Linwood Laughy, PhD, a Harvard National Scholar for four years. Dr. Laughy has worked in public schools as a classroom teacher, a school psychologist, an elementary and secondary principal, a superintendent and a community-college president. He is the author of *The Interactive Parent*, Mountain Meadow Press, Box 1170, Wrangell, AK 99929.

How Families That Are "Too Rich" Can Qualify For College Financial Aid

The biggest mistake families with bountiful assets or high current incomes make about college financial aid is to assume that they couldn't possibly qualify for outside assistance.

Important: Don't be turned off by the advice of friends, co-workers, etc., in similar circumstances who say that they tried—and failed—to get aid. The application process is complex. And the precise formulas used to decide whether or not a family will receive aid are not made public. You won't know if you qualify unless you try.

Opportunities:

The formulas used to determine how much a family can contribute to college expenses take into account about 30 variables. Included: Family size, age of the older parent, number of children in school, unusual medical expenses and the form in which assets are held.

It's not impossible for a family earning $120,000 a year to qualify legitimately for aid if it has more than one child in college, in graduate school or in high-tuition private secondary school at the same time. And families rich in assets sometimes do exceptionally well under some state aid programs that use different criteria from the so-called "Congressional methodology" formulas used in other financial-aid applications.

Example: In New York state, the formula is based on taxable income. College students whose parents own millions of dollars in tax-free municipal bonds or breeding farms, apartment houses or other real estate that shelters income may be eligible for the full amount of state financial aid.

Don't disqualify yourself:

Parents often make mistakes in filing financial-aid forms that reduce the aid they get or disqualify them from any aid at all.

Example: They list assets they don't have access to—funds in Keoghs, IRAs or pension accounts. Or they forget about certain expenses, such as medical insurance premiums automatically deducted from their paychecks.

Information provided on the financial-aid forms is audited and verified to detect income or assets that are not reported. But these audits do not uncover errors that overstate income or assets.

Don't forget to plan:

Another major mistake wealthier families often make is failing to plan far enough in advance.

Example: A family's income and assets for the current calendar year is the base that will be used to determine eligibility for students entering college in the fall of the next calendar year. Since these students are now juniors in high school, few of their parents are giving much thought now to what they can do to qualify for aid.

There are several things parents should not do during the base year (or during the next three years while the child is in college, because financial-aid packages are considered each year). Included:

• Don't sell securities and take capital gains before the child enters his/her junior year of high school. Capital gains are considered income and reduce eligibility for assistance.

• Don't take money out of pension programs—401(k) plans, IRAs, profit-sharing, etc.—in anticipation of meeting college expenses. You will have to pay taxes (and perhaps penalties) on the money. And it will increase the income that the financial-aid formulas take into account in figuring eligibility for aid.

Better: Borrow the money while the child is in school and then pay back the loan by taking assets out of pension accounts after the child graduates.

As your child approaches junior year in high school, your investment, savings and tax strategies should all take into consideration the impact on your family's eligibility for financial aid.

Some actions necessary to increase the family's chances of obtaining financial aid make no sense from any other standpoint.

Sad but true: Encouraging your child to earn and save by holding a part-time job during high school may be wonderful for the child's character...but the money earned will reduce the child's eligibility for aid.

Income earned by the child in the prior year is assessed heavily—up to 70% of that income is considered available to meet college expenses. So if a child earned $3,000 the year before college, the family may qualify for $2,100 less in financial aid than if the child had not worked.

Warning: Many accountants advise their clients to put assets in a child's name once he reaches 14 so that income will be taxed at the child's rate. But this tactic can cause you to lose financial aid.

Don't procrastinate:

Get the financial-aid applications filed by the deadlines determined by the college. Don't wait until a child is accepted at a school.

Financial aid is granted on a first-come first-served basis, and the amount of money available at any particular school is limited. You may be as qualified as the family whose application was received just ahead of yours...but they may have gotten the last buck.

The process begins by completing a financial need analysis document—in most cases the *Financial Aid Form (FAF)* or the *Family Financial Statement (FFS).* Copies of these forms are available from high school guidance counselors. The catalogs of schools your child is interested in will say what form is required.

Send your form in as soon as possible after January 1 of the year your child will enter college. That means if you aren't able to get your taxes completed by the deadlines, use estimated information.

Schools have different deadlines. Be sure you know what they are. And send the forms by certified mail, return-receipt requested—even if the form says it's not necessary to do so. It's important to have proof of the date on which you mailed the form.

If you get a financial-aid package from one school that is much better than the one offered by the school your child really wants to attend, don't hesitate to negotiate for a better package. The strategy is often successful.

And don't be discouraged because you read that financial aid is getting tighter and tighter. Reality: The budget compromise struck between Congress and the administration in late 1990 actually increased the amount of college financial aid available from the federal government.

Source: Kalman Chany, president, Campus Consultants, 338 E. 67 St., New York 10021. The company guides families and students through the financial-aid process.

Better Test Scores

Changing initial answers on multiple-choice tests improves students' scores. Recent study: 54% of changes were from wrong to right, 20% were from right to wrong and the remaining answers were from wrong to wrong...70% of students increased their overall test scores, 13% lowered their test scores. These findings contradict common expectations that students lower their scores by changing test answers.

Source: Study by Marshall A. Geiger, University of Maine, published in *Psychological Reports*, Box 9229, Missoula, MT 59807.

Questions To Ask Your Child's Preschool Teacher

Does my child seem happy? Does he/she play well with the other children? Who are his friends? What activities does he seem to like best? What signs of maturing do you see? Is he having trouble in any particular area? Does he use the bathroom by himself? What can I do to help him at home?

Source: *The School Book* by Mary Susan Miller, PhD, St. Martin's Press, 175 Fifth Ave., New York 10010.

Counteracting Learning Myths

Learning myths are passed on to us when we're young—and we don't find out the truth until we are adults. Common myths: Learning is boring...learning deals only with a formal school curriculum...we must be passive to "absorb" knowledge...to learn, you need a teacher...learning has to be systematic, logical and planned...learning needs to be thorough or it's not worth doing.

Source: *Peak Learning: A Master Course in Learning How To Learn* by Ronald Gross, co-chairman of the University Seminar on Innovation in Education at Columbia University, New York, Jeremy P. Tarcher, Inc., 5858 Wilshire Blvd., Suite 200, Los Angeles 90030.

Video College Hunting

Some colleges and independent producers are now offering campus tours on videotape—saving the cost of long-distance trips to look at schools. College-made tapes are usually free for the asking from admissions offices—but may not show all of a school's faults. Independent sources of college videos include:

- *Collegiate Choice*, Tenafly, NJ (201-871-0098)—dozens of video profiles available in libraries in New York, New Jersey and Connecticut.
- *College Home Videos*, Philadelphia (800-248-7177)—more than 100 colleges on tape at $4 each, plus $2.75 postage and handling (per order).
- *Learning Resources Network*, Durham, NC (800-225-5576)—$8 rental fee plus $2.10 postage and handling for each college.

Source: *The New York Times*.

12

You and Your Family

How To Have Fun As A Family...And Learn Too

Having fun as a family is just as important as doing chores or homework. But family fun involves more than playing games or going places. It brings the family together...and prepares it to deal with hard times—as well as good times.

In planning a fun event, a family is really training its children how to cope with the challenges of human relationships.

Planning:

When it's time to plan a vacation or other family event, each person should prepare a list of ideas and personal interests. Everyone should be involved. Even the youngest children need to realize that their desires are being recognized.

When the lists are done, the ideas should be presented to the entire group. Then everyone should vote to see if one idea or another is a clear winner.

If none are—which is often the case—open a discussion to find out what people are objecting to. Work toward a compromise solution where no one is left out.

Example: If one person wants to go to the beach, another wants to go fishing and another wants to see Disney World, plan a week in Florida that includes a few days of each.

Start your meeting with the understanding that there will be disagreement. This is part of the learning process.

Children learn through planning that differences are inevitable whenever two or more people are involved...that people shouldn't hide their differences...that they should compromise and negotiate...and that people who work together can find solutions.

What's fun:

Fun means different things to different people. For some it's being stretched out on a hammock and reading. For others, it's renting a house at the beach, hiking in the mountains, having a picnic in the backyard, watching a movie on the VCR or playing softball.

For a change of pace, families can do things together that most people think of as solitary pursuits.

Example: One year, we bought canvas, easels and paints—it's all quite inexpensive—and the four of us spent our vacation painting. It was the first time any of us had ever painted, and it was a joy to help each other and share and critique each other's work.

Family fun does not have to be expensive at all...

Examples: Strolling in the park...walking on the beach...making music together...playing games...doing crafts.

One way to increase the family fun level is to build in some kind of fun every day.

Example: At the dinner table, don't just ask your kids, "What happened in school today?" Share something interesting or amusing that happened to you. The kids will soon get into the swing of things.

Even discussing serious issues can be fun, if everyone is involved and excited. How to start: Ask questions to elicit your children's opinions about an issue they've read about or heard on the news. Avoid lecturing or arguing about who's right or wrong. And, most important, avoid ridiculing anyone.

Even chores can be fun, if they're done in a social, cooperative way.

Example: Make it a habit for the family to sing favorite songs in harmony while clearing off the dinner table and washing and drying dishes.

How not to have fun:

Some families seem to have fun all the time, while others can make having fun into work. Traps to avoid:

• Imposing things on the family. When kids—or even your spouse—are made to do something, it automatically ceases to be fun.

Example: An overbearing father forces his city-loving family into a week of hiking, telling them, "It's good for you."

• Not respecting the wishes and schedules of children. This is especially true of teenagers, who need to have time with their peers.

Remedy: Letting teens decide what they will do with the family, and when.

• Not allowing yourself to enjoy things. Some parents find it difficult to let themselves have fun. They were programmed at an early age that work is virtuous...pleasure is sinful.

Remedy: Recognize that's how you feel... and fight these feelings, for the good of your family.

• Being passive and indecisive. This results in a demoralized family moping at home because nothing has been planned.

Remedy: Plan ahead.

• Acting dissatisfied about a plan. When a child gripes, it may be just a way of getting attention.

Remedy: Don't let it stop you. Ask for the child's input, but insist you're going ahead with your plans.

Make sure, however, that even the gripers get a chance. If you don't do what they want to do this time around...schedule it for next weekend. Emphasize: Taking turns.

Source: Milton Schwebel, PhD, professor emeritus of psychology at the Graduate School of Applied and Professional Psychology at Rutgers University. He is the co-author—with his wife (a social worker and teacher), his two sons (both psychologists) and his daughter-in-law (an expert in early childhood education)—of *A Guide to a Happier Family: Overcoming the Anger, Frustration and Boredom that Destroy Family Life*, Jeremy P. Tarcher, distributed by St. Martin's Press.

How To Teach Kids To Tell The Truth

Ironically, the very skills that help children develop into adults—the ability to remember, plan, control their emotions and consider another person's point of view—also lay the foundation for lying.*

That's why it shouldn't surprise many managers that the reasons why kids bend the truth are often similar to the reasons employees lie in the work place. Many managers may be helped in spotting deception among their subordinates by understanding the psychology of lying in children.

*There are such things as necessary lies. Example: A stranger comes to the door and asks, "Are your parents at home?" A child might be safer saying, "Yes," than admitting he is all alone.

Why kids lie:

Understanding the reasons why children lie can help parents know how to respond. Key reasons:

• To gain an advantage the child can't get any other way. Example: Cheating on a test at school.

• To avoid punishment. Example: A teenager who has broken curfew says her friend's car broke down.

• To enhance status. Examples: Name-dropping, bragging.

• To spare someone else's feelings or get out of an awkward situation. Example: A child is invited to a party and her best friend isn't. When the friend invites her to play the day of the party, the girl tells her she's going out of town with her family.

• To protect privacy. Example: A teenager is evasive in response to a parent's endless grilling about how and with whom he spends his time.

Important: The age when kids are most likely to get in trouble is the same age when they feel the need to be trusted. A parent, however, has the right to know about issues that could involve breaking the law or might endanger the child or others.

• To gain power. Controlling others by putting something over on them is a form of adolescent rebellion.

Prizing the truth:

It's important to help kids understand the consequences of lying. How much they understand depends partly on how old they are. Suggested:

• Show a young child how lying keeps things from working. Example: You can't enjoy a game if one person is always lying about his roll of the dice.

• Use the newspapers to teach about actions and consequences. Examples: Athletics on drugs who forfeit their medals...politicians who break the rules and fall from public esteem.

• Develop rules of thumb about lying. Example: Before telling someone a lie, ask yourself, "How will she feel when she learns of the lie?" Most people would feel taken advantage of.

What to do when your child lies:

There are several constructive things parents can do when a child lies...

• Think about whether you played a role in the lie. Are you so harsh or unreasonable that the child is afraid to tell you the truth...or so permissive that he thinks he can get away with murder?

• Act as a teacher, not a policeman. Overly punitive parents unwittingly encourage their kids to be better liars next time, since the consequences of being caught are so dire. Instead: Make telling the truth an easy, constructive habit.

• Don't act out of anger. It's natural to feel hurt and angry when you're lied to, but acting on those feelings won't help you recover your trust.

Source: Paul Ekman, PhD, professor of psychology University of California Medical School in San Francisco. His research on lying has been supported by the National Institute of Mental Health, from which he has received four Research Scientist Awards. Dr. Ekman has written or edited nine books on lying, most recently, *Why Kids Lie*, Penguin, 1633 Broadway, New York 10019.

How To Help Your Spouse...and Yourself If Your Spouse Develops A Chronic Illness

A person whose spouse develops a chronic illness—serious heart disease, Alzheimer's, multiple sclerosis, back trouble, etc.—faces many difficult challenges. Not only must he/she help his spouse...he must learn to keep his own bearings. Otherwise the caregiver may break under the weight of the very difficult and tedious situation. There are several important things a spouse can do when chronic illness strikes.

Coping skills:

• Confront your emotions. Both you and your spouse need to be able to share everything you feel. If you don't express your emotions, your spouse won't feel free to express his. People are frequently shocked by the intense resentment they feel toward a sick spouse. But even these feelings must be faced.

Example: A man whose wife was chronically ill thought that her illness had gypped him out of the life they once shared. When he told her this, she admitted she felt the same way. Result: Together, they were able to work through their feelings.

Many people find that writing down their emotions helps to clarify them. Also helpful: List the concerns that you think are on your spouse's mind. Then go over the list together.

• Let yourselves laugh. Although it may seem macabre to outsiders, people can find humor in any situation.

Example: I know a woman who had a stroke when the oldest of her four children was less than 14. When they act up, she teases them by saying, "Don't aggravate me...or my next stroke may be the Big One."

Strange as it may sometimes seem, nothing releases tension like laughter.

• Live as normal a life as you can. Although your life can't be what it was, you can establish new routines and develop what I call a New Normal.

Hobbies provide creative and emotional outlets. Look for things your spouse can enjoy, and that will help him stay connected to the outside world.

Examples: Art, operating a ham radio.

Some people who are chronically ill still enjoy travel...although it requires a high level of planning.

Find a travel agent who's willing to help. He can tell you about tours set up especially for people who are ill. If you prefer to travel by yourselves, tell him how mobile your spouse is and what facilities and equipment your spouse requires.

• Ask for help. There are many people who need outside assistance to bear up emotionally. This is nothing to be ashamed of.

If you can't afford private counseling, many state and county mental-health centers offer free or low-cost assistance.

There are many support groups for people with various diseases. Some of the best involve both patients and spouses. Support groups allow people to share their experiences with others who understand what they're going through and can offer advice.

To find a support group: Call the local branch of an association that deals with your mate's illness. Also: Newspapers' weekend editions frequently list support group meetings.

In addition to emotional help, you will also need assistance in taking care of day-to-day needs. Look for people—relatives, friends or paid outsiders—who can help you care for your spouse and keep your home and the rest of your life on track.

• Don't give up on sex. Make an appointment to talk about sex. Pick a time that's convenient for both of you, when you won't be disturbed by phone calls, children, etc. Choose a time with a definite beginning and end. Away from the house is ideal—meet for lunch or refreshments in the afternoon.

Prepare for your conversation by reading about the topic. There's a chapter in my book. And many magazine articles are printed on the subject.

When you and your partner meet, start off by saying what you're going to talk about. Admit if you are uncomfortable with the subject. Then...just start to talk about it.

Express your feelings openly and honestly. Talk about what's happening, what you miss and what you think is still possible.

Ask open-ended questions, such as, "How do you feel about this?" Open-ended questions give your partner a chance to think and respond, not just reply with a simple yes or no.

Conclude the conversation with reassurances of caring and love, and make another appointment to continue the conversation at a later date.

If you don't discuss the emotional and physical changes affecting your sex life, it may quietly disappear. This situation could lead to depression for both of you. There are many ways to have satisfying sex.

Source: Beverly Kievman, the author of *For Better or For Worse: A Couple's Guide to Dealing With Chronic Illness*, Contemporary Books, 180 N. Michigan Ave., Chicago 60601. She is also an international speaker, consultant and president of the Atlanta-based Marketing Innovations Corp., and Beverly Kievman Enterprises, 5775 Peachtree Rd., Building E, Suite 200, Atlanta 30342.

Talk About Your Day

Tell children about your day after asking them about theirs. It's important that they understand what you do everyday and be able to explain it to others...it helps them feel proud of you. Also: When you talk about problems you may have solved at work and how you helped co-workers in the process, it teaches them to be helpful to others.

Source: *Letitia Baldrige's Complete Guide to the New Manners For the '90s*, Macmillan, 866 Third Ave., New York 10022.

Better Ways To Soothe Fussy Babies

While there's no single surefire way to soothe a fussy baby, experienced parents know that the more soothing techniques in your repertoire, the better your odds of getting the job done. Most effective:

• Rhythmic motion. Babies in our culture cry more than those in other cultures—simply because we spend too little time holding and cuddling them.

Remedy: Hold your baby as much as possible. Cradle him/her in your arms and sway or rock at a rate of 70 cycles a minute, that frequency corresponds to the adult heartbeat and walking pace. Caution: Babies should never be jostled until they can support their heads—usually at about four months.

• Breast-feeding. Nursing not only calms the baby, but also encourages the mother to be more sensitive to her baby's needs.

• Soothing sounds. Sounds with a tempo of 60–70 cycles a minute can be soothing. Examples: Metronome, grandfather clock, running water, tape recordings of a heartbeat, white noise from a blank TV channel.

• Visual distractions. Ceiling fans, surf, waterfalls, clock pendulums, trees swaying in the breeze and almost anything else with a rhythmic motion and a constant, monotonous sound are often effective.

• Warm baths. Fill the tub halfway, open the drain and leave the water running to maintain a constant 100°F. Lie in the tub with your baby on your chest. Many babies like to nurse while bathing.

• Car rides. An automobile's motion and its droning tires help put babies to sleep.

Source: William Sears, MD, of the pediatrics faculty of the University of Southern California and a pediatrician in private practice in San Clement, CA. A father of seven, Dr. Sears is author of several books on infant care, including *The Fussy Baby*, Plume, 375 Hudson St., New York 10014.

A Parent's Guide To Much Happier Adolescence

The biggest mistake most people make in dealing with teenagers is expecting them to be rebellious and moody...even to dabble in drugs, crime and risky sex. Too many adults all too frequently expect the worst.

But as research has shown over and over again, the conventional wisdom is dead wrong.

By focusing on ordinary, everyday kids—as opposed to delinquents and dropouts—researchers are now seeing teenagers with new and less-jaundiced eyes.

Facts about adolescence:

• Fact: Adolescence is not an inherently difficult period. It produces no more psychological or behavioral problems, and no more family conflict, than any other stage of the life cycle.

The great majority of adolescents (almost 90%) steer clear of serious trouble. Good kids don't suddenly turn "bad" at the age of 12 or 13.

• Fact: The evils of peer pressure have been overrated. Although adolescents need to fit in, their peer groups are more apt to be a force for good than evil.

Example: Peers may push a teenager to excel in sports—or in school.

Adolescents generally choose friends whose values, attitudes and families are similar to their own.

• Fact: The decline of the family has been overstated. Despite neighborhood decay, high divorce rates, the youth culture and the media, parents remain the major influence on their children through adolescence and into young adulthood.

What's going on:

Unfortunately, cultural stereotypes die hard. Too many parents withdraw their affection (to help their maturing children "grow up")...or rigidly control the adolescent's life (as if to deny that the child is changing)...or become excessively permissive (teenagers are teenagers, after all).

None of these strategies are helpful to the child. At worst, they may push a teenager into the negative behaviors the parents had hoped to avoid.

Better: Like all children, adolescents need what psychotherapist Carl Rogers called "unconditional positive regard." They seek reassurance that nothing—not their growing maturity, their moods, their misbehavior—can shake their parents' basic commitment to them.

Adolescents no longer view their parents as all-knowing and all-powerful. But they need their parents nonetheless.

A healthy parent-child relationship evolves into a partnership. The senior partners (the parents) have more expertise in most areas, but look forward to the day when the junior partners (the adolescents) will start running their own lives.

Goal: A lifelong friendship between two independent but loving parties.

What to do:

Achieving that goal requires a systematic effort on the part of the parent. Recommended:

- Spend more time together. Although teenagers show a heightened interest in friends, parents are wrong to assume that they are less interested in the family.

Studies consistently show that most teenagers want to share more time with their parents. Especially valuable: Time spent alone between the adolescent and one parent, when neither spouse nor siblings compete for attention.

- Discuss the adolescent's interests and concerns. Almost all teenagers like to talk. If you show genuine interest in their lives, they open up.

Favorite teenage topics: Family problems (money or job pressures)...controversial issues (sex, drugs)...current events...what their parents were like at their age.

Least-favorite topics: Household chores... the teenager's schedule...grooming.

- Share your own feelings and concerns. It's unfair to dump all of your problems on teenage children. But it's positive to reveal yourself as a whole person—with feelings, hopes, dreams and frustrations.

- Trust your child. If you look for trouble, you may find it.

Example: If you tell your son that his friends are a bunch of good-for-nothings, he may stop bringing them home—and wind up in places you don't want him.

If something does go wrong, always believe your child had good intentions.

- Treat your child with respect. Parents who would never belittle or bully another adult routinely mistreat their adolescent children. Adolescents deserve the same civility their parents extend to strangers.

- Be supportive. A teenager's problems—a poor grade on a math test, a spat with a friend, etc.—may seem small when compared with adult troubles. It's a very big mistake, however, to trivialize their worries.

Adolescents lack adult experience and perspective. From their point of view, their problem is the end of the world.

- Don't be alienated by gender. As children mature, parents tend to slip into sex stereotypes. Fathers become distant with their adolescent daughters, while mothers assume they have nothing in common with their sons.

These parents miss the point—that their teenage children remain, above all, their children.

- Set reasonable limits. Contrary to popular myth, teenagers are not automatic rebels. Most are willing to accept parental authority—as long as it is based on reason, and not on arbitrary power.

Discuss why you are setting a rule, and consider the teenager's point of view. Be willing to negotiate—unless the child's safety or deeply held family values are at stake.

Negotiable: Curfews...housekeeping... homework schedules.

Non-negotiable: Not riding in a car with a driver who has been drinking.

• Tie privileges to responsibilities. Teenagers who use the family car should be expected to refill the gas tank, and to check the oil and tires periodically.

• Stand back. Unless health or safety is at stake, let adolescents make their own mistakes. If you consistently intervene, you'll prevent your teenager from developing a sense of personal responsibility.

• Don't think punishment is the only answer. When teenagers go astray, it can be more effective to express your disappointment than let them suffer the consequences of their actions. Save stiff penalties for major infractions—and make sure that they fit the "crime."

Example: An adolescent who chronically stays out past curfew will be grounded.

Physical punishment is never effective. Studies have repeatedly shown that beatings do not stop undesirable behavior—on the contrary, they promote adolescent rebellion and aggression.

Source: Laurence Steinberg, PhD, a professor of psychology at Temple University. Author of the leading college textbook on adolescence, Steinberg is also coauthor of *You & Your Adolescent*, HarperPerennial, 10 E. 53 St., New York 10020.

The Secrets Of A Good Marriage

A good marriage doesn't just happen—it evolves over time. Trap: Marriages that were once exciting become boring because one or both partners are too afraid to confront the problems.

Couples in dull marriages avoid meaningful discussions, meeting new people, participating in challenging activities and even thinking about their problems. Since boredom isn't a malignant problem, like alcoholism or spouse battering, there's a delusion that it can be safely ignored. But boredom is the greatest threat to a fulfilled life.

To revive a dull marriage, you must recognize that only you and your mate have the power to make your marriage interesting. There's no magical formula. You need to take the risk of really confronting the longstanding problems in your marriage.

Signs of a troubled marriage:

• You don't look forward to time with your spouse. You find the time you spend with your spouse less interesting than most any other thing you do.

• The time you spend together as a couple feels like withdrawal from life.

• You're either passive or irritable around your spouse. You either become couch potatoes or constantly bicker.

Typical scenario: She's on the phone while he's watching TV and clicking the remote control.

• The activities you do together are monotonous and routine, even if there are a lot of them.

Misconception: It means you have a good marriage if you and your spouse spend a lot of time together.

What really counts: Whether you really enjoy that time.

• You don't reveal your inner feelings to each other anymore.

• You don't deal with difficult issues. Least-talked-about issue between couples today: Money.

• There's an inner sense of terror that the marriage would come apart if something provocative was brought up.

• You complain about your mate to friends or family, but you've stopped complaining to him/her.

Humdrum is a way of life:

The major reason marriages lose their dynamics is because of change. The relative levels of maturity and power in a marriage constantly change, depending on factors such as kids, careers, moves, etc. All of those major events rearrange the relationship and need to be talked through and worked out.

If, instead, a couple deals with change by avoiding those topics, differences grow...and grow...and grow. A couple that isn't sharing their lives anymore quickly gets bored with each other.

Example: Larry and Jennifer married while in college, finished graduate school together and both got university teaching jobs. Their marriage was stimulating because both brought home their interest in their work. Then Jennifer quit to have kids, and Larry was offered a great opportunity across the country. The move resulted in Jennifer dropping out of her career pursuit, losing all her friends and support, and becoming a lonely, full-time mom. Larry, meanwhile, did brilliantly at each new level of responsibility.

For fear of wrecking completely what had become an increasingly fragile structure, Larry and Jennifer never talked about the growing disparity between them. Larry wound up not talking much about work because it made Jennifer feel bad. Jennifer wound up not talking much about her problems with the kids because he'd blown up a few times listening to her complain. Neither talked about how to make it as a couple when they had become so different.

A few years later, the children started school and Jennifer went back to work, but it didn't make a difference. She and Larry hadn't had a conversation about anything substantive in years and were bored to death with each other. Larry was having an affair with a graduate student and Jennifer had lost interest in sex.

In dull marriages, there's an accumulation of dissatisfaction, resentment and problems that are not discussed.

Each partner is terrified of being the one to bring up his/her feelings and being responsible for destroying the marriage. Consequently, each partner finds himself with no energy, no creativity and no joy. Always simmering under the surface is the fear of what they ought to be talking about. The creative energy that should go into the relationship goes into keeping themselves suppressed.

The result is a gradual drifting away, until each one gets the feeling that he/she doesn't know the other person anymore. The likelihood that one or both will have an affair rises. Once one does have an affair, the specter of a real conversation is even more terrifying.

How to revive a marriage:

Stop pretending that everything is okay. Acknowledge to yourself first that you are bored...and that the marriage has become dull. Take the risk of initiating a conversation about it.

A good way to begin the conversation is by saying, "I think we've gotten into a troublesome routine." Reopen some basic questions. Ask yourself:

- Who am I?
- Who am I in this relationship?
- What do I want from this other person?

Those questions can provoke meaningful discussions—if the two of you are willing to share the answers. The conversation may be difficult, painful, unexpected and anxiety-provoking, but it's not likely to be boring.

Recognize that reviving a dull marriage isn't a safe procedure.

But having a dull marriage isn't safe, either. It just seems that way. There is no way of knowing what will happen once you open up the marriage.

Perhaps you have ducked this talk for too long and your mate is already involved elsewhere. Maybe your spouse has grown so blasé about marriage that he/she won't acknowledge that you two have problems or readily join you in solving them. Then again, your mate may be relieved that you took the initiative and be willing to join forces with you to bring the marriage back to life. You have to take the chance of putting your marriage on the line in order to save it.

Do something about a dull marriage early on. People are often bored with each other for so long that by the time they do something about it it's too late—all the good feeling is gone.

Do it slowly. Usually the way people bring up boredom is by blowing up the marriage with an affair or a divorce.

Acknowledge that you need support. Decide whether advice from good, able friends is enough or if you need to see a counselor.

If the two of you see the problem very differently or aren't both committed to solving it, a counselor can help you past these barriers so that you can cooperate as a couple to save the marriage.

Frequently, people in dull marriages grow

bitter, angry or resentful toward each other. If these emotions are present, a counselor can help you and your mate to move beyond such feelings and develop constructive ways to end the boredom and revive the love.

Talking in front of a counselor makes it more likely that you both will open up. It makes the process safer because there's someone to provide structure, support and guidance.

Attend a weekend couples workshop. If you can't get out of a rut alone, you may be able to do it in a group where it's part of the program.

Decide that the opening-up process is important. It's not just a temporary fix. Some couples think that all they need to do is talk a little, plan a trip and then their marriage is fixed. It doesn't work that way.

Reassure yourself that every time you go through this process successfully, it's likely you'll be able to succeed at it again. You will slowly build communication skills, mutual trust, a sense of safety and the confidence that you can work things out together.

Source: Martin G. Groder, MD, a psychiatrist and business consultant in Chapel Hill, NC. His book, *Business Games: How to Recognize the Players and Deal With Them,* is available from Boardroom Classics, Box 736, Springfield, NJ 07081.

How Not To Spoil Children

It's a myth that parents spoil children by giving them too much...time, attention or material goods. Real problem: Parents who don't teach children the rules and limits of acceptable behavior.*

Spoiled children often grow up to be spoiled adults who are so self-centered and immature that they find it difficult to be happy or to form positive interpersonal relationships. Guidelines for parents:

*Note: An estimated 5%–10% of all children who may seem spoiled really suffer from a condition called attention deficit disorder. They talk excessively, have trouble taking turns and act impulsively without considering the consequences of their actions. Helpful: Drug therapy with stimulants, including methylphenidate or pemoline.

• Set rules and limits. And enforce them consistently. Age-appropriate limits:

• No manipulative crying. In the first few months, children can be held and cuddled as much as they want without fear of spoiling. But after six months, they learn how to cry to gain more attention than they really need.

• No hitting. Children should be taught from a very young age not to hit others.

• No temper tantrums. Despite the ferocity of some tantrums (children can hold their breath until they turn blue), parents shouldn't acknowledge or reward them with attention. If tantrums are ignored, they will eventually disappear.

• Punish wisely. Spank a child as seldom as possible. Better: Practice time-out behavior. How it works: When the child misbehaves, he/she must spend a short amount of time—anywhere from a minute for a two-year-old to a half hour for a five-year-old—sitting in a special time-out chair.

Parents who consistently use time-outs early in the course of their child's misbehavior are rewarded with a child who learns to obey rules.

Source: Bruce J. McIntosh, MD, director, Family Practice Residency Program, St. Vincent's Medical Center, Jacksonville, FL 32204.

Talk With Kids About Sex

Talking openly about sex with your children protects them from potential conflicts now—and possible dysfunction later in life. Goal: Your children should know that you always tell them the truth so they will confidently ask you about the things that they don't understand. Silly concern: That children will discuss sex with their friends and the friends' parents may not approve. Children will discuss sex with their friends, but you can ensure that your kids will at least have the facts straight.

Source: *Talking With Your Child About Sex* by Mary S. Calderone, MD, Ballantine Books, 201 E. 50 St., New York 10020. Dr. Calderone is adjunct professor in the Human Sexuality Program for the department of health education at New York University.

Kids And Business Trips

Help your child adapt when you're away on a business trip. Develop rituals around your departure and return. These can include plotting your trip on a map or going out for ice cream when you return...having your spouse maintain the family's daily rituals... giving your child permission to have fun and not worry while you're gone...recording several favorite bedtime songs and stories on tape...bringing back a memento...spending time with your child within a day of your return.

Source: Group of experts, quoted in *The New York Times.*

Teenagers And Telephones

Most teens find it scary to interact with their peers face to face. The telephone is a safe way for them to get to know each other and allows them to try out various ideas, attitudes and feelings—almost anonymously.

Source: *I'm On Your Side* by Jane Nelsen, EdD, Prima Publishing, Box 1290, Rocklin, CA 95677.

How To Make Up After An Argument

To make up after a domestic argument, apologize with a note if you're not ready to talk...call your spouse at the office (the distance may help)...make a special dinner at home with or without children (they may be reassured that adults who love each other can fight and make up)...choose a special word that signals you are ready to make up...hug your spouse and say, "I'm sorry that we had such a terrible fight"—you don't have to admit that you were wrong.

Source: *How to Stay Lovers While Raising Your Children* by family health and psychology writer Anne Mayer, Price Stern Sloan, 11150 Olympic Blvd., Los Angeles 90064.

Add Years To A Dog's Life

Add years to a dog's life by brushing its teeth each day. Dogs are susceptible to gum disease, and if it goes unchecked, a dog will lose his teeth. Worse: Bacteria from gum disease can spread to the heart and kidneys. Technique: Gently lift the dog's lip on one side of his mouth and insert a wet toothbrush. Don't use toothpaste—it isn't good for dogs. Use gentle up-and-down strokes on the upper and lower teeth. Repeat on the other side. Alternative: Wrap wet cotton gauze around an index finger and rub around the teeth and gums to remove deposits.

Source: Michael Fox, DVM, vice president of the Humane Society, and author of *The New Animal Doctor's Answer Book*, Newmarket Press, 18 E. 48 St., New York 10017.

If Your Dog Wanders Off

If your dog wanders away in a strange area, stay in the spot where it left you. Dogs generally return to the freshest scent, so it may be able to track its way back to you.

Source: *Supertraining Your Dog* by Paul Loeb and Josephine Banks, Pocket Books, 1230 Ave. of the Americas, New York 10020.

Washing Your Cat

Washing your cat significantly reduces the major allergy-causing substance on a cat's skin. Basics: Put cotton in its ears and protective ointment (available from your veterinarian or a pet-supply store) in its eyes to keep out soap...wash in a sink filled with four to six inches of lukewarm water...use baby shampoo or pet shampoo designed for cats...towel-dry the cat (blow dryers are scary) and keep it indoors for several hours afterwards to be sure its coat is completely dry.

Source: Research by H. James Wedner, MD, Washington University, St. Louis, and recommendations from the American Society for the Prevention of Cruelty to Animals, reported in *Woman's Day*, 1633 Broadway, New York 10019.

Win-Win Parenting: The Basics

For too many parents, no stress or problem at work is as overwhelming as daily power struggles with their children. These few—and precious—hours before and after work are soured by crisis, chaos and commotion.

Three basic rules will give you a good start toward making the changes that can lead to more cooperation and peace.

Start with structure:

Structure provides an atmosphere of safety, security and predictability for children of any age. It encourages their independence while assuring them you care. And structure is one of the easiest ways to eliminate the cycle of frustration, struggle, threats and tears that often accompanies the everyday tasks of dressing, eating, getting homework and household tasks finished and going to sleep at a reasonable time.

Most parents understand the need for structure, but they often make the mistake of imposing rules and structure as a punishment. Then they wind up endlessly repeating the rules and trying to control their children's actions in ways that produce more friction than peace and more dependence than independence.

A good place to establish a structure is with a morning routine—it sets the tone for the whole day. What works best:

• Use a clearly stated routine to enforce the rules. Instead of constantly reminding the child what his/her responsibilities are, put the emphasis on actions you are taking to make sure the routine is followed.

Example: Buy your child an alarm clock and set it for his wake-up time.

• Point out the benefits of the routine. Don't use it as a threat.

Example: "Your new clock will be a lot better than you having to listen to me hound you all morning."

• State the facts as the morning routine progresses—without blaming or criticizing your child's performance.

Example: "It's 7:45. The school bus will be here in 30 minutes."

• Follow the rules yourself. If everyone is supposed to be dressed before breakfast, that applies to you, too—without exception.

• Make whatever changes are necessary in the physical setup of the household so the environment—not you, personally—dictates the rules and structure.

Examples: A snack drawer with fruit, raisins and other nutritious food that kids can help themselves to—without asking—between meals. Everything else that might tempt them is out of their reach...A comforter for your child to cover the bed when it's not being used for sleeping—rather than wrangling with him about making the bed before leaving the house.

Basic peacemaker: Avoid threats or lectures to enforce the rules and structures. Reinforce your seriousness by making clear what you will do.

Example: Don't say, "You have to be in bed by 8:30." Say, "I'll read you a story after you brush your teeth and are in your pajamas, as long as it's before 8:30."

Once your family begins to have some success with rules and structure, you can begin involving your children in negotiations to adapt the rules, or in discussions about what kind of structure is necessary to solve a new problem.

Kids who contribute to developing order in the household generally have a commitment to maintaining established rules.

Build responsibility:

You don't want your children to be compliant little rule-followers. Your challenge as a parent is to take their natural independence—a healthy trait—and move it toward personal responsibility and self-reliance rather than toward conflict with the household.

Don't use independence as a threat to your child because you're too busy to help.

Example: "If you can't undress faster than that, you'll have to take a bath without me there." Better: Teach them to act responsibly on their own.

Basic tactics for teaching self-reliance:

• Break a task down into small step-by-step pieces, which the child can tackle and accomplish.

• When appropriate, allow your child to

make decisions while you continue to take charge of the outcome.

Example: "Would you like to take your bath now or after that TV program?"

• Be specific. And only offer choices you're willing to accept. You don't want to teach your child that his choices are "wrong" when they're different from yours. And there's nothing to be learned by a choice that's really a threat.

• Avoid getting hooked into the role of rescuer, director or savior when your child tries to hand the responsibility back to you. But don't withdraw in anger, either. That often sets up a scene where the child feels abandoned and focuses on how uncaring, mean and terrible you are.

Better: Remain supportive (take on a limited, specific task as your child's assistant)... offer suggestions without being a bully...encourage your child to pinpoint his own goals (in a difficult homework assignment, for instance)...admit you don't have all the answers. Important: Show faith in your child even though he handles the situation quite differently than you would have.

Short-circuit power struggles:

Conflict can be a good vehicle for creating or changing rules, developing independence, improving relationships and solving problems. But many family struggles have no redeeming value. Make them less frequent and intense by...

• Diffusing the fight before it builds up steam. When children are young, you can often avoid a conflict by re-directing their attention. Eventually, that doesn't work anymore. But something as simple as silence might stop a flareup. It's okay to simply let your child have the first, last and only word sometimes. You don't have to respond to every complaint or accusation.

And you don't have to be quick to say "no" to a child's request. Answer by explaining when he can go visit a friend or have a cookie. When your child suffers a miserable disappointment, you don't have to convince him that second best—or nothing at all—is all right or that he or she will soon forget about it.

• Being realistic about what children are capable of.

Example: A young parent trying to work at home with a three-year old is continually interrupted by his demands for her attention. The virtually inevitable result will be a parent disappointed in her powerlessness and a child who feels he can never satisfy a parent. Better: Satisfy his needs first with something like—"I'll color with you for five minutes and then I'll have to do my own work for a bit while you finish it up."

• Replacing angry punishment with consequences, to help your child see his responsibility for the misbehavior. Never set the consequence while tempers are still flaring. Make it clear, time-specific and as closely related to the wrong behavior as possible. Old punishments like, "No TV for a week" are less effective.

Better: A boy breaks a garage door by repeatedly opening and closing it with the control device and hanging from the door as it comes down. The penalty is that he cannot play with any of the sports equipment that's stored in the garage for two weeks. And, if he's old enough, he also has to call the repairman and make arrangements for the garage door to be fixed.

When children feel powerless in relating to their parents, when they feel that they can't affect what happens by cooperating, they usually try to make an impact by arguing and making power plays. Parents criticize and correct them endlessly. As a result, the children's self-esteem drops still further—and the power struggles increase.

It's unrealistic to expect you to muster up positive things to say to your children in the midst of a battle. So you have to make maximum use of quiet time—to recognize and say something about the simple everyday actions your children do well...petting the cat gently ...putting on the right clothes for the weather ...keeping their teeth clean...reminding you that an oven timer went off.

Source: Evonne Weinhaus, a counselor in psychology and education, and Karen Friedman, a clinical social worker, founders of Stop Struggling, which conducts parenting workshops on-site for companies, Box 9138, St. Louis 63117. Their latest book is *Stop Struggling with Your Child*, HarperPerennial, 10 E. 53 St., New York 10022.

Real-Life Lessons For Every Child

Life is tough...not everybody is going to like you...there really is no free lunch. Once these are understood, a child won't feel crippled by false expectations. Whenever something unfair happens, he'll be able to shrug his shoulders, say, "That's normal"...and move on from there.

Source: *Pieces for Puzzled Parents* by Ray Maloney, founder of the Self-Esteem Center, 725 S. Adams, Birmingham, MI 48009.

Understanding Love And Marriage

When deciding to marry, people expect their feelings to be completely clear, completely unambiguous. "I don't really love him/her enough to marry him/her" is a common statement.

To dispel some of the confusion about how much you should love in order to marry, we spoke with Dagmar O'Connor, a well-known psychologist and sex therapist.

What is the biggest mistake that people make in choosing a marriage partner?

The choice of a mate is usually based on early parental influences. Problem: Many of us grew up in dysfunctional homes where parents impeded rather than enhanced children's emotional growth, or treated each other with such disrespect and unkindness that they created a negative role model for adult love relationships. People raised in such environments often develop feelings of sexual attraction toward people who resemble their parents.

Example: A woman whose father verbally or physically abused her may only be attracted to abusive men. In a room full of wonderful men, she will have an attraction for the "wrong" man.

Lesson: Whom we love and how much we love them is determined by our early experiences of love interactions with our parents and siblings. If you don't love someone enough to want to marry him, listen to your feelings. If you never feel like committing to anybody, it may be useful to investigate your childhood through therapy.

One common reason for rejecting marriage is not feeling turned on by a partner. Yet physical attraction can also be a sign of these old dysfunctional influences and you must therefore evaluate its importance carefully.

Sexual attraction should only be a part of the package along with friendship. If the attraction isn't strong in the beginning, but the other elements are there, sexual feelings may develop as the emotional intimacy deepens, unless you have learned in childhood to separate love from sex.

Some couples who hate each other and wind up divorced have good sex all the way through their marriage—and even after the divorce. Their problem is that sex becomes a substitute for emotional intimacy.

What should you look for in a marriage partner?

A companion. Not a parent figure to fill needs that were not met in childhood. Use friends or therapists to meet those needs. For the emotionally mature person, the criteria for love are that you enjoy being with the person...you feel comfortable with him/her... and you can totally trust him. Look for qualities you'd want in a friend: Honesty, generosity, integrity, sense of humor, similar values, sensitivity and similar interests.

Why is companionship so difficult to maintain in a marriage?

Because 90% of being "in love" is the feeling that you've finally found the parent you didn't have as a child. Then if your mate refuses to act like your parental fantasy, you get furious.

Companions accept each other as separate individuals with often conflicting needs. They don't demand unconditional love or approval.

Example: When Mary has a hard day at work, she expects her husband Joe, to be comforting and sympathetic. But sometimes Joe is too exhausted from his own day and just wants to be left alone. Mary goes into a rage and accuses him of not caring about her. If she viewed Joe as a companion rather than as a parent, she would back off, recognizing his need to be alone, and take care of her own needs by calling a friend.

It's important for couples to listen to each other, instead of each partner defending his own innocence so vehemently that the other partner's message is drowned out.

What are good reasons for rejecting someone you might marry?

If you have any reason to believe that you cannot trust this person...or if you suspect the person has destructive habits he's not willing to change.

Examples: Someone who has a problem with drugs or alcohol, is unfaithful, lies to you or has hit you a few times—even though he has promised never to do it again.

Also: Don't marry someone because of "potential." You need to accept someone the way he is. If you marry someone with potential, the person is a fantasy in your own head and the reality is bound to disappoint you.

A prospective mate might be a perfectly nice person, but have a quality you just don't think you can live with.

Example: A successful female executive dates a sweet, generous fellow who totally lacks ambition. She doesn't think she could accept that over the long run.

What would people who are considering a serious commitment look at in themselves?

Background patterns. Is this the first person you feel you don't love enough to commit to, or have there been several others? If so, delve deeper and investigate your difficulty loving or committing to anybody.

Trap: If you have a pattern of getting into uncomfortable or abusive relationships and you're with someone who is loving, you may find this person boring. It's important to work out your own attraction to "excitement." Excitement can at times be a way to avoid your underlying feelings.

Helpful: Ask yourself, "Who in my family does this person resemble? How does that make me feel?"

Bottom line: Any time that you feel like rejecting someone or protecting yourself, it's because your unconscious computer is talking to you. No matter what the underlying reasons are, it's important to respect that.

I don't believe that you should go against your instincts. But discovering where they are coming from can help you to make healthier decisions about your love relationships.

The most important component of a healthy love relationship is self-knowledge. Before you can decide wisely about marriage, you must learn about yourself as an individual and strive to understand your feelings.

How do you learn to trust your judgment about the opposite sex?

You make mistakes and learn from them. People who are too afraid of making mistakes don't learn much about life.

Nowadays, divorce and premarital sex and living together are permitted, so we're allowed to learn and profit from mistakes about love relationships.

Many people, unfortunately, do not learn. As a therapist, I see people who have had three or four marriages and they marry the same type of person each time—making exactly the same mistakes. They don't realize that they can only change themselves—not their partner.

What should you do if you're unsure of your decision?

I think premarital counseling is an excellent idea.

Source: Dagmar O'Connor, PhD, author of *How to Make Love to the Same Person for the Rest of Your Life and Still Love It*, Bantam Books, 666 Fifth Ave., New York 10103. She is in private practice in New York City.

How To Help Your Children Cope With Super-Parents

Children of accomplished parents are lucky to be blessed with the best of everything. But by giving them the best of everything, their parents may not be giving them everything that is best for them.

As a society, we are not accustomed to looking at the downside or pitfalls of money.

But they do exist and if we want our children to be happy, productive adults, we have to deal with them.

Children of the baby-boomers:

Fast-track parents are part of the baby-boom generation—born between 1945 and 1965. The booming economy of the 1960s, 1970s and 1980s was able to offer them the affluent lives they sought, provided they were willing to totally devote themselves to getting ahead.

But then came parenthood and things got tougher. Children had to be equipped for more competitive lives than their parents and grandparents had.

Fast-track parents, many of whom went to public schools and state colleges, want to give their children the "edge," through expensive educations. Their children have to go to the right schools from age two on.

It soon becomes a frantic race. Help has to be hired to take care of the children. Fast-track parents can't let up at work because there are massive bills to pay for their extremely expensive lifestyle. Spending money on toys and vacations soon replaces spending enough time at home.

Before they know what's happening, fast-track parents recreate for their children an upbringing that is very close to that of the old money class. And soon some of the same problems emerge—namely spoiled, overly dependent children who don't know the value of money and have little motivation to succeed in today's highly competitive environment.

This doesn't mean that fast-track parents are not necessarily bad or neglectful parents. But it does mean they need to be aware of and deal with the pitfalls in childrearing created by their own success.

Dealing with caregivers:

Fast-track parents almost always hire a caregiver to take care of their children from an early age. Despite what some experts say, having a full-time caregiver isn't necessarily harmful to children.

What is harmful: Not dealing with the kinds of problems that inevitably arise when someone else takes care of your child eight to 10 hours a day.

Parents don't deal with caregiver problems because they suffer from latent guilt for leaving their child with a caregiver to begin with. They unsuccessfully try to fit a 1950s ideal into a 1990s world. Key: Get over your guilt and confront caregiver problems directly.

Don't treat your caregiver the way you would a servant or babysitter. Do treat him/her like a professional surrogate parent.

Trap I: To undersupervise. Professional parents who easily supervise their staff at the office shrink from supervising their caregiver. They're afraid she'll quit or take out her resentment on the children.

Trap II: Your caregiver is responsible for teaching your child the basics of caring for himself, but her natural tendency is to do things for him.

Example: If a child balks at feeding himself, eventually a parent will refuse to feed him, telling him not to eat lunch if he doesn't want to. But the caregiver is worried that if the child doesn't eat lunch for a few days she'll be fired. Result: Children don't develop the self-care skills they should. Remedy: Make it clear to your caregiver that you want her to treat your child as you would, including disciplinary measures.

The burdens of too much:

Guilt is often a major factor in affluent families. When you feel that you may not have spent enough time with your child, one "socially accepted" way to make up for it is to shower the child with expensive gifts.

Result: Family tension and resentment. Your children stop feeling that gifts are special so they stop being grateful. You then feel they're ungrateful and unappreciative and start resenting them. They don't see the need to work to achieve what they've already got.

Example: Old-money kids who turn out to be dilettantes. They feel they'll always have money no matter what they do, so why bother to accomplish anything?

How to handle it: Don't always rush in with whatever the child wants. Learn how to say no. Important: Explain to the child why you're not buying him the Nintendo game or the gift from Paris.

Ask yourself: "Would I be better off spending $50 in the airport gift shop or spending the time and money talking to my child on the phone?" A phone call is a better investment.

Lesson from the Rockefellers: Bring your children up in a Spartan fashion. Teach them that if you're privileged, your life shouldn't be devoted to yourself—rather, it should be devoted to others.

Self-esteem problems:

You would expect high-achieving parents to have children who also believe in themselves. But paradoxically, low self-esteem is a major problem in many affluent families.

One reason is workaholism. Even though poor immigrant parents also worked long hours, in the immigrant family, the kids always knew they worked hard so they could have a better life. In an affluent family a child is apt to think that if his parent's career is taking 18 hours a day and he's getting less time, maybe he's not so special.

To give your children the sense that they matter without slowing down:

• Keep in closer touch with their daily lives. Call them during the day. If your job requires extensive travel, leave an itinerary so that your children can know where to reach you. Designate a consistent pattern of "at home" nights or a certain hour set aside for listening to your children.

• Be a good listener. Don't use the little time that you have together to grill your children on how they did on this test or that tryout. Kids love to talk to their parents, but they don't want to be interrogated or judged. Better: Ask gently about things such as friends and activities.

• Don't toot your own horn too often. Fast-track parents think that if they tell their son or daughter how well they did, the child will follow in the parental footsteps. But the message often backfires. Fast-track kids are terrified of failing. They see their parents as never having failed or made a mistake, and are terrified of disappointing their parents.

Example: One affluent teen told me the worst thing about her mother was her always mentioning that she was valedictorian of her class.

• Have realistic expectations. Understand that there's no guarantee that your children will be as smart as you are, let alone smarter. Most at risk: The average child who becomes overwhelmed. This kind of child would be acceptable in other families, but his achievements are too pedestrian for the fast-track family.

• Recognize that your children need to feel good about what they do. Instead of constantly making demands, give them a chance to have a lot of little victories.

• Be nurturing and compassionate about the sense of inadequacy your child may have.

Source: Andree Aelion Brooks, journalist, parent educator and author of *Children of Fast-Track Parents: Raising Self-Sufficient and Confident Children in an Achievement-Oriented World,* Viking Penguin, 40 W. 23 St., New York 10010. Ms. Brooks gives workshops and seminars on this topic for parents, teachers, adolescents, counselors and financial advisors. For more information write to 15 Hitchcock Rd., Westport, CT 06880, or call 203-226-9834.

Dealing With Dinnertime

A disproportionate number of incidents of child abuse occur during dinnertime—when exhausted parents are trying to prepare dinner with children underfoot. Better ways: Start early and prepare as much food in advance as possible...have one parent take the children out for a walk or drive while the other finishes preparations...take the phone off the hook while making dinner...when both parents work, divide dinnertime duties to fit each parent's needs and skills.

Source: *The Mother's Survival Guide* by Shirley L. Radl, Steve Davis Publishing, Box 190831, Dallas 75219. She is founder of the Parental Stress Hotline, Palo Alto, CA.

Teaching Decision-Making

Don't make it too easy for kids to dump their problem-solving on you. When they can't figure out what to do, what to wear, how to settle a dispute, introduce them to the "bring me three" rule. Tell them you'll be glad to help them find a solution, but first they must bring three suggestions of their own. Soon you'll find they're settling many problems by themselves.

Source: *Working Parent—Happy Child* by child development specialist Caryl Waller Krueger, Abingdon Press, Cokesbury Service Center, Box 801, Nashville 37202.

Plastic Bead-Filled Pillow Danger

Newborn infants have died from the use of these pillows. Danger: The air they exhale becomes trapped in a pillow's polystyrene-bead filling and is rebreathed. It is too low in oxygen content to support them, and they suffocate while appearing to breathe normally. Infants and toddlers are probably better off without any pillow. Important: The bead-filled ones must be avoided.

Source: Ron Ariagno, MD, professor of pediatrics and associate director of newborn nurseries, Packard Children's Hospital, Stanford University Medical Center, Stanford, CA 94305.

Better Transition From Work To Home

Psych yourself up for meeting your family. Helpful: Get work problems out of your system by writing them down and telling yourself you won't think about them until after the children are in bed.

Source: *The Mother's Survival Guide* by Shirley L. Radl, Steve Davis Publishing, Box 190831, Dallas 75219. She is founder of the Parental Stress Hotline, Palo Alto, CA.

In-Law Advice

Parents of married children should take the first step to keep lines of communication open with daughters-in-law and sons-in-law. Important: Apologize if you have irked your child's spouse, even if you feel innocent. In-law relationships are tender and dealing with any negatives immediately will prevent festering wounds in the family.

Source: *Letitia Baldrige's Complete Guide to the New Manners For the '90s* by the manners expert and former chief of staff for the First Lady Jacqueline Kennedy, Rawson Associates, 866 Third Ave., New York 10022.

Marriage...Divorce... Marriage

When a spouse who has initiated a divorce proceeding wants to make up and save the marriage, the other spouse must answer some tough questions before agreeing...

- How satisfying was the marriage at best?
- Are the good memories worth trying to recapture?
- How strained was the marriage before the split?
- Are there children involved?
- Was it a relief when you thought it was over?
- How seriously will your spouse take marriage counseling?

Source: *Divorce Recovery: Healing the Hurt Through Self-Help and Professional Support* by psychiatrist Allan J. Adler, MD, and director of Divorce Anonymous Christine Archambault, PIA Press, 19 Prospect St., Summit, NJ 07902.

13

Sexual Secrets

All You Wanted To Know About Intimacy... But Were Afraid To Ask

In today's super-competitive world, we all need to feel that there's one person who is 100% on our side...someone we can be completely open with, who accepts us and won't betray us in any way.

Trap: Even though most of us desperately want such a close and loving relationship, intimacy is the one thing many successful people find elusive.

Because intimacy involves taking the risk of really trusting someone, it can be quite frightening. Common fears: If you love him/her, he might reject you or try to control you. If you confide in him, he might betray you. If you give too much, he might drain you.

There are many different ways people avoid intimacy. If your relationship is not as close as you'd like, it helps to recognize what type of intimacy-avoider you're dealing with. It's also important to look at yourself...you may be the intimacy-avoider.

Distancers:

Distancers are the most obvious intimacy-avoiders. Examples:

- Fickle Lovers can't commit to one person. They want a little of this person...a little of that one. Affairs dilute intimacy, preventing Fickle Lovers from feeling too vulnerable.
- Fun-Seekers want immediate gratification. Quite prevalent today, they're after money, possessions, even drugs. They don't want long-term commitments.
- Loners are more seriously disturbed distancers. They're so afraid of people, they can't sustain a relationship.
- Narcissists are completely involved with themselves.
- Perfectionists, believe they want a relationship...but no one is ever good enough.
- Romanticists adore from afar. As long as the beloved remains aloof, the Romanticist

stays. But if the other person responds, the Romanticist loses interest—he wants the unattainable.

Pseudo-intimates:

Pseudo-intimates often get married or live with someone...but their intimacy problems are quite subtle. Examples:

• Constant Competitors, typical among yuppies, are couples who compete with each other in every area. Each raise or promotion is perceived by the other as a threat. They even compete over whom the children love more.

• Devoted Children and Devoted Parents are quite common. Devoted Children run to parents before spouse to confide something. A typical Devoted Parent is a divorced man who gets so attached to his children that he can't make the transition to the next woman. Although the Devoted Person claims he is needed, it's really the other way around.

• Intellectualizers do everything right. But they don't express emotions and they think the only way to deal with life is through reason and logic.

• Mr. Macho has to appear strong and super-independent. He expects a tremendous amount from everyone around him and can be very controlling. Important: Today, women can also be Mr. Machos.

• Rescuers are very good at caring for others. But they never become vulnerable themselves, which is necessary for true intimacy. Note: Rescuers are common among therapists and other helping professionals, including doctors and lawyers.

• Social Butterflies always have a crowd around them. They rarely spend time alone with their mate.

• Status-Seekers are also typical among yuppies. They worry about what other people think and if what they're doing looks good on the surface.

• Workaholics say that they love their family so much, they have to work hard so they all can prosper.

Intimacy-Saboteurs:

Intimacy-saboteurs don't try to avoid closeness. Rather than backing away from their mate, they hold on too tightly, forcing the other one to back away.

Examples:

• Clingers are classic overdependent types. They need constant reassurance and want to be with their partner all the time. They don't really want intimacy...they want to merge. And this means they have little sensitivity to the other person's needs.

• Constant Critics want to get close, but they're too busy finding fault with their mate. Everything he does is wrong.

• Passive Procrastinators appear to go along with whatever their mate wants, but they fail to follow through. They forget to do what they've promised...fall asleep rather than having sex...and avoid confrontations at all costs.

• People-Pleasers are very subtle intimacy-avoiders who eluded my categorization for a long time. The female counterpart of the Passive Procrastinator, they're so busy trying to please everyone—their boss, parents, children, friends, etc.—that they never get close to anyone.

• Sensitive Sulkers are the opposite of Constant Critics. They're so afraid of criticism that they make their mate feel guilty when he says anything even remotely critical (Sensitive Sulkers are usually female).

Common combinations:

Pseudo-Intimates or Distancers often get involved with Saboteurs. In old-fashioned terms, this would be expressed in the traditional male versus the traditional female, but I now see these types in both sexes.

Clingers and Mr. Machos are also a popular duo. The Mr. Macho puts up with the Clinger because he likes being in control and thinks that the clinging is attractive. The Clinger likes to feel taken care of.

Workaholics often marry Social Butterflies who won't put big demands on their time. Sometimes these duos don't know there's anything wrong until the kids leave home and they realize they don't really have a relationship.

Overcoming fear of intimacy:

• Examine your relationship in the context of your complete extended family. Intimacy-

Avoiders are often the children of Intimacy-Avoiders.

• Confront your fears.

Example: You may be afraid of being overwhelmed by another person.

If so, you have to figure out what you really want and you must learn how to stand your own ground. This will help you overcome your fear of being controlled.

• Work on your sense of independence and self-esteem. People who lack these attributes frequently get involved with Intimacy-Avoiders. Reason: A person with low self-esteem will be attracted to anyone who seems to want him.

Living with an Intimacy-Avoider:

• Realize that you and your mate are two different people. Relationships with Intimacy-Avoiders create problems because many people base their self-esteem on how their mate acts. Typical statement: How could I stay with someone who acts like that?

Solution: Separate your identity from your mate. Then recognize that love doesn't mean always saying yes. Intimacy happens when two different people with separate wants and needs come together.

• Examine your own behavior. You may be doing something to encourage your Intimacy-Avoider.

Example: If you complain that your mate is always controlling you, you may be presenting yourself as someone who is unable to take care of himself.

• Open discussions with your mate. Although you can't force someone to be intimate, discussions can help to let him know how you feel. Important: Avoid attacking, listen to his side and give him a chance to express himself.

• Adjust to your mate's version of intimacy.

Example: Most men don't like to talk about their feelings. Women who want to promote an intimate relationship with a man may have to learn to share his interests—no matter how they really feel about football.

Source: Clinical psychologist Rosalie Reichman, PhD, who practices in Roslyn Estates, NY. She is the author of *The Stranger in Your Bed*, John Wiley & Sons, 605 Third Ave., New York 10158.

How To Overcome Premature Ejaculation

Premature ejaculation (PE) is one of the most common—and most neglected—sexual problems experienced by men. In the past, men who climaxed too fast were stuck with their problem for life.

But today, through advances in sexual therapy, 90% of men who suffer from PE can be cured with an average of 14 weeks of treatment.

What is premature ejaculation?

A sexually normal male has a reasonable amount of control over his ejaculatory reflex. This means he can continue to thrust at a high level of pleasure until he chooses to "let go." The quality of this control is natural, easy and voluntary.

A man who suffers from PE hasn't learned this kind of control. He ejaculates rapidly and involuntarily—sometimes as soon as he reaches a high state of arousal—whether he wants to or not.

Some men with PE simply accept their lack of control and try not to let it spoil their sexual pleasure.

In the same way, some women accept their partner's rapid ejaculation and take pleasure from other aspects of love-making. But, far more often, PE is a source of distress to the man and his partner. Reason: In our society, men often measure their self-worth by their "staying power."

As a result, those who suffer from PE often lack sexual confidence and are anxious about their ability to perform. This can lead to chronic psychological impotence.

Since a man suffering from PE may refuse to discuss the problem with his partner, he can come across as selfish or insensitive.

A woman who is herself insecure may think that her partner's problem means that he is hostile and uncaring.

Such misunderstandings lead to pressures that can only worsen the couple's relationship.

What causes PE?

PE is most often caused by psychological

troubles. In certain cases, physical problems* can be involved—particularly if a man who has had adequate control in the past begins to come rapidly.

The problem may be complex or rooted deep in the person's past. Perhaps the person received anti-sexual messages during his childhood...he grew up in a troubled environment where the parents behaved in an inappropriately sexually seductive or competitive manner...or he had a disastrous first sexual experience.

But most of the causes of PE are easier to diagnose. Common problems: The man...

...gets too intensely excited to register penile sensations.

...is too concerned about performing and pleasing his partner.

...feels so guilty about sex that he isn't able to allow himself to register any feelings of pleasure.

No matter what it is that actually causes PE, the person never develops a normal sense of what his genitals feel like when he is highly excited and about to come.

Treatment: The man must learn to focus on the pleasurable feelings that emanate from his sexual organs during the intense state of sexual excitement that precedes orgasm.

To help yourself:

In their efforts to control their ejaculatory response, many men with PE try doing things that reduce their desire, pleasure and excitement while making love—they think about taxes, bite the insides of their cheeks, drink alcoholic beverages before, etc.

Better: Learn how to stay in control while highly aroused and excited.

The exercises described below can be done by men on their own as well as by couples.

Note: We have found the solo approach so beneficial that we now ask even married men to start the exercises alone before bringing in a partner.

*This could mean he is becoming impotent because of some illness or drug with sexual side effects. Late-occurring PE is sometimes the first sign of more serious problems—diabetes or a neurological disease (multiple sclerosis, etc.). However, many of the physical conditions that cause sexual symptoms can be successfully treated if detected in time.

However you choose to begin the exercises, the first step is to communicate with your partner. Honestly admit your problem and enlist her cooperation in resolving it. It is also important to be interested in and understand her feelings and concerns.

During the solo exercises, men should abstain from any other sexual outlet. Exercises should be done one to three times a week... and never under tense or anxious conditions.

Step 1. Masturbate in your usual manner, but slow down just a little and try to focus on the pleasurable sensations emanating from your penis as your excitement rises. Concentrate on what it feels like just before you reach the emission phase. Then leg go and enjoy your climax.

Step 2. A day or two later, masturbate again, using only your hand (no lubricants). Stop when you reach a high level of arousal—near orgasm—but only for a few seconds (to let your excitement ebb a little). Then start the rhythmic stroking again. Interrupt three times...then let yourself come the fourth time as freely as you can.

During this whole experience, try to concentrate completely on your pleasurable penile sensations—don't try to hold back. Repeat this every few days until you become familiar with pre-orgasmic sensations and feel a bit more in control.

Step 3. Repeat Step 2 standing in the shower and using soapy suds as a lubricant... or skip the shower and use Vaseline. When you are able to make the pleasure last for about three minutes before you have to stop, you are ready for the next step.

Step 4. Repeat Step 2 again (stop-start) either in the shower or with Vaseline. This time, however, don't stop stimulating yourself when you reach a high level of excitement. Instead, just slow down the pace of your stroking.

Step 5. Rate the degree of your sexual excitement from 0–10 (0 is no excitement at all and 10 is when you reach your orgasm.) Go back to the shower or Vaseline and stimulate yourself until you reach 6 or so, then slow down until your excitement ebbs to 5. Speed up again to 7 and try to keep between 5 and 7 for about two minutes.

Important: Do not try to hold back. You will find you can control the level of arousal by merely changing the speed with which you stimulate yourself and the pressure you exert.

After you have stayed aroused for about two minutes, increase the speed and let go and enjoy your orgasm. Practice this until you can keep yourself at high levels of excitement without coming for about five minutes.

Involving your partner:

Once you reach this point in the exercises described above, your partner now can join you in the exercises, starting with the partner-provided penile stop-start stimulation. (These exercises are described in further detail in my book).

Note: It's very important that you keep the lines of communication open with your partner at all times, even when you are practicing the exercises by yourself.

Be sure to let your partner know what is happening, when you are making progress... and also when you are having difficulties.

Once you both start on the joint exercises, which can be somewhat mechanical at first, you can still make the experience pleasurable for your lover through sensuous foreplay and clitoral stimulation.

Source: Helen Singer Kaplan, MD, PhD, clinical professor of psychiatry at the New York Hospital-Cornell Medical Center and the founder and director of its Human Sexuality Program. Dr. Kaplan is the author of several books, including *PE: How to Overcome Premature Ejaculation*, available from Brunner/Mazel Publishers, 19 Union Square West, New York.

Dr. Joy Browne Talks About Sex

During my nationally syndicated daily call-in show on ABC Talk-Radio, people ask all kinds of questions about sex. What they ask most often:

What can I do when my partner says I'm too tired?

The first time it happens, don't take it personally. Just listen, and offer solace and maybe a back rub. But if a pattern emerges, it's time to go on a fact-finding mission. Tiredness can stem from overwork or depression. Or it can be a way of saying "I'm angry with you." Note: Don't raise the subject in the bedroom, where your partner is likely to feel defensive.

What to say: "You seem to be tired a lot lately. Are you having problems at work? Are you angry with me? Or is something else making you tired?"

Once you track down the cause, you can start to work on the real problem.

I fantasize about being with someone else when I make love with my partner. Is this normal?

There is nothing wrong with fantasizing. Everyone does it. And fantasy can be useful because it helps us discover the discrepancy between what we have and what we want.

Example: If you often fantasize about someone who is more aggressive in bed than your partner, it is probably time to talk about either your spouse's or your passivity.

If you fantasized about a situation—a place where you have sex, for instance—you might want to share this with your partner. It could increase your mutual enjoyment. But if you fantasize about another person, don't tell your partner. It will only cause pain.

How much is too much: If your sex life is 10% fantasy, that's okay. But if it's 90% fantasy, it's not healthy. Reason: Part of the joy of lovemaking comes from the intimacy you establish with your partner. If you constantly distance yourself by fantasizing, you miss out on the benefits of that relationship.

My spouse flirts a lot. What can I do about it?

First, examine your marriage. Ask yourself: "Is this a symptom of a larger problem?" If it is, you and your partner should seek counseling.

If, however, you are generally happy with your relationship, look at the context of the flirting. Does it always happen at parties? In public? A certain amount of flirtation is natural in social situations—as long as it's not carried beyond that level.

Flirting in a happy marriage can become a problem if it is used in a manipulative way, to say, "Look—other people find me attractive!" This is an early sign of instability.

Note: If you're unhappy with yourself—if you've gained a few pounds, for instance—you may be especially sensitive to your partner's flirting. It may seem worse than it really is.

I found out that my partner is having an affair. What should I do?

Most affairs are a symptom of a greater problem in the marriage. Ask yourself: "Do I want to stay with this person? Am I willing to let it go on indefinitely? Am I willing to leave?"

If you try to ignore the affair, say nothing and hope that it will burn itself out naturally, you will become angry and your trust in your spouse will be destroyed.

Better: Tell your partner that you understand that these things happen, but that you can't live with him/her under the circumstances. He must move out until he decides what he wants. Don't guarantee that you'll be there if he decides to come back.

He may decide to break off the affair and try to save the marriage. But if he leaves, you must decide if you want to wait, or separate.

We don't have as much sex as we once did. Is this unusual?

Most couples experience great passion when they first become physically involved. They spend weekends in bed and delight in making love in strange and wonderful places.

But a sexual relationship, like anything else, loses some of its novelty over time. And many things—a new job, a baby, etc.—can affect the libido and disrupt a sexual pattern.

At the beginning of a relationship, some people try to adapt their behavior to fit the other person's sexual tastes. As the relationship continues, however, they gradually begin to reassert their own wishes. And old patterns may no longer be acceptable.

Example: Early in their relationship, Andy took the initiative sexually. But once they had been married for a few months, he grew tired of always being the instigator and relaxed his efforts. Carolyn began to think he wasn't interested in her anymore.

If the change is not comfortable for either partner, the couple should talk about why things have changed and what measures each can take to alter the pattern.

Changes could involve being more seductive, going away for weekends, balancing sex in the morning (which many men prefer) with sex in the evening or even remembering the power of an occasional quickie.

What can we do to make our sex life more interesting?

Figure out what things can be changed, what you've both outgrown, what has become a stale habit. Key ingredient for good sex: Making each other feel appreciated.

We remember our first sexual experiences as being quite wonderful—when they probably weren't—because someone made an effort to make us feel needed and special.

Good sex has very little to do with positions. It has to do with what's in our head, and that's easy to change.

Examples: Put some adventure into your sex life—show up in a trench coat and nothing else, slip a sexy note into your partner's pocket or purse, wear fun clothes...send a different kind of flower than usual...go back to the restaurant where you had your first date.

Your surprises should show your partner your special knowledge of his likes and dislikes. A hot fudge sundae by candlelight will speak volumes to a spouse with a sweet tooth.

Source: Psychologist Joy Browne, PhD. She is the author of *Why They Don't Call When They Say They Will and Other Mixed Signals,* Simon & Schuster, 1230 Ave. of the Americas, New York 10020.

All About Relationships: Monogamy...Adultery...

Although many species of animals are monogamous, just like many human beings, they also cheat on the side—according to the latest studies from all over the US.

To find out more about why adultery is so common in so much of the animal world, we asked a leading anthropologist and expert on human sexual behavior...

What exactly is monogamy?

It basically means one person has one spouse...but it doesn't mean that the person has just one sex partner.

Forming pair bonds and raising children as man and wife is a hallmark of the human species, as much as language is. But we also follow the laws of nature. And the conflicting drives to form pair bonds and be adulterous is built into both animal and human nature.

Example: A male and female beaver form a pair bond and build their dam and lodge and create their territory, just the way we create our home and maintain our lawn. But naturalists have seen male beavers slip out of their lodges at night and into a neighboring female's lodge. It's the same among some birds, like chickadees and ducks, and other creatures.

Is polygamy the answer?

Polygamy has been a custom in many societies...but that arrangement doesn't work, either. Co-wives fight, husbands show favoritism and the divorce rate is extremely high.

There are polygamous animals, such as horses, where one male travels with a harem of females. I would suspect that there's no jealousy in a harem-building species. But we're not a harem-building species. For the past four million years we've been monogamous.

This is why open marriages and communes have never worked. Within a few months after joining a commune, a man and a woman fall in love and want to be exclusive. It's natural.

Are men more likely to commit adultery than women?

No. In societies without a double standard, women avail themselves of extramarital sex just as often as men do.

We believe that men are more sexual than women, so our polls bear out that belief. Men like to brag about sex, women deny it. But in fact, the most recent polls show that women are just as adulterous as men are.

I wouldn't be surprised to see that in a society where women controlled the money and the power they were more adulterous than men. It's the sex that needs the other sex more that puts all its eggs in one basket.

Is adultery more acceptable now than at other times in history?

Polls say no, but the consequences today are nowhere near as harsh as they used to be. We haven't changed our negative opinion about adultery, but you're not put to death for it anymore or forced to wear the letter "A" branded on your head. Women today don't lose alimony or custody of their kids because of adultery.

We're much more relaxed about it and will probably become even more relaxed as women become less and less dependent on men economically.

Why do some people have a drive to cheat?

There are all kinds of psychological reasons—a desire for more attention, excitement, intimacy or sex—but none of those is the underlying reason.

The real reason dates back to the grasslands of Africa four million years ago where male and female hunter-gatherers formed pair bonds to raise their young.

A man who formed a pair bond with one woman and occasionally had sex with another was likely to have more children. Since the more children a man had the more likely it was that his genes would live on, by being adulterous he increased the number of genes he put into the gene pool. An adulterous ancestral man survived and passed to modern man whatever it is in the male spirit that makes men pursue extramarital affairs.

A woman, on the other hand, can't have more than one child every nine months. So it might seem as if she wouldn't have a motive for adultery. But adulterous women also have a slight reproductive edge.

If an ancestral woman took a husband and sneaked around on the side, she got extra food and extra protection. If her husband died or was injured, her lover could step in and help her raise her children. Or if she ended up with a husband with, say, lousy eyesight, she could have a child by a lover who had better genes.

Even though having children is the last thing people have in mind today when they commit adultery, from a Darwinian perspective, what occurs in an adulterer's brain is an old, unconscious pattern that drives us to look for variety.

Does adultery have to cause tremendous social upheaval?

No. That depends mostly on the individual culture.

Examples: According to Eskimo tradition, a woman is at liberty to offer sex to her mate's hunting partner or to a guest in the igloo in order to extend kinship and hospitality. And among the Kurkuru, a group of Amazon Indians, everyone in the village has between four and 12 lovers.

Americans are exquisitely prudish compared with world cultures. In a study of 139 cultures, 39% permit adultery at certain times of the year with certain relatives.

In some cultures, a man is permitted to have sex with his wife's sister, because if his wife ever dies she could legitimately become his wife. Some societies have puberty rituals with nights of sexual license.

The closest we get to that is Mardi Gras, which we borrowed from the French, who are much less prudish than Americans. They have a long tradition of mistresses, where adultery—if practiced discreetly—is overlooked.

If adultery is genetically ingrained, do we really have a choice about committing it?

Absolutely. There is something called the triumph of culture over the human spirit. Since 50% of all people are adulterous, that means 50% are not.

The most important thing the human animal does is reproduce, but we also have thousands of years of people believing in and practicing celibacy. We're genetically programmed for survival, but we will sacrifice ourselves for our country or a cause we believe in. Culture regularly triumphs over biology.

People can decide to be faithful and stick to it. But not always without a struggle. One has to appreciate that struggle and not think it's going to be easy.

Source: Helen Fisher, PhD, research associate, department of anthropology, American Museum of Natural History, New York. She is the author of *The Sex Contract: The Evolution of Human Behavior*, William Morrow, 105 Madison Ave., New York 10016.

Sex Fantasies Are Healthy

Eighty-five percent of those surveyed said they fantasize during sex and one in four said they do so often. Most think about their actual lover while fewer fantasize about attractive strangers. Nearly 75% said their thoughts were "bizarre, forbidden or kinky." Surprising: Those with the most active imaginations reported more satisfying relationships and fewer problems with arousal and performance.

Source: Harold Leitenberg, PhD, professor of psychology, University of Vermont, reported in *GQ*, 350 Madison Ave., New York 10017.

"Not Tonight, Dear" How To Cure Desire Disorder

Over the past 10 years there has been a great change in the field of sex therapy.

Where physical problems—including impotence, frigidity and premature ejaculation—once brought most people to therapy, today the most common problem is lack of desire... known as desire disorder. It's a problem Masters and Johnson never mentioned.

I interviewed 22 of the top sex therapists in the country to find out how they are dealing with desire disorder among their patients... and how people can help themselves.

Who suffers from desire disorder:

Although low sexual desire was always considered a woman's problems, more and more men are coming in for treatment.

What's happening: The problem was there all along for men...it was just easier to mask. Today, however, men are under increased pressure to perform. Added pressures: Many men are threatened by today's more assertive women.

Another surprising finding is that career women are less interested in sex than housewives are. One sex therapist found that women who are dedicated to their careers have more problems with sexual desire than homemakers do. On the other hand, they have fewer problems with sexual satisfaction.

Related finding: Women who work but who aren't devoted to their careers are more like homemakers than career women in their sexual response.

Underlying social causes:

Sexual desire may be one casualty of the pace of modern life. Most people with desire disorder say they enjoy sex once they get around to it...they just don't seem to get around to it anymore.

Common statement: "I'm exhausted from working, taking care of the kids and the house. You expect me to do *that*, too?"

Sex becomes one more chore, rather than a source of pleasure.

Our sexually enlightened attitudes may also make for less rather than more sex. Although it's good that we are aware of what good sex is and the importance of pleasing our partners, we've been too imbued with the idea of the proper way to have sex.

We've been told we have to have preliminary atmosphere, adequate time for foreplay, stimulation, orgasm and affection afterwards. It becomes such a production, people wonder if they should even bother.

Ideas of proper sex extend to what's politically correct. It's not, for instance, correct to have certain kinds of sexual fantasies. Problem: Sex isn't just about kindness, consideration and communication...it's about what turns you on.

Dropping the stereotyped roles of males and females has been another mixed blessing. In the days when men and women were stuck in roles, relations might have been more mechanical, but at least people had sex.

And the fantasy aspect of sex was embodied in those roles. Women were turned on by macho, take-charge men...and men were turned on by the submissive, adoring woman.

Another part of the problem is the number of distractions we now have available. Sex used to be called "the grand opera of the poor" because people who couldn't afford opera could afford sex.

But today we've got TVs, VCRs and video games, which can make sex look pretty tame by comparison, especially sex that has become routine and mundane.

Types of desire disorder:

There are several different kinds of desire disorder. Included:

• Relationship. If there are problems in a relationship, there are going to be problems with desire.

Common problems: Too much underlying anger...failure to live up to each other's expectations.

• Situational. Certain stressful situations during a marriage tend to affect desire.

Examples: After a baby is born...when one partner loses his/her job...during a major illness.

• Personal. Certain types of childhood experiences can cause desire disorder in adulthood.

Examples: Being raised in a puritanical environment...being a victim of sexual abuse.

Helpful techniques:

I've found several things people can do to help themselves get over desire disorder. Examples:

• Fantasize. Consciously fantasize about anything sexual, even things you think may turn you off. Fantasy will help open your mind to sexual feelings that you may have blotted out.

Barrier: Some people feel guilty fantasizing about someone other than their partner or are ashamed of fantasies that seem sick or perverted.

But fantasy has been given the seal of approval by the best sex therapists. Rather than wrecking, it can revitalize a marriage.

• Keep a fantasy diary. Include negative as well as positive fantasies. Fantasies do more than just turn us on. They can help us get in touch with attitudes and inner feelings that we feel uncomfortable expressing directly.

Examples: After a big promotion at her job, Glenda lost sexual interest in her husband, Vic. Although he had been encouraging and supportive of her ambitions, he withdrew emotionally after her promotion. In sex therapy, Glenda came up with a fantasy about seducing Tonto and rejecting the Lone Ranger. Since her husband was a Lone Ranger fan who collected old tapes of the show, her fantasy expressed her anger at him for being subtly controlling.

• Keep a sex log. Write down any physical correlations that you uncover.

Example: Women should keep track of any correlation between sexual desire and their menstrual cycle. Men should record any correlation to time of day, specific activity, number of drinks, etc.

• Experiment with different scenarios. Sexual desire tends to wane after marriage. Common: Men get turned off when their wives have a baby.

Helpful: Let your more adventurous side come out. Don't be afraid of experimenting to make your sex life more exciting. Wives can buy sexy lingerie and act seductively. Husbands can act sexually dominant or macho.

• Remember back to when sex was good. Turn-ons rarely involve a particular sex act. They're more commonly built around the preliminaries, including where you were and what you did before. See if you can recapture that.

All too often, sex becomes predictable and routine. Suggestion: Try necking in the back seat of your car.

• Use self-hypnosis. If your problem stems from the past, think about times in childhood when you had negative experiences that involved sex.

Fantasize that you're going back in time and confronting those people who hurt you or gave you negative sexual messages.

Enlist the aid of an authority figure. Imagine a teacher or priest or rabbi saying it's okay to have sex.

Source: Anthony Pietropinto, MD, chief psychiatrist of the Postgraduate Center for Mental Health and supervising psychiatrist for Manhattan Psychiatric Center. He is coauthor of *Not Tonight, Dear: How to Reawaken Your Sexual Desire*, Doubleday, 666 Fifth Ave., New York 10103.

Better Sex

Vaginal dryness during sexual intercourse often results from inadequate foreplay. It takes an average of 20 minutes of sexual stimulation for a woman to become fully aroused and lubricated enough for intercourse. Other causes: Lower-than-normal levels of key hormones—particularly estrogen...certain forms of the Pill...an allergic reaction to spermicidal creams used with a diaphragm or condom. In these instances, using a water-based lubricant, such as K-Y jelly, will ease intercourse. Also: Consider changing spermicidal creams.

Source: Jonathan Scher, MD, assistant clinical professor of gynecology, Mount Sinai School of Medicine, quoted in *Mademoiselle*, 350 Madison Ave., New York 10017.

Contraception Wars

There are hundreds of different contraceptives on the market today, each claiming to be more effective—and have fewer side effects—than the next. In fact, Dr. Robert Morris, director of obstetrics and gynecology at New York University Hospital, explains that different contraceptives are right at different times in life and for people with different lifestyles, medical histories and sexual habits.

Cervical cap. A small plastic or rubber cap that is placed over the cervix.

• Effectiveness: 71% to 98%. The effectiveness of the cervical cap depends on how carefully it is positioned over the cervix.

• Side effects: Risk of toxic shock syndrome if left in place too long. Sometimes it irritates tissues surrounding the cervix. It is not yet known whether these changes increase the risk of cervical cancer.

• Popularity: Widely used in Europe, but only recently available in the US.

• Other advantages: May be left in place for 48 to 72 hours.

• Other disadvantages: Smaller than the diaphragm, and therefore more difficult to insert and more easily dislodged during intercourse.

• Best for: Women in stable relationships where insertion before sex is not a problem. Women using either the cervical cap or the diaphragm should be well-informed about the correct insertion and removal of these devices.*

Condom. Placed over the erect penis, it

*The effectiveness of all methods described here varies depending upon how carefully and consistently the methods are applied.

physically prevents sperm from reaching the cervix. Typically used together with spermicidal foams or jellies.

• Effectiveness: 85% to 97%.

• Side effects: None.

• Popularity: Use of the condom has risen sharply during the AIDS epidemic, although condoms are not 100% effective in preventing the spread of the disease. Used by 12.2% of couples, the condom is exceeded in popularity only by sterilization and the Pill.

• Other advantages: No prescription is needed...readily available almost anywhere... reduces transmission of venereal diseases and AIDS.

• Other disadvantages: May break or leak. Must be put on just prior to intercourse. Reduces sensation for the male.

• Best for: Anyone concerned about venereal disease or AIDS should use (or insist a partner use) a condom. Easy availability without a prescription makes the condom, used together with spermicides, the best choice for those having infrequent coitus and in situations where individuals have not decided on a long-term contraceptive solution.

Diaphragm: A hemispherical cup that is filled with spermicide and inserted over the cervix.

• Effectiveness: 71% to 98%. As with the cervical cap, effectiveness depends heavily on how carefully it is positioned over the cervix.

• Side effects: Increased incidence of urinary tract infections.

• Popularity: Used by 8.3% of couples, it is the fourth-most-popular contraceptive method in the US.

• Other disadvantages: A consultation with a physician is needed for prescription and fitting. The diaphragm must be inserted before beginning intercourse. Its position must be checked and additional spermicide must be added prior to each coital episode.

• Best for: Many women who are concerned about potential side effects of the Pill and intrauterine device (IUD) have turned to the diaphragm. As with the cervical cap, it is best for women in stable, supportive relationships where insertion before sex is not a problem.

IUD. There are currently two types of intrauterine devices that can be inserted into the uterus by a physician. One has progesterone incorporated into the plastic material. It can be used for a limited time before it must be removed.

The other type utilizes copper that adheres to the plastic and can be left in place for several years. IUDs produce an inflammatory reaction in the uterine wall and, in some unknown way, prevent implantation and pregnancy.

• Effectiveness: 95% to 98%.

• Side effects: Menstrual periods often last longer in IUD users, and some users experience cramping and increased menstrual flow. Infections, including those leading to pelvic inflammatory disease, may cause sterility.

• Popularity: Fifth-most-popular form of birth control. It is used by 7.3% of all couples.

• Other advantages: A single visit to the doctor is all that's needed. Insertion of an IUD provides contraception for up to two years (at which time the IUD should be replaced).

• Other disadvantages: Because of the heightened risk of pelvic inflammatory disease, doctors are not as eager to prescribe IUDs as they once were. Recent legal action has also caused IUD prices to soar.

• Best for: Women older than 30 who have decided against having children but wish to avoid sterilization. Note: Women in monogamous relationships are less likely to get pelvic inflammatory disease.

The Mini Pill. Contains the hormone progestin, which causes the formation of a thick mucous barrier in the cervix that prevents sperm from reaching the uterus. The Mini Pill also inhibits the release of eggs by the ovaries and makes implantation of fertilized eggs more difficult.

• Effectiveness: 96% to 98%. The Mini Pill is not quite as effective as the standard estrogen-containing Pill.

• Side effects: Irregular menstrual bleeding, increased rate of ectopic pregnancy, depression.

• Popularity: Only 1% as popular as the standard Pill.

• Best for: Women who are breast-feeding, and women who for medical reasons cannot take the standard Pill but want to use an oral contraceptive.

Norplant. Match-stick-sized rods are surgically implanted beneath the skin of the woman's upper arm. These rods, which slowly release the hormone progestin, remain effective for up to five years.

• Effectiveness: 99%.

• Side effects: 30% to 40% of women using Norplant experience irregular menstrual cycles, especially during the first three months of use. Although Norplant uses the same hormone found in many oral contraceptives, it generally causes fewer side effects because its dosage is lower.

• Popularity: Became available in this country just six months ago. Growing in popularity.

• Other advantages: Just as effective as oral contraceptives.

• Other disadvantages: Requires minor surgery to implant—and later, to remove—the six contraceptive rods. The procedure, which can be performed in a doctor's office in less than 10 minutes. Relatively expensive—$350 for the device, plus $250 to $750 for the implant surgery.

• Best for: Women who want a highly reliable form of birth control without the bother of having to take a daily Pill.

Oral Contraceptives for Men. Despite intensive research in this field, no male contraceptive pills are yet available in the US. Researchers hope to develop a pill that prevents production of viable sperm.

• Drawback: There would be no way for a woman to determine whether or not her partner was consistently taking these pills.

The Pill. Several different types available, in a variety of dosages. All work by preventing the release of eggs from the ovaries.

• Effectiveness: 97% to 99.9%.

• Side effects: Some women experience nausea, breast tenderness, weight gain, yeast infections, hair loss and depression. The more serious side effects of the Pill are especially common in women who smoke and women who are over 35 years old. These side effects include heart attacks, strokes, blood clots in the lungs and high blood pressure.

Note: Most side effects are related to the dosage of hormones estrogen and progestin contained in the Pill. Women should find out from their doctors if they can get by with a lower-dose Pill—many equally effective formulations are available.

• Popularity: The most popular reversible contraceptive method. It is used by 28.6% of couples practicing birth control today.

• Other advantages: Doesn't interrupt lovemaking...the most effective method for preventing pregnancy, aside from sterilization... reduces pain during periods for some women.

• Other disadvantages: Requires a doctor's prescription. Must be taken every day even when no sexual activity occurs.

• Best for: Women under 35 with regular periods and who suffer no undesirable side effects during use. Not recommended for women who are forgetful or who have erratic daily schedules. Also not recommended for smokers.

Progestin Shots. An injection every two or three months prevents eggs from being released.

• Effectiveness: Up to 99.7%.

• Side effects: Irregularity or loss of periods. The shots sometimes make it harder for women to have children even after the injections have been stopped.

• Popularity: Used commonly throughout developing countries. They are not currently FDA-approved in the US.

• Other advantages: Very convenient—four to six shots per year provide continuous contraception.

• Best for: So far these shots have been used mainly for women living where other contraceptive methods are too expensive or unavailable. Because of their convenience and high rate of effectiveness, they may gain wider acceptance in the next few years.

Spermicides. Includes foams, creams, jellies and vaginal suppositories. Inserted into the vagina several minutes prior to coitus. These agents kill sperm.

• Effectiveness: 70% to 92%.

• Side effects: Few. Rarely, allergic reactions may occur.

• Popularity: Used by 2.4% of couples as the sole method of birth control.

• Other advantages: No prescription needed. Provides some protection against venereal diseases.

Sex Hormones... The Basics

Sex hormones are high-octane juices that flow through our bodies in quantities so tiny (measured in billionths of a gram) as to be barely detectable. Yet their influence over our bodies is enormous. They determine our sexual characteristics (body hair, sexual organs), our inherent psychology (from aggressive to nurturing), our mood swings (from the anguished premenstrual syndrome to intervals of well-being) and our sex drives (from lusty to indifferent or even impotent).

Until a few decades ago, little was known about these subtle chemicals, which are produced in our endocrine glands. But today doctors are using sex hormones in ways never before dreamed of—to cure illnesses and to fine-tune our bodies and states of mind. Some ways they are used:

- To ignite the sexual drive for those with seriously impaired libidos.
- As contraceptives for women (the Pill).
- To stop bone loss (osteoporosis)—common among older, post-menopausal women.
- To ease the discomforts of menopausal women (hot flashes).
- To develop breasts for men who undergo sex-change surgery.

The three leading sex hormones are estrogen, progesterone and testosterone. Most people think of estrogen as the female chemical and testosterone as the male's. In reality, both men and women share testosterone and estrogen.

However, women have far more estrogen in their bodies, which is what gives them the female characteristics...less body hair, a layer of fat under the skin—giving them a smooth, soft texture—and protection from heart attacks by commanding the liver to rid their bodies of accumulated cholesterol.

Men, on the other hand, have about six times more testosterone than women. That hormone bounty generates the male characteristics—particularly aggressiveness and sex drive. And, because men have so little estrogen, their blood vessels are not protected against the buildup of dangerous cholesterol, making them far more vulnerable to heart attacks.

Early research indicates that women who receive small doses of supplemental testosterone also experience an increase in both libido and aggressiveness. However, if a man receives extra testosterone, his sex drive will not increase—but his testes will be fooled into stopping sperm production.

Supplemental hormones are often given to women when they enter menopause because their own estrogen-producing system begins to slow down, causing a series of discomforting symptoms, including vaginal dryness and hot flashes.

Estrogen-replacement therapy received a bad rap a few years ago when it was discovered that high doses were sometimes responsible for cancer and strokes. Now, when the therapy is used in conjunction with progesterone, that risk is virtually gone. Yet many doctors continue to be biased against the therapy even when it's indicated to relieve post-menopausal problems.

Exceptions: If a woman has a history of breast cancer, strokes, blood clots or liver diseases, any estrogen-replacement therapy is dangerous.

Two areas of hormone research that have stumped scientists are a male contraceptive and a treatment for premenstrual syndrome (PMS). Work in these areas continues.

Source: Andrea Dunaif, MD, an endocrinologist and associate professor at Mount Sinai School of Medicine, New York. Dr. Dunaif specializes in the regulation of reproductive function.

Secrets Of Staying Sexually Active

Question: *What are the best ways for people over 40 to keep sexually active?*

Answer: Make sex a priority. Too many people assume their sex lives will decline as they age. Unfortunately, simply having this attitude often brings about this unfortunate situation. But people who set aside time for sex, who fantasize about it and look forward to it continue to be sexually fulfilled into their 70s and 80s. Of course, a healthy attitude alone isn't enough. Also important: Taking care of the body. Best: Don't drink or smoke...but do get plenty of exercise.

What do older people want from sex?

The same things that younger people want. Sexual contact is important, of course, but so is the sense of reassurance about one's lovability and attractiveness that sexual contact brings.

Why are so many older people sexually inactive?

Often it comes down to a problem of finding a partner. Since women usually outlive men, the ratio of older women to older men is quite high. This makes it difficult for older people to find a suitable partner...and some widowed people feel so guilty about enjoying themselves sexually following the death of a spouse that they simply avoid sex entirely. Occasionally, older people start avoiding sex because they are self-conscious of the signs of aging in their bodies—extra fat, wrinkles, etc.

How do men and women change sexually as they age?

Both men and women do slow down sexually as they age. They take longer to become aroused and longer to climax. A man often experiences a lengthening of his refractory period (the time required after an orgasm before he can get another erection). Older men are less responsive to erotic photographs and other visual stimuli than are younger men. They may feel aroused, but they are slower to develop an erection. Some men experience a diminished sex drive or ejaculatory troubles and impotence is a problem for others.

Doesn't menopause signal the beginning of the end for a woman's sexuality?

No. Menopause does bring about a major change in the vagina. It becomes drier and less supple and is slower to become lubricated upon sexual arousal. This can lead to pain during intercourse—which, in turn, leads many older women to avoid sex altogether. However, this anatomical change in no way precludes the continuation of an active sex life—especially if women and their partners are sensitive to this potential problem.

What can be done to ease vaginal dryness?

Lubricants, such as KY jelly, help. Far better, however, is an estrogen cream available by prescription. Lubricants only ease friction a little. Estrogen cream actually helps repair dried-out vaginal tissues.

What about impotence?

While it is more common among older men, impotence is by no means inevitable. And help is available.

Is impotence a result of physiology or psychology?

Up to as recently as five years ago, we thought most sexual problems, including impotence, had psychological causes. We estimate that up to 50%–75% of all cases of impotence result from organic (physical) problems, including conditions caused by common prescription medications. The problem gets complicated because a man for whom impotence is a chronic problem is likely to develop psychological difficulties, regardless of the problem's original cause. Fortunately, impotence is now treated as the complex problem it really is, with input from specialists in psychology, urology, neurology and so on. Men need to be aware that good treatment for impotence is available.

Which medications can cause impotence?

The list is long. In addition to alcohol, it includes: Anticholinergics, Antidepressants (including Elavil, Desyrel, Nardil, Parnate), Antihypertensives (including Inderal, Minipress, Catapres, Tenormin), Antipsychotics (such as Thorazine, Prolixin, Haldol, Mellaril), Atromid-S and other hypolipidemics, Barbiturates, Cocaine, Digitalis and other congestive-heart-failure drugs, Dilantin and other anti-convulsion drugs, Diuretics (such as Hygroton and Hydrodiuril), H2 antihistamines (such as Tagamet and Zantac), Levodopa and other drugs for treating Parkinson's disease, Marijuana, Morphine, Progestins like Provera, Sedatives/anxiolytics (antianxiety drugs, including Xanax and Librium).

What if a doctor prescribes a drug that has a history of causing impotence?

Any man taking one or more of these drugs who experiences impotence or some other sexual problem (decreased libido, ejaculatory problems, etc.), should discuss the problem with his doctor. Reassuring: These drugs do not create sexual problems for all men. Key: Ask about the possibility of reducing the dose or discontinuing the medication altogether—or switching to an alternative drug that has not been linked to sexual problems. If you aren't experiencing any sexual problems, there is no need to switch the medication.

What are some of the physical causes of impotence?

Circulatory problems, including an inability of the blood vessels in the penis to retain blood, are the primary culprit. Alternatively, there may be a lack of testosterone, or neurological problems. Diabetics are at special risk for impotence, as the disease involves damage to both the nerves and the circulatory system. Surgery on the rectum, prostate or bladder occasionally results in nerve damage that causes impotence.

What is widower's syndrome?

That's the name used to describe a condition in which a man is so anxious about his ability to perform sexually that he is unable to get or maintain an erection. The condition is common among elderly men who resume sexual activity following a long period of abstinence. It's particularly common among men whose wives have died, hence its name. To minimize the problem: Men should realize that they don't have to "perform" right away with women—and women should try to help men relax. Couples should take their time in getting to know one another. Instead of focusing on penetration, for example, they can lie nude on a bed and caress each other. They can shower together. By waiting to attempt intercourse until after they become comfortable with one another, they can avoid the "performance anxiety" that often leads to impotence and other sexual problems. Essential: Openness, honesty, willingness to discuss sexual issues directly.

What can an older man do to prevent impotence?

Get plenty of exercise, don't smoke—and it pays to keep a diet low in fats. Fats, like anything bad for the heart or blood vessels, are bad for erections, too. In fact, while there's no such thing as a "penis attack," the penis can be starved for blood in much the same way that a heart attack starves the heart. Certain sexual positions also seem to help men get good erections. The traditional missionary position, with the man on top, can induce blood flow out of the man's pelvic area and into his extremities. This reduces the strength of the erection. To prevent this from occurring, try a position in which the woman is on top or partners are on their sides.

Can a man satisfy his partner even if he's impotent?

Of course. Some of the most satisfied couples we know are ones in which the man has been impotent. There are many ways to have an exciting and satisfying sex life without intercourse. The key is adding variety and being willing to experiment with different ideas.

Source: Dr. E. Douglas Whitehead, assistant clinical professor of urology, Mount Sinai School of Medicine, New York, and Dr. Shirley Zussman, a leading New York sex therapist. Drs. Whitehead and Zussman, leading experts on the treatment of sexual problems, are the editors of *Sex Over 40*, a monthly newsletter that addresses the sexual concerns of mature adults.

Good Sex: How One Partner Alone Can Revive A Couple' Sex Life

Good sex begins while your clothes are still on. The same with bad sex.

Probably no more than 10% of couples with sexual dysfunction can truly lay blame on the partner's problem. For the rest, the dysfunction is rooted in their emotional states and how well the partners relate to each other.

While an improvement in a couple's psychological state is a sure route to a happy sex life, one partner can take the necessary steps alone to ensure that they will both have more fun in bed...while they are also improving other parts of their life together.

Couples should ignore most surveys on how often couples have sex. Men rarely want to divulge how frequently it occurs. They want to protect their macho image. And women are reluctant to admit how little sex they are actually getting because they fear it says something about their own sexual allure.

Such statistics aren't important, anyway—it's how much sex you would ideally like to have and how much sex your partner finds fulfilling.

Obstacles to sex:

Men's most frequent grievance: Women are too critical of them—always trying to fine-tune the relationship.

Next comes lack of appreciation—wives focusing on what husbands fail to do rather than on what they do.

Third is a woman's need to analyze the relationship in such a way that it appears to be a lecture and the husband comes out the bad guy.

Fourth is sexual timing...men prefer sex in the morning when their testosterone (sex hormone) is highest, while women like it in the evening, when they are more relaxed.

And, finally, men find their most intimate moments are after sex, while women like to experience intimacy as a prelude to sex.

Women's top grievance: Their partners avoid emotional intimacy, and their efforts to make a relationship closer are often interpreted by husbands as criticism and nagging.

Next comes one-sidedness in caring for partners' emotional needs. While women take that responsibility seriously, my research shows that men generally tend to ignore their role in fulfilling that need. That failure expresses itself in many ways—from not touching or not expressing his love for her to taking little interest in her concerns.

Also, many women complain that their husbands are too passive in both the sex role and in decision-making—even in such minor matters as what's for dinner.

Both men and women let these complaints build up until they are finally expressed in bad sex...or in no sex. Result: Sex is used as a weapon and a punishment.

Removing the barriers:

The first rule in overcoming the barriers is letting go—not making a big issue out of every irritation and complaint: "Let's agree to disagree...our differences shouldn't ruin our sex life." To overcome these barriers:

- Listen carefully to your partner—as much for getting a handle on his/her concerns as for opening the door to intimacy. Men should realize that unless they invite intimacy they will forever keep their partner at a distance and the relationship will never progress—emotionally or sexually. Women should realize that dropping the barriers to intimacy is usually hard for men...so it's important to give them time.
- If a man is too passive sexually, guide him by words and actions. Again, the key is to go slowly. If, on the other hand, a man is too abrupt in getting his sexual needs met, meet him half way: "Okay, let's make love...after we spend some time caressing and kissing first."
- If your husband is passive-aggressive—doing what makes him happy and conveniently forgetting your needs—ignore the act. Firmly, but without anger, point out the missing ingredient—that you have needs, too. Avoid nagging or criticizing.

Don't forget: Good sex starts with a fair exchange of small favors and sharing concerns.

Source: Doris Wild Helmering, author of *Husbands, Wives & Sex*, Bob Adams, Inc., 260 Center St., Holbrook, MA 02343. A psychotherapist who specializes in relationship counseling, she also hosts a television program, *Dear Doris*, and writes a weekly newspaper column on psychological issues.

How To Buy Sperm

People considering artificial insemination should be wary of sperm banks. Many of them are popping up across the country, and some are not approved by state health departments. Protection:

- Call the local health department and ask if the sperm bank has been approved by the state's health department.
- Ask for proof that a sperm donor has been retested for the HIV virus six months after giving the sperm...and ask to see a copy of a permit, license or letter from the state health department indicating that the sperm bank tests the semen or donor for hepatitis B, sexu-

ally transmitted diseases, blood group and RH and any genetically transmitted diseases.

• Inquire about the donor's sperm count. It should be 30–50 million sperm per milliliter in order to increase odds of successful insemination.

Source: Dr. Jeanne Linden, director of the blood and tissue resources for New York State's Health Department.

Impotence: The Miracle Treatment

Almost any impotent man can again have erections if, with a urologist's help, he learns to self-inject special drugs into his penis. The treatment's success rate: 80%.

Better drug mix:

Since the 1980s, two medications have been used together. Papaverine causes erections. Phentolamine helps sustain them. Papaverine, though, can cause internal scars of penile tissue, adding to erectile problems. It can also lead to erections that last too long (more than four hours) and can damage the penis.

New addition: Prostaglandin E-1 (PGE-1) augments papaverine's effect. Less or no papaverine need be used, so fewer side effects occur.

Finding the correct dose of the two- or three-drug mixture requires several office visits. The urologist also teaches the man, or his partner, how to inject the drugs into the base of the penis. (The needle is tiny and the injection virtually painless.)

The patient reports how the drugs work when he is alone with his partner (such erections frequently are firmer and longer-lasting than erections he has at the doctor's office). Then the final dose is determined and the man takes home a one- to three-month supply of the drugs. (With time, a higher dose may be needed.) The injections are to be used no more than every two days.

Vital: A man must immediately call his doctor or an emergency room if he has a rigid erection for more than four hours. (This situation can be life-threatening.)

Twice yearly, the patient must also have a blood test to check his liver function, which may be affected. Periodic visits to his urologist are also advised to make sure no internal scars have developed.

Note: Because this drug program is new, some doctors allow its use for only two years. Most allow longer use because the drugs are used in tiny amounts.

Also, the treatment does not work on men with severe atherosclerotic penile vascular problems, and many men drop out after treatment is started due to lack of spontaneity, reduced quality of erections with time and fear of unknown long-term complications.

Rate of complications, mainly prolong erections: Less than 5%.

Cost: About $1,000–$3,000 per year. Insurers may not pay. Those interested should consult with their insurance company.

Source: E. Douglas Whitehead, MD, FACS, a New York City urologist in private practice and a Director of the Association for Male Sexual Dysfunction, 520 E. 72 St., New York 10021.

14

Shrewd Career Planning

The Secrets Of Career Success

After more than two decades of research on the subject of career success, I have concluded that people on the "fast track"* are made, not born.

As a group, fast-trackers are not any brighter than their slow-track colleagues. They didn't attend better colleges. And, biggest surprise of all, they don't work any harder.

The main difference: Fast-trackers advance within their companies because they know how to tap into critical resources. Slow-trackers often aren't even aware that these resources exist.

Companies don't inform people about critical resources in their orientation materials. In fact, more than 90% of what you need to know to succeed is not published anywhere.

*A career path of highly enriched professional growth opportunities.

If you want to thrive in today's competitive corporate environment, you cannot simply play by the rules and keep your nose clean. Horatio Alger is dead, and he has been replaced by a fast-track breed that has mastered the hidden code for success.

The foundation:

In virtually every case, fast-trackers are launched by bosses who invest in their subordinates' future careers.

This goes beyond training a person to do the present job well. When a boss invests in a worker, the goal is to help the person outgrow the present job and move on to increasingly responsible positions within the company.

Are you on the fast track?

On average, the bosses studied engaged in these critical actions with 64% of their fast-trackers, but with only 27% of their slow-trackers. You can be confident you're on the fast track if your boss...

- Provides you with special information that allows you to learn how the company really operates.

- Assigns you challenging tasks.
- Warns you about changes to be made within the organization.
- Advertises your strengths to higher management.
- Prepares you to handle more difficult assignments.
- Helps plan your long-range career.
- Gives you enough authority to complete important assignments.
- Notifies you of promotion opportunities.
- Warns you in advance—and in confidence—about your career problems.
- Asks for your input in decisions for which only the boss is responsible.

Getting your boss to invest in you:

In deciding which of their subordinates to select for the fast track, bosses seek several qualities above all others:

- Decision-making similarity. Given the same complex problems, the boss and subordinate will make the same decision. They view the company, its markets and its constituents from similar perspectives.
- Dependability. In an emergency, the boss can count on the subordinate to complete an assignment the boss started. The subordinate rises to the occasion in times of crisis.
- Positive collaboration. The boss and subordinate have an effective working relationship. They communicate well and coordinate their efforts efficiently.

Beyond excelling in these critical areas, potential fast-trackers can boost their chances of selection and investment by:

- Learning about their organization beyond their job requirements.
- Telling their boss they want extra work.
- Making their boss look good.
- Giving their boss extra credit in the presence of other people.

How fast-trackers advance:

Fast-trackers engage in several activities more often than their slow-track colleagues. To get (or stay) on the fast track:

- Demonstrate initiative. Show the boss that you're eager to outgrow your job. Identify problem areas and act to correct them.
- Exercise leadership. Help co-workers perform their jobs more efficiently, and provide direction when necessary. Offer to take charge of special projects, such as interdepartmental task forces.
- Take risks. Let your boss know about problems in the work unit. Take stands you think are correct, even if you're bucking the tide. Admit your mistakes—and show what you've learned from them.
- Add value to your work. Go beyond your job description. Write unsolicited reports that can help your boss make improvements in your unit.
- Persist on a project. If an assignment appears to be going nowhere, try to view it in a new way.
- Seek opportunities for self-improvement. Request special training, or take on assignments that require the use of new skills. Ask your managers to define your strengths and weaknesses so that you can improve.
- Build competence networks. Find out who is responsible for getting things done in the organization. Then initiate relationships with these people by offering favors or providing information. Result: You'll compile credits with these people that can translate into critical resources down the road.
- Influence others. When co-workers come to you for help or advice, deal carefully with each person's problems.
- Resolve ambiguity. When a boss makes an ambiguous request, gather as much information as possible from other sources. Make educated assumptions (when necessary), and approach the boss for brief feedback regularly throughout the assignment.
- Seek wider exposure. Learn more about the company by associating with managers outside your department.
- Build up—and on—existing skills. Keep up with technical advances in your field.
- Develop a close working relationship with the boss. This cannot be overemphasized. Volunteer favors and information. Take an interest in the boss's family and career. To avoid being obvious or causing resentment: Show an interest in your co-workers as well.
- Help the boss. When you help make your boss look good, the boss will be more likely

to take you along as he/she advances through the organization.

Source: George B. Graen, director of the Center for International Competitiveness Studies at the University of Cincinnati. He is the author of *Unwritten Rules for Your Career*, John Wiley & Sons, Dept. 0-1006, Box 6793, Somerset, NJ 08875.

Job Hunting After 40

In today's economic climate, job insecurity is becoming accepted as a fact of life.

Hidden advantage: With so many highly qualified people out of work, unemployment no longer carries the stigma it used to. It's widely understood that job loss may have nothing to do with performance or skills.

Many employers are realizing that the old myths about hiring workers 40 years old and older are obsolete. Older workers are not slower to learn. Their skills are current. And they're not more expensive.

Midlife job seekers have the benefit of maturity and experience...qualities they can use to their advantage during the job hunt.

Key: Approaching the job search as a business problem—systematically and thoroughly.

If you're helping a friend or colleague who is launching a job search, here is some constructive advice you can give him/her...

- Deal with the emotions of unemployment. Depression is a common reaction to job loss. If depression becomes immobilizing, get help—from an industrial psychologist or other mental-health professional who understands the specific effects of job loss.
- Address your financial situation and apply immediately for unemployment benefits. Decide where you can cut your expenses. Investigate emergency resources—accounts you can cash in, sources of low-interest loans, etc.

Hold a family conference. Be honest about the change in family finances. Discuss ways other family members can be of assistance.

- Appearance is important. It is crucial for a job seeker to look like a winner. Remember, first impressions count. When pursuing job leads, act upbeat.

Getting started:

Fight the "Let's fix the bathroom now" syndrome—the temptation to put off the job search in favor of other tasks. Treat the job hunt like a job...get dressed and spend six hours a day on steps related to the search.

Make a written plan. Many of the following steps can be done concurrently. The important thing is to start them now.

- Prepare an interim résumé. Use the simple, traditional format—brief job descriptions arranged in reverse chronological order and printed on good paper stock. Include information that shows a proven track record of achievement and the value of skills that may be pertinent to prospective employers.

Examples: Managed 40 people...Created a new inventory management system that saved the company $50,000 a year.

Later, you can prepare a more hard-hitting résumé after assessing the job market in a specific field—and the skills in demand. In the meantime, the interim résumé can be sent out immediately.

- Evaluate. Make a list of your strengths, accomplishments and interests. What have you done that you have enjoyed most? Have previous jobs really been appropriate?

Example: Many people in the computer industry have been promoted from working with computers, which they love, to management, which they hate. You might be better off in a job that pays less than your old one but is more satisfying.

- List contacts. Tell everyone you know that you're looking for work—from your dentist to your accountant. Send a résumé and brief note to people you know professionally, especially those who have helped in the past.
- Conduct exploratory interviews. Using leads provided by professional and social contacts, consult experts in your industry.

Important: Consider these contacts sources of useful information, rather than prospective employers. Take no more than 15 minutes of their time, and leave a résumé.

Additional leads: Directories of professional organizations...annual reports...trade journals...clipping files. These and other materials can be found at a library.

• Conduct a mail campaign. Send résumés and cover letters to people who might be in a position to hire—whether they have advertised job openings or not. Address letters to a specific person, not the "human resources department" or "marketing director."

Important: Confirm the person's name and title by calling the company switchboard.

Make letters as specific as possible. If answering a newspaper ad, explain why you qualify for the job. If you are sending a résumé cold to a company listed in a directory, indicate that you are familiar with the industry and the company's products or services.

Aim: Send out 15 to 20 résumés a day. This may sound like a considerable amount, but as in any other direct-mail campaign, a 5% return is considered excellent. The more prospects contacted, the greater the chances of success.

• Interview like a pro. Concentrate on your interviewer's point of view. Your questions should probe for ways that you can be of assistance to the company. Try to keep your style in line with the interviewer's.

Example: If the interviewer is impatient, give short, concise answers. If the interviewer is more painstaking, give plenty of detail.

Relax. Don't treat any interview as a life-and-death matter. There will be others. And don't assume failure if the interview doesn't result in an immediate offer. Look at every interview as a learning experience, and remember that in some companies, hiring decisions can be put on hold for a year or more.

Evaluate the offer:

Too many people panic and take the first job they're offered, whether it fits their needs or not. Failing to consider the job in the context of your long-term career goals may produce further unhappiness. Issues that should be considered before you take a job:

• Corporate culture. You will want to know if you will feel comfortable in the corporate environment. Is it a rigid bureaucracy or an informal, team-oriented organization?

• Your prospective supervisor. Find out as much as you can about the person you'll be working for from others in the company.

• Level of authority. Will you be independent in carrying out your responsibilities, or will you need approval from a higher-up?

• Salary, perks, vacations, commuting time and other lifestyle issues. These are important considerations, but they shouldn't be the first criteria.

Source: F. Patricia Birsner, a business consultant based in New Jersey. Birsner has developed and taught professional training programs for the American Management Association and chapters of the Forty Plus Club—the country's oldest self-help, job-seeking organization for executives. She is the author of *The 40+ Job Hunting Guide: Official Handbook of the 40+ Club,* Facts on File, Inc., 460 Park Ave. South, New York 10016.

Check Résumé Credentials

Résumé credential checking becomes more important than ever during periods of high unemployment. About 80% of résumés contain some untrue or misleading information. Management should take the time to check information. The cost of a hiring mistake can be high—not only because an unqualified person may be mistakenly hired, but also because mistakes made by an unqualified employee can trigger costly negligence lawsuits and other problems for the company.

Source: Peter LeVine, president, Professional Reference Checking, Box 2552, Framingham, MA 01701.

How To Deal With Being Smarter Than Your Boss

When an employee thinks he/she is smarter than the boss—and lets the boss know it in subtle and not-so-subtle ways—destructive problems surface. Instead of putting their brains together and working as a productive team, they fall into power struggles that destroy any possibility of such productivity.

It is a common problem in business. It is also difficult to handle. Helpful:

• Never oppose the boss in public. This is true in all relationships, personal and business. People are relatively comfortable being challenged in private, but they want to be supported in public. This is a reasonable expectation for an employer. A boss deserves this respect.

• Include the boss in new ideas. Tell him the idea germinated in conversation with him, or that it came out of working on a mutual project.

This makes your concept less threatening—and more likely to be implemented. Secondly, it emphasizes to your associates that you believe in teamwork—an important instrument to the success of any business.

• It pays to share. If it's not practical to give your boss direct credit for your idea, it's often a good idea to offer him some general verbal strokes. Express to him your appreciation for having given you the opportunity to work on a particular project. You can always find something to credit the boss with.

Source: Dr. David Phillips, director of social work at the Postgraduate Center for Mental Health in New York.

Stop Selling... Start Helping

Successful salespeople don't sell at all. They help. They zero in on clients' needs and then fulfill them. It's this helping spirit that separates the super salespeople from the mediocre, pavement-pounding people who wonder why sales aren't higher.

The word "sell" has negative connotations. If you don't believe me, look it up in the dictionary. You'll find any one or more of the following definitions for the word...*

• "To deliver or give up in violation of duty, trust or loyalty: *betray*—often used with out."

• "To give up in return for something else, especially foolishly or dishonorably."

• "To deliver into slavery for money."

• "To impose on: *cheat* ('realized that he had been sold')."

*From *Webster's New Collegiate Dictionary*, G. & C. Merriam Co.

It's no wonder that buyers have such negative images of the people who come to sell them something. They're immediately on the defensive, reluctant to answer questions, just waiting for the salesperson to get lost.

Helping is something you do *for* people. Selling is something you do *to* them. Go into each sale with the intention of helping, rather than selling. Buyers are more likely to answer questions when confronted by people who are out to help them.

Condition yourself to help:

• Build a trusting relationship. Show customers that you care about them and their needs and that you're not just interested in making a sale. Relate your product's benefits to the customer's needs.

• Ask questions. The reasons the customers will buy are in their heads, not yours. Ask: What? Where? How? When? How? Why? Who?

• Listen! Sales only move forward when the buyers are doing the talking, not the sellers. One of the barriers to completing a sale is the salesperson's inability to remain silent. You can listen your way into a sale.

• Observe. Learn to be sensitive to buyers' body language. Are they fidgeting? Are they smiling? Body language can tell you when to back off and when it's time to close the sale.

Source: Alan Cimberg, noted sales trainer and consultant, 83 Tilrose Ave., Malverne, NY 11565.

Job-Hunting Action Plan

To help you change careers—whether you're currently employed or not. Key: Organization. Set up specific things to do each day...changing them week to week as the search progresses. Sample week: Sunday—read classified ads...Monday—answer ads and set up appointments...Tuesday—write letters and/or go on appointments...Wednesday—network by phone or in person...Thursday—visit employment agencies...Friday—do library research.

Source: *Marketing Yourself: The Ultimate Job Seeker's Guide* by Dorothy Leeds, HarperCollins, 10 E. 53 St., NY 10022.

Better Job Interviews

Be prepared...be ready to turn negatives into positives...ask questions to keep control...listen actively to content and intent of questions you are asked...don't answer any question until you fully understand it...ask for the job...follow up...practice so much that you can do all this while being relaxed and comfortable, so that your best self will come through.

Source: *Marketing Yourself: The Ultimate Job Seeker's Guide* by Dorothy Leeds, HarperCollins, 10 E. 53 St., NY 10022.

Flexibility Is Key To Finding A Job Now

The fast-changing job market—plus a downturn that has removed 1.5 million jobs from the nation's economy—requires: Developing several disciplines...being ready to change jobs frequently...being ready to work for a smaller company or move to a less desirable geographical area...lowering expectations for salary and benefits.

Source: Samuel Ehrenhalt, Middle Atlantic regional commissioner for the United States Labor Department's Bureau of Labor Statistics.

Networking Power

Meet people who can help you before you need them. Learn to be genuinely interested in other people. Always be polite. Follow up whenever someone gives you information or a name to call, and call back to let the person know how things worked out—people like being appreciated and knowing they've helped. Don't ask for favors, and don't keep count of who "owes" you. Keep in touch with people, and never stop building your contacts.

Source: Belinda Plutz, partner, CareerMentors, New York, quoted in *Successful Meetings*, 633 Third Ave., New York 10017.

Headhunter Relations

Cultivate a relationship with a headhunter, even though the first job offered was not right for you. Suggest a possible candidate for the job, name sources who can suggest candidates, send clippings on topics the headhunter is researching. Advantage: You establish yourself as a worthwhile contact and your file remains active so that the next suitable opportunity is sent your way.

Source: *Career Makers* by John Sibbald, HarperCollins, 10 E. 53 St., New York 10022.

Consider Consulting

Working as a consultant is good for people who lose their jobs. Discharged managers who do consulting work have the best chances of being rehired. Best: Consult only at companies for which you'd like to work. Consulting for less desirable firms delays the job search. Important: Don't assume that employers know you want full-time work—let them know.

Source: James E. Challenger, Challenger, Gray & Christmas, Inc., outplacement consultants, 150 S. Wacker Dr., Chicago 60606.

When Not To Ask For A Raise

Out of anger or frustration (for instance, because a co-worker recently got a raise)—a threatened boss is not likely to be a generous one...at a social occasion (especially if people have been drinking)—raising business at a social event is awkward for the boss, and puts your judgment in question...by saying you need the money—everyone needs money. Better way: Back up your case for a raise by showing how you've earned it.

Source: Laurie Maynard, management consultant, Arlington, MA, quoted in *Executive Female*, 1041 Third Ave., New York 10021.

Training Your Replacement

Leaving a job on a good note means thoroughly training the person who takes your place. Make sure that you: Explain to your successor the basic job duties, company policies and expectations...review status reports of all projects, including background information...go over your filing system and where resource materials are located...offer advice on efficient ways you found to complete your work...introduce others in the company and make a list of key personnel and their job titles...give a tour of the company and point out locations of key people and supplies... make a list of all job contacts, addresses and phone numbers.

Source: *Before You Say "I Quit"* by Diane Holloway, PhD, Macmillan, 866 Third Ave., New York 10022.

How To Make Your Career Dreams Come True

Many people who are unhappy in their careers think that a counselor or someone else can tell them what they really should be doing. Trap: You're the only person who knows what's right for you.

Although many great thinkers, from William Shakespeare ("to thine own self be true") to Joseph Campbell ("follow your bliss"), have advised us to look within ourselves for guidance, most people don't listen.

Reason: There's no social reinforcement for doing the things we really want to do. We get approval only for doing what our parents and peers expect of us.

Many people are so used to doing what others want them to do that they've lost sight of just what it is they really want. To get back in touch with yourself...

Use your imagination:

When people come to me for help, I ask them to perform several exercises: Examples:

- Pretend your boss just told you he was giving you a one-year fully funded sabbatical to go anywhere and do anything. The catch: You have to write out your plan for the year in the next 15 minutes. What will you do?
- Pretend you've been given a large, prominent billboard, and you can write anything you want on it. It's an unparalleled opportunity to get your message across to the community. What will you say? And how will you say it?
- Pretend you're expecting weekend guests. You've cleaned the house and bought everything you need...but they call at the last minute and cancel. You're left with two free days, totally unstructured. How will you spend that time?

The information that exercises such as these produce will help you to determine what you consider to be truly important.

Look at your history:

Analyze both work and non-work experiences—everything from editing the high-school yearbook to earning your most recent promotion. In each case, think about the skills you used to accomplish what you did. Then write each skill on an index card, one per card.

Keep looking over your life and writing down skills until the stack piles up. In the groups I work with, each member accumulates a stack of 300 to 1,000 cards.

Example: Hal, a lawyer for a big energy company, also collected classic cars. The skills on his cards ranged from "negotiating land acquisitions among adversarial parties" to "locating hard-to-find car parts."

Doing this exercise will help you redefine who you are and what you want from your career.

Example: Hal started seeing himself as not just another lawyer, but a multifaceted, rather interesting person.

Don't sell yourself short:

Many people think it would be impossible to accomplish what they really want. They relegate it to the realm of "if I could only..."

There is actually nothing more practical than living your dream. Because you're willing to give it all your energy and all your skills, you stand a good chance of succeeding.

Example: Marylou, a 40ish divorcée with two young children, had worked as a graphic designer before she was married. She always assumed she'd be a graphic designer again after her kids were grown. But in the course of writing her life history and doing her skill cards, her strong leadership skills and social conscience clearly emerged. Marylou found she had the drive and the skills to become a successful lobbyist on environmental issues.

How to get where you want to go:

Once you've figured out where you want to go, start moving in that direction by surveying, which includes gathering information from people in your field of interest. Surveying can have some unexpectedly positive results.

Example: John, a lawyer for a small subsidiary of a large multinational firm, wanted to get involved with mergers and acquisitions. He started researching the possibilities with people in the company, which attracted the attention of the company's CEO. He was eventually transferred to the main office and given a change to do what he had always wanted.

Unfortunately, it's not enough to just zero in on what you want. You have to be able to convince someone—an employer, a publisher, a department-store buyer, etc.—that he/she needs what you've got.

To find someone who needs your skills, think of how you could market these skills—like a new product.

Example: Anna, a producer for a local TV news program, wanted a slower-paced job that would also help society. She realized that the same skills she used in producing the news could be used to produce dinners and other charity events that would raise money for charities. She convinced several groups that her skills could help them improve their fundraising...and she now has her own company that produces such events.

Source: Nella Barkley, president of the Crystal-Barkley Corp., 111 E. 31 St., New York 10016. For many years a partner of the late John Crystal, Barkley has been at the forefront of career-counseling research. Crystal-Barkley's pioneering ideas have been popularized in the best-selling book *What Color Is Your Parachute?* by Richard Nelson Bolles, Ten Speed Press, Box 7123, Berkeley, CA 94707.

Career Moves: Key Questions To Ask Before You Sign On

Does this sound familiar? Just when a person is burdened with the financial responsibilities of a home and family, he comes to realize that he's not happy in his job. He has chosen the wrong company...or even the wrong career.

It is familiar, and in almost all cases, the problem arises because the person didn't stop and ask himself tough questions about himself, his career path or the company that hired him.

These questions are important if you're changing jobs now or counseling a child on a first job. They can prevent heartache or financial loss in the future.

Probing the hirers:

These days, in an effort to attract good employees, even the best firms sometimes cross the line between matching people with the right jobs and promoting themselves. To cut through the sales pitch, you've got to do some investigating of your own before you even go on an interview.

Start by going to a library that has computer databases on US companies. Today, most libraries do.

These databases are likely to contain both official financial reports and outside news reporting about the company. They can be an important source of both good and bad information that you should be aware of before the interview. Examples:

- Financial reports may indicate a pattern of growing or declining earnings, reveal the company's standing within its industry, and show whether it is surpassing or falling behind its competitors.
- Trouble may be reflected in news reports of takeover rumors, high employee turnover, labor unrest or dissension among managers, shareholders or operating divisions.
- Opportunities may be found in reports of business expansion and management innovation.

Trap: The worst information source is usually the company itself. Drexel Burnham Lambert, for instance, was hiring up until two days before it asked for bankruptcy protection. And several years ago, E.F. Hutton issued a glowing annual report just after, believe it or not, it was indicted on mail-fraud charges.

Being well-informed about the company can pay big dividends at an interview. It enables you to ask the right questions about a job that might have hidden liabilities. But it also enables you to make a very favorable impression when seeking a job you really want.

An applicant who shows up knowledgeable and enthusiastic about a growing line of business is likely to strike the company as just the right person for that business. Get as much information as you can from as many sources as possible before going on an interview.

At the interview:

When you arrange an interview by letter or phone, ask about the type of job opening that will be discussed.

Be wary if the company wants to see you before talking about specific openings or reviewing your résumé. The firm may have jobs that are so unattractive it has to sell them to applicants face to face. When you get to the interview, ask:

- Not just about the starting salary, but about the wage scale in the company from top to bottom—and the promotion rate.
- Not just about benefits, but about which health-care provider the company uses, so you can judge the quality of service to expect.
- Not just about the pension, but also whether the firm offers a 401(k) plan allowing for voluntary tax-favored savings, and whether low-interest loans from a credit union are available.

Be wary about a company that doesn't...

- Organize a thorough on-site visit and follow through with details. You should be allowed to see the surroundings you'll be working in and see whether you will work in an office or a cubicle, whether the setting will be formal or relaxed, etc.
- Let you talk with people who aren't on your interview schedule, including people you will work with and the person who previously held the position you're applying for.
- Allow you to visit the cafeteria and other business spaces you will use.
- Remember information about you or your application.
- Return your telephone calls promptly. This is not just a point of courtesy. Failure to return your calls may be a sign that the company is hiding something, or that it doesn't want to field follow-up questions.

Probing yourself:

Though salary is important, so is a sense of personal fulfillment. If you're changing jobs in mid-life, you probably know fulfillment by its absence. It doesn't come unless you enjoy the day-to-day work activities and fit into the lifestyle and culture of the business you work for.

Some businesses have strong corporate cultures with which you won't necessarily fit. (High-paying bank jobs like investment banking and international finance often have an especially rigorous lifestyle.) The conflict may be obvious from an on-site visit, but if you have doubts, ask someone who knows both you and the business. Others are often quicker to see a problem than we can ourselves.

If you're considering a switch from one field to another, it can also pay to do some part-time or consulting work in it. For your children, suggest that they consider interning for a summer or two to see whether they "fit" into a business's corporate culture.

Helpful: The Strong-Campbell Interest Inventory test. It isn't an aptitude test. Rather, it's a probe into whether your likes and dislikes are similar to those of people who have been successful in various careers.

The test isn't 100% accurate, of course. But it's very useful because, if you test negatively for a prospective job, you'll know it's time to ask more questions about it. Negative results can also steer you to a related field to which you're more suited. For instance, if you want a medical career, but test results show that you dislike dealing with sick people or death, you can steer yourself into a specialty like genetics or ophthalmology.

The test is available from most education institutions.

Source: William Corwin, associate director of career services, Princeton University, Princeton, NJ 08544.

Trick Interview Question

Beware of this line: "If we were to make you an offer today, would you accept it?" Useful response: I'd be thrilled. I think this job is right for me. However, I feel obligated to keep the other appointments I've made this week. I can tell you there's a 90% chance that your offer would be accepted.

Source: *Hot Tips, Sneaky Tricks & Last-Ditch Tactics* by Jeff B. Speck, John Wiley & Sons, 605 Third Ave., New York 10158.

How To Be Hunted By Headhunters

A headhunter—more formally known as an executive recruiter—is a job broker hired and paid by a company to fill vacancies for management positions. It's not likely that these jobs would be advertised or heard about through the grapevine. Headhunting firms operate in two different ways:

Contingency firms are paid only if they fill the position. They usually handle low- and middle-management jobs with salaries of $20,000 to $50,000, but, depending on the firm and the industry, salaries can range up to $100,000. Drawbacks:

- If you've spoken to several contingency firms, they could all send your résumé to the same employer, which may raise a question about your credibility and risk confidentiality. Protection: Firmly state that your résumé may be sent only after your approval.
- Some contingency recruiters may feel they can't afford to spend too long on one search, so they try to fill a position even if it's not best for the candidate.

Retainer firms are paid whether or not the firm actually fills the opening. These positions are usually high-level, with salaries that start around $50,000.

Because costs are so high, with the client company usually paying about one-third of the first year's salary as a fee, companies usually hire only one retainer firm per search. As a result, they provide a better guarantee of confidentiality, and there is less risk of having your résumé submitted by two recruiters for the same job.

Both types of firms may occasionally suggest job candidates to a client company—even when they are not doing a search—if the recruiter feels the candidate is a good fit for that company.

To find a headhunter:

No matter how great you are, a headhunter won't call you if you're hidden.

In order to be hunted, you have to maintain a visible profile in your industry—write articles in industry publications...stay active in your professional association...do consulting outside your job...volunteer for interdepartmental projects at work...stay in touch with former associates, etc.

If you've done all of this, you probably won't need to contact a headhunter because one will probably have found you. But if they haven't found you yet...

- Consult one of the many recruiter directories. Use them to research the firms that operate in your industry. These can be found at your local library.

Also: A listing of some recruiter directories as well as recruiter associations is included in the back of my book.

- Get recommendations. Talk to colleagues and friends or people in your professional association. Ask what recruiters they've worked with.
- Attend career-development programs sponsored by your professional association. Follow a recruiter's lecture with a note commenting on the presentation and introducing yourself.
- Ask friends in the industry to introduce you to headhunters they know. Best: Have that person call the headhunter to say that you are a good person for him to know. The recruiter will probably follow up with a call to you.

When a headhunter calls:

Many people are turned off by a cold call from a headhunter.

Better attitude: It's worth five minutes of your time to listen to what the headhunter has to say—it could be a great opportunity.

During the initial conversation with the recruiter, be sure to ask about...

- The job opening and the company. What is the level of responsibility? Salary? Corporate culture? If none of these are right, tell the headhunter what would be right for you.

Advice for women: Because some companies still carry anti-female prejudices, it's important to find out about a potential employer's views towards women to rebut any stereotypes.

- The recruiting firm. If you've never heard of the firm or the person calling you—or if the caller's questions sound suspicious—politely offer to call back when it's "more convenient," and check the firm out. How:

1. Maintain a headhunter file. Include articles, advertisements or advice from friends and colleagues on headhunters and their firms.
2. Consult an executive recruiter directory. Note: Not all firms will be listed—this is a very fluid industry and new firms open all the time.
3. Consult a professional association for executive recruiters. These groups also are listed in executive recruiter directories.
4. Contact your professional association. Many associations have a career committee that can offer information on recruiters.
5. Call the firm or ask the headhunter directly. Find out: How long has the firm been in business? What is its track record? Has it done searches for this company before (a repeat search shows confidence in the headhunter)? Does it work on retainer or contingency? Does it specialize in your field? Request a copy of the informational company brochure.

Handling the headhunter interview:

People often assume that if a headhunter contacts them about a position, they're as good as hired and can be passive in the personal interview that follows. Reality: The headhunter is probably interviewing many other candidates. You must actively show that you are the best choice. To do this...

- Be knowledgeable and enthusiastic about your field of expertise or your industry. This is especially important if you are not currently employed.
- Prepare questions for your interview. This shows that you are actively interested in developing your career. Issues to cover: Job responsibilities, basic information about the company (its corporate culture, etc.), potential pitfalls of the position, possible career opportunities, what happened to the person previously holding the job.

What turns off a headhunter:

- Prevarications. A good headhunter does thorough reference checks...lies are eventually uncovered.
- Negative attitude.
- Being unfocused about career interests and goals.
- Long-windedness. When a headhunter says, "Tell me about yourself," he expects you to talk for three to five minutes about your career. He does not want a 20-minute personal history.
- Short-windedness. Providing one-word answers shows you have little enthusiasm or interest in a new position...or in yourself.
- People in the middle of major life changes. Personal crises (divorce, death or serious illness in the family, etc.) may raise the question, "Can this person handle his problems and the stress of a new job at the same time?"

To keep on being hunted:

If this opportunity doesn't work out, others may arise in the future. Declining a position won't damage your relationship with a recruiter as long as you were professional and honest during the process. To keep the headhunter hunting you...

- Offer to be an inside-the-industry source for future searches. If you're helpful, the headhunter will think of you when other openings arise.
- Stay in touch. Follow a meeting with a thank-you note. Periodically drop a line about your latest accomplishment or promotion.

Source: Diane Cole, a contributing editor of *Psychology Today* and author of *Hunting the Headhunters: A Woman's Guide*, Simon & Schuster, 1230 Ave. of the Americas, New York 10020.

Questions Millington McCoy Asks Job Candidates

Recent research suggests that the ability and willingness to learn and gain from experience is a characteristic common to most successful executives. Locating individuals who possess this quality is important to all companies.

But probing for that quality in a recruiting interview is not easy.

What are the best questions to ask?

How can an interviewer rate the candidates' learning abilities? There is a superb new method of assessing an individual's ability to learn from practical experience.* I've adapted this method to my process of selecting executives in recruitment.

Questions that probe a candidate's ability to learn new patterns of behavior from experience...

• Tell me about a time when you have tried to help someone else change. What strategy did you use? How did it turn out?

• Tell me about your most challenging—and least challenging—job.

• Tell me about your most and least admired persons.

• Tell me about a time when you tried to do something but failed.

• Tell me about a time when something bad happened to you.

• Tell me about a mistake you made in dealing with people.

• Tell me about the best course you've ever taken.

• Tell me about the last time you made a major change? Why did you do it? How did it work out?

Critical follow-up:

After getting the answer to each question, ask the candidate to tell you what he/she learned.

Then, rate each candidate, on a scale of one to five, on how he/she measures up to these yardsticks...

• Generalization. The weaker candidates are more likely to generalize. It's difficult to determine exactly what they learned or why they learned it. The stronger candidates have specific learnings and don't generalize much.

• Texture of learning. The weaker candidates tend toward extremes. They may give bland or socially acceptable descriptions of a least-admired person, for instance. Or, at the other extreme, they may overdo blaming that person or circumstance. They don't show much texture to what they learned from their mistakes. Stronger candidates are candid. They talk about mistakes and weaknesses openly. They may be quite judgmental of themselves, situations or even other people, but quickly move on to discuss what they did differently, how they responded.

• Complexity. Weaker candidates have a simpler view of people and jobs. They describe fewer nuances. The stronger candidates, on the other hand, describe experience with deeper analysis. They see more in everything than weaker candidates do.

• Why things happened. Weaker candidates focus more on what happened and much less on why it happened. They often don't offer that they've learned differently or that they've learned at all. Stronger candidates focus less on what happened and more on why it happened, what they learned, and what they would do differently.

• Recognize ambiguities. Weaker candidates often talk about doing things right and describe others in terms of what they did to them or what they got them to do. They use words that indicate that they like to control tasks and other people. Stronger candidates do not emphasize controlling others or perfectionism. They recognize the ambiguities of life.

• Curiosity. Strong candidates ask many questions about the content of the job. Weak candidates ask questions about the context of work (chance of promotion, fringe benefits, etc.).

*Questions making up the methodology are contained in program materials for *Tools For Developing Successful Executives*, a course designed and conducted by the Center for Creative Leadership, Greensboro, NC.

• Analytical honesty. Strong and weak candidates both can analyze a failure. But strong ones are more willing than weak ones to admit their role in it. Strong candidates, however, uniquely analyze successes and admit when they were due to pure luck.

• Self-awareness. Stronger candidates are aware of their strengths, weaknesses and limits. They're more interested in developing and deploying strengths and compensating for weaknesses. Weaker candidates are not particularly self-aware. They tend to overstate their strengths, invest too much energy in correcting their weaknesses and are often unaware of their limits.

Source: Millington F. McCoy, managing director, Gould & McCoy, executive search consultants, 551 Madison Ave., New York 10022.

15

Fitness and Exercise

How To Prevent Sports Injuries

A great many of the sports injuries suffered by fitness-minded individuals could easily have been prevented. Five-step program for safety...

1. Warm-up. Common misconception: Stretching and warm-up are the same. They are not. Warm-up involves elevating the body's temperature 1.5 or 2 degrees before beginning athletic activity.

Result: Muscle fibers and tendons become more fluid. Stretching a cold muscle tears it, but warming it will allow it to be more flexible so it can stretch properly. How to warm up: The same warm-up exercises can be used for almost any sport. You can jog, you can do jumping jacks, you can ride a stationary bike. When you break into a sweat, you'll know that you have elevated your body temperature properly. This normally takes between five and 10 minutes.

2. Stretching. It must be static. Don't bounce. Go into the stretch slowly and maintain it for 15–30 seconds, then relax slowly. Here you must be sports specific. If you are a jogger, you must stretch your legs and lower body...golfers should concentrate on the torso...tennis players and swimmers should stretch the entire body.

Recommended: 10 minutes minimum. If your muscles are "tight," stretching will take longer. Note: Stretching without warming up beforehand will do nothing to prevent sports injuries.

3. Participate in your activity.

4. Warm-down. This involves movement and effort just like warm-up.

Example: If you have just run two miles, walk for five minutes. Don't stop and sit down. The idea is to get your heart rate back to normal. You want to prevent "puddling" of blood into your legs. Fainting and even a heart attack could result from an immediate cessation of an athletic activity without a proper warm-down.

5. Restretching. This is even more important than the stretching when you began. Reason: When you overuse a muscle, it tends to shorten. Stretching each part of the body for two to three minutes will bring the muscles back to normal and will prevent soreness the next day.

Warning: Don't take a hot shower or go into a sauna immediately after exercise. It is the worst thing you can do. Reason: Circulation to the exercising muscles has been increased by the body, so there is a great deal of blood in the muscles. If you heat the skin, you dilate the blood vessels in the skin and you pull more blood out of the general circulation. You may not have enough left to supply the heart and the brain. Better: Take a lukewarm to cold shower.

Also helpful:

- Get enough sleep at night. You are more likely to suffer an injury when you are fatigued.
- Drink liquids both before and during exercise. This is especially important in warm and humid climates. Before beginning to exercise, drink eight to 12 ounces of water. While exercising, stop every 15 minutes for water or one of the drinks that raises the electrolytes* in the body. If you wait until you're thirsty, you'll never catch up.

*Substances (including sodium, potassium and chloride) that become ionic conductors when dissolved in suitable solvents.

- Eat a proper diet. Best foods for exercise periods: Large amounts of complex carbohydrates, such as bread, pasta and rice. Reason: These supply the fuel to run your engine.

After a layoff:

If you've been away from exercising for any period of time, go slow the first few sessions. If you used to jog two miles a day before, do only one mile the first time back. Build up approximately 10% each time until you feel comfortable. Biggest cause of sports injuries: Too far, too fast, too soon.

Specific sports injuries:

Leg problems: If you suffer from shin splints, knee problems or ankle injuries from jogging, most likely the cause is improper foot strike. Solution: Purchase an over-the-counter arch support.

One of three things will happen once you put the support in each shoe. Your injury will get better, it will get worse or nothing will happen. If it gets better, you have solved your problem. If it gets worse, you know it is a biomechanical problem and you should then consult a good sports podiatrist to get the right arch support fitted. If nothing happens, it's not biomechanical and you should immediately check with a physician.

For knee problems, consider bike riding or swimming. These sports put less stress on the knee.

Tennis elbow can be cured by changing how you hit your serve and backhand. Put less spin on your serve and straighten your elbow on the backhand. Also, exercise programs are available for tennis elbow.

Shoulder problems resulting from swimming, golf or tennis can be similarly helped with a specific exercise regimen.

Safest exercise: Fast walking. It also helps cardiovascular conditioning and can aid in weight loss.

Source: Alan Levy, MD, team physician for the New York Giants football team and chief of the Department of Sports Medicine, Pascack Valley Hospital, Westwood, NJ 07675. Dr. Levy has 38 years of experience in sports medicine.

Whole Truth About Walking Shoes

A few years ago, as fitness walking began to boom, the major athletic-shoe companies announced that walkers had different needs than runners and developed a new category—the walking shoe.

The truth: Many walkers don't need walking shoes...and some walkers would be even better off with another kind of shoe.

Whether you are a casual fitness walker or a dedicated power walker (with a focus on technique, pace and heart rate), you can probably be well-served by tennis shoes, cross-trainers or running shoes—as long as they are of high quality. Running shoes can be very well-suited to walkers. Reasons:

- As you age, there is some atrophy of the fat in your foot pads—the heel pads, in particular. If you walk on hard surfaces, you will benefit from the extra cushioning in running shoes.
- People who over-pronate (roll in excessively) need the support of a straighter last (the form the shape of the shoe is built around) and stronger support features—which running shoes have.

The most important criterion in choosing a shoe is to find a good fit—for both length and width. Since most athletic shoes are not sized for width, the more options you have, the better.

Bottom line: When buying a shoe for walking, seek out the model that best suits your needs. Don't restrict yourself to a specific category.

Source: Tom Brunick, director of the Athlete's Foot Wear Test Center at North Central College, Napierville, IL.

Exercise Doesn't Waste Time

Minding your health—including staying fit—is a vital step toward increasing longevity...and is as important as anything else you may want to do with your time. Big payoff: Exercise provides the energy to accomplish more in less time.

Source: *Age Less: Living Younger Longer* by Ben H. Douglas, PhD, Quail Ridge Press, Box 123, Brandon, MS 39043.

Walking Can Cause Injuries, Too

Bunions and heel spurs can be aggravated—see a podiatrist to correct these problems before you begin a fitness-walking program. Pinched nerves on the ball of the foot can develop if walking shoes are too tight or cushioned inadequately. Knee or hip pain can occur from poor posture or body alignment—so make sure your stride is even, head is held erect, shoulders are level, upper body is relaxed. Shin splints can occur if you do too much too soon—don't increase intensity more than 10% per week.

Source: Roundup of walking and sports medicine experts in *The Walking Magazine,* 711 Boylston St., Boston 02116.

A Teaching Ball

Learn balance, eye-hand coordination and peripheral vision and improve reaction time. The six-sided rubber Z ball bounces in unpredictable directions, forcing the user to cover a lot of ground, strengthening arms and legs, and giving a cardiovascular workout. Available: In sporting goods and toy stores.

Aerobics And Older People

Men and women (average age: 67) were randomly assigned to an aerobic exercise group, a yoga/flexibility group or a control group. After four months, the aerobic group showed improvement in oxygen consumption, blood pressure and cholesterol level. The yoga and control groups showed no improvement in these areas. Workout: Riding a stationary bike for 30 minutes, three times a week. Extra benefit: Men in the aerobic group were less depressed and women were less anxious. The aerobic and yoga groups thought they looked better, had more energy and slept better.

Source: Research at Duke University, reported in *Behavior Today,* 2315 Broadway, New York 10024.

Bench-Stepping Dangers

Knee injuries can develop from this new low-impact aerobic exercise in which you step up and down between the floor and a platform four to 12 inches high. To step safely: Beginners, short people and anyone prone to knee injury should use a platform no more than six inches high...look down at the beach every four to six seconds to remain aware of its location...plant your heel firmly in the center of the bench...don't bend your knees more than 90°...don't pivot on a bent knee.

Source: *Shape*, 21100 Erwin St., Woodland Hills, CA 91367.

High-Impact Aerobics

Long periods of jumping and bobbing up and down can cause damage to the delicate inner-ear structure. Symptoms: Imbalance, vertigo, ringing in the ears and hearing loss. Problem: Symptoms sometimes persist long after aerobic activity has stopped. Unknown: If damage mends itself after activity is stopped permanently.

Source: Michael A. Weintraub, MD, clinical professor of neurology, New York Medical College.

How To Walk Much More Healthily

To get aerobic benefits from walking, you have to plan and monitor your workouts. Walk at least three times a week and raise your heart rate to a specified target for 30 to 60 minutes.

To find your target heart rate,* subtract your age from 220. Then multiply that number by .65...and also by .85.

Example: If you are 55 years old, the math would look like this:

220 – 55 = 165
165 × .65 = 107
165 × .85 = 140

Your target heart rate is between 107 and 140 beats per minute.

*The best way to accurately determine your target heart rate is to consult your doctor. He/she can also advise you on the types of exercise programs that are best for you.

To take your pulse while walking, pause and count your wrist or neck pulse for 10 seconds. Then multiply that number by 6. Start by aiming for the lower end of your target heart rate and work gradually toward the higher end.

Use your arms and legs right:

- Legs: When you try to pick up speed, take quicker steps...don't use a longer stride. Also: Don't kick out your heels or use an exaggerated goose step.
- Arms: Keep them close to your body, bent at a comfortable 90° angle. Don't pump.

Source: Mark Fenton, a research engineer at the human performance laboratory run by Reebok International. A race walker on the US National Team, he specializes in the 50-kilometer walk (32 miles), the longest foot race in the Olympics.

Biking Danger

Blunt trauma to the groin—such as falling onto the crossbar of a bicycle—can cause blockages in the arteries of the penis, restricting blood flow and ultimately causing impotence. Treatment: Surgery to bypass the blocked areas is about 70% successful in treating impotence in these patients.

Source: Irwin Goldstein, MD, professor of urology, Boston University School of Medicine, and co-director, New England Reproductive Center, University Hospital, Boston.

Walk...Walk...Walk... Walk...Walk...Walk... Walk...Walk...Walk...

How would you like to shed those pounds that you've been trying to lose, without running a single mile, without learning anything about step aerobics and without ever having to hear some muscle-bound trainer advise you to "feel the burn?"

Well...the next time you get up from watching TV and head for the refrigerator, keep on walking—out the door, around the block, to the newspaper stand, to a neighbor's house—anywhere. Just walk. Doctors will tell you that walking is the safest way to burn fat (and keep it off). And unlike running, walking is a low-impact activity and that means much lower risk or injuries to joints, bones and muscles.

You can burn as many calories walking as you can jogging—it just takes a little longer. Walking briskly (at about four miles per hour), you burn 100 calories per mile. At that rate, a three-mile walk every day will amount to a loss of 35 pounds over the course of a year. And you get both short- and long-term cardiovascular benefits.

Important extra benefit: As those pounds drop off and you improve the overall health and functional ability of your heart, you'll find that your outlook on life improves, too—for exercise not only burns calories, but also works off stress.

Starting at square one:

Before you start your fitness walking program—or any new exercise program—it's important to check with your doctor. If you have an existing or chronic medical condition—diabetes, arthritis, high blood pressure or heart disease—you should make sure that your new exercise plan will not make it worse.

Minimum: Have a resting electrocardiogram. And if you're over 45, or a smoker or have known cardiovascular problems, a cardiac stress test is strongly advised. After you pass these tests—and there's every likelihood that you will—you'll know that you're up to the demands of and introductory program in fitness walking.

Initial goal: Three to five 15- to 60-minute exercise periods per week.

During these exercise periods, you should be able to increase your heart rate to more than 70% of maximum capacity.

To determine maximum capacity: Subtract your age from 220...this is your maximum heart rate. Take your pulse, at rest, for 60 seconds. Subtract your pulse rate from your maximum heart rate. Multiply the answer by 0.6. This number is your target zone. Add your pulse rate to your target zone. The answer is your target heart rate.

As you walk, take your pulse for 10 seconds and multiply that number by six. If your pulse is less than your target heart rate, step up your pace. If you're exceeding your target, slow down.

Before you begin your walk: Do five minutes of stretching exercises. Stretch your calf muscles by placing both hands against a wall and leaning into the wall with your left leg straight and your right knee slightly bent. Both feet should be flat on the floor. Hold this position for about 30 seconds. Repeat with your right leg straight and your left knee bent.

Stretch the muscle in the front of your thigh (the quadriceps) next. From a standing position, reach behind your back and grab your right foot with your left hand. Pull the foot toward your buttocks while keeping your right knee pointed toward the floor. (Steady yourself by holding onto a chair or railing.) Hold the position for about 30 seconds and repeat with the opposite hand and foot.

Finally, stretch the muscle in the back of your thigh (the hamstring). Again, from a standing position, place your right heel on an elevated surface (e.g., a stair). Keep your right knee slightly bent, and lean forward from the hips, extending your hands toward your right ankle. Hold the position and repeat with your left leg.

Do these exercises gently. Don't bounce, and don't force your muscles if they don't do what you want them to do immediately.

The walk:

Start out at a slow to moderate pace for the first five minutes, then walk briskly for about 25 minutes. After 10 minutes at your faster pace, check your pulse. Are you at or near your target heart rate? Adjust your pace to stay within your target range.

As you walk, relax your shoulders and swing your arms to match your stride. End your walk with a five-minute "cool-down" period in which you slow your pace, and finish off the session with another five minutes of stretching exercises to prevent stiffness.

A word to the wise: If you're not a 16-year-old high-school athlete, make a mental adjustment to the popular "Just do it" slogan. Just do it—gradually. Do to your limit gradually and enjoy it. You don't have to leap tall buildings in a single bound your first time around the block.

And don't get tricky with your basic walking gait. Never wear ankle weights to "increase the load." You might as well hang a bowling ball off your elbow. Ankle weights will exert stresses on your joints that Mother Nature never designed into the plan—and you will suffer for it.

Fitness walking basics:

- Drink eight to 10 glasses of water a day.
- Wear light-colored or reflective clothing at night or in the early morning.
- Battle boredom by listening to music or a recorded book on a portable tape player.
- If you have a blister or sprain that can be made worse by walking, don't walk.
- If you become dizzy or develop pains in your chest or your arms, stop walking immediately and go to the nearest emergency room.

If the shoe fits:

Part of the fun of starting a new sport is "suiting up." Selecting a new pair of shoes for your fitness walking program can help to reinforce your commitment to exercise. But how do you know which shoe is right for you?

Faced with the array of athletic shoes currently on the market, let common sense be your guide. Don't buy a pair of shoes designed for running, sprinting, basketball, high-impact aerobics, etc. Buy walking shoes. Take your exercise socks to the store with you, and put them on before trying on the new shoes. Important: Always shop for shoes in the afternoon. Feet swell as the day wears on, and shoes bought in the morning can pinch in the afternoon.

What to look for: Comfort, cushioning and an appropriate degree of ruggedness. Select a lace-up shoe with good heel and arch support, a flexible sole and a good overall fit. Look inside the shoe—and feel with your hand—for any irregularities (seams, lumps, etc.) that could trouble your foot.

Once you have the shoe on, check the length by pinching the front of the shoe by your big toe. If the empty space is wider than your thumb, the shoe is too long. Check shoe width by examining the shoelace holes. When the shoe is snugly laced, the holes should be about a thumb's width apart. If the distance is greater—or less—than that, the shoe is not for you.

What about skipping the shoelace option and going for the Velcro fasteners. Bad idea. Laces allow a shoe to conform to your foot at a number of points, but Velcro straps hold, vise-like, as your foot expands.

If, after you've worn your new shoes for a while, you find that they work for you, buy another pair just like them. You'll prolong the life of your shoes if you alternate pairs. Also, shoes will have extra drying time between wearings, which decreases your risk of developing athlete's foot and other fungal conditions.

Too busy to exercise?

Stressed-out executives with a crammed schedule and a sedentary lifestyle are among the people who could benefit most from exercise—but there are only 24 hours in a day, no matter how big the numbers are on your paycheck. No time for an exercise program? Make exercise a part of the workday.

If you're stuck at the office day and night—use the stairs. When you need to go over some numbers with someone whose office is a few floors above you, skip the elevator and get there the old-fashioned way. Or just hit the stairs for a 10-minute fitness break.

Good-quality men's business shoes are also excellent walking shoes, so, if you're a commuter, park the car a 15-minute walk from the train or bus station. You'll get your half-hour walk in every day. Women commuters will probably need to carry a change of shoes, but many do anyway.

And if you find that you've arrived early for an appointment, don't sit in the lobby looking at old magazines. Walk around the block, explore the neighborhood. You have everything—fitness, health and well-being—to gain, and nothing to lose but a few extra pounds.

Source: Daniel M. McGann, DPM, author of *The Doctor's Sore Foot Book*, William Morrow & Co., 1350 Ave. of the Americas, New York 10019.

Cleaner, Dryer Running Shoes

Spray them every few months with Scotchgard to keep feet dryer on wet surfaces and keep shoes dirt resistant.

Source: *Running & Fitness*, 9310 Old Georgetown Rd., Bethesda, MD 20814.

Exercise Enhancer

Music therapy helps elderly patients cope with disabilities. Patients in groups for which music is played often respond better with physical and occupational therapy, exercises designed to increase an elderly patient's range of motion, renew motor skills and ease pain.

Source: Registered music therapist Mary Rudenberg, University of Texas Medical Branch at Galveston.

All About Physiatry: The New-ish Medical Specialty

A physiatrist is a physician who's been trained in both the ordinary aspects of movement and the therapeutic use of exercise to improve physical functioning and health.

Physiatry, a medical specialty, deals with the treatment of diseases by physical means and by restoration—using the body's own potential—and working to improve it.

Conventional medicine depends on drugs or on surgery. It doesn't ask for much participation from the patient. A conventional physician typically gives a patient a pill for symptomatic relief—a high blood pressure pill, for example. That patient will get some advice in addition...use less salt, lose weight, and so on. But the patient participates much less in his recovery than he does in physiatrics or rehabilitation medicine.

How it works:

Let's say you have some osteoarthritis of the knees or hip. You're not quite ready for surgery—or surgery is not indicated if you simply want to continue playing golf. However, you're seventy years old and golf is your favorite pastime. A physiatrist will help you to develop your joints so well that eventually you can play golf. He/she will show you how to increase the range of your hip movement, alter your golf swing and how to increase the rotation of your spine. Your game won't be perfect—even if you are in great health—but you will be able to play.

The physiatrist will also tell you point-blank that the muscles and joints don't respect the doctor's academic degrees. The patient himself has to exercise.

Physiatry grew out of rehabilitative medicine. They are basically the same thing, except that physiatry is a somewhat broader term.

Rehabilitative medicine to most people means dealing with fairly severe physical problems—usually crippling. The term physiatry is just the Greek word for using physical means.

Sports medicine is also included to some degree, but sports medicine is not an official specialty. If a doctor wants to call himself a sports medicine specialist, he is one. There's no special examination or training program..

Physiatry is an officially recognized medical specialty, with a very demanding training program—including one year of internship or residence in internal medicine or surgery, followed by three years training in an approved program.

During this training, there is an examination every year. When it's over, the doctor has to pass a written examination. After another year of practice, there is an oral examination.

On the horizon:

The number of physiatrists in the US has doubled in the past decade. But there are still relatively few. Many of today's medical students want to go into physiatry. For every one of the limited number of places, there are over 100 applicants. This generation of young people is very interested in exercise and physical functioning.

Wars and other tragedies have given the field a big boost. But what we have now is much better...a generation that's interested in physiatry without the pressure of a lot of war-related injuries. The increased longevity of our population is going to increase the need for physiatrists, too.

How to find a physiatrist:

Right now, there are so few physiatrists, and they're mostly concentrated in large urban areas. If you want to find a physiatrist, you could call a large medical center for names.

A rehabilitative medicine institute sometimes is limited to one or two diseases—they take care of strokes, for example—so that isn't necessarily the best source.

For more information: There is also a national association of physiatrists, the American Academy of Physical Medicine and Rehabilitation, 122 S. Michigan Ave., Suite 130D, Chicago 60803. 312-922-9366.

Source: Willibald Nagler, MD, chief physiatrist-in-chief, department of rehabilitative medicine, New York Hospital–Cornell Medical Center. Dr. Nagler is the author of *Dr. Nagler's Body Maintenance and Repair Book*, Fireside, an imprint of Simon & Schuster, 1230 Ave. of the Americas, New York 10220.

Health, Anxiety, Ideas And Walking

Exercise doesn't have to be strenuous or punishing to be effective. Despite its economy of muscle use, walking is considered by most experts to be one of the best exercises.

Benefits:

- Preventative and remedy for respiratory, heart and circulation disorders.
- Weight control. Walking won't take off pounds, but it keeps weight at a desirable level. (Particularly effective in keeping excess pounds from coming back, once they have been dieted off.)
- Aids digestion, elimination and sleep.
- Antidote to physical and psychological tensions.

Walking works as a second heart. Expanding and contracting foot muscles, calves, thighs and buttocks help pump blood back to the heart. This aid is crucial. The heart can propel blood very well on its own, but the body's muscles are essential to the return flow from lower regions (legs, feet, stomach). When the blood transportation system becomes sluggish because of lack of exercise, the heart compensates by doing more work. Heart rate and blood pressure rise. (Elevated pressure can be helped to return to normal by a regimen of walking.)

Best daily walking routine:

- Time. Whenever it can be fit into your daily routine. (A mile takes only 20 minutes.) People doing sedentary office work usually average a mile and a half in a normal day. Stretch that by choosing to walk down the hall to a colleague instead of picking up the interoffice phone.
- Place. Wherever it's pleasant and convenient to daily tasks. Walk at least part of the way to work. If you're a commuter, walk to the train. Walk, not to the nearest, but to the second or third bus or subway stop from the house. Get off a stop or two away from the usual one. Park the car 10 blocks further away. Walk 10 blocks to and from lunch. Walk after dinner, before sitting down to a book, TV or work.
- Clothes. Comfortable and seasonal, light rather than heavy. Avoid thin-soled shoes when walking city pavements. It may be desirable to use metatarsal pads or cushioned soles. (The impact on concrete weakens metatarsal arches and causes calluses.)
- Length. Walk modest distances at first. In the city, the number of streets tells the beginner how far he has gone. But in the country, a walker can go farther than he realizes. Consequences: Fatigue on the return trip. Instead: Use a good pedometer.
- Pace. Walking for exercise should feel different from other kinds of walking. Some useful suggestions about pace...

Set out at a good pace. Use the longest stride that's comfortable for you. Let arms swing and muscles stretch. Strike a rhythm and keep to it.

Don't saunter. Sauntering can be tiring.

Walking at a good pace allows the momentum of each stride to carry over into the next.

Lengthen the customary stride by swinging the foot a little farther ahead than usual. Lengthening the stride speeds the walking pace with no additional expenditure of energy. It also loosens tense muscles, puts other neglected muscles to work and provides continuous momentum that puts less weight on the feet.

Most comfortable pace: Three miles per hour. It generally suits the average male and is the US Army pace for long hikes. With the right shoes and unconfining clothes, most women will be comfortable at that pace, too.

Source: Aaron Sussman, an advertising pioneer, who recently died at the age of 87. He was an inspiration, in many ways, to the many people who were privileged to know him.

Walking Off Anxiety

Walking is an excellent technique to drain off panic and dangerous impulses and to prompt solutions to difficult problems. The steady, rhythmic action of walking helps thinking, both conscious and unconscious. (This is not true of more strenuous exercise.)

To encourage problem-solving while walking: Prior to the walk, clearly identify the problem. Then begin walking and put the problem aside. Think of anything else —or preferably nothing. Well into a walk, a fresh solution to the problem may spring to mind.

Diet/Fitness Traps

• Expecting immediate results. Most problems do not disappear overnight, but any progress is better than none.

• Expecting change to occur magically. Change requires thought, action, commitment.

• Getting discouraged. Long-term success is a gradual process with uneven progress.

• Expecting no pain, no gain. You need not punish yourself to be successful.

Source: *The Duke University Medical Center Book of Diet and Fitness* by Michael Hamilton, MD, Fawcett/Columbine, 201 E. 50 St., New York 10022.

Exercise/Digestion Connection

Food in the stomachs of men who exercised by walking 1.5 miles per hour moved into the intestines 40% faster than in men who were sedentary. Those who walked at 3 mph (a fairly brisk pace) cut their stomach transit time in half. Lesson: Mild exercise after eating helps relieve minor indigestion.

Source: Study conducted at the Veterans Affairs Medical Center, Salt Lake City, reported in *Body Bulletin,* 33 E. Minor St., Emmaus, PA 18098.

Exercise And Colds

Daily exercise speeds recovery from common colds by boosting the immune system. Women who walked 45 minutes a day recovered twice as fast (five days versus 10 days) from colds than women who did not exercise during a 15-week period.

Source: Study by David Nieman, exercise physiologist, Appalachian State University, Boone, NC, reported in *The Walking Magazine,* 711 Boylston St., Boston 02116.

Shaping Up For Summer Made Simple

At the first signs of spring, many of us who spend the winter hibernating get our sweatsuits out of the closet, eager to get back into shape.

Warning: Too much enthusiasm can be dangerous. Just as regular exercise gradually conditions the body, a break from exercise deconditions it. Picking up your exercise program at the point where you left off months ago could make you vulnerable to injury.

Many people fall prey to the "Three F's"—they push themselves too far, too fast, too frequently.

Don't try to match last summer's performance right away. Treat your warm-weather fitness program as though it were a brand-new activity—at least for a few weeks—and work up gradually to former levels.

Get in shape safely:

• Prepare mentally. Before you commit yourself to an exercise regimen this season, look at any mental obstacles that might have caused you to quit working out in the past.

If you keep stopping and starting fitness programs, repeated deconditioning will make you a prime candidate for injury. Common obstacles: Lack of time, inconvenience, fatigue, injury or illness, dissatisfaction with progress.

One you've identified your obstacles, find ways around them.

Example: If time is a problem, try walking during your lunch hour.

You're more likely to stick with exercise that you enjoy. If running bores you, try squash. Or vary your workouts. Walk for an hour on Monday, go for a bike ride on Wednesday, play tennis on Saturday.

• Set up the right physical conditions. Have the proper shoes, clothing and equipment. Make sure you understand the correct mechanics of the sport, including ways to guard against back and knee strain or other possible injuries. Take a brush-up lesson if you're not sure. Ask yourself:

• Where do I plan to exercise?

• How will I get there?

• What gear do I need to bring with me?

• Will I work out by myself or with a partner or team?

To keep on track, write yourself an exercise prescription—a specific workout plan for each week.

• Follow the "FIT" principle. That stands for frequency, intensity and time.

For each of these three areas, start at a level or two below the point where you left off last season. After two to three weeks, gradually begin to increase your training level.

Frequency. For aerobic exercises, such as jogging or swimming, three to five days a week is a safe schedule. If you plan to work up to more than five days a week, make sure some of those training days are easy—your body won't tolerate a hard workout every day.

For weight training, start with two and work up to no more than three or four days a week. Your muscles need at least one day of rest after each session.

As for flexibility training, such as dance or yoga, many people can work out daily without undue stress.

Intensity. During an aerobic workout, aim to get your heart rate into the aerobic training zone—60% to 85% of predicted maximum heart rate.

To find this heart rate, subtract your age from 220, then multiply that number by 60% and 85%. Take these target heart-rate numbers and divide them by six to get your 10-second heart rate. Take your pulse for 10 seconds in the middle of your workout. A good aerobic heart rate is between 20 and 28.

If you're out of shape, keep your pulse close to 60%. Aim higher as fitness improves.

For no-aerobic exercise, such as weight training (or pushups and situps, which use gravity, not weights, as resistance), stop at the point where you feel muscle fatigue.

Don't try to push through the pain. And don't increase your weight load until you can do three sets of 12 repetitions at your current weight.

During flexibility training, stretch slightly beyond the easy point of tension. You should feel tightness but not pain. Lean into the stretch steadily for 10 to 20 seconds—never bounce.

Time. Keep your workout 20 to 60 minutes long. As always, start at the low end of the range and increase duration over a period of weeks.

• Warm up and cool down. No matter what your fitness level, spend at least three to five minutes before every workout warming up your muscles and your cardiovascular system.

At the beginning of the season, warmup time is especially important. To get the blood moving, march in place or twist from side to side. Gently stretch out the muscles you're going to be using, holding each stretch 10 to 20 seconds.

Examples: Swimmers and tennis players should do arm reaches and rotations to stretch the shoulder muscles...runners and cyclists should stretch hamstrings, quadriceps and calves.

Walking, twisting and stretching are important after a workout, too. The blood vessels in the legs widen during vigorous exercise—a cool-down period allows them to return to normal so that blood can flow back to the upper body. Skipping this step leaves some people feeling faint or dizzy. Stretching keeps just-worked muscles from becoming tight and stiff.

Overriding rule: Listen to your body and don't push it past its limits. Your body will tell you better than any formula how much it's ready to handle.

Source: Susan Johnson, EdD, director of continuing education at the Institute for Aerobics Research, a nonprofit research and educator center, 12330 Preston Rd., Dallas 75230. 800-635-7050. She is author of *The Walking Handbook*, published by the Institute.

Exercise Is Good For Skin, Too

Reason: It increases the amount of collagen and elastic fibers that keep skin looking younger...and sweating allows nutrients to flow to the surface and removes skin's metabolic waste products.

Source: *Ageless: Living Younger Longer* by Ben H. Douglas, PhD, Quail Ridge Press, Box 123, Brandon, MS 39043.

Hot-Weather Workout Guidelines

Hot-weather workouts should be done with less intensity—it takes four to 10 days for your body to adjust to exercise in the heat. As you feel yourself adjusting, gradually build back up to your normal workout. Recommended: Swimming—good exercise that helps control body temperature in hot weather.

Source: *Get in Shape, Stay in Shape* by the editors of Consumer Reports Books, 101 Truman Ave., Yonkers, NY 10703.

Mistakes Hikers Make And How To Avoid Them

When it's done right, hiking is a serene soul-warming pursuit—an opportunity to see nature with fresh eyes and to rediscover the joy of one's own company. When it's done wrong, however, hiking can be miserable, frustrating, painful...even injurious.

What makes the difference is preparation, equipment, trail smarts and common sense. You don't need a vast amount of technical knowledge, equipment or experience to enjoy hiking. But you do need to avoid these common errors:

- Mistake: Buying equipment without doing your homework. Not all packs, sleeping bags, boots, tents and stoves are created equal. For reliable product review, check the annual spring ratings issue of *Backpacker* magazine.
- Mistake: Hitting the trail without a dress rehearsal. Lace up and load up before you take your first hike.

Load your pack, then adjust the straps and belts for a comfortable fit. Find uneven terrain where you can test your pack and boots. A paved road, no matter how steeply inclined, will not tell you what you need to know.

- Mistake: Buying unsuitable boots. For most beginners, lightweight fabric boots are preferable to leather ones. The fabric boots (which are comparable to tough nylon sneakers) are more comfortable, and don't require a break-in period. They also have less negative impact on the trail, since they don't drag so much soil.

Leather boots, however, are more durable and provide more support, and are more sensible for cold-weather hiking.

To buy the right size: Try the boots on while you are wearing two thick pairs of socks. Reason: When hiking, your feet will swell by a half size...and the extra pair of socks simulates that.

• Mistake: Carrying too much weight. Beginners should limit themselves to a maximum of 25% of their body weight. That means a 160-pound hiker should pack no more than 40 pounds.

To lighten your load: Buy a nylon mummy sleeping bag, rather than a heavier cotton bag. Carry food that is boxed or bagged rather than canned.

• Mistake: Packing unnecessary items. You won't have any need for a hatchet or Bowie knife (a pocket knife will serve you well)...an oversized, high-powered flashlight (keep it small)...or several changes of clothes (one change should suffice for any hike up to 10 days).

• Mistake: Hiking in too large a group. Large groups damage the trail ecologically. Best: No more than eight people.

• Mistake: Backtracking needlessly. Many hikers dislike covering the same ground twice to get back to their car.

Solution: Split your group into two parties. Drop one party off at one end of the hike, then park the car at the other end. The car key is exchanged when the two parties pass on the trail. Note: This method also works with two cars...the parties trade keys when they pass.

• Mistake: Failing to limber up. By investing a few minutes in stretching your hamstrings, calves, feet, shoulders and back muscles, you can do much to avoid muscle strains down the trail.

• Mistake: Moving too fast. Most hikers will be comfortable with an average pace of two miles per hour.

At three miles per hour (the pace favored by some hiking clubs), many hikers will experience premature fatigue. They will also risk a wide range of injuries, from blisters and sore feet to knee problems and sprained ankles.

• Mistake: Competing within your group. A hike should be a cooperative venture. To keep the group together, set the pace by your slowest member. You may also need to shift some heavy gear from someone who's lagging to someone who's shooting far ahead.

• Mistake: Forgetting to rest enough. I recommend a 10-minute rest every hour, and a break of 30 to 60 minutes every three hours. There is no absolute formula...when you're tired, stop.

• Mistake: Being inflexible. Always consider the possibility that you may not reach your goals. Someone in your party might get hurt...bad weather might slow you down. Plan a bail-out route or a shorter schedule—just in case.

Source: Cindy Ross, a contributing editor to *Backpacker* magazine, and the author of *A Woman's Journey on the Appalachian Trail*, Appalachian Trail Conference, Box 807, Harper's Ferry, WV 25425, and *Journey on the Crest: Walking 2600 Miles from Mexico to Canada*, The Mountaineers, 306 Second Ave. West, Seattle 98119.

Exercise And Caffeine

Abstain from coffee at least four hours before exercise if you have a family history of hypertension...or if your resting blood pressure is mildly elevated. Problem: The combination of exercise and caffeine is twice as likely to elevate blood pressure in those at risk.

Source: A study by the Veterans Affairs Medical Center, Oklahoma City, reported in *Working Mother*, 230 Park Ave., New York 10169.

For The Most Oxygen

To maximize oxygen flow in your body, inhale deeply—and exhale deeply—while you exercise. Avoid rapid, shallow breathing. Don't hold your breath. Don't be afraid to breathe deeply in cold weather...the air will be warmed by the time it gets to your lungs (it may feel uncomfortable because it is dry).

Source: *Immune Power Boosters: Your Key to Feeling Younger, Living Longer* by medical-nutrition reporter Carlson Wade, Prentice-Hall, Route 9W, Englewood Cliffs, NJ 07632.

Telling Good Pain From Bad

Safe levels of pain that result from exercise include a general heaviness, fatigue or mild burning in your muscles while you exercise, or an overall soreness that strikes 24 hours later. It's all right to continue exercising unless the pain interferes with your ability to control movement. Bad pain: Localized pain—an area of the body that crackles, pops, pulls, swells or limits motion. Eight times out of ten, that localized pain requires medical attention.

Source: Peter Francis, PhD, San Diego State University, and William Grana, MD, Oklahoma Center for Athletes, quoted in *Self*, 350 Madison Ave., New York 10017.

Don't Exercise First Thing In the Morning

When you lie down, the discs of the spine take in fluid, which makes them tense and more prone to irritation. Best: Wait at least two hours after you get out of bed to exercise.

Source: *Your Aching Back: A Doctor's Guide to Relief* by Augustus A. White III, MD, Fireside Books, 1230 Ave. of the Americas, New York 10020.

Best Time To Exercise: Before A Meal

Vigorous exercise suppresses appetite, and it speeds up your metabolism, so that you can burn up more of the food calories you take in.

Source: *New Aerobics for Women* by Kenneth H. Cooper, MD, MPH, and Mildred Cooper, Bantam Books, 666 Fifth Ave., New York 10103.

The Right Way To Stretch

Wear comfortable, non-binding clothing...stretch only one muscle group at a time...stretch to the point where you feel mild tension and hold for 10 to 30 seconds...stretch as often as you can, preferably every day...be patient. Don't stretch to the point of pain...don't bounce...don't stretch in ways that force the joints beyond their normal range of motion.

Source: *If It Hurts, Don't Do It* by Peter Francis, PhD, and Lorna Francis, PhD, Prima Publishing & Communications, Box 1260F, Rocklin, CA 95677.

Soccer Danger

Repeated heading (bouncing the soccer ball off the head) can cause brain damage similar to that seen in some boxers. Twenty-five percent of first-division players studied showed slightly abnormal brain waves, and 7% showed more severely abnormal waves. Likely: The damage is permanent. Most common victims: Players 12–24 years of age.

Source: Study by A.T. Tysvaer and O.V. Storli, reported in *American Journal of Sports Medicine*, Box 830259, Birmingham, AL 35283.

Hiking Preparation

Limber up before you go hiking to prevent muscle problems from developing later on. Stretch your hamstrings, calves, feet, shoulders and back muscles using slow—not bouncy—stretching movements.

Source: *Backpacker*, 33 E. Minor St., Emmaus, PA 18098.

Exercise Allergies

Allergies to exercise can cause itching, hives, swelling and fainting spells. Exercise-induced anaphylaxis (EIA) is most frequently brought on by jogging and aerobic exercising. Some people can induce EIA simply by walking briskly. Helpful: Don't eat before you exercise—some foods increase the risk of an attack—and avoid taking aspirin and ibuprofen. If you are prone to EIA, don't work out alone...stop exercising at the first sign of itchiness or faintness...and bring along an adrenaline kit.

Source: Research by Matthew Liang, MD, and Albert L. Sheffer, MD, Harvard Medical School, reported in *Omni*, 1965 Broadway, New York 10023.

Prescriptions For Walking

If you are overweight or have diabetes: Distance is more important than speed. Try to walk for 45 minutes to one hour at a self-selected pace. Heart or lung disorders: Exercise indoors in a climate-controlled, pollution-free environment, especially if the temperature is above 88° and humidity is greater than 85%. Sports injuries or arthritis in the back or lower extremities: Avoid steep hills. They stress or improve aerobic fitness: Increase intensity of exercise, aiming for a 15-minute mile or better. To increase heart rate, use handheld weights, walk up stairs or hills, and pump your arms.

Source: *Walking Medicine: Lifetime Guide to Preventative & Therapeutic Exercisewalking Programs* by Gary Yanker and Kathy Burton, McGraw-Hill, 1221 Ave. of the Americas, New York 10020.

Walking Mistakes

Although we've all been walking since we were toddlers, at least 30% of all people still don't know how to walk correctly.

Whether you're walking for pleasure, walking for exercise or just walking to get from one place to another, it's important to do it right.

• Mistake: Not maintaining proper posture. Poor posture puts extra stress on joints, vertebrae and muscles, causing pain.

Correct: Tuck your chin into your neck so your ear, shoulder, hip and ankle form a straight line perpendicular to the ground when you're standing still. Then hold this position as closely as possible when you walk. This avoids unduly stressing any one joint or part of your body.

Avoid arching the back. This causes lower back pain and shortens the length of your steps.

Correct: Do a pelvic tilt. Tuck your buttocks under your body and hold in your stomach while you walk. This will take conscious effort at first, but after a while, your stomach and buttocks will stay in automatically. Walking this way strengthens the back and the stomach muscles, which redistributes weight away from the lower vertebrae, eliminating back pain.

• Mistake: Keeping your arms still. You lose almost half the exercise value of walking—increasing your heart rate and working your shoulder, back and arm muscles—by not moving your arms.

Correct: Pump your arms. Bend your elbows slightly for regular walking, and 90° for aerobic walking.

Guide the arms straight forward and back, hands rising as far as the chest—at least to the waist. Let the inside of your arms rub the sides of your body—you should hear your clothing rubbing.

Pumping your arms is an upper-body calisthenic—your shoulders, upper back and chest all get exercised. If you pump your arms during brisk or aerobic walking, it doubles the exercise value.

• Mistake: Walking duck-footed (with the knees pointed out) or pigeon-toed (with the knees pointed in). This puts stress on the knees and ankles. They are hinge joints—made for forward, not side-to-side, motion. Stress causes knee and ankle pain.

Correct: Walk with your feet parallel. And use the heel-toe roll. Land heel first and turn the ankle out slightly (the width of a finger). Then roll on the outer edge of the foot until you reach the toe. This aligns the lower and upper leg.

• Mistake: Walking with your feet too close together. This makes it easy to trip and fall.

Correct: Keep your feet hip-width to shoulder-width apart.

• Mistake: Taking short steps. This also reduces the exercise value of walking, and causes the leg and hip muscles to tighten.

Correct: By reaching further with each step—and using arm pumping and the heel-toe roll—most people can lengthen their average step three to eight inches. Longer steps burn more calories...work leg muscles...raise heart rate...increase circulation...make you feel more energetic...and increase walking speed.

Source: Gary Yanker, author of many books and audiotapes about walking. He is the founder of Walking World, a publishing and marketing company that specializes in walking. Among Yanker's books: *Walking Medicine: The Lifetime Guide to Preventive and Therapeutic Exercise Walking,* McGraw-Hill, 1221 Ave. of the Americas, New York 10020.